Foodservice in Institutions

BESSIE B. WEST and LEVELLE WOOD

Sixth Edition Revised by:

VIRGINIA F. HARGER, M.S., R.D.
Professor Emeritus, Food Systems Management Department,
College of Home Economics, Oregon State University

GRACE S. SHUGART, M.S.
Professor Emeritus,
Hotel, Restaurant, Institution Management, and Dietetics Department
College of Human Ecology, Kansas State University

JUNE PAYNE-PALACIO, PhD., R.D.
Associate Professor, Nutritional Science,
Natural Science Division, Pepperdine University, Malibu, California

MACMILLAN PUBLISHING COMPANY
NEW YORK

Collier Macmillan Publishers
LONDON

Earlier editions copyright © 1938, 1945, 1955, 1966 by John Wiley & Sons, Inc. Fifth Edition
copyright © 1977 by John Wiley & Sons, Inc., and copyright © 1986 by Macmillan Publishing
Company.

Macmillan Publishing Company
866 Third Avenue, New York, New York 10022

Collier Macmillan Canada, Inc.

LIBRARY OF CONGRESS CATALOGING-IN-PUBLICATION DATA
West, Bessie Brooks.
    Foodservice in institutions.

    Rev. ed. of: Food service in institutions / Bessie B.
West . . . et al. 5th ed. ©1977.
    Includes index.
    1. Food service. I. Wood, LeVelle. II. Harger,
Virginia F.   III. Food service in institutions. IV. Title.
TX946.W415   1988   647'.95'068   87-11091
ISBN 0-02-425940-3

Printing: 1 2 3 4 5 6 7   Year: 8 9 0 1 2 3 4

ISBN 0-02-425940-3

Preface

Nearly fifty years have passed since the first edition of this text appeared in 1938. During those years many changes have occurred in our world and society that have had a profound effect upon the foodservice industry and ways of accomplishing activities within its establishments. New types of food-services and foodservice systems, new forms of food, new developments in equipment, especially those designed for conservation of energy, and the introduction of computer technologies and applications have all aided managers in accomplishing the never-changing goal: to provide the best possible food and service within the policies of the foodservice organization.

These changes have made it important to revise *Foodservice in Institutions* throughout the years. The two original authors, Bessie Brooks West and LeVelle Wood, wrote the first edition in response to a need for a basic college text to aid in teaching courses in foodservice administration. There were no other comprehensive texts on the market at that time. The wide acceptance of this work was due in large part to the reputation of these two women for setting and maintaining high standards of authenticity and excellence in their writing and in their teaching at Kansas State University. As a result, five editions previous to this one were prepared and widely used in the United States and other parts of the world. The fourth edition was translated into both Spanish and Japanese.

Mrs. West continued her guidance of revisions of the text through the fifth edition. She died in December 1984 at age 93. Miss Wood, who currently resides in a retirement home in Portland, Oregon, has been an inspiring advisor in the preparation of this sixth edition. It is the hope of the present authors that the text continues to meet the needs of today's students (as well as teachers) who are preparing to become qualified administrative dietitians and/or professional foodservice managers. Also, we hope this book will serve as a ready reference for those presently engaged in the planning, production, and service of food in all types of foodservice operations.

Information presented in the sixth edition has been updated and the material completely revised. Some reorganization has taken place. Four sections are included: Foodservice Organizations, Quantity Food Production and Service, Physical Facilities, and Organization and Administration of Foodservices. Three new chapters have been added: Types of Foodservice Systems (Chapter 2) introduces the foodservice operation as a system; Work Improvement and Productivity (Chapter 14) emphasizes the need for more effective and cost-containing practices in today's economy; Management Information Systems (Chapter 16) presents the use of computer technologies in providing information for management decision making and discusses computer applications in foodservice operations. The former chapter (Quantity Food Production) has been divided into two chapters: Production Planning and Control (Chapter 5) and Quantity Food Production (Chapter 6). Two former chapters (Equipment for Kitchens and Serving Rooms, and Furnishings and Equipment for Dining Rooms) have been combined into Chapter 10, Equipment and Furnishings. Several chapter titles have been renamed to reflect current terminology. An attempt has been made to broaden our concept of foodservice to include other than institutions both in text and in the applications and illustrations.

As with previous editions, this sixth edition is intended as a basic, comprehensive coverage of the field of foodservice management. The intention is *not* that all schools and universities will use the material in the same sequence, nor necessarily in the order presented, but that each teacher will organize it into the individual courses offered. This text can be used for several courses in foodservice systems management and includes subject matter appropriate to: Introduction to Foodservice Management; Quantity Food Production; Purchasing for Foodservices; Organization and Management of Foodservices; and Facility Design and Equipment Arrangement.

It is expected that users of this text will supplement the subject matter by more in-depth reading on specific topics. Supplementary references at the end of each chapter provide a ready source of pertinent information. However, the use of current journals and trade magazines as well as research reports, seminars, and exhibits will be required for students and teachers alike to keep up-to-date with the latest developments in this field of study. The time lag between preparation and publication of any textbook makes this an advisable practice even though the basic principles presented do not change.

We are deeply appreciative of the wide acceptance of former editions of this text. We hope that this newly revised edition will continue to meet the needs of the present generation as it has in the past.

Acknowledgments

Many people in addition to the present authors have been involved in the preparation of this, the sixth edition of *Foodservice in Institutions,* and all deserve our recognition. To the two women, Bessie B. West and LeVelle Wood, the original authors of this text and pioneers in the field of institution management, we owe a debt of gratitude. Without the success they achieved with earlier editions, this revision would not be necessary!

The continuing coauthors, Virginia Harger and Grace Shugart, were fortunate to have worked with, and learned from, West and Wood. Now we are pleased to introduce a new and younger writer, Dr. June Palacio, as a third author. Her desire to continue this book as a needed text and the enthusiasm and fresh perspectives she has brought to this revision have been invaluable, and we welcome her with heartfelt thanks.

Several colleagues have been gracious and generous with their time and input to help us bring the subject matter up-to-date. Dr. Ann Messersmith, head of the Department of Food Systems Management, College of Home Economics, Oregon State University, wrote parts of Chapter 9 on Facility Design and Layout, and assisted us in locating and making available various resource materials as well as giving encouragement to the project; Dr. Margy Woodburn, head of the Department of Foods and Nutrition, College of Home Economics, Oregon State University, whose doctoral work was in microbiology, reviewed and helped edit Chapter 8 on Sanitation and Safety; Mrs. Madelyn L. Wheeler, Coordinator of Research Dietetics, Diabetes Research and Training Center, School of Medicine, Indiana University, Indianapolis, who has been involved with computer committees for The American Dietetic Association, and Dr. Zoe Ann Holmes, Professor of Foods and Nutrition, Oregon State University and chairman of the American Home Economics Association's Electronic Technology Committee, reviewed and helped word the text in Chapter 16 on Management Information Systems; Mary Molt, administrative dietitian, Kansas State University Residence Halls, and Instructor, Department of Hotel, Restaurant, Institutional Management, and Dietetics reviewed and assisted in updating Chapter 3 on Menu Planning,

Chapter 5 on Production Planning and Control, and Chapter 6 on Quantity Food Production; Mrs. Pat Henderson, consultant dietitian, Seattle, Washington, and former regional manager of Hillhaven Nursing Homes, read and gave helpful advice and provided illustrations for Chapter 15 on Financial Management. To all of these willing assistants, we express our sincerest appreciation.

To the several colleagues chosen by the Macmillan editor to critique the manuscript, we express our gratitude for pointing out changes and additions, or giving suggestions that have helped us make the information most meaningful to students and other users of the book. James L. Matthews, Jr., a free-lance writer of Oak Park, Illinois, deserves a vote of thanks, too, for editing some of the writing in its early stages.

And to Christina Pyle, faithful typist and editorial advisor whose assistance has been beyond the "call of duty" in completing the manuscript into its final form, and to our understanding and sympathetic families and friends who have endured endless hours of our work on the revision and have given moral support and encouragement, we give our heartiest thank yous. Without all of these people, our task would have been impossible.

Virginia F. Harger

Grace Shugart

June Palacio

Co-Authors, Sixth Edition

Contents

SECTION I

Foodservice Organizations

CHAPTER 1

History and Development

Introduction

The history and development of foodservice organizations presented in this chapter is intended to give the reader a perspective of, and appreciation for, foodservices as they are today. This overview from early times to the present includes the many types of establishments that serve food to groups of people, and are those that make up the foodservice industry. The background information included should be of special interest to those who are or who are preparing to become foodservice managers or administrative dietitians. Trends that are shown provide some basis for anticipating the future and should alert the manager to the demands that new developments and changes in this field may bring and so prepare to meet them.

Information in the succeeding chapters is basic to the successful operation of all types of foodservice, whatever their philosophy and objectives. All are concerned with providing good food to meet specific needs of groups of people served outside the family home.

Early-Day History

Foodservice organizations in operation in the United States today have become an accepted way of life and we tend to regard them as relatively recent innovations. However, they have their roots in the habits and customs that characterize our civilization and date back before the Middle Ages. Certain phases of foodservice operations reached a well-organized form as early as feudal times in countries that have exerted the most influence on the development of American food habits and customs: England, France, Germany, and Sweden. In each of those countries, partaking of food was a social event in which the entire family, and often guests, shared. There was no withdrawal for eating that characterizes the customs of certain peoples, no religious beliefs barring participation from meals with others. Their economic level and type of food eaten also fostered serving food to groups. Instead of the few grains of parched wheat or corn or the bowl of rice and a bit of raw fruit that satisfied some races, these people ate meat or a variety of other protein foods from various sources. Since these foods could not be transported without danger of spoilage, immediate preparation and cookery in well-established kitchens and with good supervision were required. These countries, then, have contributed to the evolvement of institutional foodservices.

Some of the types of foodservices that existed long ago are contrasted in this chapter with their present-day counterparts. Although in medieval times religious orders, royal households, colleges, and inns were the most prevalent types of organizations in which quantity food production was the rule, other types of foodservice organizations and their development are considered also. These include clubs and other social organizations, schools, hospitals and health care facilities, employee feeding in industrial plants or offices, retirement homes and residences for other groups of people, and commercial foodservice establishments, including transportation companies. Foodservice to military personnel also constitutes a large segment of the present-day foodservice industry.

Religious Orders

Religious orders and royal households were among the earliest practitioners of quantity food production, and although these foodservices were far different from those we know today, each has made a contribution to the evolvement of institutional foodservice.

Abbeys that dotted the countryside, particularly in England, served not only the numerous brethren of the order, but also thousands of pilgrims who flocked there to worship. The space provided for food preparation indicates the scope of their foodservice operations. In one, Canterbury Abbey, a favorite site of innumerable pilgrimages, the kitchen measures 45 feet in diameter.

Records show that the food preparation carried out by the brethren reached a much higher standard than food served in the inns at that time. The vows they took did not diminish the brothers' appreciation for good food. Food grown on the abbey's grounds and lay contributions provided liberally for the institution's table. The strong sense of stewardship in the abbeys led to establishing a detailed accounting system. These records showed that a specified per capita per diem food allowance was in effect. Thus, an effective, early-day cost accounting system came into use.

Royal and Noble Households

The royal household, with its hundreds of retainers, and the households of nobles, often numbering as many as 150 to 250 persons, also necessitated an institutional-size foodservice. There was wide variance in rank and in the subsequent food allowances within these groups. In providing for the various needs, strict cost accounting was necessary, and here, perhaps, is the beginning of the present-day scientific food cost accounting. The cost record most often cited is the *Northumberland Household Book*. For this household of more than 140 persons, 10 different breakfasts were recorded, the best for the earl and his lady, the poorest for the lowest workman or scullion. A similar range is presumed for the other meals.

The kitchens in these medieval households would appall the present-day dietitian or foodservice manager by their disregard for sanitary standards in food storage, preparation, and handling. A clutter of supplies overflowing from inadequate table and shelf space to the wooden plank floors, handled by children and nosed by dogs, commonly comprised the background for the preparation of elaborate creations for the table. A notable example is shown in Fig. 1.1. Since labor was cheap and readily available, a large staff of workers was employed to prepare the food. Rank was evident in the division of labor. The head cook might wear a gold chain over handsome clothing and present his culinary creations to his employer in person. The pastry cook and the meat cook did not rate as high, but were esteemed for their contributions. The meanest scullion often had scarcely a rag to wear and received broken bread and the privilege of sleeping on the hearth through the chilly winter nights as his wage.

With the passage of time, discovery of the causes of food spoilage led to improved practices in food storage and preparation in these noble households. Advances in the understanding of the laws of physics resulted in replacing open hearths with iron stoves and refining much of the kitchen equipment. A more convenient equipment arrangement led to a reduction in the number of workers required, helping to relieve disorder and confusion. Employees' dress changed to show some regard for the tasks they performed.

The United States has no equivalent of these royal households. However, the White House, as the president's residence, is the scene of official entertainment in this country. Whereas the feasts of the royal households in the past were of "formidable proportions," observers have noted that the White

FIGURE 1.1   The kitchen, Windsor Castle at Christmas time.   *Courtesy, Arnold Shircliffe.*

House kitchen staff could prepare anything from "an egg to an ox." And although there may be little in common between the menu and food for a present-day banquet and those of centuries ago, an early day state diplomatic dinner at the White House included seven courses, each with many accompaniments. The present trend is toward simplification of menu pattern even for the more formal occasions, which is in harmony with current American food consumption habits (Fig. 1.2).

   Notable among the other early foodservices were the inns and taverns and the hostels established by European colleges. From these have evolved the foodservice in schools and colleges, hospitals and other health care facilities, retirement communities and the wide variety of commercial and industrial foodservices as we know them today.

Development of Present-day Foodservices

Colleges and Universities

Providing meals as well as rooms for college and university students has been the custom over many years. However, responsibility for the adminis-

FIGURE 1.2   White House State Dining Room set for formal service.   *Copyright ©*
*White House Historical Association. Photograph by George F. Mobley, National Geographic
Society.*

tration of these living situations and the kinds of services offered have changed
considerably during those years.

From the twelfth century through the medieval ages, hostels were set up
at European colleges and universities as the accepted arrangement for student living. On the continent, students managed these hostels. At Oxford,
England, however, hostels were endowed to provide board and lodging for
students unable to pay these costs for themselves. The university managed
these endowed hostels, at least to some degree, a policy that continues today.

Colonial colleges in the United States provided residence halls with dining
rooms for all students. Administrators, generally clergymen, were responsible for their operation. They dispatched their duties prayerfully and
thriftily—not always with student approval! Later, with a shift toward and
interest in German educational procedure, which did not include housing as
a school responsibility, some colleges lost interest in student living situations.
As a result, sororities and fraternities without faculty supervision assumed
the feeding and housing of large groups of students. In many cases this also
led to problems of providing adequate dietaries for all students.

The twentieth century has witnessed many changes in foodservices of colleges and universities in the United States. A shift occurred from the laissez faire policy of early-day administrators to a very strict one in the late nineteenth century. Until World War II, colleges provided separate dining halls for men and women, and they trained students in the "social graces" as well as satisfying their dietary needs. Seated table service with students serving in rotation as hostess/host and as waiter/waitress was in vogue in many residence hall dining rooms. And although this service may still be found in some college and universities today, it is the exception rather than the rule.

Gradually, with the influx of G.I. students into American schools of higher education during and after World War II, the more formal seated service and leisurely dining gave way to the speedy informality of cafeteria service. This service style makes it possible to meet student demands for greater menu variety and to cater to the food preferences of various ethnic groups that make up the student body. Also, with coeducational residences and dining halls now commonly found on the college campus, dietary requirements of both men and women in the same dining hall can be met by cafeteria or self-service. Student food habits have also changed as a result of today's concern for physical fitness and weight control. Foodservice managers have attempted to comply with this need through suitable menu selections.

Other trends in residence hall dining are longer hours of service, fewer restrictions on the number of servings allowed, and greater flexibility in board plans, including a "pay as you eat" plan, rather than a set rate paid in advance.

In addition to residence hall dining, a diversity of other campus foodservices is a familiar pattern today. Student union buildings have, for example, set up creative and innovative units catering to students' changing food interests and demands. Commercial fast food companies have been a major competitor for student patronage in many college towns. In some, therefore, the university has contracted with these companies to set up and operate one of their food units on campus.

Management of college and university foodservices usually is under the direction of well-qualified dietitians or foodservice managers employed directly by the university, or by a contract foodservice company. Both plans are found in colleges today.

The use of college and university dining facilities as laboratories for foodservice management classes is a common practice. This, no doubt, has helped establish high requirements for foodservice directors on such campuses. Directing the students' laboratory experiences and the work of numerous part-time student employees used in most campus foodservices presents unique situations not common in other types of foodservice organizations.

School Foodservice

The history of the school lunch is inevitably a part of the larger story of the rapid development of public education. As reforms stemming from the Industrial Revolution began to free society from the supposed necessity of child labor, unemployment among children of school age increased, and soon public concern with education became evident. To encourage school attendance, parents and civic-minded townspeople in some European countries banded together to provide low-cost school lunches. It is reported that canteens for schoolchildren were established in France in 1849 and that in 1865 Victor Hugo started school feeding in England by providing warm luncheons in his own home for children from a nearby school. At some time between these dates, school foodservice began in the United States. The Children's Aid Society of New York City opened an industrial school in 1853 in an effort to persuade the children of the slums to seek "instruction in industry and mental training," and offered food to all comers.

Growth in the knowledge of nutrition some decades later placed emphasis on the importance of wise food selection and the need for nourishing school lunches at little or no cost. Under the notable leadership of Ellen H. Richards, the Boston school committee passed an order that "only such food as was approved by them should be sold in the city schoolhouses." Fig. 1.3 shows an early day school lunchroom kitchen. About this same time, other men and women likewise concerned with child welfare sponsored similar developments in several urban centers, and the two decades that followed brought significant developments in the school lunchroom movement throughout the country. Although the program went forward most rapidly in large cities where sustaining organizations and concerned leaders were prevalent, the cause of rural children also was championed by such groups as the Extension Service and PTA councils. Improving the nutrition of school children through adequate foodservices in schools was the goal.

World Wars I and II again brought into focus the need for improved nutrition among young people since so many were rejected from military service for reasons related to faulty nutrition. Concern was expressed for the future health of the nation if such a trend continued. As a direct result, the first federal legislation designed to assist and direct school foodservices was enacted in 1933. This provided loans enabling communities to pay labor costs for preparation and service of lunches in schools. In 1935, additional assistance came when the federal government was authorized to donate surplus farm commodities to schools. With these aids, a noon meal became a common part of school activities.

The *major* legislation governing the school lunch program, however, was the National School Lunch Act of 1946 (Public Law 79-396). Through it,

FIGURE 1.3   Preparation for a school lunch in an early-day institutional kitchen in the U.S.   *Reprinted by permission of* School Food Service Journal, *The American School Food Service Association, Denver, Colorado, 1986.*

funds were appropriated "as may be necessary to safeguard the health and well-being of the nation's children, and to encourage the domestic consumption of nutritious agricultural commodities and other food by assisting the states through grants in aid and other means, in providing an adequate supply of funds and other facilities for the establishment, maintenance, operation and expansion of non-profit school lunch programs." States were required to supplement federal funding as set forth in Section 4 of the Act, and lunches served by participating schools were obligated to meet the nutritional requirements prescribed. Although the 1946 Act allowed Types A, B, and C meals, the Type A lunch is the only one now served under the federal school foodservice program and is referred to as "the school meal pattern" (see Chapter 3 for specifics).

Other legislation and amendments have changed the funding policy and circumstances for offering free or reduced price meals to students, revamped the commodity distribution plan, or provided for supplemental feeding programs. The Child Nutrition Act of 1966 authorized the School

Breakfast Program and the Special Milk Program to further help alleviate inadequate nutrition. The Omnibus Reconciliation Act of 1980 reduced the reimbursement rate to schools for the first time and changed the income eligibility standard for students who would receive free or reduced price meals. Further adjustments were made in 1981 and 1982 to help achieve reductions in federal spending. School foodservice managers work creatively to adjust to these changes while maintaining an attractive meal program to meet nutritional guidelines and appeal to students.

The rapid development of the school foodservice program since 1946 gives testimony to its importance. Data obtained in a survey,[1] the National Evaluation of School Nutrition Programs, conducted from 1979 to 1981 by the USDA's Food and Nutrition Service revealed that over 90,000 schools were participating in the program. Of all public schoolchildren in the United States, 98 per cent had daily access to the lunch program and 39 per cent to the Breakfast Program. Approximately 25 million lunches and 4 million breakfasts were served every school day. This represented enough lunches to feed 60 per cent of those attending public schools and enough breakfasts to serve 10 per cent of those students. A desired goal is to increase student participation in the program.

School foodservice is most effective when nutritionists, school authorities, food managers, and allied groups such as the PTA all recognize its value in the child's mental and physical development. Then they can work together to make the foodservice not just a "feeding program," but rather a nutrition program for all students as part of their learning experience.

The type of organization and management found in school foodservices varies as much as the size and location of schools involved. Small independent schools may have simple on-premises food preparation and service supervised by a cook/manager with one or two employees and/or part-time student helpers. Large city school systems often use a centralized production kitchen and deliver meals for service to individual schools in the system. Centralized management with unit supervisors characterizes this system. In 1984, *Restaurants and Institutions* magazine[2] reported that school foodservice ranked fourth among all types of organizations in terms of dollar expenditures. School foodservice truly is "big business" while serving the nutritional needs of children.

Clubs and Other Social Organizations

Clubs formed by people with a common interest have existed for decades. They were especially prominent among the wealthy society class in England in the 1800s. Member dues and assessments in some clubs provide funds to establish a "club house" or building that usually includes foodservice facili-

FIGURE 1.4   One of the early plans for an institutional kitchen made by Alexis Soyer for the Reform Club of London about 1850.

ties. As early as 1850, one Alexis Soyer worked closely with the Reform Club of London to provide a sanitary and efficient foodservice setup that would utilize the then fairly recent innovations of stoves, water baths, and refrigeration (see Fig. 1.4)!

Today, city clubs, athletic clubs, faculty clubs, and country clubs among others attempt to rival the settings of better hotels with a similar standard for foodservice. Few modern homes are spacious enough or adequately staffed to serve meals to 25 or more guests. Clubs do provide such facilities and cater to such functions as receptions and banquets in addition to regular meal service for their members. Sometimes the foodservice helps subsidize the cost of other services such as swimming pools or recreational rooms offered by the club. The number of meals served may be irregular and the stability of income somewhat uncertain, making club foodservice management a real challenge.

Hospitals

The evolution of foodservices in hospitals is as interesting as that of colleges and schools. The first hospital established in the United States was the Philadelphia General in 1751. Meals in early-day hospitals were simple to the point of monotony and with no attempt to provide any special foods or therapeutic diets. Menus in an eighteenth-century American hospital, for example, included mush and molasses for breakfast on Monday, Wednesday, and Friday, varied by molasses and mush for supper on Monday, Wednesday, Thursday, and Saturday. Oxtail soup and black bread appeared on occasion.[3]

Accounts of the Pennsylvania Hospital in the year 1804 stated that milk, butter, pork, and soap were produced on the hospital grounds for consumption in the hospital.[4] Also, cows, calves, and pigs were sold for income. Salary for a husband and wife serving as steward and matron was $350 for nine months of service.

Dietetics as one of the hospital services made its beginning at the time of the Crimean War (1854–1856). In 1855, Florence Nightingale, whom dietitians as well as nurses revere and honor as the pioneer of their profession, established a diet kitchen to provide clean, nourishing food for the ill and wounded soldiers in Scutari (now Uskudar) in Turkey. Until then, foods of questionable quality were poorly cooked in insanitary conditions and served at irregular intervals.

Alexis Soyer, a noted chef of the times (who, as noted earlier, had worked with the Reform Club of London), contributed greatly to Nightingale's efforts when he offered to serve gratuitously as manager of the barracks hospital kitchen. Soyer's plan for operating it was as efficient as modern-day practice.

Changes over the next 100 years in hospital foodservice included introducing centralized tray service and mechanical dishwashing, establishing a separate kitchen for special diet preparation and later eliminating such kitchens, and the advent of frozen foods and their use in food preparation. Also, pay cafeterias for staff and employees and separate dining areas for these two groups were introduced during this period. Employing qualified dietitians to administer dietary departments, and "therapeutic" dietitians for "special diet" supervision became the usual practice.

Today hospitals comprise a large group of institutions operated and funded by various governing bodies, such as federal, state, county, and city governments, by religious orders, or are privately owned. Regardless of source of support, the main objective of hospital foodservice is to improve patient health and restore patients to normal activity and state of well-being. A secondary objective for most hospitals is to provide foodservice for staff, employees, and guests in order to maintain happy, well-nourished personnel and good public relations.

The past 30 years have brought more innovations and changes for greater operating efficiency to hospital dietary departments. Separate dining rooms for professional staff and employees have given way to one dining area for all in most hospitals. Vended foods, used to supplement regular meal service, provide round-the-clock food availability. Many hospitals provide a dining room for ambulatory and wheelchair patients in recognition of the therapeutic value of mealtime social contacts with others.

Technological advances have influenced foodservice systems, with the introduction of new methods of food production, holding, distribution, and service; computer use for many routine tasks; and use of robots in some hospital foodservice.

Federal policy has influenced trends in hospital procedures and budgeting as is true with school foodservices. Medicare and Medicaid reimbursement payments for certain patients' hospital and nursing home costs constitute a major source of their income. In March 1983, Congress approved Medicare-mandated rates for reimbursement of Diagnosis Related Groups (DRGs) of illnesses and medical service for hospital inpatient services. This represents a strict set of cost controls for health care and has created financial incentives for hospitals to contain or reduce health care costs.

Assuring quality care and service has been the focal point in hospitals and health care facilities in recent years. The Joint Commission on Accreditation of Hospitals has established standards to enforce quality assurance programs for accrediting its member facilities. These are published in AMH/85 Accreditation Manual for Hospitals. One section is devoted to dietetic services to assure that these services shall meet the nutritional needs of patients. Hospital foodservice today is unique and complex requiring a well-qualified dietetic staff to coordinate activities that assure optimum nutritional care.

Nursing Homes and Other Health Care Centers

Nursing homes and other health care facilities have come into prominence only in relatively recent times so their history is short compared with that of hospitals. However, the increase in demand for nursing home care has been phenomenal in the last 50 years due to several factors, among them population growth, longer life span, increasing number of elderly persons that make up our population, urban living with condensed family housing units, increased incomes, and greater availability of health care insurance benefits.

The history of nursing homes tends to follow federal legislation enacted to help provide funds to care for individuals in such facilities. The modern nursing home era and the development of the nursing home as a distinct type of health care institution began in 1935 when federal funds to pay for nursing home care for the elderly were made available to the states by the passage of the Social Security Act.

In 1951 the Kerr-Mills bill made available federal matching funds for nursing home care to states establishing satisfactory licensing and inspection programs. An amendment to the Hill-Burton program in 1954 provided financial aid to construct facilities for skilled nursing care to meet specified requirements. Many large nursing homes were built, and older small ones were forced to close or modernize and expand in order to meet the standards of the new program.

Medicare and Medicaid legislation (1965) and amendments (1967) established minimum standards and staff requirements for, as well as inspection of, nursing homes to permit using those funds by their patients. Federal

Conditions of Participation Regulations[5] (1974) spell out in detail standards that skilled nursing facilities must meet.

General guidelines for all nursing homes include licensure, meeting standards of specific government programs to be certified by them, and one or more levels of care such as nursing care and related medical services, personal care, and residential care.

Nursing homes provide different categories of nursing care and are classified as:

Skilled Nursing Facilities. Skilled nursing facilities offer 24-hour nursing care and provide other professional services as prescribed by the physician. Emphasis is on rehabilitation, and the facility is eligible for both Medicare and Medicaid reimbursement.

Intermediate Care Facilities. Intermediate care facilities provide basic medical, nursing, and social services in addition to room and board. Patients need some assistance but not intensive care. These facilities are eligible for Medicaid program only.

Other Facilities. In contrast to skilled nursing and intermediate care facilities, which are certified under specific government programs, many nursing homes do not participate in these programs. Therefore, they are not classified as such, even though they may provide the same quality of care and categories of services. A facility may provide more than one category of care. The patients may be any age. Many facilities specialize in child care or care of the mentally ill or mentally retarded.

Food plays a major part in the lives of most nursing home patients. For many, it may be the one thing they have to look forward to each day. The quality and amount of food offered as well as the care and supervision given to foodservice are important to any nursing home's success and effectiveness. Dining rooms are provided for patients who are ambulatory and able to participate in group dining. Others are served in their own rooms. Many require assistance with eating.

The 1974 federal Conditions of Participation Regulations, mentioned previously, stated these general "conditions" related to *dietary* services:

> Condition of participation dietetic services: The skilled nursing facility provides a hygienic dietetic service that meets the daily nutritional needs of patients, ensures that special dietary needs are met, and provides palatable and attractive meals. A facility that has a contract with an outside food management company may be found to be in compliance with this condition provided the facility and/or company meets the standards listed herein.[5]

The services of qualified (registered) dietitians (RD's) are required to ensure that dietary service regulations are adequately met and administered.

Part-time or consultant dietitians may be employed by small nursing homes. Full-time RD's are needed in the larger skilled nursing homes.

Other Health Care Centers

Homes for specialized groups such as physically or mentally handicapped, orphaned, or runaway children, and abused and battered women; short-term residences for parolees, drug-abuse victims, or other groups during a rehabilitation period; and corrective institutions come under this category. These organizations usually serve low-income groups and may be supported by the state, county, private charities, or fraternal orders. Residents may or may not qualify for government assistance.

Trained foodservice supervisors are important to the success of these institutions in rehabilitating their residents to good health or for maintaining a healthy body. A well-balanced, nutritious diet that is acceptable to the group served and within the constraints of the budget should be provided.

DAY CARE CENTERS Day care centers for children of working parents, the underprivileged, and, more recently, for elderly persons who otherwise would be isolated and lonely offer an excellent opportunity for the foodservice to provide at least one nutritious meal a day in an attractive, friendly atmosphere. Facilities for special groups, such as camps for diabetics, include social and recreational activities and proper nutrition.

SENIOR CITIZEN CENTERS Many senior citizen centers employ trained supervisory personnel with leadership abilities to guide and assist volunteers who plan and carry out programs of value to the members. Primary among these is a limited meal service, usually a noon meal five days a week. In addition, a dietitian may give talks and advice on meal planning and good nutrition. Eating the noon meal together offers participants an opportunity to socialize. Often the meals served to senior citizen groups are subsidized in part by church, fraternal, or philanthropic organizations within the community. Free meals for those unable to pay is a common practice.

Meals-on-Wheels, a program for delivering meals (generally once a day for five days a week) to the homes of persons unable to go to a center or to prepare their own food, usually is funded through local charities. A large number of volunteer workers are involved in the program to help make it possible. Food for such meals may be prepared by contract with a senior citizen center, a school, a college, or a restaurant.

Health care of ill, disabled, and needy persons in the United States, whether at home or in hospitals or other health care facilities, holds unprecedented attention by legislative groups, patients, administrators, and the general public. Recent government cuts in federal spending, the somewhat depressed state of the American economy for a period of time, together with the high cost of health care have tended to slow the growth of and census in nursing homes and hospitals. Also, some of the available funds for long-term care have been diverted to home care or to newly organized, cost-containing alternate care delivery entities. Among the latter are Health Maintenance Organizations (HMO's), whose emphasis is on preventive care; immediate care centers for urgent situations; surgicenters for surgical procedures not requiring hospitalizations; birthing stations; cardiac rehabilitation centers; and similar specialized units. Foodservice is a necessary part of such facilities. These developments have occurred over a short time span and more changes are certain. This requires constant alertness on the part of all concerned to any pending or new legislation that may affect our present ways of health care.

Retirement Residences and Adult Communities

During the past few decades, many persons reaching retirement age expressed interest in an easier type of living than that required for total upkeep of their own homes. The result was the development of group living and dining facilities for retirees. These provide comfortable, congenial, independent living with minimal responsibility, and offer freedom from coping with a large house, its taxes and maintenance problems, and no, or less, food preparation.

Many types of residences or adult communities are available at various price levels. Some are high-rise apartment-style buildings; others are on the cottage plan. Either type may have individual kitchenettes, central dining facilities, or both. Fig. 9.5, Chapter 9, shows a lovely retirement home dining room. Other variations include purchase or rental units with full meal service, one meal a day, or no meals included in the monthly charge. Usually housekeeping, recreation and social activities, and medical and emergency nursing care units are provided. Access to public transport is a factor, but adequate health care is considered the most important provision.

Foodservice for this older clientele should be directed by a well-qualified dietitian or foodservice manager who is knowledgeable about their dietary needs and food preferences, and who can help contribute to the group's good health and relaxed, happy, gracious living.

Industrial and Business Foodservice (Employee Feeding)

Providing food for employees at their workplace has been necessary since early times when labor was forced, or hired, to work in fields or on the monuments of antiquity such as the pyramids and the great walls of the world. The apprentices and journeymen in the guilds and manor houses of the Middle Ages had to be fed by their owners, like the slaves of ancient Greek and Roman households.

The Industrial Revolution brought changes in social and economic systems. The plight of child laborers, in particular, resulted in legislation in England that forced managers to provide meal periods for their youthful workers.

Robert Owen, a Scottish mill owner near Glasgow in the early nineteenth century, is considered the "father of industrial catering." He so improved working conditions for his employees that his mill became a model throughout the industrial world. Among other things, it contained a large kitchen and eating room for employees and their families. Prices for meals were nominal, and so began the philosophy of subsidizing meal service for employees. In the United States in the 1800s, many employers provided free or below-cost meals to their employees, a practice that continues today.

The importance of industrial feeding was not fully realized, however, until the World War II period. A large percentage of workers in plants at that time were women, who demanded facilities for obtaining a hot meal while at work. Since new plants often were in isolated locations and since the competition for workers was keen, plant managers complied with worker demands and provided meal service facilities. Many plants have continued this service as an indispensable part of their operations, either under plant management or on a contract/concessionaire basis. Serving units within an industrial facility may include a central cafeteria, vending machines, canteens throughout the plant, and mobile carts to carry simple menu items to workers at their stations. Some also include a table-service dining room for executives and guests.

A newer segment of employee feeding, for office building workers, has mushroomed into existence since the 1970s. Enterprising contract foodservice caterers or companies have found this a ready market in larger cities. Many office workers enjoy the time-saving convenience of having meals delivered to them at their desks, eliminating the need to find an eating place during their brief meal period. This type of employee feeding appears to be increasing in popularity.

Commercial Foodservices

Historically the evolution of public eating places was stimulated by people's desire to travel, for both spiritual enrichment and commercial gain. Religious pilgrimages played an important role in establishing the inns of France and England. Merchants traveling from country to country to buy or sell their wares also created the need for places to stop for food and rest. These early inns and taverns, providing for the needs of travelers, were perhaps the forerunners of our present commercial foodservices. However, many of them were primitive and poorly organized and administered. The literature of the time describes unsanitary conditions under which food was prepared and served, monotonous menus, and poor service.

Stagecoach travel in colonial America, tedious at best, created the need for inns where travelers could rest and eat. They were much like those in England, but proprietors gave more attention to pleasing the guests. Many inns were largely family enterprises located in somewhat remote areas. The food offered was the same as for the family, plain, hearty, and ample. In urban centers during the early decades of the nineteenth century, hotels and inns presented extremely extensive and elaborate menus to attract guests to their facilities. Since revenues from these meals frequently did not cover preparation costs, the bar and lodging income was needed to make up the deficit. This type of subsidy is prevalent today in some operations.

Introducing the European hotel plan, which separated the charges for room and board, and later the a la carte food service were steps toward a rational foodservice in hotels. Through these measures, much of the waste that characterized their foodservice was abolished, opening the possibility that hotel and inn foodservice could be self-supporting. This led proprietors to establish foodservices separate and distinct from lodging facilities.

Origin of the restaurant concept, however, has been traced to the cook shops of France. They were licensed to prepare *ragouts,* or stews, to be eaten on the premises or taken to inns or homes for consumption. The shops had *ecriteurs,* or menus, posted on the wall or by the door to whet the interest of the passerby. The story goes that one Boulanger, a bouillon maker, added a meat dish with a sauce to his menu, contending that this was not a *ragout* and, therefore, did not violate the rights of the *traiteurs.* In the legal battle that followed, the French lawmakers sustained his point, and his new business was legalized as a restaurant. The word *restaurant* comes from the French verb *restaurer,* which means "to repair." It is said that the earliest restaurants had this Latin inscription over their doorway: *Venite ad me qui stomacho laoratis et ego restaurabo vos*—Come to me all whose stomachs cry out in anguish, and I shall restore you!

The cafeteria was a further step in the simplification of commercial foodservices. This style of self-service came into being during the gold rush days of 1849 when the "forty-niners" demanded speedy service. Regarded as an American innovation, its popularity extended all over the United States. Today commercial cafeterias still represent an important part of the foodservice industry.

Another innovative foodservice was the automat, first opened in Philadelphia in 1902 by Horn and Hardart. Patterned after a "waiterless" restaurant in Berlin, it combined features of a cafeteria with those of vending. Individual food items were displayed in coin-operated window cases from which customers made their selections. This "nickel-in-a-slot" eatery provided good food and high standards of sanitation for nearly fifty years, drawing customers from every walk of life. For many people, it became a haven, especially during the Great Depression years beginning with the stock market crash in 1929, the years of the automat's greatest success. After World War II, the automat's popularity declined as a more affluent society sought greater sophistication in dining. Competition with other types of foodservices became keen.

The 1960s brought the advent of the "fast food" concept when a midwestern chain of hamburger "drive ups" went public. Competition in the fast food field has brought many innovations and creative foodservice outlets throughout the United States, as well as around the world, many specializing in one particular food. This is the fastest growing segment of the industry today.

Perhaps the baby boom generation of World War II and the resulting population bulge have influenced the growth of the foodservice industry as much as any other factor in recent years. As this generation raised on "fast food" matures, it continues to seek more sophisticated fast food dining. Many foodservice trends that seem to be new at the time are in reality "one more repeat in a cyclic phenomenon, wrapped up in a new language and viewed by a new generation."[6]

The commercial foodservice industry today is defined in its broadest sense to mean all establishments where food is served, for a profit consideration, away from home. Included are the formal a la carte or table d'hote restaurants and hotel/motel dining rooms, coffee shops, tea rooms, soda fountains, department store dining rooms, specialty and ethnic restaurants, and the myriad of informal fast food outlets. Some are small and simple, catering to a "coffee and doughnut" trade; others are exclusive and charming in atmosphere and service. Many have expanded their services to include sales of "take home" products such as bakery goods, jams and jellies, sauces, and salad dressings. Every imaginable style of service is found among them: cafeteria, counter, table, drive-in, stand up.

The type of management of commercial foodservice operations ranges from the small, independent owner/manager to the complex franchises and chain operators, to executives of large corporations where mergers and acquisitions abound. Foodservice managers in today's complex commercial field must be highly motivated and knowledgeable to compete and survive.

Transportation Companies

A major segment of today's foodservice industry—titled "food on the move"—is provided by airlines, trains, and cruise ships. For all three, food and food-service make up a marketing tool used to "sell" travel on a particular line. Both airlines and railroads face the unique problem of planning foods that will "go the distance"; the logistics of food they serve is a challenge. Management must test the market to determine who the travelers are and what they want or like to eat. Keeping up with changing fads and fluctuations in food preferences is an important aspect of meal service on trains and planes.

Most cruise ships offer such a wide variety of foods, styles of service, and presentations that their passengers can find their preferences well met. Usually there is more good food available than any person can consume. Food storage and preparation facilities on these ships are adequate to make them self-sufficient for the length of the cruise or ocean voyage.

Career opportunities in foodservice management with transportation companies offer many possibilities for the future, especially for those with good business backgrounds in addition to their training in foodservice.

Summary

This brief history of the development of quantity foodservices should give readers an appreciation for the industry as it is today. The present status of foodservice is impressive. National Restaurant Association statistics[7] indicate the dramatic growth in the foodservice industry: a sales increase from $42.7 billion in 1970 to $185.8 billion in 1986! This represents nearly 5 per cent of the U.S. gross national product. Individuals in the United States today eat out an average of 3.7 times a week, and indications are that this figure is on the increase. Foodservice is the number one employer among all retail business, with some 8 million persons employed, of whom two-thirds are women and one-fourth are teenagers.

The large patronage given the commercial food enterprises greatly exceeds any casual estimate. Statistics on the number of persons in the military services, in hospitals, and in federal, state, or municipal institutions show the enormous scope of necessary foodservices. There are also the thousands of students whose nutrition the schools, colleges, and universities accept as a major responsibility. Industry, too, recognizes the importance of feeding its millions.

All citizens of the United States will have direct personal contact with foodservices in institutions at some time during their lives. By paying taxes, they support federal, state, county, and municipal institutions that serve food to their residents. All persons will probably have meals at school, some in college dining halls, and others at their workplaces. Some people will enjoy dining at their clubs; others may have meals "en route" as they travel, perhaps even on a space craft. At some time a high percentage of U.S. citizens will require the services of a hospital or nursing home; still others may choose retirement home living for later years. Whatever our involvement, we expect that the food served will be of high quality, prepared to conserve its nutritive value, and served in the best condition and manner possible.

Essentials in attaining this goal are knowledge of menu planning, food purchasing, preparation, delivery systems for service, successful personnel direction including delegation and supervision, wise planning and clear-cut organization, a good system of financial control, and efficient facility design and equipment arrangement. These are the responsibilities of the foodservice director and are discussed in the following chapters.

Notes

1. Radzikowski, Jack: Final report: The national evaluation of school nutrition programs. School Food Service Journal 38 (6):72, 1983.
2. The nation's "400" leading foodservice/lodging companies: Restaurant and Institutions annual honor roll. Restaurants and Institutions 94(13): 104 (Aug.), 1984.
3. Editorial. J. Am. Diet. Assoc. 9: 405, 1934.
4. Barber, Mary I.: History of the American Dietetic Association. Philadelphia: J. B. Lippincott, 1959, p. 12.
5. Social Security Administration: Skilled nursing facilities: Standards for certification and participation in Medicare and Medicaid programs. Federal Register 39: 2241, 1974.
6. Woodman, Julie: Twenty years of "400" translates into light years of change for foodservice. Restaurants and Institutions 94(15):98, 1984.
7. 1985–86 Foodservice Industry, National Restaurant Association Pocket Factbook. 311 First Street, NW, Washington, DC: National Restaurant Assoc.

Supplemental References

Barber, Edith: A culinary campaign. J. Am. Diet. Assoc. 11:89, 1935.
Berkman, Jerome: A decade in hospitals. Food Mgmt. 18(1): 44, 1983.
Child nutrition programs: A legislative history. School Food Service Journal 37(6):62, 1983.

Cohen, Daniel: For food both cold and hot, put your nickels in the slot. Smithsonian 16(19): 50 (Jan.), 1986.

Lane, H., and Van Hartesvelt, M.: Essentials of Hospital Administration. Reston, VA: Reston Publishing Co., 1983.

Leonard, Rodney: The next decade in foodservice. Food Mgmt. 18(1):79, 1983.

Lundberg, Donald A.: The Hotel and Restaurant Business, 4th ed. New York: Van Nostrand Reinhold Co., 1984.

Senior care comes of age. Food Mgmt. 20(8), 1985.

Smith, Terrance, and Schechter, Mitchell: Feeding on the next frontier. Food Mgmt. 19(1):54, 1984.

CHAPTER 2

Types of Foodservice Systems

Introduction

The foodservice industry is complex, fast-growing, and ever changing. Many factors affect its growth and status, including socioeconomic conditions, demographic shifts, and changing food habits and desires of the American people. Being alert to these changes will help foodservice managers adapt their operations to meet the demands of the times. This background information, together with a classification of the many types of foodservice markets, is provided in this chapter.

The systems approach to management is introduced. This concept is based on the idea that complex organizations are made up of interdependent parts (subsystems) that interact in ways to achieve common goals. Application of the systems concept is made to foodservice organizations.

Managers face decisions about how to organize foodservice departments for the efficient procurement and production of their food and meals. Many options are available based on the form of food purchased, where the food is prepared in relation to where served, the time span between preparation and service, and the amount and kind of personnel and equipment required.

Foodservices with like characteristics are grouped together as a particular type of system. Each of four types of foodservice systems found in the United States today is described with its identifying features, advantages, disadvantages, and typical foodservice organizations that use each system. This description should provide a basis for managers to decide on the system suitable for a particular situation.

Scope and Status of Foodservices

Foodservice in the United States today is a complex and fast-changing industry and one that has expanded rapidly in the last half century. It ranks as the number one retail employer with more than 8,000,000 workers. A conservative estimate is that one of every four meals consumed is planned, prepared, and served outside the home in the variety of establishments described in Chapter 1. Today there are approximately 561,000 foodservice units in the United States. Foodservice received 40 per cent of all consumers' expenditures for food, and those sales equaled nearly 5 per cent of the 1985 U.S. gross national product, or some $185.8 billion.

Factors Affecting Growth

The growth in patronage of foodservices may be attributed in part to socioeconomic trends and other demographic changes of the times. The *changing status of women* has had an influence on the work force. In 1970 approximately 43 per cent of women over 16 years of age were working, and in 1982, 53 per cent of women in that age group were in the work force. Two-thirds of the industry's employees in 1984 were women.[1] This indicates a dual income for many families and may contribute toward making an affluent society. More people can afford to dine out; more women are lunchtime customers.

Another factor influencing the foodservice industry is the increasing number of *single-person households* and the potential for people living alone to eat out. They tend to spend a larger portion of their food budget on meals away from home than do family groups. Also, the population growth in the United States seems to be slowing. If this trend continues there will be fewer young people and an increasing number of older persons in our society. The *average age of the U.S. population,* now nearly 31 years, will continue to go up as the number of babies born remains low and the life span of adults continues to lengthen. These facts seem to indicate a need for more retirement and health care facilities, an older target market for restaurants, and a change in the age groups in the labor market. Recent *changes in the American workplace* also have had far-reaching effects on the foodservice market. With the shift toward a high technology and computer industry, there are more office-bound jobs and white collar workers. Inplant feeding is down and contract foodservice in business offices is increasing. The shortened work week of recent years has added leisure time and promoted the recreational foodservice segment of the industry.

The awakened *interest in the health and well-being* of people and a concern to improve the nutritional status of individuals has also had an impact on foodservice. Events such as the 1984 summer Olympics in Los Angeles helped highlight the importance of good physical fitness. One result has been a change to lighter food items on the menu selections in most types of food-services, from schools and colleges to airline and commercial operations.

All of these and more have helped shape the foodservice industry into what it is today. Managers must be ever alert to societal trends and must have the ability to adjust their operations to the changing situation in order to be competitive and successful in this market.

Classification of Foodservices

The foodservice industry is broad in scope and encompasses a wide range of establishments. *Restaurant Business*[2] classifies them into three major groups:

- Commercial/Contract
- Institutional/Internal
- Military (continental U.S. only)

Further, these three are described according to their various market segments.

MAJOR SEGMENTS OF THE FOODSERVICE MARKET

EATING AND DRINKING PLACES

- Full menu restaurants and lunchrooms
- Limited menu restaurants
- Public cafeterias
- Social caterers
- Ice cream, frozen yogurt, and custard stands, etc.
- Bars and taverns

HOTEL AND MOTEL DINING ROOMS
THE RETAIL MARKET

- Department stores
- Variety and general stores
- Drugstores, supermarket dining

- Convenience food stores
- Other specialized retail stores (take-outs and gourmet foods as in shopping malls and kiosks)

BUSINESS/INDUSTRIAL MARKET (EMPLOYEE FEEDING)

- Contract foodservices in plants
- Contract foodservices in business offices
- Internal (company operated) foodservice—plants and business
- Waterborne employee foodservice
- Mobile-on-street catering
- Food vending machines
- U.S. defense personnel (military foodservices)
- Meals furnished for food service employees

TRANSPORTATION MARKET

- In-transit air and rail
- Terminal facilities
- Passenger and cargo ships
- Interstate highway foodservices

HEALTH CARE MARKET (INTERNAL AND CONTRACT)

- Hospitals
- Nursing homes
- Specialized care homes (retirement homes, orphanages, etc.)

STUDENT MARKET (INTERNAL AND CONTRACT)

- Schools—public and parochial, elementary and secondary
- Colleges and universities

LEISURE MARKET

- Theme parks, arenas, stadiums, tracks and museums
- Drive-in movie theaters
- Bowling lanes
- Summer camps and hunting facilities

Each of the establishments within this classification has its own objectives and goals and types of organization and management. And although they may seem widely divergent, each is concerned with providing a foodservice to some segment of the public. There is a commonality among them that can be identified for grouping into specific types of foodservice systems.

Foodservice Systems

The Systems Concept and Approach

Before discussing foodservice organizations as "systems," this section briefly reviews the systems *concept* and systems *approach* and how they have evolved from other theories of organization and management. This review will establish a common basis of understanding and make application of the systems concept to foodservice an easy transition.

The word *systems* is used freely and in many different contexts. We read and speak of the solar system, defense system, transportation system, school system, and even the human body as a system. A system has been defined in many ways and with so many different words that it may seem confusing. However, this commonality is found among systems: a system is a set of interdependent parts that work together to achieve a common goal. Coleman[3] states it most succinctly: "A system is a set of interrelated parts with a purpose." The interrelated parts are known as subsystems, each dependent on the others for achieving its goals. For example, a train cannot achieve its goal of transporting passengers from one destination to another if the wheels are off the track even though all parts of the train are in good working order. All elements must be coordinated to function together for success.

Organizations are systems. This concept has evolved gradually from earlier theories of organization and management. Traditional views in prominence in the late nineteenth and early twentieth centuries included the Scientific Management theory, which put emphasis on efficient work performance. Workers were trained to perform a task in what was perceived to be the *one* best way. If all performed efficiently, the goals could be reached. Another theory was the Bureaucratic or authoritarian view, with boss-directed activities considered the only way to reach the goals.

Modifications of these views came about gradually, and by the mid-1960s the Management Science theories of exact mathematical methods and computer-assisted management were viewed as the preferred method for achieving goals. At the same time, behavioral scientists were raising concerns about the psychological, sociological, and cultural aspects of the work environment and the interactions of people in the work group. Emphasis was then given to human behavior and needs of people in organizational management.

Each of these theories contributed toward the development of the systems concept as it is today, that is, viewing the organization as an entity composed or made up of interdependent parts, the subsystems. Each subsystem contributes to the whole and receives something from the whole while working to achieve common goals. Management's role is considered a "systematic endeavor," one that recognizes the needs of all of the parts, and decisions are made in light of the overall effect on the organization as a whole and its objectives. This type of leadership is the systems approach, that is, an acceptance of the systems theory of management and the use of it as a style of managing. Johnson, Kast, and Rosenzweig[4] identify these three areas of common usage of systems approach as:

- Systems philosophy, which is described as a way of thinking about phenomena in terms of wholes—including parts, components, or subsystems and with emphasis on their interrelationships
- Subsystems analysis, as a method for problem solving or decision making
- Systems management, as the application of the systems theory to managing organizational systems or subsystems.

Luchsinger and Dock[5] say that the word *systems* has five fundamental implications that should be understood and accepted. They are:

- A system must be designed to accomplish an objective.
- The elements (subsystems) of a system must have an established arrangement.
- Interrelationships must exist among the individual elements of a system, and these interrelationships must be synergistic in nature.
- The basic ingredients of a process (the flows of information, energy, and materials) are more vital than the basic elements of a system.
- Organization objectives are more important than the objectives of its elements, and thus there is a de-emphasis of the parochial objectives of the elements of the system.

Organizations perceived as systems are made up of a variety of subsystems. Burch, Strater, and Grudnitski[6] have grouped these into three major subsystems found in all organizations:

- Operations subsystems—the activities and people who perform primary functions
- Management subsystems—all people and all activities that plan, control, and make decisions
- Information subsystems—the collection of people, machines, ideas, and activities that gather and process data to provide formal information needed

These subsystems operate within the environment of the organization and with supporting resources: money, materials, time, equipment, utilities, fa-

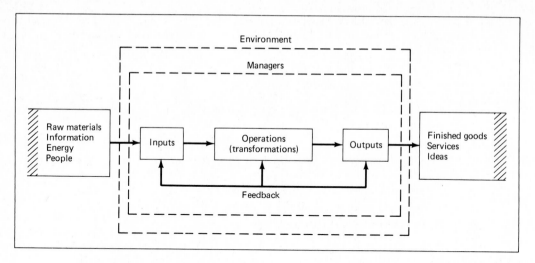

FIGURE 2.1   The organization as a system.   *Reprinted by permission from* Management, *Second Edition, by Edgar Huse; copyright 1982 by West Publishing Company, St. Paul, Missouri. All rights reserved, p. 60.*

cilities, and personnel. These together with information necessary are the *inputs* into the system. The work that is performed, known as *operations*, transforms the raw material into the finished product or services. These are the *outputs*. The outputs provide the information on how the operations worked or failed, or how they should be changed or modified. This information is known as *feedback* and provides management with data as bases for decision making.

Various diagrams may be used to illustrate an organization as a system with its inputs, subsystems performing the operations, and the outputs, together with their interactions with the environment. One that is clear, simple, and easily adaptable to specific organizations is given by Huse[7] in Fig. 2.1.

Adapting this diagram to a foodservice organization, the raw materials are, of course, the food and supplies; the operations are procurement, food preparation, delivery and service, and "clean up." Outputs are the meals or food served, and consumer, employee, and management satisfaction in relation to objectives desired. Ideas generated from results of operations are the feedback to managers for use in improving the process as necessary. The functions of subsystems of foodservice systems are diagrammed and shown in Fig. 2.2.

Of the three major subsystems—operations, management, and informa-

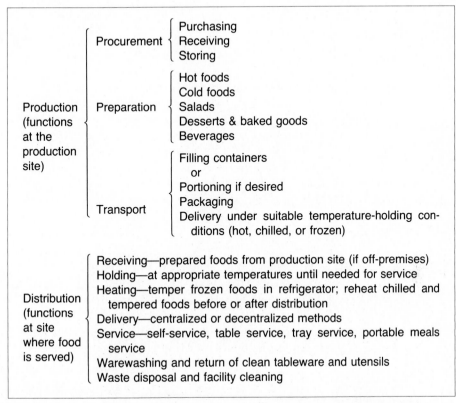

FIGURE 2.2   Function of foodservice subsystems.   *Adapted from Livingston and Chang (11) with permission from Gay Livingston. Reprinted from* Food Technology, *Vol. 20:76, 1966. Copyright © by Institute of Food Technologists; used by permission.*

tion—named by Burch, Strater, and Grudnitski, only the organization of operations is considered in this chapter. Specific operations in the foodservice system, procurement, food preparation, delivery and service, and clean up are discussed in Chapters 4, 6, 7, and 8 in Sections II and III. Management and Information subsystems are discussed in Section IV.

Types of Foodservice Systems

Those foodservices that operate in a like manner or with common elements give the basis for grouping them into specific types of systems. One group of researchers defines a foodservice system as:

The facility where large quantities of food intended for individual service and consumption are routinely provided, completely prepared. The term includes any such place regardless of whether consumption is on or off premises and regardless of whether or not there is a charge for the food.[8]

Although it is not specifically stated in this definition, it is implied that activity or operations must occur to "provide" large quantities of food.

According to this definition, four major types of foodservice systems appear to be in operation in the United States today. The systems differ in **where** the food is **prepared** in relation to where it is served, the **time span** between preparation and service, the **forms of foods** purchased, **methods of holding** prepared foods, and the amount and kind of **labor and equipment required.** These four types of foodservice systems are: conventional, commissary (central production kitchen), ready prepared (cook/chill or cook/freeze), and assembly/serve.

CONVENTIONAL   As the name implies, the conventional system traditionally has been used throughout the years. Menu items are prepared in a kitchen on the premises where the meals are served and are held a short time, either hot or cold, until serving time. In earlier years, all preparation as well as cookery took place on the premises and foods were prepared from basic ingredients. Kitchens included a butcher shop, a bakery, and vegetable preparation units.

Over the years a modified conventional system has evolved because of labor shortages and high labor costs and the technological developments in the form of foods available. In order to reduce time and labor costs, foodservice managers began to purchase some foods with "built-in" labor. Butcher shops where meats were cut from prime cuts and bake shops are gone from most "conventional" kitchens today. Meats are purchased ready-to-cook or portion-ready; bread and many bakery items are purchased from a commercial bakery or prepared from mixes; and produce is available in prepeeled, frozen, or canned forms, all of which reduce the amount of production and labor required on premises. Foods with varying degrees of processing are now used in conventional foodservice systems.

This system is most effective in situations and locales where the labor supply is adequate and of relatively low cost, where sources of food supplies, especially raw foods, are readily available, and when adequate space is allocated for foodservice equipment and activities.

Advantages. The conventional system has many advantages. Quality control is considered of primary importance. Through the menus, recipes, and quality of ingredients selected by the manager, the foodservice achieves its individuality and standard of quality desired. It is not dependent on the availability and variety of frozen entrees and other menu items commercially prepared. This system is more adaptable to regional, ethnic, and individual preferences of its customers than is possible with other systems. From an economic standpoint, greater flexibility is possible in making menu changes to take advantage of good market buys and seasonal fluctuations. Also, less freezer storage space is required than with the other systems and distribution costs are minimal, both of which save on energy use and costs.

Disadvantages. The conventional system produces an uneven, somewhat stressful workday caused by meal period demands. Because the menu differs each day, the workloads vary, making it difficult for workers to achieve high productivity. Skilled workers may be assigned tasks that could be done by nonskilled employees just to fill their time between meal periods. When three meals a day are served, two shifts of employees are required to cover the 12–15 hour or more workday. Scheduling workers may be difficult with overlapping shifts.

Typical users of the conventional system are smaller foodservice operations such as independent restaurants, schools, colleges, hospital and health care facilities, homes for specialized groups, and inplant employee feeding.

COMMISSARY (CENTRAL PRODUCTION KITCHEN)   The commissary foodservice system is described as a large, central production kitchen with centralized food purchasing, and delivery of prepared foods to service (satellite) units located in separate, remote areas for final preparation and service. This system came about with development of large, sophisticated equipment for preparing and cooking large quantities of food from the raw, unprocessed state that performs specialized processes such as making sandwiches, or cooking and turning pancakes. Most food items are completely processed from that raw state in the central kitchen. Foodservice organizations with many serving units, sometimes widely separated as in a large city school system, sought ways to consolidate operations and reduce costs. The commissary system is the result.

> Economies of large scale purchasing and production realized from utilizing one central facility often justify procurement of expensive, multi-function foodservice equipment which has been developed and may be automated for preparation of foods from the unprocessed state. Consequently, food may be procured before processing expenditures within the food industry have occurred.[9]

Prepared food may be stored frozen, chilled, or hot-held. Menu items may be distributed in any one of several forms: bulk hot, bulk cold, or frozen for reheating and portioning at the satellite serving units; or proportioned and plated for service and chilled or frozen before delivery.

Advantages. The commissary foodservice system can realize cost savings due to large volume purchasing and reduced duplication of labor and equipment that would be required if each serving unit prepared its own food. Some facilities where food is served may not have adequate space for a production kitchen, or the space can be better utilized for some other purpose. Quality control may be more effective and consistent with only one unit to supervise than with many.

Disadvantages. Food safety and distribution of prepared foods may be concerns. There are many critical points in mass food production where contamination could occur. Employment of a food microbiologist or someone knowledgeable about safe techniques in mass food handling with specialized equipment is highly desirable yet may be costly.

Food must be loaded and transported in such a manner that it maintains correct temperature for safety and is of good quality and appearance when received for service. This requires specialized equipment and trucks for delivery. Poor weather conditions, delivery truck breakdowns, or other such catastrophes may result in food arriving late, causing irritating delays in meal service.

Another disadvantage is the high cost of purchase, maintenance, and repair of the sophisticated and specialized equipment needed for this type of production and distribution.

Typical users of this system are airline caterers, large city school systems, franchised or chain restaurant organizations that provide food for their various outlets, and vending companies.

READY-PREPARED (COOK/CHILL OR COOK/FREEZE) In the ready-prepared system, foods are prepared on premises, then chilled or frozen and stored for use at some later time. Thus, foods are "ready," prepared well in advance of the time needed. This is the distinct feature of ready-prepared foodservice systems—the separation between time of preparation and service—and also that the food is not for immediate use as in the conventional system. Foods *are* prepared on premises, however, unlike the commissary system, where there is separation between place of preparation and of service.

After preparation, the food may be handled in one of two ways, giving variation to this system. The names *cook/chill* and *cook/freeze* imply this variation. In the cook/chill method, prepared foods are quickly chilled and either preplated for service or put into bulk containers for later portioning. In either form, the food is held in refrigerated storage for a day or two until time for use.

In the cook/freeze method, a blast freezer or cryogenic freezing system must be available to freeze foods quickly and so prevent cell damage. Foods for freezing may be preplated, but more often they are stored in bulk, which requires less freezer storage space.

It should be noted that the ready-prepared system entrees and vegetables undergo two heating periods, first, when foods are prepared, and second, after storage to reheat them for service to the consumer. Ready-prepared systems were developed to offset the critical shortage and high cost of skilled foodservice employees. Also, it was seen as a way of evening out the workload from day-to-day and within each day because only a large quantity of certain menu items are prepared on any given day to build up an inventory for future use.

Advantages. Ready-prepared system advantages are related to reducing the "peaks and valleys" of workloads that may be found in the conventional system. Production scheduling to build up the menu item inventory can be on a 40-hour week, 8-hour day, without early morning and late evening shifts. Many employees are freed from work on weekends and holidays.

Other advantages are reductions in labor costs; fewer highly skilled employees are needed and with the more even workday, the workers become more efficient and productive. There can be more balanced use of equipment when preparation is spread over eight hours, rather than at mealtime only.

Management has close control over menu selections, the quality of ingredients, and quantity and portion size. This is not always true in other systems, especially with the assembly/serve system. Menu variety is potentially greater with this system, as many items may be prepared and stored for future use.

One advantage of the ready-prepared system over the commissary system is the lack of worry over delivery from the central production kitchen. When foods are prepared and stored on premises, menu items are available on call and no waiting is involved.

Disadvantages. There is need for large cold storage and/or freezer units, which take space and add to energy costs. If the cook/freeze method is used, a blast freezer is required and is expensive to purchase and operate. Control for food safety is especially essential with the cook/freeze method. Longree[10] warns that "the production of precooked frozen foods must not ever be handled in a haphazard fashion; unless the freezing operation can be a continuous, streamlined, bacteriologically controlled, short-time process, the bacteriological hazards could be formidable." (See Chapters 4 and 8 for more information on food safety.)

Because frozen foods are prone to structural and textural changes, extensive modifications in the recipe and ingredients usually are necessary to offset cell damage and to assure high quality products.

Appropriate and adequate equipment for rethermalizing foods prior to service is essential and may be costly. Microwave and/or convection ovens are the equipment usually used in service units located near the consumers.

The ready-prepared system has been used primarily in hospitals and also in restaurant chains, schools, and colleges.

ASSEMBLY/SERVE   The assembly/serve system has no on-premises food production. Fully prepared foods are purchased and require only storage, final assembling, heating, and serving. Assembly/serve systems evolved with the advances in food technology that led to development of high quality frozen entrees and other food products, and the wide variety of such items that have appeared on the market in recent years. Also, foodservice managers confronted with high labor costs and few skilled employees available for food production turned to this system to relieve the labor situation. Often with this system, "single use" disposable tableware is used, thus eliminating the need for a dishwashing unit.

Advantages. A minimal investment is required for equipment. Operating costs for gas, electricity, and water are lower than for the other three systems. Portion control is absolute, and little, if any, waste occurs.

Disadvantages. There is limited availability in some markets of a good selection of desired menu items or those that have regional appeal. However, more and better quality frozen entrees are becoming available. The higher cost of these prepared foods may not be offset by the labor savings realized. Dietitians and food managers must carefully weigh the overall cost effect of this system.

Another disadvantage may be the quality of available prepared products and customer acceptability. The proportion of protein food (meat, fish, seafood, etc.) to sauce or gravy in some menu items may not be adequate to meet nutritional requirements of the clientele. For example, two ounces of protein is required in Type A meals in the school foodservice program. Many frozen entrees may contain much less than that. Evaluation of products under consideration for use in the assembly/serve system is essential.

A manager considering a change from another system to the assembly/serve should carefully evaluate the change in amount and kind of equipment needed. It may be excessively high in cost and in energy used to operate the duplicate pieces of heating equipment. Additional freezer space required for storage of the inventory of frozen entrees may not be available or may be too costly to install. Disposal of the large quantities of packaging materials and single-use tableware, if used, must be part of the total concern.

The primary users of this system are hospitals. Some health/care institutions and restaurants have been reported to use it also. Although foodservices of all classifications may use some prepared entree items, few have adopted them exclusively. Hotels employing unionized chefs may be prohibited from using frozen entrees.

Each type of foodservice system has proved successful in providing acceptable quality food in specific organizations with the conditions described for each. However, foodservice managers attempting to decide on one system over another should undertake an extensive investigation and study before making any decision. Among the factors to consider are cost comparisons, availability of foods in all forms, quality, and nutritional value of fully prepared items, customer needs and acceptability, equipment and space requirements, energy use as estimated by the amount and kinds of equipment needed for each system, and availability and cost of labor. Livingston and Chang[11] present a detailed discussion of cost factors involved in foodservice systems that may be helpful to those seeking such information.

A summary of the major characteristics of each system is given in Fig. 2.3. A flow chart of the processes, step by step, for the four foodservice systems is shown in Fig. 2.4.

Summary

Today's foodservice managers should view their organization as a system made up of various elements or subsystems that are united by a common goal and are interdependent and interact so that the processes or functions involved will produce outcomes to meet stated objectives.

An overall definition of foodservice systems as well stated by Livingston and Chang: "A food service system is an integrated program in which the procurement, storage, preparation and service of foods and beverages, and the equipment, methods (and personnel) required to accomplish these objectives are fully coordinated for minimum labor, optimum customer satisfaction, quality, and cost control."

The arrangement of subsystems, procurement, food preparation, delivery and service, and sanitation into varying ways is the basis for grouping foodservices into types of systems, each with common elements and procedures. Four major types of foodservice systems found in the United States are conventional, commissary, ready-prepared, and assembly/serve. An evaluation of the merits of each system based on its characteristics, advantages, and disadvantages should be made before any one is adopted for use in a specific foodservice organization. The North Central Regional research group[8] has stated the rationale for each of the four systems, which should be helpful in this decision making:

Summary

	Conventional	Commissary	Ready Prepared Cook/Chill	Ready Prepared Cook/Freeze	Assembly/Serve
Location of Food Preparation Kitchen in Relation to Where Served:	On premises where food is served	Central production kitchen in building separate from service units. Food transported to satellite serving units.	On premises where food is served		Off premises (Commercially prepared foods are purchased)
Form of Food Purchased:	Raw; some convenience foods	Primarily raw ingredients	Raw; some convenience foods		All convenience and pre-pared foods-frozen, canned dehydrated, or prepeeled fresh
Food Procurement:	Purchase for its own unit	Centralized purchasing for all service units	Purchase for its own unit		Purchase for own use
Time span between preparation and service, and method of holding:	Food prepared for immediate service (may be held hot, or chilled for a few hours)	Food prepared and may be: a) distributed to satellite units for immediate service b) chilled and either pre-plated or put into bulk c) chilled and frozen and stored for later use either pre-plated or in bulk	Food prepared & cooked then chilled and held for 1–3 days. Portioned cold and distributed for reheating in units close	Food prepared and fast frozen; held for later use later use up to 3–4 months	No on-premises preparation. Foods purchased pre-prepared are stored and ready for reheating and service at any time needed
Amount and kind of equipment required:	All pre-preparation cooking and serving equipment needed. Both	Large, sophisticated equipment for pre-preparation and cooking. Some robots may be	All pre-preparation and cooking and serving equipment.		Equipment for reheating as steamers, st. jacketed kettles, convection or microwave

skilled and un-skilled employees needed	used—can be repro-grammed for various tasks. Suitable contain-ers for packaging and delivery; trucks to deliver prepared foods to ser-vice units; reheating equipment if foods fro-zen or chilled	Large amounts of refrigerated storage space.	A "blast" or cryogenic freezer—large amounts of freezer hold-ing space.	ovens. Equipment for setting up and serving Reheating equipment as convection or mi-crowave ovens and kettles for immersion heating
Labor Needs:	Skilled cooks and preparation work-ers as well as less skilled for pre-para-tion and serving	Highly trained in techno-logical aspects of food production in mass quantities. Food micro-biologists to assure food safety. Employees must be able to operate highly specialized equipment used for food production	Fewer highly skilled cooks needed compared with con-ventional because of "produc-tion line" type of work and only one or two items prepared per day; workers needed to reheat foods, operate that equipment, and to assemble & serve meals	No skilled cooks nor other pre-preparation employees needed. Workers for assem-bling salads, and des-serts, etc. Workers for reheating and serving foods must be able to operate equipment.
Typical Foodservices Using This:	Independent res-taurants and cafe-terias; hospitals and health care fa-cilities; homes for specialized groups; in-plant foodser-vices; colleges and universities; schools	Airlines; chain restau-rants; large school dis-tricts; commercial cater-ers and vending companies	Large hospitals, some large colleges and universities	Hospitals and nursing homes. Some com-mercial foodservices and colleges

FIGURE 2.3. Summary: Characteristics of four types of foodservice systems.

Conventional	Commissary	Ready-Prepared	Assembly/Serve
Purchase raw basic foods and limited convenience items	Purchase raw basic foods for all units	Purchase raw basic foods and limited convenience items	Purchase fully prepared foods in frozen, canned, dehydrated form; salad ingredients pre-prepared
Receive goods			
Store foods: Refrigerator at 40° or lower Drystores 65–70° F.			Store in freezer, 0° F. or refrigerator 40°F or lower until serving time.
Prepreparation: washing, sorting peeling, cutting, etc.			(none required)
Preparation and cooking: small to large batch & short order	Large batch cookery	Large batch cookery	(none required)

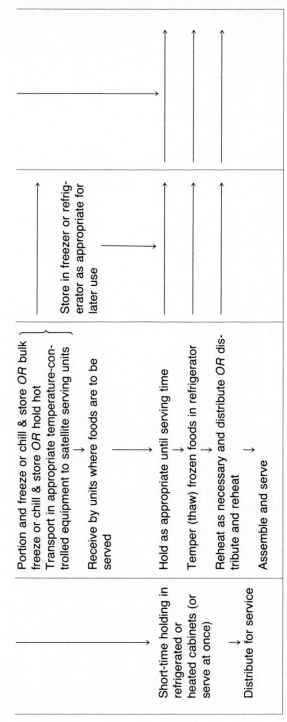

Store in freezer or refrigerator as appropriate for later use

Portion and freeze or chill & store *OR* bulk freeze or chill & store *OR* hold hot

Transport in appropriate temperature-controlled equipment to satellite serving units

Receive by units where foods are to be served

Hold as appropriate until serving time

Temper (thaw) frozen foods in refrigerator

Reheat as necessary and distribute *OR* distribute and reheat

Assemble and serve

Short-time holding in refrigerated or heated cabinets (or serve at once)

Distribute for service

FIGURE 2.4 Flowchart: processes, step-by-step, of the four foodservice systems.

Rationale for Conventional Foodservice Systems. Traditionally, effective foodservice administrators with conventional foodservice systems have utilized a skilled labor force for food production 13–14 hours per day. Given adequate food production equipment and available skilled labor, foods may be procured with limited amounts of processing. However, with constantly rising labor costs within the foodservice industry, the current trend in conventional foodservice systems is to procure more extensively processed foods.

Rationale for Commissary Foodservice Systems. The commissary foodservice principles have been adopted in systems where service areas are remote from, yet accessible to, the production center. This concept can be applied to reduce the duplication of production labor and equipment which occurs if production centers are located at each foodservice site. Space requirements at the service sites are minimized because limited production equipment is required. By centralizing food procurement and production, the economies of volume purchasing may be realized. Commissary foodservice concepts are employed to meet various operational objectives related to effect use of resources.

Rationale for Ready-Prepared Foodservice Systems. Mass producing and freezing food may reduce labor expenditures by more effective use of labor in selected situations. Peak demands for labor may be removed because production is designed to meet future rather than daily needs. Furthermore, fewer skilled employees can be trained to heat and serve menu items, thus reducing the number of highly skilled workers required by the system. Food procurement in volume may decrease food costs for the system. A foodservice system based on ready-prepared products is contraindicated if additional expenditures for storage facilities, equipment, and food inventory cannot be absorbed by the organization.

Rationale for Assembly/Serve Foodservice Systems. Assuming a lack of skilled food production employees, and an available supply of highly processed, quality food products, an assembly/serve foodservice operation may achieve operational objectives to provide client satisfaction. Managerial decisions to adopt this form of foodservice system should consider the availability of these resources to the foodservice operation.

Recent research studies on foodservice systems in relation to time and temperature effects on food quality have been summarized and reported in another North Central Research bulletin.[12] These microbiological safety, nutrient retention, and sensory quality studies provide specific data useful to persons deciding on a system to install or to those contemplating a change in systems. Further investigations are needed to advance understanding of the interrelationships among food products, resources, processes, and management in foodservices and so improve food quality in foodservice establishments.

The vast and ever-changing foodservice industry continues to be shaped by socioeconomic changes, demographic shifts, and the changing food habits and desires of the American people. Foodservice managers must keep abreast of these conditions and adapt their operations to the changing times in order to be competitive and successful.

Notes

1. 1984 Foodservice Industry Pocket Factbook. Washington, DC: National Restaurant Assoc.
2. 17th Annual Restaurant Growth Index. Restaurant Business 83(14):120–153, 1984.
3. Coleman, R. J. and Riley, J. J.: MIS: Management Dimensions. San Francisco: Holden-Day, Inc., 1973, p. 3.
4. Johnson, R. A., Kast, F. E., and Rosenzweig, J. E.: Theory and Management of Systems, 3rd ed. New York: McGraw-Hill Book Co., 1973, p. 19.
5. Luchsinger, V. P. and Dock, V. T.: The Systems Approach. Dubuque: Kendall/Hunt Publishing Co., 1976, p. 1.
6. Burch, J. G., Strater, F. R., and Grudnitski, G.: Information Systems: Theory and Practice, 3rd ed. New York: John Wiley and Sons, 1983, p. 10.
7. Huse, E. F.: Management, 2nd ed. St. Paul: West Publishing Co., 1982, p. 60.
8. Foodservice Systems: Product Flow and Microbial Quality and Safety of Foods. North Central Regional Research Publication No. 245. Columbia: University of Missouri Agriculture Experiment Station Research Bulletin 1018, 1977, pp. 11, 12, 15, 17.
9. Ibid., p. 10.
10. Longree, K.: Quantity Food Sanitation, 3rd ed. New York: John Wiley and Sons, 1980, p. 346.
11. Livingston, G. E. and Chang, C. M., eds.: Food Service Systems: Analysis, Design and Implementation. New York: Academic Press, 1979, p. 3.
12. Foodservice Systems: Time and Temperature Effects on Food Quality. North Central Regional Research Publication No. 293. Illinois Bulletin 779. Urbana-Champaign: University of Illinois Agricultural Experiment Station, 1984.

Supplementary References

Axler, B.: Food Service: A Managerial Approach. Indianapolis: D. C. Heath and Co., 1979.

Cook it here, serve it there: Control kitchens grow more attractive as USDA bows out. Restaurants and Institutions 95(4):147, 1985.

Palmer, J. D.: Logic and logistics of commissaries. Cornell HRA Quarterly 25(1):104, 1984.

Spears, M. and Vaden, A.: Foodservice Organizations: A Managerial and Systems Approach. New York: John Wiley and Sons, 1985.

Quantity Food Production and Service

CHAPTER 3

Menu Planning

Introduction

The production and service of food begins with the menu, which is a detailed list of foods to be served at a meal or, in a broader sense, a total list of items offered by a foodservice. The term *menu* also applies to the printed list given to the patron.

The menu, as an essential control in the foodservice system, determines the foods to be purchased, the personnel and equipment needed for production and service, and their work schedules. It is closely tied to financial management and marketing and, in a new foodservice, influences the design of the kitchen and selection of equipment. Ultimately, the menu determines to a large extent customer satisfaction and thus the success of the foodservice.

In this chapter the factors involved in planning foods that will appeal to the clientele and meet the goals of the foodservice are discussed. Identifying the clientele is one of the first steps. The nutritional requirements, cultural and economic backgrounds, food habits, and preferences of the clientele, as well as the philosophy and objectives of the organization, are considered.

Production and service constraints in menu planning are also discussed in this chapter. In addition, the various types of menus are identified and a step-by-step planning procedure is outlined.

Factors Affecting Menu Planning

The major goal of most foodservices is to serve food that is acceptable to its clientele. It is important to be familiar with the target market—who the consumers are, their identifying characteristics, and their food preferences. They

47

may be located in a variety of settings, such as schools, hospitals, or restaurants; and the menus for each type of organization and its patrons will be different.

Certain management factors must be considered also, and in many cases a compromise must be made between what a foodservice would like to offer and what it is capable of producing and serving. A discussion of the various factors affecting menu planning follows.

The Target Market

A profile of the clientele for which menus are being planned would include age, sex, state of health and activity, cultural and economic environment, and nutritional requirements and food habits and preferences.

NUTRITIONAL REQUIREMENTS Meeting the nutritional requirements of individuals in the group to be served is important in meal planning, especially in foodservices that are responsible for providing the total daily nutritive requirements. These menus should fulfill the latest recommended dietary allowances (RDA) defined by the National Research Council, which specify nutrient needs for various age groups by sex. Schools participating in the National School Lunch Program are required to meet certain nutrition requirements, as are many hospitals and government-sponsored nutrition programs.

The general public is becoming more health conscious and more interested in nutrition than in the past. In response to this changing attitude, restaurants and other foodservices are featuring foods that enable patrons to follow their established eating patterns. Many people are observing the dietary guidelines issued by the U.S. Department of Agriculture (USDA) and the U.S. Department of Health and Human Services: (1) eat a variety of foods, (2) maintain desirable weight, (3) avoid too much fat, saturated fat, and cholesterol, (4) eat foods with adequate starch and fiber, (5) avoid too much sugar, (6) avoid too much sodium, and (7) if you drink alcoholic beverages, do so in moderation. Many foodservices are offering selections that will permit patrons to follow these recommendations and are providing and publicizing light foods, low sodium foods, salad bars, low-fat dairy products, and other items directed to the health-oriented patron.

FOOD HABITS AND PREFERENCES The clientele of a foodservice generally is composed of individuals from different cultural, ethnic, and economic backgrounds, most of whom have definite food likes and dislikes. The menu planner must keep this in mind when selecting foods that will satisfy this diverse group.

Food habits are based on many influences, the most direct being the attitude of the parents in the home about food and eating. The family's ethnic and cultural backgrounds, as well as its economic level, all combine to determine the foods served and enjoyed. These habits are passed down from generation to generation, and when several different cultural or ethnic backgrounds are represented in one group for which a menu is to be made, the task of planning presents a challenge.

In today's mobile society, however, people are becoming more knowledgeable about ethnic and regional foods, and interest in Mexican, Oriental, Italian, and other international foods is evident from the number of specialty restaurants today. Many schools, colleges, and similar foodservices include these foods in their menus to add variety and to contribute to the cultural education of the students. The menu planner should be aware of local and regional food customs and religious restrictions as well.

In addition, the traditional three-meal-a-day pattern with the entire family eating together has changed. People are eating fewer meals at home, and they are eating more frequently and at less regular hours. To accommodate this change in eating habits, a more flexible meal schedule is evident in most institutional foodservices, and continuous service is available in many restaurants. Breakfast has increased in importance, and brunch, a combination of breakfast and lunch, has in many cases replaced the luncheon as a business meal. In spite of the desire for fast-paced services, however, some experts predict that with the variety of prepared foods available today, many people will eat frozen and other easily prepared foods at home and will seek a restaurant with interesting decor and atmosphere when they eat out. The person planning menus for any type of foodservice should monitor these trends.

Organizational Goals

The planned menu must be appropriate for the foodservice and must be consistent with its organizational goals. Whether the objective is to provide nutritionally adequate meals at a reasonable cost, as in school foodservice, or whether profit is the major goal, the menus must reflect the organization's stated purpose. Whatever the specific goals are, most foodservices are offering food choices that reflect the current emphasis on nutrition.

Production and Service Constraints

AMOUNT OF MONEY AVAILABLE   Before any menu is planned, the amount of money that can be spent for food must be known. That amount is based on anticipated income from the sale of the food. The money available from food sales constitutes the potential income to be budgeted for the foodservice department. This income must give adequate revenue to cover not only the cost of the raw food used, but also the cost of labor and operating expenses, and in commercial foodservices must allow for reasonable profit. Management determines the percentage of the income to be spent for each of these items. Food, usually the most costly and variable expense, must be closely controlled.

In a school, college, health care facility, or other nonprofit organization, a raw food cost allowance per person per meal or per day may be determined, and menu items having portion costs that are within that food allowance are selected. This does not mean that the cost of every item must fall below the budgeted figure. The planner looks at the total week's or month's food costs and not merely the day-by-day calculations. This cumulative average is readily available in a computer-assisted system. By balancing more costly items with less expensive foods, a more interesting variety may be offered and still stay within the budget. For example, the raw food cost of rib roast or beef tenderloin steak may be offset by lower cost poultry or ground beef items. In menus in which there is a choice, a well-liked lower cost item should be offered with a more expensive food. For example, tacos or burritos are popular and relatively lower cost entrees that could be offered as a choice with baked pork chops. Costs, then, may determine what the choices are, but it is important to remember that variety in the menu may be enhanced by balancing high- and low-cost items.

In commercial foodservices, the selling price is based on the cost of food plus labor, operating costs, and profit. The selling price of items selected for the menu must fall within the guidelines of the foodservice and the amount the customers are willing to pay. The price must be low enough to compete with other restaurants, but not so low that the foodservice loses money. The type and location of the foodservice and the extent of its service and atmosphere help determine the price the clientele is willing to pay.

Commercial foodservices establish a percentage of food cost in relation to selling price, usually between 30 and 35 per cent. This would allow for a markup of 65 to 70 per cent to cover labor, operating costs, and profit. This markup is an overall goal and is not necessarily the same for each menu item because of differences in the cost of preparation. Steaks, for example, require less preparation time than do stuffed pork chops or spaghetti and meatballs. Ice cream or fresh fruit are less costly to prepare than cream pies or fruit cobblers. The raw food costs of the steaks, ice cream, or fresh fruit, therefore, could represent a higher percentage of the selling price. For table d'hote menus, a pricing schedule usually is determined for the different types of menus or for various entrees, and menu items are selected that can be served for the established selling price.

In all types of foodservice operations, the person planning menus must know what the budgeted allotment for food is and should have information about raw food costs and portion costs of prepared menu items. The planner must be alert to current prices and foods available that can be included profitably on the menu.

EQUIPMENT AND PHYSICAL FACILITIES   The menu plan for the day must be one that can be produced within the work space available and with the number and capacity of large and small equipment. Care should be taken to distribute the workload evenly for ovens, ranges, mixers, and other large pieces of equipment. The ovens are especially vulnerable to overuse. Including too many foods at one meal that require oven use may cause an overload or complicate production schedules. For example, it may not be possible to bake Swiss steak, potatoes, and a vegetable casserole at the same meal. If equipment must be shared, the menu should not include items that will cause a conflict. Unless separate ovens are available to the bakery unit, for example, hot breads may not be possible if other menu items must be baked just prior to serving.

The planner should be aware of restrictions on equipment and space and should be familiar with the methods of preparation, the equipment used, and pans or other utensils needed before choosing the menu items. Refrigerator and freezer space must be considered. A chilled dessert, molded gelatin salad, and individual cold plates may be difficult to refrigerate if planned on the same day's menu. If the refrigerator and freezer space are inadequate, the frequency of delivery becomes a determining factor in the planning of the menu.

The amount of china, glassware, or silverware available may prevent the serving of certain menu items at the same meal. For example, fruit cobbler and a creamed vegetable may both require sauce dishes. Foods such as parfaits or shrimp cocktail should not be placed on the menu unless there is appropriate glassware for serving. For hospital patient and other tray service, the type and number of dishes required for service of the menu must fit on the tray.

PERSONNEL   The number and skill of employees are factors to consider when determining the variety and complexity of a menu. Understanding the relationship between menu and personnel will help the planner develop menus that can be prepared with the available staff. Work schedules must be considered for all days because some foods require advance preparation, whereas others are prepared just prior to service. Menu items should be planned that will enable employees' workloads to be spread evenly throughout the day and that will not result in too much last-minute preparation.

AVAILABILITY OF FOODS   The location of the market or other sources of food may have a limiting effect on the menu. This is especially true of fresh foods. A knowledge of fresh fruit and vegetables and their seasons enables a planner to include them on the menu while they are at their peak of quality and at an affordable price. Whether the menu planner is responsible for ordering or purchasing the food, it is important to keep abreast of new items on the market and to be alert to foods that would add interest to the menu or that would improve the variety and quality of menu items offered.

SERVICE   The style of service influences food item selection and the number of choices on the menu. Some foods are more adaptable to seated service than cafeteria; cherries jubilee, for example, requires tableside preparation. Baked Alaska would be difficult to manage in cafeteria service because of last-minute preparation and the need for immediate service.

The distance between the point of preparation and the point of distribution should be considered, as well as the time elapsing between the completion of preparation and service. The menu should not include foods such as souffles that will change during their transportation if the food is prepared in a central kitchen and sent to service areas in remote locations. Foods transferred in bulk to a service unit must be of a type that will hold up well and that will be appetizing when served. If the meals are served directly from a central unit to patients' trays or to a dining room, more emphasis may be placed on garnishing.

FOOD CHARACTERISTICS AND COMBINATIONS   When planning menus, one must visualize how the food will look on the plate, tray, or cafeteria counter and sense the combinations of foods presented, how the flavors will combine, whether there is contrast in texture, shape, and consistency; in other words, an overview of the final menu as it is served.

Color gives eye appeal and helps to merchandise the food. At least one or two colorful foods should be included on each menu. A green vegetable adds color to an otherwise colorless combination of broiled fish and creamed potatoes; or serving parsley-buttered potatoes and glazed carrots improves the appearance on the plate. Other green vegetables, tomatoes, and beets also add color as do garnishes of fruit, watercress, or radishes. It is just as important to have pleasing color combinations on the cafeteria counter as on the individual plate.

Texture refers to the structure of foods and can best be detected by the feel of foods in the mouth. Crisp, soft, smooth, and chewy are adjectives describing food texture. A variety of textures within any one meal should be included. A crisp vegetable salad accompanying a chicken and rice casserole with fruit cobbler or other fruit dessert would offer more contrast in texture than would a gelatin salad and a chocolate pudding served with the casserole meal. For cafeterias, contrasts in texture usually are offered within each menu category.

Consistency is the way foods adhere together, their degree of firmness, density, or viscosity and may be described as firm, thin, thick, or gelatinous. Serving two creamed foods on the plate would be unattractive. A menu including baked ham with cherry sauce, escalloped potatoes, and creamed peas would be unappetizing when the foods are intermingled on the plate.

Shape of food plays a big part in eye appeal, and interest can be created through variety in the form in which foods are presented. One way to add interest to the menu is to vary the way in which vegetables are cut; for example, carrots cut into julienne strips or circles, cubed or shredded; green beans served whole, cut, or French cut. Dicing and cutting machines provide an easy method for obtaining different forms and sizes. Variation in height of food also aids in eye appeal for the customer.

Flavor combinations are important in menu planning. In addition to the basic flavors of sweet, sour, bitter, and salty, vegetables may be thought of as strong and mild flavored; chili or other foods as spicy or highly seasoned. A variety of flavors within the meal is more enjoyable than duplication of any one flavor. Foods with the same basic flavors, such as spaghetti with tomato sauce and sliced tomato salad, should be avoided in the same meal.

Certain food combinations complement each other, such as turkey and cranberries, roast beef and horseradish sauce, or pork and applesauce. The planner should avoid exclusive use of stereotyped combinations, however, and explore other accompaniments to make menus more interesting. Red currant jelly instead of mint with lamb is an example.

Variety in preparation should be considered in menu planning, and two foods prepared in the same way should not be included in the same meal. Variety may be introduced by marinating or stir-frying foods in addition to the traditional fried, broiled, baked, braised, or steamed. Foods can be varied further by serving them creamed, buttered, or escalloped, or by adding a variety of sauces.

Planning Procedures

Menus should be planned well in advance of use, preferably at a regularly scheduled, uninterrupted time. Files of standardized recipes with portion size and cost, previous menu files, market quotations, suggestions from patrons, lists of food items classified for easy reference, and trade publications may all provide inspiration and new ideas.

Information on consumer preference is important in menu planning. The relative popularity of a food may serve as a guide to the frequency that a given item appears on the menu. A file of previous menus with comments concerning the reactions of guests, the difficulty or ease of preparation, and the cost will help prevent repetition and will indicate combinations found satisfactory and profitable.

An inherent liking for good food, a lack of prejudice, a flair in planning based on creativity and imagination, and the ability to merchandise food attractively are traits that aid the menu planner. If one individual is responsible for menu planning, it is helpful to have input from purchasing, production, and service personnel. Many foodservices assign this responsibility to a committee rather than to one individual, a practice that is especially appropriate for a multiunit foodservice. Input from the public through marketing research, food preference studies, test marketing, and participation of food or menu committees can be of assistance. The planner should be alert to new products and to trends in consumer preferences and should be aware of menu items that are offered successfully by the competition, whether it is a nonprofit or commercial situation. Menu planning should be ongoing and current and flexible enough to respond to changing conditions.

Types of Menus

The menu may take different forms, each written for the needs of the particular market it serves. Patrons may be offered an extensive list of items from which to select a meal or they may be given a menu that offers little if any choice.

A **selective menu** includes two or more choices in each menu category, the exact number of options varying with different types of foodservices. The menu mix, or the selection of food items to be offered in each category, is important to the success of a selective menu.

A **nonselective menu** offers no choices, but in many schools and health care facilities where these are used there may be two or three options in certain items, such as salads, desserts, and beverages. A single entree may be offered, with a choice of tossed salad or molded fruit salad, and fresh fruit or ice cream may be available as an alternative to a baked or other prepared dessert. In some cases, the choice may be between a full meal and a soup and salad combination. Some foodservices having a nonselective menu provide certain items daily, in addition to the planned menu; for example, cottage cheese, tossed salad, ice cream, and fresh or canned fruit.

Menus may be **static** or **set,** in which the same menus are used each day. This type of menu is found in restaurants and other foodservices where the clientele changes daily or where there enough items listed on the menu to offer sufficient variety. Some flexibility may be built into the menu by changing an item or two daily or offering daily specials. The static menu may be quite limited in choice, as in most fast service restaurants. Changes in these menus are made only after careful development of a new product and extensive market research and testing. With a set menu, the purchasing, production, and service can be simplified.

A **single-use menu** is one in which the menu is planned for a certain day and is not repeated again in exactly the same form, although some food combinations may be used again in future meals.

The **cycle menu** is a carefully planned set of menus that is rotated at definite intervals, the length of cycle depending on the type of foodservice. Hospitals, with a three-day average patient stay, could have a seven-day cycle but may prefer 8 or 12 days to avoid repetition of foods on the same day each week. A three-week cycle, however, would accommodate a wider variety of foods and result in greater patient satisfaction. Most hospitals add additional choices for the employees' cafeteria and may use a longer cycle for that service. An extended care facility normally has a longer cycle because of length of stay of the residents.

There are many advantages in using a cycle menu. After the initial planning has been completed, time is freed for the planner to review and revise the menus to meet changing needs such as holidays, vacations, changes in personnel, or unavailability of a food item. Repetition of the same menu aids in standardizing preparation procedures and efficient use of equipment. Forecasting and purchasing are simplified, and with repeated use of the menus and needed adjustments, employee workloads can be equalized and distributed fairly.

There are disadvantages in using cycle menus. They may become monotonous if the cycle is too short of if the same food is offered on the same day each week. It may not include well-liked foods often enough or unpopular items too frequently. Some variety may be added by specifying certain changes in the second and third rotations. For example, spice cake may be substituted for a white layer cake in the second week, or pot roast with vegetables for beef stew. The cycle menu may not provide for foods that come into the market at varying times of the year, but many foodservices solve this problem by developing summer, fall, winter, and spring cycles; others note the seasonal alternatives on the menu. If these disadvantages can be resolved and the menu properly developed to meet the needs of a particular foodservice system, the cycle menu can become an effective management tool.

In foodservices where the clientele remains constant, a cycle for as long as three to six months may be used; or a modified cycle menu may be written in which cycles are developed for some foods and the rest of the menu filled in each week. An example would be an entree cycle of from one to six months, which would enable popular foods to be served more often and yet include for variety items that are acceptable if offered only occasionally. For example, liver and onions or spareribs and sauerkraut probably would not be acceptable once a week, but would be appreciated by many patrons if offered once in six or eight weeks. A salad cycle of 12 to 21 days or longer is appropriate, especially when a salad bar is offered. A dessert cycle is a possibility also.

Whatever the length of the cycle, the menus must be carefully planned and evaluated after each use. A cycle menu should be flexible enough to handle emergencies, to utilize leftover food, and to accommodate new ideas and menu items.

Menus may also be categorized by the method of pricing. In the **à la carte menu,** food items are priced separately. This type of menu allows the patron to select only the food wanted.

The **table d'hôte menu** offers a complete meal at a fixed price, usually with a choice of some items.

The **du jour menu** means menu of the day. It must be planned and written daily. This is a good way to utilize leftover foods and food bargains.

Menu Patterns

The menu pattern is an outline of food to be included in each meal, and the extent of this choice must be decided before menus are planned. For years, the traditional schedule has been three meals a day, with breakfast, lunch, and dinner served within a certain time span. In some cases the larger meal has been served at noon, resulting in a pattern of breakfast, dinner, and supper. In foodservice, the trend is away from this traditionally structured plan because of the desire of many patrons for fast food and instant service and because many prefer eating at different times of the day.

To accommodate this trend, some cafeterias are offering snack-type foods as part of their regular menu and are lengthening their hours of service. Some hospitals offer a light evening meal as a choice with a traditional dinner menu. Many foodservices with multiple choice menus have essentially the same menu for the noon and evening meals and some give patrons not only a choice of food items but of menu structure as well. Brunch, combining breakfast and lunch, is becoming increasingly popular.

A traditional basic menu pattern is:

- **Breakfast**—Fruit or juice
    Cereal, hot and/or cold
    Eggs and/or breakfast meat
    Toast or hot bread
    Choice of beverages

- **Lunch**—Soup (optional)
  - Entree or sandwich
  - Salad or vegetable
  - Bread/margarine or butter
  - Fruit or light dessert
  - Choice of beverages
- **Dinner**—Soup (optional)
  - Entree (meat, fish, poultry, or vegetarian)
  - Two vegetables (one may be potato or pasta)
  - Salad
  - Bread/margarine or butter
  - Dessert
  - Choice of beverages

Although menus for most institutions serving three meals a day are based on this pattern, some adjustments usually are made for different types of foodservices, as discussed later in this chapter. The number of choices offered varies with the type of foodservice; the type of service or method of delivery of the food; and the personnel, equipment, and money available.

COLLEGES AND UNIVERSITIES   The objective of most foodservices on college and university campuses is to satisfy students' nutritional requirements through service of quality food within the limitations of the budget. Many schools also consider the service of food as an opportunity to contribute to the social and cultural education of the student.

A variety of meal plans is available in college foodservice, one of the more prevalent being a plan in which a student is entitled to a certain number of meals per week for a set fee. An increasing number of schools are using à la carte or other types of operations, however. Payment may be made in cash or by a declining balance method, in which charges are subtracted from a deposit made by the student, or by some other plan. Specialty food shops and other alternative types of eating plans have in many cases met the preference of students for a less traditional foodservice.

With many housing opportunities available to students today, the competition for a share of the market has increased the pressure to attract and retain new students and has increased the importance of merchandising in campus foodservices. Managers must be on the alert for new foods and merchandising ideas to maintain the volume needed for their operations. Special theme meals, holiday dinners, and picnics are examples of "extras" offered to students in many college and university foodservices. Some are actively engaged in catering and others have set up food shops to sell their food specialties.

Cafeteria service is used in most college and university residence halls, and the menu follows the pattern noted earlier under "Menu Patterns" with two or more choices in each category usually offered. The university must assume responsibility for providing foods that meet the total daily nutritional needs of the student, as well as planning foods that are well liked.

Some foodservices offer a protein salad, a salad plate, or sandwich as one of the entree choices for students who prefer a light meal. Many provide a salad bar that includes ingredients and accompaniments for a tossed salad, two or more prepared salads, and certain items such as peanut butter, cottage cheese, and deviled or hard-cooked eggs. Ice cream, yogurt, and fresh fruit may be served daily, and when these are offered, there may be only one prepared dessert. Fast service lines that feature hamburgers, French fries, and milkshakes; soup and sandwich or salad; or specialty or international foods are popular with students for both lunch and dinner. In some residence halls a continental breakfast of assorted juices, cereals, sweet rolls or donuts, and beverages is provided after the regular line is closed.

HOSPITALS   Hospitals and other health care facilities must serve meals that meet the total nutritional needs of patients and personnel at a cost within a budgetary allowance. In addition, health care institutions must provide food that appeals to persons whose appetites may be below normal and that in many cases must contribute to the physical treatment and emotional security of the patient.

Hospital menus are complicated because of the diversity of diet needs and often widely separated service areas. The basic menu is a regular or normal diet that will supply all food essentials needed for good nutrition and may include adult and pediatric menus. Modifications of the regular menu are made to meet the various diet prescriptions, and provisions are made for between-meal nourishments. Whenever possible the foods prepared for the regular diet are used for the modified diets.

A selective menu contributes to the satisfaction of the patient and may be cyclical. Generally, two or more choices are offered in each menu category. Hospitals, like schools and other institutional foodservices, are looking to the commercial field for new ideas in menus and merchandising that will add to patient satisfaction. Some have adopted a selective menu similar to the table d'hôte menu used in restaurants, in which the patient may select from fifteen or more items or meal combinations offered daily.

Food for hospital personnel and visitors generally is provided in a cafeteria. The menu is based on the regular patient menu but usually includes a wider variety of choices. A cycle menu, if used, may be longer than that for patient menus. In addition, some provision must be made for meals for the personnel who work at night. This often is provided through vending machines or snack bars.

Many hospitals are faced with the need to generate additional income and are accomplishing this through aggressive merchandising in their cafeterias, catering for groups and special events, and selling "take home" foods for their employees.

EXTENDED CARE FACILITIES AND RETIREMENT COMMUNITIES   To meet the needs of the older adults who reside in retirement communities and who often are in the majority in nursing homes and other extended care facilities, the planner should be aware of the problems peculiar to this age group. Their fixed habits and food preferences developed through many years may influence but should not determine entirely the meals planned for them. Healthy adults regardless of age need a well-balanced diet, and in planning the day's food the basic pattern for the normal diet should be followed. Individual problems of the group members, such as difficulty in chewing solid food, special diet requirements, and their limited mobility and activity, must also be of concern.

At least three well-planned meals should be served daily, with a hot food at each meal. The menu pattern is similar to that of the regular hospital diet, with adjustments in portions and some modifications for residents with individual eating problems. The caloric intake or quantity of food eaten usually is smaller because of lessened activity.

Because plate or family service is used in many retirement complexes, a nonselective menu is more feasible than one with numerous choices. However, some modification adds to the residents' acceptance of the food and is not prohibitive in most cases. Choice may be provided by a soup and salad bar; by offering certain menu items daily, such as soup, cottage cheese, or fresh fruit, in addition to a set menu; or through a choice of two entrees for the evening meal. The second entree could be a sandwich or a protein salad. If a relatively unpopular entree is planned, a second entree might be offered as a choice. Foodservice in this type of long-range facility offers opportunity for use of the eight-week or longer cycle.

SCHOOLS   Goals for the USDA National School Lunch Program are to provide approximately one-third of the child's daily nutritive requirement at a reasonable price, to contribute to a better understanding of nutrition, and to foster good food habits. School lunch patterns for various age groups are given in Fig. 3.1. To qualify for reimbursement, schools are required to use this framework, but other foods may be added to improve student acceptability. A recent provision is "offer versus service," which allows high school students to choose less than all of the food items within the lunch pattern.

The cycle menu is used by many school foodservices, and some have a modified selective menu in which students may choose from two items of comparable nutritional value. Many feature salad bars routinely. Another

CHART 1
SCHOOL LUNCH PATTERNS FOR VARIOUS AGE/GRADE GROUPS

U.S. Department of Agriculture, National School Lunch Program

USDA recommends, but does not require, that you adjust portions by age/grade group to better meet the food and nutritional needs of children according to their ages. If you adjust portions, Groups I-IV are minimum requirements for the age/grade groups specified. If you do not adjust portions, the Group IV portions in the shaded column are the portions to serve all children.

COMPONENTS		MINIMUM QUANTITIES				RECOMMENDED QUANTITIES[1]	SPECIFIC REQUIREMENTS
		Preschool		Grades K-3	Grades 4-12[1]	Grades 7-12	
		ages 1-2 (Group I)	ages 3-4 (Group II)	ages 5-8 (Group III)	age 9 & over (Group IV)	age 12 & over (Group V)	
MEAT OR MEAT ALTERNATE	A serving of one of the following or a combination to give an equivalent quantity:						• Must be served in the main dish or the main dish and one other menu item. • Textured vegetable protein products, cheese alternate products, and enriched macaroni with fortified protein may be used to meet part of the meat/meat alternate requirement. Fact sheets on each of these alternate foods give detailed instructions for use. NOTE: The amount you must serve of a single meat alternate may seem too large for the particular age group you are serving. To make the quantity of that meat alternate more reasonable, use a smaller amount to meet part of the requirement and supplement with another meat or meat alternate to meet the full requirement.
	Lean meat, poultry, or fish (edible portion as served)	1 oz	1½ oz	1½ oz	2 oz	3 oz	
	Cheese	1 oz	1½ oz	1½ oz	2 oz	3 oz	
	Large egg(s)	1	1½	1½	2	3	
	Cooked dry beans or peas	½ cup	¾ cup	¾ cup	1 cup	1½ cup	
	Peanut butter	2 Tbsp	3 Tbsp	3 Tbsp	4 Tbsp	6 Tbsp	
VEGETABLE AND/OR FRUIT	Two or more servings of vegetable or fruit or both to total	½ cup	½ cup	½ cup	¾ cup	¾ cup	• No more than one-half of the total requirement may be met with full-strength fruit or vegetable juice. • Cooked dry beans or peas may be used as a meat alternate or as a vegetable but not as both in the same meal.
BREAD OR BREAD ALTERNATE	Servings of bread or bread alternate A serving is: • 1 slice of whole-grain or enriched bread • A whole-grain or enriched biscuit, roll, muffin, etc. • ½ cup of cooked whole-grain or enriched rice, macaroni, noodles, whole-grain or enriched pasta products, or other cereal grains such as bulgur or corn grits • A combination of any of the above	5 per week	8 per week	8 per week	8 per week	10 per week	• At least ½ serving of bread or an equivalent quantity of bread alternate for Group I, and 1 serving for Groups II-V, must be served daily. • Enriched macaroni with fortified protein may be used as a meat alternate or as a bread alternate but not as both in the same meal. NOTE: Food Buying Guide for School Food Service, PA-1257 (1980) provides the information for the minimum weight of a serving.
MILK	A serving of fluid milk	¾ cup (6 fl oz)	¾ cup (6 fl oz)	½ pint (8 fl oz)	½ pint (8 fl oz)	½ pint (8 fl oz)	At least one of the following forms of milk must be offered: • Unflavored lowfat milk • Unflavored skim milk • Unflavored buttermilk NOTE: This requirement does not prohibit offering other milks, such as whole milk or flavored milk, along with one or more of the above.

[1]Group IV is shaded because it is the one meal pattern which will satisfy all requirements if no portion size adjustments are made.

[1]Group V specifies recommended, not required, quantities for students 12 years and older. These students may request smaller portions, but not smaller than those specified in Group IV.

Food Buying Guide   June 1980

FIGURE 3.1   National school lunch menu pattern.

variation is found in multiple menus in which more than one complete meal is offered; for example, a student may choose a plate lunch or a soup and sandwich meal. À la carte menus are used in some schools in which reimbursement is not sought.

COMMERCIAL FOODSERVICES For the commercial restaurant, profit is a major objective, but customer satisfaction is an important consideration also. Merchandising and competition become important factors in this type of foodservice. Goals in commercial foodservices may differ, too, with some featuring service in a relaxed atmosphere and others stressing convenience and speed of service. Many industrial organizations believe in good food at a low cost as a means of maintaining a healthy work force whose morale is high. To assure this fringe benefit to employees, the foodservice may be partially or wholly subsidized by the company.

Menu planning for commercial foodservices varies according to the size and type of operation, its goals, and the expected check average. Menus range from the fast food chain's limited menu for high volume and speedy service to the elaborate table d'hôte menu of a formal seated-service restaurant.

In addition to the basic rules of successful meal planning and food combinations, special emphasis must be placed on choosing menu items that will sell and be profitable. With the exact number of patrons from day-to-day unknown, the menu must be flexible enough to accommodate any excess in food production. As in any other foodservice, labor is one of the largest items of expense and one of the most difficult to control. The use of pre-portioned foods, portion-ready entrees, ready-to-cook foods, and other labor-saving items is of major importance in effecting economies of time and cost.

Some restaurants have a set menu that does not vary from day-to-day; others have found the use of cycle menus to be valuable in reducing planning time and equalizing labor. The menu may be planned and presented as a listing of à la carte items rather than complete meals, or may include both. Some restaurants having a set menu feature daily specials to add interest to the menu, to enable them to take advantage of seasonal foods, and to incorporate foods on hand. In national restaurant chains, the same menu may be offered in all units and generally is limited to a few items that have been carefully developed and standardized. In commercial cafeterias, the noon and evening meals may be essentially the same with a wide selection of entrees, sandwiches, and desserts. It is not uncommon to have five to six entrees, eight to ten salads, and eight to ten desserts. Cafeteria operations may offer special food items on individual days or may serve a unique soup, salad, or dessert as their specialty.

Steps in Menu Planning

Menus should be planned for at least a week, preferably longer, but provision should be made for flexibility to effectively use supplies on hand and to take advantage of the daily food market. If a cycle menu is used, the length of the cycle should be determined.

A planning worksheet on which to record menu items is shown in Fig. 3.2. For a selective menu offering certain items daily, time is saved by having the names of these foods printed on the worksheet.

A suggested step-by-step procedure for planning menus follows.

1. **Entrees.** Plan the meats and other entrees for the entire period or cycle. If planning for a week only, select entrees for a month or longer, then complete the menus weekly or as needed. Since entrees are the most expensive items on the menu, costs can be controlled to a great extent through careful planning at this point.

   If the menu pattern provides entree choices, the selection should include at least one meat and a vegetarian entree, along with poultry, fish, and meat extenders to complete the number of items required. Fewer luncheon entrees may be offered than for the dinner meal, depending on the type of foodservice.

2. **Soups and sandwiches.** If a soup and sandwich combination is to be an entree choice, it should be planned with the other entrees. In a cafeteria a variety of sandwiches may be offered, and these may not change from day-to-day. If more than one soup is included, one should be a cream or other hearty soup and one a stock soup.

3. **Vegetables.** Decide on the vegetables appropriate to serve with the entrees. Potatoes, rice, or pasta may be included as one choice. On a selective menu, pair a less popular vegetable with one that is well accepted.

4. **Salads.** Select salads that are compatible with the entrees and vegetables. If a protein-type salad such as chicken, tuna, or deviled egg is planned as an entree choice, it should be coordinated with the other entree selections. If only one salad is to be offered, choose one that complements or is a contrast in texture to the other menu items.

   On a selective menu, include a green salad plus fruit, vegetable, and gelatin salads to complete the desired number. Certain salads, such as tossed salad, cottage cheese, deviled egg, or cabbage slaw, may be offered daily; or a salad bar that includes a variety of salads and relishes may be a standard feature.

5. **Desserts.** If no choice is to be offered, plan a light dessert with a hearty meal and a richer dessert when the rest of the meal is not too filling. On a selective menu, the number of choices may be limited to two or three

Menus				
Week of _____				
	Monday	Tuesday	Wednesday	Thursday
Breakfast				
Fruit	1.			
Fruit juice	1.			
	2.			
Cereal	1.			
	2. Assorted dry	Assorted dry	Assorted dry	Assorted dry
Entree	1.			
Bread	1. Toast	Toast	Toast	Toast
	2.			
Beverages	C.T.M.	C.T.M.	C.T.M.	C.T.M.
Lunch				
Soup	1.			
Entrees	1.			
	2.			
Vegetable	1.			
Bread	1. Assorted	Assorted	Assorted	Assorted
Salads	1. Salad bar	Salad bar	Salad bar	Salad bar
	2.			
Desserts	1.			
	2.			
Beverages	1. C.T.M.	C.T.M.	C.T.M.	C.T.M.
	2.			
Dinner				
Soup	1.			
Entrees	1.			
	2.			
Potato or	1.			
pasta				
Vegetables	1.			
	2.			
Salads	1. Salad bar	Salad bar	Salad bar	Salad bar
	2.			
Desserts	1.			
	2.			
	3.			
Beverages	1. C.T.M.	C.T.M.	C.T.M.	C.T.M.

FIGURE 3.2   Suggested worksheet for menu planning.

plus a daily offering of fruit, ice cream or sherbet, and yogurt. For a commercial cafeteria, it may be quite extensive and include a two-crust pie, a soft pie, cake or cookies, pudding, fruit, ice cream or sherbet, and gelatin dessert.

6. **Breads.** Vary the kinds of breads offered or provide a choice of white or whole grain bread and a hot bread. Many foodservices use homemade breads as one of their specialties.

7. **Breakfast items.** Certain breakfast foods are standard and generally include fruit juices, hot and cold cereals, and toast. It is customary to offer eggs in some form and to introduce variety through the addition of other entrees, hot breads, and fresh fruits.

8. **Beverages.** A choice of beverages that includes coffee, tea, milk, and low-fat milk is offered in most foodservices. Decaffeinated coffee and tea generally are provided, and soft drinks and a variety of juices also may be included.

Menus for the entire day should be considered as a unit and checked for adequacy and for repetition of food items. The day's menus are then compared with those for the previous and following days to be sure they are compatible. The selective menu should be so planned that a customer, by choosing from the various menu categories, may select combinations that are pleasing and that offer contrasts in flavor, color, and texture.

Menu Evaluation

Menu evaluation is an important part of menu planning and should be an ongoing process. The menu as planned should be reviewed prior to its use and again after it has been served. The use of a checklist aids in making certain that all factors of good menu planning have been met.

CHECKLIST FOR MENU EVALUATION

1. Does it meet nutritional guidelines and organization objectives?
2. Are the foods offered in season, available, and within price range?
3. Do foods in each menu offer contrasts of color? texture? flavor? consistency? shape or form? type of preparation? temperature?
4. Can these foods be prepared with the personnel and equipment available?
5. Are the workloads balanced for personnel and equipment?
6. Is any one food item or flavor repeated too frequently during this menu period?
7. Are the meals made attractive with suitable garnishes and accompaniments?

8. Do the combinations make a pleasing whole, and will they be acceptable to the clientele?

Periodic assessment of the popularity of various menu items is valuable to the menu planner and may be accomplished through observation of plate waste, informal customer comments or customer comment cards, and formal or informal surveys. Methods often used for these surveys are food preference studies, in which food likes and dislikes are rated on a sliding scale by clientele (Fig. 3.3). Children's reactions to food are often measured by a facial hedonic scale (Fig. 3.4). Another approach is the frequency of acceptance in which clientele are asked how often they would be willing to eat individual menu items.

The Printed Menu

As indicated at the beginning of this chapter, the menu is an itemized list of foods served at a meal. From it a working menu and production schedules evolve. The term also refers to the form on which the menu is printed to present to the restaurant customer, the hospital patient, or other clientele. The menu may also be posted on a menu board, as is the custom in most cafeterias and fast service restaurants.

Menu Design   A menu card must be designed and worded to appeal to the guest and to stimulate sales and often to influence clientele to select items that the foodservice wants to sell. The menu card should be of a size easily handled, spotlessly clean, simple in format with appropriate print size and type and with ample margin space. The menu should be highly legible and interesting in color and design to harmonize with the decor of the foodservice. The printed menu is a form of merchandising and an important marketing tool. It should not be thought of as a price sheet alone but as a selling and public relations device.

Descriptive Wording. Menu items are listed in the sequence in which they are eaten and should present an accurate word picture of the foods available so that the patron knows exactly what the menu items are. It is disappointing for the guest to visualize one thing and be served something entirely different.

Giving misleading names to menu items is unfair to the customer and is illegal where truth in menu legislation has been enacted. In general, these laws require that the menu accurately describe the foods to be served. If Baked Idaho Potatoes are listed on the menu, they must indeed be Idaho potatoes. The same is true when listing Maine Lobster or the **point of origin** for other foods. **Fresh** foods listed on the menu must be fresh, not frozen

Please circle the word that best describes how you feel about the food today:

Food Item			
1. _____	2. _____	3. _____	4. _____
Like Extremely	Like Extremely	Like Extremely	Like Extremely
Like Very Much	Like Very Much	Like Very Much	Like Very Much
Like Moderately	Like Moderately	Like Moderately	Like Moderately
Like Slightly	Like Slightly	Like Slightly	Like Slightly
Neither Like Nor Dislike	Neither Like Nor Dislike	Neither Like Nor Dislike	Neither Like Nor Dislike
Dislike Slightly	Dislike Slightly	Dislike Slightly	Dislike Slightly
Dislike Moderately	Dislike Moderately	Dislike Moderately	Dislike Moderately
Dislike Very Much	Dislike Very Much	Dislike Very Much	Dislike Very Much
Dislike Extremely	Dislike Extremely	Dislike Extremely	Dislike Extremely
Comments:	*Comments:*	*Comments:*	*Comments:*

FIGURE 3.3   Hedonic rating scale may be used for evaluating menu items.

or canned. If the word **homemade** is used on the menu, it means that the food was made on the premises. If a menu lists a grade such a U.S. Choice beef and indicates portion size, the meat must be of that grade and size.

Descriptive words do enhance the menu, and, if accurate, may influence

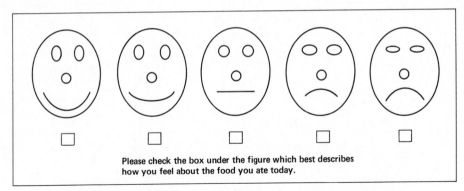

FIGURE 3.4   Rating scale for evaluating children's food likes and dislikes.

the customer selections. Examples are slices of red ripe tomato on Bibb lettuce, fresh spinach salad with bacon-mayonnaise dressing, old-fashioned beef stew with fresh vegetables, chilled melon wedge, and warm peach cobbler with fluffy hard sauce. The menu should not include recipe names that are unknown to the customer or do not indicate the contents. Even where truth in menu legislation is not in effect, accuracy in menu wording helps to ensure customer satisfaction.

Prices. It is important that the customer understands what food items he or she will receive for the money paid. Menus may be **à la carte,** in which food items are priced separately; or **table d'hôte** when a complete meal is offered at a fixed price. The menu card may include both. If a daily special is offered, it may be typed and clipped to the menu.

Summary

The menu is the focal point from which many functions and activities in a foodservice organization start. It determines the foods to be purchased, it is the basis for planning production and employee schedules, and it is an important factor in controlling costs.

In planning foodservice menus, many factors must be considered: the nutritional requirements, food habits, and preferences of the individuals in the group for which menus are being planned; the goals of the organization; the amount of money available; limitations on equipment and physical facilities; the number and skill of employees; and the type of service. The menu must offer a selection of foods that is satisfying to the clientele, but it must be one that can be produced within the constraints of the physical facility and limitations dictated by management policies.

The menu may take different forms, each written for the needs of a particular type of foodservice. The static or set menu, in which the same menu items are offered each day, is found mainly in commercial foodservices. A selective menu offers two or more choices in each menu category and is widely used in many types of foodservice. A nonselective menu offers no choice, but in schools and health care facilities where this type of menu often is used, there may be limited choices in some categories. A cycle menu is a carefully planned set of menus that are rotated at definite intervals. The single-use menu is planned for a certain day and is not repeated in the same form.

Systematic planning procedures that include continuous evaluation of the menus as served should be followed. The menu planner should keep abreast of new products on the market and should be alert to the preferences of the clientele and the need for changes in the menu. Innovation is a key word in today's menu planning. New menu ideas and marketing techniques must be developed if the foodservice is to satisfy a clientele that is becoming increasingly sophisticated about food.

Supplementary References

Axler, B. H.: Foodservice: A Managerial Approach. Lexington, MA: D.C. Heath & Co., 1979.

Eckstein, E. F.: Menu Planning, 3rd ed. Westport, CT: AVI Publishing Co., 1983.

Fanelli, M.T. and Stevenhagen, K. J.: Characterizing consumption patterns by food frequency methods: Core foods and variety of food in diets of older Americans. J. Am. Diet. Assoc. 85:1570, 1985.

Food and Nutrition Service, USDA: Menu Planning Guide for School Food Service. PA No. 1260. Washington, DC: U.S. GPO, 1980.

Gisslen, W.: Professional Cooking. Ch. 6 The Menu. New York: John Wiley and Sons. 1983.

Kelley, S. M., Jennings, G. E., Funk, K. Gaskins, C. T., and Welch, G. B.: Edible plate waste assessment in a university dining hall. J. Am. Diet. Assoc. 83:436, 1983.

Khan, M. A. and Lyke, L. K.: Snacking and its contribution to food and nutrient intake of college students. J. Am. Diet. Assoc. 81:583, 1982.

Kirks, B. A. and Wolff, H. K.: A comparison of methods for plate waste determinations. J. Am. Diet. Assoc. 85:329, 1985.

McConnell, P. E. and Shaw, J. B.: Developing school lunch menus using food preferences and frequency of preference. School Food Serv. Res. Rev. 4:125, 1980.

Mahaffey, M. J., Mennes, M. E., and Miller, B. B.: Food Service Manual for Health Care Institutions. Ch. 7 Menu Planning. Chicago: Am. Hosp. Assoc., 1981.

Menu census: A 15-year retrospective. Restaurant and Institutions 96:4, Feb. 19, 1986.

National Research Council: Recommended Dietary Allowances, 9th ed.: Washington, DC: National Academy of Sciences, 1980.

Nelson, M. B. and King, P. C.: Snack and beverage preferences of university students. J. Am. Diet. Assoc. 81:65, 1982.

Peterkin, B. B., Patterson, P. C., Blum, A. J., and Kerr, R. L.: Changes in dietary patterns: one approach to meeting standards. J. Am. Diet. Assoc. 78:453, 1981.

Price, D. Z.: Developing a food preference instrument. School Food Serv. Res. Rev. 4:101, 1980.

Reid, R. D.: Foodservice and Restaurant Marketing. Ch. 7 Planning and Designing the Menu. Boston: CBI Publishing Co., 1983.

Seaburg, A. G.: Menu Design, Merchandising and Marketing. Boston: Cahners Books, 1973.

Shugart, G., Molt, M., and Wilson, M.: Food for Fifty, 7th ed. Part 3 Menu Planning. New York: John Wiley and Sons, 1985.

Stokes, J. W.: How to Manage a Restaurant. Ch. 4 Planning the Menu. Dubuque, IA: Wm. C. Brown Co., 1982.

Tastes of America. Restaurants and Institutions: 95:97, Dec. 11, 1985.

U.S. Department of Agriculture and U.S. Department of Health and Human Services: Nutrition and Your Health: Dietary Guidelines for Americans, 2d ed. Washington, DC: Office of Governmental and Public Affairs, 1985.

VonEgmond-Pannell, D.: School Food Service, 3d ed. Westport, CT: AVI Publishing Co., 1985.

Welsh, S. O. and Marston, R. M.: Review of trends in food use in the United States, 1909 to 1980. J. Am. Diet. Assoc. 81:120, 1982.

Wenzel, G. L.: Wenzel's Menu Maker, 2d ed. Boston: CBI Publishing Co., 1981.

CHAPTER 4

Purchasing and Storage

Introduction

Purchasing is an essential function in the foodservice system and is the first step in the production and service of quality food. Although the procurement process for an institutional or commercial foodservice involves food, supplies, and equipment, major emphasis in this chapter is on the buying of food.

Today's market offers a large variety of products from which selections must be made to meet the needs of a particular foodservice. Whether the buying decisions are made by the dietitian or manager or by a purchasing agent, they must be based on an awareness of the quality standards and economic structure of the institution and a thorough knowledge of the marketing system.

Procedures for the selection of vendors, determining food needs, and writing specifications are discussed, as are the methods of purchasing. Emphasis is on information that will assist the buyer in making purchasing decisions rather than an in-depth discussion of individual food items.

An important part of the purchasing process is the receiving, storage, and issuing of food and supplies. Requirements for storage facilities and records needed for inventory control are included here.

The Market

The market is the medium through which commodities are moved from the producer to the customer. Markets are classified according to the type of food sold, their location, and the marketing channels involved. A **primary** market is the basic source of supply and might be found in the principal fruit and vegetable growing areas of California, Florida, and Texas, the poultry producing areas of Arkansas, the fresh seafood markets along the coasts, or the food processing plants in various parts of the country.

The raw agricultural products are delivered to primary markets where they are processed or prepared for distribution to **secondary** markets located in different marketing areas throughout the country. In these markets, middlemen (wholesalers or purveyors) purchase in large quantities from primary markets and redistribute in smaller quantities to local buyers. Full-service wholesalers handle all of the items normally required by their customers, whereas specialty wholesalers restrict their sales to only three or four items within a particular line, such as fresh and frozen meats, fresh produce, or canned foods and groceries.

Food also may be distributed through brokers, who act as agents between buyers and sellers without assuming ownership of the commodity, or through commission agents, who buy the merchandise and then, with a guaranteed source of supply, sell the products for a price named by them.

The third type of market available to the food buyer is the **local** market. Farmers' markets may offer savings on seasonal products, and local supermarkets may be a good source of supply for the restaurant or small foodservice operator who has money and storage space to buy only what is currently needed.

Thus, involved in the system are the growing, harvesting, transporting, processing, packaging, storing, selling, financing, and supplying of market information for the many foods and food products available. Each process and transfer of ownership adds to the cost of the end product so that the final consumer cost is far in excess of the amount paid to the original producer of the commodity. The tendency today is to bypass as many individual marketing agents as possible and thus reduce the marketing cost contributed by these agents' charges. For example, large volume buyers may be able to purchase directly from the food processor, thus saving the middleman's charges for handling, storing, and selling the product.

The market is dynamic and ever changing and the food buyer must be alert to trends and conditions that affect it. Foods in plentiful supply, new market forms of food, and fluctuations in price are but a few of the factors that demand the attention of the buyer. Exchange of information between seller and buyer is an important function of the market and is made possible through various channels, such as trade association newsletters, local and federal market reports, and the press. Other sources of market information are technical and trade association meetings and magazines, research reports, talks with sales representatives, and visits to the produce markets and wholesale distributors.

Adverse growing conditions can affect food prices, as can unusual consumer demands and seasonal variations. Some foods are relatively stable in price and follow general economic conditions. Others are more perishable and have greater price fluctuations during the year. Most fresh fruits and vegetables are considered best at the height of the production season, particularly those grown within a given market area. However, treatment of fresh foods and improved transportation, refrigeration, and storage facilities have greatly reduced the so-called seasonability of foods. Stocks of processed foods may be high or depleted at times, which will affect both price and availability.

Regulatory Agencies

Quality in food as purchased is assured to a large extent by the standards that have been established by government agencies to protect consumers. Such standards give definitions and descriptions of the food product, including its appearance, quality factors, and, in some cases, its composition. Federal agencies establish quality standards and provide regulatory control over such standards. All foods shipped in interstate commerce must meet the requirements of one or more federal laws and regulations.

FOOD AND DRUG ADMINISTRATION   The Food and Drug Administration (FDA) is responsible for enforcement of the **Federal Food, Drug, and Cosmetic Act** covering production, manufacture, and distribution of all food involved in interstate commerce except meat and poultry, which are regulated by the United States Department of Agriculture. This act, which was passed in 1938 and amended in 1958, defines adulteration and misbranding and clarifies certain definitions and standards.

If a food product contains substances that are injurious to health, if it has been prepared or held under unsanitary conditions, or if any part is filthy or decomposed or contains portions of diseased animals, it is considered **adulterated.** The product is considered to be **misbranded** if the label does not include the information mandated by law or if it gives misleading information.

Standards of identity define what a food product must contain to be called by a certain name, such as preserves, salad dressing, or mayonnaise. **Standards of quality** apply chiefly to canned fruits and vegetables and describe the ingredients that go into the product. These standards limit and describe the number and kinds of defects permitted. They do not provide a basis for comparing foods as grades do, but establish minimum quality requirements. **Standards of fill** regulate the quantity of food in the container. They tell the packer how full the container must be to avoid deceiving the consumer. If the standards of fill requirements are not met, the product may be marketed but only with the label "below standard in fill" and an accompanying explanation. All are mandatory for foods in interstate commerce and may be used voluntarily for others.

Labeling requirements for food made mandatory by the Fair Packaging and Labeling Act of 1967 are the common or usual names of all ingredients, listed in descending order of their predominance by weight; the name and address of the manufacturer, packer, or distributor; a statement of the quantity of the contents in weight, measure, or numerical count; and the name of any artificial flavoring, coloring, or chemical preservative.

Descriptive labeling such as brand names, number of servings, or recipes may be added voluntarily by processors. Nutrition labeling provides the consumer with information concerning the nutritional quality of a defined serving of the food. It is voluntary for most foods but is mandatory for foods to which nutrients have been added and foods for which nutritional claims are made.

UNITED STATES DEPARTMENT OF AGRICULTURE   The Agricultural Marketing Service, United States Department of Agriculture (USDA), has grading and inspection programs designed to certify quality and condition of agricultural commodities and food products. The USDA has developed grade standards for several types of food, including fruits and vegetables, dairy products, eggs, poultry, and meat products. For most agricultural products, grading is voluntary. However, inspection of commodities for wholesomeness is mandatory for meats, poultry, and other processed foods. An inspector from the appropriate federal or other agency must give approval that the product is of high quality and processed under sanitary conditions before the official inspection stamp can be affixed.

The **Wholesome Meat Act,** passed in 1967, is an extension of the **Federal Meat Inspection Act of 1906** and provides for establishing a uniform standard for state and federally inspected meats. Under this law, meats that do not cross state lines are required to be inspected in programs "at least equal to" federal inspection. In addition, the amendment provides for inspection of foreign processing plants exporting meat to the United States.

The act mandates that standards of identity, which specify the kinds and proportions of ingredients in a product, be established; that meat and meat products be clean, wholesome, free from disease and adulteration, and truthfully labeled; and that official establishments where meat products are slaughtered and processed be inspected to assure that animals are free from disease and that products are packed under sanitary conditions.

Label requirements include the name of the product and of the packer or distributor, the inspection mark, net weight, and where applicable the ingredients listed in descending order of weight. Meat product standards are regulated by the Animal and Plant Health Inspection Service, USDA, and are used as a guide by manufacturers of these foods to ensure the proper quality.

The **Poultry Products Inspection Act,** effective in 1959, requires that fresh and frozen ready-to-cook poultry, canned poultry, and canned and frozen poultry products with two per cent or more of cooked poultry meat be inspected for wholesomeness by the Animal and Plant Health Inspection Service, USDA, if sold in interstate or foreign commerce. The act was amended in 1968 to require states to set up poultry inspection programs equal to the federal programs.

The act also requires the official mark of inspection to appear either on the immediate container in which fresh or frozen poultry is shipped or on the shipping container. Other labeling requirements are the same as for meat and meat products. Standards of quality have been established for poultry, and minimum requirements also have been specified for processed poultry products defining the percentage of meat in items such as chicken pie or chicken à la king.

The **Egg Products Inspection Act,** passed in 1978, provides for mandatory inspection of egg processing plants and requires that all liquid egg for freezing and drying be pasteurized.

USDA Quality Grades. The USDA has established standards for most agricultural products and many of these are used voluntarily by growers, canners, and processors. USDA grades, which vary with different categories of foods, are discussed in more detail later in this chapter under "Food Quality."

Grading and Acceptance Services. The Agricultural Marketing Service, in cooperation with state agencies, offers official grading or inspection for quality of meat and meat products, fresh and processed fruits and vegetables, poultry and eggs, and manufactured dairy products. Grading is based on U.S. grade standards developed by the USDA for these products.

Included in the grading and inspection programs is an **Acceptance Service** available to institutional food buyers on request. This service provides verification of the quality specified in a purchase contract. The product is examined at the processing or packing plant or at the supplier's warehouse by an official of the Agricultural Marketing Service or a cooperating state agency. If the product meets the specifications as stated in the contract, the grader stamps it with an official stamp and issues a certificate indicating compliance. If the purchases are to be certified, this provision should be specified in contracts with vendors. The inspection fee is then the responsibility of the supplier.

NATIONAL MARINE AND FISHERIES SERVICE   A voluntary inspection system for fish and fish products and grade standards for some products are controlled by the National Marine and Fisheries Service, an agency of the Department of Commerce. If the product carries a U.S. grade designation, the purchaser is assured of continuous inplant inspection during processing by federal inspectors. An ungraded product may or may not have been inspected during processing.

UNITED STATES PUBLIC HEALTH SERVICE   The Public Health Service is concerned primarily with control of infectious and contagious disease but is also responsible for the safety of some foods. This agency is responsible for the inspection of some shellfish and advises state and local governments on sanitation standards for production, processing, and distribution of milk. The PHS standard for Grade A fresh milk is a standard of wholesomeness, which means that it has met state or local requirements that equal or exceed federal requirements.

The Buyer

Food and supplies for a foodservice organization may be purchased by an individual, by a purchasing department, or through a cooperative arrangement with other institutions, depending on the size and ownership of the organization and its procurement policies. In a small operation the buying may be done by the manager or dietitian as part of his or her responsibilities.

Whatever the arrangement, it is the responsibility of the foodservice or the individual units of a foodservice to communicate its needs to the buyer to assure delivery of the needed amount of food and supplies at an appropriate time and of the desired quality. This requires cooperation on the part of the buyer as well as the foodservice personnel and a willingness to honor the quality standards set by the foodservice.

To purchase the amount and quality of food required for the foodservice within the limitations imposed by the budget and financial policies of the organization requires knowledge of the marketing system, quantities of food needed, food standards, what is available on the market, purchasing methods, and storage requirements.

The buyer represents the institution in negotiations with market representatives and should have some knowledge and understanding of legal requirements, especially as they relate to orders and contracts. There should be a clear understanding as to the extent of the buyer's decision-making authority and of the institutional policies within which the buyer must operate.

Buying demands integrity, maturity, bargaining skills, and maintenance of a high standard of ethics. Acting as an agent for the institution, the buyer is entrusted with making decisions concerning quality, prices, and amounts to purchase and cannot afford to compromise either money or position. Buyers may be subjected to bribes and other kinds of inducements to influence a buying decision, but no gifts or other favors should be accepted that might obligate the buyer.

A buyer must be able to deal successfully with sales representatives, purveyors, and other marketing agents. Courtesy and fair treatment contribute to establishing a satisfactory working relationship with these agents who can be valuable sources of information on new products and the availability of foods on the market. If orders are placed through a salesperson, scheduling regular office appointments or a specific time for telephoning saves time for both the buyer and seller.

Products should be evaluated objectively and buying decisions made on the basis of quality, price, and service. Information received in confidence from one company should not be used to obtain an unfair advantage in competitive negotiations.

CENTRALIZED PURCHASING   Centralized buying, in which a purchasing department is responsible for obtaining needed supplies and equipment for all units in the organization, is used in many universities, schools, multiunit restaurants, and hospitals. By relieving the individual units of responsibility for interviewing sales representatives, negotiating contracts, and placing orders, this system has proven to be cost effective and time-saving for the foodservice, especially if the system also has central storage. Where centralized purchasing is used, the authority to buy fresh produce or other perishables may be delegated to the foodservice, or in multiunit organizations to the individual units.

One disadvantage of centralized purchasing is that excessive paper work may result; also, friction can develop between the purchasing department and the foodservice unit if there is not a clear understanding about authority for decision making, especially on quality standards. This possibility for friction may exist in all large scale purchasing unless the limits of authority are well defined and the lines of communication kept open.

GROUP PURCHASING   It is obvious that buyers must increase volume and/or lower service requirements to improve leverage with suppliers and thus buy at lower prices. The efforts to increase volume have led some foodservice directors to consolidate their buying with that of other organizations in cooperative purchasing arrangements. For example, several hospitals in a metropolitan area may combine their purchases to obtain lower prices and possibly more favorable service arrangements; or in smaller communities, two or more unlike foodservices, such as a school, hospital, and nursing home, may join in a group purchasing agreement. Central warehousing may or may not be part of a group purchasing plan, and if the volume is large enough vendors may agree to deliver merchandise to the individual units.

Group buying differs from central purchasing in that members of the group are independent organizations and are not under the same management; in central purchasing the members usually are units of a larger system, such as schools in a city or countywide school system. The main advantage of group buying obviously is the price advantage gained by increased volume, which in turn may attract more prospective vendors.

The buyer is selected by the group and usually maintains an office independent of the participating organizations. The purchasing service generally is supported by a fee paid by each institution determined by the percentage of its orders. To be effective, all members of the group must commit their time and the majority of their purchase orders to the group's efforts. Participating agencies must agree on common specifications and establish a bid schedule. Food preferences may differ from system to system so members must occasionally be willing to compromise their requirements for the benefit of the group.

The Vendor

The selection of suppliers is one of the most important decisions that must be made in a purchasing program. Management and the buyer should work together in establishing quality standards for foods to be purchased and in conducting a market search for reliable vendors that are able to furnish products of the desired quality.

Information about vendors should include delivery schedules, their reputation for reliability, their ability to furnish the quantities needed, and their policies concerning credit and terms for payment. Some suppliers, for example, extend credit for 30 days but offer a discount for payment within 10 days. Visits to the vendors' establishments and past experience with them, as well as talks with other buyers, will supply much of this information.

The location and size of the foodservice are important factors in the selection of a supplier. If the operation is located in or near a large metropolitan area, there may be several suppliers that could meet its quantity and quality needs and whose delivery schedules are satisfactory for the foodservice.

For an operation in a small or remote location, part or all of its supplies may be purchased locally. In this case, the buyer should be sure that the vendors carry adequate stocks and are able to obtain replenishments quickly. If there are not enough local suppliers to offer competitive prices, the buyer may prefer to purchase certain products, such as dairy products, bakery items, and fresh produce locally and place orders for canned goods and groceries on a less frequent basis from a larger wholesaler. It may be necessary for small organizations to buy from a wholesaler that will break down food packages to quantities the foodservice can use.

Large volume operators may be able to purchase canned foods or other nonperishable items directly from the processor and work out satisfactory arrangements for delivery of their products. Since the quantity of foods purchased would be large, the amount and kind of storage space and the financial resources may be determining factors in whether direct buying is possible.

Methods of Purchasing

The two principal methods of buying are **informal or open market** and **formal competitive bid** buying. Both may be used at various times for different commodities. Variations of these methods or alternative buying arrangements may be preferred by some foodservices or may be used during uncertain market conditions.

Purchasing is a management function and as such the foodservice administrator will have policies and procedures to guide him or her in setting up a course of action. The method of buying selected depends on these institutional policies, on the size of the organization, the amount of money available, location of the vendors, and the frequency of deliveries.

Informal or Open-Market Buying

Informal purchasing probably is the most commonly used method of buying. The system basically is one of ordering needed food supplies from a selected list of dealers based on daily, weekly, or monthly quotations. These prices are based on a set of specifications furnished to interested dealers. The buyer may request daily prices for fresh fruits and vegetables but may use a monthly quotation list for grocery items. The order is placed after consideration of price in relation to quality, delivery, and other services offered.

Contact between the buyer and vendor is made by telephone, a visit to the market, or through sales representatives who call on the buyer. The use of price quotation and order forms on which to record the prices submitted by each seller (Fig. 4.1) is an aid to the buyer. If the quotations are given by telephone, the prices should be recorded. For large orders of canned goods or groceries or where the time lapse between quotations and ordering is not important, requests for written quotations may be made by mail, as shown in Fig. 4.2.

Informal buying requires less lead time than formal competitive buying and is appropriate for foodservices that are too small to justify more formal procedures or when immediate delivery is required. It does have some disadvantages, however. Prices often are not compared with two or more vendors, and because the procedure usually is completed in one day, the buyer does not have an opportunity to negotiate or take advantage of seasonal trends.

Introducing new dealers from time to time and visiting the market when possible enables the buyer to examine what is available from other vendors and note the prices for the current week. When using informal purchasing, the buyer and vendor must agree on quantities and prices before delivery. Only vendors who give reliable service and competitive prices should be considered for open-market buying.

Formal Competitive Bid Buying

In formal competitive bid buying, written specifications and quantities needed are submitted to vendors with an invitation for them to quote prices, within a stated time, for the items listed. The request for bids may be quite formal and advertised in the newspaper, copies may be printed and widely distributed, or less formal with single copies supplied to interested sellers. Bids are opened on a designated date, and the contract generally is awarded to the lowest responsible bidder.

Purchasing agents for local, state, or federal government-controlled institutions usually are required to submit bids to all qualified vendors, especially those bids over a certain dollar limit. Buyers for private organizations, however, may select the companies whom they wish to invite to bid and the buyer may include on the list only those vendors whose performance and reliability are known. The procedure for competitive bid buying is discussed in more detail later in this chapter under "Purchasing Procedures."

		Name of Food Service						
		Fruit and Vegetable Quotation and Order Sheet						

For Use on_____   Delivery Date_____

	Specs	Amount Needed	Amount on Hand	Amount to Order	Price Quotes			
					Vendors			
					A	B	C	D
Fruits:								
Vegetables:								

FIGURE 4.1   A suggested form for recording telephoned price quotations for fresh produce. Combines a listing of total needs, the inventory on hand, and the resulting quantities to order. When order is placed, price quotation from vendor from whom it is to be purchased is circled.

_____ **University**
Food Stores Department

INQUIRY NO.

_____
(Date)

To:

Quote on this sheet your net price f.o.b.
for the items specified below. We reserve
the right to accept or reject all or part of
this proposal.
Quotations received
until 4:00 P.M. _____

Important: Read instructions on reverse side before preparing bid.

Quantity	Unit	REQUEST FOR QUOTATIONS—This is NOT an order	Price Unit	Total Price
		Return—TWO COPIES—To: Food Stores Department		

We quote you f.o.b. _____   Delivery can be made { immediately
                                                                _____ days.

_____
Sign Firm Name Here

Cash Discount: _____

_____   Per _____
Date

FIGURE 4.2   Suggested form for requesting price quotations by mail.

ADVANTAGES AND DISADVANTAGES OF FORMAL BID BUYING   Bid buying usually is required in government procurement systems and is found to be advantageous by large foodservices or multiple unit organizations. The formal bid, if written clearly, minimizes the possibility of misunderstanding as to quality, price, and delivery. The bid system is satisfactory for canned goods, frozen products, staples, and other nonperishable foods. Food that is purchased by standing order, such as milk and bread, is appropriate also for this type of buying, but it may not be practical for perishable items because of the day-to-day fluctuation in market prices.

There are two main disadvantages to formal competitive bidding. The system is time-consuming, and the planning and requests for bids must be made well in advance so that the buyer has time to distribute the bid forms and the suppliers have time to check availability of supplies and determine a fair price. Although this type of buying was designed to ensure honesty, it does lend itself to manipulation when large amounts of money are involved, especially if the buyers and the purchasing department are open to political pressure.

COMPETITIVE BIDDING VARIATIONS   Many variations and techniques are found in formal competitive bidding, depending on the type of institution, financial resources of both vendor and buyer, and storage facilities of the foodservice and delivery capabilities of the vendor. Bids may be written for a supply of merchandise over a period of time at prices that fluctuate with the market; for example, a six-month supply of flour may be required, with 500 pounds delivered each month, at a price compatible with current market conditions.

In a firm fixed price contract (FFP), the price is not subject to adjustment during the period of the contract, which places maximum risk on the vendor and is used when definite specifications are available and fair and reasonable prices can be established at the outset. A buyer may request bids for a month's supply of dairy products, to be delivered daily as needed. Another variation involves the purchase of a specific quantity of merchandise, such as a year's supply of canned goods, but because of inadequate storage the foodservice may wish to withdraw portions of the order as needed within the year.

Many different forms are used in the written bidding system and the terms may differ in various parts of the country, but all of them basically are invitations to bid with the conditions of the bid clearly specified. Attached to the invitation is a listing of the merchandise needed, specifications and quantities involved, and any conditions related to supply and fluctuations in the market. (See the example of a bid request later in this chapter in Fig. 4.8.)

A bid can be written so that the buyer pays for the entire order at the time of purchase, or the merchandise can be paid for as it is withdrawn, with a suitable arrangement to cover the cost of storage and the cost of carrying the inventory in storage.

Other Types of Purchasing

COST-PLUS PURCHASING   In cost-plus purchasing, a buyer agrees to buy certain items from a purveyor for an agreed upon period of time based on a fixed markup over the dealer's cost. The time period may vary and could be open for bid among different dealers. Such a plan is most effective with large volume buying and when deliveries are restricted, preferably to one location.

The dealer's cost generally is based on the cost of material to the purveyor plus any costs incurred in changes in packaging, fabrication of products, loss of required trim, or shrinkage from aging. The markup, which must cover overhead, cost of billing or deliveries, or other expenses that are borne by the vendor, may vary with the type of food being purchased. When negotiating a cost-plus purchasing agreement, there should be a clear understanding of what is included in the cost and what is considered part of the dealer's markup. Some way of verifying the dealer's cost should also be part of the agreement.

PRIME VENDOR OR ONE-STOP PURCHASING   A system of purchasing that is gaining acceptance among restaurant and institutional buyers is prime vendor buying, which is based on an agreement to purchase the majority of specified supply categories from one vendor at an agreed upon price. For example, a vendor may bid on supplying the foodservice with meats, frozen foods, canned goods, cheese, and prepared entrees, to be delivered as needed at regularly scheduled times. When this type of agreement is negotiated, the buyer may request line-item prices, cost-plus percentages, or cost-plus percentages with reflected prices. A prime vendor agreement usually is for a definite period and normally covers a specified quantity of items.

Prime vendor purchasing saves time for the buyer, and the overhead, delivery costs, and selling and billing costs can be less than when dealing with several purveyors. One disadvantage is the loss of a reliable backup vendor; another could be an increase in prices due to lower competition. This type of purchasing is similar to cost-plus buying except that the buyer is dealing with fewer vendors.

BLANKET PURCHASE AGREEMENT (BPA)   The blanket purchase arrangement is used sometimes when a wide variety of items are purchased from local suppliers, but the exact items, quantities, and delivery requirements are not known in advance and may vary. Vendors agree to furnish on a "charge account" basis such supplies as may be ordered during a stated period of time. BPA's should be established with more than one vendor so that delivery orders can be placed with the firm offering the best price. Use of more than one vendor also allows the buyer to identify a "price creep," which is possible if only one vendor is involved.

Product Selection

Market Forms of Foods

Deciding on the form in which food is to be purchased is a major decision that requires careful study. Several different products may be available, all of which will produce an acceptable menu item. Costs involved in purchase and use of fresh or natural forms of food versus partially prepared or ready-to-eat foods and the acceptability of such items by the consumer are major factors to consider.

Because of lack of space, equipment, or personnel, some foodservices are faced with a decision to convert to a convenience system in which all prepared foods are purchased. Before making this decision, the cost, quality, and acceptability to patrons of the purchased prepared food should be compared with the same menu item made on the premises. If the decision is to buy the prepared product, the dietitian or manager and the buyer must establish quality standards for these foods. Standards of identity have been developed for some, but there is wide variation in quality.

For foodservices preferring the preparation of products in their own kitchens, there are alternatives in purchasing that save preparation time. The market offers a variety of processed ingredients from which to choose. Dehydrated chopped onions, frozen lemon juice, cooked chicken and turkey, and the various baking, soup, sauce, and pudding mixes are examples. Casserole-type entrees, often requiring time-consuming processes, may be made by combining several convenience items, such as frozen diced chicken, sauce made from a mix or from canned soups, and pasta or vegetables.

Choices among fresh, frozen, and canned foods depend on the amount of labor available for preparation, comparative portion costs, and acceptability by patrons. The high cost of labor has caused many foodservices to limit the use of fresh fruits and vegetables except for salads or during times of plentiful supply when costs are lower. There may be times when a menu change must be made because of the price differential among fresh, frozen, and canned food items.

Keeping in mind the quality standard established for the finished product, the dietitian or manager must find the right combination of available foods in a form that will keep preparation to a minimum yet yield a product of the desired quality.

Food Quality

Before food can be purchased, the quality of foods most appropriate to the foodservice operation and their use on the menu must be decided. The top grade may not always be necessary for all purposes. Foods sold under the lower grades are wholesome and have essentially the same nutritional value, but they differ mainly in appearance and, to a lesser degree, in flavor.

Foods that have been downgraded because of lack of uniformity in size or that have broken or have irregular pieces may be satisfactory to use in soups, casseroles, fruit gelatin, or fruit cobblers, for example. Also, more than one style or pack in some food items may be needed. Unsweetened or pie pack canned peaches may be satisfactory for making pies, but peaches in heavy syrup would be preferable for serving in a dish as a dessert.

QUALITY STANDARDS   Quality may refer to wholesomeness, cleanliness, or freedom from undesirable substances. It may denote a degree of perfection in shape, uniformity of size, or freedom from blemishes. It may also describe the extent of desirable characteristics of color, flavor, aroma, texture, tenderness, and maturity. Assessment of quality may be denoted by grade, brand, or condition.

GRADES AND INSPECTION   Grades are market classifications of quality. They reflect the relationship of quality to the standard established for the product, and they indicate the degree of variation from that standard. Grades have been established by the United States Department of Agriculture for most agricultural products, but their use is voluntary. Inspection of commodities for wholesomeness is mandatory for meats, poultry, and other processed foods.

USDA grades are based on scoring factors, with the total score determining the grade. The grades vary with different categories of food as noted in the following list.

• *Meats:* U.S. Prime, U.S. Choice, U.S. Good, and U.S. Standard. Quality grades are assigned according to marbling, maturity of the animal, and color, firmness, and texture of the muscle. Yield grades of 1,2,3,4, or 5 are used for beef and lamb to indicate the proportion of usable meat to

fat and bone, with 1 having the lowest fat content. Veal and pork are not
graded separately for yield and quality.

- *Poultry:* Consumer grades are U.S. Grades A, B, and C, based on confor-
mation, fleshing, fat covering, and freedom from defects. Grades often
used in institutional purchasing are U.S. Procurement Grades 1 and 2.
The procurement grades place more emphasis on meat yield than on appearance.
- *Eggs:* U.S. Grades AA, A, and B. Quality in shell eggs is based on exterior factors (cleanliness, soundness, shape of shell, and texture) and interior factors (condition of the yolk and white and the size of the air cell, as
determined by candling). Shell eggs are classified according to size, as Extra Large, Large, Medium, and Small.
- *Cheddar cheese:* U.S. Grades AA, A, B, and C. Scores are on the basis of
flavor, aroma, body and texture, finish and appearance, and color.
- *Butter:* U.S. Grades AA (93 score), A (92 score), B (90 score), and C (89
score), based on flavor, body and texture, color, and salt.
- *Fresh produce:* U.S. Fancy, U.S. Extra No. 1, U.S. No. 1, U.S. Combination, and U.S. No. 2. Fresh fruits and vegetables are graded according to
the qualities deemed desirable for the individual type of commodity, but
may include uniformity of size, cleanliness, color, or lack of damage or
defects. Grades are designated by name or by number. Because of the
wide variation in quality and the perishable nature of fresh fruits and
vegetables, visual inspection may be as important as grade; or a buyer
might specify that the condition of the product at the time of delivery
should equal the grade requested.
- *Canned fruits and vegetables:* U.S. Grade A (or Fancy), U.S. Grade B (or
Choice for fruits and Extra Standard for vegetables), U.S. Grade C (or
Standard), and U.S. Grade D (or Substandard). The factors for canned
fruits and vegetables include color, uniformity of size, absence of defects,
character, flavor, consistency, finish, size, symmetry, clearness of liquor,
maturity, texture, wholeness, and cut. In addition to these factors, general requirements must be met, such as fill of container, drained weight,
and syrup density. The grading factors vary with individual canned fruits
and vegetables, but the scoring range is the same. Fig. 4.3 shows suggested standards for canned foods. Following is a summary of the total
scoring ranges for grades of canned fruits and vegetables:

Grades	Scores
A (Fancy)	90–100
B (Choice, Extra Standard)	75–89
C (Standard)	60–74
Substandard	0–59

- *Frozen fruits and vegetables:* U.S. grade standards are available for many

Standards for Canned Foods

Fruits

Grade	Quality of Fruit	Syrup
U.S. Grade A or Fancy	Excellent quality, high color, ripe, firm, free from blemishes, uniform in size, and very symmetrical	Heavy, about 55%. May vary from 40 to 70%, depending on acidity of fruit
U.S. Grade B or Choice or Extra-Standard	Fine quality, high color, ripe, firm, free from serious blemishes, uniform in size, and symmetrical	About 40%. Usually contains 10 to 15% less sugar than in Fancy grade.
U.S. Grade C or Standard	Good quality, reasonably good color, reasonably free from blemishes, reasonably uniform in size, color, and degree of ripeness, and reasonably symmetrical	About 25%. Contains 10 to 15% less sugar than in Choice grades
Substandard	Lower than the minimum grade for Standard.	Often water-packed. If packed in syrup, it is not over 10%.

Vegetables

Grade	Quality of Vegetable
U.S. Grade A or Fancy	Best flavored, most tender and succulent, uniform in size, shape, color, tenderness; represents choice of crop.
U.S. Grade B or Extra-Standard (sometimes called Choice)	Flavor fine; tender and succulent; may be slightly more mature, more firm in texture, and sometimes less uniform than Fancy grade.
U.S. Grade C or Standard	Flavor less delicate; more firm in texture, often less uniform in size, shape, color; more mature.
Substandard	Lower than the minimum grade for Standard.

FIGURE 4.3 Suggested standards for USDA grades of canned fruits and vegetables.

frozen fruits and vegetables but not standards of identity, quality, or fill of container. Fruit may be packed with sugar in varying proportions such as four of five parts of fruit to one part of sugar by weight or without sugar. Fruits or vegetables may be individually quick frozen (IQF) or frozen in solid blocks.

(a)   *(b)*   *(c)*

FIGURE 4.4   Federal meat stamps. (a) Round stamp shows that meat was federally inspected and passed as wholesome food; the number identifies the establishment in which meat was inspected. (b) Shield-shaped stamp shows that meat was federally graded. (c) Yield stamp denotes amount of usable meat in carcass.

Designation of U.S. grades and marking in the form of a shield are permitted only on foods officially graded under the supervision of the Agricultural Marketing Service of the USDA. Fig. 4.4 shows examples of inspection and grade stamps.

BRANDS   Brands are assigned by private organizations. Producers, processors, or distributors attempt to establish a commodity as a standard product and to develop demand specifically for their own brands. The reliability of these trade names depends on the reliability of the company. Brand names may represent products that are higher or lower in quality than the corresponding government grade, and some brand name products are not consistent in quality. Private companies may set up their own grading system, but such ranking may show variation from season to season.

Some knowledge of brand names is essential in today's marketing system. USDA grades are used for most fresh meats and for fresh fruits and vegetables, but very few canners use them, preferring instead to develop their own brands. If USDA grades are specified and bidders submit prices on brand products, the buyer should be familiar with USDA grades and scores in order to evaluate the products. The buyer may wish to request samples or, if the order is large enough to justify it, request a USDA grading certificate, as described earlier in this chapter under "Grading and Acceptance Services," which verifies that the food is of the quality specified.

Purchasing Procedures

The complexity of the purchasing system depends on the size and type of organization, whether the buying is centralized or decentralized, and established management policies. Procedures should be as simple as possible, with record keeping and paper work limited to those essential for control and communication.

Good purchasing practices include the use of appropriate buying methods, a systematic ordering schedule, maintenance of an adequate flow of goods to meet production requirements, and a systematic receiving procedure and inventory control.

The process of purchasing, using the informal and formal methods of buying, is shown in Fig. 4.5 and discussed in the following sections.

IDENTIFYING NEEDS   Quantities of food needed for production of the planned menus are identified from the menus and from recipes used to prepare them. Added to this are staples and other supplies needed in the various departments or production and service areas. Ingredients that are in stock are requisitioned from the storeroom, as explained in more detail later in this chapter under "Storeroom Issues."

Inventory Stock Level. A system of communicating needs from the production areas and the storeroom to the buyer is essential. Establishing a minimum and maximum stock level provides a means of alerting the buyer to needs. The minimum level is the point, established for each item, below which the inventory should not fall. This amount will depend on the usage and time required for ordering and delivery. If canned fruits and vegetables, for example, are purchased every three months through the formal bidding procedure, the time lapse would be longer than for fresh produce that is ordered daily or weekly through informal buying.

The **minimum stock level,** then, includes a safety factor for replenishing the stock. The **maximum inventory level** is equal to the safety stock plus the estimated usage, which is determined by past experience and forecasts. From this information, a reorder point is established.

Another factor to be considered in the amount to reorder is the quantity most feasible economically. For example, if five cases of a food are needed to bring the stock to the desired level, but a price advantage can be gained by buying ten cases, the buyer may consider purchasing the larger quantity.

Quantity to Buy. The amount of food and supplies purchased at one time and the frequency of ordering depend on the amount of money on

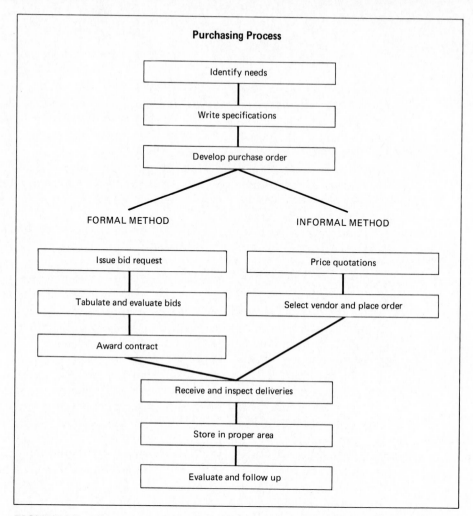

FIGURE 4.5   The process of purchasing, using the informal and formal methods of buying.

hand, the method of buying, the frequency of deliveries, and storage space. With adequate and suitable storage, the purchase of staples may vary from a two- to six-month supply, with perishables weekly and/or daily.

Meat, poultry, fish, fresh fruits and vegetables, and other perishable foods may be purchased for immediate use on the day's menu or more likely are calculated for two or more days, depending on delivery schedules and storage facilities, and preparation requirements. Quantities are based on the portion size and projected number of servings needed, taking into consideration the preparation and cooking losses. If the recipes are stored in a computer, it is a simple task to calculate the amount needed for the desired number of servings.

Some products such as milk and bread are delivered daily or several times a week, and the orders are based on the amount needed to keep the inventory up to a desired level. The price may be determined by a contract to furnish certain items as needed for a period of a month or longer. A stock level of butter and margarine, cheese, eggs, lettuce, celery, onions, and certain other fruits and vegetables may be established and maintained, whereas other produce is ordered as needed from the menu. Fig. 4.6 is a suggested form for recording supplies on hand and the amounts to order.

Canned foods and groceries generally are purchased less often than are perishable foods, the frequency depending on storage space and money available. A year's supply of canned goods may be purchased at one time if bought on competitive bid or if growing conditions indicate a possible shortage or a rise in prices. In some cases, an arrangement may be made for the supplier to store the food and deliver as needed. A projection is made of the quantity that will be needed for the designated period, based on past purchases. That amount less the inventory is the quantity to purchase.

WRITING SPECIFICATIONS Many foodservice operations have a set of specifications that have been developed as different food and supply items have been purchased. If specifications do not exist for the items being purchased, they should be written before bids or quotations are sought.

A specification is a detailed description of a product stated in terms that are clearly understood by both buyer and seller. Specifications should be brief and concise but should contain enough information so that there can be no misunderstanding. Certain information is included in all specifications for food products:

- **Name of the product.** The common or trade name of an item generally is simple, but the name of some products may vary in different parts of the country.
- **Federal grade or brand.** As already noted, the USDA has established federal grades for most agricultural products, but many packers or food processors have developed their own brands or trade names for canned, frozen, or other processed foods. If a bidder submits a quotation on a brand name product in lieu of a federal grade, buyers may request verification of quality by the USDA Acceptance Service; see earlier in this chapter under "United States Department of Agriculture—Grading and Acceptance Service."

Daily Purchase Order

Date _____

ON HAND		ORDER	ON HAND		ORDER
Dairy:			*Fresh Vegetables:*		
_____	gal whole milk	_____	_____	Cabbage	_____
_____	cs ½ pt whole	_____	_____	Carrots	_____
_____	cs ½ pt choc	_____	_____	Cauliflower	_____
_____	cs ½ pt B. milk	_____	_____	Celery	_____
_____	cs ½ pt skim	_____	_____	Celery cabbage	_____
_____	lb cot. cheese	_____	_____	Cucumbers	_____
_____	Ice cream	_____	_____	Egg plant	_____
Bread:			_____	Head lettuce	_____
_____	White bread	_____	_____	Leaf lettuce	_____
_____	Wheat bread	_____	_____	Onions	_____
_____	Rye	_____	_____	Parsley	_____
_____	Sandwich white	_____	_____	Peppers	_____
_____	Sandwich wheat	_____	_____	Potatoes	_____
_____	Sandwich rye	_____	_____	Spinach	_____
_____	Crumbs	_____	_____	Squash	_____
Sweet Rolls:			_____	Tomatoes	_____
_____	Raisin bread	_____	*Frozen Vegetables:*		
_____	Cinnamon	_____	_____	Asparagus	_____
_____	Butterscotch	_____	_____	Green beans	_____
_____	Raised donuts	_____	_____	Lima beans	_____
_____	Bismark	_____	_____	Broccoli	_____
_____	Twist	_____	_____	Brussel sprouts	_____
_____	Pecan strip	_____	_____	Cauliflower	_____
_____	Stick donuts	_____	_____	Peas	_____
_____	Jelly donuts	_____	*Fresh Fruits:*		
Meats:			_____	Apples	_____
			_____	Bananas	_____
			_____	Berries	_____
			_____	Cantaloupe	_____
			_____	Grapefruit	_____
			_____	Grapes	_____
			_____	Lemons	_____
			_____	Oranges	_____
			_____	Peaches	_____
			_____	Pineapple	_____
			_____	Plums	_____
Fish:			_____	Watermelon	_____
			Poultry:		
			_____	Chicken	_____
Miscellaneous:			_____	Turkey	_____
			_____	Eggs	_____
			Frozen Fruits and Juices:		
			_____	Apples	_____
			_____	Cherries	_____
			_____	G. fruit sections	_____
			_____	Lemon juice	_____
Potato Chips:			_____	Orange juice	_____
			_____	Peaches	_____
			_____	Rhubarb	_____
			_____	Strawberries	_____

FIGURE 4.6   Daily purchase order form.

- **Unit on which price is quoted.** This refers to the size and type of unit, such as pound, gallon, can, bunch, or other unit in common use.
- **Name and size of container.** Examples of container size are: a case holding 6 no. 10 cans, a 30-pound can of frozen cherries, or a 30-pound lug of tomatoes.
- **Count per container or approximate number per pound.** Examples are: 30/35 count canned peach halves per no. 10 can; 8 per pound frankfurters; size 36 grapefruit, which indicates the number of fruit in a 4/5 bushel box. Sizes 27 through 40 are acceptable for half grapefruit servings. Oranges and apples also are sized according to the number in the box. Apples 80 to 100 are large, 113 to 138 medium, and 150 to 175 small.

Additional information may be required for different categories of food:

- **Fresh fruits and vegetables:** variety, weight, degree of maturity, geographical location; for example, Jonathan apples, Indian River grapefruit, or bananas turning ripe, pale yellow with green tips; if needed immediately, specify fully ripe, bright yellow flaked with brown, and no green.
- **Canned foods:** type or style, pack, size, syrup density, drained weight, specific gravity. Examples are: cream style corn; whole vertical pack green beans; no. 4 sieve peas; apricot halves in heavy syrup or 21–25 degrees brix (syrup density); diced beets, drained weight 72 ounces (per no. 10 can); tomato catsup with total solids content of at least 33 per cent.
- **Frozen foods:** variety, sugar ratio, temperature during delivery and upon receipt; for example, sliced strawberries, sugar ratio of 4:1, or delivered frozen, 0°F or less.
- **Meats and meat products:** age, market class, cut of meat, exact cutting instructions, weight range, fat content, condition upon receipt.
- **Dairy products:** milk fat content, milk solids, bacteria count, temperature during delivery and upon receipt.

A well-written specification includes all of the information needed to identify the food item and to assure the buyer of getting exactly the quality desired. It should be identifiable with products or grades currently on the market and capable of being checked by label statements or USDA grades. Information for use in writing specifications is available from the USDA and from material published by industry such as the National Association of Meat Purveyors. Names and addresses are included in the list of supplementary references at the end of this chapter.

DEVELOPING PURCHASE ORDERS The procedure for authorizing purchases differs in various foodservices. The process may begin with a purchase request, to be used along with quality specifications, as the basis for a purchase order and bid request to be issued by an authorized purchasing agent. A foodservice director who is also the buyer may develop a market order or purchase order that has been compiled from requisitions from the various production and service units or from individual units in a school system or other multiunit organization. In central purchasing for these operations, the requisitions originating in individual units do not necessarily need to include specifications, since the quality is determined at a central point and is uniform throughout the system.

Regardless of the method used, there should be a clear understanding of who is authorized to issue purchase requests or orders and the vendors should be aware of the name or names of authorized purchasing personnel. Authorization to sign for goods received and to requisition supplies from the storage areas should also be understood.

The purchase order specifies the quantity of each item needed for the bid period, quality specifications, and required date of delivery. The order must include the name of the organization, the individual making the request, and the signature of the person officially authorized to sign the order. Purchase order forms may be prenumbered or the number may be added at the time of final approval, but a number, as well as the date of issue, is essential for identification. Fig. 4.7 is a suggested purchase order form.

ISSUING BID REQUESTS   An invitation to bid provides vendors with an opportunity to submit bids for specific items advertised. Bid requests originate in the office of the purchasing agent or the person authorized to purchase for the foodservice. A bid request includes quantities required and purchase specifications for each item. In addition, the general conditions of acceptance are outlined, including the date and method of delivery, terms of payment, willingness to accept all or part of the bid, discounts, the date of closing bids, and other terms of the negotiations. Fig. 4.8 is a sample bid request that includes general requirements and that would be used with Fig. 4.9, which would list needed items and specifications.

The bid request may also ask for samples to be tested. This is especially important when large quantities are involved and often is requested when purchasing canned foods. Testing of canned foods is done by "can cutting," which involves opening of the sample cans and evaluating the products according to USDA scoring factors, as noted earlier in this chapter under "Grades and Inspection—Canned fruits and vegetables." If samples from more than one company are being tested, the labels on the cans should be covered so the test will be impartial.

Copies of USDA specifications and score sheets are available from the Government Printing Office. An example of a score sheet for canned foods

Purchase Order

Name of Institution _____ Date _____

_____ Purchase Order # _____
Address   *(Please refer to above number*
                                           on all invoices)
_____
Address   Requisition No. _____

Department _____ Date Required _____

To _____

_____

_____

_____

Instruction for Completing Order. Prepare in triplicate for the
vendor, business office, and the manager.

Shipped to: _____ FOB _____ Via _____ Terms _____

Unit	Total Quantity	Specification	Price per unit	Total cost

Approved by _____

FIGURE 4.7 Suggested purchase order form.

Bid Request for Frozen Fruits and Vegetables

Issued By _____   Date _____

_____   Date to be Delivered _____

Address _____

_____

Bid Request for _____

Notice is hereby given that the Board of Education of _____ County, _____ State (hereinafter referred to as the Board) requests written and sealed bids on the following items to be submitted to said Board on or before 10:30 a.m. on _____, 19___ and on each subsequent bidding period date indicated in the bid specifications. Sealed bids will not be opened until 10:30 a.m. _____, 19___ if the outside is marked: Do not open until _____. Respond on attached bid form.

Contract Period: The bid covers the period from date of award through _____, 19___, inclusive and vendors receiving awards shall be the sole suppliers to all schools for items for the period.

Samples: Bidders will be required to submit samples of the items bid upon. Samples are to be furnished without cost to _____ and are to be sent to _____ on _____ by _____.

Quality: Successful bidders must furnish United States Department of Agriculture Grade Certificates indicating each fruit and vegetable item to be U.S. Grade ___.

Grade Certificates: A U.S. Grade Certificate shall be submitted for required items prior to delivery. These certificates must cover the specific brand name of items being delivered. The code numbers on the item being delivered shall be the same as the codes listed on the certificate.

Estimated Quantities: Quantities indicated on Bid Proposal Forms are estimated total requirements based on anticipated use. They will provide the basis for determining the total low bid complying with specifications for each group of items and are submitted as information.

Actual Quantities: Quantities on attached Bid Sheet are estimated to cover the period from date of award to _____, 19___, inclusive. The School Food Service Department will furnish the successful bidder with actual quantities as are needed. Purchaser guarantees to purchase during contract period only, the actual requirements needed.

Delivery (Equipment): Carrier shall utilize only properly insulated, mechanical or thermostatic temperature control refrigeration equipment. Such equipment must be capable of maintaining temperature to protect the product. All products must be delivered in a hard frozen state, 0°F. or below.

The Board of Public Education reserves the right to reject the use of any equipment by a carrier if it is not in a clean, sanitary condition and suitable for hauling of all goods.

Each carrier shall furnish a Certificate of Insurance issued by an insurance company showing that the Board of Public Education will be protected from loss or damage to property of third persons or to the carriers' own property, loss or damage to Board of Public Education commodities, and injury or death to third persons or to the carrier's employees. Carrier will assume full common liability for all shipments.

FIGURE 4.8a and 4.8b   Sample bid request.   *From* Food Buying Guide for School Food Service. *PA 1257, USDA.*

Orders: All orders will be placed directly with awardees by telephone by the individual qualified purchasing official who in some cases may be the individual lunchroom manager. They may order fractional cases. Regular orders should be placed at least seventy-two (72) hours (3 work days) before the delivery time requested; but each emergency order should be filled within two (2) hours after the order is placed. ALL VENDORS MUST SUBMIT SEPARATE DELIVERY TICKETS AND/OR INVOICES FOR NONBID ITEMS.

Deliveries: Deliveries shall be made to the receiving area of individual schools between the hours of 7:00 a.m. and 2:15 p.m. These deliveries must be made in mechanically refrigerated trucks maintaining a temperature below freezing at all times.

Invoices & Statements: Invoices for the purchases of food and miscellaneous supplies made by schools are paid by the central accounting department. In order to facilitate the handling of these invoices, ALL VENDORS MUST ADHERE TO THE FOLLOWING INSTRUCTIONS:

Code number for each school listed on each invoice. (A list of schools with code number is attached.)

All items on delivery tickets MUST be billed according to description of item quoted on bid. Unit prices for all items shall be recorded and invoices shall be accurately extended. SEPARATE DELIVERY TICKETS AND/OR INVOICES SHALL BE MADE FOR ALL NONBID ITEMS.

All vendors must issue delivery tickets and credit memos in QUADRUPLICATE, and all four (4) copies must be signed by qualified purchasing official.

> 2 copies (original and 1 carbon) left with proper person at time of delivery.

> 2 copies to be returned to vendor.

The vendor shall forward as per attached list, weekly statements, with one signed delivery ticket attached, directly to the School Food Service Department.

All delivery tickets supporting weekly statements must be in exact agreement with copy of delivery tickets left with manager. If for any reason it is necessary to make a change on the delivery ticket, MAKE AN ADDITIONAL CHARGE OR CREDIT MEMO.

All cancellations or merchandise returns must be recorded by driver on all FOUR COPIES of delivery tickets, or "pick-up tickets."

> 2 copies left with manager at time of pick-up.

> 2 copies to be returned to vendor.

> Do not mail statement to individual schools.

A monthly statement for each school should be sent to the official responsible for paying bills by the 10th working day or by the 10th calendar day of every month, following date of purchase.

is shown in Fig. 4.10. Scores from different samples would be summarized on a form similar to Fig. 4.11. Product evaluation forms may be developed for testing of other foods and should include specific qualities to be judged. A panel composed of persons who are involved in foodservice quality control should participate.

A bid schedule outlining the bid periods and delivery frequency should be established and when possible planned to take advantage of new packs of processed fruits and vegetables usually available in October and January.

This step is omitted in informal buying. Quotations are requested from two or more vendors, usually by telephone or from price sheets.

TABULATING AND EVALUATING BIDS Bids should be kept sealed and confidential until the designated time for opening. Sealed envelopes containing the bids should be stamped to indicate the date, time, and place of receipt. Bids received after the time and date specified for bid opening must be rejected and returned unopened to the bidder.

Specifications For Frozen Fruits and Vegetables

Bid Form

Name of School District _____ Date _____

Item no.	Quantity	Unit size	Item and specification	Brand quoted	Quantity quoted	Unit price	Total price

FIGURE 4.9 Bid form to be used with Fig. 4.8 to list items and specifications.

The opening and tabulation of bids should be under the control of an appropriate official. When schools and other public institutions are involved, the quotations and contents of bids should be open to the public. The bids and low bids should be carefully examined. In most instances public purchasing laws specify that the award be made to the lowest responsible bidder. The following points should be considered, however, before accepting bids:

1. Ability and capacity of the bidder to perform the contract and provide the service
2. Ability of the bidder to provide the service promptly and within the time specified
3. Integrity and reputation of the bidder
4. Quality of bidder's performance on previous contracts or services
5. Bidder's compliance with laws and with specifications relating to contracts or service
6. Bidder's financial resources

When the award is not given to the lowest bidder, a full and complete statement of the reasons should be prepared and filed with other papers relating to the transaction.

Score Sheet for Canned Tomatoes

Number, Size, and Kind of Container

Label

Container Mark or Identification	Cans/Glass		
	Cases		
Net Weight (oz)			
Vacuum (in.)			
Drained Weight (oz)			

Factors	Score Points			
I. DRAINED WEIGHT	20	(A) 18–20 (B) 15–17 (C) 12–14 (SStd) 0–11		
II. WHOLENESS	20	(A) 18–20 (B) 15–17 (C) 12–14		
III. COLOR	30	(A) 27–30 (B) 23–36 (C) 19–22 (SStd) 0–18		
IV. ABSENCE OF DEFECTS	30	(A) 27–30 (B) 22–26 (C) 17–21 (SStd) 0–16		
TOTAL SCORE	100			
NORMAL FLAVOR AND ODOR				
GRADE				

FIGURE 4.10 Government score sheet for grading canned tomatoes.

Kind	Code	Label Net Weight	Actual Weight	Sp. Gr. or Drained Weight	Brix	Count	Remarks and Ratings (Defects, Color, etc.)	Price Per Dozen	Price Per Can	Price Per Piece

FIGURE 4.11   Suggested form for recording data on samples of canned products.

AWARDING CONTRACTS   The contract should be awarded to the most responsive and responsible bidder with the price most advantageous to the purchaser. Buying on the basis of price alone can result in the delivery of products that are below the expectations of the foodservice. Purchasing should be on the basis of price, quality, and service.

The general conditions of the contract should include services to be rendered, dates and method of deliveries, inspection requests, grade certificates required, procedure for substitutions, and conditions for payment. The following information should also be provided: name and address of the foodservice, a contract number, type of items the contract covers, contract period, date of contract issue, point of delivery, quantities to be purchased, and the signature of an authorized representative of the firm submitting the bid.

A contract that is issued represents the legal acceptance of the offer made by the successful bidder, and it is binding. All bidders, both successful and unsuccessful, should be notified of the action. When the contract is made by a purchasing agent, the foodservice should receive a copy of the contract award and specifications.

This step is omitted when using informal purchasing.

RECEIVING AND INSPECTING DELIVERIES   When purchases are delivered, they should be inspected for condition and checked against the invoice or delivery slip for shortages or omissions. Containers of fresh produce should be opened and inspected for quality when received. The delivery slip from the vendor should be signed only after making sure all goods ordered are received and in good condition. Each item should be counted, measured, or weighed, then stored in the appropriate area. Scales should be standard equipment in every receiving room. A chart posted in the receiving room near the scales showing the average weights of perishable food items aids in checking deliveries.

Merchandise that is received in damaged condition or gives an indication that it has been exposed to higher temperatures during delivery should be rejected and the vendor notified immediately. The invoice or delivery slip, which has been prepared by the vendor, should be checked to see if it agrees with the purchase order and that extensions are correct.

STORING IN PROPER AREA   Shipments received should be stored in the appropriate storage areas as soon as possible after delivery and their receipt recorded on inventory records. Storage is discussed in detail in the following section.

EVALUATING AND FOLLOWING UP   Evaluation of products should be continued as they are issued for use because some discrepancies may not be detected until the item is in use. When products are found to be defective, some type of adjustment should be made. If the products are usable but do not meet the specifications, the buyer may request a price adjustment. The manager may refuse to accept the shipment or, if some of the food or supplies are used but found to be unsatisfactory, the buyer may arrange to return the remaining merchandise or request some type of compensation. The purchasing agent or other proper official should be notified of deficiencies in quality, service, or delivery.

Storage

The flow of materials through a foodservice operation begins in the receiving and storage areas. Careful consideration should be given to procedures for receiving and storage as well as to the construction and physical needs of both areas. In planning, there should be a straight line from receiving dock to the storeroom and/or refrigerators and preferably on the same level as the kitchen. A short distance between receiving and storage will reduce the amount of labor required, lessen pilferage, and cause the least amount of deterioration in food products.

The proper storage of food immediately after it has been received and checked is an important factor in the prevention and control of loss or waste. When food is left unguarded in the receiving area or exposed to the elements or extremes of temperature for even a short time, its safekeeping and quality are jeopardized.

Adequate space for dry, refrigerator, and freezer storage should be provided in locations that are convenient to receiving and preparation areas. Temperature and humidity controls and provision for circulation of air are necessary to retain the various quality factors of the stored foods. The length of time foods may be held satisfactorily and without appreciable deterioration depends on the product and its quality when stored as well as the conditions of storage. Suggested maximum temperatures and storage times for a few typical foods are given in Fig. 4.12. The condition of stored food and the temperature of the storage units should be checked frequently.

Security measures in the receiving and storage areas include the employment and training of qualified reliable personnel, immediate moving of products from receiving to storage, and scheduled hours for receiving. Storage areas should be kept locked, and daily stores and refrigerator areas should be locked when responsible personnel are not present.

Receiving Area

The receiving area should be located near the delivery door and should be convenient to the storage areas. The space should be large enough so that an entire shipment of food can be inspected before being moved to storage areas. Minimum equipment should include platform (Fig. 4.13) and counter scales, a table for inspection of deliveries, a desk, and hand trucks or carts as needed for moving the merchandise.

Cleanliness and pest control are important in the receiving room and loading dock, just as they are in the storage areas. The floor should have a surface that is easily cleaned and ideally has floor drains and water connections to enable scrubbing. Adequate screening should be provided to protect the area from flies and other insects. Electrical devices for destroying insects are sometimes mounted on the wall near the delivery entrance.

Dry Storage

The main requisites of a food dry-storage area are that it be dry, cool, and properly ventilated. If possible it should be in a convenient location to the receiving and preparation areas.

Dry storage is intended for nonperishable foods that do not require refrigeration. Paper supplies often are stored with foods, but a separate room should be provided for cleaning supplies, as required in many health codes. The separation of food and cleaning materials that could be toxic prevents a possible error in identification or a mixup in filling requisitions.

TEMPERATURE AND VENTILATION   The storage area should be dry and the temperature not over 70°F. A dark, damp atmosphere is conducive to the growth of certain organisms such as molds and to the development of unpleasant odors. Dry staples such as flour, sugar, rice, condiments, and

Food	Suggested Maximum Temperature (°F)	Recommended Maximum Storage
Canned products	70	12 months
Cooked dishes with eggs, meat, milk, fish, poultry	36	Serve day prepared
Cream filled pastries	36	Serve day prepared
Dairy products		
Milk (fluid)	40	3 days In original container, tightly covered
Milk (dried)	70	3 months In original container
Butter	40	2 weeks In waxed cartons
Cheese (hard)	40	6 months Tightly wrapped
Cheese (soft)	40	7 days In tightly covered container
Ice cream and ices	10	3 months In original container, covered
Eggs	45	7 days Unwashed, not in cardboard
Fish (fresh)	36	2 days Loosely wrapped
Shellfish	36	5 days In covered container
Frozen products	0 (to −20)	
Fruits and vegetables		1 growing season to another Original container
Beef, poultry, eggs		6–12 months Original container
Fresh pork (not ground)		3–6 months Original container
Lamb and veal		6–9 months Original container
Sausage, ground meat, fish		1–3 months Original container
Fruits		
Peaches, plums, berries	50	7 days Unwashed
Apples, pears, citrus	50 (to 70)	2 weeks Original container
Leftovers	36	2 days In covered container
Poultry	36	1–2 days Loosely wrapped
Meat		
Ground	38	2 days Loosely wrapped
Fresh meat cuts	38	3–5 days Loosely wrapped
Liver and variety meats	38	2 days Loosely wrapped
Cold cuts (sliced)	38	3–5 days Wrapped in semimoisture-proof paper
Cured bacon	38	1–4 weeks May wrap tightly
Ham (tender cured)	38	1–6 weeks May wrap tightly
Ham (canned)	38	6 weeks Original container, unopened
Dried beef	38	6 weeks May wrap tightly
Vegetables		
Leafy	45	7 days Unwashed
Potatoes, onions, root vegetables	70	7–30 days Dry in ventilated container or bags

FIGURE 4.12   Suggested maximum storage temperatures and times.

FIGURE 4.13 Weighing-in scale with dial visible from both sides. *Courtesy Dietary Department, Ohio State University Hospital.*

canned foods are more apt to deteriorate in a damp storage area. The storeroom is more easily kept dry if located at or above ground level, although it need not have outside windows unless required by code. If the storage area does have windows, they should be equipped with security-type sash and screens and painted opaque to protect foods from direct sunlight.

Ventilation is one of the most important factors in dry storage. The use of wall vents, as shown in Fig. 4.14, is the most efficient method of obtaining circulation of air, but other methods are possible. The circulation of air around bags and cartons of food is necessary to aid in the removal of moisture, reduction of temperature, and elimination of odors. For this reason, containers of food are often cross-stacked for better air circulation.

STOREROOM ARRANGEMENT Foods and supplies should be stored in an orderly and systematic arrangement. A definite place should be assigned to each item with similar products grouped together. The containers are dated and usually left in the original package or placed in tightly covered contain-

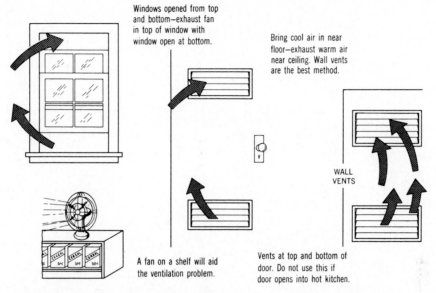

Windows opened from top and bottom—exhaust fan in top of window with window open at bottom.

Bring cool air in near floor—exhaust warm air near ceiling. Wall vents are the best method.

WALL VENTS

A fan on a shelf will aid the ventilation problem.

Vents at top and bottom of door. Do not use this if door opens into hot kitchen.

FIGURE 4.14   Suggestions of possible ways to provide circulation of air in a dry storage area.   *Courtesy, Ohio Department of Health.*

ers if the lots are broken. All items should be stored on racks or shelves instead of directly on the floor or against walls.

Cases and bags of food may be stacked on slatted floor racks, pallets, or wheeled metal platforms. Hand or power lifts are useful for moving loaded pallets from one location to another, but the aisles between shelves and platforms should be wide enough for the use of such mobile equipment.

Shelving, preferably metal and adjustable, is required for canned goods or other items that have been removed from cases. Shelves should be at least ten inches above the floor and two inches away from the wall to permit a free flow of air. Broken lots of dry foods like sugar and flour should be stored in metal containers with tightly fitted lids. The items may be arranged according to groups, and foods in each group may be placed on the shelves in alphabetical order—for example, *canned fruits:* apples, apricots, etc. New shipments should be placed in back to ensure use of the oldest stock first. Alphabetical arrangement facilitates counting when the physical inventory is taken and locating items when filling storeroom requisitions.

A chart showing the arrangement of supplies is helpful to storeroom personnel. It should be posted near the door or other place where it can be easily seen. Following is a suggested classification of food supplies.

FOOD STORES INDEX

A. Beverages
B. Cereals, prepared
C. Cereals, flour, cereal products
D. Crackers, cookies
E. Chocolate, cocoa
F. Condiments, seasonings, spices
G. Extracts, colorings
H. Fats, oils
I. Fish, canned
J. Fruits, canned
K. Fruits, dried or dehydrated
L. Fruit and vegetable juices (including soft drinks)
M. Gelatin, prepared desserts
N. Meats and poultry, canned
O. Milk products
P. Nuts, nut products
Q. Pickles, olives, relishes, sauces, salad dressings
R. Prepared mixes
S. Preserves, jams, jellies, candied fruit
T. Soup and soup bases, canned and dehydrated
U. Sugar, syrups, candy
V. Vegetables, canned
W. Vegetables, dried

CLASSIFICATION OF PERISHABLE FOODS

Breads, rolls, other baked products
Butter, margarine
Cheese
Eggs, fresh, frozen, and dried
Entrees, frozen
Fats, oils
Ice cream, ices, sherbets
Milk, cream
Meats: beef, lamb, pork, ham, bacon, veal, variety meats
Poultry, fresh and frozen
Fish, fresh, frozen, and smoked
Shellfish, fresh and frozen
Fruits and fruit juices, fresh
Fruits and fruit juices, frozen
Vegetables, fresh
Vegetables, frozen

SANITATION   Food in dry storage must be protected from insects and rodents by preventive measures, such as the use of proper insecticides and rodenticides, the latter under the direction of persons qualified for this type of work. Floors in the dry storage area should be slip resistant and easily cleaned. A regular cleaning schedule designed according to the volume of traffic and other activity in this area is vital to the maintenance of clean and orderly storage rooms. No trash should be left on the shelves or floor, and spilled food should be wiped up immediately.

Refrigerated and Freezer Storage

The storage of perishable foods is an important factor in their safety and retention of quality. Fresh and frozen foods should be placed in refrigerated or frozen storage immediately after delivery and kept at these temperatures until ready to use. Recommended temperatures for fresh fruits and vegetables are 40 to 45°F and 32 to 40°F for meat, poultry, dairy products, and eggs. Frozen products should be stored at 0 to −20°F.

In some foodservices separate refrigerators are available for fruits and vegetables, dairy products and eggs, and for meats, fish, and poultry. Fruits and vegetables, because of their high moisture content, are susceptible to freezing so should be kept at a slightly higher temperature than meats or dairy products. As in dry storage, foods under refrigeration should be rotated so that the oldest is used first. Fruits and vegetables should be checked periodically for ripeness and decaying pieces removed to prevent further spoilage. Some vegetables, like potatoes, onions, and squash, may be kept at temperatures up to 60°F and in some foodservices are placed in dry storage. Foods that absorb odors must be stored away from those that give off odors.

In many operations walk-in refrigerators are used for general and long-term storage, with reach-in units located near work stations for storage of daily perishables and foods in preparation and storage. All refrigeration and freezer units should be provided with thermometers, preferably the recording type. Walk-in refrigerators may have remote thermometers mounted outside the door so that temperatures may be read without opening the door, as shown in Fig. 4.15. Temperatures should be checked twice daily and any irregularity reported to the appropriate supervisor. Prompt action can result in saving food as well as money. Employees should be aware of the correct temperatures for the refrigerators and should be encouraged to open the doors as infrequently as possible.

Cleanliness is vital to food safety, and refrigerators should be thoroughly cleaned at least weekly and any spillage wiped up immediately. Hot food should be placed in shallow pans to chill as soon as possible after preparation unless it is to be served immediately. Cooked foods and meat should be

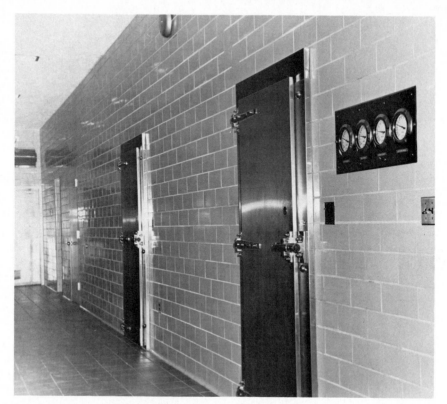

FIGURE 4.15   Individual refrigerator units in a large foodservice grouped for
convenience to receiving and preparation areas and for servicing. Separate cooling
equipment makes it possible to control and maintain the proper temperature for
the food stored in each unit. Floors on the same level as the corridor, easily visible
temperature indicators outside the unit, and tight-fitting, well-hinged doors with
locks that will release from the inside are only a few of the built-in features of a
refrigerated walk-in storage area.   *Courtesy Kent State University.*

covered to reduce evaporation losses and to limit odor absorption and damage from possible overhead leakage or dripping. Some health codes require
that cooked meats be stored above raw meats in the refrigerator. Daily checks
on the contents of refrigerators is advisable so that leftover and broken package
foods will be incorporated into the menu without delay.

Self-contained refrigeration units are used for ice makers, water dispensers, counter sections for display of salads, and storage for individual
milk cartons. Each is adjusted to maintain the temperature needed. Freezer

storage generally is in walk-in units, which may open from a walk-in refrigerator or the dry storage area. Ice cream and other frozen desserts may be kept in separate freezer cabinets.

The maintenance of refrigeration equipment requires the regular inspection by and services of a competent engineer to keep it in good working order. However, the manager and other employees must be able to detect and report any noticeable irregularities, since a breakdown in the system could result in heavy loss of food and damage to equipment. In most installations the refrigerator system is divided into several units so that failure in one will not disrupt the operation of the others.

Inventory Records and Control

Accurate records are essential to inventory control and provide a basis for purchasing and for cost analysis. The exact procedure and forms used will vary according to policies of the institution, but an adequate control system requires that a record be made of all food products and supplies as they are received and stored and again as they are issued for use in production or other areas of the foodservice.

Receiving

All incoming supplies should be inspected, as explained earlier under "Receiving and Inspecting Deliveries," and recorded on a receiving record form such as the one shown in Fig. 4.16. A journal in which to list the items received, with date of receipt, may also be used as a receiving record. Whatever form is used, the information should be checked with the purchase order, the delivery slip, and the invoice to be sure that the merchandise as ordered has been received and that the price is correct.

Storeroom Issues

Control of goods received cannot be effective unless storerooms are kept locked and authority and control over the merchandise is delegated to one person. Even if the foodservice is too small to justify the employment of a full-time storekeeper, an employee may be made responsible for receiving, putting away, and issuing goods from the storeroom in addition to other assigned duties.

No food or other supplies should be removed from the storeroom without

Receiving Record

Date _____

Quantity	Unit	Description of item	Name of vendor	Inspected and quantity verified by	Unit price	Total cost	Distribution	
							To kitchen	To store room

FIGURE 4.16   Sample receiving record form.

authorization, usually in the form of a written requisition. An exception may be perishable foods that are to be used the same day they are received and are sent directly to the production units. In that case they are treated as direct issues and are charged to the food cost for that day. All foods that are stored after delivery are considered storeroom purchases and in most operations may be removed only by requisition.

A list of supplies needed for production and service of the day's menu is compiled by the cook or other person responsible for assembling ingredients. If the foodservice uses an ingredient room for weighing and measuring ingredients for all recipes, the personnel in this unit are responsible for requesting supplies. (The ingredient room is discussed in more detail in Chapter 5.) The list of needed supplies is then submitted to the storekeeper, who completes the requisition. The order is filled and delivered to the appropriate department or section. The exact procedure for issuing supplies var-

Storeroom Requisition

Issue following items to

Date:

_____ Department

Signed:

Item	Description	Quantity Ordered	Quantity Received	Unit Price	Total Cost	Signature of Person Checking Out Food

FIGURE 4.17   Requisition for storeroom issues.

ies with the size of the operation and whether there is a full-time storekeeper.

Requisitions should be numbered and made out in duplicate or triplicate as the situation requires. Prenumbering of the requisitions makes it possible to trace missing or duplicate requisitions. An example of a storeroom requisition is shown in Fig. 4.17. Columns should be included for unit price and total cost unless a computer-assisted program is used, in which case the data will be available from the stored information in the computer. An inventory number is needed for each item on the requisition if a computer is used in calculating costs.

The requisition should be signed by a person authorized to request supplies and should be signed or initialed by the individual who fills the order.

The requisitioning of food and supplies is an important factor in controlling costs and in preventing loss from pilferage, and it should be practiced in some form even in a small foodservice.

Perpetual Inventory

The perpetual inventory is a running record of the balance on hand for each item of goods in the storeroom. The use of electronic data processing has simplified the process of maintaining the perpetual inventory and is used by many foodservices. In organizations where data processing is not used, the inventory information usually is recorded on cards. Standard forms for perpetual inventory are available from suppliers, or the foodservice manager may design forms that are best for an individual operation. An example is given in Fig. 4.18.

The perpetual inventory provides a continuing record of food and supplies purchased, in storage, and used. Items received are recorded on the inventory from the invoices, and the amounts are added to the previous balance on hand. Storeroom issues are recorded from the requisitions and subtracted from the balance. Additional information usually includes the date of purchase, the vendor, the brand purchased, and the price paid.

If minimum and maximum stock levels have been established, as discussed earlier under "Identifying Needs—Inventory stock level," these figures should be indicated on the inventory. When electronic data processing is used, the reorder point is included in the program. If cards are used, a colored marker or some other method of flagging will alert the storekeeper or manager to reorder the item when the inventory reaches that level.

These inventory records are recommended for all items except perishable foods that are delivered and stored in the production area. A physical inventory taken at the time perishable foods are ordered is more realistic. However, if there is a need for purchasing information on prices or total amounts of these foods used during a certain period of time, a purchase record as illustrated in Fig. 4.19 may be used to record the date of purchase, amounts, prices, and vendors. In Fig. 4.20, a purchase record and summary of purchases are combined with a perpetual inventory.

Time and strict supervision are required if the perpetual inventory is to be an effective tool, but it is a useful guide for purchasing and serves as a check on irregularities such as pilferage or displacement of stock. It also provides useful information on fast-moving, slow-moving, or unusable items.

Physical Inventory

An actual count of items in all storage areas should be taken periodically, usually to coincide with an accounting period. In some organizations an in-

SPECIFICATIONS

NO.	FIRMS	NO.	FIRMS
1		4	
2		5	
3		6	

Date	Firm	Brand	Size	Amt. Rec'd	Cost Doz	Cost Unit	Date	Firm	Brand	Size	Amt. Rec'd	Cost Doz	Cost Unit

PERPETUAL INVENTORY

Date	In	Out	Bal.	Date	In	Out	Bal.	Date	In	Out	Bal.	Date	In	Out	Bal.

PERPETUAL INVENTORY

Food Classification	Item	Description	Size	Maximum/Minimum

FIGURE 4.18 Perpetual inventory card.

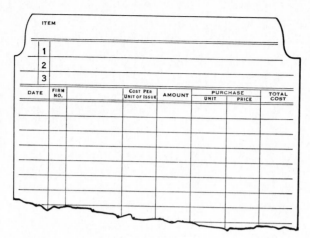

FIGURE 4.19 Purchase record.

ventory is taken at the end of each month, in others two or three times a year. The inventory is simplified if two people work together, one in a supervisory position or not directly involved with the storeroom operation. As one person counts the number of each item on hand, the other enters it on the inventory.

The procedure for taking a physical inventory is simplified by developing a printed form on which are listed the items normally carried in stock and their unit sizes, as shown in Fig. 4.21. For convenience and efficiency in recording, the items on the inventory form may be classified and then arranged alphabetically within the group or listed in the same order as they are arranged in the storeroom and in the perpetual inventory. Space should be left on the form between each grouping to allow for new items to be added.

After the physical inventory is completed, the value of each item is calculated and the total value of the inventory determined. Inventory figures are used to calculate food costs by adding the total food purchases to the beginning inventory and subtracting the ending inventory. The physical count also serves as a check against perpetual inventory records. Minor differences are expected, but major discrepancies should be investigated. Carelessness in filling requisitions or in record keeping is the most common reason for these errors, which may indicate a need for tighter storeroom controls or more accurate record keeping.

Both perpetual and physical inventories should be kept of china, glassware, and silverware. These items should be revalued at least once a year on the basis of physical inventory, although it may be desirable to revalue them

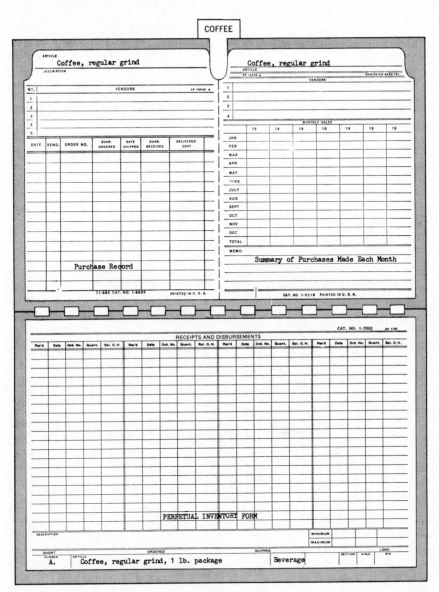

FIGURE 4.20 Form for purchase and summary records combined with perpetual inventory.

The Student Union Food Division

Physical Inventory _____ 19 _____

Page 1

Classification	Item	Unit	Quantity	Unit Price		Total Cost	
Beverages:							
	Coffee	14 oz pkg					
	Tea, iced	1 gal					
	Tea, individual	100/Box					
Cereals:							
	Assorted individual	50/carton					
	Corn Flakes	100/cs					
	Cream of Wheat	1# 12 oz box					
	Hominy grits	1# 8 oz box					
	Oats, Rolled	3# box					
	Ralstons	1# 6 oz box					
	Rice, white	1# box					
Cereal Products and Flour: Cornmeal		Bulk/lb					

TOTAL PAGE 1 _____

FIGURE 4.21   Physical inventory form.

at more frequent intervals. An inventory of other kitchen and dining room equipment and furniture normally is taken once a year.

Management of inventory both as to quantities to keep on hand and the security methods used to control the stock influences overall foodservice costs. Each organization should decide on maximum and minimum quantities desirable to maintain in the storeroom. This decision is based on storage facilities and capacities, delivery patterns, and the volume of business. Established standards for quantities desirable to keep on hand aid in purchasing—both as to quantity to order and when to order.

Carrying an inventory is costly, and some thought should be given to the total value of such an investment. Carrying costs normally range from 15 to 35 per cent of the inventory value, but can be as high as 50 per cent, and fast food operations with a minimum of inventory and rapid turnover may be as low as 2 to or 4 per cent of the inventory value. This percentage includes capital invested in inventory that prevents the use of money for other purposes; storage costs of space, personnel, materials handling, records and utilities; deterioration and spoilages; obsolescence of items no longer in use; and insurance on this asset.

Summary

Purchasing is an essential function in the operation of a foodservice organization and is vital to maintaining an adequate flow of food and supplies to meet production and service requirements.

Informal or formal methods of buying may be used, sometimes varying for different commodities. The buyer should be knowledgeable about the market and should understand the legal implications of contracts and bid buying. Purchasing may be the responsibility of the foodservice administrator or may be done centrally through a purchasing department. Group buying, in which several organizations combine their purchasing volume, has been successful in many cases.

The safety of food products is protected by several federal agencies, and quality grades have been established for many products. Detailed specifications should be used to ensure the purchase and delivery of products of the desired quality. Decisions must be made by the foodservice on the market form preferred, the quality to buy, and whether to make or buy prepared foods.

Good purchasing procedures include the use of appropriate buying methods, establishment of ordering schedules, and a system of communicating needs from production and service areas to the buyer. Foods and supplies should be received and checked by trained personnel and properly stored at appropriate temperatures. A storeroom control system that includes authorized issuing of supplies and complete inventory records is essential, but the procedures and paper work should be limited to those necessary for control and communications.

Supplementary References

Almanac of the Canning, Freezing, Preserving Industries: Westminster, MD: Edward E. Judge & Sons (published annually).

Axler, B. H.: Foodservice: A Managerial Approach. Ch. 8 The Purchasing System. Lexington, MA: D.C. Heath & Co., 1979.

Food and Nutrition Service, USDA: Food Buying Guide for School Food Service. PA No. 1257. Washington, DC: U.S. GPO, 1981.

Food Safety and Quality Service, USDA: FSQS Facts—Federal Food Standards. FSQS 19. Rev. Oct. 1979.

Food Safety and Quality Service, USDA: FSQS Facts—Food Acceptance Service. May 1978.

Foodservice Purchasing Managers: Code of Ethics. Chicago, IL: National Restaurant Assoc.

Human Nutrition Service, USDA: Food Purchasing Guide for Group Feeding. Agriculture Handbook No. 284.

Jacobs, J. A.: Codes of ethics and the courts. Food Mgmt. 16:16 (Apr.), 1982.

Knight, J. B. and Kotschevar, L. H.: Quantity Food Production, Planning and Management. Ch. 6 Purchasing and Receiving. Boston: CBI Publishing Co., 1979.

Kotschevar, L. H.: Quantity Food Purchasing, 2d ed. New York: John Wiley and Sons, 1975.

Levine, A. S., Labuza, T. P., and Morley, J. E.: Food technology: A Primer for physicians. New Engl. J. Med. 312:628, 1985.

Livestock Division, Agricultural Marketing Service, USDA: Institutional Meat Purchase Specifications. Washington, DC, 1975.

Livingston, G. E.: Prepared food. Part 2: Make or buy? Hospitals 46:95, Sept. 16, 1972.

Longree, K.: Quantity Food Sanitation, 3d ed. New York: Wiley-Interscience, 1980.

Mahaffey, M. J., Mennes, M. E., and Miller, B. B.: Food Service Manual for Health Care Institutions. Chicago: Am. Hosp. Assoc., 1981.

Mayfield, B. K.: Line-item versus prime vendor purchasing. J. Am. Diet. Assoc. 84:685, 1984.

Morin, T. H., Bloom, T., and Zaccarelli, H.: The Nifda Canned Goods Spec Manual. West Lafayette, IN: Purdue Univ. Rest., Hotel and Institution Mgmt. Institute, 1984.

Morrison, L. P. and Vaden, A. C.: Foodservice purchasing practices in small hospitals. Hospitals 52:94, Feb. 1, 1978.

National Association of Meat Purveyors: The Meat Buyers Guide, 7th ed. McLean, VA: National Association of Meat Purveyors, 1984.

National Live Stock and Meat Board: Meat in the Foodservice Industry. Chicago: National Live Stock and Meat Board, 1975.

Ninemeier, J. D.: Purchasing, Receiving, and Storage: A Systems Manual for Restaurants, Hotels, and Clubs. Boston: CBI Publishing Co., 1983.

Nix, M.: Purchasing, purchasing, purchasing! School Food Serv. J. 37:161 (June/July), 1983.

Oakley, H., ed.: The Buying Guide, 7th ed. Hagerstown, MD: Blue Goose, 1980.

Pedderson, R. B.: Foodservice and Hotel Purchasing. Boston: CBI Publishing Co., 1981.

Spears, M. C. and Vaden, A. G.: Foodservice Organizations: A Managerial and Systems Approach. New York: John Wiley and Sons, 1985.

Stefanelli, J. M.: Purchasing Selection and Procurement for the Hospitality Industry. New York: John Wiley and Sons, 1984.

Stokes, J. W.: How to Manage a Restaurant. Dubuque, IA: Wm. C. Brown Co., 1982.

VanEgmond-Pannel, D.: School Foodservice, 3d ed. Westport, CT: AVI Publishing Co., 1985.

Warfel, M. C. and Cremer, M. L.: Purchasing for Food Service Managers. Berkeley: McCutchan Publishing Corp., 1985.

Zenz, G. J.: Purchasing and the Management of Materials, 5th ed. New York: John Wiley and Sons, 1981.

CHAPTER 5

Production Planning and Control

Introduction

Production of high-quality food involves a number of interrelated steps, each dependent on the other. The transformation of raw or processed foods into an acceptable finished product ready for service is an essential operation in the overall foodservice system. It requires the purchase of food products of good quality, initial storage and "holding" at optimum temperatures at various points in its production, and, generally, one or more processing procedures under controlled conditions.

Traditionally, these procedures have been carried out in the individual foodservice and menu items were prepared "from scratch." Today, however, there are alternatives to this conventional system. Foodservice organizations composed of several individual units may centralize all or part of their food production in a commissary or central production kitchen. Preparation in these facilities may range from controlled production of items such as desserts and baked goods; preparation of meats ready for cooking; preparation of fruits and vegetables for salads or for final cooking in the individual foodservice units; or complete preparation and cooking of menu items, packaged in individual or bulk containers, and chilled or frozen for delivery to serving units.

Many foodservices prepare either all or part of the food for immediate service, but in some, food is cooked then chilled or frozen for later service. Others purchase certain menu items in ready-to-cook or ready-to-serve forms, and most use some type of convenience ingredients or components. These foodservice systems—conventional, commissary (central production kitchen), ready prepared (cook/chill or cook/freeze), and assembly/serve—are discussed in detail in Chapter 2.

Regardless of the system used, production planning and control are vital to the successful production of high-quality food. Forecasting the quantities to prepare and scheduling of production are discussed in this chapter, as are the various elements of production and quality control.

Production Planning

Forecasting

Production planning starts with the menu and the production forecast, which is a prediction of the food needs for a day or other stated period. Forecasting not only is vital to production planning, but it serves as a basis for purchasing and provides data for budgets and other financial reports. For this reason, forecasting is especially important in a computer-assisted foodservice system because it is the point from which other activities are generated. Accurate forecasting not only is vital to cost control, but it lessens the problem of leftover food to be reused or customer dissatisfaction when not enough food is prepared.

HISTORICAL DATA   Common to all forecasting methods is the use of historical data to determine needs and to establish trends. To be of value, this information must be recorded in some way or entered into the computer, whether it be as a record of meals served, a daily census record, a listing of food left after a meal, or a tabulation of the various menu items served.

The number to be served is based on a known population, such as a hospital patient census, the number of paid residents in a college foodservice, the number of students enrolled in a school, or an estimate of potential customers in a restaurant, and on past meal records. Where the population is known, a pattern of meals served by day and by meal usually develops. In a residence hall foodservice, for example, a fairly accurate meal participation percentage becomes evident. This information, along with knowledge of scheduled special events, holidays, weather conditions, and unusual circumstances, assists the planner in making a valid estimate.

The food selection prediction is an estimate of the percentage of the total number to be served who will select each menu item. This information is based on past records and on known popularity of menu items. In a hospital using selective menus, choices are made by patients in advance and tallied to give the quantity needed for patient service.

Quantities to Produce

The forecast is the basis for determining quantities of menu items to be prepared and foods to be purchased or requisitioned from the storerooms. An estimate at the time the major food orders are placed is later adjusted, one or two days prior to the day of production, for more accurate decisions on amounts of food to be prepared. The amount of food needed is based on the number of persons to be served, portion size, and the amount of waste and shrinkage loss in the preparation of foods.

Recipes adjusted to the predicted number of portions needed will provide much of this information. Most quantity recipes for noncomputer systems are calculated in modules of 50 or 100 or, in foods like cakes or casserole-type entrees, to pan sizes and equipment capacity. For example, if a recipe produces two sheet cakes, which can be cut into 30 or 32 servings each, three cakes (or one and one-half times the recipe) would be required for 75 portions. Where very large quantities are produced, the amount to prepare in one batch is limited to the capacity of the production equipment.

In foodservices using a computer, recipes are printed daily and, where appropriate, provide recipes for the exact number of individual portions or are adjusted to the number of pans or other modules required to serve the predicted numbers. To be effective, computer-assisted programs include recipes for all menu items offered, including fresh vegetables and fruits, salads, relishes, and meats such as a beef roast or baked pork chops. Quantities to purchase or requisition are readily available from these computer-generated recipes. In foodservices not having a computer-assisted system, standardizing and calculating recipes for more than one amount lessens the need for refiguring the quantities for each day's forecast.

A general procedure for determining amounts of meats, poultry, fruits, and vegetables follows.

1. Determine the portion size in ounces.
2. Multiply portion size by the estimated number to be served and convert to pounds. This is the edible portion (EP) required. EP may also be given in the standardized recipe.

$$\frac{\text{ounces} \times \text{number of portions}}{16 \text{ oz}} = \frac{\text{number of pounds edible}}{\text{portion (EP) required}}$$

3. To determine the amount to order, divide the edible portion (EP) weight by the yield percentage (or the weight in decimal parts of a pound of

ready-to-eat or ready-to-cook product from 1 pound of the commodity as purchased). The USDA Food Buying Guide for School Food Service PA 1257 is a good source for yield information.

$$\frac{EP \text{ weight}}{\text{yield}} = \text{amount to order}$$

4. For foods to be purchased, convert the amount needed to the most appropriate purchase unit (e.g., case, crate, or roast). If the food is to be used for other menu items, combine the amounts and then convert to purchase units.

As an example, if 3-ounce portions of fresh asparagus are needed for 50 people, you would calculate the amount to purchase this way:

1. $\dfrac{3 \text{ ounces} \times 50 \text{ portions}}{16 \text{ oz}} = \dfrac{150 \text{ oz}}{16 \text{ oz}} = 9.375$ lb edible portion needed

2. $\dfrac{9.375 \text{ lb needed}}{0.53 \text{ lb yield from}} = 17.68$ lb to purchase
   1 lb as purchased

3. Convert to purchase unit, 18 to 20 lb

In a computer system, these figures would be calculated automatically from the forecast, portion size, and yield data.

Scheduling

Once the needed quantity of food is known and recipes are obtained from the file or from the computer, supplies are requisitioned or ordered, as discussed on p. 109. The next step in production planning is scheduling of food preparation. Careful planning assures the efficient use of employee time and a minimum of production problems. Foods that are ready for service at the scheduled time without undue holding will be superior in quality to those that are prepared too early.

Production planning and scheduling require a knowledge of the steps through which a product must go and the time required for each, as well as the steps that can be completed early without affecting the quality of the food. Most menu items go through part or all of the following steps:

- Storage: dry, refrigerated, freezer
- Assembly: weighing or measuring ingredients
- Prepreparation: vegetable cleaning, peeling, cutting, chopping, preparing pans
- Preparation: mixing, combining ingredients, panning

- Cooking: baking, frying, broiling, steaming, simmering
- Finishing: setting up salads, portioning desserts, slicing meat, packaging food for freezing
- Storage prior to serving: heated, refrigerated, or frozen

Up to the point of final cooking, many steps can and should be scheduled early, possibly the day before. Each recipe should be broken down into production stages to determine which steps may be done in advance. Preparation of casserole-type entrees should be scheduled so that the cooking of all recipe components is completed in time for final assembling and baking; for example, browning the beef cubes, dicing and cooking the vegetables, and preparing the topping for beef pot pie; or cooking ground beef, tomato sauce, and pasta for a casserole.

For some foods, it may be better to assemble the product in batches as needed for final cooking and serving. Combining the entire amount may reduce the flexibility of the individual ingredients if there is an overproduction. For example, the ground beef could be used for tacos, the pasta for a salad, and the tomato sauce in chili. These would be "new" menu items rather than "leftovers." In commercial cooking where food may be prepared in relatively small quantities because of the uncertain number of portions needed or if the menu includes a large selection of items, the finished product may be cooked to order or in amounts compatible with the anticipated patronage.

Cheese balls, croquettes, and similar foods must be shaped and chilled for several hours before deep-fat frying. Other procedures, such as breading of chicken, cutlets, or fish prior to cooking; shaping of meat balls; and filling of deviled eggs are examples of time-consuming procedures that can be scheduled early. Some menu items or ingredients can be prepared two or three days ahead, but care must be taken not to schedule early preparation if the quality or safety of the food is endangered. If frozen foods are to be defrosted, time must be allowed for thawing in the refrigerator.

When scheduling the cooking of foods in quantity, allowances must be made for the time required for heat to penetrate. It will take longer for heat to reach the center of a pan with 50 servings of scalloped potatoes than a casserole serving six, for example. Sheet cake baked in an 18 × 26-inch pan needs more cooking time than the same amount of batter baked in 9-inch layer cake pans. Four beef roasts in an oven will require more time than cooking only one. Size of container, then, and oven load affect the total cooking time.

Final cooking should be scheduled so that only food needed for immediate service is cooked at one time. Batch cooking of vegetables in small amounts, baking of pans of entrees at intervals, and continuous deep-fat frying "to the line" or to order are examples. Some cooks are more comfortable if all food is cooked at once, but batch cooking should be scheduled and employees encouraged to recognize that the quality of the prepared food is better when it has not been held for long periods.

Because of the variation in complexity of menu items from day-to-day, production should be planned several days ahead to distribute the workload evenly. An increasing number of foodservices are using advance production to equalize workloads. Food preparation is scheduled during slack periods, and the food is frozen for later use. Such a program should not be attempted, however, without adequate freezing and refrigeration equipment and without some knowledge of foods that freeze well and the effect of storage length on different foods. Proper cooling, packaging, and freezing are especially important to the quality and safety of the finished products. The foods, of course, should be prepared under close supervision so that adequate sanitation and processing precautions are observed. If the product will be stored for any length of time, a system of inventory control of the frozen prepared foods should be implemented.

PRODUCTION SCHEDULES   A production schedule, sometimes called a production sheet or work sheet, lists in detail the items to be produced for the current day's menu plus any advance preparation needed. This schedule should include as a minimum the menu items, amounts to prepare, cooking times, special instructions for preparation and serving, and the name of the employee assigned to prepare each item. Some production schedules include space for recording quantities of food prepared and amounts left after the serving is completed. This information is important to the menu planner or production supervisor who must plan for incorporating these foods into the menu for the next meal or the next day or to freeze for later use. Also added on some production schedules is information concerning weather, holidays, or special events that might assist in explaining the quantities prepared and served.

A single schedule for a small foodservice may include preparation and cleaning assignments for all employees, with production times by hour of the day to assist employees in planning their work. In a large, more complex operation, schedules are made for each department and usually are quite detailed. Fig. 5.1 is an example of a production schedule that also serves as a production record. If cycle menus are used, time is saved by setting up orders and production schedules for each cycle as a "package" to be used with the cycle. Adjustments, of course, may be needed if there are changes in menus or the numbers to be served.

PRODUCTION MEETINGS   A meeting with appropriate staff and employees to discuss the menu and production plans heightens the effectiveness of the

PRODUCTION SCHEDULE

DATE _____ AREA _____

Special Events _____

Meal Count _____

Weather _____

PERSON	MENU ITEM	QUANTITY TO PREPARE	ACTUAL YIELD	DIRECTIONS	TIME SCHEDULE	LEFT OVER AMOUNT	RUN OUT TIME	SUBSTITUTION	CLEANING ASSIGNMENT

PRE-PREPARATION:

PERSON	MENU ITEM	QUANTITY	PERSON	MENU ITEM	QUANTITY

Form 4.1

F.S. Form 60

FIGURE 5.1 Production schedule for a large residence hall food center. Information useful for production forecasting also is recorded on this form. *Courtesy Kansas State University Residence Halls.*

written production schedule. Such meetings generally do not need to be long, but they should be held regularly and at a time when activity in the production area is at a minimum. At meeting time, the menu can be explained and special instructions given for the items where needed. Employees also have an opportunity to discuss the schedule and any production problems they may anticipate.

No amount of "paper work" can replace the human element in food production. Food must be prepared by people, and no matter how carefully plans are made and how many instructions are written, there must be "follow through" to be sure that the menu as served measures up to the menu as planned.

Production Controls

Quality Standards and Control

Food quality is a primary objective of foodservice systems and its control is a major function of management. Quality is closely related to consumer acceptability, which may vary with the expectations and needs of customers, patients, students, or other patrons in different types of foodservices. Each person has his or her own perception of what constitutes quality food based in part on personal likes and dislikes.

Traditionally, quality has referred to sensory characteristics, such as flavor, texture, appearance, and temperature, and is measured by the response of the clientele to the food. Assurance of quality food has been through purchase of quality ingredients, use of standardized recipes, continuous supervision of food production, and critical tasting of the finished product. In addition, many foodservices have established quality standards for each product to use in evaluating the purchased ingredients and/or the cooked product.

Although sensory characteristics are vital to consumer acceptance of food, a broader definition of quality includes nutritional and microbiological attributes, according to Bobeng and David[1]; in other words, food that is nutritious and safe as well as satisfying to the consumer. The Hazard Analysis Critical Control Point (HACCP), used successfully by the food processing industry, has been recommended as a preventative approach to quality control in foodservice systems. The HACCP concept and safeguards in food production are discussed later in this chapter under "Safeguards in Food Production."

PRODUCT EVALUATION   One useful tool for quality control is product evaluation. Products generally are evaluated when a new product or recipe is being tested, but product evaluation should be a continuing process to make certain that the original high quality is maintained. Responsibility for this important part of quality control should be assigned to a person or a committee, but staff, employees, and consumers often participate. Many large foodservices and most commissaries have facilities for product development and laboratories for product evaluation.

Subjective or **sensory** methods are used most often to evaluate menu items or new products for such qualities as flavor, odor, texture, tenderness, and color. Foods are evaluated by a panel, composed of several persons who are knowledgeable about product standards and who have been trained to judge quality characteristics and differences among food items. The evaluations should be made in an area that is quiet and free from distractions, well lighted, and ventilated. Each panel member should, if possible, be provided with an individual booth or table. Samples to be tested are coded, and a score card, such as that illustrated in Fig. 5.2, is provided.

Objective methods, which include chemical and physical tests, are used to measure certain qualities in foods, as already noted, such as nutritive value, color, texture, and flavor. Most foodservices do not possess instruments for objective testing of foods, but if the occasion warrants it usually is possible to arrange for these tests in a research laboratory.

Standardized Recipes

An important tool for production control is the standardized recipe. It enables the manager to predict the quality, quantity, and portion cost of the finished product, and it simplifies purchasing. Use of standardized recipes is helpful in training new or substitute production employees and makes management less dependent on the whims of and changes in personnel. Accuracy in the use of standardized recipes and in weighing and measuring ingredients takes the guesswork out of quantity food production. Clientele expect to and should be able to depend on having a food item the same each time it is selected.

Standardized recipes are required if ingredients are assembled in a central area and are essential in a computer-assisted production system because the recipe is the starting point for many procedures. Each recipe and each ingredient has an identification number that is essential for purchasing, inventory, and cost records. Production scheduling is simplified if recipes include all essential information needed to produce the menu item.

The standardized recipes must be **used** by the employees, too, if the system is to be effective. For example, if the daily cost report is calculated on

Score Card for Cake

Date _____

Factor	Qualities	Standard	1	2	3	Comments
			Sample No.			
I. External appearance	Shape, symmetrical, slightly rounded top, free from cracks or peaks	10				
	Volume, light in weight in proportion to size	10				
	Crust, smooth uniform golden brown	10				
II. Internal appearance	Texture, tender, slightly moist, velvety feel to tongue and finger	10				
	Grain, fine, round, evenly distributed cells with thin cell walls, free from tunnels	10				
	Color, crumb even and rich looking	10				
III. Flavor	Delicate, well-blended flavor of ingredients. Free from unpleasant odors or taste	10				

Directions for use of score card for plain cake:

Standard	10	No detectable fault, highest possible score
Excellent	8–9	Of unusual excellence but not perfect
Good	6–7	Average good quality
Fair	4–5	Below average, slightly objectionable
Poor	2–3	Objectionable, but edible
Bad	0–1	Highly objectionable, inedible

Signature of evaluator

FIGURE 5.2   Suggested score card for evaluating cake or muffins.

the basis of standardized recipes provided by the production personnel, but employees change the amounts and ingredients, there will be a discrepancy in figures that will not give a true financial picture.

FORMAT   A suitable recipe form or format that provides all information needed for production of the menu item should be selected. An orderly arrangement of this information should be developed and the same general pattern followed for all recipes in the file. Each foodservice should decide on the format best suited to its operation and use this form consistently.

In most recipes, the ingredients are listed in the order in which they are used. A block arrangement, in which ingredients that are to be combined are grouped together, is helpful, and separating these groups with space or lines above or below them makes following recipes easier and faster. Listing the procedures directly across from the ingredients involved simplifies preparation and enables clear directions to be written in a minimum number of words. Fig. 5.3 illustrates this suggested format. Some recipe writers like to number the steps in the procedure.

Certain information is essential, regardless of the form in which the recipe is written. Following are suggestions for material that should be included.

Recipe Title. The title should be printed in large type and either centered on the page or placed on the left or right side at the top of the page as shown in Fig. 5.3. The recipe identification code for ease in filing is also placed here.

Yield and Portion Size. The total yield may be given in measure, weight, number of pans, or number of portions. The portion size may be in weight, measure, or count.

Baking Time and Temperature. This information is listed at the top of the page so the preheating of the oven and the scheduling of baking can be determined without reading the entire recipe. Some recipe writers repeat the baking time and temperature in the instructions so the cooks can see them while working with the ingredients.

Ingredients and Quantities. The amounts of ingredients may be listed first followed by the names of ingredients, as in Fig. 5.3, or the ingredients may be given first with the quantities arranged in one or more columns to accommodate different yields (Fig. 5.4) For the sake of accuracy, however, there should not be more than three ingredient amount columns on one card. Too many columns increase the chances of error in reading amounts and crowd the space needed to give complete directions for preparation.

Names of ingredients should be consistent. Descriptive terms are used to define clearly the kind and form of each ingredient. In some recipes, the term **before** the name of the ingredient designates the form as purchased or that the ingredient has been cooked or heated before using in the product.

Chicken Pie with Batter Crust

Oven: 400°F (205°C)
Bake: 20–25 minutes

Yield: 50 portions
2 pans 12 × 20 × 2 in.
Portion: 8 oz

Amount	Ingredient	Procedure
12 oz 14 oz	Margarine or butter Onions, chopped	Sauté onions in margarine.
1lb 6oz ½ t	Flour, all-purpose Pepper, black	Add flour and pepper. Stir until blended. Cook 30 minutes.
1¼ gal	Chicken Stock (p. 495)	Add chicken stock, stirring constantly. Cook until thickened, stirring often. Check for seasoning. Add salt if necessary.
6 lb	Chicken, cooked	Cut chicken into ½–¾-in. pieces. Add to sauce.
1lb 8oz 2 lb	Celery, sliced Carrots, sliced	Cook celery and carrots until partially done. Drain. Fold into sauce.
2 lb	Peas, frozen	Add peas uncooked to chicken mixture. Mix carefully. Scale into 2 12 × 20 × 2-in. counter pans, 12 lb per pan.
6 qt	Batter Crust (p. 382)	Make 1 recipe Batter Crust. Pour 3 qt batter over each pan. Bake at 400°F for 20–25 minutes, or until batter crust is done.

Notes:
1. 18-20 lb chickens AP will yield approximately 6 lb cooked meat.
2. Pastry (p. 199) may be substituted for Batter Crust. Roll out 1 lb 8 oz for each pan.
3. Chicken mixture may be topped with Baking Powder Biscuits (p. 84).
4. For individual pot pies, scale 8 oz hot chicken pie mixture into each of 50 casseroles. Pour ½ c (4 oz) batter crust over each. Bake as above.

Variation: **Turkey Pie.** Substitute turkey for chicken.

FIGURE 5.3   Recipe format showing block arrangement. Notes and variations are given at the end of the recipe.   *From* Food for Fifty, *seventh edition, Macmillan Publishing Co., 1985.*

Applesauce Cake

Desserts No. Ck-3
Portion: 2 x 2¾ in.
Cut 6 x 8

Oven temperature: 350 °F
Time: 30–35 minutes

Ingredients	2 pans	3 pans	Procedure
Shortening	1 lb 7 oz	2 lb 3 oz	Cream 5 min. on
Sugar	2 lb 14 oz	4 lb 5 oz	medium speed, with paddle.
Eggs	2 cups	3 cups	Add and beat 5 min. on medium speed.
Applesauce	2 qt + ½ c	3¼ qt	Add gradually on low speed. Beat 1 min. on medium speed after last addition. Scrape down.
Cake flour	2 lb 14 oz	4 lb 5 oz	Sift dry ingredients
Salt	4 tsp	2 Tbsp	together and mix
Soda	1 oz	1½ oz	with raisins.
Cinnamon	1 Tbsp	4½ tsp	Add to creamed
Nutmeg	1½ tsp	2¼ tsp	mixture gradually
Cloves	1½ tsp	2½ tsp	on low speed.
Raisins	12 oz	1 lb 2 oz	Beat 2 min., medium speed, after last addition. Scrape down once.
Total wt	13 lb 6 oz	20 lb 2 oz	Weigh into greased baking pans, 12 x 22 x 2 in., 6 lb 8 oz / pan.

FIGURE 5.4   Recipe format with columns for three quantities. Total weight of batter is helpful in adjusting recipes. Preparation steps may be numbered, if space permits.

Examples are: *canned* tomatoes, *frozen chopped* broccoli, *hot* milk, *boiling* water, *cooked* turkey. The descriptive term is placed **after** the ingredient to indicate processing after the ingredient is weighed or measured as: onions, *chopped;* eggs, *beaten;* or raw potato, *grated.* It is important in some recipes to designate AP (as purchased) or EP (edible portion). For example, 15 pounds (AP) of fresh broccoli would be 10 pounds (EP) or less. Whatever system is used, it should be consistent and understood by those using the recipes. Abbreviations should be consistent and easily understood, as qt for quart or lb for pound.

Procedures. Directions for preparation of the product should be divided into logical steps and are most effective when placed directly across from the ingredients involved. Procedures should be clear and concise so that employees can easily read and understand them. It is helpful if basic procedures are uniform in all recipes for similar products. For example, white sauce is basic to many other sauces and is an ingredient in many menu items. The procedures on the recipe should be worded the same in each recipe. Likewise, there are several basic procedures in baked products, such as creaming fat and sugar or combining dry and liquid ingredients that should be the same on all recipes using them.

Timing should be given for procedures in which mixers, steamers, or other mechanical equipment is used, as "Cream shortening and sugar on medium speed for 10 minutes" or "Cook on low heat until rice is tender and all water is absorbed, about 15 to 20 minutes."

Panning instructions should include the weight per pan to help in dividing the product equally into the required number of pans. For example: "Scale batter into two prepared $12 \times 18 \times 2$-inch baking pans, 4 lb 10 oz per pan." When layering ingredients in baking pans for a casserole type entree, it is helpful if the weight or measure of each layer is given. For example: "Place dressing, sauce, and chicken in two $12 \times 20 \times 2$-inch counter pans, layered in each pan as follows: 4 lb 8 oz dressing, 1½ qt sauce, 3 lb chicken, 1¼ qt sauce."

The size dipper to use in portioning meatballs and similar foods ensures uniform portions. Instructions for serving are needed in many recipes, too. Such directions are especially important in baked products that are cut into portions or where a ladle is used for serving soups, sauces, or puddings.

Additional information not essential to the recipe but that may be helpful in substituting ingredients, alternate methods of preparation, or comments about the appearance of the product, such as "These cookies puff up at first, then flatten out with crinkled tops," may be added as footnotes. Variations of a basic recipe usually are included at the end of the recipe.

The size and form of the recipe card or sheet, the format to be followed, and the manner of filing the recipes are optional. Cards $4'' \times 6''$ and $5'' \times 8''$ are popular sizes, and heavy typing paper, $8½'' \times 11''$, is used in some operations. In deciding on a size and format, keep in mind that the recipes will be used by cooks and other employees who will be busy weighing and mixing ingredients and may not be able to read a small crowded card easily. Recipes should be typed or printed and should be readable at a distance of 18 to 20 inches. Recipes that are used in the production or ingredient assembly areas should be placed in clear plastic covers to keep the copy clean.

In foodservices using a computer-assisted system, recipes are printed as needed and for the quantities required for the day's production. Because the printout is generated each time the recipe is used, it is considered a working copy and does not need a protective covering. An example of a computer-generated recipe is shown in Fig. 5.5. The format for recipes in this type of system will depend on the software purchased, so the format should be considered when comparing different software packages.

RECIPE FILES   A master file of all recipes used by the foodservice should be maintained, with at least two complete sets available, one to be kept on permanent file in the office of the dietitian or foodservice manager and the other to be available for production employees. Additional sets may be needed by other key personnel.

A system of classification and filing enables recipes to be located easily. Recipes may be coded by number or filed alphabetically under appropriate headings, such as appetizers, beverages, breads, desserts, eggs and cheese, fish, meat, pasta, poultry, salads, sandwiches, sauces, soups, and vegetables.

STANDARDIZING RECIPES   A recipe is considered **standardized** only when it has been tried and adapted for use by a given foodservice operation. **Tested** quantity recipes are available from many sources, such as cookbooks, trade journals, materials distributed by commercial food companies from their own experimental kitchens, and from other foodservice managers. Regardless of the source, each recipe should be tested and evaluated, then standardized for use in a particular situation.

The first step in standardizing a new recipe is to analyze the proportion of ingredients and clarity of instructions, and to determine whether the recipe can be produced with the equipment and personnel available. The recipe should then be tested, being sure ingredients are weighed and measured accurately and that procedures are followed exactly. The yield, number and size of portions, and problems with preparation should be recorded, and the finished product evaluated for acceptability. A suggested evaluation form is shown in Fig. 5.6. If the product is judged suitable for use, the recipe is then adjusted to the quantities needed and tested again. If other changes are needed, they are made and the recipe retested, but only one change should be made at a time. When the testing is completed, the recipe is ready to be set up in finished form for the permanent file. Some foodservice managers use cards of one color for recipes during testing and standardizing and a different color for the final completed copy.

Recipe standardization need not be used entirely for new recipes. There

CHILI CON CARNE

RECIPE CODE — 14-01-0-023-7   STATUS – STANDARDIZED   1

EQUIPMENT-STEAM KETTLE
COUNTER PANS-LIDS

RECIPE SOURCE-
04/16/86 10:20 AM   751124

*** NUMBER OF PORTIONS	68
PORTION SIZE / COST	.560 LBS. / $0.3044
MEAL PATTERN ALLOWANCE	1 PORTION
SUGGESTED SERVING UTENSIL	6 OZ LADLE
PAN SIZE	10X12X6
NUMBER OF PANS	
WEIGHT PER PAN	LBS.
HANDLING LOSS	
MINIMUM BATCH	6.00 PERCENT
MAXIMUM BATCH	
FORECAST UNIT	
*TOTAL RECIPE WEIGHT / COST	40.5 LBS. / $20.6992
TOTAL RECIPE VOLUME	

CODE	PERCENT	INGREDIENT	WEIGHTS AND MEASURES	AP/EP	STEP	PROCEDURE
0012113719	22.49	GROUND BEEF CHILI BULK	9.1 LBS 13.6 LBS	EP AP	A	1. COOK MEAT IN KETTLE UNTIL IT LOSES ITS COLOR. STIR OFTEN TO PREVENT LUMPS FROM FORMING. DRAIN OFF FAT.
0052001211	1.68	ONIONS CHOPPED FRESH	0.68 LBS		B	2. COMBINE WITH MEAT.
0052000826	0.02	GARLIC MINCED FRESH	1.0 TSP			
0082054100	0.34	SALT	0.14 LBS			
0082060401	0.57	CHILI POWDER	0.23 LBS			
0082093008	0.34	SUGAR GRANULATED	0.14 LBS			
0082060801	0.08	CUMIN GROUND	0.03 LBS			
0082063109	0.02	PEPPER BLACK GROUND	1.8 TSP			
0072011602	17.12	TOMATOES DICED CND	6.9 LBS		C	3. ADD TO MEAT MIXTURE.
0072011751	15.40	TOMATO PUREE CND	6.2 LBS			4. SIMMER 1 HOUR OR MORE. STIR FREQUENTLY.
0072010363	33.90	BEANS RED CND	13.7 LBS			5. TAKE UP IN SOUP PANS. COVER.
0000000001	8.05	WATER	3.3 LBS			

FIGURE 5.5 Example of a computer-generated recipe. *Courtesy Kansas State University Residence Halls.*

Recipe Evaluation Card

Please Return This Card to the Test Kitchen as Promptly as Possible.

Product _____   Residence Hall _____
                                      Date _____

Quantity prepared _____
Did you obtain yield as stated in recipe? _____
If not, what quantity was obtained? _____
Do you consider size of portion adequate? _____
If not, what change would you suggest? _____

Was product generally well accepted? _____

Further comments on recipe—for example—ease of using recipe; problems encountered; suggestions for changes in procedure, kind and/or amount of ingredients, etc.:
   (Consult cooks for suggestions) _____

_____
_____
_____
_____
_____

                                      _____
                                      Reporting Supervisor

FIGURE 5.6   Recipe evaluation card.   *Courtesy, Central Food Stores, University of Illinois.*

may be recipes in the file that produce food of satisfactory quality but that yield more or less food than is needed. The product may lack proper seasoning or the consistency may need improvement. In some cases an ingredient change is made that necessitates some adjustment in the recipe; for example, catsup may be substituted for tomato puree or cream of mushroom soup for white sauce and mushrooms. The manager may wish to implement a program for standardizing these recipes by testing each time the item is on the menu until the recipe is satisfactory.

ADJUSTING RECIPES   Three methods commonly used to adjust recipes are the factor method, the percentage method, and direct-reading measurement tables.

Factor Method. In the factor method, the quantities of ingredients in the original recipe are multiplied by a conversion factor, as explained in the following steps.

1. Convert all volume measurements to weights, where possible. For example, 3 cups of water would weigh 1 pound 8 ounces. For ease in figuring, weights should be expressed in pounds and decimal components of pounds; 1 pound 8 ounces would be 1.5 pounds. Add together the weights of all ingredients.
2. Divide the desired yield by the known yield of the original recipe to obtain the conversion factor. For example, if you have a recipe for pie crust for 12 two-crust pies that you wish to change to 66 two-crust pies, as shown in Table 5.1, divide the desired yield (66) by the known yield (11) to obtain the factor of 5.5.
3. Multiply the amount of each ingredient in the original recipe by the factor, which in the example would be 5.5.
4. A check on the accuracy of the figures can be made by multiplying the

TABLE 5.1   Pastry   Adjusting Yield *from* 12 2-Crust Pies *to* 66 2-Crust Pies

Ingredients	Original Recipe 12 2-Crust Pies	Step 1 Original Recipe in Weight	Step 2 Original Recipe in Ounces	Step 4 Each Amount in Step 2 Multiplied by Factor	New Recipe in Weight	Step 5 New Recipe Rounded Weight and Measure
Pastry flour	5 lb	5 lb	80	440.0	27 lb 8 oz	27 lb 8 oz
Salt	1¼ oz	1¼ oz	1¼	6.9	6.9 oz	7 oz
Shortening	3 lb	3 lb	48	264.0	16 lb 8 oz	16 lb 8 oz
Water	3 c	1 lb 8 oz	24	132.0	8 lb 4 oz	1 gal ½ c
Total weight		9 lb 9¼ oz	153¼	842.9	52 lb 9 oz	52 lb 11 oz

Step 3: Conversion Factor

$$\frac{66 \text{ (new)}}{12 \text{ (original)}} = \frac{11}{2} = 5\frac{1}{2} = 5.5$$

Total Weight in Step 2 × Factor
153¼ oz × 5.5 =
    $153.25 \times 5.5 = 842.875 = 842.9$ oz

Essential information needed:
    Water: 1 c = 8 oz
             4 c = 1 qt = 2 lb
             4 qt = 1 gal = 8 lb

    1 lb = 16 oz

SOURCE: Procedure for Adjusting Recipe Yield, Department of Institution Administration, Michigan State University.

total weight of ingredients in the original recipe by the factor and comparing with the total weight of ingredients in the new recipe. If the two are not the same, check the calculations before preparing the product.

5. Change weights back to pounds and ounces and convert to quarts, cups, or other volume measures ingredients that are more easily measured than weighed.

6. Round off unnecessary or awkward fractions that would be difficult to measure or weigh as far as accuracy permits.

Percentage Method. In the percentage method, the percentage of the total weight of the product is calculated for each ingredient, and once this percentage has been established, it remains constant for all future adjustments. Recipe increases and decreases are made by multiplying the total weight desired by the percentage of each ingredient.

The percentage method is based on weights expressed in pounds and decimal parts of a pound. The total quantity to be prepared is based on the weight of each portion multiplied by the number of servings needed. The constant number used in calculating a recipe is the weight of each individual serving. Following is a step-by-step procedure as used at Kansas State University and reported by McManis and Molt (NACUFS J. 35, 1978) for adjusting a recipe by the percentage method follows.

Step 1. Convert all ingredients in the original recipe from measure or pounds and ounces to pounds and tenths of a pound. Make desired equivalent ingredient substitutions such as frozen whole eggs for fresh eggs and powdered milk for liquid milk.

Step 2. Total the weight of ingredients in the recipe. Use edible portion (EP) weights when a difference exists between EP and as purchased (AP) weights. For example, the weight of onions or celery should be the weight after cleaning, peeling, and ready for use. The recipe may show both AP and EP weights, but the edible portion is used in determining the total weight.

Step 3. Calculate the percentage of each ingredient in relation to the total weight. Repeat for each ingredient.
Formula:

$$\frac{\text{Individual ingredient weight}}{\text{Total weight of ingredients}} = \frac{\text{percentage of each}}{\text{ingredient}}$$

Sum of percentages should total 100 per cent.

Step 4. Check the ratio of ingredients, which should be in proper balance before going further. Standards have been established for ingredient proportions of many items.

Step 5. Determine the total weight of the product needed by multiplying the portion weight expressed in decimal parts of a pound by the number of servings to be prepared. To convert a portion weight to a decimal part of a pound, divide the number of ounces by 16 or refer to a decimal equivalent table (Table 5.2). For example, a 2-ounce portion would be 0.125 pound. This figure multiplied by the number of portions desired gives the total weight of product needed. The weight is then adjusted, where necessary, to pan size and equipment capacity. For example, the total weight must be divisible by the optimum weight for each pan. The capacity of mixing bowls, steam-jacketed kettles, and other equipment must be considered in determining the total weight. Use the established portions, modular pan charts, or known capacity equipment guides to determine batch sizes to be written.

Step 6. Add estimated handling loss to the weight needed. An example of handling loss is the batter left in bowls or on equipment and will vary according to the product being made and preparation techniques of the worker. Like items, however, produce predictable losses, which with some experimentation can be accurately assigned. The formula for adding handling loss to a recipe follows.

$$(100\% - \text{Assigned Handling Loss }\%)\,X = \text{Desired Yield}$$
$$X = \frac{Desired\ Yield}{100\% - \text{Handling Loss }\%}$$

Example: Butter cake has a 1% handling loss. Desired
yield is 80 lb (or 600 servings)
$$(100\% - 1\%)X = 80\ \text{lb}$$
$$.99\ X = 80$$
$$X = 80/.99$$
$$X = 80.80\ \text{total lb of ingredients to}$$
produce 80 lb of batter

Step 7. Multiply each percentage number by the total weight to give the exact amount of each ingredient needed. Once the percentages of a recipe have been established, any number of servings can be calculated and the ratio of ingredients to the total will be the same. One decimal place on a recipe is shown (e.g., 8.3 lb) unless it is less than one pound, then two places are shown (e.g., 0.15 lb).

Tables 5.3 to 5.5 illustrate the expansion of a recipe for muffins from 60 to 340 servings.

TABLE 5.2   Ounces and Decimal Equivalents of a Pound

Ounces	Decimal Part of a Pound	Ounces	Decimal Part of a Pound
¼	0.016	8¼	0.516
½	0.031	8½	0.531
¾	0.047	8¾	0.547
1	0.063	9	0.563
1¼	0.078	9¼	0.578
1½	0.094	9½	0.594
1¾	0.109	9¾	0.609
2	0.125	10	0.625
2¼	0.141	10¼	0.641
2½	0.156	10½	0.656
2¾	0.172	10¾	0.672
3	0.188	11	0.688
3¼	0.203	11¼	0.703
3½	0.219	11½	0.719
3¾	0.234	11¾	0.734
4	0.250	12	0.750
4¼	0.266	12¼	0.766
4½	0.281	12½	0.781
4¾	0.297	12¾	0.797
5	0.313	13	0.813
5¼	0.328	13¼	0.828
5½	0.344	13½	0.844
5¾	0.359	13¾	0.859
6	0.375	14	0.875
6¼	0.391	14¼	0.891
6½	0.406	14½	0.906
6¾	0.422	14¾	0.922
7	0.438	15	0.938
7¼	0.453	15¼	0.953
7½	0.469	15½	0.969
7¾	0.484	15¼	0.984
8	0.500	16	1.000

NOTE: This table is useful when increasing or decreasing recipes. The multiplication or division of pounds and ounces is simplified if the ounces are converted to decimal parts of a pound. For example, when multiplying 1 lb 9 oz by 3, first change the 9 oz to 0.563 lb, by using the table. Thus, the 1 lb 9 oz becomes 1.563 lb which multiplied by 3 is 4.683 lb or 4 lb 11 oz.

TABLE

5.3   Original Recipe for Muffins   *Yield: 60 muffins*

Ingredients	Amount
Flour, all-purpose	2 lb 8 oz
Baking powder	2 oz
Salt	1 Tbsp
Sugar	6 oz
Eggs, beaten	4
Milk	1½ qt
Shortening	8 oz

TABLE

5.4   Percentage Calculated on Original Recipe   *Yield: 60 muffins*

Percentage	Ingredients	Measure	Pounds
35.79	Flour	2 lb 8 oz	2.500
1.79	Baking powder	2 oz	0.125
0.67	Salt	1 T	0.047
5.37	Sugar	6 oz	0.375
6.27	Eggs	4	0.438
42.95	Milk	1½ qt	3.000
7.16	Shortening	8 oz	0.500
100.00	Total		6.985

6.985 lb divided by 60 = .116 lb per muffin

TABLE 5.5   Expanded Recipe for Muffins   *Yield: 340 muffins*

Percentage	Ingredient	Pounds
35.79	Flour	14.26
1.79	Baking powder	0.713
0.67	Salt	0.267
5.37	Sugar	2.14
6.27	Eggs	2.50
42.95	Milk	17.11
7.16	Shortening	2.85
100.00	Total	39.84

.116 lb per muffin $\times$ 340 = 39.44 lb with 1% handling loss, 39.84 lb batter needed 39.84 lb $\times$ % each ingredient = weight of ingredient

If using pounds and ounces, change decimal parts of pounds to ounces by using Table 5.2. If using measures for some ingredients, adjust to measurable amounts.

Direct Reading Measurement Tables. The use of tables showing ingredient amounts for different numbers of portions saves time and simplifies recipe adjustment. Conversion charts have been developed that give amounts in weight and measure in increments of 25 for from 25 to 500 portions. Measurement tables are included in *Quantity Food Preparation: Standardizing Recipes and Controlling Ingredients* by Buchanan, and *Food for Fifty* by Shugart, Molt, and Wilson.

ADAPTING HOME-SIZE RECIPES   Many quantity recipes can be successfully expanded from home-size recipes, but their development involves a number of carefully planned steps. Before attempting to enlarge a small recipe, be sure that it is appropriate to the foodservice and that the same quality can be achieved when prepared in large quantity and possibly held for a time before serving. Procedures should be checked because many home recipes are lacking in detailed directions for their preparation. Before preparing the product, the extent of mixing, time, and temperature used in cooking or baking should be known; also special precautions that should be observed and any other details that may have been omitted.

Enlarging the recipe in steps is more likely to be successful than increasing from a small quantity to a large quantity without the intermediate steps. Following are suggestions for a step-by-step approach for expanding home-size recipes.

Step 1. Prepare the product in the amount of the original recipe, following exactly the quantities and procedures, noting any procedures that are unclear or any problems with the preparation.

Step 2. Evaluate the product, using a written form such as shown in Fig. 5.6, and decide if it has the potential for the foodservice. If adjustments are necessary, revise the recipe and make the product again. Work with the original amount until the product is satisfactory.

Step 3. Double the recipe or expand to appropriate amount for the pan size that will be used and prepare the product, making notations on the recipe of any changes you make. For example, additional cooking time may be needed for the larger amount. Evaluate the product and record the yield, portion size, and acceptability.

Step 4. Double the recipe again, or if the product is to be baked, calculate the quantities needed to prepare one baking pan that will be used by the foodservice. If ingredients are to be weighed, home-size measures should be converted to pounds and ounces or to pounds and tenths of a pound before proceeding further. Prepare and evaluate the product as before.

Step 5. If the product is satisfactory, continue to enlarge by increments of 25 portions or by pans. When the recipe has been expanded to 100 or a specific amount that would be used in the foodservice, adjustments should be made for handling or cooking losses. Handling loss refers to losses that occur in making and panning batters. About 3 to 5 per cent more batter, sauces, and puddings will be required to compensate for the handling loss. Cooking losses result from evaporation of water from the food during cooking. Soups, stews, and casseroles may lose from 10 to 30 per cent during cooking. The actual yield of the recipe should be checked carefully. Mixing, preparation, and cooking times should be noted because these may increase when the product is prepared in large quantity. Preparation methods should be checked to see if they are consistent with methods used for similar products. An evaluation of the product should be made and its acceptance by the clientele determined before it becomes a part of the permanent recipe file.

Ingredient Assembly

Central assembly of ingredients for food production has been found to be cost effective in many operations. In this system, the ingredients needed for recipes for the day's production and for advance preparation are weighed, measured, and assembled in a central ingredient room or area. If prepreparation equipment and low temperature storage are available, certain other procedures, such as peeling, dicing, and chopping of vegetables; breading and panning of meats; opening of canned goods; and thawing of frozen foods, may be completed in the ingredient room. The extent of responsibilities will depend on the space, equipment, and personnel available.

After ingredients have been weighed or measured and the preparation completed, each ingredient is packaged in a plastic bag or other container and labeled. The ingredients for each recipe are assembled and delivered, with a copy of the recipe, to the appropriate production unit. In some operations, the assembled ingredients are distributed when needed according to a predetermined schedule.

There are many advantages to an ingredient room, the term used most often for this activity. Increased production control, improved security, more consistent quality control, and more efficient use of equipment, especially if prepreparation is included in this area, are possible with central ingredient assembly. Because cooks are not involved in the time-consuming job of weighing and measuring ingredients, their time and skills can be more effectively used in production.

There are some disadvantages, the main one being the lack of flexibility.

The ingredients must be weighed the day before, or earlier in some cases, which does not provide for last-minute changes in menus or quantities needed. Cooks may feel restricted by not being able to add their own touches to the food they are preparing. This attitude usually changes when they are satisfied that the recipes as written will result in a product of the desired quality and once the cooks have confidence in the person who weighs the ingredients.

PERSONNEL AND EQUIPMENT   Accuracy in measuring ingredients contributes to the acceptability of the finished product, so it is important that the ingredient room personnel be well qualified and that they be provided with adequate equipment.

Personnel assigned to the ingredient room must be able to read and write and perform simple arithmetic with at least minimal ease and accuracy. Honesty, accuracy, and dependability are desirable traits for this person or persons. Safety precautions and sanitation standards should be stressed in their training.

Weighing is the quickest, easiest, and most accurate means of measure in most cases so good scales are essential. A scale that accurately weighs up to 25 pounds usually is adequate and if more than that is required the ingredients are divided in two or three lots for easier handling. Some foodservices have separate scales for very small amounts such as spices. If scales that accurately weigh small amounts are not available, volume measurement may be preferable for those foods. Scales that are calibrated to pounds and tenths of a pound instead of pounds and ounces are useful with a system that uses a computer for calculating recipes.

The equipment needed depends on the functions performed in this area. Suggested minimum equipment for weighing and measuring includes:

- Worktable, 6 to 8 feet long, with one or two drawers
- Counter scales, with gradations of 1 ounce minimum to 25 pounds
- Mobile storage bins for sugar, flour, and other large volume staples
- Shelving for bulk staples and spices
- Mobile racks for delivery of foods to production areas
- Refrigeration (and freezer if frozen foods are distributed)
- Sink and water supply
- Can opener
- Trash containers
- Counter pans with lids if canned foods are opened
- Trays for assembling ingredients
- Rubber spatulas

- Measuring utensils (gallon, quart, pint, cup measures; measuring spoons)
- Scoops for dipping flour and sugar
- Packaging materials (paper and plastic bags, paper cups)
- Masking tape and marking pens to label ingredients

If vegetable preparation is part of the ingredient room responsibilities, the following additional equipment is needed:

- Double or triple sink
- Waste disposer
- Peeling, slicing, and/or dicing equipment
- Cutting board
- Assorted knives and sharpening equipment
- Plastic tubs or bags for cleaned products

Portion Control

An early step in recipe standardization is a decision on the size of portions to be offered. Standardized portions are important not only in the control of costs, but also in creating and maintaining consumer satisfaction and good will. No one likes to receive a smaller serving than other customers for the same price.

Food is portioned by weight, measure, or count and really begins with the purchase of foods according to definite specifications so that known yields can be obtained from each food. Portioned meats, fish, and poultry; fresh fruits ordered by size (count per shipping box); canned peaches, pears, pineapple slices, and other foods in which the number of pieces is specified are examples. Also helpful in portion control is the purchase of individual butter and margarine pats and individually packaged crackers, cereals, and condiments.

During food production, portions are measured by scoop or dipper or are weighed on portion scales. For example, the recipe for meatballs may call for dipping the mixture with a size 16 dipper (or scoop), which means ¼ cup or 2 ounces. The numbering system for scoop sizes is based on the number of scoops per quart. Table 5.6 shows approximate dipper and ladle sizes. Dippers range from size 6 (10 tablespoons/6 ounces) to size 100, which holds a scant 2 teaspoons. Muffins are also measured by dippers, but bread and roll doughs are weighed. A roll cutter provides equal portions without the necessity of weighing each roll. Each recipe should indicate the yield expected in number of portions, total weight or measure, and the size in weight or measure of each serving.

TABLE 5.6   Dipper (or Scoop) Equivalents

Dipper No.*	Approximate Measure	Approximate Weight	Suggested Use
6	10 T (⅔ c)	6 oz	Entree salads
8	8 T (½ c)	4–5 oz	Entrees
10	6 T (⅜ c)	3–4 oz	Desserts
12	5 T (⅓ c)	2½–3 oz	Muffins, salads, desserts
16	4 T (¼ c)	2–2¼ oz	Muffins, desserts
20	3⅕ T	1¾–2 oz	Sandwich fillings, muffins, cup cakes
24	2⅔ T	1½–1¾ oz	Cream puffs
30	2⅕ T	1–1½ oz	Large drop cookies
40	1½ T	¾ oz	Drop cookies
60	1 T	½ oz	Small drop cookies, garnishes
Ladles	⅛ c	1 oz	Sauces, salad dressings
	¼ c	2 oz	Gravies, sauces
	½ c	4 oz	Stews, creamed foods
	⅔ c	6 oz	Stews, creamed foods
	1 c	8 oz	Soup

These measurements are based on level dippers and ladles.
*Portions per quart.

The appropriate utensil and its size for serving the product should be indicated. Ladles, which are used for serving sauces, soups, and similar foods, are sized according to capacity (1 ounce/⅛ cup to 8 ounces/1 cup). Although spoons are used for serving some foods, they are not as accurate as ladles unless the employees have been instructed in their use and know how full the spoon should be. For cakes and other desserts baked in a pan, instructions for cutting should be included. Many foodservices have pie markers or other marking devices to assure equal portions of baked products.

Employees should know the number of servings expected from a certain batch size and should be familiar with the size of the portion. In addition to the information included on recipes, a list of portion sizes for all foods should be made available to employees either in an employees' manual or posted in a convenient location (see Fig. 5.7).

Portion Guide

Breakfast Items

Bacon	2 strips	1 oz
Cereal, hot	1 portion	4-oz ladle
Eggs, scrambled	No. 8 dipper	4 oz
Fruit, canned, frozen, or dried	No. 12 dipper	2½ oz
Juices	1 glass	8 oz

Luncheon Entrees

Bacon, lettuce, tomato sandwich	1 sandwich	2 slices bread, 2 slices tomato, 3 strips bacon, 1 lettuce leaf
Barbecued meat sandwich	No. 16 dipper	1½ oz on 4-in. bun
Casserole entree	1 portion	cut 24 per 12 x 20-in. pan or 4 oz ladle meat on No. 12 dipper of rice or pasta
Chili	1 dipper	6-oz ladle
Soup or chowder	1 dipper	4-oz ladle
Tacos	1 portion	2 shells, No. 12 dipper meat, 2 oz salad mixture

Dinner Entrees

Beef roast	1 slice	2½ oz E.P.
Fried chicken	2 pieces	1 breast and 1 wing OR 1 thigh and 1 leg
Fish	1 portion	5 oz A.P.
Meat loaf	1 slice	cut 10 per 5 x 9-in. pan
Pork chops	1 chop	6 oz A.P.
Roast pork, dressing	1 portion	2 oz meat, No. 16 dipper dressing

Vegetables and Pasta

Broccoli spears	3–4 spears	3 oz
French fries	1 portion	3 oz
Noodles or spaghetti	Tongs	2½ oz lunch; 4 oz dinner
Whipped potatoes	No. 12 dipper	3½ oz

Desserts

Bar cookies	1 portion	18 x 26-in. pan cut 6 x 10
Cake, sheet	1 piece	cut 6 x 10, 18 x 26-in. pan
Ice cream	1 scoop	No. 12 dipper
Pies	1 piece	9-in. pies cut in 6

FIGURE 5.7   Portion guide for use by production and service employees. This is a partial listing but includes portion sizes for some typical foods.

Guidelines for Food Production Employees

Efficient Work Habits

Efficient work habits and organization of the preparation area will simplify the job for employees and will contribute to the attainment of high standards in food production. Observance of certain basic rules for foodservice workers will aid greatly in promoting efficient work habits.

- Check assignment to be sure that there is no question as to what is to be done or how it is to be accomplished.
- Plan work so that everything can be done within the time limit. Often several preparation procedures can be carried on simultaneously, but those that are preliminary or require the longest time should be started first.
- Assemble any equipment or ingredients not at hand and arrange them conveniently for use before beginning work. If ingredients are weighed and measured in a central ingredient area, ingredients will not need to be assembled, but they should be checked with the recipe to be sure all items have been delivered.
- Prepare equipment (preheat oven, line baking sheets).
- If prepreparation has not been done in another area, wash, trim, cut, prepare, and measure raw materials.
- Use proper equipment for the job. Employees should master the technique of using a French knife and should be aware of time-saving equipment available.
- Use power equipment whenever possible. Economy of effort and time can soon pay for additional conveniences.
- Arrange equipment and materials in the work area so that tasks can be accomplished in logical sequence with minimum movement of the worker. For example, for efficiency in breading chops, arrange pans containing the chops and dipping mixtures on the worktable from left to right.
- Use of smooth, continuous motions will keep fatigue to a minimum. Use both hands simultaneously whenever possible. Comfortable working heights and good lighting also reduce fatigue.
- Make each motion rhythmic. For example, portion meat balls by dipping and placing on baking sheets at regular intervals (count if necessary); stir mixtures evenly, taking each stroke in the same direction.

- Carry through one step in a procedure before beginning the next for speed in accomplishing a task.
- Accomplish something each time you pass one part of the kitchen to another. For example, when soiled dishes are taken to the pot and pan sink for washing, clean mixing bowls may be brought back on the return trip.
- Keep the work area clean and orderly. Use of a tray on which to work or to place soiled equipment simplifies the cleaning of the table or counter. For example, place a cutting board on the tray when peeling citrus or other juicy fruits. If responsible for measuring ingredients, place soiled measuring cups and spoons on a tray as soon as the ingredients for a recipe have been weighed or measured.

Energy Saving Suggestions

Both foodservice management and employees should assume responsibility for conserving energy whenever possible. Managers should keep electrical and other power equipment in good working order and should stress energy conservation in employee training programs. Some suggestions follow.

OVENS

1. Determine how long it takes to preheat ovens and do not begin preheating until necessary.
2. When preheating, set thermostat at the desired temperature; it will not preheat faster if set higher.
3. Check oven thermostats to be sure they register correctly.
4. Many foods can be placed in the oven and the cooking started while the oven is warming.
5. Do not open oven doors during operation. Food will cook faster and lose less moisture if door is opened at scheduled times.
6. Schedule baking or roasting so that oven capacity can be fully utilized, thereby reducing operating hours.
7. Load and unload ovens quickly to reduce heat loss.

RANGES

1. When using a gas range, the top of the flame should just touch the bottom of the pan or kettle.
2. Electric range burners should always be smaller than the kettle or pot placed on them.
3. Place kettles and pots close together on range tops to decrease heat loss.
4. Use the smallest piece of cooking equipment possible; for example, use a small hot plate to melt butter rather than a large burner or an oven.
5. Turn off unneeded cooking and heating units.

REFRIGERATORS

1. Defrost frozen food in the refrigerator. Food will thaw easily and will help reduce power demand of the refrigerator.
2. Plan ahead so that an employee entering the walk-in refrigerator or freezer can fill many needs at one time.
3. Close doors immediately after items have been removed from refrigerator.
4. Do not store food in front of refrigerator coils in a manner that would restrict air flow.
5. Turn off lights in walk-in refrigerator when leaving. Units should have pilot lights on switches to warn if lights are left on.
6. Defrost freezers frequently. Ice should not be allowed to build up more than ⅛ inch on the walls and shelves.

SERVING COUNTERS AND WARMERS

1. Do not turn heat on before it is necessary.
2. Turn on food warmers and hot plates only as needed; don't let them run when not in use. Also, run at the lowest temperature permissible for safe food handling.

In general, develop a schedule for equipment use. Equipment should be turned on at a specific time, to a specific temperature, and turned off at the designated time. When possible, stagger the turn-on times for heavy duty electrical equipment at 30-minute intervals to reduce the demand load. Do not use more equipment than necessary by filling equipment item to its capacity before using another.

Safeguards in Food Production

An important part of quality control is the recognition that food must not only be cooked so that it is served at its peak of quality and seasoned so that it is acceptable to the consumer, but it also must be safe to eat. Microbiology and food-borne illnesses are discussed in Chapter 8, but some precautions that should be taken in scheduling and producing food are noted here.

The Hazard Analysis Critical Control Point (HACCP) concept, recommended for use by the foodservice industry, emphasizes microbiological control and identifies process stages where loss of control could present a safety risk. As defined by Bauman,[2] hazard analysis is concerned with identifying microbial-sensitive ingredients, critical control points during processing, and human factors that may affect the microbiological safety of the product. The original HACCP model was modified by Bobeng and David[3] to include nutritive and sensory quality. Four critical control points in the production of entrees in conventional, cook/chill, and cook/freeze hospital foodservice systems were identified as ingredient control and storage, equipment sanitation, personnel sanitation, and time-temperature relationships.

It is the responsibility of management to provide for inspection of food at the critical control points. Management must establish quality standards for the finished product and then monitor its production at critical points during procurement, storage, preparation, heating, holding (hot, chilled, or frozen), thawing when necessary, portioning, distribution, and service.

Precautions for Safe Food Production

Proper handling throughout the purchasing, storage, production, and service of food is critical in safeguarding the food against contamination. As discussed in Chapter 4, legal safeguards are provided by federal, state, and local regulatory agencies, who are responsible for setting and enforcing standards for raw and processed foods. Minimum standards for sanitation in foodservice establishments are monitored by city and state agencies, but managers and dietitians are responsible for the maintenance of sanitation standards in their respective foodservices.

Inadequate refrigeration practices (46 percent) have been major contributors to reported outbreaks of food-borne illness, most of which occurred from foods prepared in foodservice establishments, according to Bryan.[4] Other major factors have been identified as the time lapse between preparing and serving food (21 per cent), inadequate thermal processing or cooking (16 per cent) improper hot storage (16 per cent), inadequate reheating (12 per cent), and infected persons touching cooked foods (20 per cent). Personnel must be made aware of critical points in the production and service of food and must be trained in the use of safe procedures related to these areas.

Temperature is an important factor in the control of harmful organisms. Their growth can be slowed by refrigeration or freezing, and they can be destroyed by sufficient heat. As shown in Fig. 5.8, the danger zone favoring bacterial growth is the temperature range of 45 to 140°F, and the period of time during which food is allowed to remain in this critical temperature zone largely determines the rate and extent of bacterial growth. It is imperative, therefore, that the internal temperature of potentially hazardous food be kept **below** 45°F or **above** 140°F to ensure their safety. This means that the temperature of the refrigerator should be colder or the holding equipment hotter to maintain the proper internal temperature in the food. Temperature controls on walk-in and other refrigerators should be in good working

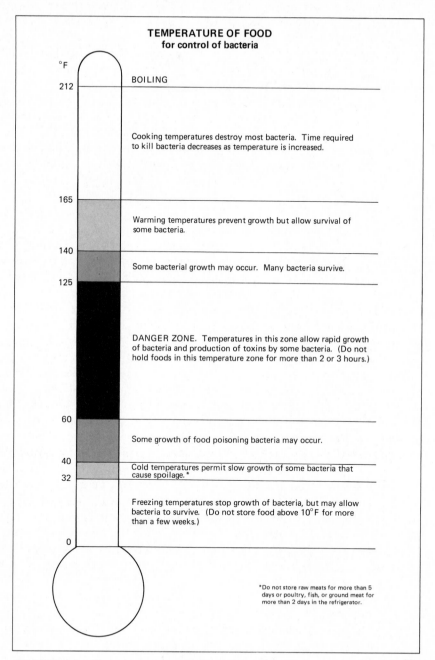

FIGURE 5.8 Temperature guide for food safety. *From* Keeping Food Safe, *Home and Garden Bulletin No. 162, USDA.*

order and checked daily to make certain that temperatures are maintained below 45°F, as appropriate for the specific foods stored in them.

POTENTIAL HAZARDS IN FOOD PRODUCTION   Foods that are potentially hazardous include meat, poultry, and fish. These products are frequently contaminated with food-borne pathogens, which can be spread to surfaces of equipment, to the hands of workers, and to other foods. If frozen turkeys are to be cooked whole, they should be thawed completely in the refrigerator before being cooked, and if cooked the day before, they should not be refrigerated without first reducing their bulk. The practice of cooking, chilling, and then reheating beef roasts is also potentially hazardous because reheating may not produce a temperature high enough (165°F) to destroy any bacteria that may have survived in the meat.

Food requiring preliminary preparation, which may include cooking prior to the final steps in their preparation, should be refrigerated following the preliminary steps. This includes items such as sandwich and salad mixtures; sliced, chopped, cut, and boned poultry and meats; ground, mixed, and shaped cooked meats; cream pie fillings and puddings; and sliced ham and similar items.

Cream pie fillings, puddings, and other products made with eggs, if not served hot, should be refrigerated as soon as possible after cooking. Attempting to cool at room temperature to save refrigeration is a practice to be discouraged. Masses of hot food cool slowly, even in large walk-in refrigerators. To be cooled quickly, the food should be poured into shallow containers to a depth of no more than two inches and refrigerated, as shown in Fig. 5.9. Other suggestions for cooling large amounts of food quickly include stirring the food and placing the pan of food into an ice bath or vat of cold running water.

Mishandling of food by cooks and other production workers also constitutes a hazard. Cooked ingredients in potato salad, for instance, can be contaminated by persons during peeling, slicing, chopping, or mixing operations in its preparation. Cross-contamination by a worker or equipment that has been in contact with raw meat or poultry and then with the cooked product is to be avoided.

Following is a summary of basic standards for safeguarding the preparation and storage of food:

• Select clean, wholesome food from sources approved or considered satisfactory by the health authority.
• Specify that frozen products be maintained at 0°F or lower during delivery.
• Wash thoroughly all raw fruits and vegetables before using.

FIGURE 5.9   Portable wire racks facilitate rapid cooling
of food in shallow pans.   *Courtesy, Metropolitan Wire Goods
Corporation.*

- Scour and sanitize all cutting boards, knives, and electric slicers immediately after use with raw or cooked meats, fish, or poultry.
- Cook food to recommended temperatures.
- Maintain all potentially hazardous foods at **safe** temperatures, 45°F or below, or 140°F or above, except for brief periods necessary for preparation.
- Check internal temperature of cooked foods to be held on a serving counter or in a holding cabinet; should be 165 to 170°F before taking to the serving unit in order to maintain 140°F during the serving period.
- Refrigerate immediately any cooked foods to be used later; refrigerate in shallow containers; center of food mass should reach 45°F within four hours. Place pans in refrigerators so that air circulation is not blocked.
- Discard any questionable food.
- Protect food from contamination or cross-contamination during preparation, service, and storage through precautionary measures such as use of

clean properly sanitized equipment; optimum refrigerator temperatures, proper handling of food by healthy personnel who wash hands thoroughly after touching any food or objects that may be contaminated; and storage and use of poisonous or toxic materials away from the food.

FOOD HANDLING PROCEDURES Correct work habits of employees and sanitary food handling procedures to be followed by the foodservice personnel include:

- Wash hands with soap and water on reporting for work and after handling raw poultry and meat, smoking, sneezing, and use of handkerchief, and, above all, after each visit to the toilet.
- Keep work surfaces clean and the work area well organized and orderly.
- Refrigerate unused foods and clean up any spillage promptly.
- Use only clean utensils in preparing, cooking, and serving food.
- Keep fingers and hands out of food as much as possible. Use spoons, forks, tongs, or other appropriate utensils. Wear disposable gloves for handling food that will not be further cooked before serving.
- Always grasp utensils such as spoons, spatulas, tongs, and forks by the handles.
- Use a clean spoon each time for tasting food.

Summary

Basic to production planning and scheduling is the forecast, which is a prediction of the number of persons to be served for a meal or a day and, for a selective menu, an estimate of the number who will choose each menu item. Quantities of food to prepare are based on the predicted number of servings needed and the portion size to be offered. This information, plus special instructions for preparation and work assignments, are included in a production schedule.

Management's responsibility for serving high quality food starts with the setting of standards and ensuring that employees are aware of them. The use of standardized recipes, good quality ingredients, and proper supervision of food production are vital to quality control. The dietitian or manager must also be aware of the critical points in food production that affect food safety and insist on personal and work habits of employees that will minimize the danger of food contamination.

Notes

1. Bobeng, B. J. and David, B. D.: HACCP models for quality control of entree production in foodservice systems. J. Food Protection 40:632, 1977.
2. Bauman, H. E.: The HACCP Concept and Microbiological hazard categories. Food Technol. 28:30, 1974.
3. Bobeng, B. J. and David, B. D. HACCP models for quality control of entree production in foodservice systems. I. Development of Hazard Analysis Critical Point models. II. Quality assessment of beef loaves utilizing HACCP models. J. Am. Diet. Assoc. 73:526, 1978.
4. Bryan, F. L.: Factors that contribute to outbreaks of foodborne disease. J. Food Protection 41:816, 1978.

Supplementary References

Bryan, F. L.: Foodborne diseases in the United States associated with meat and poultry. J. Food Protection 43:140, 1980.

Bryan, F. L.: Hazard analysis of food service operations. Food Technol. 35:78, 1981.

Bryan, F. L.: An inspectional form to evaluate temperatures in foodservice establishments. J. Food Protection 47:127, 1984.

Bryan, F. L. and Lyon, J. B. Critical control points of hospital foodservice operations. J. Food Protection 47:950, 1984.

Buchanan, P. W.: Quantity Food Preparation: Standardizing Recipes and Controlling Ingredients. Chicago: The Amer. Diet. Assoc., 1983.

Chandler, S., Norton, L., Hoover, L., and Moore, A.: Analysis of meal census patterns for forecasting menu item demand. J. Am. Diet. Assoc. 80:317, 1982.

Cullen, K., Hoover, L. and Moore, A.: Menu item forecasting systems in hospital foodservice. J. Am. Diet. Assoc. 73:640, 1978.

Dougherty, D.A.: Forecasting production demand. *In* Rose, J. C.: Handbook for Health Care Food Service Management. Rockville, MD: Aspen Systems Corp., 1984.

Gerlach, N.: Food production controls. *In* Rose, J. C.: Handbook for Health Care Food Service Management. Rockville, MD: Aspen Systems Corp., 1984.

Klein, B. P., Matthews, M. E., and Setser, C. S.: Foodservice systems: Time and temperature effects on food quality. North Central Regional Research Publication No. 293. Urbana-Champagne, IL: University of Illinois, June 1984.

Knight, J. B. and Kotschevar, L. H.: Quantity Food Production. Boston: CBI Publishing Co., 1979.

Longree, K.: Quantity Food Sanitation, 3rd ed. New York: Wiley-Interscience, 1980.

Longree, K. and Blaker, G. G.: Sanitary Techniques in Foodservice, 2nd ed. New York: John Wiley and Sons, 1982.

McManis, H. and Molt, M.: Recipe standardization and percentage method of adjustment. NACUFS J. 35, 1978.

Rose, J. C., ed.: Handbook for Health Care Food Service Management. Rockville, MD: Aspen Systems Corp., 1984.

Shugart, G. S., Molt, M., and Wilson, M.: Food for Fifty, 7th ed. New York: John Wiley and Sons, 1985.

Skelton, M.: Sensory evaluation of food. Cornell Hotel and Rest. Admin. Q. 24:51 (Feb.), 1984.

Thorner, M. E. and Manning, P. B.: Quality Control in Foodservice, rev. ed. Westport, CT: AVI Publishing Co., 1983.

U.S. Department of Agriculture. Food Buying Guide for School Food Service. PA 1257. Food and Nutrition Service, USDA. Washington. DC: U.S. GPO, 1980.

U.S. Department of Health, Education, and Welfare: Food Service Sanitation Manual. DHEW Publication No. (FDA) 78-2081. Washington, DC: U.S. GPO, 1978.

CHAPTER 6

Quantity Food Production

Introduction

The principles of food preparation in large quantity are much the same as in small quantity except that there are differences in procedures because of the larger amounts of food involved. Mechanized equipment is essential for heavy processes and for time-consuming procedures, especially in the larger operations. Steam-jacketed kettles with stirring paddles in which food can be cooled after cooking; timers on steam-cooking equipment; metering devices on steam-jacketed kettles for measuring water; and high-speed vegetable cutters are examples of labor-saving equipment in use. Convection ovens and high-pressure steamers, used in many foodservices, reduce the time required for cooking. No-transfer cooking, in which foods are cooked in the same pans used for serving, saves time and possible damage to the food quality through additional handling.

Basic cookery processes and their application to quantity production are discussed in this chapter. Emphasis is on general procedures used in institutional and commercial food production. Types of equipment used for the various procedures are noted; for more details about the equipment, see Chapter 10.

Basic Cooking Processes

Objectives of Cooking

The objectives of cooking food are to develop and enhance the flavor and attractiveness of the original color, form, and texture, to destroy harmful organisms and substances, to improve digestibility, and to conserve nutritive value. Cooking is accomplished by the transfer of heat from an energy source to and through the food.

Heat Transfer

For food to be cooked, heat must be transferred from the energy source by one of these three methods: *conduction,* in which heat moves directly from one item or substance to something touching it; *convection,* in which heat is spread by the movement of air, steam, or liquid; or *radiation,* in which energy is transferred by waves from the source to the food. These methods of heat transfer usually involve some intermediary such as the air in the oven, the water, steam, or fat that may surround the food and/or container, or the metal, glass, or ceramic that is the food container itself. A brief discussion of these processes follows.

AIR AS A COOKING MEDIUM

Baking. Food is cooked by dry heat, usually in an oven. Baking temperatures may vary from 250 to 500°F.

Roasting. The term roasting is commonly applied to the baking of meats. Cooking uncovered is essential to roasting because if the meat or poultry is covered with a lid or aluminum foil, the steam is held in, changing the process from dry-heat to moist-heat cooking.

A variety of ovens may be used in foodservice operations. In addition to those that are part of range units, deck ovens are used extensively. Pans are placed directly on the oven deck rather than on wire shelves. The deck oven may be a single oven or may consist of two or three individual units stacked one above the other, with temperatures usually adjustable for each separate unit.

In a convection oven (Fig. 6.1), circulation of air speeds the baking process, resulting in decreased cooking time of 30 to 40 per cent and at temperatures 25 to 50 degrees lower than in a deck oven. Shelves can be placed closer together without blocking the heat flow, so more food can be accommodated in these ovens. The forced heat cooks more quickly, but it tends to dry out some foods excessively if they are overcooked. A combination convection/steam oven bakes or roasts with moisture or can be used as a standard convection oven or as a pressureless steamer.

Revolving or reel ovens, in which pans of food go around on shelves or trays arranged on a ferris-wheel arrangement, and conveyor ovens, in which pans of food are loaded onto a belt that is moved through the ovens, are used in bakeshops and in high-volume operations. In a new type of oven, based on the technology of air impingement, hot-air jets focus heat on the

FIGURE 6.1   Convection oven. Space-saving rack shelves
and forced air heat accomplish more cooking in less time
than in conventional oven.   *Courtesy, Market Forge Company.*

food from above and below as it moves on conveyor belts. Illustrations of
the impingement and other types of ovens are included in Chapter 10.

LIQUID AS A COOKING MEDIUM   Methods using water or other liquid as
the cooking medium are known as moist-heat methods.

Boiling. Food is cooked in a liquid that is bubbling rapidly. The temperature of boiling water is 212°F. This point is raised by the presence of solids in the water and lowered by higher altitudes. At 5,000 feet, water boils at about 203°F, so it takes longer to boil foods at high altitudes because the temperature is lower.

Simmering. Food is cooked in liquid at temperatures ranging from 185°F to a few degrees below the boiling point. Most foods cooked in a liquid are simmered because the higher temperatures and intense bubbling of boiling liquid may be detrimental to the texture and appearance of the food.

Stewing. Food is cooked in a small amount of water, which may be either boiling or simmering. Whether a food is to be simmered, stewed, or boiled, the liquid usually is brought to a full boil first. This compensates for the lowering of the temperature when the food is added. The heat is then adjusted to maintain a steady temperature.

Poaching. Food is cooked by immersion in hot liquid maintained at simmering temperatures. Poaching is used to cook foods such as fish, poultry, and eggs out of the shell.

When cooking food in water, the amount of heat, and indirectly the amount of time required to raise the temperature of the kettle and its contents to the desired degree, depends on the size and density of the food and the temperature of the food at the start of cooking. Some foods will conduct heat rapidly from the walls of the kettle to the center portions of the food, but others are poor conductors. Regardless of whether the food is immersed in water, the size of the pieces and the manner in which they pack together, as well as the kind of food, all bear on its conductivity. In large masses of food of poor conductivity, the outer portions are commonly overdone by the time the center is cooked.

Since food in institutional and commercial foodservices is cooked in greater quantities and in larger containers than in home cookery, more heat and time are needed to bring the food to the cooking temperature. The amount of heat required also will depend on whether the food is at room temperature when put into the cooker or has just been removed from the refrigerator and whether the container has been preheated or not. When the food has reached the cooking temperature, only heat enough to keep the container and the food at cooking temperature need be supplied. Food will cook no faster in rapidly boiling than in slowly boiling water.

The mass of substance to be heated is one of the factors determining the length of time required to raise the whole quantity to a given temperature. Therefore, food cooked in large amounts is subjected more to conditions that destroy vitamins and lessen attractiveness than is food cooked at home. For this reason, it has been suggested that vegetables and other foods of high vitamin content be cooked in small batches of five pounds or less to avoid overcooking.

The major equipment used for cooking in liquid includes steam-jacketed kettles and stock pots on top of the range. However, some products such as eggs, rice, or pasta may be covered with water and heated in the steamer; others that involve stewing, braising, or poaching may be done in the oven.

STEAM AS A COOKING MEDIUM   In steaming, foods are cooked by exposing them directly to steam. Steam cookers provide for controlled cooking in constant temperatures that range from 212 to 250°F. Most steamers are designed to accommodate standard-size pans that can be used in the serving counter. The temperature depends on whether the steamer is pressure operated and on the altitude at which the cooking is done.

Free-venting steam cookers operate without pressure in the cooking compartments and maintain the temperature of boiling water, 212°F. A pressure steamer is a cooker that holds in steam under pressure. A low pressure steamer uses about 5 pounds per square inch (psi), with the steam reaching about 227°F. At 10 psi, the steam temperature is 240°F and at 15 psi, the temperature reaches 250°F.

High pressure steam cookers are used primarily for fast cooking of vegetables. The shortened cooking period possible in the pressure steamer is due partly to the quickly penetrating heat characteristic of live steam, but chiefly to the instantaneous start of the cooking process. Pressure steaming is an extremely rapid method of cooking and must be carefully controlled and timed.

Pressureless convection steamers, in which heat transfer is accomplished by steam interacting with the food through forced convection, are being used in many foodservices. This type of steamer can be used for defrosting frozen foods as well as for steaming fresh and frozen foods.

Food properly cooked in a pressure steamer is evenly cooked, retains a high vitamin content as well as its natural color and flavor, and suffers less of the usual cookery losses, such as shrinkage caused by prolonged cookery, boiling over, or burning. Overcooking results from reaching too high pressure or from holding the food at a given pressure for even a few minutes overtime.

Steam is the source of heat in jacketed kettles. The heat is transferred through the walls of the inner lining of the kettle by conduction, but no contact between food and steam is possible. The temperature is higher than in a double boiler because the steam is under pressure. The temperature increases with increase in pressure.

FAT AS A COOKING MEDIUM   Fat serves as a medium for heat transference in deep-fat frying, panfrying, and sautéing.

Deep-fat Frying. Food is cooked by submerging in hot fat. Proper temperature is important in deep-fat frying to cook and brown the food with a minimum fat absorption. Foods may be dipped in a breading or batter before frying to form a protective coating between food and fat and to give the product crispness, color, and flavor. In this type of cooking, the medium becomes part of the food during the cooking process. It is not unusual for foods to absorb 10 to 20 per cent fat during frying.

The best temperature for the deep-fat frying of cooked foods, such as cheese balls, is 375 to 385°F and of uncooked foods, 350 to 375°F. Table 6.1 shows deep-fat frying temperatures for different food products. The fryer basket generally is filled half full, never more than two-thirds of its capacity. Overloading results in an improperly cooked product. Food should not be salted over the fat because the presence of salt in contact with the frying fat helps break it down and shorten its life.

The choice of fat used as a frying medium is an important factor in the production of good quality deep-fat fried foods. The fat should have a relatively high decomposition point, a smoking point well above temperatures best for cooking, and should have no undesirable odor or flavor. The smoke point varies with the type of fat. Those with the highest smoke point usually are the vegetable oils or hydrogenated vegetable fats to which no emulsifier has been added. Emulsifiers that improve the quality of fats for baking lower their smoke points.

Frying in fat with a low smoking point causes greater fat absorption by the food than occurs when fat of higher smoking temperature is used. Particles of food, such as flour or other cooking residue, lower the smoking point as does an increase in the surface of the fat, which explains the use of a deep kettle with a relatively small surface.

The frying life of the fat is important to the foodservice that uses large quantities of this relatively high-cost food. The fat should be heated only to the temperature and for the time required for cooking. The heat should be turned off immediately after completion of the frying; in continuous operations the thermostat should be lowered to 200°F during slack periods.

The fryer should be cleaned daily and the fat strained to remove crumbs and food particles. The type of frying kettle now used in most foodservices is so constructed that the particles of food fall into the lower layer of relatively cool fat and are drawn off before decomposition takes place. In such kettles only the upper part of the fat is heated to the desired temperature, which is thermostatically controlled. Such a method cuts the cost of deep-fat frying considerably. The fryer may be equipped with a strainer, but if it is not, the fat can be strained through several layers of cheesecloth.

The fryer should be replenished with fresh fat to replace that lost during frying. Fat turnover is one of the most important factors in determining the life of the frying fat. The more rapid the turnover, the longer the life of the

TABLE 6.1   Deep Fat Frying Temperatures

Type of Product	Temperature (°F)	Frying Time[a] (min)
Bananas	375	1–3
Cauliflower, precooked	370	3–5
Cheese balls	350	2–3
Chicken, disjointed,		
1½–2 lb fryers	325	10–12
2–2½ lb fryers	325	12–15
Chicken, half,		
1½–2 lb fryers	325	12–15
Croquettes (all previously cooked foods)	360–375	2–5
Cutlets,		
¼ in. thick	325–350	5–8
Doughnuts	360–375	3–5
Eggplant	370	5–7
Fish fillets	375	4–6
Fish sticks	375	3–4
French toast	360	3–4
Fritters	370–380	2–5
Onion rings	350	3–4
Oysters	375	2–4
Potatoes, ½ in.		
Complete fry	365	6–8
Blanching	360	3–5
Browning	375	2–3
Frozen, fat blanched	375	2–3
Sandwiches	350–360	3–4
Scallops	360–375	3–4
Shrimp	360–375	3–5
Timbale cases	350–365	2–3

[a]The exact frying time will vary with the equipment used, size and temperature of the food pieces, and the amount of food placed in the fryer at one time. If the kettle is overloaded, foods may become grease-soaked. If food is frozen, use lower temperatures listed and allow additional cooking time.

fat. In some foodservices that operate continuously, it may never be necessary to discard the fat, but where maximum production is not maintained, the fat will need to be discarded at some point. If undesirable flavors develop in the fried food or if the fat foams excessively, the fat is no longer suitable for frying.

Panfrying. Food is cooked in a moderate amount of fat in a pan over moderate heat. The amount of fat depends on the food being cooked. Only a small amount is used for eggs, while more may be needed for panfried chicken. Most foods must be turned at least once for even cooking. Some larger foods may be removed from the pan and finished in the oven, to prevent excessive surface browning.

Sautéing. Food is cooked quickly in a small amount of fat. The pan should be preheated before adding the food, which should be seared rapidly.

Braising and Fricasseeing. The methods of braising and fricasseeing combine cooking in fat with the addition of moisture. The first step in braising is browning in a small quantity of fat, and then cooking slowly in liquid in a covered utensil. Fricasseeing is browning in fat and simmering in gravy. Steam-jacketed kettles and tilting frypans are used extensively for these methods. After the moisture is added to the browned food, the product may also be finished in the oven at a low temperature.

DIRECT HEAT CONDUCTION   In direct heat conduction, heat is transferred directly from the source of heat to the food.

Broiling. A rapid, high-heat method, broiling uses radiant heat from above, generally only for tender meats, poultry, and fish.

Grilling. Food is cooked on an open grid over a heat source, which may be charcoal, an electric element, or a gas-heated element.

HEAT CONDUCTION THROUGH THE CONTAINER   Methods in which the transference of heat is direct from the container include griddling and panbroiling.

Griddling. Food is placed on a griddle, which is a solid cooking surface, and cooked with or without a small amount of fat. The temperature is adjustable and is lower than on a grill (usually around 350°F). Meats, pancakes, and eggs are commonly cooked on a griddle.

Panbroiling. The method of panbroiling is similar to griddling except that it is done in a frypan. Fat should be poured off as it accumulates, or the process would become panfrying. No liquid is added and the pan is not covered.

RADIATION   Radiation occurs when ultrahigh-frequency energy waves penetrate directly into the food and set up a rapid rate of molecular activity. The waves themselves are not actually heat energy, but they are changed into heat energy when they strike the food being cooked. Applications of radiation used in foodservice operations are microwave and infrared.

Microwave Cooking. Friction between food molecules produces heat in the food. Microwaves penetrate food from all directions to a depth of one to one and one-half inches. They cause no chemical change in the food, but the vibration of the food molecules causes heat in the area of penetration. These areas begin to cook, and heat spreads through conduction to other parts of the foods, as it does in conventional cooking. Food usually is cooked in oven glass, paper, or china utensils, since these materials are transparent to the microwaves. Metals reflect the waves and, therefore, cannot be used in many microwave ovens.

Foods in a microwave oven cook in one-third to one-tenth of the time required in a conventional oven. However, the oven capacity is limited, and there is no browning of food unless the oven is equipped with a conventional high-speed broiler. Microwave ovens for foodservice are best adapted for cooking foods rapidly from the frozen state and are often found in serving areas of hospitals, where they are used for heating individual plates of cooked foods from the chilled or frozen state for service to patients. Microwave ovens are used in restaurants also for heating rolls or individual portions of frozen entrees.

Some foods cannot be heated successfully in the microwave and menu items can easily be overcooked. Some items tend to heat unevenly, so the plating of food becomes important if two or more foods are to be reheated at the same time. Employees who are responsible for use of microwave ovens should be trained for this function, and there should be a continuous monitoring of food quality and safety.

Infrared Broiling. A broiler is used in which an electric or ceramic element heated by a gas flame becomes so hot that it gives off infrared radiation, which cooks the food. There are also high-intensity infrared ovens designed to heat food rapidly, and infrared lamps are often used to hold foods at serving temperatures.

FREEZING AND RECONSTITUTING

Freezing. The freezing process is used extensively for frozen desserts, for preservation of fruits and vegetables, and for storing prepared foods for later service. Some prepared foods to be frozen require special treatment, and all should be properly packaged and quick frozen at −10°F or lower temperatures to maintain their quality during storage.

The main problems in frozen cooked foods are damage to texture or structure and the development of off-flavors. Much of this damage can be reduced or eliminated by substituting more stable ingredients, adding stabilizers, and exercising greater control of storage time, temperature, and packaging. Examples are substitution of at least 50 per cent waxy rice flour for wheat flour in sauces and gravies to overcome the loss in smoothness after thawing. Substitution of waxy rice flour in custards and cream puddings also helps to solve the problem of separation and curdled appearance in these foods. A number of freeze-resistant starches made by modifying waxy corn or maize starches also have been developed.

The stability of souffles and soft pie meringues can be improved by an increase in sugar or flour content, and souffles are most satisfactory if baked before freezing, reheated from the frozen state, and covered during reheating to avoid loss of moisture. Hard-cooked egg white does not freeze well, although the yolk can be frozen. Most meats freeze satisfactorily, but they lose freshness and develop stale or rancid flavors if cooked or packaged improperly and if stored too long.

Most types of bread, rolls, cakes, cookies, and pies can be frozen, stored, and thawed without marked change if properly packaged, but most custard pies "weep" after thawing and, without a marked change in formula, are not very satisfactory. Moisture vapor-proof packaging is of great importance for baked goods to be frozen.

Reconstituting or Rethermalizing. Reconstituting frequently refers to returning a food to its original form. The addition of water to dry milk or frozen orange juice is an example. Rethermalizing refers to the use of heat to bring a product to serving temperature, usually in a microwave, convection, conventional, or reconstituting oven, or in a steamer.

Applications in Quantity Food Production

Certain basic procedures for production of menu items are used in quantity cooking regardless of the type or size of the foodservice. Broiling, frying, baking, and stewing are standard processes in food preparation, but there may be some variation in exact procedures because of size and character of the operation and the available equipment and personnel. For example, in a restaurant steaks and chops probably are broiled or grilled to order, while in a hospital where all food must be ready at one time to send to patient areas, the same meat might be browned, then finished in the oven. In school foodservices having no deep-fat fryers, fish fillets would be breaded and placed on baking sheets and cooked in the oven, whereas a commercial foodservice no doubt would deep-fat fry them.

Following is a discussion of the application of cookery principles to quantity preparation for foods grouped according to major menu categories and customary areas of production in a foodservice kitchen: soups, stocks, and sauces, meat, fish, poultry, pasta and cereals, eggs and cheese, fruits and vegetables, salads, sandwiches, and bakeshop production. Coverage is not comprehensive, and no attempt has been made to include recipes. It is necessary and expected that this material be supplemented with standardized recipes, basic food preparation texts, and current research.

Soups, Stocks, and Sauces

The popularity of soups today has focused attention on their preparation and their basic ingredients of stock and sauces. Most soups can be classified as clear or unthickened and cream or thick.

CLEAR OR UNTHICKENED SOUPS   **Clear** soups are based on a clear, unthickened broth or stock. Vegetables, meat, or poultry products may be added. **Bouillon** refers to clear soups without solid ingredients. **Consommé** is a concentrated flavorful broth or stock that has been clarified to make it clear and transparent.

Broth or **stock,** the basic ingredient for all clear soups, is made by simmering meat, poultry, seafood, and/or vegetables in water to extract their flavor. Brown stock, made from beef that has been browned before simmering, and white or light stock, made from veal and/or chicken, are the stocks used most often.

To prepare stock, cover the meat and bones or poultry with cold water in a stock pot or steam-jacketed kettle. Salt usually is not added at this point because when the stock is concentrated or combined with other ingredients, it may be too salty. Onions, celery, and carrots often are added, as are herbs and spices in moderation. Bay leaves, thyme, peppercorns, and parsley are commonly used. Bring to a boil, lower heat, and simmer for 3 to 4 hours. Strain and cool, then remove fat. When cold, the fat will congeal on top and may be skimmed off. To clarify the stock after it has been chilled, add egg whites and crushed eggshells, boil for 15 to 20 minutes, then strain. Stock is highly perishable. If it is not to be used immediately, it may be reduced in volume by boiling to one-half or one-fourth its volume and frozen for later use.

Because the making of stock is so time-consuming, many foodservices use concentrated bases, which are mixed with water to make flavored liquids similar to stocks. Bases vary in quality, with the best products being composed mainly of meat or poultry extracts. These are perishable and must be refrigerated. Many bases have salt as their principal ingredient, so it is important to read the list of ingredients on the label. The best way to judge the quality of a base is to compare a sample made with a base to a well-made stock. When using these bases, the salt and other seasonings in the soup recipe may need to be adjusted.

CREAM OR THICK SOUPS   **Cream** soups are made with a thin white sauce combined with mashed, strained, or finely chopped vegetables, chicken, fish, or meat. Chicken stock may be used to replace part of the milk in the sauce to enhance the flavor. **Chowders** are unstrained, thick soups prepared from seafood, poultry, meat, and/or vegetables. **Bisques** are mixtures of chopped shellfish, stock, milk, and seasonings, usually thickened. **Purées** are soups that are naturally thickened by puréeing one or more of their ingredients.

SAUCES Basic to many sauces is a **roux,** which is a cooked mixture of equal parts by weight of fat and flour. Melt fat in a heavy sauce pan or steam-jacketed kettle. Add flour and stir until fat and flour are thoroughly mixed. Cook until roux is of the desired color. A roux may range from white, in which the fat and flour are cooked only for a short time, to brown, cooked until it is light brown in color and has a nutty taste and aroma.

Many meat and vegetable sauces are modifications of basic recipes, such as white sauce, bechamel sauce, and brown sauce. **White sauce** is made with a roux of fat, usually margarine or butter, and flour, and with milk as the liquid. Its uses in quantity food preparation are numerous, as a basis for cream soups, as a sauce for vegetables, and as an ingredient in many casseroles. **Bechamel sauce** and its variations use milk and chicken stock as the liquid and generally are served with seafood, eggs, poultry, or vegetables. **Brown sauce** is made with a well-browned roux and beef stock and is used mainly with meat.

To make these basic sauces, the liquid usually is added to the roux and may be hot or cooled. A very cold liquid will solidify the fat in the roux. The liquid is added slowly while beating with a wire whip to prevent lumps from forming. If the liquid is hot, it will be necessary to beat vigorously because the starch will gelatinize quickly. If making more than one gallon of sauce, the mixture will be less likely to become lumpy if about one-fourth of the liquid is added and stirred until smooth, then the remainder of the liquid added gradually. Stir until mixture reaches the boiling point, then reduce heat and cook, stirring occasionally, until the starch is fully swollen and transparent and the starchy taste is gone. This will take from 10 to 20 minutes. Viscosity decreases if the swollen starch granules are broken by continued heating or excessive stirring. Therefore, the products should be heated quickly and stirred during the thickening process but discontinued, except to prevent sticking, after the particles are well disbursed. Table 6.2 gives basic proportions of ingredients for white sauce.

The roux may also be added to the liquid, a method used when the roux is made in amounts to last for several days. A small amount of roux is added to the hot liquid and beaten vigorously with a wire whip to break up all lumps. Continue to beat small quantities into the simmering liquid until the desired consistency is reached.

Other sauces may have a butter, mayonnaise, or tomato base or may be made from concentrated canned soups. Many mixes and seasoning combi-

TABLE 6.2 Basic Procedure of Ingredients for Making White Sauce in Quantity

| | Milk | Flour | | Salt | Fat[a] | |
	(gal)	(lb)	(c)	(T)	(lb)	Uses
Thin	1	¼	1	1	½	Soup, scalloped potatoes
Medium	1	½	2	1	½	Creamed and scalloped dishes, gravies
Thick	1	¾	3	1	½	Soufflés, creamed watery vegetables (i.e., celery and onions)
Heavy	1	1	4	1	½	Croquettes

Directions:

   1. Scald the milk in covered container in a steamer or steam-jacketed kettle or on top of the range.
   2. Make a roux of the fat and flour.[b]
   3. Add to the heated milk while stirring briskly; continue to stir until mixture is thickened.
   4. Continue to cook, stirring only occasionally, until the starch is thoroughly cooked and the desired thickness is obtained.

[a] Often increased in thick and heavy sauces.

[b] An alternative method is to make a paste of the flour and ¼ of the milk (cold). Add to remainder of hot milk, cook, then add fat. For quantities larger than 1 gallon, ¼ of the milk may be added to the roux and stirred with a wire whip until smooth; then add this mixture to remainder of the hot milk.

SOURCE: Ruth M. Griswold, *The Experimental Study of Foods,* Boston: Houghton Mifflin, p. 295, 1962.

nations are available, but as with other convenience products they should be purchased only if their use results in a menu item that is acceptable. Commercial bases are often substituted for the chicken or beef stock called for in sauces, but salt and seasonings in the recipe may have to be reduced.

Meat

The methods of cooking meat and meat products depend on the quality and cut of meat, the facilities available for its preparation and service, and the quantity that must be prepared at one time.

In general, dry heat (broiling, roasting) is more satisfactory for tender cuts, and moist heat cookery (braising, stewing, simmering) for the less tender cuts. Table 6.3 suggests methods of cooking appropriate for various cuts and grades of beef. In veal, pork, and lamb, practically any cut but the shank may be cooked by dry heat, although broiling is not as desirable for pork or veal as it is for lamb or beef. Veal, because of its delicate flavor and lack of fat in the tissues, combines well with sauces and other foods.

The lower grades of meat and the less tender cuts of higher quality meat may be tenderized by scoring, cubing, grinding, or by the addition of en-

TABLE 6.3   Suggested Cooking Guide for Beef

The use of an appropriate method of cooking is essential to bring out the desirable eating qualities of the specific cut and grade selected. Below is a guide suggesting the most generally accepted method of cooking retail cuts of beef of each grade.

Flank, plate, brisket, foreshank, and the heel of the round should be prepared in the same manner for all grades of beef. These less tender cuts are used for stewing, braising, pot roasting, or boiling, or are ground for use in meat loaves and similar dishes.

Cut	Prime	Choice	Good
Top round and sirloin tip (steaks and roasts)	Braise, broil, pan fry, pot roast, or roast	Braise, broil, pan fry, pot roast, or roast	Braise, pan fry, pot roast, or roast
Bottom round (steaks and roasts)	Braise, pan fry, pot roast, or roast	Braise, pan fry, pot roast, or roast	Braise, pot roast, or roast
Rump roast	Roast or pot roast	Roast or pot roast	Roast or pot roast
Sirloin (steaks and roasts)	Broil, pan fry, or roast	Broil, pan fry, or roast	Broil, pan fry, or roast
Porterhouse, T-bone, club and rib steaks	Broil	Broil	Broil
Rib roast	Roast	Roast	Roast
Chuck, round bone and blade (roasts and steaks)	Roast, pot roast, or braise	Roast, pot roast, or braise	Roast, pot roast, or braise

SOURCE: "U.S. Grades of Beef," *Marketing Bulletin No. 15,* U.S. Department of Agriculture, Washington, D.C.

zymes. Adding tomatoes or vinegar to a meat mixture also has a tenderizing effect.

The quality of the cooked meat at the time of service influences to a marked degree its acceptability by the consumer, who is looking for palatability factors such as tenderness, flavor and aroma, juiciness, and color. Since meat represents a large part of the food dollar, the manager wants meat that is highly acceptable to the patron and that provides a satisfactory yield. Reduction in yield may occur as cooking losses and carving or serving losses. Shrinkage usually is the major loss involved and it may range from 15 to 30 per cent. Some shrinkage occurs regardless of the cooking method, but the cooking temperature and the cooking times have a direct bearing on the amount of shrinkage.

Low temperatures usually are preferred for meat cookery, resulting in fewer cooking losses and the most palatable product. It is obvious that the higher the cooking temperature, the more rapid the conduction of heat. The effect of higher temperatures on palatability and on the amount of shrinkage, however, is such as to make their use undesirable except perhaps in the case of broiling steaks "rare."

If cooked too long, the meat dries out and tends to be less tender. Even meat that requires moist heat and a comparatively long cooking time to become tender will be less tender when overcooked. Tenderness is increased by the softening of connective tissue when cooking with moist heat, but when overcooked, the muscle fibers do not hold together and the meat becomes stringy.

ROASTING   Only tender cuts of meat should be roasted. The meat is placed fat side up in an uncovered roasting pan without water and cooked at a moderate (325°F) temperature until it reaches the desired degree of doneness. This is a dry-heat method of cooking. In pot roasting, which is a moist-heat cooking method, the meat is browned, a small amount of water is added, and the meat covered for cooking.

Cooking time-weight relationships expressed in minutes per pound are reasonably dependable for home-size quantities, but they can be used only as guides in quantity preparation. The most accurate way to determine the doneness of a roast is with a meat thermometer that registers the internal temperature. The thermometer is placed in the roast so its bulb is in the center of the thickest part, but not in contact with bone or a pocket of fat.

Table 6.4 shows recommended internal temperatures for large beef roasts. Recent findings indicate that pork is juicier and more palatable when cooked to an internal temperature of 170°F, lower than the previously recommended 185°F, and these temperatures are high enough to destroy any trichanae that might be present. Lamb usually is cooked to the medium or well-done stage (160 or 170°F) and veal to the well-done stage (170°F).

The cooking time is influenced by the size of the cut; normally the larger the cut, the longer the total cooking time required and the fewer minutes per pound. However, the shape and style of the cut, the number of cuts in a pan, and the oven load also affect the total cooking time. The more cuts there are in the oven at one time, the greater the total time required for cooking. A thin, wide roast will cook in less time than a boned and rolled

TABLE 6.4   Internal Temperatures of Large Beef Roasts for the Different Degrees of Doneness

Degree of Doneness	Color of Inside of Roast	Meat Thermometer Reading When Roast Comes from Oven[a] (°F)
Rare	Bright pink	120 to 125
Medium	Pinkish brown	135 to 145
Well done	Grayish to light brown	150 to 160

[a] The temperature at which color changes take place in beef as it cooks is considerably higher than the temperatures above indicate; however, large roasts continue cooking for some time after they are removed from the oven. Therefore, to prevent overcooking, roasts should be removed from the oven when the thermometer shows several degrees lower than the temperature at which the actual color change takes place.

SOURCE: From "Cooking Meat in Quantity," National Live Stock and Meat Board, Chicago.

roast because in boning and rolling the distance from the outside of the roast to its center has been increased. Most roasts, except standing ribs, are boned before cooking to conserve oven space and to make machine slicing possible. For ease in roasting and handling, it is advantageous to specify uniform size roasts (10 to 15 pounds, for example). Frozen meat generally is thawed in the refrigerator before cooking to reduce both time and heavy drip losses during preparation.

Roasts will continue cooking for a period of time after removal from the oven, and the internal temperature of the roast may rise as much as five degrees. The roast should be allowed to set or rest in a warm place for 15 to 20 minutes before it is carved. The roast becomes more firm, retains more of its juices, and is easier to carve. Slicing losses are minimized if the production personnel are adequately trained and if the portions are standardized and weighed.

When cooking a number of roasts, it is possible to offer meat at different stages of doneness by staggering the times that roasts are placed in the oven. The well-down roasts are started first and, when done, are removed from the oven, allowed to stand 20 minutes, sliced, and placed in pans in the warmer or in the oven at low heat. The rare meat is put in the oven last and, when the thermometer reaches 125°F, is removed from the oven, sliced, and sent directly to the serving area.

For optimum quality, roasts are cooked and sliced just prior to serving. However, this may not be possible in some foodservice operations. If the meat must be cooked the day before or several hours prior to serving, the quality is better if the cooked roasts are stored in the refrigerator, then sliced and reheated before serving rather than refrigerating and reheating the sliced meat.

BROILING　　Steaks or chops are broiled by placing on the rack in a broiling oven, with the top of the meat at least three inches from the source of heat. When browned on one surface, the steaks or chops are turned, browned on the opposite side, and cooked to the desired degree of doneness, if rare, 130 to 135°F internal temperature. A steak 2 inches thick will require approximately 10 minutes of cooking on each side. Broiling is done to order or just prior to service, so it presents problems in large quantity production. One solution is to prebrown steaks and refrigerate or freeze prior to final cooking.

PANBROILING　　The meat is placed on a sizzling hot metal griddle or frypan and turned at frequent intervals to provide for even cooking and to prevent burning. Neither water nor fat is added, and excess fat is drained off. When the meat is satisfactorily browned on one side, it is turned, and the cooking process is continued until the desired degree of doneness is reached. In panbroiling a thick steak, it will be necessary to reduce the temperature after browning.

GRILLING　　The grilling method is used for cooking steaks on an open grid over charcoal, gas, or electric heat. However, the term is also used when referring to cooking on a griddle, which is a flat, solid surface. Portioned meats such as cube steaks, breaded pork or veal cutlets, liver, or hamburger patties are often grilled this way. Meat is cooked in a small amount of fat on a griddle at a moderate temperature and when browned on one side, it is turned and cooked on the other side until done. The meat may be grilled to order or may be browned, then finished in the oven. Cutlets or patties may also be placed on baking pans that have been covered with a pan coating and baked in a moderate oven.

BRAISING　　In braising meat, the first step is to brown it in a small quantity of fat. When browned, moisture may or may not be added, the pan is covered tightly, and the cooking continued at a low temperature in the oven, in a tilting frypan, in a heavy kettle on top of the range, or in a steam-jacketed kettle.

STEWING　　Meat prepared for stewing is cut into small pieces, which may or may not be browned. The meat is covered with hot liquid, the pan is covered tightly, and cooking is continued at a simmering temperature until the meat is tender. A steam-jacketed kettle, a tilting frypan, or heavy kettle on top of the range is used.

Fish and Shellfish

The connective tissue of fish is small in quantity and is comprised largely of collagen, which readily softens during cooking. The high protein content indicates that low to moderate heat is desirable. It is important to remember that fish should be cooked only until the flesh may be easily separated from the bones. Fish too often is overcooked.

The basic rules for cooking fish are few, although the flavor, texture, appearance, and size of the fish to be cooked vary according to the species. The variation in the fat content is the most important difference to be considered when choosing the best method of cooking. Fat fish such as salmon, trout, and whitefish are best for baking or broiling because the fat content tends to keep them from becoming dry. Lean fish such a haddock, halibut, and sea bass are considered best by many when poached, simmered, or steamed, although they may be successfully broiled or baked if basted frequently. All types of fish are suitable for frying. Whatever the method selected, fish should be served as quickly as possible after cooking for optimum quality. Table 6.5 suggests cooking methods for the various purchase forms of fish and shellfish.

Frozen fish may be completely thawed before cooking, but need not be unless it is to be breaded or stuffed. Fish fillets and steaks and dressed whole frozen fish may be cooked as if they were in the fresh, chilled form, if additional cooking time is allowed. However, fish fillets or sticks that have been breaded or batter-dipped and cooked prior to being frozen are not thawed before cooking.

Frozen fish may be thawed at refrigerator temperature but only long enough to permit ease in preparation. Whole or drawn fish may be thawed quickly by immersion in cold running water. Thawing at room temperature is not recommended. Fish once thawed should be cooked immediately and never refrozen.

FRYING   Much of the fish cooked in quantity food operations is deep-fat fried. When properly fried, fish and seafoods have an attractive brown color, a crisp, nongreasy crust, a thoroughly cooked interior without being overcooked, and the characteristic flavor of the specific fish. Uncooked fish should be fried at 350 to 375°F to assure cooking before browning. Precooked fish may be fried at a slightly higher temperature to brown and reheat. To prepare fish for frying, dip pieces in seasoned flour, then in an egg-milk mixture, and finally in cornmeal, bread crumbs, or fine cracker meal.

TABLE 6.5 Suggested Methods of Cooking Fish and Shellfish

Species	Approximate Weight or Thickness	Baking Temperature (°F)	Baking Minutes	Broiling Distance From Heat (in.)	Broiling Minutes	Boiling, Poaching or Steaming Method	Boiling, Poaching or Steaming Minutes (per lb)	Deep-Fat Frying Temperature (°F)	Deep-Fat Frying Minutes	Pan Frying Temperature	Pan Frying Minutes
Fish											
Dressed	3 to 4 lb	350	40 to 60			Poach	10	325 to 350	4 to 6		
Pan dressed	½ to 1 lb	350	25 to 30	3	10 to 15	Poach	10	350 to 375	2 to 4	Moderate	10 to 15
Steaks	½ to 1¼ in	350	25 to 35	3	10 to 15	Poach	10	350 to 375	2 to 4	Moderate	10 to 15
Fillets		350	25 to 35	3	8 to 15	Poach	10	350 to 375	2 to 4	Moderate	8 to 10
Portions	1 to 6 oz	350	30 to 40					350	4	Moderate	8 to 10
Sticks	¾ to 1¼ oz	400	15 to 20					350	3	Moderate	8 to 10
Shellfish											
Clams—live, shucked		450	12 to 15	4	5 to 8	Steam	5 to 10	350	2 to 3	Moderate	4 to 5
Crabs—live, soft-shell				4	8 to 10	Boil	10 to 15	375	2 to 4	Moderate	8 to 10
Lobsters—live	¾ to 1 lb	400	15 to 20	4	12 to 15	Boil	15 to 20	350	2 to 4	Moderate	8 to 10
Spiny lobster tails—frozen	¼ to ½ lb	450	20 to 30	4	8 to 12	Boil	10 to 15	350	3 to 5	Moderate	8 to 10
Oysters—live, shucked		450	12 to 15	4	5 to 8	Steam	5 to 10	350	2 to 3	Moderate	4 to 5
Scallops—shucked		350	25 to 30	3	6 to 8	Boil	3 to 4	350	2 to 3	Moderate	4 to 6
Shrimp—											
Headless, raw						Boil	3 to 5				
Headless, raw, peeled		350	20 to 25	3	8 to 10	Boil	3 to 5	350	2 to 3	Moderate	8 to 10

SOURCE: "How to Eye and Buy Seafood," National Marine Fisheries Service, U.S. Department of Commerce, 1970.

Panfrying is a good method for preparing small, whole fish, steaks, or fillets and is feasible when a small quantity is prepared. Ovenfrying is an alternative method for preparing large quantities of fish. The fish portions are prepared with the desired coating and placed on baking sheets that have been covered with melted butter or other cooking fat. The tops may be dipped in the fat, or additional melted fat may be poured sparingly over the fish. Bake 10 to 15 minutes in a hot over (400°F).

BROILING   Frozen fish usually is thawed before broiling. Fresh or thawed fillets and steaks are placed in a preheated broiler 3 to 4 inches from the broiling unit. The distance from the source of heat for split fish varies from 2 to 6 inches. Frozen fish or fish of a delicate texture is placed about 4 inches from the direct heat. The fish is brushed several times with oil, melted butter, or margarine. Steaks are turned once; thin fillets do not need to be turned.

BAKING   Whole fish, steaks, and thick fillets may be baked successfully. Whole dressed fish may be sprinkled with salt, pepper, and lemon juice before baking and may or may not be stuffed. For fish low in fat content, bacon strips may be laid across it to add moisture during cooking, or it may be basted frequently as it bakes. Steaks and fillets are dipped in a mixture of melted butter or margarine and lemon juice, placed on greased baking pans, and seasoned. Mayonnaise may be brushed on the fish before cooking. Bake at 350°F until the fish flakes easily when tested with a fork.

MOIST HEAT COOKING METHODS   Steaming, poaching, and simmering are closely related, the difference being in the amount of cooking liquid used. In steaming, the fish is placed on a rack over the liquid, covered tightly, and cooked. In poaching or simmering, the fish is covered with the liquid, usually lightly salted water, seasoned broth, or a specially prepared stock called court bouillon. Bring to a boil, reduce heat, and simmer gently until the fish is cooked. Poaching is done in a flat pan on top of the range, in a tilting frypan, or in the oven. Fish cooked in moist heat requires very little cooking time and usually is served with a sauce.

SHELLFISH

Oysters. Thawing oysters in the refrigerator is advised if it is necessary to thaw them for preliminary preparation. In the preparation of shucked oysters, washing is rarely regarded as necessary, since something of the flavor of the sea is said to be lost in washing. Inspection of the pack allows for removal of any bits of shell that may be included. Use of a fork should be discouraged, as should overhandling, to prevent a bruise or break in the membrane. If oysters are to be served cooked, care should be taken that they are heated through and the cooking continued only until the edges begin to curl. If the application of heat is continued beyond this point, the product will be tough.

Clams. Where clams are available fresh, they are steamed, roasted, and dipped in butter, prepared as bouillon, or made into chowder. Most food-services use canned clams for chowder, however, and purchase breaded clams for deep-fat frying. If clams are purchased raw, care should be taken to obtain live ones, as indicated by the tightly clasped shell. To prepare, the clams are scrubbed and rinsed, then opened and the meat washed. To cook clams in the shell, roast or steam 5 to 10 minutes until they open, remove the meat from the shells, and wash. Serve immediately or remove meats and cool in cold water; otherwise they will be tough.

Crustaceans. It is necessary that fresh crustaceans be alive at the time they are cooked. They cannot live at a temperature that exceeds 98.6°F. A usual method of preparing crabs or lobsters is to plunge them head down into boiling salted water and cook for approximately 20 minutes. A second recommended method is to place the crabs or lobsters into cold fresh water and gradually raise the water temperature to lukewarm (about 104°F), then simmer 15 to 20 minutes. Coagulation of crustacean protein occurs at about 126°F. Under such treatment crustaceans die quickly and easily, and the flavor of the meat is reported superior to that cooked by the former method.

Soft-shell crabs are cleaned, parboiled, and then fried in butter.

Cooked **hard-shell crabs** are chilled, the claws and apron removed, the shells broken apart, and the spongy substance removed from between the halves of the body and next to the shell. The meat is removed from the back and cracked claws, either in preparation for cooked dishes or salads, or at the table if the crab is served as an entree.

The stomach, lungs, and intestinal tracts of cooked **lobster** are removed before serving. If it is to be broiled, it may be boiled first for 5 minutes, or it may be killed by cutting down between the body shell and the tail segment, severing the spinal column. It is then split from head to tail and the intestinal tract removed. The claws are cracked and the flesh brushed with melted butter and seasonings and spread out in the broiler pan, flesh side up. Broil for 10 minutes, then turn and continue cooking for another 10 minutes. The meat regarded as most delicate is that of the claws.

Washed green **shrimp** are plunged into salted boiling water and cooked for 15 to 20 minutes, or they may be peeled and cooked as any fresh fish. If cooked first, the meat, now pinkish white, is removed from the shell, which has been opened on the underneath side. The intestinal tract, a black cord on the pink mass of the muscle, is removed, and the shrimp is ready for use.

Canned and frozen shrimp need examination and sometimes extra cleaning before final preparation.

Poultry

Chicken and turkey, popular menu items, are the two types of poultry used most often in foodservices, although roast duck or goose and Cornish game hens appear on some menus. Cooked chicken or turkey meat is used in many menu items; ideally, the whole chicken or turkey would be cooked, the meat removed from the bones, and the broth saved for use in the recipe. However, the loss in weight through processing, cooking, and boning of poultry is relatively high, as reflected in the yield of only 30 to 35 per cent of usable cooked meat from chicken and 40 to 45 per cent from turkey. Because of this and the amount of labor involved, most poultry used in foodservice operations is purchased in portioned ready-to-cook form, as chicken parts, turkey roasts or rolls, or as frozen cooked cubed chicken or turkey meat.

Poultry should be cooked at moderate heat so the meat will be tender, juicy, and evenly done. Most poultry purchased today is young, so it can be broiled (if not too large), fried, roasted, braised, stewed, or barbecued.

BROILING   Small birds only are used for broiling. Adjust rack to position bird about 4 inches under the heat. As the chicken or turkey browns, brush with melted butter, turning about every 10 minutes. Cook until tender (35 to 60 minutes, depending on the size and thickness of the piece). Season and serve immediately.

FRYING   Young poultry may be pan-or ovenfried successfully if special care and attention is given to time and temperature relationships. The meat may be brushed with melted butter or coated with a seasoned flour or crumb mixture, or dipped in a thin batter if it is to be fried in deep fat. Dipping poultry pieces in cold milk or water prior to dredging aids the mixture in adhering closely to the meat.

To *panfry,* brown poultry pieces in heavy skillets or tilting frypan containing one-half inch of hot fat. Turn until the pieces are well browned on all sides. Reduce heat and cook slowly until tender, about 45 to 60 minutes, or place in counter inset pans and finish in the oven at 325 to 350°F.

Ovenfrying is a time-saving method of preparing chicken and is especially well suited to large quantities. Butter or cooking fat is melted to cover the bottom of each baking pan. Dredge chicken pieces in seasoned flour and roll in fat on the pan. Place pieces close together in one layer, skin side up. An alternative method is to place the chicken on a greased pan or a pan lined with silicone-coated paper. Brush top of chicken pieces with melted fat. Bake 1 to 1¼ hours at 350°F. For crisp backed chicken, coat with crushed potato chips or cornflakes.

Deep-fat frying is preferred by many large foodservices because of ease of preparation and the uniform, golden brown color of the chicken. The pieces are dipped in a crumb mixture or a thin batter and allowed to drain for 10 to 15 minutes, then fried at 325°F for 12 to 15 minutes. Chicken may be browned in the deep-fat fryer, placed in serving pans, and finished in the oven at 325°F for 20 to 30 minutes. Poultry may also be poached before dipping in the batter, then fried until golden brown and the batter is fully cooked.

The process of cooking poultry pieces in deep fat under pressure is known as *broasting*. Special equipment has been developed for this process that reduces the cooking time to less than that for conventional frying.

ROASTING   Rub skin of turkey or chicken with softened or melted cooking fat, season inside and out, and place on rack in shallow roasting pan breast up. Bake at 325°F and maintain this temperature throughout the roasting process. The breast meat tends to be drier than the darker meat of the legs and thighs and is improved by some protection during roasting. The top and sides of the bird may be covered with a fat-moistened cloth and remoistened as needed, or left uncovered and basted occasionally with a mixture of equal parts of water and melted fat. A foil "tent" that loosely covers the turkey but does not form a complete wrap may also be used. This method speeds up roasting time and eliminates the necessity for basting, but does not result in the disadvantages of a tight wrap. In poultry cooked in an aluminum foil wrap, the juice cooks out and the muscles tend to pull away from the bone. During the last half hour of cooking, remove cloth or foil tent if used. Fat birds, such as geese and ducks, need no basting, and the fat is poured off as it accumulates.

The importance of proper temperature in the cooking of poultry can hardly be overstressed. High temperatures inevitably result in stringy, tough, and unappetizing meat. The poultry is done when the leg joints move easily and the meat of the drumstick is soft when pressed. For turkey or other large birds, a meat thermometer is the surest test for doneness. It is placed in the heaviest part of the breast or the inner part of the thigh muscle (Fig. 6.2) and inserted to a point where the bulb will not be resting against a bone. A thermometer placed in the breast should reach 170 to 180°F, depending on the degree of doneness desired. Poultry usually is cooked well done, but overcooking is undesirable because it results in loss of juiciness. Cooked tur-

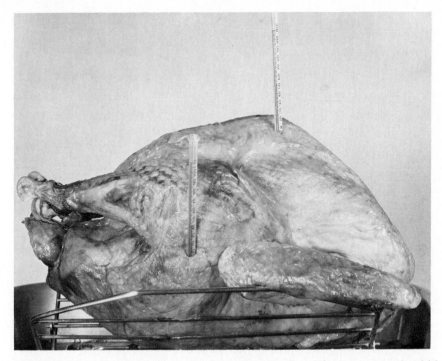

FIGURE 6.2   Use of thermometers in roasting turkey. Thermometers should be inserted in the heaviest part of thigh and breast to determine when the turkey is cooked to the desired degree of doneness.   *Courtesy, College of Human Ecology, Kansas State University.*

key should stand 20 to 30 minutes before carving to allow the juices to be reabsorbed into the muscles, making the meat easier to slice.

See Table 6.6 for cooking times for roasting turkey. Sliceable roast meat is limited almost entirely to that on the breast and thighs, the remainder being removed from the carcass for use in casserole-type entrees, soups, salads, or sandwiches. For this reason, the breasts and thighs of large turkeys are sometimes boned, rolled, and tied before roasting, as shown in Fig. 6.3, and the bony parts simmered or stewed for other uses. The roasting time for the smaller pieces is reduced to about half of that required for a whole bird of similar size, and the cutting yield is increased. Also it is possible to slice such roasts on a machine.

Many foodservices prefer to purchase boneless turkey roasts or rolls for convenience in roasting, slicing, and portion control. Cooking time for ready-

TABLE 6.6   Time Table for Roasting Turkey

Form of Turkey	Weight of Turkey, Whole or Piece (lb)	Oven Temperature (°F)	Cooking[a] Time (hr)
Turkey, whole, ready-to-cook	12 to 16	325	3½ to 4½
	16 to 21	325	4½ to 6
	21 to 26	325	6 to 7½
Turkey parts			
Breast	8 to 12	325	3 to 4
Leg (drumstick and thigh)	3 to 8	325	1¾ to 3
Halves	8 to 12	325	2¼ to 4
Quarters	3 to 8	325	1½ to 3½
Turkey roasts, boneless			
Frozen	9½ to 11½	350	4 to 4½
Thawed	9½ to 11½	350	2¾ to 3½

[a]Turkey is done when thermometer registers 180 to 185°F in inner thigh or 170 to 180°F in breast of whole turkeys; or 170°F in turkey roasts.

SOURCE: Adapted from "Quantity Recipes for Type A School Lunches," PA-631, U.S. Department of Agriculture, revised 1971.

to-cook rolls has been found to be longer in minutes per pound than for whole turkeys, but the total cooking time is less. The rolls compare favorably to whole turkeys in flavor and tenderness.

It is recommended for large quantity preparation that the stuffing or dressing be baked separately and served with the roasted sliced meat. This eliminates the possibility that the dressing will become contaminated by bacteria if it stays too long, or is inadequately heated or chilled, in the body cavity of the bird.

OTHER METHODS   Mature but not old cut-up poultry may be *braised* in the oven or tilting frypan. The pieces are browned, a small amount of water added, covered, and cooked until tender. Larger compact and sliceable pieces may be *poached* by simmering in a steam-jacketed kettle, in a deep pan in the oven, or in a heavy kettle on top of the range. Usually older birds or bony parts are simmered or steamed and the meat separated from bones for various uses. The chicken or turkey may be cut in pieces or left whole. Poultry is *stewed* in a steam-jacketed kettle or stockpot. Cover with cold water and bring to simmering temperature if the purpose is to produce soup stock. If more flavor in the meat is desired, start with boiling water. Season and simmer until tender, about 2½ to 3 hours. Poultry to be steamed is placed in

FIGURE 6.3   The roasting of boned turkey breasts and thighs reduces cooking time, oven space, and waste, and provides for easy slicing by machine.   *Courtesy, National Turkey Federation.*

solid steamer pans, covered with water and seasonings, and cooked until tender, about 2 to 2½ hours. Poultry should be removed from broth as soon as cooking is completed and placed on trays or sheet pans. When poultry is cool enough to handle, remove meat from bones.

Pasta and Cereals

The cooking of pasta and cereals is similar. Water and heat are applied, and cooking is continued until gelatinization of the starch granules is completed.

PASTA   The term *pasta* refers to a basic dough mixture of durum or other high-protein wheat flour and water. With the exception of noodles, which contain eggs, the various pasta or macaroni foods are made of the same dough. There are many different types and shapes of pasta. Dry pasta will approximately double in *volume* after cooking, except egg noodles, which remain about the same. The *weight* of egg noodles and most pasta will triple when cooked.

Pasta is cooked in a large amount of boiling water in a stock pot or steam-jacketed kettle. Pasta is added gradually to the boiling salted water while stirring. A small amount of oil may be added to prevent foaming and sticking. It is cooked uncovered at a fast boil until tender, about 10 minutes, then drained and rinsed with hot or cold water. The use of hot water shortens the time of oven cooking if combined into an item like macaroni and cheese.

Pasta should be tender but firm *(al dente),* and if it is to be used with other ingredients in a casserole, it should be undercooked slightly.

If the pasta is not to be served immediately, it should be drained and covered with cold water. When pasta is cold, drain off water and toss lightly with a little salad oil. This will keep pasta from sticking or drying out. Cover tightly and store in the refrigerator. To reheat, place pasta in a colander and immerse in rapidly boiling water just long enough to heat through; or reheat in a microwave oven.

RICE   Rice is cooked until all of the water is absorbed, so the right proportion of rice to water and the correct cooking time are important. Converted or parboiled long-grain white rice requires slightly more water and a longer cooking time than does regular long-grain or medium-grain rice. The cooking time for brown rice is almost double that of white rice. Rice may be cooked in a steamer, the oven, or in a kettle. When cooked, rice should be fluffed with a fork before serving.

Steaming. Weigh rice into solid steamer pans and add salt and margarine or cooking oil (optional). Pour hot water over rice and stir. Steam uncovered for 30 to 40 minutes (50 to 60 minutes for brown rice).

Oven Cooking. Proceed as for steamed rice, but cover pans tightly with aluminum foil and bake at 350°F for 1 hour (1½ hours for brown rice). Remove from oven and let stand covered for 5 minutes.

Boiling. Add rice and salt to boiling water in a large kettle or steam-jacketed kettle, and stir. Cover tightly and cook on low heat until rice is tender and all water is absorbed, about 15 to 20 minutes. Remove from heat and let stand covered 5 to 10 minutes.

BREAKFAST CEREALS   The objectives of cereal cookery are to soften the cellulose and render it palatable, to retain the distinct form of the cereal, and to change the starch to a more digestible form. Moisture and heat are essential to accomplish these objectives. They soften the cellulose and cause the starch granules to swell and gelatinize. Flavor is thus improved also.

The amount of water used for cooking cereals largely determines the volume of the finished product. Cereal swells to the extent of water used until the limit of the grain is reached. As a rule, granular cereals absorb more water than whole or flaked. The fineness of the cereal and the amount of bran or cellulose are factors that determine the length of time a cereal should be cooked. Table 6.7 gives proportions and cooking times for cereals and cereal products.

Cereals in quantity generally are cooked in a steam-jacketed kettle or steamer, but they may be prepared in a heavy kettle on top of the range. Add cereal and salt to boiling water, using a wire whip. Stir until some thick-

TABLE 6.7   Cooking of Cereals and Cereal Products

Cereal or Cereal Product	Number of Portions	Amount of Cereal (lb)	Amount of Water (gal)	Amount of Salt (c)	Cooking Time Steam-Jacketed Kettle (min)	Cooking Time Pressure Steam Cooker (min)	Increase in Volume	Size of Portions (oz)
Breakfast cereals								
Corn meal	100	4	4	1/3	45	30	2	5
Cracked wheat— unprocessed	100	5	4	1/3	120	60	3	5
Cream of Wheat and Farina	100	4	4	1/4	20	15	1	5
Grits, hominy	100	5	4	1/4	20	15	1	5
Grits, wheat	100	4	4	1/4	20	15	1	5
Pettijohns	100	6	4	1/3	20	15	2½	5
Rolled oats	100	5	4	1/3	20	15	2½	5
Rice	100	7½	4	1/3	50–60	30–40	3½–4	5
Macaroni and spaghetti[a]	100	6	6	½	30	20	2	2½–3
Noodles[a]	100	5	6	½	20	15	1	2–2½

[a] Extended with other foods, i.e., sauces and meats.

ening is apparent, then reduce the heat and cook until cereal reaches desired consistency and the raw starch taste has disappeared. Cereal should be thick and creamy but not sticky. Overstirring or overcooking produces a sticky, gummy product.

Eggs and Cheese

EGGS   The physical properties of eggs, such as thickening, binding, coating, leavening, emulsifying, and coloring, determine their cooking functions. Egg proteins are coagulated by heat, thus making possible the thickening of custards, the binding together of particles of foods in croquettes, and the coating of foods.

The temperature at which coagulation occurs depends on whether the whole egg, the white only, or the yolk only is used. The addition of sugar to egg protein in solution raises the temperature of coagulation, the effect being proportional to the amount used. The addition of acid, such as vinegar or lemon juice, tends to produce a stiffer coagulation and likewise to lower the coagulation temperature. Beyond the point of coagulation, continued appli-

cation of heat to a lemon juice or vinegar mixture with egg results in pepti-
zation of the protein and consequent thinning of the coagulation mass.

The amount of air beaten in and retained during preparation determines
the effectiveness of egg as a leavening agent. The white forms a more stable
and elastic foam than either the yolk or the whole egg. Overbeating causes
loss of some elasticity, and addition of sugar retards the rate of coagulation.

Egg yolk, a stable emulsion, is a more efficient emulsifying agent than
either whole egg or egg white. Use is made of this quality in making mayonnaise. Egg yolks contribute color to such foods as mayonnaise, noodles,
and some bakery products.

Processed Eggs. Although fresh shell eggs are used extensively for table
service, processed eggs are convenient for quantity food production and
eliminate the time-consuming task of breaking the eggs. Frozen eggs are
available as whites, yolks, or as whites and yolks mixed and are required to
be pasteurized. Freezing does not alter the egg white, and after defrosting it
is similar to the unfrozen white and can be used in the same way. The egg
yolk on thawing tends to form a pasty, rubbery gel, and often does not mix
well with other ingredients such as sugar and milk. The mixing of sugar or
salt with the liquid yolk or whole egg prior to freezing helps to reduce the
degree of gelation. Such additions to frozen eggs should be known to the
user when purchased so that appropriate adjustments in recipes can be made.
Frozen egg once defrosted is an excellent medium for bacterial growth and
should be refrigerated and used within one to two days after thawing.

Dried eggs are used less often in institutional cooking than the frozen
product. Pasteurization is required also for dried eggs, but if they are recon-
stituted into a liquid they become highly perishable, so they should be used
in powdered form wherever possible.

Methods of Cooking Eggs. The most important point to remember in the
cooking of eggs is to avoid high temperatures and long cooking times. Egg
should be cooked as close to service as possible or cooked to order. If egg
are to be held on a hot counter, they should be undercooked slightly t
compensate for the additional heating that will occur.

Basic methods of preparing eggs for serving include poaching, frying
scrambling, and cooking in the shell, either soft or hard. When *poaching* i
large quantity, use a counter pan deep enough to permit 2 to 2½ inches o
water to cover the eggs. Eggs should be broken onto saucers and slid int
the water toward the side of the pan. The water should be simmering whe
the eggs are dropped in. The addition of 2 tablespoons of vinegar and
tablespoon of salt to 1 gallon of water prevents whites from spreading
Poaching may be done in a shallow pan on the range top, in the oven, in
tilting frypan, or in a steamer.

Eggs generally are *fried* to order and may be cooked in frypans or on griddle. Eggs cooked on a griddle are more apt to spread than those cooked in a small frypan, and so are less attractive. For large quantities, eggs may be ovenfried. To prevent toughening, eggs should not be fried at a high temperature.

Scrambled eggs are easily prepared in quantity in the steamer or oven. The addition of milk to the eggs keeps them from drying, and medium white sauce added in place of milk prevents the eggs from separating and becoming watery when held on the serving counter.

Shell eggs may be cooked in a pan on top of the range, an automatic egg cooker, a wire basket in the steam-jacketed kettle, or in a steamer. If eggs are brought to room temperature before cooking, the shells will not crack when heat is applied. Eggs are covered with water and simmered approximately 3 to 6 minutes for soft-cooked eggs and 16 to 20 minutes for hard-cooked eggs.

If hard-cooked eggs are cooled at once by plunging into cold running water, the cooking process is stopped, thus helping to eliminate the development of a ferrous sulfide (greenish) ring around the yolk, which develops when eggs are overcooked or allowed to cool slowly in the cooking water. Hard-cooked eggs are also used in sandwiches and with other foods in various entrees. Unless slices are required, fresh eggs may be broken into a greased counter pan (egg depth not to exceed 2 inches) and cooked uncovered in the steamer to the desired degree of doneness (usually about 20 minutes). The same procedure can be followed for baking in the oven, except the pan should be covered and set into a larger pan containing boiling water. Approximately 40 minutes at a 400°F oven should be adequate for hard-cooking the eggs. After cooking, the eggs can be chopped, thus eliminating the time-consuming task of shelling each egg.

CHEESE Careful preparation of cooked dishes in which cheese is used is necessary for satisfactory results. The degree of ripening, the acidity, and the method of manufacture affect the plasticity of cheese when heated for blending with liquid. In the process of ripening, cheese loses its tough, rubbery qualities and becomes soft and mellow. During this change as much as 50 per cent of the nitrogenous material may be converted to a soluble form, producing a well-aged or ripened cheese that blends more readily than a green cheese does and results in a product of higher quality.

Processed cheese is a blend of fresh and aged natural cheeses that have been melted, pasteurized, and mixed with an emulsifier. It has no rind or waste and melts readily, making it easy to use and satisfactory for cooking. During processing, however, it loses some of the characteristic flavor of natural cheese, so a natural cheese with a more pronounced flavor may be preferred for cheese sauce and as an addition to other cooked foods where a distinctive cheese flavor is desired. Cheese usually is added to other foods in a finely divided form by grinding, shredding, or dicing.

Cheese softens and finally melts as it is heated. Relatively high temperatures and long periods of heating cause it to curdle, string, or become hard and tough. Cheese melts at 324°F, and baked products containing cheese should be cooked at a temperature no higher than 350°F. Temperatures of 105 to 120°F are usually preferable for blending cheese with a sauce. When making a soufflé, the best results are obtained if the beaten egg yolks are added to the white sauce before the grated cheese is added. This procedure cooks the eggs and aids in emulsifying the fat of the cheese. The added moisture and the emulsification of the fat in processed cheese causes it to combine readily with a sauce.

Fruits and Vegetables

Flavor, color, texture, and form of fruits and vegetables are the characteristics that make up quality. The basic physical and chemical attributes determine this to a large degree. The flavor is due to sugar, organic acids, mineral salts, and aromatic compounds and, in some instances, to the pungent, astringent evidence of tannin content found in green or immature fruit. The colors of fruits and vegetables are due to the various pigments they contain.

Among the substances responsible for certain strong flavors in foods are the volatile sulfur compounds found in vegetables of the onion and cabbage families. These may hydrolyze by enzymatic action or by long heating in the presence of acid to yield a product both unpleasant and strong smelling. It is important to choose a preparation method that will minimize as far as possible the undesirable development of these compounds.

The characteristic structure of fruits and vegetables is largely determined by the cellulose, which forms the walls of the plant cells, in combination with pectin and some other substances. The water content within the plant cells determines the crispness of the tissue. Lacking water, the structure wilts. The cellulose is altered by cooking, being partly broken down by steaming or long-continued boiling. This action is accelerated by the presence of alkalis and retarded by the addition of acids.

PREPREPARATION   Many foodservice operations have taken the preliminary preparation of fruits and vegetables out of the individual kitchens; they either centralize this function or buy convenience products that have some or all of the prepreparation completed. Peeled potatoes and carrots, washed spinach and other leafy vegetables, cut vegetables ready for cooking, and peeled and sectioned citrus fruits and fresh pineapple are examples. With modern processing of vegetables, it is unnecessary to spend costly labor time for preliminary preparations, and the use of convenience vegetable forms has eliminated the need to purchase expensive equipment for prepreparation in many foodservices.

On the other hand, many foodservice directors prefer to maintain control of quality standards from the very beginning and to purchase produce in its natural state if they have ample supervisory staff to ensure good control throughout production. Therefore, following is a brief review of some of these preliminary procedures.

The time required for preparation of fresh fruits and vegetables will vary with the type of product, its quality, the equipment available, and any preparation needed beyond the preliminary, such as cutting potatoes for French frying, slicing carrots, or chopping onions. The relationship of the weight of the vegetable as purchased to the edible portion obtained is important. Variations in waste are influenced by many factors, such as the skill of the worker, the condition, quality, maturity, size, and shape of the vegetable, the length and conditions of storage, the season, and the producing district. Because of the wide variations in the amount of waste, the cost of the edible portion rather than the cost as purchased should be the basis for determining the serving cost of vegetables.

Figures on preparation losses may be found in various sources, but there is some variance among them. Table 6.8 gives the approximate yield in preparation of some fruits and vegetables. Each food unit will find it necessary to make studies of its own and record actual preparation losses and costs under the particular conditions of operation and with varieties of foods used. Fig. 6.4 suggests a form that would be suitable for collection of such data.

Fruits and vegetables should be handled as little as possible. Convenient arrangement of the work area and its location close to the cooking unit help prevent undue loss of time. Equipment for washing, peeling, slicing, and chopping conveniently arranged for efficient work should be provided for the employees. Some general suggestions follow for fruit and vegetable prepreparation.

Fruits. All fruits should be washed to remove surface soil, sprays, and preservatives (such as wax on apples) before they are served raw or cooked. Apricots, cherries, grapes, pears, and plums most often are washed in a colander, dried, and served whole without further preparation as desserts or cut and used in salad.

Apples, bananas, and peaches discolor rapidly after peeling so should be immersed in pineapple, orange, or diluted lemon juice. Fruits also may be treated with ascorbic acid or other preparations that prevent oxidation. Berries deteriorate rapidly, so washing should be scheduled as near service as possible or a small amount of sugar sprinkled over the berries after cleaning.

TABLE 6.8 Approximate Waste in the Preparation of Fresh Fruits and Vegetables

Fruits	Average Percent Waste	Vegetables	Average Percent Waste
Apple	27	Asparagus	49
Avocado	40	Beans, green	16
Banana, peeled	42	Broccoli	38
Blueberries	16	Cabbage, green	21
Cranberries	3	Carrots	24
Cherries, pitted	21	Cauliflower	69
Cantaloupe, with rind	63	Celery	29
Cantaloupe, peeled, served without rind	39	Chicory	29
		Cucumber	28
Grapefruit, sections and juice	52	Eggplant	22
Grapes, seedless	5	Lettuce, head	31
Honeydew, served without rind	46	Onions, mature	11
		Peas, green	63
Orange sections	43	Peppers, green	22
Peaches (average)	20	Potatoes	16
Pears	33	Potatoes, sweet	20
Pineapple	52	Radishes	40
Plums	7	Spinach	64
Strawberries	16	Squash, acorn	34
Watermelon	54	Squash, Hubbard	41
		Squash, zucchini	2
		Tomatoes	14
		Turnips	20

NOTE: To change the prepared raw food weight to as purchased weight: (1) Subtract the percent waste from 100 to obtain percent yield. (2) Divide the known prepared raw food weight by the percent yield obtained in (1), then multiply by 100, to obtain the A.P. (as purchased) weight.

SOURCE: Adapted from Elsie H. Dawson, Elsie F. Dochterman, and Ruth S. Vettel, "Food Yields in Institutional Food Service," *Journal of the American Dietetic Association, 34,* 267–272 (1958).

The quality of most fruits is better if the preparation is completed as near the time of service as is practical.

Vegetables. All leafy and stem vegetables should be washed thoroughly, drained, and crisped by placing in covered containers in a refrigerator for at least two hours before use.

Vegetables to be cooked unpeeled are scrubbed well with a stiff brush.

Root and tuber vegetables put through a vegetable peeler need not be

Product: Amount:				
Date				*Average*
1. A.P. weight				
2. E.P. weight				
3. Weight of waste				
4. Per cent waste				
5. Unit cost of ingredient				
6. Cost of added ingredients				
7. Total cost of product				
8. Average weight of serving				
9. Estimated servings				
10. Estimated cost per serving				
11. Selling price (40% food cost)				
12. Time of preparation				
13. Pay rate of worker				
14. Labor cost per serving				
Comments:				

FIGURE 6.4   Suggested form for fruit and vegetable preparation and cost study.

washed prior to peeling. Vegetables such as carrots, turnips, and potatoes are pared for approximately one to two minutes, the exact time depending on the size of the vegetables, the number put into the peeler at one time, and their condition. Vegetables should be sorted for uniformity of size to minimize waste. Peeled vegetables are placed in containers of clean cold water and then trimmed or eyed as necessary. Cutting into desired shapes for cooking may be done with a French knife on a cutting board, or by machine.

The practice of preparing vegetables, particularly root vegetables, some hours before they are to be cooked and soaking them in cold water for a long period of time results in the leaching of flavor and nutrients. The size of the pieces and the length of the soaking period influence the losses, small pieces and long soaking causing the largest loss. It is, therefore, important from the standpoint of palatability and food value that preparation be scheduled as close to cooking the food as possible and that soaking of fresh vegetables be eliminated or sharply limited. It often is necessary, however, to soak wilted vegetables briefly in cold water to restore their crispness.

COOKING OF FRUITS   It is generally agreed that there is little need for concern about fruit cookery because the methods of preparation are limited mainly to stewing or baking. The method used is determined by the character of the desired final product, although the selection of a variety of fruit suitable for a specific use may be as important as the cooking method used. For example, some varieties of apples are better for cooking than others, and within the many kinds of cooking apples, those that hold their shape are to be preferred for baking, whereas apples that become soft when cooked are used for sauce.

When the shape of the fruit is to be retained, it may be baked whole with the skin on, or gently cooked in a sugar syrup without stirring. The concentration of sugar should be about the same as the concentration of soluble materials in the fruit for it to hold its shape; if too high, the water is drawn from the fruit by osmosis, leaving the fruit shrunken and tough. The optimum concentration varies for each fruit, so a standard recipe should be consulted for best results. If a sauce is desired, the fruit is cooked in water or steam until soft, and sugar to flavor is added at the end of cooking.

There is little loss of nutrients in fruit cookery, since fruits are cooked for a relatively short time and the juices are not discarded but served with the fruit. This promotes retention of both nutrients and flavor.

COOKING OF VEGETABLES   One of the main purposes of cooking vegetables is to change the texture. During the cooking process, however, the color and flavor may be altered and there may be some loss in nutrients. How much these characteristics change determines the quality of the cooked vegetable. An understanding of the effects on vegetables of different conditions and cooking methods is essential.

Effect of Cooking on Texture. The fiber structure of vegetables, consisting largely of cellulose and pectins, is softened by cooking. The amount of fiber varies in different types of vegetables and in different stages of maturity. In some, the amount of fiber may even vary in different parts of the vegetable, as in the stalks and tips of broccoli and asparagus. Fiber is made firmer by acids, so lemon juice, vinegar, or tomato products added to vegetables extends the cooking time.

Many factors affect cooking time, including the type and maturity of the vegetable, the presence of acids, the size of the pieces, and the degree of doneness. Vegetables are considered done when they have reached the desired degree of tenderness. This stage varies with different types of vegetables. Winter squash, for example, is considered done when it is quite soft, but most vegetables are best cooked very briefly, until they are tender-crisp. Vegetables at this stage of tenderness are not only more palatable, but they retain maximum color, flavor, and nutrients.

The starch in vegetables also affects texture. Dry starchy foods like beans or lentils must be cooked in enough water so that the starch granules can absorb moisture and soften. Moist starchy vegetables like potatoes and yams have enough moisture of their own, but they must still be cooked until the starch granules soften.

Effect of Cooking on Color. Color is a major factor in consumer acceptance of vegetables, so methods of cookery that retain color as well as nutritive value should be selected.

The *green* pigment chlorophyll is the least stable of food pigments, and considerable attention is given to ways of preserving this color in vegetables. Chlorophyll is affected by acid to produce an unattractive olive-gray color. Vegetables are slightly acid in reaction, and when cooked, the acid is liberated from the cells into the cooking water. Fortunately, much of the acid is volatile and given off in the first few minutes of cooking. If an open kettle is used for cooking green vegetables, the volatile acids may escape easily, aiding in the retention of the green pigment.

Steaming is an acceptable method of cooking green vegetables. Steam cooks food rapidly, lessens the loss of nutrients and flavor, and does not break up delicate vegetables. However, overcooking can occur very rapidly in steamers, so the timing must be carefully controlled. Length of cooking time probably has more effect on the color and flavor of vegetables than any other one factor. Overcooking of green vegetables particularly, or holding them too long before serving, will cause a change from the bright attractive color to one that is dull, drab, and unappealing.

Yellow and *orange* pigments, called carotenoids, found in carrots, sweet potatoes, corn, winter squash, rutabagas, and tomatoes, are very stable. They are little affected by acids or alkalis, but long cooking can dull the color.

Flavones, the *white* pigments in potatoes, cauliflower, and onions, stay white in acid but turn yellow in alkaline water. A small amount of lemon juice or cream of tartar added to the water when cooking cauliflower will keep it white. Cooking for a short time, especially in a steamer, helps maintain color and flavor. Overcooking or holding too long in a steam table turns white vegetables dull yellow or gray.

Vegetables owing their *red* color to anthocyanins may become more attractive in the presence of acids. These pigments are present mainly in beets and red cabbage (the red color in tomatoes is due to the same pigment found in carrots). Some vegetables, such as beets, contain enough acid to preserve their red color if cooked in a covered container. However, the addition of acid enhances the color of red cabbage, which often is cooked with tart apples for this reason. If vinegar is used to enhance the color and flavor, as in sweet-sour red cabbage, only a small amount is added at first and the rest after the vegetable is tender. If the full amount needed for a strongly acid vegetable is added at the beginning of the cooking, the acid toughens the vegetable and extends the cooking time. Because red pigments are exceedingly soluble, beets are cooked whole and unpeeled with the root and an inch of stem attached to protect the color. The skins may be slipped off the cooked beets easily. When steaming red vegetables, use solid instead of perforated pans to retain the red juices, and do not overcook. Whereas acids enhance the color of vegetables with anthocyanins, alkalis turn them an unattractive blue or blue-green.

Effect of Cooking on Flavor. Flavor in vegetables is due primarily to sugar and essential oils present; some vegetables contain sulphur compounds and acids. Strong-flavored vegetables such as onions and cabbage will lose some of their undesirable flavor in the steam if cooked in an open kettle. These vegetables retain a good flavor, however, when cooked in a high-pressure steamer for the short time required.

Other factors believed to influence the effect of cooking on flavor and palatability are the hardness of the water and the presence of salt. The use of hard water in cooking may have an undesirable effect on the product. Calcium and magnesium dissolved in the water may combine with the cellulose, thus hardening the structure of the food. The addition of salt either at the beginning of or at least early in the cooking period is regarded as important in developing and maintaining a good flavor, although it may have an effect on certain nutrients.

Effect of Cooking on Nutritive Value. Nutritive losses are those resulting from the solubility of nitrogenous compounds, sugar, mineral salts, and vitamins. In general, losses are less if the cooking of the vegetables is begun in boiling water and if the vegetable is cut into fairly large chunks.

Investigators sometime ago found that the greatest amount of minerals and vitamins were retained when vegetables were cooked without added water. The least amount was retained when water covering the vegetables was used, which resulted in the leaching of minerals and vitamins. Vitamin A is almost completely retained in vegetables cooked by most methods because the carotenoids are insoluble in water and resistant to oxidation. Destruction of vitamins A and C takes place more rapidly at high temperatures, and the greater the length of cooking time, the most loss. The higher temperature of steam at five or more pounds pressure over boiling water might be expected to cause greater loss of nutritive value. However, the short time required to cook vegetables in this manner may be less destructive than boiling for a long time. Ascorbic acid and the B vitamins are soluble in water, and since ascorbic acid is susceptible also to oxidation, they are not as well retained as the carotenoids in vegetable cookery.

From this discussion of the effect of cooking on various characteristics of vegetables, several general rules are evident.

- Do not overcook. Cooking time should be as short as possible, consistent with the type of vegetable. Cook until tender but slightly crisp for best color, texture, flavor, and nutritional value.
- Cut vegetables in uniform pieces for even cooking.
- When boiling vegetables, start with boiling, salted water.
- Cook green and strong-flavored vegetables uncovered.
- Never use baking soda with green vegetables.
- Handle vegetables carefully to avoid mashing.
- Cook in small quantities and as close to service time as possible.
- Supply freshly cooked vegetables to the serving counter at frequent intervals and hold none longer than 20 minutes for optimum quality.
- Do not mix batches of cooked vegetables.
- Avoid holding cooked vegetables for long periods on a steam table.

COOKING PROCEDURES FOR FRESH VEGETABLES   Boiling and steaming are the most commonly used methods of cooking fresh vegetables, although stir-frying and deep-fat frying are used to some extent.

Boiling. Boiling may be done in a steam-jacketed kettle, a tilting frypan, or in an open kettle on the range. To boil vegetables:

1. Add required amount of water to small pot or steam-jacketed kettle. Most vegetables are cooked in just enough water to cover, although strong-flavored vegetables and some green vegetables may benefit from an increased quantity of water so the plant acids can be more quickly diluted and driven off.
2. Add salt (about 1 to 2 tablespoons of salt to each gallon of water) and bring to a boil. Do not add soda.
3. Add vegetables and return the water to a boil.
4. Reduce heat to a simmer and cook vegetables, covered or uncovered as

indicated below, to the required degree of doneness. The cooking time should be as short as possible, consistent with the type of vegetable.
   a. Cook green vegetables and strong-flavored vegetables *uncovered.*
   b. Cook other vegetables *covered.*
5. Drain vegetables quickly to avoid overcooking.

Steaming. Steaming may be in a pressurized or nonpressurized compartment steamer. An advantage of using a steamer is that the vegetables can be cooked in the serving counter inset pans, thus eliminating the transfer of food after cooking. To steam vegetables:

1. Arrange prepared vegetables in thin layers, not over 2 inches in depth, in shallow pans. Use perforated pans for best steam circulation; solid pans if cooking liquid must be retained.
2. Insert pans or baskets in steamer and close door.
3. Steam for required time. Check timing charts supplied with steamer.
4. Remove vegetable from steamer and season or finish according to recipe, and serve at once.
   Stir-Frying. Stir-frying is done in a skillet, tilting frypan, or steam-jacketed kettle. To stir-fry:

1. Choose vegetables for contrasts in color, texture, shape, and flavor. Cut or slice diagonally.
2. Heat small amount of oil in pan.
3. Stir in vegetables. Continue to stir for 1 minute or until vegetables are coated well with oil.
4. Add liquid (water, broth and seasonings, or sauce) to vegetables. Stir quickly, then reduce heat. Cover and steam for 3 minutes or until vegetables are tender but crisp.
5. Add cornstarch and water mixture. Cook and stir just until sauce thickens and vegetables are glazed.

COOKING PROCEDURES FOR FROZEN VEGETABLES   Frozen vegetables are cooked by the same methods used for fresh vegetables, but because frozen vegetables have been partially cooked, the final cooking time is shorter than for fresh products.

Most frozen vegetables do not need to be thawed, but they can be cooked from the frozen state and placed directly into steamer pans or boiling salted water. Exceptions are vegetables that are frozen into a solid block, such as spinach and squash. Results are more satisfactory if they are thawed in the refrigerator first for more even cooking.

COOKING PROCEDURES FOR CANNED VEGETABLES   Canned vegetables need only be heated since they are cooked when canned. Overheating, as with overcooking of fresh and frozen vegetables, results in further loss of nutrients and a soft-textured, unattractive, and poor-flavored product. Heating may be in a stock pot, steam-jacketed kettle, steamer, or oven. To heat canned vegetables:

1. Drain off half the liquid; use for soups, gravies, and sauces.
2. For **stock pot** or **steam-jacketed kettle** cooking, heat vegetables and remaining liquid only enough to bring to serving temperature (140 to 160°F).
3. For **steamer** or **oven** heating, transfer vegetables and remaining liquid to steamer pans (a 12 x 20 x 2 inch pan will hold contents of two no. 10 cans). Cover and heat in steamer for the time recommended by the manufacturer; or in a 350°F oven until serving temperature is reached.
4. Drain vegetables and add melted margarine or butter (2 to 4 ounces per no. 10 can) or other seasonings.

COOKING PROCEDURES FOR DRIED VEGETABLES   Dried legumes, such as navy, lima, pinto, and kidney beans, and peas and lentils are soaked before cooking to restore the water content to that of the fresh legume and to shorten the cooking time. Legumes will absorb enough water to approximately double their dry weight, with an attendant increase in volume. The length of the soaking period depends on the temperature of the water, with warm water cutting the soaking time about half. The use of hard water containing calcium and magnesium salts is undesirable in cooking dried vegetables, since such water has a hardening effect on them. To cook dried vegetables:

1. Sort and wash vegetables.
2. Heat required amount of water to boiling in stock pot or steam-jacketed kettle.
3. Add vegetables and boil for 2 minutes.
4. Turn off heat and allow to stand for 1 hour.
5. Add salt and cook slowly until vegetables are tender (1 to 1½ hours).
6. Vegetables may be covered with cold water and soaked overnight, drained, then cooked.

PRODUCTION SCHEDULING   Small batch or continuous cooking of vegetables throughout the meal service is the most satisfactory way to obtain high-quality products. Quantities of not more than 10-pound lots, and preferably 5-pound batches, should be cooked at intervals as needed. High-speed steamers and small tilting trunnion kettles behind the service line are the most useful kinds of equipment for batch cooking of vegetables (Fig. 6.5).

FIGURE 6.5   Rapid cooking of vegetables in small amounts is possible in high-pressure steam cooker.   *Courtesy, Market Forge Company.*

This system reduces the need for the long holding periods after cooking that cause rapid loss of color and flavor. With a batch small enough to be served within 20 to 30 minutes cooked in one kettle or steamer, there is uniformity of cooking and little chance of damaging the bottom layers of food. The vegetables should be divided into amounts equal to the size of a single cooking batch at the time of preparation and refrigerated until needed. With small-batch cooking, fewer leftovers result and better waste control is effected.

Scheduling of vegetable cooking takes good organization of the production staff and close supervision, but the results are well worth the effort. Studies by the manager or supervisor with written records of vegetable usage at frequent, stated intervals throughout the serving period will give a factual basis on which to determine the production needs.

Salads

A salad may be an appetizer, an accompaniment to the main course of a meat, may be served as a separate course, or may be an entree salad used as the main course. The salad bar, with its wide variety of salads and salad ingredients, has become a well-established part of many foodservice operations.

SALAD INGREDIENTS   In foodservices having a prepreparation room, the cleaning and preliminary preparation of salad ingredients usually are included in the responsibilities of that area.

Salad Greens and Vegetables. A variety of greens are available for tossed vegetable salad and for the salad bar: iceburg, leaf, bibb, and Boston lettuce, as well as romaine, endive, spinach, escarole, and watercress. Other raw or cooked vegetables such as celery cabbage, green and red cabbage celery, carrots, cauliflower, potatoes, and zucchini may be used. Raw vegetables should be crisp, and cooked vegetables should be steamed or simmered until just tender. Marinating improves the flavor of some salad ingredients. All should be chilled.

Greens should be clean, crisp, chilled, and well drained. It may be necessary to separate leaves for thorough cleaning. Wash in a spray of water or in a large container of water. Shake off excess moisture, drain thoroughly, and refrigerate. Draining in a colander or on a rack placed on a sheet pan will keep the greens from standing in water while chilling. Cover with a clean damp cloth or plastic to prevent dehydration.

When preparing head lettuce for garnish, remove and discard any outside leaves that are unsuitable for use. Remove the core by hitting the stem end sharply on a flat surface, then removing the loosened core. Hold inverted head under cold, running water until the leaves are loosened. Turn heads open side down to drain. Separate the leaves and stack or nest six or seven leaves to a pile. Invert and pack in a covered container or plastic bag. Refrigerate two hours or more to complete crisping.

Loose-leafed greens, such as leaf lettuce, watercress, endive, romaine, spinach, and parsley, are sorted, washed in clear water, and drained. Pack in a container, cover with a fitted lid, plastic, or damp cloth, and refrigerate for further crisping.

Fruits. Preparation of fresh fruits is discussed earlier in this chapter under "Fruits and Vegetables." Canned and frozen fruits are used for salads also, and grapefruit and orange sections may be purchased fresh or frozen. Pieces of fruit should be large enough to be distinguishable, should not be soft and mushy, and should be chilled and drained before using.

SALAD ARRANGEMENT   Proper seasoning, a simple arrangement on a pre-chilled plate or bowl, and selection of a dressing to complement its flavor add to the attractiveness of a salad. When a mixture is desired, the ingredients are tossed together as lightly as possible to avoid crushing or mangling them. If a dressing is used, all pieces should be coated with it before serving.

Usually this is done just before service, except for potato and some entree salads where flavor is improved by standing two to four hours after mixing.

The lettuce, or other underliner, on salad plates forms a frame for the salad and adds to its appeal. The liner should be of a size to fit the plate without extending over the rim. Tossed green salads usually have no underliner.

To make salads efficiently, prepare all ingredients and chill. Arrange salad plates or bowls on trays that have been lined up on a work table. Place underliners on all plates, then add the body of the salad to the plates. This may be a mixed salad, measured with a dipper or scoop, or it may be a placed salad in which individual ingredients are arranged on the underliner. Chopped lettuce is sometimes placed in the lettuce cup to give height to the salad. Top garnishes add the final touch of color and flavor contrast. The trays of salads are then placed in a refrigerator until service, but should not be held more than a few hours or the salads will wilt. Fig. 6.6 illustrates a pass-through refrigerator for convenient storage of completed salads. Dressings generally are served separately or dipped over the salad just before serving.

SALAD BAR   The basic salad bar consists of salad greens with a variety of accompaniments and dressings. Lettuce usually is the main ingredient, but other greens may be added. Accompaniments may include tomatoes, cucumbers, alfalfa sprouts, carrots, cauliflower, green pepper, onions, radishes, or other vegetables cut in various shapes. A contrast in shapes adds to the attractiveness of the salad bar. Chopped hard-cooked eggs, crumbled crisp bacon, shredded cheese, and croutons often appear on salad bars, as do cottage cheese, cabbage slaw, pasta salads, molded fruit gelatin, and other prepared salads. A variety of dressings is offered.

The salad bar should be attractively presented and the salad ingredients kept cold. A logical arrangement places chilled plates or bowls on ice first, near the greens, followed by the accompaniments, the prepared salads, and finally the dressings. The salad bar offers an opportunity for creativity and can be an effective merchandising tool.

Sandwiches

The sandwich is one of the most popular foods today and, with the wide variety of breads and fillings available, its possibilities are almost endless. Sandwiches may be served hot or cold and may be closed or open-faced.

Sandwiches may be prepared to order in commercial foodservices by pantry workers and/or short-order cooks. Fillings are made and refrigerated, margarine or butter softened, lettuce is cleaned and crisped, and other ingredients prepared ready for assembling. Ingredients should be arranged

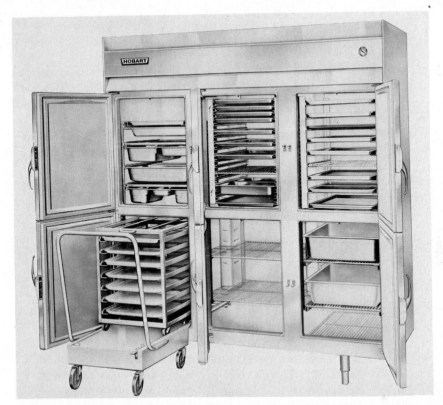

FIGURE 6.6 Storage of made-up salads and other cold foods in a pass-through refrigerator. Sliding glass doors on counter side facilitate rapid service. *Product of Hobart Corporation.*

for maximum efficiency, with everything needed within easy reach of both hands.

In large quantity, all sandwiches needed may be made and refrigerated until service, or in cafeteria service may be assembled a few at a time. Hot sandwiches may be made up and grilled or baked as needed, or for cafeteria service, the fillings may be cooked and the sandwiches assembled on the cafeteria counter.

An efficient work station should be set up for making sandwiches and an assembly line procedure should be used. Bread slices are placed on a baking sheet or tray and brushed with margarine, butter, or mayonnaise, then the filling is spread or placed, according to the type of sandwich being made, on all slices on the tray. The top bread slices are then added to all the sandwiches. For grilled sandwiches, the top and bottom slices are brushed with melted margarine or butter. Fillings are measured with a dipper or scoop and sliced meat or cheese portioned according to count or weight. The recipes or instruction sheets should include the directions for portioning.

Sanitation is especially important in the making of cold sandwiches because of the amount of handling involved and because they are not cooked. Mixed fillings containing meat, poultry, fish, eggs, or mayonnaise should be prepared the day they are to be served and only in such quantities as will be used during one serving period. Fillings should be refrigerated until needed, and if sandwiches are made ahead they should be refrigerated. Lettuce should be omitted from sandwiches to be stored for some time in the refrigerator because the lettuce will wilt and become unappetizing.

Bakeshop Production

Breads, cakes, cookies, pies, and other desserts may be produced in a separate bakeshop or may be made in an area of the main kitchen where ovens, mixers, and other equipment are available. Although some foodservices purchase all or some of these items already prepared, others prefer to make these on the premises either from mixes or "from scratch."

The choice of baking mixes influences the finished product and should be made only after testing and comparing more than one brand. Some large foodservices contract with manufacturers to make mixes to their specifications. If mixes are used, the baked product may be individualized by variations in finishing and presentation. For example, a basic white cake may be baked as a sheet cake or made into a layer cake by cutting the cake into two pieces and placing one on top of the other. A variety of icings may be used with a basic plain cake. Many possibilities exist when making up plain or sweet roll dough.

If mixes are not used for breads and cakes, balanced formulas should be developed and standardized for the pan sizes used in the foodservice. Many variations are possible if good basic recipes are developed for butter, white, and chocolate cakes, and for biscuits, muffins, and rolls. An important factor in successful bakeshop production is the weighing and portioning of batters and doughs. Each recipe should include the size pan to use and the weight of batter for each pan for products such as cakes, coffee cakes, and loaf breads; the weight of each roll or bun; and the size dipper for muffins and drop cookies.

BATTERS AND DOUGHS The classification of formulas for batters and doughs is based on the ratio of flour to liquid:

PROPORTION OF FLOUR TO LIQUID (BY MEASURE)

	Flour	Liquid	Example of Product
Pour batter	1 part	1 part	Popovers, pancakes, waffles
Drop batter	2 parts	1 part	Muffins, cornbread, cake
Soft dough	3 parts	1 part	Cookies, biscuits
Stiff dough	4–8 parts	1 part	Yeast breads, pastry

These proportions affect the character of the mixture. Further variation is produced by the leavening agent, the combination and proportion of eggs, the shortening and sugar, and the kind of flour. A greater amount of baking powder usually is needed for thin batters than for stiffer ones, since the gas is not retained so well in the thin mixture and little or no air has been incorporated in the mixing or by the addition of beaten egg whites.

INGREDIENTS   The type and quantity of ingredients affect the characteristics of the finished product. Basic ingredients in all flour mixtures are flour, a leavening agent, a liquid, flavorings like sugar and salt, and often fat and eggs.

Flour. The baking properties of any flour depend primarily on the grain from which it is ground and the processing procedure, the aging to which it has been subjected, and the possible addition of so-called flour improvers. Wheat usually is classified as hard or strong and soft or weak, depending on the variety and protein content. *Bread flour,* with its high protein content, is milled from hard wheat and is suitable for bread making. The gluten that is formed from the protein when mixed with liquid gives strength to the cell structure of the dough, an important factor in making yeast breads and rolls. For muffins, cakes, and pastries, the development of gluten strength in excess of that needed to carry the other ingredients is undesirable. *All-purpose flour* is milled from a blend of wheats, usually both hard and soft, and is lower in protein content than bread flour. It is suitable for most products. *Cake flour* is made from soft wheat, has a low protein content, and a fine uniform granulation. Cakes made with this type of flour usually have better volume and texture than those made with all-purpose flour. *Pastry flour* generally is made from soft wheat and has properties between those of all-purpose and cake flours and is designed for making pastries, cookies, and similar products.

Rye and many types of whole grain flours are available and are popular for both quick and yeast breads. These flours should be combined with white flour, since they do not have enough gluten to effect proper bread structure. Many foodservices, especially small operations, find it impractical to purchase and store more than one kind of flour; hence, all-purpose may be the only flour used. Where cakes are baked on the premises and mixes are not used, however, cake flour often is purchased for this purpose.

Leavening. The leavening of flour mixtures is accomplished by the expansion of incorporated air, production of steam, or the generation of carbon dioxide. Air is incorporated by creaming, folding, and beating the mixture, or by the addition of air in beaten egg yolks or whites. Steam is produced when the ratio of liquid to flour is high, such as in thin batters, and when the oven temperature is high so that the liquid is heated quickly and the steam formed before the structure is set. Carbon dioxide, formed by the reaction of certain ingredients in the recipe, such as yeast and sugar, baking powder and the liquid, baking soda with an acid ingredient like chocolate, molasses, or sour milk, and on application of heat in some cases, causes the product to expand.

By far the greater part of leavening is accomplished through baking powders, which are composed of an acid, an alkali (sodium bicarbonate), and a starch filler. The classification of baking powders depends on the kind of acid employed to neutralize the sodium bicarbonate. A single acid such as cream of tartar, tartaric acid, or calcium acid phosphate or a double acid such as sodium aluminum sulfate are those commonly combined with the sodium bicarbonate. The three main types of baking powder are designated by these acids.

All baking powders have the capacity to liberate approximately the same amount of gas, but this process occurs at different rates. The tartrate powders liberate a large part of their available gas as soon as moistened, the phosphate somewhat less, and the combination powders very little. Quick mixing and immediate baking in a hot oven are necessary to obtain the best results from tartrate and phosphate baking powders. It is estimated that only 20 to 30 per cent of the gas liberated from these baking powders during mixing is retained in the dough. In the combination powders, the monocalcium phosphate alone is responsible for the liberation of carbon dioxide before baking, the sodium aluminum sulfate reacting slowly at low temperature. In the higher temperature of the oven, the sodium aluminum sulfate liberates its portion of carbon dioxide. This delayed action of the combination powder makes it most satisfactory for quantity food production, and it is the most commonly used type in foodservice since its use permits the making of quick bread or cake batter some time in advance of baking.

Yeast is the leavening agent used in bread and roll doughs. Active dry yeast is used more than compressed yeast, and a quick-rising yeast is replacing both in many foodservices. Dry yeast does not require refrigeration and remains active a reasonable length of time in cool dry storage. The quick-rising yeast reduces proofing time by about half.

Liquid. A liquid in the correct amount is essential for gelatinization of starch, development of gluten, and the reaction of the leavening agent. Milk is the most commonly used liquid because it adds flavor and nutritive value. In quantity production, nonfat dry milk is often used since it incorporates easily with the dry ingredients and is low in cost. Water is added as the liquid. Buttermilk may be used, with baking soda to neutralize it, and other liquids such as fruit juices are used sometimes to give variation in products. One type of liquid should not be substituted for another without adjusting the recipe, however.

Fats. Fats give tenderness and flavor to baked products and improve their keeping qualities. The shortening for flour mixtures should be a fat with a pleasing flavor and color and a wide range of plasticity. Fats commonly used for shortening are of vegetable origin. Most hydrogenated fats lend themselves satisfactorily to this type of cookery, and the addition of emulsifiers has improved the qualities of the fat for making cakes.

Eggs. Eggs are used in flour mixtures principally for color, shortening action, flavor, and nutritive value, although in thin batters they are helpful in retaining the leavening agent. In cakes, egg white acts as a binder of other ingredients and when beaten incorporates considerable air to the flour mixture. Egg yolk tends to act as an emulsifier, separating the mass into smaller particles that influence the texture favorably. Eggs break down the gluten strength of flour, causing cell walls in the mixture to become thinner and the baked product to become more tender.

Egg whites beaten at room temperature give a larger volume than those beaten at refrigerator temperature. The whites are stabilized by the addition of an acid such as cream of tartar, which is especially effective. The use of the acid improves quality and volume of cakes in which egg white is a major ingredient.

Frozen eggs are a satisfactory substitute for shell eggs in the making of bakery products, and they save much time and labor. However, time must be allowed for their complete thawing before incorporation into a mixture. It has been found that eggs defrosted fairly quickly under cold running water produce more satisfactory products than those defrosted for a longer period of time. Frozen egg whites defrost in approximately one-half the time required for either yolks or whole eggs.

METHODS OF COMBINING INGREDIENTS   The methods used in combining ingredients in all types of flour mixtures are important. Uniform distribution of all ingredients, particularly of the fat and liquid with the flour mixture, is essential in making batters and doughs. Also, the loss of carbon dioxide must be kept to a minimum. The poor emulsion formed by the combination of a fat and water increases the problem of obtaining a uniform distribution of the fat particles with the mixture. Melted fat added to the mixture may coat the particles with fairly large globules. Products so made are most satisfactory if consumed as soon as baked. Hard fats are more often mixed with the dry ingredients, as in the making of pastry, biscuits, or shortened cakes.

Muffin Method. The muffin method of combining ingredients ordinarily is used for pancakes, waffles, muffins, and their variations. It also is used for loaf breads such as nut bread and banana bread, although some recipes with a higher proportion of sugar are mixed by the cake method. This method requires quick work and an avoidance of overmixing. In quantity products, exact timing and the mixer set at low speed are recommended to avoid overmixing. The batter may be lumpy, but such a condition is normal. This type of batter breaks and separates easily when lifted with a spoon.

As soon as mixed, the batter should be dipped into the prepared pans with as little agitation as possible. The use of an ice cream dipper for portioning muffins ensures products of uniform size, prevents "stretching" the gluten strands in the batter by cutting them off, and is faster than dipping with a spoon. If the muffins are to be baked at intervals during the serving period, the filled pans should be refrigerated until they are cooked. Muffins are baked at 375°F for 15 to 20 minutes or until golden brown; loaf breads at 350°F for 45 to 50 minutes. Muffin batter swells to approximately twice its original volume in baking. A good muffin has a pebbly, rounded top, a tender golden-brown crust, and uniform medium-fine texture, with no tunnels.

Biscuit Method. In the biscuit method the dry ingredients are combined in a mixer bowl; the fat is added and cut into the dry ingredients at low speed, using the pastry cutter or flat beater. Liquid is added all at once, and the mass is mixed until it adheres together. The length of mixing time is important, but unlike the muffin procedure undermixing must be avoided.

Biscuit dough should be light and soft but not sticky. The biscuits will tend to be smoother and finer in texture if the dough is kneaded lightly 10 to 20 times before it is rolled and cut. The kneading combines the ingredients more thoroughly than by stirring alone. After the mass of dough has been kneaded, it is rolled lightly to the desired thickness (usually about three-quarters of an inch) and cut with a floured cutter. The biscuits are placed on an ungreased baking sheet one-half inch apart for crusty biscuits, just touching for softer ones. Biscuits are baked at a temperature of 425°F for 12 to 15 minutes or until the crust is evenly browned and the inside is flaky, light, and dry. The biscuits should be regular in shape with vertical sides and fairly smooth, level tops and should have tender golden-brown crusts. The thickness should be about twice that of the unbaked biscuit. The fine flaky texture is light and fluffy; and long, thin layers can be peeled off when the biscuit is broken open.

Cake Methods. The usual methods for combining ingredients for cakes containing fat are the conventional or sugar-batter, dough-batter, and muffin methods. The *conventional* method of combining ingredients for shortened cakes consists of creaming the fat and sugar and adding the beaten eggs and then the sifted dry ingredients alternately with liquid. Best results are obtained when the fat and sugar are thoroughly creamed and the dry ingredients are well mixed before being added to the creamed mixture.

The *dough-batter* method of making shortened cakes is used successfully in quantity production. This quick-mix or one-bowl method became popular with the common usage of hydrogenated fats to which an emulsifier had been added, thus eliminating the necessity for creaming of the fat and sugar. Such fats can carry a high ratio of sugar to fat, producing a sweet, fine-textured cake. This method requires little time, few utensils, is easy to follow through, and yields a highly desirable product. The finished cake tends to be slightly smaller than those made by some other methods, but the uniformity of the cells is quite marked and the velvet texture is an outstanding characteristic. In this method, the flour, baking powder, and shortening (hydrogenated plastic fat at room temperature) are mixed at low speed for five minutes. Half of the milk is combined with the sugar and salt, added to the flour mixture, and beaten for five minutes. The remainder of the milk and eggs and vanilla or other flavoring is combined and blended into the flour mixture for an additional five minutes.

The muffin method (described earlier) of combining ingredients may also be followed in making cakes. This method is quick and most successful if the cake is to be used soon after baking.

The amount of cake batter that can be mixed successfully at one time depends on the size of the mixer bowl, provided the formula is balanced and the correct mixing techniques are used. In addition, a suitable amount of batter in the pans, correct baking temperature, and even distribution of heat in the oven also contribute to the quality of the baked cake.

A good shortened cake is uniform in thickness and attractive in appearance. The crust is delicate brown, tender, and thin with no cracks. The cake should be light, tender, and agreeably moist, but not sticky. It should have an even, find-grained texture and a delicate, well-blended flavor. An excellent shortened cake has the characteristic commonly spoken of as "velvetiness," meaning that to the tongue or fingers it feels like soft velvet. A cake with this characteristic is always light and has a fine, even grain, but these qualities do not ensure the velvety feeling.

For foam-type of unshortened cakes, the character of the egg whites and the way in which they are handled are significant to quality. Stability and a fine, uniform size of the foam, plus elasticity sufficient to swell without rupture during baking, are important for volume and tenderness. For best results, thick whites (characteristic in fresh, high-quality eggs) at room temperature when beaten should be used. Salt and cream of tartar are added to increase whiteness and stability. The egg whites are beaten to the stage of soft or rounded peaks, the sugar added when the whites are at the soft peak stage of stiffness, and the beating continued until the whites are stiff but not dry. The flour should be folded in carefully to minimize loss of air from the foam.

Pastry Method. Pie crust is a relatively simple mixture because the ingredients consist only of flour, shortening, salt, water, and sometimes sugar or baking powder, but the quality of the finished product depends on the quality and temperature of these ingredients, their ratio to each other, and the method of mixing them. The ingredients in the proportion commonly used in large quantity preparation are: 100 pounds of flour, 70 to 75 pounds of shortening, 30 pounds (15 quarts) of water, and 3½ pounds of salt. Some bakers prefer to use almost equal parts (by weight) of flour and shortening. The all-purpose flour is commonly used for pie crust, although in some large bakeshop operations pastry flour, made from soft winter wheat with low protein and ash content, is used. Bread flour, with its high gluten content important in making yeast bread, is unsuited to making good pie dough.

The fat or shortening determines in part not only the character of the dough, but also its flavor. A stable fat of a consistency to blend easily with the other ingredients and bland in flavor is preferred for this purpose.

The quantity of salt should be proportionate to the weight of the batch of dough instead of to the weight of flour used in the recipe. A satisfactory ratio of salt to dough is approximately .3 ounces of salt to each pound of dough. Best results are obtained when the salt is dissolved in the water instead of being mixed with the flour.

Water used in pie dough serves as a binder. The dough that has excess moisture is well bound, not tender; the dough that has too little water is too lightly bound and crumbles readily. The ability of water to bind dough is determined by both the quantity present and the method of mixing. If the flour and fat have been well mixed, the flour containing the gluten is sealed away from the water, and toughness cannot develop.

The method of mixing pie dough depends on the materials used, the quantity to be mixed at one time, the equipment available, and the type of crust desired. In any case, the usual procedure is to blend the fat and flour and add the water, in which the salt has been dissolved. Pie crust may be made satisfactorily in a mixer if low speed is used and the mixing is timed carefully to avoid overmixing. The type of pie crust is determined by the method of combining the ingredients and modifying slightly the amount of water in a basic recipe. The types are known as short flaky, mealy, and flaky or long flaky, and are characteristic of their names.

Short flaky pie crust is produced when a dough is made by cutting or rubbing the fat into the flour until all flour spots are broken, but not until pasty. The full amount of water is added, and the mixing is continued until the mass holds together. The result will be a tender crust with small flakes, because of the coating of fat on the particles of starch, which prevents the development of gluten. Also, the high water content will permit some oven expansion. Some bakers prefer to modify this method by combining half the fat with all the flour to a fine crumb, and then adding the remainder of the fat and mixing only until it has been broken down to lumps about the size of a pea. This mass should be mixed only long enough to combine lightly after the water has been added.

Mealy pie crust is made by mixing the fat and flour quite thoroughly, then adding approximately one-sixth less water than listed in a basic recipe. A modification of this method is to combine all the fat with half the flour and then work in the remainder of the flour before adding the water.

Long flaky pie crust requires quick careful handling and chilling for several hours before using. The fat and flour are combined lightly, leaving chunks of fat one-third to one-half inch in diameter. Approximately twice as much water is needed for this type of crust as for the mealy crust, and it should be mixed only a few turns. It can be smoothed out on a flat pan for chilling. Overmixing after the water is added toughens this type of dough because much of the flour is free to combine with the water and thus form gluten. This type of crust is best suited for use as tops on fruit pies or as baked shells for cream pies.

Approximately 6 ounces of dough are necessary for each 9-inch pie shell or crust. Some bakers prefer to use 7 ounces of dough for the bottom crust and 5 or 5½ ounces for the top crust. For hand rolling the scaled dough is worked slightly to shape it into a round mass, then rolled on a lightly floured board or pastry cloth to an even thickness. Roll from the center out in all directions without turning the dough over; or it may be given a few quick up-and-down strokes perpendicular to the edge of the table and the elongated piece of dough, just long enough for the pan, turned over and at right angels to the previous position. A few more up-and-down strokes will make it the exact shape and size for the pan. There should be few if any trimmings. Mechanical pie crust rollers (Fig. 6.7) are used in most large foodservices with great saving of time and human effort. The dough, scaled and shaped as for hand rolling, goes through two sets of rollers. The first elongates the piece of dough, which is rounded by the second set.

A shell for a one-crust pie, in which several very small holes have been made to release the steam, is baked either on the inside or outside of the pan for approximately 12 to 15 minutes at a temperature of about 450°F. Some bakers prefer to bake the shells between two pans at a temperature of

FIGURE 6.7   The use of mechanical pie-crust roller saves time and energy of employees.

500°F. Care should be taken not to stretch the dough too tightly over the bottom of the pan, or the resulting crust will be smaller than desired. The cooked filling is poured into the baked crust, and if covered with meringue, the pie is baked 10 to 12 minutes at 375°F.

Two-crust pies are made by lining the pan with a layer of dough, which has been rolled to fit the pan. The filling usually is raw, cooked, or frozen tart fruit, sweetened, and thickened slightly with corn or waxy maize starch, tapioca, or flour. The waxy maize thickens at a relatively low temperature and, on cooling, retains a consistency similar to its consistency when hot. Cover with a second crust and seal by moistening the edge of the bottom layer of crust and pressing the edges of the two layers together. If the top crust has been cut one inch larger than the pan, it can be folded over and under the edge of the lower crust. When the edge so prepared is pressed with a fork or fluted with the fingers, the pie is completely sealed, so that the juices tend to be retained in it throughout the baking period. Pie tape, carefully placed to bind the two edges of the crusts, will also seal them together to conserve the juice. This procedure may not be feasible in foodservices where preparation time is an important factor. A small fold across the center of the top crust allows for shrinkage, and several perforations permit the escape of steam from within the pie.

The temperature at which filled pies are baked depends on the filling.

They may be placed in a hot oven so that the lower crust will begin to bake before the filling has soaked into it. The baking is then continued at a lower temperature; for example, to bake fresh apple and rhubarb pies, the temperature range might be 400 to 450°F for a 10-minute period, followed by a 40- to 50-minute baking period for apple and a 20- to 25-minute period for rhubarb at 300 to 350°F. A more common practice in quantity pie production is to bake fruit pies at a constant temperature of 425°F. This makes it possible for the crust to bake before the filling boils and causes sogginess of the bottom crust or spillage onto the oven floor. In all fresh fruit pies, the length of the baking period depends on the time necessary to ensure tenderness of the fruit.

Following are possible causes for difficulties encountered in pie making (information furnished by the Bakery Research Department, Wilson and Company, Chicago):

- **Shrinkage of crust.** Not enough shortening used, not coating all the flour with shortening, hard shortening, hard-to-coat flour, excess water used, too strong a flour, overmixing.
- **Soakage of bottom crust.** Crust too rich or excess shortening, lack of bottom heat, too sweet a filling, pies taken from oven before baked, pies filled with hot filling.
- **Boiling out of fruit.** Oven too cool, excess acidity in filling, hot filling used in making the pies, not enough thickening agent used, lack of holes in top crust for vapor to escape.
- **Sticking to pans.** Dirty tins, moisture on pans, lack of bottom heat, excess bottom heat, boiling over, break in bottom crust.
- **Watery custard pies.** Hot oven or excessive baking time, excessive sugar in filling.
- **Watery meringue.** Egg whites not whipped light enough, not right percentage of sugar (three pounds per quart of whites), watery whites, baked in cool oven.

Yeast Breads. Because the making of yeast breads is a rather complex procedure and requires several steps to complete, many foodservices find it more practical to purchase these products. Others believe the offering of fresh "home-baked" breads, rolls, and other baked products is profitable and contributes to customer satisfaction.

Yeast doughs may be classified as lean, which are low in fat and sugar and are used for breads and dinner rolls, and rich, which generally contain higher proportions of fat, sugar, and sometimes eggs, and are used for rich dinner rolls, sweet rolls, and coffee cakes. Danish pastry is made from a dough in which a fat is incorporated into the dough in many layers.

For most yeast breads a straight dough method is used. This procedure consists of combining the dry and liquid ingredients and mixing until gluten has developed and a smooth dough has been formed. The mixing generally is done in a mixer with a dough hook attachment. The yeast may be added to the dry ingredients or may be softened in warm water and added with the rest of the liquid, shortening, sugar, and salt. If *compressed* yeast is used, it is softened in lukewarm water (95°F); *dry* yeast is softened in warm water (105 to 110°F); and if dry yeast is mixed with the other dry ingredients, the liquid may be heated to 120°F (very warm) because the flour particles protect the yeast from the higher temperature.

Fermentation begins when the dough is mixed and continues until the yeast is killed by the heat of the oven. The dough should be set in a warm place (80 to 85°F), free from drafts. Many foodservices have proofing boxes, in which the temperature and humidity can be controlled.

After the dough has doubled in bulk, it is punched down to its original bulk by placing the hand in the center of the dough and folding edges to the center, then turning over the ball of dough. This forces out excess carbon dioxide and incorporates oxygen, which allows the yeast cells to grow more rapidly. The yeast cells are more uniformly distributed, producing an even-textured product with a fine grain. After the dough has been punched down, it must be handled lightly to avoid breaking the small air cells that have been formed. If the dough is made with bread flour, it usually is allowed to rise a second time before shaping, although if the dough has been made with all-purpose flour, the second rising may be omitted.

The next step is scaling, in which the dough is divided into pieces of uniform weight and shaped into smooth, round balls. The dough is allowed to rest for 10 to 15 minutes to relax the gluten, which makes shaping of the dough easier.

The dough is then shaped into loaves or rolls, placed in pans or on baking sheets, and allowed to rise in a warm place until double in bulk. The dough may be retarded at any point during the fermentation process by chilling the dough. Roll doughs may be refrigerated and portions of the dough baked at intervals, but storage time should be limited to less than a week to prevent crust formation. Dough that has not risen long enough makes a small, compact product; dough that has risen too long tends to have an open, crumbly texture and reduced volume.

Most loaf breads are baked at 375 to 400°F and rolls made from plain bread dough at 400°F. Rolls and breads made from rich doughs are baked at lower temperatures (350 to 375°F) to prevent excessive browning of the crust. After baking, bread must be removed from pans and cooled rapidly on racks to allow the escape of excess moisture created during fermentation. Rolls may be left on the baking sheets, since they will have adequate air circulation. If soft crusts are desired, breads may be brushed with melted shortening before cooling.

BAKING PANS   The size, shape, and type of baking pan materials affect the quality of flour mixtures. Products baked in pans with a dark color or dull finish generally have a larger volume and better crumb quality than those baked in pans with shiny surfaces, but the center tends to be more rounded. When comparing aluminum and stainless steel, the products baked in aluminum pans have better volume and grain, although the time for cooking is greater. Cakes baked in tinned steel and aluminum pans have been found to be comparable in size and quality, but a longer time for baking is required with the aluminum. Bright, shiny pans reflect heat and the heat penetration, therefore, is slower.

Shallow pans produce larger and more tender cakes with flatter tops than do deep pans. In deep pans, the batter near the sides of the pan becomes firm during the early part of the baking period, and the softer center of the batter expands to form a humped crust that usually shows a crack. Too large a pan allows the batter to spread so thin that excessive browning results. An aluminum pan that is shallow and not shiny on the outside is a good choice.

A baking sheet 18 x 26 inches and 1½ inches deep with straight sides is a frequently used size for cakes, cookies, and some quick breads. A half size baking sheet 12 x 18 inches has proven successful also, especially for making layer cakes. Some foodservices use baking pans 12 x 18 inches or 12 x 20 inches, with 2½- to 3-inch sides. Since these pans are deeper than the 18 x 26 baking sheets, special attention must be given to the amount of batter in the pans. Recipes should be standardized for the pan sizes in use, and the weight of the batter for each pan indicated on the recipe. Loaf pans for pound cakes and quick breads and tube pans for foam cakes vary in size and should be selected according to the size serving desired.

Pans should be prepared before preparation of the products begins. Pans for angel food and sponge cakes are not greased; baking powder biscuits and cookies with high fat content usually are also placed on ungreased baking sheets. Most others are either lightly greased, greased and floured, or covered with a silicone or waxed paper liner.

PRODUCTION SCHEDULING   Scheduling of production is very important in the bakeshop area, especially when ovens, mixers, and other equipment must be shared. If possible, baking of hot breads should be scheduled so that freshly baked products are available during the serving period. Biscuits and muffins may be mixed and shaped, then refrigerated and baked at intervals. Rolls may also be shaped after the dough has risen and refrigerated, but time must be allowed for the rolls to rise the second time before baking. The time and quantity to be baked at each interval should be included on the production schedule.

All baked breads freeze well if properly cooled and wrapped, and yeast doughs can be frozen up to six weeks either before or after shaping. Sugar and yeast usually are increased slightly in doughs to be retarded or frozen. If freezer storage is adequate, pie crusts may be frozen unbaked until needed, and fruit pies can be made ahead and frozen. Most cakes and cookies freeze well but should not be iced until they have been removed from the freezer and thawed.

Summary

The processes in quantity food production are similar to those in small quantity cooking, but the procedures may differ because of the quantities involved and the management constraints imposed. Cooking of food is based on the transfer of heat to the food through the mediums of air, liquid, steam, fat, direct heat conduction, the container, and radiation.

The methods of cooking meat, fish, and poultry depend on the form in which they are purchased, the quantity that must be prepared at one time, and the facilities available for their preparation and service. In meat, the quality and cut may determine the choice. Many of these products are purchased as portion-ready items, which influences the method of cooking. Grilling, broiling, roasting, frying, braising, and stewing are the methods used in meat and poultry cooking. In general, dry heat is used for tender cuts and moist-heat cooking for the less tender cuts. Most poultry purchased today is young and, therefore, tender, so it may be cooked in any of the methods listed. Frying, baking, broiling, and poaching are the methods most often used for cooking fish, which is by nature tender and should be cooked only until the fish flakes easily when tested with a fork. The oven is used extensively not only for roasting but for "broiling" and "frying" in foodservices where it is impractical to broil or panfry because of the quantity to be prepared at once. In foodservice operations where cooking to order is possible, broiling, grilling, and panfrying are used extensively. The steam-jacketed kettle and tilting frypan are used frequently for braising or stewing meat and poultry.

With the increased interest in soups, their preparation merits attention. Clear or unthickened soups are made with a clear broth or stock base and may or may not have other ingredients added. Because the making of stock is so time-consuming, many foodservices use concentrated bases. The quality of these bases varies, so one should be selected that will result in a good quality stock, and if necessary the salt and other seasonings in recipes should be adjusted. These bases are used also for sauces and for other recipes having chicken or beef broth as an ingredient. Cream soups are prepared by combining a thin white sauce with mashed, strained, or finely chopped vegetables, chicken, fish, or meat. Chowders, bisques, and purées are thick soups that do not necessarily have a white sauce base. Many sauces are based on a roux, which is a cooked mixture of equal parts by weight of fat and flour. Many meat and vegetable sauces are modifications of basic recipes, such as white sauce, bechamel sauce, and brown sauce.

For optimum quality, vegetables should not be overcooked and should not be held for long periods on a serving counter. The method of cooking influences the texture, color, flavor, and nutritive value of the product. Small batch or continuous cooking of fresh or frozen vegetables throughout the meal service is the best way to produce the most satisfactory results. High-speed steam cookers and small tilting trunnion kettles are the most useful kinds of equipment for batch cooking. Vegetables may also be stir-fried.

Ingredients for salads should be chilled, crisp, and cut into well-defined pieces. Some fresh fruits deteriorate rapidly after being washed and peeled, so they should be treated to prevent oxidation. In many foodservices, the preliminary preparation of salad ingredients is done in a separate preparation area. When making individual salads, an assembly line procedure saves time and energy. Salads should be refrigerated until time for service, but not for so long that the salads become wilted. The salad bar is a well-established part of many foodservice operations. Ingredients and prepared salads should be arranged logically and should be attractively presented.

Sandwiches, a popular item on most menus, may be served hot or cold and may be closed or open-faced. In some foodservices, sandwiches are prepared to order, in which case the ingredients should be prepared and refrigerated and the sandwiches assembled as needed. In large quantity, all the sandwiches required may be made and refrigerated until needed; or they may be assembled a few at a time to keep up a steady supply to the serving counter; or ingredients for hot sandwiches may be prepared ahead and assembled as needed on the cafeteria counter. In any of these methods, an efficient work station should be set up and an assembly line procedure used.

Production of breads, cakes, cookies, pies, and other baked products may take place in a separate bakeshop or may be made in an area of the kitchen where ovens, mixers, and other equipment are available. Whether these products are made from commercial mixes or from original ingredients, there is opportunity for creativity in their presentation. Recipes must be consistent with the capacity of the large equipment and must be tailored to fit the pan sizes being used. Production scheduling is important in the bakeshop, and many products can be mixed and baked as needed to provide freshly baked products during the serving period. Most baked products freeze satisfactorily and some doughs may be frozen until needed.

Supplementary References

Gisslen, W.: Professional Baking. New York: John Wiley and Sons, 1985.

Gisslen, W.: Professional Cooking. New York: John Wiley and Sons, 1983.

Hoffman, C. J. and Zabik, M. E.: Current and future foodservice applications of microwave cooking/reheating. J. Am. Diet. Assoc. 85:929, 1985.

Hoffman, C. J. and Zabik, M. E.: Effect of microwave cooking/reheating on nutrients and food systems: A review of recent studies. J. Am. Diet. Assoc. 85:922, 1985.

Hotel, Restaurant, and Institution Management Department, Iowa State University: Standardized Quantity Recipe File for Quality and Cost Control. Ames, IA: Iowa State University Press, 1971.

Hotel, Restaurant, and Institution Management Department, Iowa State University: Quantity Recipes, Supplement to Standardized Quantity Recipe File for Quality and Cost Control. Ames, IA: Iowa State University Press, 1984.

Knight, J. B. and Kotschevar, L. H.: Quantity Food Production. Boston: CBI Publishing Co., 1979.

Matthews, E. M.: Microwave ovens: Effects on food quality and safety. J. Am. Diet. Assoc. 85:919, 1985.

Matthews, R. H. and Garrison, Y. J.: Food Yields Summarized by Different Stages of Preparation, rev. ed. USDA Agricultural Handbook No. 102. Washington, DC: U.S GPO (Sept.), 1975.

National Live Stock and Meat Board: Meat in the Foodservice Industry. Chicago: National Live Stock and Meat Board, 1975.

Shugart, G. S., Molt, M., and Wilson, M.: Food for Fifty, 7th ed. New York: John Wiley and Sons, 1985.

Sultan, W. J.: Practical Baking, 4th ed. Westport, CT: AVI Publishing Co., 1986.

Terrell, M. E.: Professional Food Preparation, 2nd ed. New York: John Wiley and Sons, 1979.

U.S. Department of Agriculture: Food Buying Guide for School Food Service. PA No. 1257. Food and Nutrition Service, USDA. Washington, DC: U.S. GPO, 1980.

CHAPTER 7

Delivery and Service

Introduction

Foodservice managers have responsibility for making certain that after food is prepared, it is safely transported, delivered, and served to consumers, whomever and wherever they may be. There are many methods and types of equipment available from which to choose to achieve these three goals: to maintain quality food characteristics, including desirable temperatures, to assure microbial safety of food, and to serve food that is attractive and satisfying. In addition, the delivery/service system should save steps, reduce time and labor costs, and lessen worker fatigue.

The chapter provides background information for the foodservice manager to make sound decisions about delivery and service systems and the selection of one to meet the needs of a particular situation. Styles of table service and merchandising of foods for attractive presentation also are included.

Goals and Methods

Modern technological research and development related to foodservice have brought many advances in methods of delivery and service of food and in the equipment used for those processes. These developments resulted in large part from the newer production systems discussed in Chapter 2. With the increased time and distance between production and service, the potential for loss of food quality also was increased. Newer delivery and service methods are designed to protect against such loss.

Most menu items are at their peak of goodness at the time production and cooking are completed. It is not possible to serve food at that precise time in many foodservice systems because of the need to assemble, transport, and deliver meals for service. Equipment that will maintain foods at proper temperatures for best quality and to ensure safety of the foods in transit is a necessity. Methods of delivery and service that involve the shortest possible time and distance are best able to help achieve the desired goal. It is assumed that the foods as prepared were of good quality before delivery and service begin.

Goals

Simply stated, the goals of all foodservice delivery and service systems are to:

1. Maintain quality characteristics including desirable temperature of food
2. Ensure microbial safety of the food to the consumer
3. Present food that is attractive in appearance and satisfying to the consumer

Further, the delivery/service system should be planned to:

1. Save steps and energy
2. Reduce labor time and costs
3. Lessen worker fatigue

To achieve these goals, an evaluation of the various types of equipment available, a study of routes and distances involved, and consideration of employee time and effort required should precede the adoption of any particular system.

Methods—Delivery and Service as Subsystems

The term *delivery* is used to mean making ready prepared foods and transporting them from production to place of service; *service* involves assembling prepared menu items and distributing them to the consumer. The equipment required for both delivery and service is an essential part of these subsystems. And whereas delivery and service *are* subsystems in the overall foodservice system, they are small systems within themselves and are referred to here as "systems."

Basically, there are two major *on-premises* delivery/service systems: centralized and decentralized. Although some people think of these two terms only in relation to tray service to hospital patients, they are used in relation to other types of foodservices as well.

Centralized Delivery/Service System   In the centralized method, prepared foods are portioned for individual service and meals assembled at a central area in or adjacent to the main kitchen. The completed orders are then transported and distributed to the customer. This is typical of over-the-counter service in fast food restaurants, of table or counter service in restaurants that utilize waiters or waitresses to transport and deliver meals to the patrons, of room service in hotels/motels, and of banquet service where plates are served in a central location and transported by various means to the dining areas for service. It is used also in many hospitals and health care facilities. Foods are portioned and plated, and trays for individual patients are assembled in the central serving room. Completed trays are then transported by various means to the patients throughout the facility. Soiled trays and dishes are returned to the central area for washing.

Kotschevar and Terrell[1] note a modification of the centralized service called *"centralized bulk,* in which food is sent in trucks for dispensing in corridors near patients' rooms or from a floor pantry." Trucks may have microwave ovens attached for rapid reheating of food just prior to service.

Centralized delivery/service systems are prevalent today because of the close supervision and control of food quality, portion size, assurance of correct menu items on each tray or order, and correct food temperatures at point of service that this system affords. Also, it requires less equipment and labor time than does the decentralized method. If the number of people to be served is large, however, the total time-span required for service may be excessively long.

Decentralized Delivery/Service System   In the decentralized system, bulk quantities of prepared foods are sent hot and/or cold to serving pantries or ward kitchens located throughout the facility. There the reheating (if needed), portioning, and meal assembly take place. Thus, instead of one central serving area, there are several smaller ones close to the consumers. Often these pantries have facilities for limited short-order cooking for eggs, toast, coffee and for broiling certain items. Refrigerators, ovens for reheating, temperature-holding cabinets, and a counter or conveyor belt for tray assembly are a part of the equipment provided in these serving pantries. Dishwashers also may be provided for warewashing in the ward kitchens. Or soiled dishes and trays may be returned to the central area for washing, which eliminates the need for duplication of dishwashing equipment for each pantry. If dishes are washed in the central area, the clean dishes must be returned to the pantries for use for the next meal. It is time and energy consuming to transport dishes twice each meal, soiled and clean, from and to the pantries. Over a period of time, this may be more expensive than providing dishwashing facilities for each serving unit.

Decentralized service is considered most desirable for use in facilities that are low and spread out in design or in any facility where there are great distances from the main kitchen to the consumers. It is expected that foods will be of better quality and retain desired temperatures more effectively if served near the consumer rather than plated in a central location and transported to distant locations within the facility. Also, with many serving units rather than one, meals for all consumers can be distributed within a reasonable time-span. When all meals are served from one central location, the time-span to complete service can be much greater.

Types of foodservice that utilize the decentralized system include large hospitals and medical centers; industrial plants with several serving units or that use mobile carts to travel throughout the plant to serve workers at their work stations; hotels providing room service from serving pantries on various floors, and banquets from serving kitchens within the facility.

Costs and values of centralized vs. decentralized methods should be studied and carefully weighed before deciding on which one to adopt. Both can be successfully utilized in specific situations and with given conditions.

Factors Affecting Choice of Delivery Systems

Every organization has its own requirements for delivery and service based on the type of foodservice system, the kind of foodservice, the size and physical layout of the facility, style of service used, skill level of available personnel, economic factors related to labor and equipment costs, quality standards for food and microbial safety desired, timing necessary for meal service, space requirements vs. space available for foodservice activities, and the energy use involved.

No one factor can be considered alone when deciding on a delivery/service system, for most of the factors interact with, and have an influence on, the others. They must be regarded as a whole when a choice is made.

Type of Foodservice System

The system used determines to some extent its own needs for delivery and service. Of the four types of foodservice systems discussed in Chapter 2, the commissary system, for example, is the only one requiring delivery trucks to take prepared foods to satellite serving units. In both the conventional and ready-prepared systems, foods are prepared on-premises, and the assembly-serve system has meals that are purchased and delivered by the vendor to the service facility.

As noted previously, menu items processed in the commissary are either held in bulk or portioned before storage. Three alternatives for storage following food production are: frozen, chilled, or hot-held. Each method requires different equipment.

Bulk foods may be placed in $12'' \times 20''$ counter-size pans for freezing so they may be reheated and served from the same pan. Or, if they are to be transferred to serving units in the chilled or hot state instead of frozen, they are placed in heavy containers with lids that clamp on securely. Otherwise, spillage may result during transport to the foodservice facility. Individual portions may be placed in casserolelike dishes, onto TV-like portioned aluminum tray plates, on plastic or paper plates, or wrapped in wax paper as sandwiches for a school foodservice lunch.

Carriers (Fig. 7.1a and b, for example) to hold the portioned food in their containers are filled at the commissary. At scheduled times each day, other types of carriers, which may or may not be heated or refrigerated depending on whatever is appropriate to maintain optimum food temperature, are loaded onto a truck for transfer to the service unit. In many cases, the driver is responsible for unloading the truck and taking the food carriers to the storage or service area as required. Empty carriers from the previous delivery are collected and returned to the commissary on the delivery truck.

The fleet of trucks required by the commissary will depend on geographic distances to be traveled and number of deliveries to be made by each truck driver. Timing can be crucial, especially in those situations where the food is delivered hot just at meal times. School foodservices or college residence hall service may utilize the hot food delivery system to a greater extent than other foodservices since they may not have finishing kitchens. Distances for hot foods to be transported should be short. Timing also is essential for delivery of meals to airports for loading onto planes before take-off. Heavy penalties are imposed for deliveries not meeting airline schedules.

Delivery of frozen foods requires well-insulated carriers to maintain food in the frozen state during the time it is being transported. If the service facility has adequate space for holding frozen food, there is little problem with delivery time, since meals can be sent a day or two ahead. If there is no such storage space, delivery timing must be correlated with meal periods and time for rethermalizing and assembling the menu items.

At this point, foods are on-premises, and the procedures for delivery and service within the facility may be the same for all four systems.

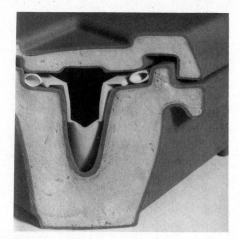

FIGURE 7.1   *(a)* An example of a carrier for transporting prepared hot food. This model has two snap-in Heat
Packs for efficient heat distribution that extends holding
time at desired temperature. NSF approved. *(b)* Cut-away
shot of same insulated carrier. Note the one-piece polyethylene, double-wall construction, thick polyurethane insulation and the design features for heat retention.   *Courtesy of Cambro Manufacturing Company,*
Huntington Beach, California.

Kind of Foodservice Organization

The type of organization determines to a large extent the delivery and service system requirements. Those where large numbers of people must be
served quickly, such as schools, colleges, and industrial plants, usually provide cafeterias for meal service. Fast food restaurants serve foods as quickly
as possible, too, but with over-the-counter or drive-by customer pick-up or
drive-in service by car hops.

Hospitals and nursing homes cater to the foodservice needs not only of
their patients but also of the employees, professional staff, and visitors. This
calls for tray service for patients who are bedfast, perhaps dining room service for ambulatory patients in some care centers, cafeteria service for staff,
employees, and visitors, and often vending machines provided as a supplemental service for between-meal hours.

Airlines have special delivery-service needs also. Food must be transported
by delivery truck from commissary to airport for loading onto the planes for
service after take-off (see Fig. 7.2). Meals may be transported preplated hot

FIGURE 7.2   Marriott In-Flite Services supplies more than 150 carriers and is typical of foodservice delivery to airlines.   *Courtesy of H. H. Gill, president, Gladieux Corporation, Toledo, Ohio (now merged with Marriott Corporation).*

or cold for reheating in the galley of the plane. Passengers are served meals or snacks on trays at their seats by flight attendants.

Table service restaurants may use differing styles of service (see later in this chapter under "Style of Service"), but all employ servers to carry meals from kitchen to dining area for service to the guests. Where customers serve themselves, buffet service is used in some restaurants. Employees replenish the food and usually serve beverages to the guests' tables.

The large hotel/motel may have several types of service within its facility, including a counter or coffee shop for fast meals and table service dining rooms, some more "exclusive" and expensive than others, and so may use more formal types of service. Since may hotels cater to conventions and group meetings, banquet service is also offered. Room service is available in most, which calls for a different means of delivery and service, by servers taking meals on tray or table on wheels to guests in their rooms.

Meal service aboard cruise ships parallels that of hotels/motels, except there is no banquet service. In the main dining room, guests are served at one or two sittings, depending on facilities and number of guests aboard. In addition to regular meals, speciality foods such as pizza and short-order menu items may be served in snack bars, around the pool, or in a lounge. Mid-morning coffee or bouillon, afternoon tea, and elaborate midnight buffets necessitate various delivery/service methods. Food service is provided almost around the clock. Food is a most important part of life on a cruise ship.

Size and Physical Layout of Facility

The size and building arrangement of the facility are other factors to consider when determining a delivery system. Some restaurants, for example, may be in a high-priced downtown location, so are generally tall and narrow, several stories in height to utilize valuable land to best advantage. In this case, the bakery may be on one level, preparation and cooking units on another, and dishwashing still another, all on different levels from the dining room. This calls for a well-coordinated system of mechanized conveyors, subveyors, and elevators to deliver food quickly to the place of service.

Hospitals and health care facilities may be constructed as high-rise buildings or low, rambling facilities with miles of corridors. Different systems are required for each to ensure tray delivery to the patient within a reasonable time. The distance and the routing from production to service areas are points for consideration.

Style of Service

Whether or not the style is *self service* as cafeteria, buffet, vended, or pick up by the consumer; *tray service,* either centralized or decentralized; *waiter or waitress service* for table, counter, or drive-in facilities; or *portable meal service* with meals delivered to home or office throughout an industrial plant, each has different equipment and delivery needs. (See later in this chapter under "Equipment Needs" and "Styles of Service.")

Skill Level of Available Personnel

The availability of well-trained or trainable personnel is essential if a sophisticated, automated, and mechanized delivery and service system is to be employed. The use, care, and maintenance of such equipment requires persons with a mechanical "bent" to use it correctly and keep it in good working order. Less skilled personnel may be employed with a centralized service that does not require the use of specialized reheating and delivery equipment.

Economic Factors

Labor and equipment required in the various delivery/service systems must be costed and evaluated in relation to budgeted allocations. Unless adequate funding is available, the foodservice would not, for example, be able to install automated electronic delivery equipment. Economic factors play a part in deciding where and how frozen or chilled foods should be reheated, assembled, and served. Decentralized service requires duplication of assembling and serving and, sometimes, dishwashing equipment, as well as personnel for the many pantries or ward kitchens throughout the facility, and so may be more expensive to install and operate than the centralized service. Cost comparisons of the numerous types of carts and trucks for transporting food should precede the selection of a specific delivery and serving system.

Quality Standard for Food and Microbial Safety

Management establishes standards for food quality and safety, then selects equipment for heating, holding, and transporting food to achieve those standards. How hot shall the food be when served to the consumer? How can that temperature be maintained through delivery and service? How hot must foods be at the time of serving and portioning to aid in achieving the desired standards?

Considerable research has been conducted to find answers for these questions; a summary is reported by a group of North Central Regional Researchers.[2] Studies relate to the four foodservice systems, microbial safety, nutrient retention, and sensory qualities. Microbial quality of menu items studied is dependent on the type of food, quality of raw ingredients, batch size, type of equipment used for cooking, and position of menu items in foodservice equipment, among others. The management of time and temperature relationships throughout all stages of product flow in every foodservice system is considered of major importance. (See Chapter 8 for more on microbial safety.) Time and temperature relationships also are important in nutrient retention and on sensory qualities of food products. Foodservice managers should be knowledgeable about these factors to improve their foodservice.

Timing Required for Meal Service

The time of day desired or established for meals is another factor influencing the choice of a delivery/service system. For example, if 1,200 people are to be served at a 7 P.M. seated banquet, all food must be ready at once and served within a few minutes to all of the guests. Many serving stations and adequate personnel for each station are prerequisites for achieving the time objective. Preheated electric carts may be loaded with the preplated meals a short time before service and then taken to various locations in the dining room for service from the carts to guests. An alternate method is to place the plates as they are served on trays and carried by servers to the dining room. This will require several trips from serving area to dining room and so takes more time than when carts are used.

If only a few people need to be served at one time, as in a restaurant where customer orders come to the kitchen over a period of a few hours, food is cooked to order or in small batches and held for short periods of time.

In school foodservice, many children are ready for lunch at the same time. To avoid long waits in a cafeteria line, however, a staggered meal period may be scheduled, which allows various grades to be dismissed for lunch at five- or ten-minute intervals.

Large hospitals have the problem of serving their many patients within a reasonable meal period time-span. Should all be served at approximately the same time as may be possible with decentralized service? Or is a one to two hour time-span acceptable as may be required with centralized service? Various systems meet specific needs.

Space Requirements or Space Available

Allocation of space for departments and their activities is determined at the time of building construction. The delivery-service system preferred should be stated early in the facility planning process so adequate space will be available for those foodservice activities. Any later remodeling to change to a different system can be disruptive and expensive, if possible at all.

Decentralized systems require less space in the main kitchen area but more throughout the facility for the serving pantries than do centralized systems. In hospitals with centralized service, tray assembly equipment as well as trucks or carts take up considerable space. Based on the number and size of the transport carts or trucks, the space needed for their storage when not in use can be calculated. Added spaced must be allocated for moving the carts through the facility with ease.

Energy Usage

A concern for energy use and its conservation plays a role in deciding on a delivery/service system. Systems that utilize a large number of pieces of electrically powered or heated equipment are more costly to operate than those that use the "passive" temperature retention equipment, such as insulated trays or pellet-heated plates.

A report of a research study[3] in 66 New York City hospitals showed that 30 per cent of the hospitals changed their meal delivery systems during the period between 1979 and 1983. There was a trend toward a decrease in decentralized and microwave systems and an increase in insulated tray meal delivery systems that use hot food assembly at a central tray line and transport portioned food in trays designed to maintain food temperatures during transport to the patient. The "active" hot food systems using hot/cold carts and rethermalizing food previously prepared decreased in use. Reasons given for this "switch" to centralized from decentralized service and to the hot food assembly with "passive" temperature retention equipment were to decrease electrical energy consumption, to decrease labor costs and increase manager's control of food and supplies, and to improve the quality of patient food.

Equipment Needs

Delivery and service of food in institutions necessitate the use of specialized equipment for each step of the procedure: reheat if necessary, assemble, transport, distribute, and serve. Every foodservice system has its own requirements. Manufacturers work closely with foodservice directors to design pieces of equipment that will best fill those specific needs. Equipment for delivery and service may be classified in several ways:

- In general: fixed or built in, mobile, and portable
- According to a specific use: reheating, assembling, temperature maintenance holding, transporting, and serving
- For each of the four foodservice systems: conventional, commissary, ready-prepared, and assembly/serve

A brief description of general and specific classification follows for an understanding of the various delivery/service systems in their entirety. For more detailed information about this equipment, see Chapter 10.

General Classification of Delivery/Service Equipment

Fixed or Built In   Equipment that is fixed or built in should be planned for at the time of building a facility as an integral part of the structure.

One such system is the automated cart transport or monorail. This has its own specially built corridor for rapid transit, out of the way of other traffic in the building. It is intended for use by all departments since it is so expensive to install. It can transport items in a few seconds from one part of the building to another and is desirable because of its speed. The carts are not seen while in transit and do not interfere with other traffic in the building. An alternate plan for tray delivery may be needed in case of power failures that could incapacitate the automated tray delivery system.

Other fixed equipment includes: elevators; manual or power-driven conveyors for horizontal movement as for tray assembly; subveyors and lifts (dumb waiters) to move trays, food, or soiled and clean dishes to another level within the facility.

Mobile Equipment   Mobile equipment is equipment that is moved on wheels or casters. This includes *delivery trucks* for off-premises use to transport food from commissary or central kitchen to the meal sites, and for "meals on wheels" delivery to home or offices.

Another type is *movable carts and trucks,* either hand-pushed or mechanized, for on-premises transport of either bulk food for decentralized service or preplated meals for centralized service. Such carts are available in many models, open or closed, insulated or not, temperature controlled for heated or refrigerated units, or combinations of both; see Fig. 7.3 for an example. Some movable carts are designed to accommodate the served plates of hot food as for banquet service, others for entire meals assembled on trays for service in hospitals, and still others for bulk quantities of food. Assembly equipment and galley units are also available as mobile, instead of built in, which permits flexibility of arrangement. An example of a galley is shown in Fig. 7.4.

Portable Equipment   Included in this category are items that may be *carried,* as opposed to mobile equipment that is moved on wheels or casters. For delivery and service, equipment such as pans of all sizes and shapes, many with clamp-on lids to prevent spillage in transit, and hand carriers (also called totes) are commonly used. Totes may be insulated to retain temperature of foods for short-time transport or delivery; see Fig. 7.5.

Also, a variety of plates and trays can keep preplated foods at proper temperatures for service. When these are used, unheated carts can be em-

FIGURE 7.3   Unitray™ is an example of a delivery cart that utilizes a single tray
with a divided design so one section fits into a heated compartment and the other
into a refrigerated unit. Cart is preheated and prechilled before both hot and cold
foods are placed on the solid tray for correct temperature for transport handling.   *Courtesy of United Service Equipment Company, Murfreesboro, Tennessee.*

FIGURE 7.4   Galley station (9½ linear feet) includes flight-type convection oven with capacity for reheating 24 frozen or chilled preplated meals.   *Courtesy of Crimsco, Incorporated, Kansas City, Missouri.*

ployed for transporting meals to consumers. Types of these plates and trays include unitized pellet disc, insulated trays, and dish reheat.

Unitized Pellet Disc. A metal disc (pellet) is preheated and at mealtime is placed in a metal base. Individual portions of hot food are plated and placed over the base and then covered. Either china or disposable dishes may be used. The hot metal pellet generates heat and keeps the meal at serving temperature for approximately 40–45 minutes (Fig. 7.6).

Insulated Trays with Insulated Covers. Insulated trays are designed with a variety of configurations for the differing types of dishes used for the menu of the day. Thermal, china, or disposable dishes may be used. After the food is served, the dishes are placed on the tray and covered with the insulated cover. No special carts are needed to transport these trays as they are nesting and stackable, and, of course, no temperature-controlled units are necessary. Meals in these insulated trays retain heat quite well for short periods of time

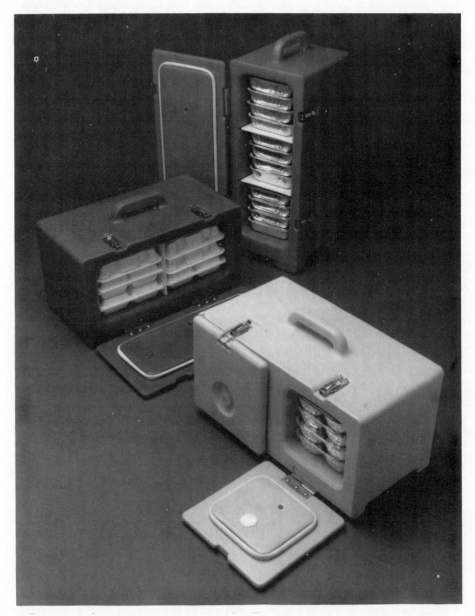

FIGURE 7.5   Portable totes are insulated for holding temperatures for short-time delivery.   *Courtesy of Cambro Manufacturing Co., Huntington Beach, California.*

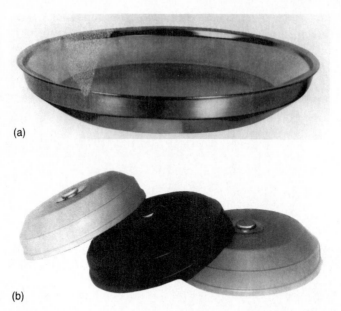

(a)

(b)

FIGURE 7.6 *(a)* Unitized base of pellet system is constructed of two 20-gauge stainless steel shells that are hermetically sealed. Bases are heated in specially designed heater/dispenser before filled dinner plate is set in it and covered. *(b)* Cover for unitized pellet. *Courtesy of Seco Products, St. Louis, Missouri.*

as during transport and distribution. It should be noted that many foods retain heat much better than others under any circumstances.

Specialized Dish Reheat Module. The module is known by various names by different manufacturers. One, called the Integral Heating System, was developed by the 3M Company to be used with the cook-chill production system. Electrical energy is converted to heat through the use of thin film resistors fused to the bottom of individual dishes, which transmit the heat to the food they contain. Hot meals can thus be served on the same dish in which they have been reheated. Dishes for the system are in two parts (see Fig. 7.7a). The interior is porcelain ceramic and the outer section is a high-quality polysulfone plastic shell on which the metal connectors or contact points for the electric current are placed. A resistor is fused to the bottom exterior of the inner dish. The metal connectors on the bottom of the dishes make electrical contact with the rods in the cart (see Fig. 7.7b). Thus, the cart not only transports food, but is a serving cart that provides electrical power to the unique 3M dishes. Virtually no convection heat is generated inside the cart, so cold foods stay cold. These carts may be transported to any area for use and service of meals. Approximately 20–24 chilled meals can be heated in one cart in 18 minutes. This is an energy-saving use of electrical power.

Equipment for Specific Uses

Reheating Frozen or Chilled Foods   Foods prepared, cooked, and then frozen or chilled for later service must be reheated at serving time. This may be done in the central serving area or in serving pantries throughout the facility. Equipment used for reheating in both cases is the same. This includes: convection ovens, conduction (conventional) ovens, microwave ovens, infrared ovens, and the integral cabinets described in the previous section. Also used are immersion equipment (for foods in pouches) such as steam-jacketed kettles or tilting frypans. Microwave ovens are the fastest for single portions, but unless a fleet of these ovens or a tunnel-type microwave is available, reheating a large number of meals may take an overly long time. Convection ovens with the forced air heat can reheat many meals at one time, the number depending on size model selected. Frozen foods usually are tempered in the refrigerator before reheating to reduce time for bringing foods to serving temperature. With any rethermalization system, "the objective is to heat the food product to service temperature and to retain nutrient content, microbial safety, and sensory quality. Prolonged holding should be avoided. The equipment used affects the rate of heat transfer. Microwave ovens, immersion techniques, and convention ovens have been proven effective."[4]

Meal Assembly   The assembling of meals for service is an important step in the delivery/service system. Methods vary for various types of establishment and the activities involved must be suited to the specific needs of each.

Meal assembly is the collecting and putting in one place the various menu items that make up a meal. This may require equipment as simple as a convenient table or counter for bagging or plating the foods cooked behind the counter in a fast food restaurant. In a table service restaurant, servers may pick up the cold foods at one or more stations and hot foods from the chef's station and assemble them all on a tray for service.

The most complex assembly is for tray service for many patients or other consumers. Trays, dishes, silverware, and food are prepositioned along a conveyor belt. Employees are stationed to place a specific item on the tray as it passes along. Conveyors of various types are commonly used for this purpose. All must be sized to the width of the trays used. The simplest is a manual or self-propelling conveyor with rollers that move trays when they

FIGURE 7.7 *(a)* The durable heating/serving dishes of the 3M system are in two parts; two sizes illustrated. Heavy duty thermoplastic covers help retain heat in the dish-ovens after meal is removed from power module. *Courtesy of Medical-Surgical Division/3M, St. Paul, Missouri.*

are pushed from one station to the next. Others are motor driven. Power-operated conveyors may be set at varying speeds for moving trays along the belt automatically; see Fig. 7.8. Conveyors may be mobile or built in.

Temperature Maintenance and Holding   Foods prepared and ready for service often must be held for short periods until needed, while being transported to another area for service, or during the serving period itself. Equipment for this short-time holding includes refrigerated and heated storage units of many types. It should be noted that heated storage cabinets will

FIGURE 7.7 (b) Trays with specialized dish reheat modules are loaded into cart where the dishes make electrical contact with the rods in the cart which heat the food. *Courtesy of Medical-Surgical Division/3M, St. Paul, Missouri.*

not heat the food, but will, when preheated, maintain for short periods the temperature of the food as it was when it was placed in them.

Heated or refrigerated cabinets may be built in, pass through from kitchen to serving areas, or mobile carts and trucks of all types, some designed with both refrigerated and heated sections. Movable refrigerated units are often used for banquet service. Salads and desserts may be preportioned and placed in them in the production area and held until moved to the banquet hall at service time. Likewise, hot foods for large groups may be portioned and placed in preheated carts close to serving time but held until all plates are ready to be served at the same time.

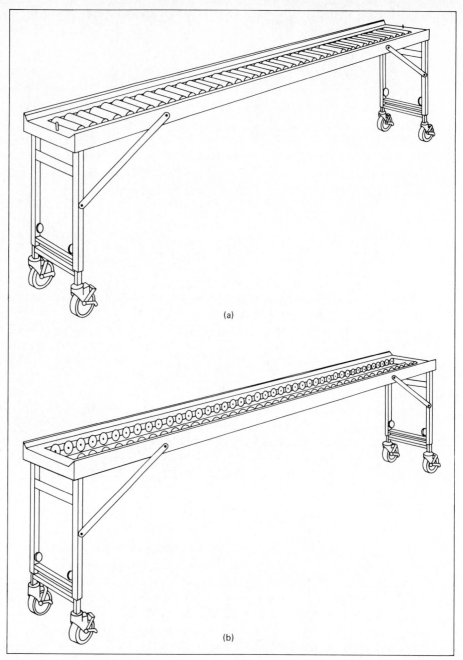

FIGURE 7.8 *(a)* Roller-type conveyor; *(b)* skate wheel conveyor. Both are mobile, stainless steel construction, adjustable in height, and NSF approved. *Courtesy of Precision Industries, Inc., Miami, Florida.*

Infrared lamps are also used to keep certain foods hot on a serving counter during the serving period.

Transporting and Delivery   Equipment for transporting and delivery is described earlier in this chapter under "Mobile Equipment" and Portable Equipment." Open or closed noninsulated carts, including monorail, are used to transport meals served on pellet- or capsule-heated dishes, or placed on insulated trays with covers. Temperature maintenance carts with heated and refrigerated sections or insulated nonheated carts are used to transport meals preplated on regular dishes and placed on noninsulated trays. Other carts are designed with heated wells and compartments for bulk amounts of soup, vegetables, meats, and so forth, as well as for cold ingredients and other food items for meal assembly in another location.

Roll-in refrigerator units serve as transport equipment also with preplated salads and desserts set up in the production area and moved later to the dining areas. Similarly, other mobile serving equipment, such as banquet carts, buffet or catering tables, may serve the dual functions of transporting and serving. Some catering carts for snack items, soups, sandwiches, and beverages are used to take foodservice to workers in plants or office buildings. Insulated totes are inexpensive yet effective means for home delivery of meals.

Many methods and pieces of equipment are available for transporting food from the kitchen to the consumer. The manager must identify the specific needs of the organization when choosing among them. Consideration must be given to the total number to be served; the distance to be traveled between production and service areas; layout of the building with routes including doors, ramps, elevators involved; and the form of food to be transported: hot, cold, bulk, or preplated.

Serving   The style of service (discussed in the next section) also determines equipment needs.

Cafeteria counters of varying configurations and with sections for hot and cold foods, buffet tables with temperature-controlled sections and sneeze guards, and vending machines all provide a means for self-service. Various methods for tray service have been described. The diagram of alternate plans for tray service shown in Fig. 7.9 provides a summary of them.

For dining room table service, trays or carts are used to carry the assembled menu items ordered to the guests. Serving stations, small cabinets often located in or near the dining room, are equipped with table setup items such as silverware, napkins, and perhaps water, ice, glasses, coffee and cups. This speeds service and reduces the distance traveled to serve guests. Other specialized serving equipment is noted under "Styles of Service."

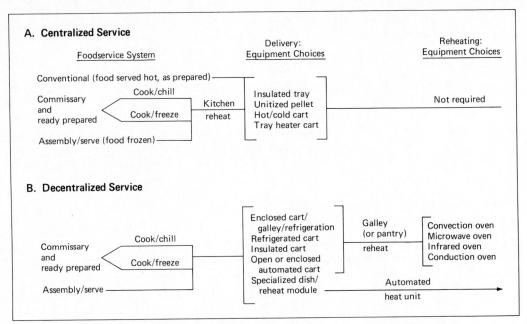

FIGURE 7.9 Alternative systems for food service to patients. *Adapted with permission, from* Food Service Manual for Health Care Institutions *by Mahaffey, Mennes and Miller, copyright 1981 by American Hospital Publishing, Inc., Chicago, Illinois.*

Styles of Service

There are many styles of services, differing widely among institutions, but all with the common objective of satisfying the consumer with food of good quality, correct temperature for acceptability and microbial safety, and attractively served.

The style of service selected, appropriate for a particular type of foodservice operation, should contribute toward reaching those objectives. Also, the style must be economically compatible with the goals and standards of the organization. The basic types or styles of service discussed are:

1. Self-service: cafeteria—traditional, free flow or scramble; machine vended; buffet, smorgasbord, salad bar; and drive-through pickup
2. Tray service: centralized or decentralized

3. Waiter-waitress service: counter, table—American, French, Russian, family, banquet; and drive-in
4. Portable meals: off-premises or on-premises delivery

Self-Service

The simplest provisions for foodservices involves guest or customers carrying their own food selection from place of display or assembly to a dining spot. The best-known example of self-service is the cafeteria, although buffet service with its variations, smorgasbord and salad bars, and vending are also popular.

Cafeteria   Cafeterias are of two types. The *traditional* is where employees are stationed behind the counter to serve the guests and encourage them with selections as they move along a counter displaying the food choices. There are many configurations for counter arrangement, from the straight line to parallel or double line, zigzag, and U-shaped. In each case, however, the patrons follow each other in line to make their selections.

The traditional self-service is used in colleges and other residences, cafeterias open to the public, school lunchrooms, inplant foodservices, and commercial operations. The emphasis is on standardized portions and speedy yet courteous service. The rate of flow of people through the cafeteria line varies according to the number of choices offered and patron familiarity with the setup. From three or four per minute in a commercial cafeteria to 12 to 15 in a school cafeteria with limited choices is typical.

The second type of cafeteria is known variously as the *hollow square, free flow,* or *scramble system.* In this, separate sections of counter are provided for various menu groups, such as hot foods, sandwiches and salads, and desserts. The sections are usually placed along three sides of the serving room, and customers flow from the center to any section desired. This may seem confusing for the first-timer, but it does provide speed and flexibility by eliminating the need to wait in line for customers ahead to be served. Also, it relieves the pressure on those who do not wish to hurry in making decisions. As many as 25 people per minute can be served in this type of self-service unit once the customers have learned the routine. In order to be successful, it is necessary to have repeat business and a mechanism for controlling the number of people who enter at one time. Fig. 9.20 in Chapter 9 shows a diagram of a free flow cafeteria.

Machine Vended   The history of vending dates back as far as 215 B.C. in Greece, but *food* vending began in this country centuries later with penny candy and gum machines. Other items such as cold drinks and coffee soon were dispensed from vending machines. Today a complexity of menu items, enough to make complete meals, are available through vending machines. Some contain heating elements to cook or reheat foods before dispensing them. Others are refrigerated, some low temperature-controlled for holding frozen foods such as ice cream.

Machine-vending foodservice skyrocketed in use and popularity in the 1950s and 1960s as it met a demand for speedy service and for having foodservice available 24 hours a day, seven days a week. Its popularity continues, and today vending is accepted as an important component of the foodservice industry, especially as a means for supplementing other styles of service. Schools, residence halls, hospitals, industrial plants, office buildings, and transportation terminals especially have used this mode of service for coffee breaks, after-meal-hour snacks, and, in some, as the sole means of providing meals. The impersonality of machine-vended food has influenced its acceptance by some individuals who prefer to patronize other types of food services.

Food for the vending machines may be prepared by the institutions using them, or by an outside catering company that delivers fresh foods at frequent intervals and keeps the machines supplied and in good working order. Fast turnover of the food and good supply service are requisites for safety and success of vended foods. Also, the foods offered must be fresh and displayed attractively. Glass-front display cases are far superior to metal-front machines for this purpose. Cleanliness and adherence to city health and sanitation codes are essential. Cooperative efforts by those concerned with packaging, production, merchandising, transportation, storage, and sanitation have brought about improvements in the quality and variety of the food offered and will continue to do so in the future. Another innovation is the "talking" machine, which "communicates" some brief statement to the customer. This may be a trend that will take some of the impersonality out of vended service in days ahead.

Buffet   Buffet service, such as the smorgasbord and the popular salad bar, is a means for dramatically displaying foods on a large serving table. Guests move around the table to help themselves to foods of their choice. Selections usually are numerous and elaborate, and eye appeal is an all-important factor in the foods offered. Foods that "stand up" during the meal hour and the proper equipment to keep them hot or cold as desired are essential to the success of this type of service. One concern that may be met through local health department regulations is for the protections foods on the buffet table against patron contamination. Portable sneeze guards placed around

FIGURE 7.10   Portable food bar with sneeze guard, adaptable for many uses.
Courtesy of Cambro Manufacturing Company, Huntington Beach, California.

the foods give some protection as customers serve themselves. Fig. 7.10 is an example of one type of buffet table.

Drive-Through Pickup   This type of service, popular with fast food establishments to speed customer service, is a variation of the drive-in service. Customers drive through the restaurant grounds in a specially designated lane, make their food selection from a large menu board posted outside, and call their order in through a speaker box (usually next to the menu board). By the time they reach the dispensing window, their order has been assembled and packaged for pick up. Parking facilities may be provided for customers who wish to eat in their cars, or the food is taken elsewhere to be consumed.

Tray Service

Meals and/or snacks that are assembled and carried on a tray to individual consumers by an employee is a type of service provided for those unable to utilize other dining facilities. Airlines, hospitals, nursing homes, and other health care facilities use this method. For persons who are ill or infirm, attractively appointed trays served by pleasant-mannered employees do much to tempt their appetites and help restore health. Airline travelers also appreciate attractive meals served to them in flight and often judge the airline company by the quality of its food and service.

The two types of tray delivery service in hospitals, centralized and decentralized, are described earlier in this chapter. After trays have been transported to serving pantries, they are carried to patients by an employee either of the nursing or dietary department. Good cooperation between the two departments is a prerequisite to coordinate timing for prompt delivery. Delays in getting trays to patients may cause loss of temperature and quality of the food. Thus a major objective of foodservice will not be attained.

Meals for airline foodservice are supplied by the airline's own commissary or on contract from caterers. Foods generally are preplated at the commissary and loaded, either hot or cold, into insulated holding cabinets that are delivered to planes at flight time. Meals loaded hot must be served soon after take-off; those chilled are reheated on the plane in either small convection or microwave ovens. The length of the flight may determine the method to be used for there must be adequate time for reheating all meals. Flight attendants assemble the meals in the galley, placing the hot entree (if one is served) on a tray with cold foods, and hand carry the trays or wheel them down the aisle on carts to serve passengers where they sit. Beverages are distributed in a like manner. Many airlines have expanded the use of cold plates, sandwiches, and snacks on shorter flights, but all continue to use good merchandising techniques to make food attractive and satisfying and so help meet the competition for business among airlines.

Waiter-Waitress Service

Counter   Lunch counter and fountain service are perhaps the next thing to self-service in informality. Guests sit at a counter table that makes for ease and speed of service and permits one or two attendants to handle a sizable volume of trade. Covers are laid and cleared by the waiter or waitress from the back of the counter, and the proximity of the location of food preparation to the serving unit facilitates easy handling of food. The U-shaped counter design utilizes space to the maximum, and personnel can serve many customers with few steps to travel.

Table Service   Most restaurants and hotel/motel dining rooms use more formal patterns of service in addition to the counter service, although both employ service personnel. Many degrees of formality (or informality) may be observed as one dines in commercial foodservice establishments around the world. Generally, there are four major styles of service classified under table service: American, French, Russian, and banquet.

American service is the one generally used in the United States, although all styles are employed to some degree. A maitre d', host, or hostess greets and seats the guests and provides them with a menu card for the meal. Waitresses or waiters, place fresh table covers, take the orders, bring in food from the kitchen serving area, serve the guests, and may also remove soiled dishes from the tables. Busers may be employed to set up tables, fill water glasses, serve bread and butter, and remove soiled dishes from the dining room. Checkers see that the food taken to the dining room corresponds with the order and also verify prices on the bill before it is presented to the guest. Characteristic of this type of service is that food is portioned and served onto dinner plates in the kitchen.

French service is often used in exclusive and high-cost restaurants. It is sometimes considered "old-fashioned" but elegant. In this style, portions of food are brought to the dining room on serving platters and placed on a small heater *(rechaud)* that is on a small portable table *(gueridon)*. This table is wheeled up beside the guests' table and here the chief waiter *(chef de rang)* completes preparation, for example, boning, carving, flaming, or making a sauce. The chief waiter then serves the plates, which are carried by an assistant waiter *(commis de rang)* to each guest in turn. This style is expensive, since two professionally trained waiters are needed to serve properly and extra dining room space is required for the *gueridon*. It is slower than other methods, but gracious and leisurely and much enjoyed by patrons because of the individual attention they receive.

Russian service is the most popular used in all of the better restaurants and motel dining rooms of the world. Because of its simplicity, it has replaced to a high degree the French style that seems cumbersome to many. In Russian service, the food is completely prepared and portioned in the kitchen. An adequate number of portions for the number of guests at the table are arranged on serving platters by the chef. A waiter or waitress brings the platters, usually silver, with food to the dining room along with heated dinner plates and places them on a tray stand near the guests' table. A dinner plate is placed in front of each guest. The waiter then carries the platter of food to each guest in turn and serves each a portion, using a spoon and a fork as tongs in the right hand and serving from the left side. This is repeated until all items on the menu have been served. Although this service has the advantage of speed, one waiter only required, and little extra space needed in the dining room, it has the possible disadvantage that the last person served may see a disarrayed unappetizing serving platter. Also, if every guest orders a different entree, many serving platters would be required.

Family style is often used in restaurants or residences of various types. Quantities of the various menu items, appropriate for the number of guests at the table, are served in bowls or platters and placed on the dining table. Guests serve themselves and pass the serving dishes to the others. This is an informal method that is popular for Sunday "fried chicken dinner specials," for example, and is used in Chinese restaurants for foods that are to be shared, family style. The possible disadvantage is that guests served first may take more than a normal portion, leaving smaller quantities for those who help themselves last. For this reason, it is used less frequently than the other styles of service. (For further details on styles of service, see Martin's *Quality Service* listed in Supplementary References at the end of this chapter.)

Banquet service, unlike other types discussed, is a preset service and menu for a given number of people for a specific time of day. Some items, such as salads, salad dressings, butter, or appetizers, may be on the table before guests are seated. Either the American style or the Russian style may be used.

For American style, dinner plates filled in the kitchen are transported to the guests in one of several different ways: preheated carts are filled with up to 96 plates each and taken to the dining room before guests arrive. Service personnel remove plates from these carts to serve their guests. Another way is for each server to obtain two dinner plates from the serving station, and with one in each hand, go, as a group, to the dining room and serve one table completely. Several trips back and forth are required to finish this service. Still another method is to use busers to carry trays of dinner plates to the dining room, place them on tray stands, and return for another load. Service personnel, working as a team in the dining room, serve the plates as busers bring them in. The head table is served first; then the table farthest from the serving area is served next, so that each succeeding trip is shorter. All guests at one table are served before proceeding to the next table.

The Russian style is used at banquets as described for restaurant service. Sixteen to 20 guests per server is a good estimate for banquet service.

Drive-In   Drive-in service requires waiters or waitresses (carhops) to serve patrons who drive up to the restaurant and remain in their parked cars. The service was most popular in the 1950s and 1960s. Today patrons seem to prefer going into a restaurant instead of eating in their cars. Most drive-ins provide dining space inside. Although many still enjoy good business as they were, others have changed to the drive-through customer pickup method described earlier.

Portable Meal

Off-Premises Delivery   One example of off-premises service is delivering meals to the homes of aged, chronically ill, or infirm individuals not requiring hospitalization. This plan, sometimes called Meals-on-Wheels, attempts to meet the need for nutritious meals for those persons who are temporarily disabled, or for the aged who may live alone and are unable to cook for themselves. In communities where such a plan is in operation, meals are contracted and paid for by the individual in need of the service or by some federal or community agency or volunteer organization for persons unable to pay. Desirably, the menus are planned by a dietitian or nutritionist working cooperatively with the organization providing the meals. Food may be prepared by restaurants, hospitals, colleges, or other foodservices and delivered by volunteer workers. Preplated meals are covered and loaded into some type of insulated carrier (see Fig. 7.5) to ensure food safety while in transit and to maintain desired temperatures until delivered to the home.

A similar service is provided by caterers for workers in office buildings or to customers in their homes by pizza restaurants or others, but on a profit-making basis.

On-Premises Delivery   Another example of portable meals often used in some industrial plants is the distribution of foods to workers at their workplace by mobile carts that move throughout the plant. Carts are equipped with heated and refrigerated sections for simple menu items such as soup, hot beverages, sandwiches, snack items, fruits, and pastries. Workers pay the cart attendant as selections are made. This provides a time-saving service for employees who might have long distances to go to a central cafeteria in a large plant during a short meal period.

An alternate-type portable service is utilized by some companies not having foodservice facilities. That is the mobile canteen provided by a catering firm and driven each day to the yard of the plant. Workers go outside to buy their meals from the canteen truck.

Although variations of these basic styles of service may be found in today's innovative foodservice systems, the types discussed here should provide understanding of the most commonly used service systems.

Merchandising

A not-to-be-overlooked aspect of service of food is that of merchandising— "to promote the sale of." In foodservice this means careful supervision of all steps of preparation and service. But beyond that it calls for creativeness and imagination to plan and present a service that will spark the jaded appetite of an elderly person, coax a schoolchild to try something new, create interest so the ill patient will want to eat, cause a traveler to remember food served on a particular airline, or use an unusual "touch" to reflect the personality of a restaurant and bring return patronage. Food that delights the eye as well as the appetite is the objective.

The final appearance of food when served begins with menu planning, the consideration given to color combinations, shape, and form of items to be served together, and how the food is to be arranged on the plate, serving counter, or buffet table.

Garnishes do much to enhance color and attractiveness of a plate, even the overused parsley sprig or maraschino cherry. Lists of inexpensive and easy-to-prepare garnishes may be compiled for reference use and included on the menu plan so they will not be omitted at service time.

Care given to avoid spillage on the edges of dishes as food is served, or wiping any drips with a clean damp cloth, makes for neatness and attractiveness of the plate. Color coordination of table or tray appointments such as place mats or tablecloths, napkins, and dishes that are in harmony with the environment likewise help to merchandise the food.

More than food quality and appearance, however, merchandising includes the manner in which foods or meals are presented to the consumer by the server. Courtesy and efficiency, a friendly smile, a word of encouragement when needed, and assistance in making selections if called for all add to the guest's sense of complete satisfaction with the meal. A good training program for all service personnel should be provided by every foodservice manager. Objectives are to instill in the employees the importance of a pleasing manner in dealing with the public and to teach correct procedures for serving. These should be a trademark of every foodservice operation.

Summary

The delivery and service of food after it has been prepared are important aspects of the total foodservice system. Consumer satisfaction depends in large part on the pleasing presentation of carefully prepared, assembled, and transported food in every type of foodservice operation.

Foodservice managers should be cognizant of the major goals of delivery and service systems. These goals are to maintain quality food characteristics including desirable temperatures, ensure microbial safety, and present food attractively. In addition, the system selected should save worker steps and energy, reduce labor time and costs, and lessen worker fatigue.

Factors affecting the selection of a particular delivery system, either centralized or decentralized, and therefore the appropriate equipment needed include: the type of foodservice system (conventional, commissary, ready-prepared, or assembly/serve); the type of organization as school, hospital, commercial, or other; the size of physical facilities and amount of space available; the style of service to be used; the skill level of personnel; the labor and equipment costs involved; the quality standards required and desired; the timing for meal service; and the energy usage involved.

The style of service used whether self-serve, tray, or waiter/waitress service must be appropriate for the type of operation and for attaining its goals. Training the workers to use correct serving procedures and to present the food to the consumers in a pleasing and courteous manner also are essential elements in achieving a successful foodservice operation.

Notes

1. Kotschevar, L., and Terrell, M. E.: Foodservice Planning: Layout and Equipment, 3rd ed. New York: John Wiley and Sons, 1985, p. 205.

2. Foodservice Systems: Time and Temperature Effects on Food Quality. North Central Regional Research Publication No. 293. Urbana-Champaign, IL: Agricultural Experiment Station (Illinois Bulletin 779), 1984.

3. Franzese, Rita: Food services survey shows delivery shift. Hospitals 58:61, August 16, 1984.

4. Foodservice Systems: Product Flow and Microbial Quality and Safety of Foods. North Central Regional Research Publication No. 245. Columbia, MO: University of Missouri-Columbia, College of Agriculture, Agriculture Experiment Station (RB 1018), 1977, p. 14.

Supplementary References

MAHAFFEY, MARY J., MENNES, MARY E., AND MILLER, BONNIE B.: Food Service Manual for Health Care Institutions. Chicago: American Hospital Publishing, Inc., 1981, p. 63.

MARTIN, W. B.: Quality Service (The Restaurant Manager's Bible). Ithaca, NY: Cornell Hotel and Restaurant Admin. Quarterly, 1986.

PALMER, J. D.: The logistics of commissaries. Cornell Hotel and Restaurant Admin. Quarterly 25: 104 (May) 1984.

POWER, T. F., AND WILLIAMSON, B. J.: Large Quantity Food Production Systems. In Power, T. F. and Swinton, J. R., eds.: Centralized Foodservice Systems, Service Management Reports. University Park: Pennsylvania State University, 1975.

SCRIVENS, CARL AND STEVENS, JAMES: Food and Equipment Facts: A Handbook for the Food Service Industry. New York: John Wiley and Sons, 1982.

SNYDER, P. O. AND MATTHEWS, M. E.: Effect of hot-holding on the nutritious quality of menu items in food service systems: A review. School Food Service Research Review 8:6 (Spring) 1984.

Your Keys to Energy Efficiency. U.S. Dept. of Energy and the U.S. Office of Consumer Affairs, Washington, DC 20585, 1984.

Physical Facilities

CHAPTER 8

Sanitation and Safety

Introduction

Providing a clean, safe foodservice facility is basic to achieving a successful operation and strategic to the health and well-being of both employees and customers. Also, it contributes to the aesthetic satisfaction that guests derive from dining and gives a feeling of personal security to all.

Sanitation and safety are closely related environmental factors, to be first considered when planning a facility and then followed in its daily operations. Maintaining high standards of cleanliness, making sure that the food served is safe for consumption and that the workplace is free from hazards are management responsibilities.

To help maintain minimum sanitation and safety standards, certain regulations have been established and enforced by city, state, and federal law. Agencies such as the United States Public Health Service (USPHS) and state and city health departments, and organizations such as the National Sanitation Foundation and the National Safety Council recommend standards. Results of research conducted at certain universities, hospitals, food, detergent, and equipment manufacturing companies, and others provide data for recommending or setting standards. These groups, individually or cooperatively, work with the foodservice industry to prepare, distribute, and interpret pertinent information in publications and exhibits. Some present seminars, classes, and programs for various foodservice groups and perhaps for the public. All are aimed at informing concerned persons of the rules, regulations, and standards to be met and/or how to achieve them.

Food safety as an integral part of food purchasing, preparation, and service is discussed previously in Chapters 3, 4, and 5. A brief review of micro-

251

biology involved with food safety and cleanliness, together with sanitation of the facility and its equipment, and the personal safety of workers and guests are discussed in this chapter.

Sanitation

Although many readers will have had a course in microbiology, the application of the principles involved too the operation of a foodservice department cannot be overemphasized. Too many establishments receive poor ratings by health department inspectors because of lack of cleanliness or improper food handling procedures. Reports of outbreaks of food-borne illnesses due to contaminated food or workers continue to appear. Such an outbreak has devastating effects on the reputation of an establishment and possibly on its success or failure. Also, the economic loss associated with food-borne disease outbreaks may be much more startling than most foodservice directors realize. Todd[1] reported an average cost per case of $788 in 17 incidents studied. Loss of business for the foodservice and lawsuits contributed the most to the cost, but loss of income for victims and infected food handlers also was considerable.

The Centers for Disease Control in Atlanta, Georgia, an agency of the United States Public Health Service, is the clearinghouse for receiving reports of food-borne illness outbreaks. These food poisoning incidents are published each week in *Morbidity and Mortality Weekly Report* (see the supplementary references at the end of this chapter).

Foodservice managers should have an understanding of the microbiological aspects involved in such outbreaks and prevent their occurrence, rather than being one of the statistics reported.

Microbiology and Food

Certain organisms such as bacteria, microscopic in size, are able to invade the human body causing more or less severe illness and hazard to life. Since food or contaminated workers are major sources for transmitting the organisms to people, it is essential that foodservice managers understand the conditions involved and insist that employees follow correct procedures to prevent such illnesses from occurring.

Bacteria whose forms are recognizable under the microscope are *cocci*, round in shape; *bacilli*, rod-shaped; and *spirilla*, corkscrewlike. The conditions necessary for bacterial growth are food, moisture, favorable temperatures, and adequate time. Most bacteria grow best in low acid food, a few in acid food. Some grow best if sugar is present in the food, others if proteins are present. Some need air for growth, and others thrive in its absence. The temperature most favorable to the growth of pathogenic bacteria is body temperature of about 98°F; temperatures below 45°F inhibit their growth markedly, and temperatures above 140°F for a period of time are lethal to many varieties of organisms. Time required for growth and multiplication depends on the other conditions present and the type of food. The foods of greatest concern in foodservices are those defined by the US Public Health Service as potentially hazardous:

> Potentially hazardous food means any food which consists in whole or in part of milk or milk products, eggs, meat, poultry, fish, shellfish, edible crustacea, or other ingredients, including synthetic ingredients, in a form capable of supporting rapid and progressive growth of infectious or toxigenic microorganisms. The term does not include clean, whole, uncracked, odor-free shell eggs or foods which have a pH level of 4.6 or below or a water activity (a_w) value of 0.85 or less.[2]

One means of transport or channel by which bacteria are communicated is from person to person through *direct contact*. This direct contact either by carriers or infected persons who harbor the disease-causing bacteria and convey them to other individuals accounts for a large part of the spread of communicable disease. According to the US Public Health Service, there are some 62 different communicable diseases, each caused by a specific kind of organism. A *carrier* is a person who, without symptoms of a communicable disease, harbors and gives off from his or her body the specific bacteria of a disease, usually without being aware of it. An *infected* person is one in whose body the specific bacteria of a disease are lodged and have produced symptoms of illness. Thus, others are aware of the possible danger of contamination.

Another route is the inclusion of fecal matter from an infected person in the water, milk, or other food consumed. Still another path of infection is by drinking raw milk drawn from cows with infected udders. A now rare source of infection is from muscle tissue of hogs infected with the parasitic organism *Trichinella spiralis*.

An infectious disorder of the respiratory system such as the common cold may be spread by the droplet spray of infected discharges of coughing and sneezing without safeguard. An *indirect route* of infection spread through respiratory discharges is the used handkerchief, the contaminated hand, and the subsequent handling of food or plates and cups in serving a patron.

The modes of transmission or locomotion for pathogens as diagrammed by Longree and Blaker are given in Figs. 8.1a and b. It should be noted that human wastes, particularly fecal material, are especially hazardous. An individual who has used the toilet is certain to have contaminated hands. If careful and thorough handwashing is ignored, the worker's hands can be a dangerous "tool" in the kitchen.

Common foodborne diseases are caused either by bacterial *infections* or by food *intoxication* or poisoning. The term "foodborne infections" means an illness caused by the ingestion of harmful living organisms into the body, usually on the food consumed. With "food intoxication or poisoning," however, the bacteria grow on the food prior to its ingestion and produce toxins or poisonous substances that cause the illness. In this case, the microorganisms themselves are not harmful, but the toxins they produce are. Illness occurs more quickly from toxins than from infection from living bacteria, which take a longer time in the body to cause symptoms of illness. In both cases, however, cramps, nausea, diarrhea, and sometimes vomiting will occur.

Microorganisms Causing Foodborne Infections   Primary organisms that cause foodborne infections are salmonellae, pathogenic *Escherichia coli, Vibrio paraehaemolyticus,* and *Campylobacter jejuni.* The first two are especially prevalent and require special care in food handling.

Salmonellae infections account for numerous cases of gastrointestinal disorders. The causative organism may be any one of the 1,300 known serotypes of salmonellae, of which the three most common are *S. enteriditis, S. typhimurium,* and *S. newport.* Infected foods most commonly reported include dairy products, custards, meats, protein salads, and eggs. Contamination of the food may occur through human carriers and animal carriers, including cats, dogs, rats, mice, and pet turtles, or it may result when edible animals infected with salmonellae are slaughtered and their flesh marketed through channels that bypass meat inspection. Milk from cows with udders infected with salmonellae, or eggs from ducks and less frequently chickens may carry the infection to human beings. In countries where duck eggs are used extensively, consumers are urged to cook them well done. A precautionary measure in the United States, even with the pasteurization of egg solids, is the recommendation that dry egg solids be restricted in their use to oven-cooked dishes where the time-temperature relationship is sufficiently high to destroy any salmonellae that might be present.

Pathogenic *Escherichia coli* has been responsible for a number of foodborne illness outbreaks in this country. Imported soft cheese was the cause of the first identified outbreak, occurring in 1971. This organism is found in feces of humans and other animals, and so may contaminate soil, water, and food plants. It is considered a moderate hazard but with potential for extensive

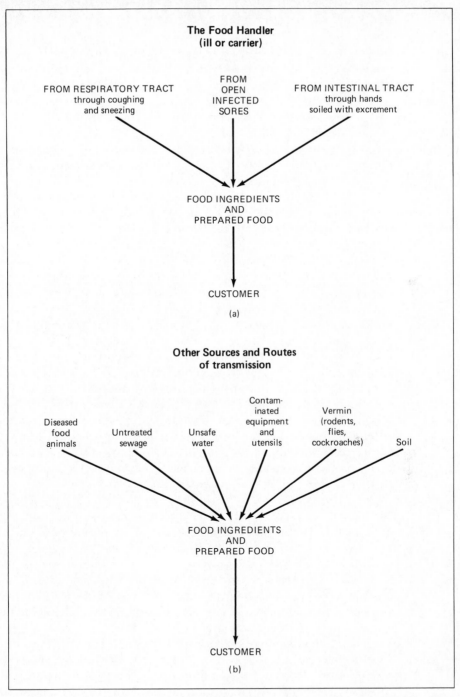

FIGURE 8.1 Transmission of pathogens through food. *(a)* From the food handler, to food, to customer. *(b)* From other sources, to food, to customer. *Reprinted with permission of Macmillan Publishing Company, from Longree and Blaker,* Sanitary Techniques in Food Service, *1982. [Originally published by John Wiley and Sons, Inc.]*

spread. The organism is easily killed by heat, but foods that have been heat-processed may be contaminated after heating, due especially to improper refrigeration and temperature control. In addition to cheese, both raw and processed shellfish, raw ground beef, and inadequately cooked ground beef have caused some outbreaks of gastrointestinal illness due to the presence of pathogenic *E. coli*.

Vibrio parahaemolyticus has been the cause of the majority of foodborne illnesses in Japan, but only in recent years has been recognized as the cause in other countries. Since this microorganism lives in salt water, contamination of fish and shellfish may occur, especially those from warm waters. Most outbreaks have resulted from eating raw or undercooked seafood or cooked seafood that has come into contact with raw products or contaminated containers. At present, *V. parahaemolyticus* gastroenteritis has not been considered a serious health problem in the United States. But if seafood, especially crustaceans, are mishandled during storage, cooking, and holding, the organism will multiply and cause mild abdominal pain, diarrhea, and often nausea and vomiting—all symptoms of various foodborne illnesses in varying degrees of severity.

Another organism, long known as an animal pathogen, has only recently been recognized for its importance and prevalence in human gastroenteritis. It is *Campylobacter jejuni* and is transmitted by the consumption of raw milk, contaminated water, undercooked chicken, beef, pork, and raw clams. Poultry has an especially high carriage rate of this contamination. "While *C. jejuni* is killed by ordinary cooking temperatures, cross contamination from knives or cutting boards onto foods that are not subsequently heated may be a source of contamination."[3] Evidence of the importance of *C. jejuni* is that it is now isolated from human diarrheal stools more frequently in the United States than are salmonella and shigella *spp*.

Microorganisms Causing Food Intoxication or Poisoning

Major organisms that cause food intoxication or poisoning are *Staphylococcus aureus*, *Clostridium botulinum*, and *Colstridium perfringens*.

Staphylococcal food intoxication, the most frequent type of food poisoning, results from the contamination with *Staphylococcus aureus* of menu items high in protein, meat, eggs, milk, and cream pie. This organism is commonly found on the human skin and is abundantly present in pimples and suppurating wounds. Major points of control of this food hazard are to exclude from work any employee with pimples, pus pockets, or suppurating wounds so that gross contamination of food may be avoided, and to keep foods potentially susceptible to the organism under refrigeration. Most reported cases of staphylococcal food intoxication are traceable to violation of one or both of these.

General estimates are that a majority of the cases of "food poisoning" are due to staphylococcal organisms. The illness is not fatal, but causes extreme pain and nausea to its victims for several hours. Usually the symptoms are evident within 1 to 7 hours after the ingestion of the infected food, which may have shown no visible indications of the contamination at the time of consumption.

Clostridium botulinum is a spore-forming organism that causes a far more serious food poisoning, known as botulism. The toxin produced in various media under anaerobic conditions is highly poisonous and usually fatal. Commonly, food contaminated with botulism show more or less marked changes from normal. The toxin can be destroyed by boiling vigorously for 20 minutes. Fortunately, botulinum poisoning is an uncommon occurrence in institution foodservices. Commercially processed foods are usually fully sterilized at high temperatures under pressure. However, the hazard is great enough to stimulate constant watchfulness of food condition and quality. One outbreak in 1978 caused by commercially prepared three-bean salad affected 34 victims. Mann, Lathrop, and Bannerman[4] reported that the resulting expenses exceeded $5.8 million in investigations and control, medical care, and settlements and legal charges. The legal expenses involved (84.4 per cent of the total) make a large societal impact of foodborne illness outbreaks.

Clostridium perfringens, which is an anaerobic, spore-forming bacteria, is often also placed in the group of organisms causing food poisoning. However, the toxin, instead of being present in the food, is produced in the intestinal tract. The incubation period varies between 8 and 20 hours, when illness then occurs.

Clostridium perfrigens is found widely distributed in the soil, water, dust, sewage, and manure, and is also found in the intestinal tracts of humans and healthy animals. Many foods purchased by institutions, especially meats, are probably contaminated with this organism. Also, foodservice workers may carry this organism into the kitchen on their hands. Extreme care must be taken to keep hands and equipment clean, especially meat slicers. Meats to be sliced should never be left to be "cut as needed" over a long serving period. *Clostridium perfringens* grows rapidly, faster than almost any other of the bacteria discussed here. Gravy, a frequent offender, should be held above 140°F.

The diagrams and information in Table 8.1 summarize the three most common of the foodborne diseases, the germ involved, source of contamination, factors that contribute to outbreaks of the illness, and preventive measures to be taken by the foodservice organization. A study of this information will indicate the potential health hazards that foodborne illnesses present. Employees *must* be trained to follow these correct procedures.

TABLE 8.1   Three Most Common Organisms Involved in Foodborne Diseases in Foodservice Establishments

Germ (Disease in parenthesis)	Source	Factor That Contribute to Outbreaks	Preventive Measures
Staphylococcus aureus (Staphylococcal food poisoning)	Workers' noses, hands, hair, intestines, boils Infected sores and cuts	Workers touching cooked foods Keeping food at room temperature Storing foods in large pots in refrigerators Holding foods at warm (bacterial growing) temperatures	Wash hands after coughing, sneezing, smoking, going to the toilet Practice good personal hygiene Cool foods rapidly Put foods in shallow pans in refrigerators Keep cold foods at 45° F or below Keep hot foods at 140° F or above Cover infections with waterproof dressing or band-aid Restrict workers with diarrhea or colds from touching foods
Salmonella (Salmonellosis)	Intestinal tract of man and animals Surfaces of meat and poultry Unpasteurized egg products	Inadequate cooking Cross-contamination of cooked foods from raw foods by contact with common equipment or with hands Keeping food at room temperature Storing foods in large pots in refrigerators Holding foods at warm (bacterial growing) temperatures Inadequate cleaning of equipment Inadequate reheating of cooked foods	Cook foods to internal temperatures of 165° F Use separate equipment for raw and cooked products Cool foods in shallow pans in refrigerators Keep cold foods at 45° F or below Keep hot foods at 140° F or above Reheat leftover foods to 160° F Clean and disinfect kitchen utensils and equipment Wash hands after visiting toilet and handling raw foods of animal origin Restrict workers with diarrhea or fever from touching foods

Germ (Disease in parenthesis)	Source	Factor That Contribute to Outbreaks	Preventive Measures
Clostridium perfringens (Clostridium perfringens gastroenteritis)	Intestinal tract of man and animals Surfaces of meat and poultry Soil Dust	Keeping foods at room temperature Storing foods in large pots in refrigerators Holding foods at warm (bacterial growing) temperatures Workers touching cooked foods Inadequate reheating of cooked foods	Cool foods rapidly Put foods in shallow pans in refrigerators Keep cold foods at 45° F or below Keep hot foods at 140° F or above Reheat leftover foods to 160° F Wash hands after going to toilet, handling raw meat, and doing activities other than food preparation Clean and disinfect kitchen equipment Restrict workers with diarrhea from touching foods

One other type of poisoning that should be included here is chemical poisoning. This results from eating food to which toxic chemicals have been added accidentally. Reports from the Centers for Disease Control for 1981 showed that 20 per cent of all foodborne outbreaks were of chemical etiology. Anderson[5] reported that a number of these health risks were related "to the use and storage of cleansers, food additives, and pesticides. . . . These included monosodium glutimate (MSG), trisodium phosphate, sodium hydroxide, heavy metals, calcium chloride, and cleaning agents. Most were due to storage of cleaners in unlabeled spray bottles."

Achieving Good Sanitation Standards

Many factors, in addition to serving "safe" food, are involved in setting and achieving high standards of sanitation and safety in foodservices. These include the physical plant and provision of supplies, facilities, and services necessary for cleanliness; the personnel and their training in proper techniques to be followed; the cleaning and maintenance of the facility and its equiment; and dish and utensil washing. All contribute to achieving a high degree of success in meeting the standards desired by the organization and its manager. Determining those standards is the first step in control.

The Physical Plant

Built-in Features. Many features that facilitate easy cleaning and maintenance of the foodservice should be built in at the time of construction. These include smooth, nonskid floors with all crevices sealed, and so laid that good drainage after scrubbing is assured, adequate and well placed floor drains, and glazed tile walls or other washable surfacing to make cleaning easy. An adequate ventilating system should be installed as needed with ducts and fans accessible for cleaning. All wiring, pipes, and ducts should be encased, if possible, to prevent having so many areas to clean, as well as to provide the esthetic value of not having them in view.

Water Supply. The adequacy and quality of the water supply available to the institution is of prime concern in the operation of a sanitary foodservice. It is relatively easy to check on the water and its safeness from the reports of the department of health. The adequacy of the hot water supply can be checked against the existing standards of consumption. At least 1.8 gallons should be allowed for each meal served. Food preparation activities require approximately one-fourth of this total, dishwashing takes one-half to one-fifth, and kitchen cleanup takes one-fifth or less. The remainder is spent on hand washing and other sanitation needs. These demands are not made simultaneously, but extend over several hours during which time there will be a number of well-defined peaks.

The source of heat and the capacity of the hot water storage tank determine the quantity of hot water that can be supplied in most small institutions. Rapid heating with a high recovery rate reduces the storage requirement greatly. With a good source of heat a 50-gallon storage tank should supply adequate hot water within the meal preparation, service, and cleanup period to provide a meal for 100 persons. However, the storage capacity of a tank heated slowly must be greater to provide adequately for the same number of patrons, because the recovery rate would be relatively slower. Some type of booster heater system may be installed to ensure a ready supply of water for heavy or unusual demands and when water of a higher temperature than 120 to 140°F is required. Water above this temperature in the pipe lines of a building would be a hazard to the safety of the workers. Larger institutions usually have an unlimited supply of hot water provided by means of the steam heating system.

Other information that may be desired is the relative hardness of the water, since this will have a bearing on the detergents selected and perhaps on the predicted time-span of useful service of necessary equipment such as that in the dishwashing area, most of which is fairly expensive to replace. If the hardness or ratio of carbonates or sulphates to water exceeds the usual maximum tolerance of 250 parts per million, undesirable precipitation may be expected and deposition on equipment will occur. If there is an unpleasant taste or odor, the quality of coffee and other foods may be impaired. If iron and manganese are present in excess, staining and discoloration will occur, with probable alteration in the flavors of food. Any organic matter present should be cause for questioning the safety of the water.

Trash and Waste Removal. Provision for the daily removal of trash and any other wastes not eliminated by mechanical means is essential for good sanitation. Until such disposal is made, garbage should be stored temporarily in metal cans with tight-fitting lids, in a well-ventilated and chilled place. The containers should be scrubbed daily, rinsed, and steam treated to sanitize them.

Sanitary Facilities: Restrooms and Locker Rooms. Adequate sanitary facilities for employees are basic requirements that must be provided in the physical plant of any food or related service. Most states have laws specifying the kind and number of facilities to be provided. Standards generally regarded as reasonable include separate toilet facilities for each sex in the general ratio of one toilet to each 10 or 12 persons; floors of toilet rooms to be of cement or tile laid in cement, or other nonabsorbent materials; toilet rooms to be separate and apart from the space devoted to food production and service, yet of a maximum distance of 150 to 200 feet; all toilet rooms to be adequately equipped with toilet paper and holders, and those for women with sanitary supplies.

Hand washing facilities must be provided in an area adjacent to the toilet rooms and be supplied with running hot and cold water, soap, paper towels, or air-drying blowers. The hot water supply for hand washing should not exceed 120°F (lower than required for dishwashing), otherwise persons could be burned. Toilet and washrooms should have self-closing doors and completely screened outside windows or built-in ventilating fan(s).

Another provision for employee cleanliness and comfort is a locker room for each sex, with ample space for changing clothes and equipped with: individual lockers with locks for storage of uniforms when off duty and street clothes and personal effects while at work; benches to sit on while changing; cots for anyone who may become ill at work and needs to lie down; and an adjacent, fully equipped shower room.

In the kitchen work areas, drinking fountains and additional hand washing facilities, separate and apart from other sinks, are required. They should be so placed as to be readily available to employees in various parts of the kitchen. Only if a lavatory is close to the work station will most employees wash their hands frequently. Otherwise, they tend to use food preparation or pot washing sinks, or go without washing soiled hands, both unsanitary practices. Sinks that are used for washing equipment or utensils or for food preparation should not be used for hand washing.

Equipment: Design and Placement   Each piece of equipment that will come in contact with food should be so designed and constructed that the food contact surfaces are nonabsorbent (like stainless steel), continuous, and smooth, free from open seams, cracks, chipped places, exposed junctions, and sharp corners. All junctions should be rounded or coved. The food contact surface should not only be readily cleanable, but also readily accessible for cleaning.

The National Sanitation Foundation has been instrumental in establishing definite acceptable sanitation standards for materials used in foodservice equipment and for equipment design, construction, installation, and maintenance. These standards, based on scientific research, are agreed on by joint committees made up of qualified representatives from research, industry, education, and the public health profession. Publications are available from the Foundation in which minimum standards are clearly and specifically defined and are adaptable to various geographical areas. Attention will be called to certain of the standards in this text, but each foodservice director should have access to a complete set of the publications for reference. (See suggested references at the end of this chapter.)

Manufacturers who meet the standards are privileged to use the seal of approval of the National Sanitation Foundation (see Fig. 8.2) on their products, and the purchaser is assured of acceptable design, materials, construction, and performance if the equipment is properly installed and operated. Recommended standards give much attention to the proper conditions for installation and use of equipment as well as construction in the factory.

Publicity of the recommended standards is given through publication and distribution of booklets and posters. Local and state public health departments make wide use of the standards in formulating and enforcing codes

FIGURE 8.2   National Sanitation Foundation's seal of approval.

FIGURE 8.3 Simple design and good construction of equipment facilitate ease of maintenance and contribute to beauty of a modern food service. Note equipment is built into the floor or is mounted on wheels.

for physical facilities and the operation of foodservices under their jurisdictions. Emphasis in the work of the NSF is on the positive approach to good health in the prevention of disease through knowledge and practice of high standards of sanitation for the community, especially in the foodservice industry.

The placement of the pieces of large fixed equipment should be determined thoughtfully to allow the worker space for necessary activity and to avoid such things as accident and spillage. Adequate space beneath and behind heavy equipment is necessary for mopping and cleaning if such items are not built into the floor or wall with proper fittings and joinings. Fig. 8.3 is an illustration of equipment of simple design and good arrangement of work to ensure that high sanitation can be maintained.

Personnel Foodservice workers carry a heavy responsibility for the health and well-being of the people they serve. The importance of their own good personal habits and of using correct food handling techniques cannot be overemphasized. An outbreak of foodborne illness among those who eat at a foodservice establishment may result from carelessness of its employees.

Food should be handled only by healthy individuals. Physical and medical examinations may or may not be a requirement in the selection of foodservice workers, although most health authorities require at least tuberculin tests, chest X-rays, and blood tests before issuing any food handlers' permits if and where required. Additional checks depend on the local health service regulations and the individual food operation. Constant observation of the health of employees and attention to their work habits are important functions in supervision. Those who have symptoms of colds, flu, or other communicable illness, such as sore throat, diarrhea, fever, or similar conditions, and those who have acne, boils, "running sores," or any pus-containing lesions should not be allowed to work in food preparation or service areas.

Standards of cleanliness and sanitation will be only as high as those established and enforced by the foodservice director. That person must create the philosophy of good sanitation and impart a sense of urgency about the matter to the employees. This is best accomplished through an intense, ongoing training program for the foodservice workers, organized and led by the foodservice administrators. This assumes that foodservice directors themselves have had some training and are knowledgeable about sanitary procedures and practices advocated in legislative measures and why they are important. In many cities, a formal training program in food protection and safety is mandatory before restaurant operators may obtain a required food sanitation certificate. In certain other cities, voluntary or mandatory certification programs for managers as well as workers have been initiated by state restaurant associations or by the state health department. A large number of foodservice directors have had college courses that teach safe and sanitary food handling procedures. Although not all foodservice directors may feel capable of conducting an employee training program in this area, they can plan for and initiate one.

A *continuous* educational program for foodservice personnel is obligatory if a high standard of sanitation is to be maintained. This program should keep the employees aware of sanitary procedures and practices and why they are important. Also, employees must continually realize the heavy responsibilities that they, as foodservice personnel, assume for the health and well-being of the people to whom they serve food. Keen awareness of the importance of their own good health, personal hygiene, and work habits, and the inherent dangers in improper care and handling of food should be emphasized. The educational program that combines the "why" with the "how to do" is usually a well-organized, systematic, and functioning program. Teaching machines have been used effectively in some organizations for self-learning of the requisite sanitation procedures.

Organized classes in sanitation may be held satisfactorily either within an organization or by an outside agency such as a city health department, and as part of the continuous on-the-job training and supervision. Sessions for presentations to groups of foodservice personnel may be repeated as often as is necessary to give all workers an opportunity to attend, or as refresher courses. The amount of training will be determined somewhat by rate of turnover of personnel and the existing sanitary conditions needing further improvement. The classes should be taught by well-qualified persons who know and can explain the technical phases of the program to the employees on a level that will be meaningful to them. There are many visual aids available in the form of films, slides, and posters that may be used to add interest and emphasis. The National Restaurant Association distributes many such materials. Also, training materials may be obtained from the Centers for Disease Control and from the National Sanitation Foundation, among others. (See supplementary references at the end of this chapter for addresses.)

Topics to be included in a training program or class in sanitation for foodservice workers are those related to the standards desired by the organization. They usually are those discussed in the Foodservice Sanitation Manual:[2]

- *Dress standards:* The wearing of hair restraints by women and men is a protective measure to be observed by all food personnel. Clean aprons, clean uniforms, and comfortable, well-fitted shoes are essential; elimination of jewelry and nail polish and avoidance of excessive makeup are common requirements of the worker.
- *Personal hygiene and cleanliness:* General good appearance includes clean, well-kept nails; clear skin with no pimples, boils, or blemishes; clean teeth; nonoffensive breath; lack of body odors; and freedom from colds or other respiratory difficulties. Hands and the exposed portion of the arms should be washed with soap and warm water on reporting for work and after handling raw poultry and meat, smoking, sneezing, and use of handkerchief, and, above all, after each visit to the toilet.
- *Correct work habits:* Keep work surfaces clean and the work area well organized and orderly so that each part of the work may be carried through to completion without hazard.
- Use only clean utensils in preparing, cooking, and serving food.
- Keep fingers and hands out of food as much as possible. Use spoons, forks, tongs, or other appropriate utensils. Wear disposable gloves for handling food that will not be further cooked before serving.
- Always grasp utensils, such as spoons, spatulas, tongs, and forks, by the handles.
- Pick up and convey glasses by the bases, cups by their handles, and plates

by their rims, being careful to avoid possible contamination of the serving surface.

- Use a clean spoon each time for tasting food; never put a tasting spoon back into a pan of food nor use a stirring spoon for tasting the product.
- Observe "no smoking" rules in all food preparation and serving areas.
- Consume food in designated dining areas only.

After the training sessions, follow-up supervision on the job is necessary to ensure that workers actually understand and observe the procedures taught. Only then will the desired high standards be maintained from day-to-day. See Chapter 4 for a detailed discussion of food handling procedures.

CLEANING AND MAINTENANCE   The total housekeeping and maintenance program of a foodservice department must be planned to reflect concern for sanitation as "a way of life" if this philosophy phrased by the National Sanitation Foundation is to pass from words to reality. Good sanitation results can be obtained through establishing high standards, rigid scheduling of assignments that are clearly understood by the workers, ongoing training, control of cleaning supplies, provision of proper materials and equipment to accomplish tasks, and frequent meaningful inspections and performance reviews.

Organization and Scheduling. The organization of a plan for housekeeping and maintenance begins with a list of duties to be performed daily, weekly, monthly, and occasionally. Most organizations believe that "sanitation is a part of every person's job," and that daily cleaning of the equipment and utensils used by each person is that person's responsibility. General cleaning of floors, windows, walls, lighting fixtures, and certain equipment is assigned to cleaning personnel. These tasks can be scheduled in rotation so a few of them are performed each day; at the end of the week or month, all will have been completed and the worker then repeats the schedule. Fig. 8.4 gives an example of such a schedule. Each of the duties on the schedule list must be explained in detail on a written work sheet or "job breakdown" for the employee to follow. This description is the procedure that management requires to be used in performing each task. The job breakdown includes the name of the task, tools, equipment, and materials to be used, and the step-by-step list of *what to do* and *how to do* it. Fig. 8.5 is an example of such a job breakdown. Longree and Blaker present a slightly different format with procedures for cleaning some 40 pieces of kitchen equipment (see the supplementary references at the end of this chapter.)

In addition to establishing procedures, a time standard for accomplishing each task is important. Based on studies of the actual time required for performing the same tasks by several different workers, an average time stan-

---

Typical Job Assignments for Heavy-duty Cleaner

MONDAY Filter grease in snack bar
Clean left side of cafeteria hot-food pass-through
Clean all kitchen windows
Clean all kitchen table legs
Vacuum air-conditioner filters; wipe exterior of air conditioner
Wash all walls around garbage cans
Complete high dusting around cooking areas
Clean outside of steam kettles
Wash kitchen carts
Clean cart-washing area

TUESDAY Snack bar: Wash inside of hood exhaust
Clean all corners, walls, and behind refrigerator
Empty and clean grease can
Wash garbage cans
Main range area: Clean sides of ovens, deep-fat fryers, grills, drip pans, and hood over ovens

WEDNESDAY Clean two refrigerators in cooks' area
Clean right side of cafeteria hot-food pass-through
Clean kettles, backs of steamers, and behind steamers
Clean walls around assembly line and pot room

THURSDAY Clean all ovens in cooks' area, bottoms of ovens, and between ovens and stoves
Clean long tables in cooks' area, including legs and underneath
Clean and mop storage area

FRIDAY Clean stainless steel behind kettles and steamers
Clean main range and tops of ovens
Clean legs of assembly line tables
Clean vents in all refrigeration equipment
Clean cart-washing area

FIGURE 8.4   Certain weekly or monthly tasks are scheduled, a few each day, for balanced workload and completion of all such tasks within the time frame of the rotation period.

dard may be set. This is used to determine labor-hour requirements for each department within the foodservice and also provides management with data to establish a realistic daily workload. A chart stating the task, cleaning method to be used, the time standard for doing it, the number of the same items to

How to Clean a Food Slicer

Equipment and supplies needed:
  Three cloths:
    One to wash
    One to dry
    One to apply rust preventative
  One-gal container for detergent
  One container with sanitizer
  One table knife

Cleaning products needed:
  Hand detergent
    In amount needed to make one gal of solution
    Usual proportion: 1 oz to 1 gal of water
  Sanitizer:
    Usual proportion: 2 oz chlorine to 1 gal water
  Rust preventative:
    In amount needed to moisten cloth for application of thin film to specified metal surfaces

Approximate time: 20 min
Frequency of cleaning: Daily, after each use.
Approximate cost: Labor _____
                  Supplies _____

What To Do	How To Do It
1. Remove parts	1. *a.* Remove electric cord from socket.
	b. Set blade control indicator at zero.
	c. Loosen knurled screw to release; remove meat holder and chute.
	d. Grasp scrap tray by handle; pull away from blade; remove.
	e. Loosen bolt at top of knife guard in front of sharpening device; remove bolt at bottom of guard; remove guard.
	f. Remove two knurled screw nuts under receiving tray; remove tray.
2. Clean knife	2. *a.* Wash circular surface with hot hand-detergent solution; rinse; dip in sanitizing solution; dry. DANGER: Keep clear of knife edge.
	b. Wring out cloth dipped in hot detergent solution, bunch thickly and wipe entire circumference of blade, wiping from center toward edge of blade; rinse; dip in sanitizing solution; dry with bunched cloth.
3. Clean and replace guard	3. *a.* Wash knife guard in hot detergent solution; rinse; sanitize; dry.
	b. Replace knife guard.

What To Do	How To Do It
	c. Tighten bolt at top; insert and tighten bolt at bottom. DANGER: Replace knife guard as quickly as possible to prevent injury.

4. Clean other parts	4. *a.* Immerse in hot detergent solution:
	        1. Meat holder and chute.
	        2. Receiving tray.
	    b. Wash; rinse, sanitize; dry.

5. Clean beneath receiving tray	5. *a.* Wash surface below receiving tray with hot detergent solution; rinse; dry. *b.* Apply *very thin* film of rust preventative to any exposed metal *under* receiving tray.
6. Clean frame and base	6. *a.* Wash frame with hot detergent solution, rinse, dry. *b.* With table knife, push damp cloth under knife of slicer; pull cloth through to remove food particles.

7. Replace parts	7. *a.* Replace meat holder and chute; tighten knurled screw.
	    b. Replace scrap tray.
	    c. Replace receiving tray; replace and tighten two screw nuts under tray.

FIGURE 8.5   A Job Breakdown is prepared by managers detailing correct procedures, one for each task performed, and are used as a tool for training employees.

be cleaned, total time required, and cleaning frequency is used for calculating the labor-hour needs. Fig. 8.6 illustrates such a chart. The chart can be used for budgetary calculations and needs as well as for number of employees or labor-hours required.

Equipment. Heavy-duty power equipment is available to foodservice managers to aid in keeping the facility clean and properly maintained. Mechanical food waste disposers, indispensable in most foodservices, eliminate the need for garbage cans, which may become unsightly and difficult to keep clean. Disposers are located advantageously where food waste originates in quantities as in vegetable and salad preparation units, main cooking areas, and the dishwashing room. In the latter, a disposer may be incorporated as a part of the scraping and prewash units of the dishwashing machine.

Compactors and can and bottle crushers (Fig. 8.7a and b) reduce appreciably the volume of trash, including items such as disposable dishes and tableware, food cartons, bags, and crates. (See Chapter 10 for details of this equipment.)

WORK LOAD DETERMINATION FORM

AREA _PROB MGMT. DEPT. 1570 SQ.FT._   QUALITY STANDARD _88_

ITEM TO BE CLEANED	CLEANING METHOD (DESCRIBE)	STANDARD TIME PER ITEM	AMOUNT OR NUMBER OF THE ITEM	TOTAL TIME (MINUTES)	CLEANING FREQUENCY	YEARLY TIME (HOURS)
WASTE BASKETS	EMPTY	17 SECONDS	15	4.3	DAILY	18.6
ASH TRAYS	EMPTY & DAMP WIPE	10 SECONDS	11	1.8	DAILY	7.8
STD. DESK GROUP—	DUST—WHISK	42 SECONDS	12	8.4	DAILY	36.4
DESK, CHAIR,	UPHOLSTERED CHAIRS					
TELEPHONE,						
MAIL BASKET, FILE						
ASPHALT TILE FLOOR	DUST MOP	8 M/1000	1570 SQ.FT.	12	DAILY	52
ASPHALT TILE FLOOR	COMPLETE BUFFING	20 M/1000	1570 SQ.FT.	30	WEEKLY	25
PROJECT WORK	WAXING,	7 M/1000	1570 SQ.FT.	11	DAILY	47.6
	FURNITURE WASHING,					
	SPOT WASHING, ETC.					

TOTAL YEARLY TIME (Area Work Load):

FIGURE 8.6   Example of method for charting work loads and time standards for specific jobs; used as a basis for determining labor-hour requirements.

Scrubbing/waxing machines are used for cleaning both kitchen and dining room floors and are available in many sizes and models. Adequate drains in the kitchen floor are essential for proper sanitizing.

Care of equipment used in food preparation, storage, and service is an essential part of the maintenance program to ensure good sanitation. All containers and utensils must be cleaned thoroughly after *each* use. This is especially true of meat grinders and slicers, cutting boards, and knives in order to prevent any cross-contamination and ensure safety against *Campylobacter perfringes, C. jejuni*, and salmonellae.

The thorough cleaning and sanitizing of stationary equipment are more difficult but quite as necessary as is the cleaning of dishes and small portable equipment. No piece of large equipment should be purchased unless the operating parts can be disassembled easily for cleaning purposes. Dishwashing machines, mixers, peelers, slicing machines, and stationary can openers are examples of equipment that should be cleaned after each use. The standard practices for hand dishwashing should be followed in the routine cleaning of such equipment. An example of the detailed daily care necessary for one piece of equipment is shown in Fig. 8.5.

Detergents. The selection of a compound to aid in cleaning the many types of soil and food residues is a complex one because so many compounds are available from which to choose. An understanding of the basic principles involved in cleaning will assist the foodservice manager in making this decision.

Detergents are defined as cleansing agents, solvents, or any substances that will remove foreign or soiling material from surfaces. Specifically listed are water, soap, soap powders, cleansers, acids, volatile solvents, and abrasives. Water alone has some detergency value, but most often it is the carrier of the cleansing agent to the soiled surface. Its efficiency for removing soil is increased when combined with certain chemical cleaning agents.

The three basic phases of detergency are penetration, suspension, and rinsing. Following are the actions and agents required for each phase.

1. Penetration: The cleaning agent must penetrate between the particles of soil and between the layers of soil and the surface to which it adheres. This action, known as *wetting*, reduces surface tension and makes penetration possible. Agents are: water, soaps, and synthetic detergents, which are rather fragile suds formers.
2. Suspension: An agent is required to hold the loosened soil in the washing solution so it can be flushed away and not redeposited. Agents (vary according to type of soil) are: *For sugars and salts,* water is the agent since these are water-soluble and are easily converted into solutions. *For fat* particles, an emulsifying action is required to saponify the fat and carry it away. Soap, highly alkaline salts, and nonionic synthetics may be used. *For protein* particles, colloidal solutions must be formed by *peptizing* (known also as sequestering or deflocculating). This action prevents curd formation in hard water, which settles out as a "ring" and leaves glassware dingy. Sudsy water, solvents, and sometimes abrasives are needed.
3. Rinsing: The agent used must remove and flush away soils and cleaners so they are not redeposited on the surfaces being washed. Agents: clean, clear, hot water is usually effective alone. With some types of water, a *drying* agent may be needed to speed drying by helping the rinse water drain off surfaces quickly. This eliminates alkaline and hardwater spotting, films, and streaks on the tableware or other items being cleaned.

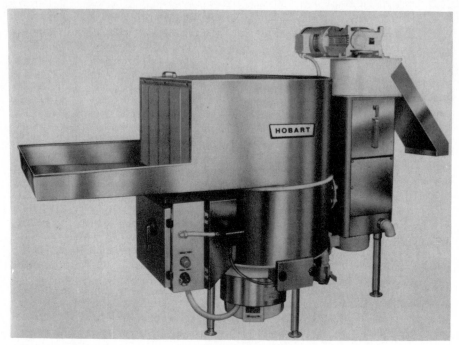

FIGURE 8.7   *(a)* Trash compactor. Courtesy of Hobart Corporation, Troy, Ohio.   *Courtesy of Lois Jackson.*

Basic alkalis such as caustic soda and soda ash produce saponification, but they have poor water-softening and rinsing qualities and high corrosive properties. The addition of sodium metasilicate improves the cleansing power and reduces the corrosive qualities. Trisodium phosphate makes a good cleaning solution and acts as a water softener, but it precipitates the calcium and magnesium salts in the water as a film on surfaces. None of these alkalis has complete satisfactory rinsability, and all are harsh to the hands.

The development of polyphosphate detergents has provided a wide variety of highly satisfactory cleaning compounds. Film deposit from precipitation, poor rinsability, and harshness to hands no longer are problems, and the selection of cleaners can be made to meet the needs for particular uses in the institution foodservices; for instance, a suds-producing hand wash with high wetting action would be satisfactory as such but entirely unsatisfactory for machine dishwashing where a nonsuds-producing detergent is needed.

Certain of the detergents have nontoxic germicidal properties, and some operate best at a relatively low temperature, because their solubility decreases with increased temperature. However, heat hastens action and makes

FIGURE 8.7   *(b)* Under counter model, Hobart's Ecolo-Line™ waste equipment system installed at Louisiana State University Medical Center. *Courtesy of Lois Jackson.*

most detergents more effective. Synthetic detergents are classified according to the production of electrically negative (anionic) or positive (cationic) charged, or neutral (nonionic) organic particles in water. The cationic synthetics are usually good bactericides, but some have limited detergency values. The quarternary compounds come within this group. The nonionics are often in liquid form and are good wetters. There seems to be no perfect product for all conditions of use.

Selection of the right detergent for the job of cleaning in any situation is determined in large measure by the hardness of the water. The sequestering of the lime and magnesia of hard water by the polyphosphates produces a clear, not muddy, solution with insoluble precipitates, as is the case when some of the phosphates and silicates are used.

Foodservice sanitation is concerned mainly with china, crockery, glass, and metal surfaces. Common soils to be removed are saliva, lipstick, grease, and carbohydrate and protein food particles that may adhere to dishes, glassware, silverware, cooking utensils, worktable tops, floors, or other surfaces. Some types of food soil such as sugars, starches, and certain salts are water soluble. The addition of a wetting agent to hot water will readily remove most of these simple soils. The soils that are insoluble in water, such as animal and vegetable fats and proteins, organic fiber or carbon residues, and mineral oil, are more difficult to remove. Abrasives or solvents may be necessary in some cases to effect complete cleanliness.

The use of a "balanced" detergent or one with a carefully adjusted formula of ingredients suitable for the hardness of the water and the characteristics of the soil is advised in order to produce the best results. The properties of the detergent must cause complete removal of the soil without deposition of any substance or deleterious effect on surfaces washed.

Detergents for *dishwashing machines* must be a complex combination of chemicals that will completely remove the soil in a single pass through a high-speed machine. It must soften the water, solubilize and emulsify greases, break down proteins, suspend soil, protect the metal of the machine, increase wetting action, and counteract minerals in the wash water. Other characteristics desired in some situations are defoaming action where excess sudsing is a problem, and chlorination action where a chlorine-type detergent is used to remove stains and discolorations.

It is the phosphate in dishwashing compounds that reacts with the minerals in the water. Many different types of phosphates are used, from the crude ones, such as trisodium phosphate, and the more refined, such as pyrophosphates; but the most efficient is the highly refined polyphosphate ingredient that completely cancels out the mineralization of the water and "conditions" water in the wash tank for the cleansing task.

Managers responsible for purchasing dishwashing and other cleaning compounds should be aware of the chemicals they contain and the suitability for use in a particular situation. The effectiveness of the product instead of the price should be the primary factor in the selection of any cleaning compound. In evaluating the cost of a rinse agent, for example, consider the concentration required (parts per million) for effective drying in relation to the price to get a true usage cost.

The quality of service offered by the company selling detergents is an important factor in selecting a particular brand. Sales representatives know their products' capabilities and can give good assistance in selection of items for the foodservice's specific needs. For example, the salesperson should know as much or more about the operation of various dishwashing machines than do the managers. Since the company representative is accustomed to making quantitative and qualitative tests under differing circumstances and conditions, that person can wisely recommend the amounts of a compound to use. Since it is to the company's advantage to have its products do the best job possible, the representative will not want to recommend using too much as it may be an ineffective as too little.

Dishwashing machines should be equipped with automatic detergent dispensers. Also, a water softener more than pays for itself and is recommended for use in hard water areas.

Rodent and Insect Control. The importance of rodent and insect control cannot be minimized. Rats, mice, flies, roaches, grain insects, fruit flies, and gnats all facilitate the transmission of communicable disease; therefore, it is essential for any foodservice to try to effect complete elimination of resident pest infestations and then to correct conditions within the establishment so that such pests cannot gain entrance in the future.

Two conditions, food and a place to "harbor" or hide and live, are required for these pests to survive. Adherence to strict rules for proper food storage and maintenance of high standards for cleaning the nooks and corners, such as drawers in cooks' tables, around sink pipes and drains, as well as the general overall sanitation and cleaning program, provides good preventive maintenance against pests.

Many roaches and insects gain entrance to a building on incoming foodstuffs and packages, which makes their control difficult. Their reproduction is rapid, and they thrive in the warm, damp hiding places afforded in many foodservices. Screens to help keep out flies, covered trash and garbage cans, closed cracks and crevices in walls and around equipment and areas around pipes, and clean storerooms are preventive measures to try to block the entrance and reduce the hiding places of such pests. The use of certain residual insecticides is effective treatment when there is no danger of polluting food, whereas the use of less toxic insecticides is recommended for contact spraying.

Ratproofing the building to make it impossible for rodents to gain entrance is the best preventive measure for making it free of the rodents. This means the closing of openings as small as one-half inch in diameter, placing rat guards on all wires on both inside and outside of pipes leading into the building, and careful joining of the cement walls and foundations of the building. Trapping and the use of rodenticides are part of a rodent-control program and are used either inside or outside the building. However, the most effective rodenticides are also the most dangerous to humans and pets; therefore, they must be used with care and caution.

Constant attention and alertness to signs of the intruders and an effective program for their destruction by a trained person within the organization or an outside agency are usually required. Specialized entomological services may be scheduled, as often as once a month. The effectiveness of such an effort depends on its scope, regularity, and intelligent administration of a cleaning program and proper care of foodstuffs to eliminate the environmental factors conducive to the harboring of pests.

DISHWASHING/WAREWASHING   Dishwashing requires a two-part operation, that is, the cleaning procedure to free dishes and utensils of visible soil by scraping or a water flow method, and the sanitizing or bactericidal treatment to eliminate the health hazard. Dishwashing for pubic eating places is subject to rigid regulations.

The two groups of equipment and utensils that are commonly considered for discussion under dishwashing are: kitchen utensils, such as pots, pans, strainers, skillets, and kettles soiled in the process of food preparation, and eating and drinking utensils, such as dishes, glassware, spoons, forks, and knives.

Kitchen Utensils. Mechanical pot and pan washing equipment is relatively expensive; therefore, in many foodservices this activity remains a hand operation. A three-compartment sink is recommended for any hand dishwashing setup (see Fig. 8.8). Public health authorities recommend that sinks used for manual washing and sanitizing operations be of adequate length, width, and depth to permit the complete immersion of the equipment and utensils.

The soil may be loosened from the utensils by scraping and then soaking them in one compartment of the sink, well filled with hot water, previous to the time of washing. A forced-flow pump system unit, such as shown in Fig. 8.9, facilitates the cleaning of pots and pans. It can be installed onto the end of any sink and is relatively inexpensive to install and operate, and highly effective in the loosening and removing of cooked-on food.

After the surface soil has been removed from the utensils, the sink is drained and refilled with hot water to which a washing compound is added. The utensils are washed in the hot detergent solution in the first compartment; rinsed in the second compartment, the outlet and inlet of which are so ad-

FIGURE 8.8   Three-compartment stainless steel pot and pan sink with sliding platform. Note rounded corners for ease of cleaning and good sanitation.   *Courtesy of S. Blickman.*

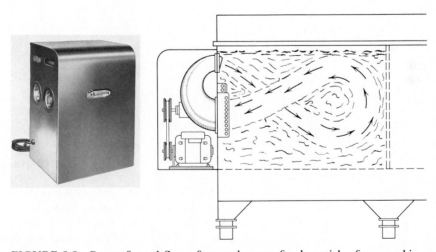

FIGURE 8.9   Pump-forced flow of water loosens food particles from cooking utensils in a pot and pan sink. Easily installed on end of sink.   *Courtesy of Kewanee Washer Corporation.*

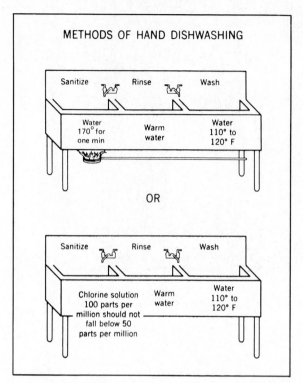

FIGURE 8.10 Sink arrangement and U.S. Public Health Service recommended temperature and sanitizing methods for hand dish or pan washing.

justed as to keep the water level constant if hot water is kept running throughout the process; and sanitized in the third compartment.

There are several methods for sanitizing both dishes and utensils. One recommended method is by immersing them for at least one minute in a lukewarm (at least 75°F) chlorine bath containing a minimum of 50 ppm available chlorine. Dishes and utensils must be thoroughly clean for a chlorine rinse to be an effective germicidal treatment. Another method of sanitizing hand-washed dishes or utensils is immersion in clean soft water of at least 170° for one minute. When hot water is used for sanitizing, an integral heating device or fixture must be installed in, on, or under the sanitizing compartment of the three-unit sink. The water may be heated by a booster heater on the hot water line or by a thermostatically controlled heater arrangement, by burners placed directly under the sink compartment (see Fig. 8.10), or by installation of steam injectors into or closed coils within the vat.

Utensils also may be successfully sanitized by subjecting them to live steam in an enclosed cabinet after washing and rinsing (see Fig. 8.9). The steam must be free of materials or additives other than those specified by the USPHS,[2] Section 5-103. The hot, clean utensils should be air-dried before stacking upside down on racks or hanging for storage.

Dishes, Glassware, Silverware. Washing of these items may be accomplished by hand or by use of mechanical dishwashers. Steps for these are outlined in Figs. 8.11, 8.12. In either case, *prewashing* or *preflushing,* which applies to any type of water scraping of dishes before washing, is recommended to prevent food soil in the wash water. The usual types of water scraping equipment include: (1) a combination forced water stream and food waste collection unit built into the scraping table, by use of which dishes are rinsed under the stream of water before racking, (2) a hose and nozzle arrangement over a sink for spraying the dishes after they are in racks, and (3) a prewash cabinet through which the racks of soiled dishes pass and are jet-sprayed to remove food particles prior to their entering the wash section of the dishwashing machine (see Fig. 9.18 in Chapter 9). The prewash cabinet may be built in as a part of the large model machines or, in small installations, may be a separate unit attached to the wash machine in such a way that the water used is the overflow from the wash tank. The prewash water should be at a temperature of 110 to 140°F to provide for the liquefying of fat and the noncoagulation of protein food particles adhering to dish surfaces. The installation and use of a prewash system lessens the amount of organic waste and the number of microorganisms entering the wash tank, removes fat that might otherwise result in suds formation, reduces the number of washwater changes, cuts the costs for detergents, and results in cleaner dishes.

There are many dishwashing machines on the market. Various types are discussed in Chapter 12, but Fig. 8.13 illustrates the general principles of *how* dishes are washed in a single-tank, spray-type machine. Large machines have divided tanks (Fig. 8.14) so that the wash and rinse waters are kept separate and the dilution of the wash water is less rapid.

After the prerinse, the dishes are loaded into racks or on conveyor belts in a way that food-contact surfaces will be exposed to direct application of the wash water with detergent and to the clean rinse waters. Cups, bowls, and glasses must be inverted and overcrowding or nesting of pieces avoided if dishwashing is to be effective. Wash water shall not be less than 120°F, and if hot water is the sanitizing agent, the rinse water shall be 180°F. The pressure of the rinse water must be maintained at a minimum of 15 pounds per square inch (psi) but not over 25 psi to make the sanitizing effective.

China, glassware, and silver may be washed in the same machine, but it is preferred wherever possible to subject glasses to friction by brushes so that

HAND DISHWASHING

Important Steps (in Doing the Job)	Key Points [a]
1. Get ready (materials and equipment)	Sinks Hot water Washing powders (chlorine, or other bactericidal treatment, if used) Scraper Garbage can Drying racks
2. Scrape dishes and prewash	Use scraper Garbage in can or disposer
3. Wash dishes	Each piece separately Hot water, 110–120° F Use detergent (washing powder)
4. Rinse	Place in basket Set in hot rinse water
5. Sanitize	Place basket in vat In hot water (170° F for one min or 212° F for 30 sec) [b] 2 min in chemical solution (chlorine of approved strength)
6. Dry	Lift out basket Place on drain board Air dry
7. Store	Cups and glasses bottoms up Stack dishes on mobile carts In clean protected place
8. Clean vats	Stiff brush Washing powder
9. Use separate baskets for dishes, cups, and glasses	
10. Silver may be air-dried or by use of clean towel	
11. Fingers should not touch surfaces which come in contact with food or drink	
12. All multiservice eating and drinking utensils must be thoroughly cleaned after each usage	
13. Single-service containers must be used only once	

[a] Key points are those things which will make or break the job, injure the worker, or make the job easier to do.
[b] This standard may vary with local or area regulations.

FIGURE 8.11   Job breakdown details procedure for hand dishwashing.

MACHINE DISHWASHING

Important Steps (in Doing the Job)	Key Points[a]
1. Get ready (materials and equipment)	Sort dishes, cups, glassware, and silver Water temperature: 140° F wash, 170° F rinse [b] Check washing powder and dispenser, wash and rinse sprays
2. Scrape and prerinse	Use brush to scrape off garbage
3. Rack dishes, etc.	Place in separate racks Do not pile dishes, cups, etc. Cups and glassware bottoms up One kind at a time, separately
4. Place racks in machine	Every dish, etc., under spray
5. Wash	Start machine Turn on wash spray 140° to 160° F Do not hurry machine if it is manually operated Keep washtank water clean
6. Rinse	10 sec 170° F [b]
7. Dry	Remove racks Allow dishes, etc., to dry in racks on drain table or if flight type machine, do not remove dishes before they reach end of conveyer
8. Store	Fingers should not touch surfaces which come in contact with food In a clean, dry place above floor Away from dust and flies Dishes stacked Cups and glasses bottoms up—leave in racks in which they are washed
9. Clean machine	Take out scrap trays and clean Clean wash sprays Use clean water Add new washing powder as required

[a] *Key points are those things which will make or break the job, injure the worker, or make the job easier to do.*
[b] *This means temperature of 170° F at the dish, and requires 180° F water in the line. This standard may vary with local or area regulations.*

FIGURE 8.12   Job breakdown details procedure for machine dishwashing.

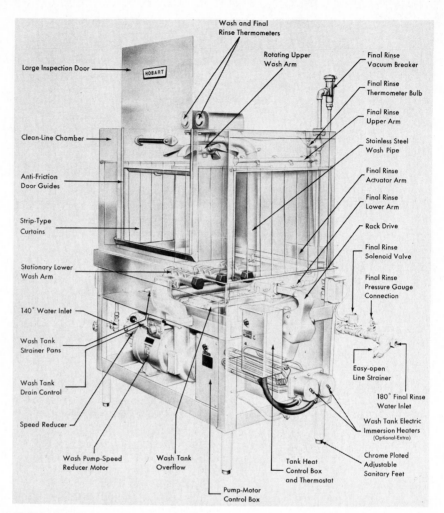

Wash and Final
Rinse Thermometers

Large Inspection Door

Rotating Upper
Wash Arm

Final Rinse
Vacuum Breaker

Final Rinse
Thermometer Bulb

Clean-Line Chamber

Final Rinse
Upper Arm

Stainless Steel
Wash Pipe

Anti-Friction
Door Guides

Final Rinse
Actuator Arm

Final Rinse
Lower Arm

Strip-Type
Curtains

Rack Drive

Final Rinse
Solenoid Valve

Final Rinse
Pressure Gauge
Connection

Stationary Lower
Wash Arm

140° Water Inlet

Wash Tank
Strainer Pans

Easy-open
Line Strainer

Wash Tank
Drain Control

180° Final Rinse
Water Inlet

Speed Reducer

Wash Tank Electric
Immersion Heaters
(Optional-Extra)

Wash Pump-Speed
Reducer Motor

Wash Tank
Overflow

Tank Heat
Control Box
and Thermostat

Chrome Plated
Adjustable
Sanitary Feet

Pump-Motor
Control Box

FIGURE 8.13   Design and identification of parts of a single-tank dishwashing machine.   *Product of Hobart Corporation, Troy, Ohio.*

all parts of the glass are thoroughly cleaned, which means the use of a special machine designed for that purpose (Fig. 8.15). This is especially important in soda fountains, bars, and similar establishments where glasses are the primary utensils used. To prevent water spotting, it is advisable to use a suitable detergent for the washing of silver and also a drying agent with high wetting property in the final rinse water to facilitate air drying. The intro-

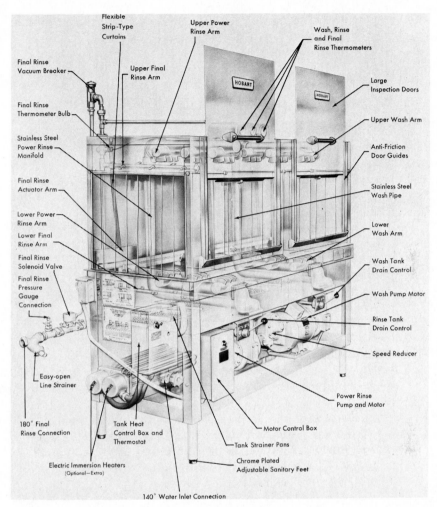

FIGURE 8.14 Phantom view of a two-tank dishwashing machine and identification of ports. *Product of Hobart Corporation, Troy, Ohio.*

duction of a drying agent with low foam characteristics into the sanitizing rinse promotes rapid drying of all types of tableware.

Provision for the storage of clean glasses and cups in the racks or containers in which they have been washed reduces the possibility of hand contamination.

Some machines are designed for a chemical solution rinse rather than the

FIGURE 8.15   Glasswasher installed for convenient use in a back-counter unit.

high-energy use of the 180°F temperature water. In this case the rinse water used with the chemical sanitizer shall not be less than 75°F nor less than that specified by the manufacturer. Chemicals used for sanitizing shall be dispensed automatically to make sure that the proper amount and concentration are used.

Dishes can be dried by hot air blast within the machine or allowed to air dry. If the hot water rinse is used, dishes should be hot enough to air dry within a minimum of 45 seconds before they are removed for storage.

Unklesbay and Unklesbay[6] note a high-energy usage in mechanical dishwashers. All steps require energy except air drying. For this reason, the low-temperature models are preferred by many operators. To minimize energy use, only fully loaded racks or conveyors should be put through the machine.

The National Sanitation Foundation (see the supplementary references at the end of this chapter) offers acceptable standards for wash and rinse cycles of three types of dishwashing machines: (1) single tank, stationary rack, hood, and door types, (2) single tank, conveyor type, and (3) multiple-tank conveyor type with dishes in inclined position on conveyor or in rack. These standards may be obtained and used as a check on specifications of various makes of dishwashers and by managers for ensuring that the specified conditions such as water temperature and pressure are met. Employees, too, should be trained to follow proper procedures in the use and care of the dishwashing machine, or hand washing of dishes if no machine is available.

Any machine can fail in its function if it is not kept clean and properly maintained, and dishwashing equipment is no exception. Corrosion or lime deposits in nozzles can alter the jet or spray materially. Also, detergent sanitizers can be inactivated by contact with soiled surfaces and lose their power of penetration. The removal of microbial contamination is necessary; otherwise, the washed surfaces of dishes will have deposited on them bacterial populations and soil proportionate to that in the washing solution.

Procedures for the cleaning and care of dishwashing machines are:

- Clean dishwashing equipment thoroughly at the end of each washing period.
- Wash dish tables with detergent and rinse with fresh water. During this operation, scrap trays should remain in place in the machine.
- Turn off heat on wash or rinse tanks.
- Drain water from tanks and pumps.
- Remove racks from door-type machines and curtains from curtain-type machines.
- Remove wash arms or end caps where arms are not removable and clean with brush provided for this purpose.
- Check and clean final rinse sprays, if necessary.
- Remove and clean scrap trays.
- Close tank drain; hose and scrub the entire inside of machine thoroughly. Refill tank and then flush out pump and pump lines by running the machine at least one minute.
- Scrub and wash down curtains and hang in place for drying.
- Replace scrap trays, wash arms, and rinse arms.
- Check machine for next operation, leaving all inspection doors open.
- Clean and refill detergent dispenser.
- Check filler opening, final rinse, and pump-packing glands for leakage.
- Make sure periodic checks are made by authorized manufacturing personnel or manufacturer's authorized distributor every six months.

Good maintenance also includes frequent examination and lubrication where needed by a qualified maintenance person to ensure the continuing satisfactory operation of motors, nozzles, pumps, thermostats, thermometers, and all moving parts of a dishwashing machine.

The installation of elaborate equipment, however, offers no real security for good sanitation, since the efficiency of the machines depends almost entirely on the operator, the availability of an adequate supply of hot water at the proper temperature and pressure, the selection and concentration of detergent used for the hardness of the water, and the length of time the dishes are subjected to treatment. In the small, hand-operated, single-tank machines, the process and length of washing time are under the control of the operator and are followed by the rinsing process, also under manual control. Other machines have automatic controls that regulate the length of times for washing and rinsing. Thermometers that record the temperatures of both wash and rinse waters and thermostatic controls, except for the final rinse, are included as standard parts of dishwashing machines. Booster heaters with temperature controls are available and necessary to provide the sanitizing rinse temperature, because 180°F water in the pipe lines of a building would be a hazard to personnel safety. The installation of electronic detergent dispensers makes it possible to maintain optimum detergent concentration in the wash water and sanitizing chemical rinse in low-temperature machines. Each of these mechanical aids is most helpful in reducing the variables due to the human element and ensures clean, properly sanitized dishes and pots and pans.

CHECKS AND INSPECTIONS   Maintaining high standards of sanitation is essential in *all* foodservice establishments regardless of type or size. Consumers expect and demand a clean facility. In fact, it is one of the first criteria they use for judging an eating place. A sound basis of understanding and cooperative effort, and interest on the part of management, personnel, and control officials is necessary to carry out an effective program in food department sanitation. Management can operate successfully and happily under its own high and established standards and more than meet requirements that might be effected through legislation; hence, the emphasis on the importance of management's attitude. However, most personnel will do only what they believe management stands for and will expect. If managers fail to train employees and to supervise and check on their work, official control measures will be enforced.

Inspections. The U.S. Public Health Service has developed the *Food Service Establishment Report* as part of its 1976 Food Service Sanitation Ordinance,[2] which is designed as a model for local regulatory agencies. It recommends that inspection of a foodservice establishment be performed at least every six months or as often as necessary to enforce the regulations. Findings are recorded on the report form and the rating score made known to the manager. These inspection reports are public documents and may be revealed upon request. Fig. 8.16 shows one such rating form.

Many local public health departments issue a rating sticker to be placed on the door or window of a restaurant for the public's information. An "A" rating assures customers of a clean sanitary establishment. Lower ratings indicate that there are some infringements that management must correct within a given time period.

State of Oregon
OREGON STATE HEALTH DIVISION
Department of Human Resources
Environmental Health Services
FOOD INSPECTION REPORT

FAC. TYPE | CTY. NO. | ESTAB. NO. | INSPECT TIME | TRAVEL TIME

ESTABLISHMENT NAME: ______

STREET ADDRESS: ______

CITY/COUNTY: ______

NAME OF LICENSEE: ______

INSPECTION DATE
MO. DAY YR.

Semi-Annual ______ Complaints ______
Critical Items ______ Reinspection ______

SCORE: ______

Public Notice of Restaurant Sanitation
☐ EXCEEDED THE SANITATION STANDARDS
☐ MET THE SANITATION STANDARDS
☐ FAILED TO MEET THE SANITATION STANDARDS

AN EVALUATION OF SANITATION ON YOUR PREMISES HAS THIS DAY BEEN MADE AND YOU ARE HEREBY NOTIFIED OF THE VIOLATIONS FOUND. SUCH VIOLATIONS MAY RESULT IN DENIAL, SUSPENSION, OR REVOCATION OF YOUR LICENSE; OR CLOSURE OF THE RESTAURANT MAY RESULT FROM UNCORRECTED CRITICAL VIOLATIONS OR FAILURE TO MAINTAIN THE MINIMUM ACCEPTABLE SCORE. YOU MAY OBTAIN A CONTESTED CASE HEARING FOR ANY DENIAL, SUSPENSION, REVOCATION OR CLOSURE BY CONTACTING THE LICENSING AGENCY. SUCH HEARINGS ARE IN ACCORDANCE WITH ORS CHAPTER 183.

ITEM NO./PT. OAR/ORS	SPECIFIC PROBLEM	REQUIRED CORRECTION & TIME LIMIT

OPERATOR ______ SANITARIAN ______

FIGURE 8.16 An example of one state's sanitation inspection report form for foodservice establishments. *Oregon State Health Division.*

FOOD SOURCE

01	Approved source; unadulterated; no spoilage (OAR 32-026)	5
02	Approved milk dispensing; original container for shellfish (OAR 32-026)	1

FOOD PROTECTION

03	Potentially hazardous food meets temperature requirements during storage, preparation, display, service, transportation (OAR 32-024,-026,-028)	5
04	Dependable, spirit stem thermometers provided and located (OAR 32-024)	1
05	Potentially hazardous food properly thawed, cooked, preheated before hot-holding, rapidly reheated and cooled (OAR 32-024,-026)	4
06	Unwrapped and potentially hazardous food not reserved; self-service foods effectively protected (OAR 32-026,-028)	4
07	Food protection during storage, preparation, display, service, transportation (OAR 32-028)	2
08	Handling of food (ice) minimized (OAR 32-026,-024)	2
09	In use, food (ice) dispensing utensils properly stored (OAR 32-022)	1

PERSONNEL

10	Personnel with infections and sores restricted (ORS 624.080)	5
11	Hands washed and clean, good hygienic practices, no smoking in food preparation and service areas (OAR 32-030)	5
12	Clean clothes, hair restraints, no unauthorized personnel (OAR 32-030,-028)	1

FOOD EQUIPMENT AND UTENSILS — SANITIZING

13	Food (ice) contact surfaces of equipment; designed, constructed, maintained, installed, located (OAR 32-018)	2
14	Non-food contact surfaces of equipment; designed, constructed, maintained, installed, located (OAR-018)	1
15	Dishwashing facilities; designed, constructed, maintained, installed, located, operated (OAR 32-020)	2
16	Accurate thermometers, chemical test kits provided (OAR 32-020)	1
17	Pre-scrape, soak, wash, rinse water; clean, proper temperature (OAR 32-020)	2
18	Sanitization rinse; clean, temperature, concentration, exposure time; equipment, utensils sanitized (OAR 32-020)	4
19	Wiping cloths; clean, use restricted, stored in sanitizing solution (OAR 32-020)	1
20	Food contact surfaces of equipment and utensils clean, free of abrasives, detergents (OAR 32-020)	4
21	Non-food contact surfaces of equipment and utensils clean (OAR 32-020)	2
22	Protected storage, handling of clean equipment/utensils (OAR 32-022)	1
23	Single-service articles, storage, display, no re-use (OAR 32-022)	1

WATER, SEWAGE AND PLUMBING

24	Water source approved, safe, at least 20 P.S.I. (OAR 32-014)	5
25	Approved sewage and waste disposal (OAR 32-023)	4
26	Sewage disposal violations which do not directly or indirectly effect food service operations inside the restaurant (OAR 32-023)	2
27	Plumbing installed, maintained (OAR 32-023)	1
28	Cross-connection, back siphonage, backflow (OAR 32-023)	5

TOILET AND HANDWASHING FACILITIES

29	Number, convenient, accessible, designed, installed (OAR 32-012,-16)	2
30	Clean, enclosed, self-closing doors, fixtures good repair, hot and cold water, hand cleanser, sanitary towels/hand drying devices, provided, proper waste receptacles, handwashing signs posted (OAR 32-023,-012,-016)	2

GARBAGE AND REFUSE DISPOSAL

31	Containers or receptacles, covered; adequate number insect/rodent proof, frequency, clean (OAR 32-023)	1
32	Outside storage area enclosures properly constructed, clean (OAR 32-023)	1

INSECT AND RODENT, ANIMAL CONTROL

33	Approved and effective control of insects/rodents, outer openings protected, no birds, turtles, other animals (OAR 32-006,-028)	4

FLOORS, WALLS AND CEILINGS

34	Floors; installed, constructed with sealed junctures, smooth, easily cleanable, good repair (OAR 32-002)	1
35	Walls and ceilings; installed, constructed; washable up to splash level in food preparation, utensil washing and toilet areas (OAR 32-004)	1
36	Floors and junctures; clean, dustless cleaning methods (OAR 32-002)	2
37	Walls, attached equipment, ceilings; clean (OAR 32-004)	2

LIGHTING AND VENTILATION

38	Uniform lighting provided in food preparation and storage areas (OAR 32-008)	1
39	Adequate, designed ventilation systems in food preparation, dishwashing and restroom areas; filters cleaned (OAR 32-010)	1

HOUSEKEEPING

40	Toxic items properly stored, labeled, used (OAR 32-028,-032)	5
41	Premises maintained free of litter, unnecessary articles, cleaning/maintenance equipment properly stored (OAR 32-032)	1
42	Complete separation from living/sleeping quarters, personal items separate (OAR 32-032)	1
43	Clean, soiled linen properly stored (OAR 32-032)	1

Other Areas (do not affect grade)
_____ Employes certified in First-aid for choking victims (ORS 624.130)
_____ Smoking area comply with ORS 433.845 (effective July 1, 1983)
_____ Food Sanitation Training _____

100% - 92% and no uncorrected critical violations:
EXCEEDED THE SANITATION STANDARDS

91% - 60% and no uncorrected critical violations:
MET THE SANITATION STANDARDS

59% or below:
FAILED TO MEET THE SANITATION STANDARDS

All 4 and 5 point critical violations must be rectified immediately with an approved alternative procedure and must be corrected within the designated time period. Previously cited 1 and 2 point items which have not been corrected are considered repeat violations and will accumulate 1 or 2 penalty points respectively each time they are observed on semi-annual inspections. Failure to correct critical violations as described above or two consecutive complete inspection sanitation scores below 60% may result in the closure of the restaurant or the revocation, suspension or denial of the license.

Because of the heavy load for agency inspectors, many types of foodservices are exempt from this inspection. Directors of such foodservices will find the details of the U.S. Public Health Service model code an excellent reference. Any foodservice may use it as is or as a basis for developing a check sheet appropriate for its own operation.

Some institutions have found check sheets for each separate unit of the foodservice useful in directing various workers' attention to the major points on which maintenance of sanitary and desirable working conditions depends. Another check and inspection used by many managers is a bacterial count on dishes to test the effectiveness of the dishwashing procedure. The cleanliness of dishes and utensils may be checked for visible soil deposited on their surfaces or, more exactly, by bacterial counts determined by the swab test; procedures are outlined in *U.S. Public Health Service Bulletin 37.* Counts of 100 or less are acceptable, but those showing 30 to 100 colonies indicate that something should be done to improve the situation. Counts above 100 mean unclean dishes and utensils and indicate poor or faulty methods. The form shown in Fig. 8.17 was designed for use in reporting the bacterial counts on the dishes and eating utensils in each of the foodservice units on one university campus, made monthly by the school's department of microbiology. Such reports indicate where procedures in dishwashing or handling need revision and are of interest to both manager and employees in maintaining a good record of clean tableware.

In summary, the combined efforts of all concerned with foodservices— managers, employees, and representatives of regulatory agencies and industries—have one broad objective: to protect the health of the consumer. All of the topics addressed in this chapter and certain ones in Chapters 4 and 5 on food purchasing and production planning and control are involved in achieving this goal. In a well-operated sanitation program, primary attention should be given to those things that most directly affect food protection. Although esthetic considerations play a most important role in a food sanitation program, managers must not overlook the more critical items related to food safety procedures and personnel food handling techniques. Maintaining a good perspective is important for obtaining desirable results in a good sanitation program.

Safety

Physical safety of workers and customers alike is a major concern of foodservice administrators. A work environment free from hazards that cause accidents and a dining facility in which customers are safe and secure should

REPORT OF BACTERIA COUNTS IN DINING HALLS

Date_____

Location	Date of Sample	Time Sample Taken	Storage Consult Code	*I *W Water Glass	Dinner Plate	Salad Bowl	Cereal Bowl	Coffee Cup	Silver-ware Knife	Fork	Spoon	Trays	Steam Table Inset
Baker Hall	5/26	9:00		0	0	1	25	1	0	0	0	0	
Women's Res.		9:30		0	0	S	0	0	7	4	3	S	
Neil Hall		9:50		0	0	0	0	0	0	0	0	1	
Stadium		11:50		S	S	S	0	S	1	3	0	40	
Pomerene		9:15		0	0	18	1	0	0	0	0	0	
University School		8:15		—	0	0	0	1	0	0	1	0	
Faculty Club		8:00		0	0	0	0	0	8	1	0	0	
Main D. R.		8:40		0	2	S	S	0	0	0	0	S	
Cafeteria		8:30		0	0	0	0	0	0	3	1	0	

NOTE: Code letters used in table:
S   Spreading type of colony
TMC   Innumerable colonies (too many to count on plate)
C   Closed storage
O   Open storage
*I   Water glass inverted—no air space
*W   Water glass inverted—with air space
D   Immediately after washing
      Silver racked: yes_____ no_____.

RATING according to City Regulations:
      0–10   Excellent
      11–29 Good
      30–49 Fair
      50–99 Poor   Counts by_____
      Over 100 Very poor   Approved by_____

FIGURE 8.17 Summary record of bacterial counts on dishes makes it easy to detect problem areas.

be aims of all managers. However, because some managers have shown a lack of interest or a disregard for this area of their business, federal legislation was enacted in 1970 to force compliance with certain safety standards.

The Occupational Safety and Health Act (OSHA), which became effective April 28, 1971, makes it illegal *not* to have a safe establishment. It is administered by the U.S. Department of Labor (see the supplementary references at the end of this chapter). The Act mandates action on the part of management to ensure safe and healthful working conditions for all of the nation's wage earners. It states, among other things, that each employer has a duty to furnish the employees a place of employment that is safe and free from any hazards that may cause serious physical harm or death. The organization set up to enforce this act has the authority to inspect any place of business and to penalize those who do not comply with the provisions of the law. Managers must strictly comply with correcting specific potential hazards and furnish written records of any accidents that have occurred.

The National Safety Council, although not a regulatory agency but a nonprofit service organization, is devoted to safety education. Through its research, reports, and printed materials available to the public, the Council provides valuable assistance to managers of numerous types of businesses, including foodservice.

Worker Safety

The provision of a safe workplace through a well-designed facility (see Chapter 9) with equipment that meets National Sanitation Foundation standards is a first step in ensuring worker safety. However, safety is more than a building with built-in safe features. Safety can never be *assumed,* for accidents can and do occur. Managers and employees must work together on a safety awareness program to attain a good safety records.

"Accidents don't happen; they are caused"—and can be prevented. The National Safety Council has defined an accident as any suddenly occurring, unintentional event that causes injury or property damage. An accident has become a symbol of inefficiency, either human or mechanical, and usually represents a monetary loss to the organization. The injured individual loses not only time at work and wages, but also incurs indirect costs such as medical and insurance expenses, cost of training new workers, waste production resulting from inexperienced substitute workers, administrative costs for investigating and taking care of accidents, and cost of repair or replacement of broken or damaged equipment. Not only from the humanitarian standpoint, therefore, but also from the economic should dietitians and other foodservice managers be aware of the advantages of good safety measures. All should seek ways to improve working conditions and employee performance that will reduce accidents with their resulting waste, and maintain low accident frequency and severity rates. *Severity rate* is computed by the number of working days lost because of accidents, and *frequency rate* by the number of lost-time accidents during any selected period, each multiplied by 1,000,000 and the result divided by the total number of hours worked during the same period. National Safety Council statistics rank the food industry about midway among all industry classifications in terms of severity rates. However, in terms of frequency rate, it is nearly twice as high as the average for all industries reporting.

Foodservice managers must organize for safety and develop a wholesome regard for safe procedures among the entire staff.

Safety Program

Specific topics for a safety campaign may be centered around the "three E's" of safety: engineering, education, enforcement.

The *engineering* aspect refers to the built-in safety features of the building and equipment, and the manner in which the equipment is installed to make it safe to use. Encased motors, safety valves on pressure steamers, easily manipulated spigots on urns, and guards on slicing and chopping machines are examples of safety features. A maintenance program to keep equipment in good working order is the responsibility of management, as is all other phases of providing a safe environment.

A study of traffic patterns in kitchen and dining areas and the placement of equipment and supplies in locations to avoid as much cross traffic as possible, and the arrangement of equipment within a work unit to provide for logical sequence of movement without backtracking are a part of the engineering phase of the safety program.

Education for safety is a never-ending process. It begins with the establishment of firm policies regarding safety, which then should be discussed with each new employee during the orientation period. "Safety from the first day" is an appropriate slogan for any organization.

Because safety is an integrated part of every activity, it should be taught as a component of all skills and procedures. Written procedures for tasks to be performed by each employee must include the safe way of doing each task, and the written outline then used to train the employee in the correct steps to follow. These written, step-by-step procedures provide a follow-up, on-the-job reference for the employee, and may be used by managers as a check against employee performance.

Safety education, however, is more than training each employee in the procedures for a particular job. An ongoing group program based on *facts* about safe and unsafe practices keeps employees aware of safety. The National Safety Council, the Bureau of Vital Statistics, and various community safety councils, as well as trade and professional organizations, can provide statistics and materials for planning such a program. Data obtained from records kept on accidents *within* the organization are invaluable and more meaningful than general statistics.

A form for reporting accidents should be provided by management (see Fig. 8.18 as an example). These written records should include the type of

---

Board of Education
Office of Assistant Supervisor of Home Economics
in Charge of Cafeterias

Department Report of Personal Injury Involving
the Employees of the City Schools

School _____   Date _____
Name _____   Title _____
Address _____   Date of accident _____
Sex _____   Time of accident _____
State fully in your own words how accident occurred: _____
_____
_____

Exact part of person injured and extent of injuries: _____
_____
_____

Probable period of disability _____
Was medical attention necessary? _____
Name and address of Physician _____
_____

Give location where accident occurred _____
Will employee lose any time? _____
If not able to work, give probable date of recovery _____
Are there any indications of permanent injury? _____
State monthly salary of employee _____
How long in our employ? _____

IMPORTANT: Fill out report in *duplicate* on day of accident and mail immediately
to above office.

_____
Employee

FIGURE 8.18   Example of a typical accident report form; to be filled in and filed immediately.

accident, kind of injury that has occurred and to whom, when it occurred, the day and hour, and where it took place. In foodservices most accidents occur at rush hours when it is especially difficult to take care of the injured, find replacement help, and continue efficient customer service. This fact alone should provide incentive enough for the manager to do all that is possible to promote safety.

An analysis of the causes of accidents provides further data for preventing them. Causes may be classified into "unsafe acts" and "unsafe conditions." Usually it is found that unsafe acts outnumber unsafe conditions three to one. From this, there is an immediate indication of the need for proper training to reduce accidents.

In the foodservice industry, falls cause the largest number of food-handling accidents, with cuts second, and burns and strains from lifting next in order. Falls and strains result in the greatest loss of time from the job and monetary loss to the institution.

It is estimated that 85 to 90 per cent of all accidents could be prevented. Curley[7] reports that "insurance industry studies have determined that fully 85 per cent of all occupational injuries result from human error, while the remaining 15 per cent are caused by faulty equipment and other unsafe conditions. Inadequate training, meager experience, and improper supervision all contribute to the conditions that allow for human error."

It is management's responsibility to ferret out the reasons, remove the hazards, and then train the employees to prevent recurrence of the same accident. Good housekeeping procedures, such as storing tools and materials in proper places and keeping aisles and pathways clear, optimum lighting of work areas, prompt repair of broken tools and equipment, replacement of worn electrical cords, and proper care and removal of broken china and glassware, are only a few of the things that can be done to correct unsafe conditions. Employees should be encouraged to report to the manager any unsafe conditions they may notice. A simple form could be developed and made available to the employees for such reporting. Having the information in writing is helpful to the manager who must then follow up to correct the situation.

The possibility of fires is an ever-present threat in foodservice establishments, making it essential that all employees follow good procedures in use of equipment and cooking techniques. Further, they should know the location of fire extinguishing equipment and how to use it. Directions for and practice in the use of fire extinguishers, fire blankets, and other first aid equipment, necessities in every institution kitchen, are included in training meetings, for supervisory personnel particularly. Information about the various types of fire extinguishers and which should be used for grease, paper and wood, and other types of fires is important. Fig. 8.19 give this informa-

KNOW YOUR FIRE EXTINGUISHERS

	WATER TYPE				FOAM	CARBON DIOXIDE	DRY CHEMICAL			
							SODIUM OR POTASSIUM BICARBONATE		MULTI-PURPOSE ABC	
	STORED PRESSURE	CARTRIDGE OPERATED	WATER PUMP TANK	SODA ACID	FOAM	CO2	CARTRIDGE OPERATED	STORED PRESSURE	STORED PRESSURE	CARTRIDGE OPERATED
CLASS A FIRES — ORDINARY COMBUSTIBLES — WOOD, PAPER, TRASH HAVING GLOWING EMBERS	YES	YES	YES	YES	YES	NO (BUT WILL CONTROL SMALL SURFACE FIRES)	NO (BUT WILL CONTROL SMALL SURFACE FIRES)	NO (BUT WILL CONTROL SMALL SURFACE FIRES)	YES	YES
CLASS B FIRES — FLAMMABLE LIQUIDS — FLAMMABLE LIQUIDS, GASOLINE, OIL, PAINTS, GREASE, ETC.	NO	NO	NO	NO	YES	YES	YES	YES	YES	YES
CLASS C FIRES — ELECTRICAL EQUIPMENT — ELECTRICAL EQUIPMENT	NO	NO	NO	NO	NO	YES	YES	YES	YES	YES
CLASS D FIRES — COMBUSTIBLE METALS — COMBUSTIBLE METALS	SPECIAL EXTINGUISHING AGENTS APPROVED BY RECOGNIZED TESTING LABORATORIES									
METHOD OF OPERATION	PULL PIN-SQUEEZE HANDLE	TURN UPSIDE DOWN AND BUMP	PUMP HANDLE	TURN UPSIDE DOWN	TURN UPSIDE DOWN	PULL PIN-SQUEEZE LEVER	RUPTURE CARTRIDGE-SQUEEZE LEVER	PULL PIN-SQUEEZE HANDLE	PULL PIN-SQUEEZE HANDLE	RUPTURE CARTRIDGE-SQUEEZE LEVER
RANGE	30'-40'	30'-40'	30'-40'	30'-40'	30'-40'	3'-8'	5'-20'	5'-20'	5'-20'	5'-20'
MAINTENANCE	CHECK AIR PRESSURE GAUGE MONTHLY	WEIGH GAS CARTRIDGE ADD WATER IF REQUIRED ANNUALLY	DISCHARGE AND FILL WITH WATER ANNUALLY	DISCHARGE ANNUALLY -RECHARGE	DISCHARGE ANNUALLY -RECHARGE	WEIGH SEMI-ANNUALLY	WEIGH GAS CARTRIDGE-CHECK CONDITION OF DRY CHEMICAL ANNUALLY	CHECK PRESSURE GAUGE AND CONDITION OF DRY CHEMICAL ANNUALLY	CHECK PRESSURE GAUGE AND CONDITION OF DRY CHEMICAL ANNUALLY	WEIGH GAS CARTRIDGE-CHECK CONDITION OF DRY CHEMICAL ANNUALLY

FIGURE 8.19 Types of fire extinguishers.

tion. Group training in precautionary procedures to be followed in everyday work and instructions in what to do in case of an accident should be part of the overall safety program. Be certain that all employees know where and to whom to report an accident and that the phone numbers to use for emergencies are posted on or near the telephone.

Many aids are available to foodservice managers to use in setting up a training program. The National Restaurant Association's *Safety Operations Manual*[8] is an excellent resource. The National Safety Council[9] has posters, pamphlets, and other materials available for use in training sessions. These are invaluable sources of information and illustration for foodservice managers. Clear eye-catching posters that create favorable impressions and serve as reminders of good, safe practices are effective supplements to other types of training. The safety rules given in Fig. 8.20 may be used as topics for training sessions. However, each foodservice organization should establish its own similar list of safety rules to be adhered to in its own department.

FIGURE 8.20   Safety rules—a basis for safety training programs.

General Restaurant Safety Rules

(*please post*)

- Report *every* injury *at once,* regardless of severity, to your Supervisor for first aid. *Avoid delay.*

- Report all *unsafe conditions,* broken or splintered chairs or tables, defective equipment, leaking radiators, torn carpeting, uneven floors, loose rails, unsafe tools or knives, broken china and glass, etc.

- Understand the *safe way* to perform any task assigned to you. If in doubt, see your Supervisor. Never take unnecessary chances.

- If you have to move over-heavy objects, ask for help. *Do not overlift.* When lifting any heavy object, keep your back straight, bend your knees and *use your leg muscles.* Your back has weak muscles and can easily be strained.

- Aisles, passageways, stairways must be kept clean and free from obstructions. Do not permit brooms, pails, mops, cans, boxes, etc., to remain where someone can fall over them. Wipe up any grease or wet spots from stairs or floors or ramps *at once.* These are serious falling hazards.

- Walk, do not run, in halls, down ramps or stairs, or around work areas. Be careful when passing through swinging doors.

- Keep your locker clean and the locker top free from all loose or discarded materials, such as: newspapers, old boxes, bottles, broken equipment, etc.

- Wear safe, sensible clothes for your work. Wear safe, comfortable shoes, with good soles. Never wear thin-soled or broken-down shoes. *Do not wear high-heeled shoes for work.* Ragged or over-long sleeves or ragged clothing may result in an injury.

- If you have to reach for a high object, use a ladder, not a chair or table or a makeshift. There is no substitute of any kind of a good ladder. *Never overreach.* Be careful when you have to reach high to fill coffee urns, milk tanks, etc.

- Horseplay or practical jokes on the job are forbidden.

- Do not argue or fight with fellow employees. The results are usually unpleasant and dangerous.

- Keep floors clean and dry. Pick up any loose object from the floor immediately to prevent someone from falling.

- Do not overload your trays. Trays should be loaded so as to give good balance. An improperly loaded tray can become dangerous.

- Dispose of all broken glass and china immediately. Never serve a guest with a cracked or chipped glass or piece of china. Check all silverware.

- Take sufficient time to serve your guests properly. Too much haste is liable to cause accidents to your guests and to yourself. *Haste makes waste.*

- Remove from service any chair, table or other equipment that is loose, broken or splintered so as to prevent injury.

- *Cashiers.* Close cash registers with back of hand. Do not permit fingers to hang over edge of drawer.

- Money is germ-laden. Keep your fingers out of your hair, eyes, and mouth after handling. Wash hands carefully before eating. Report the slightest cut or sore *at once* for treatment.

- Help *new employees* to work safely on the job. Show them the right way to do the job—the safe way.

The third "E" in the overall safety campaign is *enforcement.* This represents the follow-up or constant vigilance required to prevent carelessness and to make certain that the rules and prescribed procedures are observed. Enforcement can be accomplished in many ways. In some organizations, safety committees are set up among the employees, who observe and report unsafe conditions and practices. Membership on this committee may be rotated so that everyone will be personally involved in a campaign against accidents. In other places, contests among departments serve as incentives for keeping accident rates low. Honor rolls for accident-free days or months help call attention to safety records. If possible, one person in each organization should have the overall responsibility for developing and supervising the safety program, after being specifically trained for the task.

Probably the most effective overall enforcement plan, however, is a periodic inspection of the department by someone on the supervisory staff. The use of a checklist as a reminder of all points to be observed is helpful. Any foodservice manager could develop a form for use in a specific operation. The comprehensive checklist illustrated in Fig. 8.21 includes both food safety and sanitation and may serve as a model for developing a checklist for a specific department.

Customer Protection

"Customers" of foodservices deserve the same careful concern given employees in regard to safety. They expect and should have assurance that the food served will be "safe" for consumption and that the facility for dining is also safe. This includes everything from a safe parking area that is well lighted and free of any stumbling "block," to furniture that is in good condition and will not cause snags or splinters. The flooring must be kept in good repair to prevent tripping and falls, and any spillage should be wiped up at once so that no one will slip and fall.

Dining rooms should be adequately lighted and ample aisle space provided between tables so diners can see to make their way through the room without tripping.

Servers must be well trained in correct serving procedures so they will not spill any hot food on the customers or anything on the floor that could cause accidents. Any spillage must be cleaned up at once.

Managers are liable for accidents that may occur on the premises. Lawsuits could result that are costly and certainly are hard on the reputation of the establishment. Therefore, extreme care should be taken so none will occur.

Summary

In summary, the steps to safety in any foodservice include awareness, involvement, and control. The first step is *awareness* on the part of managers for the need to provide a safe environment for employees and patrons, and to assume the responsibility for and positive attitude toward accident prevention. *Involvement* includes initiating a safety education program or campaign that keeps employees safety conscious. A training program that indoctrinates employees with the philosophy of working safely and instructs them in how to do so is a major part of being involved. Seeking employee suggestions about safe procedures and forming safety committees in which they participate are other forms of involvement. *Control* is insisting on safety, checking on safety codes and meeting them, analyzing accident records as a

Check Sheet
Safety in the Kitchen

(Rating Scale: 5—1; 5 points is highest and 1 point the lowest.)

Burns
1. Are handles of pans on the stove turned so the pans cannot be knocked off? _____
2. Are flames turned off when removing pans from stove? _____
3. Are dry pot holders used for lifting hot pans? _____
4. Are fellow workers warned when pans are hot? When pans of hot food are to be moved? _____
5. Is steam equipment in proper working order to avoid burns from leaks? _____
6. Is hot water regulated at proper temperature so it will not scald? _____
7. Are lids lifted cautiously and steamer doors opened slowly to avoid steam burns? _____

Cuts
1. Are broken dishes and glasses promptly cleaned up and disposed of in special container provided? _____
2. Are knives stored in the slotted case provided for them? _____
3. Are knives left on the drain board to be washed, and not dropped into the sink? _____
4. Is the safety hood put over the slicer after each use and cleaning? _____
5. Is the can opener in good repair so it cuts sharply and leaves no ragged edges? _____
6. Are safety devices provided on slicers and choppers? _____

Electricity
1. Are electric cords in good repair? _____
2. Are sufficient outlets provided for the equipment in use? _____
3. Are hands always dry before touching electrical equipment? _____
4. Are there extra fuses in the fuse box? _____

Falls
1. Are spilled foods cleaned up immediately? _____
2. Are corridors and stairways free from debris? _____
3. Are articles placed on shelves securely so they will not jar off? _____
4. Are step ladders sturdy and in good repair? _____
5. Are brooms and mops put away properly after use and not left out against a wall or table to trip someone? _____
6. Are hallways well lighted and steps well marked so no one will trip? _____

Fires and Explosions
1. Are gas pipes free from leaks? Have they been checked by the gas company? _____
2. Are matches kept in a covered metal container? _____
3. Are fire blankets and extinguishers provided? _____
4. Has the fire extinguisher been checked in the last month? _____
5. Is the first-aid box fully supplied? _____
6. Is hot fat watched carefully, and is cold fat stored away from flame? _____

Please Report Immediately Any Fires or Accidents to the Food Manager
or Dial _____ to Report a Fire

FIGURE 8.21 Example of a kitchen safety check sheet to be used by managers to help identify unsafe practices.

basis for improvement, and, above all, good consistent supervision of employees' work. This assumes that the institution has established safety policies, written procedures for job performance, and adopted a procedure for reporting and handling accidents that are known to all in the organization.

Benefits of a safety program include: a reduction in accidents, improvement in employee morale, patron satisfaction and feeling of security, and fewer workers' compensation claims, resulting in reduced costs and better financial performance for the foodservice. The objective is to keep injuries to a minimum and the working force at maximum efficiency.

Notes

1. Todd, Ewen C. D.: Economic loss from foodborne disease outbreaks associated with foodservice establishments. Journal of Food Protection 48(2):169, 1985.
2. U.S. Department of Health, Education and Welfare, Public Health Service, Food and Drug Administration: Food Service Sanitation Manual. DHEW Publication No. (FDA) 78-2081, 1976, p. 21.
3. Abram, Debra, and Potter, Norman: Survival of Campylobacter jejuni at different temperatures in broth, beef, chicken and cod supplemented with sodium chloride. Journal of Food Protection 47(10):795, 1984.
4. Mann, Johnathan M., Lathrop, George, and Bannerman, John A.: Economic impact of a botulism outbreak. JAMA 249(10):1299, 1983.
5. Anderson, Steven R.: Assessment of the health risks and handling of products used in foodservice establishments. Journal of Environmental Health 47(4):200, 1985.
6. Unklesbay, Nan, and Unklesbay, Kenneth: Energy Management in Foodservice. Westport, CT: AVI Publishing Co., 1982, p. 354.
7. Curley, David P.: Preventing employee injuries. Cornell HRA Quarterly 25(3):13, 1984.
8. National Restaurant Association: Safety Operations Manual. Suite 2600, One IBM Plaza, Chicago, IL 60611.
9. National Safety Council, 425 N. Michigan Avenue, Chicago, IL 60611.

Supplementary References

American Hospital Association: Safety Guide for Health Care Institutions, 3rd ed. Chicago: AHA, 1983.

American Society for Hospital Food Service Administrators: OSHA Reference for Food Service Adminstrators. Cat. No. 1420. Chicago, IL: Am. Hosp. Assoc. 1976.

Centers for Disease Control: Morbidity and Mortality Weekly Report. Atlanta, GA: US Dept. HEW, PHS.

FRAZIER, W. C. AND WESTHOFF, D. C.: Food Microbiology, 3rd ed. New York: Mc-
Graw-Hill Book Co. 1978.

LONGREE, K.: Quantity Food Sanitation, 3rd ed. New York: John Wiley and Sons,
1980.

LONGREE, K., AND BLAKER, G.: Sanitary Techniques in Foodservice, 2nd ed. New
York: John Wiley and Sons, 1982.

National Institute for the Foodservice Industry: Applied Foodservice Sanitation (a
course of study), Chicago, IL 60606.

National Sanitation Foundation, P.O. Box 1468, Ann Arbor, MI 48106:

EDUCATIONAL MATERIALS

Clean Dishes. Slide/tape program (25 min.), 1974. Food Service Facility Plan Preparation and Review—A Sanitation Guide, 1979. (Keyed to use with Reference Guide.)
Sanitation Aspects of Food Service Facility Plan Preparation and Review—A Reference Guide. (Keyed to the 1976 revision of Food Service Sanitation Manual, US Dept.
HEW, PHS, FDA.)
Instructional Guide, 1979. (Reference Guide and Instructional Guide are compan-
ions.)

STANDARDS

No. 1. Soda Fountain and Luncheonette Equipment, 6/84.

No. 2. Food Service equipment, 6/82.

Supplement. Descriptive details for Standard No. 2.

No. 3. Commercial Spray-Type Dishwashing Machines, 6/82, under revision.

No. 4. Commercial Cooking and Hot Food Storage Equipment, under revision.

No. 5. Commercial Hot Water Generating and Heat Recovery Equipment, 11/83.

No. 6. Dispensing Freezers (for Dairy Dessert-Type Products), 11/82.

No. 7. Food Service Refrigerators and Storage Freezers, 11/83.

No. 8. Commercial Powered Food Preparation Equipment, 5/80.

No. 12. Automatic Ice Making Equipment, under revision.

No. 18. Manual Food and Beverage Dispensing Equipment, 6/81.

No. 20. Commercial Bulk Milk Dispensing Equipment and Appurtenances, 7/80.

No. 25. Vending Machines for Food and Beverages, 12/80.

No. 26. Pot, Pan, and Utensil Washers, 12/80.

No. 29. Detergent/Chemical Feeders for Commercial Spray-Type Dishwashing Machines, 6/82.

No. 35. Laminated Plastics for Surfacing Food Service Equipment, under revision.

No. 36. Dinnerware, 3/81.

No. 37. Air curtains for Entranceways in Food Establishments, 7/80.

No. 51. Plastics Materials and Components Used in Food Equipment, under revision.

No. 52. Supplemental Flooring, under revision.

CRITERIA

C-2. Special Equipment and/or devices (Food Service Equipment), 11/83.

Occupational Safety and Health Act. Office of Assistant Secretary of Labor for OSHA,
200 Constitution Ave., NW, Washington, DC 20210.

Subcommittee on Microbiological Criteria, Committee on Food Protection, Food and
    Nutrition Board, National Research Council: An Evaluation of the Role of Mi-
    crobiological Criteria for Foods and Food Ingredients. Washington, DC: Na-
    tional Academic Press, 1985.
Tools of the Trade: How to Select, Use, Clean and Maintain Foodservice Equipment
    (a 75-slide learning program). Write to: Director, Restaurant, Hotel, and Insti-
    tution Management Institute, Stewart Center, Purdue University, West Lafay-
    ette, IN 47907.

CHAPTER 9

Facility Design and Layout

Introduction

Food managers are involved in facility design and layout as part of their position responsibility. The involvement can range from a large project for planning a new foodservice facility, remodeling an existing facility, or a minor change within an existing work area such as adding or replacing equipment.

This chapter is intended to assist the student in learning how to organize thoughts and plans regarding foodservice design and layout. Planning concepts presented serve as an aid to the foodservice manager in:

1. Gaining understanding of preliminary preparation desirable before undertaking a facility designing project
2. Developing a prospectus (written plan) for remodeling or building a new facility
3. Understanding his or her role as a member of the planning team and the contribution each is prepared to make
4. Preparing a floor plan that supports the goals, objectives, and procedures of the design prospectus
5. Arranging the required equipment for greatest efficiency in work

The planning concepts in this chapter are applicable to all planning projects regardless of size and scope. However, each person must identify his or her own goals and needs, and work to maximize a project's attributes and plan around any constraints that may exist. The desired outcome, common to all foodservice, is to provide an appropriate and efficient facility for the production and service of high quality, attractive food acceptable to consumer demands.

Goals and Definitions

Facility design and equipment layout planning present a real challenge to the foodservice manager. An understanding of the many decisions required in such a project and how to meet them intelligently make it essential for the planner to prepare well for the task ahead. The finished project, based on the design and layout plans, may result in success or failure for the foodservice operation involved.

Physical facility requirements for the many and varied types of organizations that make up the extensive foodservice industry are as diverse and numerous as the individual units themselves. All must maximize the attributes and plan around constraints that exist in the facility. Each foodservice is planned with its own individual goal, objectives, budget, location, menu, equipment, and skilled personnel available to the foodservice. Also, the type of foodservice selected—conventional, commissary, ready-prepared, or assembly/serve, or a combination of these systems—must be identified so that the plans made will support the system.

The outcome goal that is common to all foodservices is to provide an appropriate and efficient facility for the production and service of high quality, attractive food that meets the consumers' needs.

For good understanding, certain definitions and examples of terminology to be used are provided:

- Physical: having material existence measured by weight, motion, and resistance.[1] Therefore, anything that takes up space in a facility must be accounted for and planned in the space available.
- Design: scheme in which means to an end are laid down.[1] Thus, it refers to the broad function of developing the facility, including site selection, menu, equipment requirements, and other pertinent planning functions that will guide the design into reality.
- Layout: the act or process of planning or laying out in detail.[1] This process deals with the arrangement of the physical facilities, including equipment, and dictates operational efficiency.

In practical application when developing a project plan for a foodservice facility, the physical design is drawn on paper to show the material existence of walls, doors, windows, and other major structural components. Then within this plan, work areas are designated, and equipment and other facilities are arranged and drawn. Conceptually, the design will reflect the use of physical space as though a person were looking at the floor area from the ceiling.

The foodservice manager must be involved with the development of the physical design throughout all phases of planning to ensure desired outcomes. Other professionals will be involved at various stages of planning to design the electrical, water and plumbing systems, lighting, heating and ventilation, and elevations required to make the facility functional.

Preliminary Preparation for Planning

Much preparation is preliminary to the development of a final design. The first thing the manager should do is to make a study of trends that may have an effect on foodservice design. Other suggestions for preliminary preparation include: learning about new developments in design and equipment, building a file of reference materials and ideas, becoming familiar with regulatory codes affecting building projects, and studying the special requirements of specific types of foodservices.

Trends in Foodservice Planning

INCREASE IN DINING OUT   Changes in foodservice, and thus design, have been prompted by more people eating away from home. Children are beginning to eat away from home at an early age in day centers and preschools. Eating away from home then continues for people throughout their life cycles at preschool, schools, universities, camps, workplaces, leisure dining restaurants, and often on to retirement and convalescent homes. Meals eaten away from home have prompted the foodservice industry to meet the needs of the increasing customer load through style of foodservice, types of food, and accepted selling prices of the prepared food. These in turn all influence the design of the facility to accommodate the changes indicated.

CHANGE IN DESIRED MENU ITEMS   Customer preferences for type of meals eaten away from home continues to change, and these preferences affect the foodservice facility design. Customers do want their "money's worth" when purchasing meals, and foodservices provide this while keeping alert to consumer changing desires for certain foods. A concern for physical fitness and well-being on the part of the American people in the 1980s, for example, has brought a change in the menus of most foodservices from heavy caloric foods to lighter food selections, limited desserts in many cases, and a trend toward specialty or ethnic foods. Marriott[2] says the "new grazers of the 80s" prefer appetizers and/or a first course and dessert and skip the main course. This is one reason for the popularity of salad bars and Chinese restaurants that offer a variety of appetizers. There has been an influx of Asian immigrants on the West Coast who have established restaurants with the appeal of their lightly cooked meals, and so draw this type of customer. This in turn changes equipment and space needs within a facility, which is a factor in remodeling or new construction to accommodate the type of foods customers prefer. Consumer demand is shaping the market.

ECONOMIC FACTORS   Economic factors such as wages, food and utility costs influence the types of foodservice and their design. Wages of skilled and unskilled employees generally continue to rise. Therefore, equipment automation, including use of robots in some places, and the purchase of convenience foods have been a trend in foodservice. Also, as costs for food and the energy to prepare it continue to rise, the foodservice design must provide for an efficient operation. Therefore, design and layout must utilize only a minimum amount of space for a maximum job regardless of the type of foodservice. This is the challenge to the foodservice manager. Each existing foodservice should be studied to determine if these objectives are being met. Also, the manager must search for the best design and layout arrangement of work centers to maximize the efficiency of the operation. The number of steps a worker must take and distances required for transport and distribution of food should be kept at a minimum.

FLEXIBILITY OF USE   One trend in facility design is to make the existing space as flexible as possible either for multiple use or for ease in remodeling or rearranging to meet future demands. This may be accomplished in part through selection of equipment mounted on wheels or by use of portable units. Also, planning matched modular units, such as the range, fryer, broiler, and oven, to make a given space flexible and the equipment easy to disconnect and transport is generally efficient. Standard-size storage units, well planned, accommodate the same size tray, and thus maximize the use of all stationary and mobile equipment. The key is to have equipment that is uniform and adaptable to numerous work activities.

BUILT-IN SAFETY, SANITATION, AND NOISE REDUCTION   In planning the total facility, the safety of the employees, safety of food, and overall sanitary conditions are considerations in new designs. These may be achieved by the type of floor covering, ventilation, building materials, lighting and equipment selected, and the method of their installation. Ease of cleaning reduces labor costs, and materials and designs chosen for safety features help reduce accidents. Both make for an attractive, safe working environment for the employees. Many of these features reduce noise and worker fatigue and so result in greater productivity.

ENERGY CONSERVATION   With the ever-rising energy costs, trends are to design and equip foodservice facilities to save energy to the greatest extent possible. Equipment manufacturers are producing equipment that gives a high yield of energy for the work accomplished. The energy used by specific pieces of equipment is stated in the specifications, and comparisons should be made by the foodservice manager before selecting a particular make or model.

Other energy conservation trends are toward better insulation, heat recapture for other uses, and recirculation of heat. Solar heat designs are used in some areas, especially for restaurants, and may be a future trend of other types of foodservices.

SPECIFIC TYPES OF FOODSERVICE ORGANIZATIONS: CHANGES AND TRENDS
   Some universities have found it economical to change from a set board plan operation to an à la carte plan. Dunlap[3] implemented such a plan to accommodate and appeal to the variety of student eating habits and patterns within the confines of the program that would be affordable both for students and the university. Also, public school foodservices have added à la carte selections for their older student customers.

Hospital foodservices are expanding to include varied revenue-generating functions. Some of these are catering, vending, home-delivered meals, and contracting meal service in other facilities such as retirement homes and day care centers. Adequate space is essential to provide for these extra services.

Commercial foodservices have shown trends toward capturing the business of the increasing older population and the affluent segment of society. Gourmet and leisurely dining and expensive, attractive decor attract many; for others, all-you-can-eat buffet-type service and lower prices have gained popularity. The increase in the number of speciality restaurants featuring one particular food, such as pizza, hamburgers, pancakes, seafoods, or ethnic foods, reflects the need to appeal to the public's changing food desires.

All of these changes must be taken into account in appropriate facility planning and design to achieve the greatest economy and efficiency in operation for whatever the type of foodservice.

Birchfield[4] identifies the following features that will be considered in facility design of the near future:

1. Food facility will be a delightful place to dine and work.
2. High technology will not replace good cookery.
3. Nutrition awareness of the public will continue to guide menu preparation and meal preparation.
4. Mini-mall foodservice design, which is a series of food shops around a common dining area, will be popular.
5. Electronic assistance will be used in the purchase, preparation, and service of food, records, operation, documents, and procedures.
6. Sanitation with minimal labor cost will be reflected in design.
7. Energy conservation will be a major consideration in all aspects of design.

Information on New Developments

Another preliminary step for the foodservice manager in preparation for working on a facility design is to learn what is new in the field. Suggestions for doing this include visiting new facilities of a type similar to the one being planned, or one where a remodeling project has recently been completed. Managers of new facilities usually are willing and eager to share their experiences. Discussion of what is good and working effectively and of ideas that were discarded can be very profitable to the planner.

Literature from equipment companies, such as catalogs, specification sheets, and descriptions of models, designs, and layouts, provides an invaluable aid to obtaining the best for the needs. Foodservice managers should contact equipment companies for such reference materials. A "library" of these material will provide a good basis for decision-making on equipment selection and arrangement. Many of these companies have representatives to assist customers with planning, and such contacts can be most helpful.

If the project involves remodeling an existing facility, another resource not to be overlooked is present employees. They often have excellent ideas and suggestions developed from their own work experience in the situation. Giving them an opportunity to express opinions should be mutually beneficial.

Regulatory Considerations

The foodservice manager will want to obtain information and become knowledgeable about national, state, and local laws, codes, and regulations that affect a building or remodeling project. These regulations have to do with zoning restrictions, building standards, electrical wiring and outlets, gas connections; health, fire and safety codes, sanitation standards related to water pollution and waste disposal systems, and for the installation of heavy duty equipment. Regulations have been established by agencies and organizations such as state, county, and local health and engineering departments, the American Gas Association, Underwriter's Laboratories, and the National Sanitation Foundation, and by federal legislation such as the Occupational Safety and Health Act (OSHA). Copies of these codes may be obtained by writing to or visiting the appropriate agency. Major libraries also usually have copies of the codes and regulations.

Other professional persons will assist in the identification and application of regulatory codes and standards. These people make up a part of the planning team discussed later in this chapter.

Special Considerations for Specific Types of Foodservices

Preliminary consideration should be given to the specialized needs of certain types of foodservice operations, having to do with location of the facility or location within a facility where foodservice is not the primary function. The physical environment has much to do with the successful operation of the individual foodservice. Thoughtful study and planning can overcome limitations often imposed by poor location or physical features inappropriate for the facility being designed. Following is a brief review of some special requirements for several types of foodservices.

COMMERCIAL   *Restaurants* that cater to downtown shoppers and business-people prefer a location near the "busiest" corner. The primary market area may be within a ten-minute walk. Rents are apt to be high in these prime locations so every inch of space must be utilized most efficiently. Reports by research studies show that when office buildings, developments, and parking areas are on one side of a major street and the restaurant is on the other side, patrons with only one hour or less for lunch are not likely to cross the street to go to that particular restaurant. Usually restaurants in a downtown location offer fast service and moderately priced menus.

Restaurants in suburban areas draw patrons from a larger radius, within comfortable driving distances. Adequate space for parking is essential. The location should have good access from roadways and good visibility when approached. Shopping centers are considered desirable locations for commercial foodservices, because they have a ready patronage and generally ample parking facilities.

Hotel and motel food units are usually located so that the coffee shop is in a conspicuous place with both street and lobby entrances, whereas the main dining, party, and banquet rooms may be more secluded and accessible only through the lobby. Usually basic preparation is done in a central kitchen, and the pre- and partially prepared items are transported to pantries adjacent to the respective service areas. The amount and arrangement of equipment needed in each instance depends on the particular situation.

SCHOOL AND UNIVERSITY   *School lunchrooms* are preferably located on the first floor of the school building, as convenient as possible to the main hallways and locker rooms. The location should be such that, in the absence of an adequate ventilating system, cooking odors that might lessen the appeal of food to the students and prove a nuisance to the classes will be eliminated. A cheerful dining room with natural light and a view does much to enhance school foodservice. Dining areas in both elementary and high schools often must serve dual purposes as for a study hall or gymnasium in addition to dining. When this is the case, a different planning situation is presented.

Foodservices for *colleges and universities* are usually located in residence halls and in student union or commons buildings. Most campuses locate residence halls on or near one side or end of the campus. The foodservice units in these halls may face a court or quadrangle. The plan of a large residence hall often includes a central kitchen and bakeshop surrounded by two, three, or four service units. A campus housing plan may include several residence halls, each with its own kitchen and dining room, but with a central bakeshop, warehouse, and laundry. Student union or commons buildings are usually centrally located and accessible from all sides, with the dining rooms prominently and conveniently located to entrances. In school and university foodservices, large quantities of relatively few menu items must be ready for service during a specified period of time so, even though a well-programmed schedule of preparation is in effect, several duplicate pieces of large equipment may be necessary. Also, adequate work space must be provided for the personnel required at peak production hours as well as for the equipment needs.

INDUSTRIAL   The *industrial food service* should be central in location with ready access from as many areas in the plant as possible. Every provision should be made to expedite service so that all workers may be accommodated quickly during a fairly short lunch break. Mobile units and vending operations may be used satisfactorily in remote areas of large plants or in those too small to justify the space and expenditure for kitchen equipment, management, and labor. Adequate passageways for such carts are essential.

HOMES FOR CHILDREN AND ADULT COMMUNITIES   Homes for children and retired persons make use of the residence hall and cottage type of planning. Because a quiet, homelike atmosphere is desirable for this type of situation, they often are located away from the busy streets of the city and surrounded by private grounds.

HOSPITALS AND HEALTH CARE CENTERS   Facility planning for hospitals and other health care centers may be more complex than for other types of foodservices because of the need to provide for staff, employees, visitors, and guests as well as for the patients. Adequate passageways for transporting patients' food on carts and trucks to various parts of the facility and space for cart storage when not in use are special considerations. Elevators or lifts designated for use only by the foodservice department can expedite meal service. Office space for the many clinical dietitians in a large hospital should not be overlooked. Group teaching of patients calls for classrooms with adequate space for teaching aids and materials. If special catering, vended food, or Meals-on-Wheels are to be provided, adequate space for these services must also be allocated.

In general, the location of kitchens and dining areas within any type of facility should be as convenient and accessible for the "customers" as possible. It is preferable for efficiency's sake to have the dining room adjacent to the kitchen. In most institutions it is desirable to have the foodservice rooms located on the first floor. Basement foodservice rooms present a perpetual problem of ventilation and lighting, and the psychological effect on patrons is less pleasing than in units located on the first floor or above, which have by virtue of their placement the advantage of more air and view. The location of the foodservice above the first floor has the disadvantage of inaccessibility to patrons and the problems relative to the necessary elevating of food supplies and the disposal of waste. In large cities the advantages of food units on the top floor of high-rise buildings, such as roof garden dining rooms, are sometimes greater than the disadvantages. Spectacular views, often seen as the dining room slowly revolves, and excellent quality food and service usually attract a high volume of business.

Steps in the Planning Procedure

After preliminary study to prepare for the facility design project, certain other steps will lead to the development of a completed layout design. In logical sequence, these steps are:

• Prepare a prospectus (a program or planning guide).
• Organize a planning team.

- Conduct a feasibility study.
- Make a menu analysis.
- Consider the architectural features desired: building materials, floors, walls, lighting, heating, cooling, ventilation, refrigeration, plumbing.
- Adjust costs and money available relationships.

Upon completion of these preliminaries, the design development process can proceed.

The Prospectus

A prospectus is a formal summary of a proposed work, that is, a written description detailing all aspects of the situation under consideration. A food-service manager or owner may spend months thinking about building a foodservice facility, remodeling, or rearranging work centers and equipment. The next step is to express these ideas on paper. Thus, a prospectus or plan is developed as a description of the elements that will affect and guide the proposed design. The prospectus is a communication tool that is shared with and used by other professionals, such as architects and consulting engineers, on the planning team. It aids their understanding of what is required and desired in the design to be developed. Prospectus development documents the conceptual thinking of the planner. The program or prospectus should give a good picture of the physical and operational aspects of the proposed facility. It might be based on questions such as:

- What type of foodservice is planned?
- What is it to accomplish?
- How many people and of what age groups are to be served? How many are to be served at one time?
- What will be the hours of service? Style of service?
- What is the menu pattern?
- In what form will food be purchased? How often? What storage facilities will be needed? How much refrigerated storage?
- What equipment and of what capacities will be required for the preparation and service of the menus?
- What are desirable space relationships?
- Will safety precautions be incorporated?
- What are the cost limitations? Projected income?
- What energy sources are available? Most economical?

The prospectus must be written clearly, concisely, yet in detail. Usually it is in three parts; these major divisions may be used as a guideline for writing the prospectus:

1. The *rationale* includes title, reason or need for project, its goal, objectives, policies, and procedures.
2. *Physical and operational characteristics* include suggested or desired architectural designs and features, all details about the menu, food preparation and service, employee and customer profiles, and anticipated volume of business.
3. *Regulatory information* includes built-in sanitation, safety, and noise control features, and energy and type of utility usage desired.

RATIONALE   This preliminary section of the prospectus needs to be defined before the remainder of the plan can be developed. It includes the project title, goal, objectives, policies and procedures, and a statement of need for the project. Perhaps these are the most difficult components to define in the prospectus document. Definitions and examples follow:

- *Title*. Description of the plan. Narrow the title to reflect actual scope of the design that is proposed. Example: Design for a warewashing area of the Coastal Restaurant Foodservice.
- *Goal*. State the single outcome of the project. Example: To develop a central warewashing area that will process all dishes, utensils, and pans of the foodservice.
- *Objective*. Specific statements that indicate what is necessary to achieve the goal. Example: The warehouse area will: (1) utilize no more than 36 square feet of floor space, (2) be operated with no more than four persons, and (3) operate with minimum energy usage.
- *Policy*. A definite course or method of action selected from among alternatives and in light of given conditions to guide and determine present and future decisions. Example: All dishes, utensils, and pans will be washed and stored within 45 minutes of use.
- *Procedure*. A particular way of accomplishing something. Example: Conveyor belts will be used to carry dirty dishes to the warewashing area, or scrapping, racking, and washing of dirty utensils and pans and storing clean ones should be accomplished with 80 per cent automation.

There is only one goal but several objectives and supportive policies and procedures. Policies are not always appropriate for each objective; however, it is very important to identify procedures in all cases. Remember, the prospectus is a guide to assist the team members in developing a foodservice facility that will meet the needs of the organization or company.

The statement of need may be simple or complex, depending on the project. An example would be: The foodservice dry and refrigerated storage areas need to be expanded 60 per cent to accommodate the increased meal census that has resulted from the recent building addition. The meal census has grown from 500 to 1,200 per day.

The rationale section should include a proposed budget for the project, although at this point it may be a very rough estimate.

PHYSICAL AND OPERATIONAL CHARACTERISTICS   Physical characteristics relate to architectural or design features such as an appropriate structural building style compatible with the type of food to be served to carry out a theme. For example, Mexican foods usually call for Mexican-or Spanish-style architecture. An example of a *design feature* to identify in a remodeling project would be an existing elevator shaft or a supporting pillar that cannot be removed. Or perhaps solar heating is desired. This need should be identified here since the desired feature may affect other considerations, such as style of roof and type of windows.

Operational data refer to the activities that go on in the foodservice department. The menu is the key item of concern in planning a foodservice facility. The menu pattern (see Chapter 3) for the foodservice being designed must be agreed on so that the type of foods to be served at each meal period will be known. Further, the forms in which the food will be purchased as fresh, canned, or frozen, and the approximate quantities of each must be estimated with some accuracy by the foodservice director. This will provide information on the amount and kind of storage space required. The methods of food preparation to be used, such as grilled hamburgers, roasted chicken, broiled steaks, and such, as well as the kind of prepreparation to be done on the premises will let the planners know the types of equipment that will be needed, and thus the amount of space required to accommodate that equipment.

The type of foodservice system to be used is included in the prospectus as the *major operational characteristic* that is basic to all design planning. Space requirements for an assembly/serve system are quite different from those of the conventional system. Another decision that must be known in advance of facility planning is whether centralized or decentralized service is to be used and the method planned for delivery and service of food. A monorail transport system, for example, must be planned for early on.

Other operational characteristics are the hours of service, anticipated volume of business, both total and per meal period, and the number of diners to be seated at any one time. These data are used to help determine the *size* of the dining area.

A *customer profile* including age, size, and mobility of people to be served is needed to determine the probable dining space required per person. For instance, children require less space than do adults; ambulatory persons require less space than do persons in wheelchairs. An *employee profile* is also necessary to identify the number of employees, the number of shifts and of employees on duty for each, the sex of the employees (for locker and rest-room space planning), and each work position as it relates to sitting, stand-ing, walking, pushing carts, and the like. All of this information is essential in planning spaces for work and movement of people and equipment.

REGULATORY INFORMATION   The regulatory information section of the prospectus should identify standards of safety, sanitation and cleanliness, noise control, and garbage and trash disposal to be met through the design plan. Guidelines for selection of type of utility and energy constraints to be used are also stated.

Every design is unique; therefore, this section may include some charac-teristics not found in the other sections. The prospectus with its identified sections and respective categories is global. However, not every project will require all parts of all sections, only those that are pertinent to the situation. For example, if the design is for dry and refrigerated storage, the customer profile would not be needed; instead, employee and equipment characteris-tics would be the focus, in addition to menu, food items, and safety and sanitation regulations.

The key in writing the prospectus is to be technical, include all pertinent data, and always comment on how data presented will affect the proposed designs. If a cocktail lounge is being designed, for example, the seating space will depend on the size of the tables and chairs selected. Generally, a com-fortable upholstered chair will take up more space than a plain straight-backed one. Such characteristics should be included, but extraneous infor-mation that has no effect on the planned design should be omitted.

The person to write the prospectus and later to help develop the design should be a professional foodservice manager who has the knowledge and authority to make decisions about the menu to be used and the space and equipment needs. That person also must be able to provide other opera-tional data required by members of the planning team.

The Planning Team

After the project plan has been identified and detailed through the prospec-tus, it is time to organize a team of persons who will work together to de-velop the design plan. The members of the planning team will vary from plan to plan according to the extent of the project. The expertise needed will be determined by the objectives and size of the design project. Typical planning team members are:

1. Owner or administrator (the person who has authority to spend money for the project and give final approval to carry it out)
2. Foodservice manager

3. Architect
4. Foodservice design consultant
5. Equipment representative
6. Business manager
7. Builder/contractor
8. Maintenance engineer/mechanical engineer

Not all team members are involved at all planning stages. Certain members will be included at intervals throughout the design development. Generally, the owner/administrator and foodservice manager will coplan an initial design and invite other team members to join them as the project develops conceptually.

The planning team formulates the floor plan, selects materials, and writes specifications cooperatively. However, the plans need to be checked and rechecked many times by team members before final proposals are submitted to builders and equipment companies for project bids. It is essential that every detail is included and is so specific that no part of the architectural features, equipment layout, and specifications are left to chance or have areas that can lead to misinterpretation. The team must allow enough time for the planning to take place. This is a very critical component to a successful foodservice.

Feasibility Study

A feasibility study is basically a research and data analysis that justifies the project under consideration. The work to be done that is proposed and defined in a prospectus should be supported by feasibility data to make sure that the project is worthy of being carried out.

The feasibility study follows the prospectus outline, and data are collected for each of the major categories. Since each project is unique, categories vary according to need. For instance, if the project is to plan a new restaurant, the feasibility study would include site selection and a marketing research of the proposed site, potential customer profiles and community growth, building trends, competition in the area, and possible revenue-generating sources such as catering functions. If the project is a small one for remodeling an existing structure, the feasibility study would reflect more operational data than community and competitive business information. In the case of a project to automate a warewashing area of a foodservice, current operational data compared to what is anticipated with the automated equipment would be included. Some of the information to be compiled would relate to labor, energy, and chemical costs, space utilization, volume of dishes, trays, pans, and the like to be processed in an identified timeframe, employee attitudes, noise generation, and quality output.

Who conducts the feasibility study? Perhaps someone on the planning team has experience as a project analyst. If not, then someone with a marketing research company could be contracted. Others with specialized knowledge may be employed to conduct parts of the study. If in-depth time/cost data are needed, an industrial engineer or management consultant may be employed. Often the foodservice director and staff can conduct the necessary surveys if their time permits.

The financial investment in most projects is so great that cost information for the building, equipping, and/or remodeling is an essential part of the feasibility study. Many people may assist in gathering data related to the costs involved, but one person should coordinate the effort. This person may be the business or financial manager who also explains the costs to the planning team. The top administrator or owner (the funding source) has authority to accept or reject the proposal.

Data sources for the feasibility study may include:

1. Operational records obtained from payroll, production, cash register, and inventory records and reports
2. City, county, state, and national regulations obtained from government documents of the respective agency involved or from library copies of those documents
3. Statistics regarding trends, average costs, and customer information obtained from regional and national trade journals as well as from independent, on-site data collection studies

Minno and Bhayana[5] have provided a chart of feasibility resources for restaurants (Fig. 9.1).

The feasibility study is a critical component to a project. If it is not well done, or otherwise vague and inaccurate, the likelihood of funding is small. If well done, however, and funds are made available to proceed, the project has every chance for success.

Menu Analysis

An important step in the preliminary planning procedure is to identify the type of menu to be served (see Chapter 3 for menu types) and the various food preparation methods involved in producing the menu items. This is the key to equipment needs, which in turn determines the amount of space required to house that equipment.

The decisions of menu, foodservice system, and style of service to be used

Restaurant Feasibility Study Resources

Sources	Available Information
1. Chamber of commerce, economic development authority or city planning office	• Population trends (historical and projected) • Age, occupation, income level, ethnic origin and marital status by census tract • Retail sales and food and beverage sales • Maps • Consumer shopping habits and patterns • Employment and unemployment statistics • Major employers and industries • Planned commercial, residential and industrial developments • Demographic and socio-economic trends • Area master plan
2. Housing and community development	• Residential occupancy and housing • Urban renewal projects • Property values
3. Building commission	• Building permits data • Planned construction developments
4. Zoning commission	• Planned uses for zoned areas • Building height, signage, parking and construction restrictions
5. Transportation department	• Road traffic patterns and counts • Proposed traffic developments • Types of public transportation and routes
6. Department of revenue	• Income and other related sales taxes • Real estate assessments
7. Convention and visitors bureau	• Number of visitors by month and spending habits/statistics • Conventions—size, type, frequency and duration • Recurring festivals and fairs
8. Utility companies	• Estimates of gas and/or electric expenses for the proposed restaurant
9. Local newspapers and magazines	• Restaurant critiques • Dining guides • Planned commercial developments

FIGURE 9.1 Resources for obtaining information needed in making feasibility studies prior to facilities planning. *Courtesy of National Restaurant Association.*

TABLE 9.1 Menu Analysis

Menu Item	Storage Type	Portion Size	Total Portions	Batch Size	Process Required	Utensils	Work Surface	Large Equipment	Holding Equipment
spinach salad	refrigerated	1 ounce	350	100	wash trim drain	knife drain pan	sink counter	sink counter	refrigerator
beef patty	freezer	4 ounces	300	50	grill	spatula	counter utility cart	grill	warming oven

A sample of a menu analysis to be made for all menu categories. When similar menu items are used, such as several salad dressings that require the same production and service treatment, only one analysis need be made. This information is the basis for determining equipment and space needs for designing a foodservice facility.

are the major planning components of the foodservice. The impact of the menu affects the design and layout of equipment. In addition, personnel skills and staffing are based on the menu. As an example, if no fried foods are included in the menu and menu pattern, no frying equipment need be purchased or planned for in the design and no cooks will be needed for this activity.

In the prospectus a sample of several days' menus and a menu pattern are included. The menu pattern defines the categories or courses of the meal, and the menu defines the respective preparation methods involved. Based on this sample typical menu, the foodservice manager makes a detailed study of the variables involved in menu item production, such as item, storage type, portion size, total portions, batch size, processing required, utensils needed, work surface, large equipment, and holding equipment (see Table 9.1). Estimated time when batch is needed and when preparation is to be done is also helpful in deciding which pieces of equipment could be shared or if duplication is necessary. The variables that the food manager selects to include must be appropriate for management decisions. Also, the manager evaluates the menu for production, service, acceptability, and feasibility. At this time, menu changes can be made to balance the equipment utilization, workload, and acceptability.

Architectural Features

Consideration should be given in the initial planning stages to certain architectural features such as style and materials of building, type of floors, walls, and ceilings with noise reduction components, provisions for lighting, heating, cooling, and ventilation, built-in refrigeration, and plumbing. Not only are decisions on these features essential for costing the project, but the right decisions can provide for ease of cleaning, good sanitation, safety in use of the facility, adequate kind and amount of lighting and temperature control for high productivity, and a reduction in noise that makes for a more pleasant work/use environment. Also, certain refrigeration units are usually built into foodservice establishments, and the amount and location of such units must be determined in advance of building construction. Likewise, if an automated monorail-type transport system is desired, plans for it must be included at this stage.

Although the food director or dietitian does not have sole responsibility for these features, some knowledge of the possibilities is desirable. Some of the components mentioned previously are included here as a basic information review.

BUILDING STYLE AND MATERIALS Geographic location, type of foodservice operation, and its menu will markedly influence the type of architecture and materials used. The Spanish influence is strong in the southwestern United States, for example, and may determine a choice for that area. The modern influence is pronounced in certain cities and brings about a marked similarity in building designs using that style.

There have been many changes in the appearance of buildings in recent years. Not only have architectural designs been changed and colors introduced to produce many different effects, but there is much change in the use of materials. Developments in metallurgy, masonry, and glass have been rapid and influential in bringing about such changes. In the selection of materials for any building, much depends on the type of architecture planned, the permanence desired, geographical location, and the likely effect of local weather conditions on the material. Certain types of architecture, such as the extremely modern, call for materials that will help to produce striking and often severe effects. The cafeteria restaurant shown in Fig. 9.2 a and b is a fine example of modern architecture, designed to take advantage of a scenic location. The interior arrangement of the dining room is planned to give diners an outstanding view.

If a building is to be constructed as a permanent structure, it is most important that the best possible materials and construction be obtained. The expense of building should be reckoned over a long period of time. Often the most expensive initial cost, when prorated over the years, will mean a lower building cost as well as lower upkeep costs. Materials of local origin, such as stone of a certain kind, will generally be used extensively because of accessibility, possible lower cost, and civic interest and pride. The action of local weather conditions on materials also influences the choice and the way they are handled. For example, a roof made of material that expands and

FIGURE 9.2 (a) The curved façade of the Top of the Falls Restaurant overlooks the whole Niagara Falls panorama. (b) The multi-level design of the restaurant interior offers every customer a spectacular view. *Both pictures courtesy of Herbert H. Gill, President, Gladieux Corp., Toledo, Ohio.*

contracts appreciably would be a poor investment in a climate of extreme changes in temperature, and moisture-resistant building materials are essential for localities where the rainy season is prolonged.

Metal, stone, brick, tile, glass, cement, marble, and wood are among the materials commonly used in the construction of buildings. The use of wood is limited in food preparation units but is often extensive in dining rooms. Comparatively low structural strength and high inflammability make wood less desirable for heavy building purposes than more durable materials.

The building engineer is particularly concerned with the chemical composition of the material, the hardness, toughness, resistance to strain, and density. All are important in determining the material best suited to the particular structure and the type of construction that will be most satisfactory. The food director, who has the responsibility of planning or remodeling a foodservice, will need to rely on the advice of experts for much of the selection of building materials and the details of construction.

FLOORS   Floors form a part of the background of rooms and should harmonize with walls and furnishings in color and type. They must also meet other requirements, chiefly utility, durability, and resiliency. Floors should be impervious to moisture, grease, and food stains; they should also be non-slippery and resistant to scratches and acid, alkali, or organic solvents. The coloring should be permanent, and the cost of maintenance and upkeep relatively low. Floors should be strong and durable to withstand the wear from the heavy traffic that is characteristic of large food units, and in kitchens to support the great weight of heavy duty equipment. Floors are commonly sloped to drains in various parts of the kitchen to permit easy cleaning. Floors under steam units are indented and fitted with their own drains.

Floors and floor coverings are available in many materials, designs, and colors, making possible interesting and pleasing decorative effects. Common among these are wood, concrete, and terrazzo floors, and clay, asphalt, vinyl, and rubber tile.

What is the best flooring for the institutional food unit? There is considerable difference of opinion about which types are most satisfactory. Hard surface flooring is fatiguing for employees and may cause accidents through slipping and falling if wet. However, this type of flooring is highly resistant to wear and soil, is comparatively easy to maintain, and is permanent. The softer, more resilient floors are likely to be less durable and more absorbent. An absolutely perfect type of floor for the foodservice in institutions remains to be discovered, although a majority of institutional kitchens use quarry tile.

WALLS AND CEILINGS, NOISE REDUCTION   Walls should intersect with floors in a coved base, and all external and internal corners and angles should be rounded to facilitate cleaning and prevent chipping. Items such as pipes, ventilator fans, radiators, and wiring conduits should be concealed in the walls.

The amounts of natural and artificial light available determines to a great extent the wall finish selected for a given room. The colors and textures of materials that may be used as wall finishes have different reflective and absorptive qualities, which must be considered in relation to the light that the room will receive.

The texture of the reflecting surface has considerable influence on the amount of light reflected. The influence that the texture of a wall surface may have on the reflection factor is indicated by the fact that light cream paint has a reflection factor of 74 and cream-colored paper has 56. Acoustical materials absorb light as well as sound, the amount varying with the material used. If such a treatment is to be given the ceiling or walls of a room, the choice of color in the finish must be carefully considered.

The walls and ceilings of institution foodservice units should provide a pleasing and sanitary background. The entire wall may be plastered and finished with enamel or enamel-type paint. This is the least expensive of the various treatments deemed even fairly satisfactory. For food preparation rooms, walls of glazed tile or masonry at least to a height of five to eight feet are commonly recommended. The remainder of the wall may then be made of a hard, smooth-finished plaster. Tile, white or colored, may be used for the entire wall if the budget permits. Regardless of the materials used, walls in all preparation units should be washable and impervious to moisture.

The height of ceilings in food units varies widely. Dining rooms with high ceilings usually produce a formal impression; those with lower ceilings give a more friendly and informal effect. Kitchen ceilings vary from 11 to 20 feet in height, with 14 to 18 feet as an average. Ceilings of both kitchens and dining rooms should be acoustically treated and lighter in color than the wall. There are many attractive, fireproof acoustical materials available for ceilings that may be mechanically suspended from or cemented to existing ceilings, or built into new installations. In dining rooms, local noises may be minimized by the use of acoustical plaster or other sound-absorbing material as wall and ceiling finishes, by heavy draperies at the windows, and by sound-absorbing finishes, such as linoleum or rubber tile, on the floors. The use in the kitchen of soundproof materials in wall, ceiling, and floor construction and finishes will reduce distracting noise levels. Acoustical ceiling materials suitable for kitchens are designed to resist deterioration from rapid temperature and humidity changes and corrosive cooking fumes. They have a low reflectance value, are fire-resistant and washable, and should be given serious consideration in the planning of all new or remodeled institution kitchens.

Fig. 9.3 shows an example of sound reduction treatment over a noisy area. Features such as automatic lubrication of the so-called noiseless power equipment that keeps it in quiet working condition, rubber-tired carts, rubber collars on openings in dish-scrapping tables, and ball bearing glide table drawers help to minimize noise in the kitchen.

Sound-absorbing materials are used not only as surface finishes in construction but also as insulators. Vents, radiator pipes, and water pipes all may act as carriers of sound, and the most effective means of noise prevention is their careful and thorough insulation with sound-absorbing material. Because of later inaccessibility and prohibitive costs, it is most important that this precaution be taken in the original construction.

LIGHTING   The amount and kind of lighting to plan for a foodservice represents a long-time investment and merits much study with the assistance of technical experts in this field, such as a lighting expert, a member of the Illuminating Engineering Society. Concern for the adequacy, efficiency, and suitability are far more important than the cost of the initial installation.

Wiring is an important consideration in the planning of lighting. It is advisable to install wiring adequate to provide an economical distribution of electrical energy for future requirements as well as for present needs. When wiring is not heavy enough to carry the specified wattage, energy is lost between meter and light, light generation is lower than rated, and cost is higher.

Wiring circuits are limited in load and length. It is economical as well as convenient to have many switches and automatic circuit breakers for control of lighting. Installation of wiring, panel boards, switches, and automatic circuit breakers should be in accordance with the requirements of the National Electrical Code. Hidden wiring with easy access to control boxes is desirable.

The foodservice design should allow for as much natural light as possible. Not only does food look more appealing in daylight, as opposed to artificial lighting, but some energy is saved and operational costs reduced. In addition, there is a good psychological effect upon workers and guests when they can look outside. Total dependence on natural illumination is not possible, however, so some knowledge of lighting and its requirements is desirable for the foodservice manager to have when working with lighting experts.

Good lighting in foodservice work areas reduces eye strain and general worker fatigue associated with improper kind and amount of illumination. Also, poor lighting produces a gloomy, depressive atmosphere, which is conducive to inaccuracy in work and lack of cleanliness, and it creates a safety hazard.

The amount or intensity of light, the kind and color of light, and type of fixtures and their placement combine to make what is called "good lighting." Reflective values of walls, ceilings, and other surfaces also affect lighting.

FIGURE 9.3   Special sound-absorbing ceiling treatments above dishwashing area. *(a)* Removable perforated accoustical panels hung from ceiling. *(b)* Boxlike corrugated aluminum sheets filled with 1 inch of fiberglass insulation suspended from ceiling in metal frame.

Light intensity is measured in footcandles, and the number required is based on the kind of work or activity to be done. The trend is toward use of better and more effective lighting, with the number of footcandles increased over earlier recommendations.[6] A light intensity of 15 to 35 footcandles is suggested for rough work; 35 to 70 footcandles are considered adequate for general work or food display area; and 70 to 150 footcandles are needed for localized work areas where recipes are read, ingredients weighed and measured, gauges and thermometers used, and for inspecting, checking, and record keeping. Fifty footcandles are sufficient for most refrigerators for good viewing of products on hand, and for detecting unsanitary conditions. Light intensity may be checked by the use of a light meter. Fig. 9.4 shows a well-lighted serving area using diffused lighting in the ceiling and supplementary lights over each serving station.

The recommended intensity of light for most institution dining rooms is

FIGURE 9.4   Example of good, diffused lighting for a scramble system cafeteria.   *Courtesy of Lois M. Jackson, Louisiana State University Medical Center Hospital, Shreveport.*

15 to 20 footcandles, which can be supplied for about 2 watts per square foot of floor area. Hallways and corridors might have less bright (10 to 20 footcandles) lighting. The desired intensity can usually be supplied if proper care is given to the choice of room finishes and to the selection of the types of lighting fixtures and their placement.

The kind and color of lights can provide varying effects on the general atmosphere, the attractiveness of the food, and the people. Two kinds of electrical lights are commonly used in foodservice. These are incandescent and fluorescent lights. Incandescent or tungsten lights generate more heat and do not burn as long as the fluorescent, rod-shaped tubed lights. Fluorescent lighting is energy saving as well as cost saving. However, certain colors of fluorescent lights make people look pale and many foods unappealing. Yellow-white incandescent lights are preferable in food display areas and dining rooms because they create a better appearance. Fluorescent lights are available in warm colors also, which are preferable to the cool blue-green hues. Selection of "good color" lights can greatly enhance a foodservice, particularly in merchandising the food.

Choice of light fixtures and their placement may be made at the planning stage, so locations for switches and outlets can be determined. The type of fixtures should harmonize with the architectural plan of the building and be so placed that the desired illumination level and balance in brightness are assured for each particular situation. Lighting systems may be either indirect, direct, or a combination of the two. The indirect has approximately 90 to 100 per cent of the light from the luminaire directed upward, whereas the direct system has a corresponding amount directed downward. A general diffusing system has about equal amounts directed either way. Diffusion of natural light through window shades or adequate shielding of artificial light by design and position of the luminaire to direct the reflected image away from the eye of the worker is necessary. Luminous ceiling lighting is an example of an allover even lighting of the entire ceiling to create the effect of natural sunlight. Care must be taken to keep the lighted-ceiling brightness low enough to prevent its becoming a source of glare and causing reflections on shiny surfaces. Light fixtures should be positioned so that employees do not stand in their own shadows while working. Shadows on work surfaces are irritating and can cause confusion for the employee. (For a detailed discussion of lighting for foodservices, see Kotschevar and Terrell.[6])

HEATING, COOLING, AND VENTILATION Providing comfortable temperatures for employees while they work and guests as they dine is the aim of the heating, cooling and ventilation system to be used. This will be planned by the architect together with engineer specialists in this field. Foodservice establishments present a somewhat different problem from other types of buildings due to the heat and moisture produced by cooking processes and the food odors that may result. A total air-conditioning system may be installed in a facility under construction, or separate heating, cooling, and ventilating control methods may be used.

Air conditioning means more than "air cooling." It includes heating, control of humidity, and the circulation, cleaning, and cooling of the air. Systems are available whereby controls for all features are in one central unit. The system may be set up to filter, warm, humidify, and circulate the air in winter, and with the addition of cooling coils and refrigeration, maintain a desirable and comfortable temperature in the summer. Dehumidification may be necessary in certain climates.

A desirable work environment for cooks is 65 to 70°F in winter, and 69 to 73°F in summer. Cooling is effected through increased circulation of the air, which provides for rapid changes of air near the body surface, dehumidification of the incoming air, and the actual cooling or refrigeration of the air to be circulated. Refrigeration may be produced by any of the usual means. It may be desirable to install air conditioning independent of the heating system, especially if conversion is accompanied by fans that regulate the velocity of the heated or cooled air. The real test of any air-conditioning system is whether or not a desirable inside temperature is maintained when the out-of-door temperature is extremely high or low and whether the relative humidity remains fairly constant at the desired degree. Summer cooling systems often present a health hazard by providing inside temperatures that differ extremely from those outside. An optimum difference between inside and outside temperature has been suggested as 1 degree for every 2.5 degrees that the outside temperature goes above 70°F. For example, if the outside temperature is 85°F, it is 15° above the desired 70°F; 15 divided by 2.5 is 6; six from 85 is 79, or 79°F as the optimum inside temperature. Local codes give specific guides for ventilating requirements in dining rooms. The average is 12 to 15 cubic feet per minute per person, or an air change every 2 to 5 minutes.

Automatic regulation of an air-conditioning system is necessary. Electric thermostatic control is favored for small installations, compressed-air control for larger units. Care should be taken to prevent wide fluctuations in air velocities; the automatic on-off cycles should be set to provide small variations that are not disturbing to guests or workers. The placement of air ducts is important to prevent direct blasts of cold air on those in the room. Fig. 9.5 shows a retirement home dining room that seats 400. It illustrates several points. The ceiling is designed with wood slats; sound absorption material is behind them. This allows enough sound to feel "friendly," but reduces the sound level enough to allow people with hearing aids to be comfortable. The lighting is excellent, with natural light on three sides and ad-

FIGURE 9.5   Distinctive treatment of a retirement residence dining room.
Courtesy of Willamette View Manor, Inc., Portland, Oregon.

equate, well-spaced ceiling lights. The row of ducts visible beside the right-hand row of lights carry the air conditioning. The room is made attractive with the suspended umbrellas and by planters surrounding the room to break up this large area.

Adequate and proper insulation of the building is necessary to obtain the best results with an air-conditioning system. Heat losses frequently run as high as 40 per cent because of such factors as poorly constructed walls, leaky windows, and improperly fitted doors.

Satisfactory ventilation in kitchens may be provided through a fan system with a special arrangement to eliminate cooking odors and fumes, moisture, and grease-laden vapors through vented hoods located over the cooking units. Cool outdoor air may be drawn into the kitchen by fans to reduce the temperature, if direct air conditioning is not installed.

Although air conditioning may be considered expensive to install and operate, it is estimated that employee productivity is increased 5 to 15 per cent in such a controlled environment. To this end, careful attention should be given to deciding on what type of temperature control system is most appropriate for a given climate and type of facility.

BUILT-IN REFRIGERATION   Planning for the adequate kind and amount of refrigeration is essential to the smooth, efficient operation of the foodservice department. Built-in, walk-in refrigerators and freezers as well as reach-in types are utilized by most foodservices. At the architectural features stage of planning, however, only the permanent built-in types are considered. Reach-in and portable types are discussed in Chapter 10.

Some knowledge of the principles of refrigeration and the types of systems used and an understanding of how to determine space needs are essential for good planning.

Cold is the absence of heat. Refrigeration by mechanical means in a food-service is the removal of heat from food or other products stored in an enclosed area such as a refrigerator, freezer, ice maker, holding cabinet, or water cooler. The use of certain refrigerants (chemical compounds), and a series of coils or evaporator, a compressor, condenser, thermostatic expansion valve, and controls are incorporated. Warm air rises from the food and moves toward the cooler surface of the evaporator coils within the refrigerator or freezer, which contains liquefied gas when at low temperature. In the beginning of the cycle, the refrigerant in liquid form flows into the coils, where it is vaporized and pressure is built up by the heat it absorbs. This starts a compressor, which pumps the heat-laden gas out of the evaporator and compresses it to a high pressure. The compressed gas flows into a condenser that is air- or water-cooled, the heat is released, the gas is reliquefied, and the refrigerant is stored until the temperature in the fixture again rises above the control level. At that time a sensor opens a thermostatic valve to admit more liquefied gas to the evaporator, and the cycle repeats itself as often as necessary to reach and maintain the desired temperature in the refrigerator, freezer, or other equipment.

The heat that is released can build up and become a deterrent to air temperature control. However, modern systems can be designed to recapture this heat and use it for heating water or similar purposes. This is energy efficient and a desirable feature to include.

Some of the common refrigerants used are sulphur dioxide, methyl chloride, dicholorodifluoromethane, known as Freon or F-12 and F-22 or Isotron. These have a relatively low condensing pressure. Desirable characteristics of refrigerants are: low boiling point, nontoxicity, nonexplosiveness, noninflammability, noncorrosiveness, stability, harmlessness to foods, inoffensive odor, high miscibility, high latent heat, and reasonable cost.

Refrigerator systems may be central, multiple unit, and single unit. In a *central* system, one machine supplies refrigeration in adequate amount for all cooling units throughout the building. This system is rarely used because of the problem of trying to maintain desirable refrigeration in all the different units and because, in case of a breakdown, *all* refrigeration is gone. In a *multiple* system of refrigeration, there is a compressor for a series of coolers, the compressor being of proper capacity to carry the load required to maintain the desired temperature in the series of coolers. A *single* unit is the self-contained refrigerating system used in the reach-in types.

The best results will be obtained if refrigeration loads are divided among units that are operated at or near the same storage temperatures.

The location and space allocations for the number of built-in units require a careful calculation of needs. Walk-in refrigerators are for large quantities of fresh or frozen products and some prepared foods. Units smaller than approximately 8 x 10 feet are considered uneconomical to install as a permanent fixture. Small establishments probably will use reach-in rather than walk-in boxes. However, factors other than size of the foodservice will also determine needs. The kind of foodservice system is one consideration. Ready-prepared systems with cook/freeze or cook/chill methods require a large amount of refrigerated storage. The frequency of deliveries is a factor. The more frequent the deliveries, the less space required. This is especially important with conventional and assembly/serve systems. The form of food purchased affects the amount as well as the kind of storage needed. If canned foods are used primarily and few fresh and frozen items are purchased, limited refrigerated storage will be required.

The amount of built-in refrigerated space to include in the facility design plan can be estimated by calculating the size of the unit of purchase (cases, boxes, bags, and so on) of the food items to be stored, multiplied by the number of units, fresh and frozen, to be stored at any one time. This will give a cubic foot total figure; walk-in units are usually 7 to 8 feet high. Three separate walk-in refrigerators are desirable, one for fresh produce, one for meat and poultry, and one for dairy products and eggs, since each grouping has a different optimum storage temperature. In addition, a walk-in freezer or freezers may also be planned. Remember to allow aisle space within the walk-ins wide enough for trucks or carts to enter. Insulation should be a minimum of 3 inches thick on all sides for coolers; 5 to 8 inches thick for freezer units that are built in. The width of shelves is based on what is to be stored, usually 2, 2.5, or 3 feet, which enters into space/size determinations.

Floors of walk-ins should be made of strong, durable, easily cleaned tile, and made level with the adjoining floor to permit easy transport of food on carts. Walls should have a washable finish impervious to moisture or should be covered with stainless steel, anodized aluminum, or vinyl. The unit should be fitted on the inside with a safety door-opening device. An outside wall-mounted recorder or gauge to indicate inside temperature of the box eliminates opening the door for checking and thus conserves some energy. Walk-ins are located close to the receiving area in most cases (see later in this chapter under "Schematic Drawing" for more about location).

Any refrigeration system selected should ensure reliable, safe, quiet, and efficient operation. It should be flexible to serve changing needs, located to save steps, and designed to do a specific job with maximum efficiency. *Flexibility* is achieved through preplanning for possible conversion from standard

(36 to 40°F) to low temperature (0 to −10°F) or vice versa, through dual controls or interchange of compressors. It is important that such an arrangement be incorporated in the initial installation instead of making revisions later on at greater expense and inconvenience.

PLUMBING   Architects and engineers have the specialized knowledge for planning plumbing for a facility. Foodservice managers must be aware of the need for kitchen and dishroom floor drains and proper drains around steam equipment; the desired location for water and steam inlets and for hand washing sinks in kitchens, in restrooms, and in various work units; and must know the pressure needs for equipment usage. Waste disposal has to be planned for with adequate drains to sewer lines. Venting of the plumbing system to allow sewer gases to be expelled into the atmosphere, traps to prevent backups of gas, and adequate size pipelines to supply steam pressures specified by manufacturers for their equipment are other plumbing components that will be planned by the specialists. Local codes as well as those established by the National Plumbers Association and by the U.S. Public Health Service provide guidelines to be followed in building and installation of plumbing.

ELECTRICITY   Food managers are responsible for providing information as to where electrical outlets will be needed and the voltage required to accommodate all of the equipment to be used. Manufacturers state power requirements in their specifications of equipment. Usually both 220v and 110v are required. Power requirements must be compatible with the power supply into the building, otherwise the equipment will not operate at full efficiency or will overload the wiring. The power supply will determine the pin configuration to be specified for the plugs on appliances purchased for the receptacles installed: single-phase power requires a three-pin configuration; three-phase power a five-pin.

   The wattage and/or horsepower of the equipment should be included in the specifications. The mechanical engineer on the planning team will be responsible for writing the electrical specifications, but the food manager will have to provide the information just described for the foodservice department's requirements. Hospitals may require special receptacles for their food carts. It should not be forgotten that these carts will be moved to various locations, which must be designated so compatible receptacles can be installed at all points of need. Fig. 9.6 shows installation of overhead electrical raceways for carts in a hospital kitchen being remodeled.

FIGURE 9.6   Overhead electric raceways to accommodate ten patient food carts. Connection plates are equipped with receptacles and point-of-use circuit breakers.   *Courtesy of Louisiana State University Medical Center Hospital, Shreveport.*

Cost/Money Available Relationship

A study of costs involved in any facility design project is an inevitable aspect of planning. Only rarely does someone have unlimited funds to proceed as desired without some monetary restrictions. In most situations, a predetermined budget is established, and spending must be kept within the limits set. Whatever the situation, the quality and features selected may affect the cost of operation. It may be better economy to spend more initially for good quality and best design that will effect savings later on rather than to "cut corners" all along the way.

Building and construction costs are affected by many factors, all interrelated. They have to do with regional price of labor and materials, quality and quantity of items selected, and overall building design. The relationship of these three factors—cost, quality, and quantity—may be diagrammed as a triangle. If the cost or amount of money available to be used is preset, there will be some restrictions on quantity, quality, or both. However, if the space

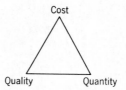

needs are the first and most important consideration, then the funds must be flexible to cover the cost of obtaining the size of building or space required. Likewise, if the quality of features and equipment is the main determinant, the cost and quantity factors must be flexible. Thus, if one factor is changed, the others are affected in some manner.

Since there are so many variables involved in the construction and equipping of a foodservice unit, especially during a fluctuating economy, it is difficult to suggest even average figures on which to base estimates of total costs for a project. Some architects base overall costs on cubic feet instead of square feet, or on the number of beds in a hospital, or the number of seats in a dining room of a school, restaurant, or industrial plant. Whatever the basis of costing, the architect and design planners will be knowledgeable about current rates and charges.

The design of the building or foodservice department determines many expenses, particularly the labor costs involved in the operation of the department. A well-planned arrangement on one floor reduces to a minimum the travel distance of food and people and lends itself to good supervision. Compact work units with the proper equipment easily accessible to the workers and arranged to reduce steps, motion, and fatigue make it possible to minimize time, labor, and operating costs. In the past it was not uncommon for at least 10 per cent of an employee's time to be spent in locating and assembling utensils and supplies. It has been estimated that in an efficiently planned department, perhaps only the dietitian or foodservice supervisor, storeroom clerk, dishroom supervisor, pot and pan washer, and janitor would need to walk about outside their work areas.

The total costs for cleaning materials, utilities, depreciation costs for building and equipment, and the amount of equipment needed are other expenses that are in direct ratio to the amount of space allocated to the foodservice department, and are often overlooked in planning.

The furnishings or items of equipment included should contribute to efficient operation and reflect the best design, materials, and workmanship to conform to established sanitary standards. The comfort of both guests and employees will depend on provisions made for them in early planning. Air conditioning, lighting, sound deadening, artistic incorporation of color and pleasing design, comfortable chairs and working surface heights, and clean, well-ventilated restrooms are some of the things to which both patrons and employees are particularly sensitive.

The cost factor cannot be overlooked as it will necessarily influence what can be done in facility designing within the budgetary allowance. However, the assumption is made in the remainder of this book that adequate funds are available for foodservice planning on a moderate scale.

Design Development

After the foodservice manager has completed preliminary preparations—the feasibility study, menu analysis, prospectus writing, and cost considerations—it is time to develop a design and layout plan. Provision of adequate facilities for all anticipated activities, incorporation of the ideas generated by the planning members, and a regard for the future growth of the facility are all involved in design development.

A logical sequence for developing a design and for completing a foodservice facility is:

1. Determine space allowances; draw a flow diagram to show space relationships of the work units to be included and routes for material and people.
2. Prepare a schematic design to scale showing space allowances and relationships and placement of equipment, preliminary to preparation of blueprints by the architect.
3. Prepare and submit the architect's complete set of blueprints and contract documents, including specifications, to reliable interested contractors, builders, engineers, and equipment representatives for competitive bids.
4. Formulate contracts with accepted bidders.
5. Make inspections of construction, wiring, plumbing, finishing, and of the equipment and its installation, as specified on blueprints and in contracts. This is the responsibility of the architect and the contractor.

These steps are detailed in the remainder of this chapter.

Space Allowances and Relationships

The amount of floor space and how it should be divided for foodservice activities is difficult to state because each operation differs. Each needs adequate space for the preparation and service of meals for the number of people to be served. Yet if too much space is allowed, inefficiency and lost time and effort can result.

From the prospectus and menu analysis, the number and kind of activities to be performed will be stated. For each activity, such as vegetable preparation, baking of bread, pastry and desserts, cooking specific menu items, service methods to be used, and so on, the equipment needed to accomplish each is listed. Consulting the equipment catalogs collected for reference, the size specification of the model to be purchased is determined. This space for equipment plus adequate aisles will give a fair estimate of space required.

One procedure often followed is to calculate dining room space needs first. Fairly accurate estimates for dining areas can be calculated if the type of service and number of persons to be seated at one time are known. Likewise, the seating capacity can be determined by use of the generally accepted standard number of square feet per seat for the different kinds of institution foodservices. Larger allowances permit room for easy waiter service and adequate table space and comfort for the diner. Variations from the following list will depend on the sizes of tables and chairs and whether spacious arrangement is desired. These are suggested guides.

School lunchrooms	9–12 (sq. ft. per seat)
Hotel and club banquet rooms	10–11 (sq. ft. per seat)
Commercial cafeterias	16–18 (sq. ft. per seat)
Industrial and university cafeterias	12–15 (sq. ft. per seat)
Residence halls	12–15 (sq. ft. per seat)
Restaurants and hotels (table service)	14–16 (sq. ft. per seat)
Lunch counters	18–20 (sq. ft. per seat)

Once the dining area is known, the kitchen size may be estimated as one-third to one-fourth of the dining room area. This is a rough estimate at best for so many variables are involved. A fast food restaurant and a school cafeteria serving the same number of persons in a given meal period have entirely different needs in both kitchen and dining rooms. The restaurant may have a turnover of three customers per hour for each seat over a three-hour meal period. In the school cafeteria, one-half of the group is seated at one time and the total number is served in a 50-minute period. Larger quantities of food would be prepared and ready at one time to serve the schoolchildren; the restaurant would use small batch preparation. In each case the size and capacity of the equipment needed would be very different. The restaurant kitchen likely would be much smaller than the school kitchen with its larger capacity equipment. Variation in menu may result in further differences in kitchen size.

Hospital foodservices have a unique situation for space determination in that only one-third to one-half of the total number to be served eat in the dining room; patients usually are served in bed. Consequently, hospital kitchens are large in relation to dining areas in order to prepare and assemble the quantity and variety of food needed for patients in addition to staff, employees, and guests served in dining rooms.

Mayfield[7] reported a study using general guidelines versus actual determination of square footage requirements for a small hospital expansion project. Data presented showed an average of 9.73 square feet per meal equivalent (American Hospital Association definition) of the hospitals studied, and the average of 36.83 square feet for each bed. A calculation of total space requirements for a foodservice facility was also made by grouping the equipment and staff into work units with reasonable space for each. Using this method, space requirements were considerably less, that is, 9.1 square feet per meal equivalent and 31.81 square foot per hospital bed.

> This method . . . allowed for the consideration of all variables such as type of food service and delivery system, number and variety of meals produced, functions and tasks of each production area, traffic aisle needs, equipment needed to meet production demands, employee scheduling, work space requirements, storage requirements, and office space needs.[7]

The author concludes that this is the preferred method for determining kitchen space requirements because the variables in each situation can be taken into account, and so give a realistic figure of space required.

FLOW DIAGRAM OF SPACE RELATIONSHIPS   The first step in designing the floor plan is to draw a diagram showing the routing or flow of work and/or materials (food and supplies) and the relationship of work units. A basic principle to follow in planning for an efficient operation is the assembly line concept to effect a continuous work flow from receiving, storing, issuing, preparing, cooking, and serving the food without backtracking and with as little cross traffic as possible. After service and consumption of the food, the direction reverses to remove dishes to be washed and trash taken back to the area where the routing began. A flow diagram may be drawn as in Fig. 9.7. Only the work units involved in a specific planning project would be shown.

Also to be considered is the relationship of one work unit to the other, that is, which areas need to be close to each other, which with the other areas of the building, and which with the out-of-doors. The example in Fig. 9.8 shows the relationship of areas in a medium-size institution using the conventional foodservice system. From the receiving area, which must be located at the back outside door, the direct routing of food is from receiving through preparation to service. Food is checked in and removed from receiving to dry long-time storage or refrigeration units if that is necessary. Otherwise, it can be moved directly from storage to the preparation or cooking

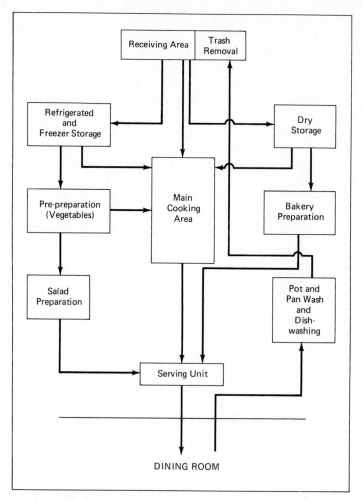

FIGURE 9.7   Flow chart diagram showing desirable work-area relationships and progression of work from receiving goods to serving without backtracking and little cross traffic.

areas. Much food is now purchased in ready-to-cook form so the preparation stations may be bypassed in some kitchens. If most foods are purchased after preliminary preparation, the vegetable preparation area may be reduced to a worktable, sink, refrigerator, and chopper, and the meat preparation area, other than refrigerated storage, may be eliminated entirely. Such diagrams are of assistance in planning kitchen arrangements to minimize traffic lines, backtracking, and crossing of traffic, all of which result in con-

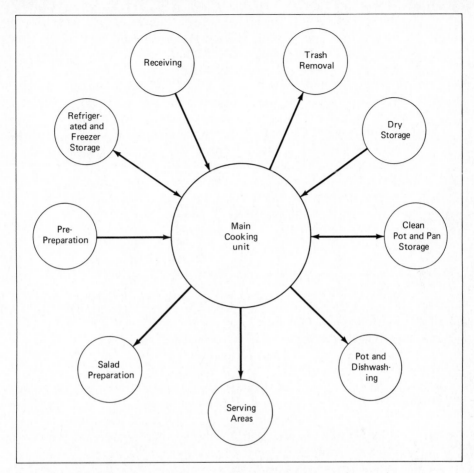

FIGURE 9.8 Relationship of main cooking unit to other work areas in a conventional foodservice system.

fusion and inefficient use of space, time, and energy. The most direct and shortest route for the workers and for food and supplies is the goal.

Schematic Drawing

Translating a flow diagram into a preliminary floor plan is the next step in design development. This is a sketch or sketches of possible arrangements of the work units with equipment within the allocated space. A brief description of various work areas, their specific equipment needs, and some general guidelines to be followed in this planning are given.

Work Areas   Seven major types of work are generally provided for in foodservice departments: receiving, storing and issuing dry and refrigerated foods, preparation, preparation/cooking, food assembly/serving, warewashing (dishes, pots and pans), and such supporting services as administrative work that requires office space, lockers and restrooms, and janitorial storage and facilities. Each of these areas may be further divided. For example, cooking may be broken down to: meats, vegetables, salads, baked goods, desserts, and beverages. Space for all or part of these units may be provided in the main kitchen. If so, these work centers often are separated with a semipartition 4 to 6 feet high. This type of partition allows for better circulation of air and ventilation than partitions to the ceiling. In larger facilities, separate rooms are desirable for certain tasks, such as preparation if done on premises, baking, and dishwashing. This ensures a more quiet kitchen, especially with dishwashing separated from other activities.

The number of units to plan in a specific foodservice depends on the volume and types of food to be prepared. A small operation may have a closely organized kitchen staffed with two or three cooks who assist each other with their work and share equipment. The shared equipment would be located nearest the area where it is used most. For example, in a small residence hall, the cook may mash potatoes or make muffins more often than the salad and dessert cook would make mayonnaise or mix a cake. Therefore, the mixing machine might be located at the end of the cook's table but near the salad and dessert area. Each person may have a work area alone to perform specific duties, but generally there are no widely separated areas. The preparation and dishwashing areas are included in the kitchen space, and a dining room and storeroom may be adjacent (see Fig. 9.9).

A larger foodservice may not have completely separated departments with duplicate equipment, but by careful grouping of the equipment, each cook has his or her own work area and may possibly share a common mixing machine and stack of ovens. Large operations are usually divided into specialized departments, each with its own equipment and short-time storage facilities. Several dining rooms may be serviced from one main kitchen. Storage space for cleaning supplies, locker rooms, and restrooms for employees, checkrooms and restrooms for guests, and sometimes a laundry and employee/staff dining rooms are included in addition to the usual major areas noted earlier.

The location of areas and their relationship to each other should be conducive to the maximum output and efficient operation of the whole organization. Specific work areas are:

The *receiving area* includes an outside platform, preferably covered, and adjacent floor space where food is checked in, examined, and weighed or counted. The height of the platform or loading dock should be that of a

FIGURE 9.9   Compact, efficient kitchen arrangement with serving and dishwashing units included within one room. Power-driven conveyor for soiled dish return is on the right.

standard truck floor above the driveway. The floor of the platform should be on the same level as the floor of the entrance to the building. Eight feet is suggested as a minimum width, and the length of the platform is determined by the number of trucks that might need to unload at one time. The service driveway should be easily accessible from the street or highway and provide space for trucks to back up to the loading platform or turn around. A ramp or steps at the end of the platform for pedestrians and a chute on which to slide canned goods to a basement storeroom would be advantageous. Products need to be examined for quality; weights need to be verified and invoices checked before the deliveryperson leaves; therefore, the receiving area needs to be large enough to accommodate the quantity of food and supplies that might be delivered at any one time. Also, there should be space to house hand trucks and platform scales and a desk or shelf on which papers may be placed while items are being checked off as they are delivered from the truck. Large institutions that process their own meat need to include an overhead track with hooks for carcass meat, to extend from the loading platform through the meat preparation department to refrigerator. The outside door should be a six-foot single or regular double size to admit hand trucks, large cartons, and any pieces of large equipment. A glass-walled office back of a double-face weighing-in scale would be convenient if someone else is responsible for examining the products for quality.

The *storage area* includes space for storing canned foods and grocery items and for the walk-in refrigerators and low-temperature boxes or rooms for perishable foodstuffs. Refrigerators used for daily supplies or leftovers in each department are usually not considered as stores. The food storage area should be as near receiving as possible and accessible to the preparation areas. In large institutions auxiliary storage space may be needed for reserve stocks of items purchased in great quantity at infrequent intervals. Dry storage rooms should be cool and well ventilated. Other requirements are moistureproof washable floors, screened windows, metal-slatted shelves for open case goods, and covered storage bins for items such as cereal products and condiments. All should be arranged so that hand trucks may be used for convenient loading and unloading. Cases of canned goods and sacks of sugar should be stacked on racks to keep them above the floor level. A desk and possibly a file should be provided for inventory records, requisitions, order lists, or other records kept in this area. Scales are a necessity. Double doors with a good lock and wide enough to admit hand trucks should open onto a corridor leading to the preparation areas. An orderly arrangement with index posted in a conspicuous place aids in locating items without time-consuming searches. (See Chapter 3 for a suggested arrangement plan.)

Walk-in storage refrigerators are usually located in close proximity to the receiving and preparation areas. Mobile units of shelves that can be wheeled into the kitchen for checking and cleaning are conducive to good order and housekeeping and limited food spoilage.

The amount of storage space needed depends on the frequency of deliveries. When deliveries of supplies are made daily, an institution may require comparatively little storage space; whereas an institution receiving less frequent deliveries may need considerable storage space. Also, storage requirements vary according to the form in which food is purchased. Foods in prepared forms, such as frozen foods, require lower storage temperatures but less storage space. Fresh potatoes and other root vegetables should be stored in a dark, well-ventilated dry room near the vegetable preparation area.

Storage space for cleaning compounds and supplies must be provided that is *separate* and *apart* from all food stores to help ensure that none of these poisonous chemicals will be mistaken for and issued as a food product. Incidences have occurred of chemical poisoning due to such errors.

Additional space is needed for paper goods and reserve supplies of china, glassware, and linens, including uniforms and aprons. The amount of space is determined by the quantities of these items that are to be stocked. Kotschevar and Terrell[6] (p. 118) provide a table of measurements of representative storage items, helpful for calculating storage space requirements.

A *central ingredient room,* if one is to be used, should be located adjacent to the storage areas and usually is connected to them. Adequate table/counter space for weighing or measuring ingredients, accurate scales, and adequate aisle space for moving carts with the assembled ingredients to the production units are basic requirements of this unit.

The *prepreparation areas* include meat and vegetable preparation units and fish and poultry units. With the general trend toward the purchase of fabricated and pan-ready meats, peeled or frozen vegetables, and ready-to-cook fish and poultry, the need for these once necessary large and important areas has decreased. However, some institutions find it to their advantage to continue these operations in their kitchens, where the use of fabricated meat cuts does not seem advisable. A well-equipped meat preparation department would include the hardwood meat tables, electric saw and grinder, sink, storage trays, and refrigeration facilities. If a meat prepreparation area is needed, it is often arranged directly in front or at the side of the meat storage refrigerator and not far from the central cooking area.

The *vegetable preparation area* should be located near refrigerated storage and the cooking and salad areas. In a large institution this unit is often set up in a square- or rectangular-shaped area with equipment arranged on the sides and down the center, and one end open to the main kitchen. The usual vegetable preparation area is equipped with a chopper, cutter, a two-compartment sink, worktables, cart, knives, and cutting boards, A peeler, if needed, may be either a pedestal or table model and placed to empty directly into a sink along a wall or at a right angle to it. A portable sink would be a convenience in many vegetable preparation units. Fig. 9.10 shows three possible arrangements for this work unit.

Two separate sinks should be provided to permit unhampered use. Food waste disposer units are placed in the drainboard or on a worktable near the end of the sink, or space for a garbage can is provided, often under an opening cut in the worktable or drainboard.

Often the preparation for the salad department is done in the vegetable preparation area; therefore, ample space is needed for many workers. Tables 30 to 36 inches wide and 8 to 10 feet long are adequate; a 36-inch-wide table permits workers to be on either side for most types of preparation. The inclusion of at least one table low enough for employees to sit comfortably while working is advisable. In an area where employees work back-to-back, a 4½ foot aisle is minimum; a 6-foot aisle is preferable where portable tables or carts and dollies are used to transport foods and utensils from one area to another.

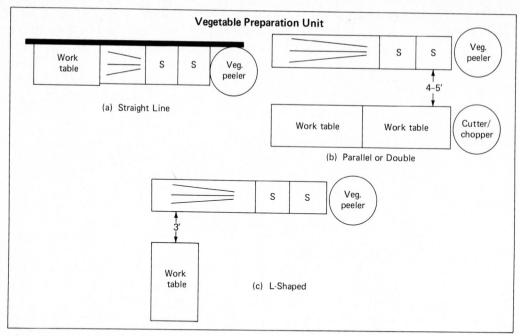

FIGURE 9.10   Three possible arrangements for vegetable preparation unit: *(a)* straight-line; *(b)* parallel; *(c)* L-shaped.

The main *cooking area* is the hub or center of the kitchen and is located adjacent to the vegetable preparation area, the pot and pan washing unit, the storage rooms, and in back of or near the serving units. It may include range, ovens, broilers, fryers, and equipment used by the cook such as the cook's table, pot and pan storage rack, mixing machine, and slicers. Some kitchens need specialized equipment such as steam-jacketed kettles and pressure steam cookers for batch cooking of fresh vegetables, grills, roast and convection ovens, and tilting fry pans, which reduce or eliminate entirely the number of heavy range units required.

In large kitchens an island arrangement of the cooking equipment near the center of the room is usually favored over a wall setup, because of its relationship to preparation units, the shortened distance to the serving units, and the sanitation factor. The grouping of equipment within an area varies with the size and shape of the room. Ranges and steam-jacketed kettles may be set up side by side in a straight-line arrangement or back to back or facing in parallel lines. The steam unit may be at the end and perpendicular to the line of the range unit, forming an L-shaped arrangement. Other modifica-

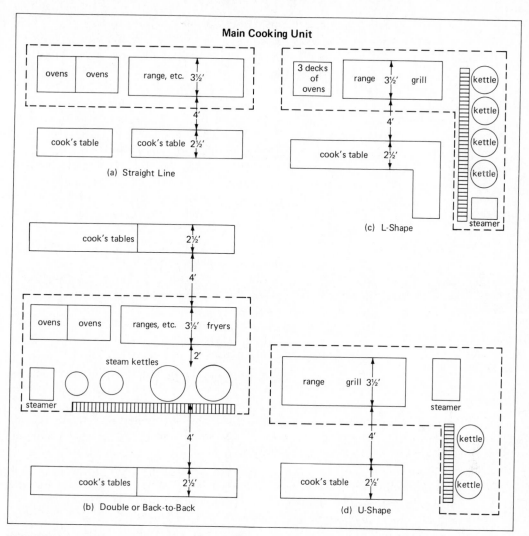

FIGURE 9.11 Four suggested arrangements for a main cooking area: *(a)* straight-line; *(b)* back-to-back or double; *(c)* L-shaped; *(d)* U-shaped. Note the amount of aisle space and total floor space required for each.

tions are the U-shaped and E-shaped kitchens. Broilers and fryers are included in the range unit. Various shaped units for a main cooking area are illustrated in Fig. 9.11. Note the amount of space required for various arrangements, including a 12- to 18-inch cleaning space between back-to-back rows of cooking equipment.

Hoods fitted with exhaust fans, vented separately, hung from the ceiling, and extending one foot down over all cooking surfaces and steam units aid materially in ventilating the kitchen by removing odors, smoke, moisture, and gas fumes. Hoods also facilitate the installation of direct lighting fixtures to illuminate cooking surfaces. Often one large hood and ventilating fan may serve the whole grouping, with consequent economy in installation. Specially designed ventilator systems with removable filters may be installed over cooking equipment and in hoods. Such filters, easily removed for cleaning, reduce fire hazards by filtering grease and dust from the air and prevent clogging of grease vent pipes. They provide a fireproof filter chamber between the cooking equipment and the exhaust duct and an automatic release valve for the bypassing of any unburned gases. Such a system provides a frequent complete change of air and improves the appearance of the room.

The cook's table, usually located directly in front of the cooking equipment, includes a rack for small equipment and, in most kitchens, a sink. A rack for clean pots and pans should be easily accessible to both the cooking unit and the pot and pan sink and power washer. A mixing machine used most in the cooking areas should be located near the pressure steam cookers. A short-time storage reach-in refrigerator and hand sink should be near the cook's unit. The length of this depends on the amount of equipment and the plan of the arrangement. Much of the equipment in the cooking area may be wall hung or mobile to facilitate cleaning. Flexible connections are available with safety valves for installation of mobile gas-fired equipment.

A modular utility distribution and control system has many advantages over fixed and permanent installations that often need to be changed after a few years. The entrance of and controls for all utilities are centered in one end-support column of the system. All pipes and wiring are enclosed, but control buttons for both operation and quick-disconnect are on the outside within easy reach of a kitchen worker or maintenance person. Water, steam, gas, and electrical outlets may be installed as desired in panels extending from the "one-point" control column along a wall or to a center room unit, directly back of equipment or from above (see Fig. 9.12). Also, pedestal or counter installations are possible. A water outlet at each point of use, such as a swing-arm faucet between each pair of steam-jacketed kettles, above or at the side of a tilting frypan, is a great convenience and timesaver for the cook. Several gas and electrical outlets along the panel permit easy interchange of mobile equipment. It is possible to move an entire system of this type to another location in the kitchen; also, such a system may be custom designed for any situation (see Fig. 9.13).

The *salad area* is often located at one side or end of the room and as close to the serving unit as practicable. This unit requires liberal allowance of table space, refrigerator space, sinks, and the usual sharp knives and cutting boards.

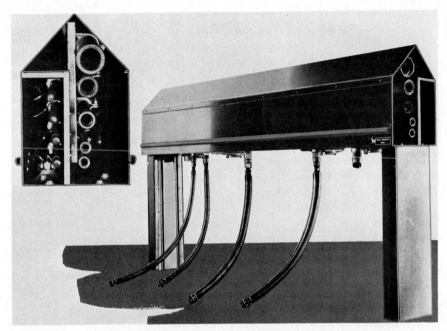

FIGURE 9.12   An overhead modular utility distribution and control system facilitates flexibility in arrangement and ease of maintenance.   *Courtesy of Avtec Industries, Inc.*

Mechanical cutters and choppers in the vegetable preparation area may be used in preparation of vegetables. Ingredients and dressings must be kept chilled. Placing bowls of ingredients on a refrigerated table while working helps to retain the crisp freshness desired in a salad. A refrigerated cabinet, with angle slides for trays or shelves for the storage of approximately one-third of the salads made up in advance, is necessary for certain types of institutions where many people are served in a limited period of time. Otherwise, it is highly desirable to make salads as close as possible to time of service. In a cafeteria, it would be advantageous to locate the salad area directly in back of the salad counter, with a pass-through refrigerator built into the separating wall. Several possible arrangements are shown in Fig. 9.14. The trays of salads may be placed in the refrigerator as soon as they are made and removed by the counter attendant as needed, thus ensuring a constant supply of freshly made salads and eliminating the necessity of persons to transport the finished product over a long distance from preparation to service. In a hospital or service restaurant operating on more than one floor, easy access to service elevators, subveyors, or dumb waiters is impor-

FIGURE 9.13   Custom-designed utility distribution system. This wall-type unit houses electrical wiring, plumbing assemblies, gas piping, and contains controls for water wash cleaning system for the exhaust ventilator. The fire control system for protection of cooking equipment is located in the exhaust ventilator which is above the utility distribution system.   *Courtesy of Louisiana State University Medical Center Hospital, Shreveport.*

tant to deliver made-up salads in good condition for service far from their preparation source.

The *bakery and dessert area* operates as a fairly independent unit. It has little direct association with the other preparation areas and may be separated from them in location. Products from this unit are transported directly to the service unit; therefore, the two units should be rather close, although the quality of pies, cakes, puddings, and rolls is not as dependent on timing and temperature for serving as is that of meats, cooked vegetables, and salads. Routing of work should be in a counterclockwise arrangement with the finished product on the side closest to the serving area.

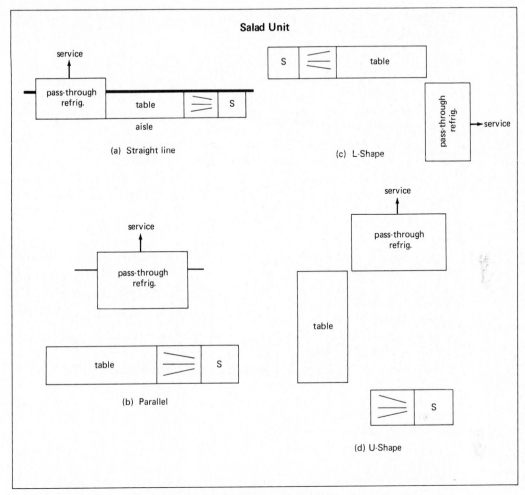

FIGURE 9.14 Four suggested arrangements for a salad unit: *(a)* straight line, *(b)* parallel, *(c)* L-shape, *(d)* U-shape. *Note:* Equipment is arranged so work progresses from left to right (preferred progression) in all except *(c)*.

Equipment for a typical bakeshop unit includes baker's table with roll-out bins, oven, pan racks, sinks, cooling racks, steam-jacketed kettle, dough divider and roller, pie crust roller, and reach-in or small walk-in refrigerator. Large units include additional items such as dough mixer, proof box, and dough trough. The routing in the performance of the tasks should provide for a direct line of procedure with little or no backtracking or crisscrossing.

The small institution may place the baker's table near the cooking unit so that equipment can be shared.

Many institutions purchase frozen desserts, especially ice creams and ices, instead of producing them within the foodservice. If the production activity is included, a separate room must be provided with specialized equipment to permit handling these products to meet the highest standards of sanitation. The production of frozen desserts must conform to the regulations established by the local department of health.

The *pot and pan area* includes the space for a work aisle allotted to this function, the three-compartment sink, mechanical washer, and storage racks for both soiled and clean utensils. The location of the area should be near the cooking unit but out of any main traffic lines. Often it is conveniently located at the end or back of the cooking unit, or in an alcove. Hand washing of pots and pans may be implemented by the use of a manually guided power scrubber and a good detergent. The three-compartment sink provides for washing, rinsing, and sanitizing either by higher temperature or a chemical rinse. The installation of a steam jet in, a gas burner beneath, or an electric immersion element in the last compartment is possible. The drainboard on the right end of the sink may be used for the temporary stacking of soiled utensils, and the left drainboard for air drying of the clean utensils. The rack for storage of clean equipment should be near and also convenient for the cook. Although mechanical pot and pan washers have been installed in many large operations, sinks are still necessary for soaking or preflushing. After hand washing of pots and pans, they may be sanitized in a steam cabinet as described in Chapter 8.

Large institutions, particularly hospitals with their serving carts for meal delivery to patients, may need a room-size cart and pan washer as illustrated in Fig. 9.15 (a) and (b). Adequate space must be allowed for such an installation.

The *dishwashing area* should be compact, light, and airy. If it is not located directly adjacent to the dining room, mechanical conveyors save time and money in transporting soiled dishes to this work unit. It is desirable to have the dishwashing area away from the dining room because of the noise. If this is impossible, the area should be surrounded by acoustical material to modify the sounds. Care must be taken in locating the unit so that the return of soiled dishes will not interfere with the routine of service. The dishwashing unit may include a prewash arrangement, a dishwashing machine, a glass washing machine, soiled and clean dish tables, waste disposers, storage carts, and carts or conveyors for transporting dishes to and from this unit (Fig. 9.16). The setup must provide space and facilities for the smooth flow of dishes through sorting, scrapping, washing, rinsing, drying, and removal to storage. In addition to space for the fixed equipment, floor space is needed

(b)

(a)

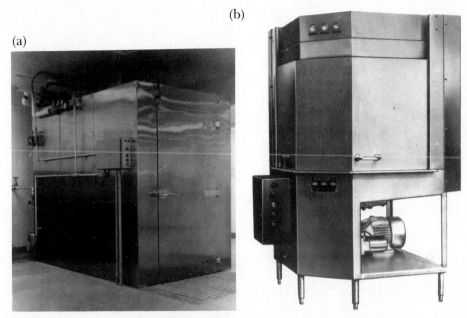

FIGURE 9.15 (a) Insulated rack, cart and pan washer with "drip off" area in front of door. (b) Mechanical pot and pan washer for corner installation. *Courtesy of Alvey Washing Equipment, Division of Alvey Industries, Cincinnati, Ohio.*

FIGURE 9.16 Dishwashing room shows incoming conveyor belts on left that merge on a double scrapping table with integral silver soak sink and waste disposer; convenient dish rack return. *Courtesy of S. Blickman, Inc.*

for aisles and as many conveyors, carts, and portable counter storage units as are needed to transport china, glassware, and silverware to and from this area.

The size and type of dishwashing machine to select and the arrangement of the dishwashing area depend on the number of pieces to be washed, the speed with which they must be returned for reuse, and the shape of the available area. Capacities and installation requirements of different size machines must be studied in order to select the one that will best meet the needs of the organization. Fig. 9.17 shows one solution to a limited length of space. The length of dish tables varies with the size of the unit, but, in general, the clean dish tables should be long enough for three to five racks for air drying and stacking space for rack-type machines. The usual division of space allotted to dish tables is 40 per cent for clean dishes and 60 per cent for soiled. Flight-type machines require comparable space for soiled dishes and adequate space for unloading clean dishes at the other end of the machine, usually directly onto carts for transport to the area of next use.

Some form of preflushing equipment should be provided. A dishwashing machine can have a built-in or attached unit for preflushing. Other types are hose and nozzle and forced spray, neither requiring more than about two feet of table space. These are illustrated in Fig. 9.18. The hose-nozzle arrangement could be near the machine, but the forced spray should be far enough away from it to permit easy racking of dishes following the preflushing operation. Food waste disposer units could be installed with either type. A method for returning emptied racks to the soiled dish table should also be provided. (See the power-driven conveyor arrangement in Fig. 9.9.)

The type of arrangement for a dishwashing area may be straight-line, L-shape around or into a corner, U-shape, open square, platform, or closed circle. The straight-line type is often installed near a side wall in small operations. Machines are designed for either right- or left-hand operations, although the usual flow direction is right to left. The U-shaped type is a compact and efficient arrangement for small operations; whereas, the open-square might be preferred for a larger unit and could easily include a glass washer. A more complex arrangement is the platform type, where two parallel tables are connected by sliding bridges over which trays loaded with soiled dishes may be transferred to the machine table. Usually a receiving table is located across the end or parallel with the soiled dish table, onto which silver, china, and glassware are deposited into their respective places or racks.

The closed-circle, or fast-rack conveyor, arrangement is shown in Fig. 9.19. In this setup, the racks are moved continuously to the soiled dish end of the washer by a stainless steel chain drive. Components such as a waste system for pulpable materials (see Fig. 8.7, Chapter 8), condenser, and blower-dryer

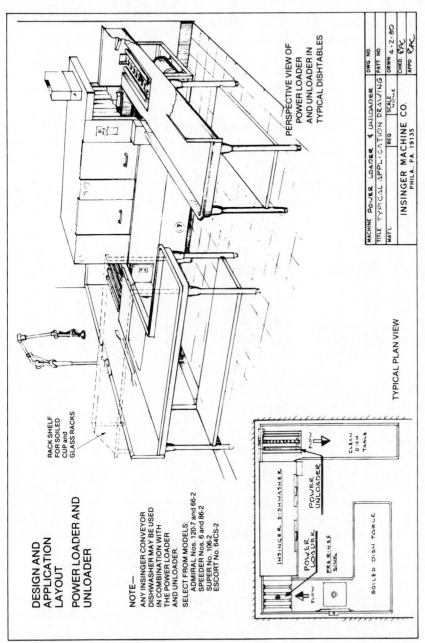

DESIGN AND
APPLICATION
LAYOUT

POWER LOADER AND
UNLOADER

NOTE—

ANY INSINGER CONVEYOR
DISHWASHER MAY BE USED
IN COMBINATION WITH
THE POWER LOADER
AND UNLOADER.

SELECT FROM MODELS:
ADMIRAL Nos. 120-7 and 66-2
SPEEDER Nos. 6 and 86-2
SUPER No. 106-2
ESCORT No. 64CS-2

RACK SHELF
FOR SOILED
CUP and
GLASS RACKS

PERSPECTIVE VIEW OF
POWER LOADER
AND UNLOADER IN
TYPICAL DISHTABLES

TYPICAL PLAN VIEW

MACHINE	POWER LOADER & UNLOADER		DWG. NO.	
TITLE	TYPICAL APPLICATION DRAWING		PATT. NO.	
MATL		REQ	SCALE NONE	DRWN. 4-2-80
	INSINGER MACHINE CO.			CHKD RAC
	PHILA. PA. 19135			APPD. RAC

FIGURE 9.17 A dishroom layout plan for a small space. This company's power
loader and unloader enables many facilities to use larger dishmachines in a small
area. The unloaders eject dishracks at a right angle to the machine, which is a
space-saving feature. *Courtesy, Insinger Machine Co., Philadelphia.*

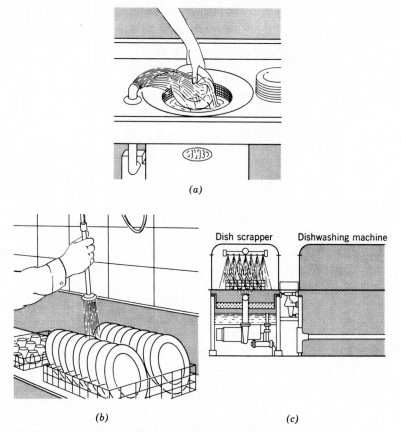

FIGURE 9.18   Three arrangments for preflushing soiled dishes. *(a)* Forced water spray. *(b)* Hose and nozzle. *(c)* Water scrapping unit on dishmachine.

may be incorporated into the system. This type requires approximately the same amount of floor space as a straight-line type, but it fits into a more compact arrangement and is operated with fewer employees, who can remain in one location.

Any type of dishwashing arrangement should be installed far enough from the wall to permit ease of cleaning. A four-foot aisle, at least, is desirable if people are to work behind the table. A booster heater should be installed adjacent to the machine to increase the temperature of the rinse water from the usual 135 to 180°F. An oversize sink may be needed for washing serving trays that are too large to go through the dishwashing machine.

Good ventilation of the dishwashing area is essential. A hood fitted with an exhaust fan should be installed over the unit or exhaust ducts should be

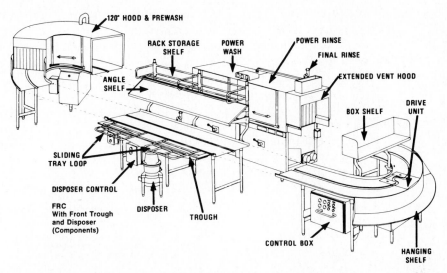

FIGURE 9.19 Fast-rack conveyor warewashing system may be custom designed to fit the space and needs of the situation. *Product of Hobart Corporation, Troy, Ohio.*

attached directly to the machines to remove steam and hot air. The ducts should be of rustproof material and must be watertight to prevent dripping of condensed vapor.

The *serving area* may be in the kitchen itself at the various preparation centers where servers pick up their orders for table service or for assembling trays for centralized hospital tray service, in a serving unit adjoining the kitchen, or in a pantry several floors above as in a hospital. A cafeteria counter may be located in a serving room between kitchen and dining room, at the end or side of the dining room, or in an alcove adjoining the dining room. The length and number of counters needed depend on the number of persons to be served, the number of menu items offered, and the speed of service desired. A 20-foot counter would be adequate for a small school lunchroom. A commercial establishment might find a 50-foot counter necessary to meet its needs, although newer installations tend toward the use of short counters, which are more easily supervised and require fewer workers. Commercial cafeterias with a seating capacity of 300 or more may find it desirable to have two counters or parallel counters with a serving station between.

The desirable rate of service for a school cafeteria is 12 to 15 students per minute. If the lunch period is limited in length, it may be necessary to plan for two or more counters, depending on the number of persons to be served.

The rate of service in commercial cafeterias is reported to be 5 to 8 persons per minute. Speed of service is increased when the cafeteria is arranged for customer movement to be from right to left, rather than left to right, down the line. This arrangement makes it easier and faster for right-handed customers to pick up and place food on the tray.

Counter designs should facilitate speedy service, reduce labor, and eliminate the necessity of guests waiting in a long line. Many configurations may be used such as those designed into short zigzag sections. A revolving counter section centered in or near the kitchen wall is well adapted to the display of cold items such as salads and desserts and is serviced easily from preparation areas in the kitchen. Another two-counter arrangement is a rounded U-shape with a central checkout. Silver, napkin, beverage, and condiment bars are often located in the dining room to help move guests quickly from the serving area.

The hollow-square type cafeteria has trays, silver, and napkins on an island arrangement in the center with counters on three sides. The separate counters offer different menu items, such as salads and cold sandwiches, hot entrees, and desserts, a central unit for duplicate self-serve beverage dispensers, and several checkout stations. This arrangement is sometimes called the "scramble" or "supermarket" system; see Fig. 9.20.

Regardless of the length of the serving unit or type of service, it should be a well-constructed piece of equipment that keeps hot food hot and cold food cold, provides storage space for dishes, and can be easily cleaned.

Steam tables, which once comprised a large part of the counter, have been replaced by electrically heated, thermostat-controlled units. Many hot foods are displayed in the pans in which they are prepared. The containers are replaced often by other containers of freshly prepared food. The hot unit should be located as near as possible to the kitchen cooking area.

Some institutions, especially school lunchrooms, prefer to place the unit of hot foods first in line arrangement so that the meal is selected in the order in which it is eaten. Commercial foodservices find that desserts and salads have a stronger psychic appeal, and provide a greater money return, and so place them first and the hot items near the end of the counter. An efficient plan is to arrange the counter so that the salad display is directly in front of the salad preparation unit in the kitchen, with pass-through refrigerated storage between. Small-size coffee makers in which a supply of fresh coffee may be prepared continuously are considered an improvement over giant urns in which a large quantity of coffee is made and kept hot for long periods of time. Icemakers at or near the point of use are recommended.

Commercial cafeteria managers find that salads and cold meats, hot meats and vegetables, desserts, and beverages need about equal display space on the counter. Since a counter is usually a fabricated piece of equipment, any

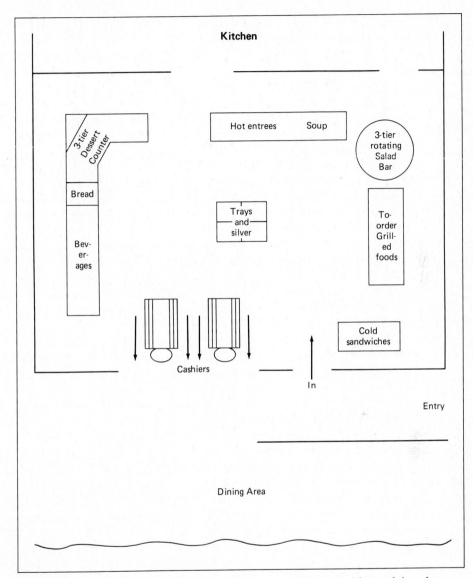

FIGURE 9.20   Typical hollow square cafeteria arrangement with revolving three-tiered salad display.

length desired may be ordered. Each serving section requires about 16 linear feet for efficient service. Costs are computed on the basis of so much per foot of counter. Mobile units provide for flexibility in counter arrangement.

The size of serving pantries, such as those in hospitals, depends on whether centralized or decentralized service is used. Refer to Chapter 7 for details of the equipment and space requirements for these two systems.

The *dining area* includes the seating facilities and small service stations. Quiet, attractive, well-ventilated, well-lighted dining areas are conducive to the enjoyment of good food and hospitality. Public dining rooms usually have many four- and two-seat tables that can be put together for larger groups. Dining rooms for college students are often arranged to seat six or eight at a table. The larger tables make for economical seating space but are difficult for waiter service and do not lend themselves to satisfactory social grouping. There should be a minimum space of 18 inches between chair backs after guests are seated; main traffic aisles of 4½ or 5 feet are advisable. See earlier in this chapter under "Space Allowances and Relationships" for dining area requirements.

Folding plastic or wood partitions are decorative and make it possible to close off parts of the dining room for special groups or when not in use. A separate dining room for employees is desirable.

Employee facilities include restrooms, washrooms, toilet rooms, locker and shower rooms, and the traffic aisles in these units. Each employee should have a locker. The need for the other facilities depends on how many people are on duty at any one time. Standards for such facilities are listed in Chapter 8. Customer restrooms should be located close to the dining area for convenience and security. Size of this area is in relation to the number of seats in the dining room.

Food waste and trash storage and removal are necessary if facilities for their disposal are not possible within the building. Many institutions have incinerators in which most trash is burned, central compactors in which waste is compressed under heavy pressure to small volume, and unit food waste disposers. If no such facilities are in use, both garbage and trash must be collected and held for frequent removal. A refrigerated room near the back entrance is satisfactory for the daily storage of garbage, but when feasible unit or central disposers should be incorporated into the system. Familiarity with, and conformance to, local sanitation regulations is an important function of the dietitian or manager of a foodservice.

The smooth flow of foods from the time they enter the building until the time they reach the consumer depends on the equipment selected and its arrangement to make a functional layout. Although space does not permit more detailed presentation of planning the specific areas, most of the points covered are basic and may be used as guides in foodservice planning.

GENERAL GUIDELINES   Several considerations should be noted in planning an institution kitchen. The main traffic aisles should be a minimum of 5 feet, or wide enough to permit passing of carts or hand trucks without interference with each other or with the workers in the area. A 10-inch clearance on either side of carts is desirable for ease of movement. Aisles between equipment and worktable must have a clearance of at least 3 feet. In front of ovens or kettles where contents of the kettle are emptied into containers on a truck, 3.5 to 4 feet are necessary. Work aisles are perpendicular to or parallel with the main traffic aisles but separated from them. Work heights are generally 36 to 41 inches for standing positions and 28 to 30 inches for sitting positions (Fig. 9.21). A *minimum* of 4 linear feet of worktable space is recommended for each preparation employee, but 6 feet is preferable.

The maximum reach over a table without stretching is 20 inches, so equipment usage should come within that arc. The highest shelf should not exceed 6 feet from the floor. Tools and equipment should have adequate storage space, convenient to the point of use. Sinks, reach-in refrigerators, and space for short-time storage of supplies should be in or near the main work areas so that employees will be at one location and have everything needed

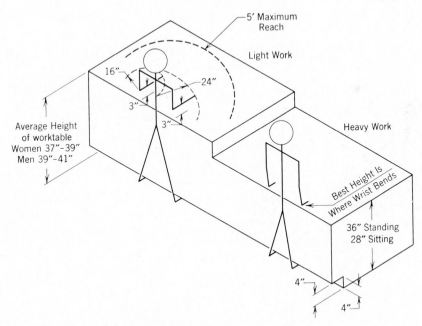

FIGURE 9.21   Optimum heights for work table and for working area.   *Courtesy of Arthur C. Avery.*

to do the job. Drinking water and hand washing facilities should be in a convenient location for all personnel. Overall integration of areas is necessary in planning.

It is generally agreed that more efficient service is possible if the dining room and kitchen are adjacent. A service pantry between the two is an effective means of reducing kitchen noise and confusion to a minimum in the dining room, but it does take extra space. If for any reason the dining room must be located a long way from the kitchen or on a different floor level, adequate provision should be made for mechanical means of conveying the prepared food in the briefest possible time and for keeping it at the proper temperature until served.

Rectangular or square kitchens are considered the most convenient. If possible the length of a rectangular kitchen should not be more than twice its width. Steps will be saved for employees if entrance to the dining room is from the longer instead of the shorter side of a rectangular kitchen. Another arrangement found efficient for some restaurants is a square dining space with the kitchen occupying a smaller square or rectangular space in one corner (Fig. 9.22). The dining area is thus on two sides and entrances to the kitchen can be located on each side. At slow periods, one section or side could be closed with a folding partition until more dining space is required. Arrangement for a counterclockwise routing of waiters through the kitchen and serving units of any seated foodservice is advisable. This provides a more efficient routing than the clockwise arrangement, at least for

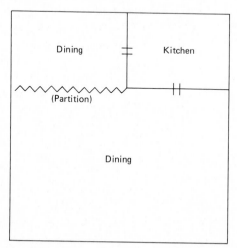

FIGURE 9.22   Efficient kitchen/dining room arrangement.

right-handed persons. An office for the manager or other person in charge should be located in direct sight of the kitchen and readily accessible to an outside entrance or to a hallway for the convenience of tradespeople and others. And as noted previously, all work and materials should move in a direct line from one process or activity to the next without backtracking and with as little crisscrossing as can be arranged. Following these suggestions in design planning will help to provide a facility that will have an efficient operation.

The planning team, supplied with all of this information, should now have a conference to discuss ideas, rejecting or discarding features and/or components of the plan until agreement is reached on what shall be included and the boundaries for the project. If it is a remodeling project, the team decides how much can be done and, perhaps, what has to be left undone. Decisions on quantity and quality within the confines of the budget will be made. Only with this agreement among all team members will each be fully committed to the project and continue to devote work time and provide the expertise needed to bring the project to a successful conclusion—to bring the menu and customers together through a planned system of time and motion.

MECHANICS OF DRAWING   The actual drawing of a plan to scale requires certain tools and techniques. The use of quarter-inch squared paper provides a good size scale to visually depict the entire plan, yet is a convenient size with which to work. A pen and India ink, or a heavy black ink pen, a good ruler, preferably an architect's ruler with various scales marked on it, and some tracing paper and masking tape are other needed supplies.

An outline of the size and shape of the space allocated is first drawn to scale with pencil on the squared paper. (If a one-eighth-inch scale is used, buy one-eighth-inch squared paper and so on.) When the location of doors and windows has been decided on, these are marked off on the outline. Then the outline of the space is inked in, using proper architectural symbols for walls, doors, and windows as illustrated in Fig. 9.23.

The next step is to obtain a set of templates, to-scale model drawings, of each piece of equipment to be used. They must be to the same scale as the floor plan. Label each template with the name and dimensions of the piece of equipment it represents; see Fig. 9.24. Sometimes a different color is used for each work unit. Templates should include overall measurements of features that require space, such as the swing of door openings, control boxes or fittings, and any installation needs as specified in equipment catalogs. The templates are then cut out, placed on the floor plan, and moved about until a good arrangement is found. Templates may then be secured to the plan with a bit of rubber cement (for easy removal if changes are made).

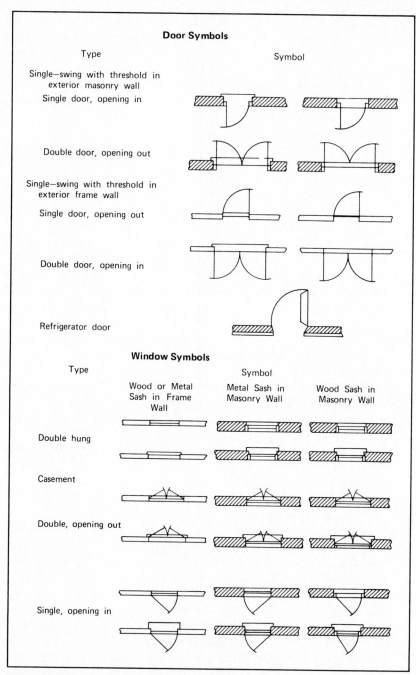

FIGURE 9.23   Architectural symbols used on blueprints to show placement and arrangement of various types of doors and windows.

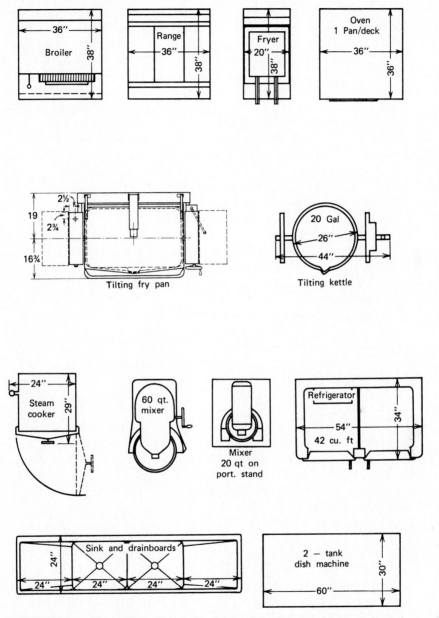

FIGURE 9.24 Templates of sample pieces of equipment drawn to floorplan scale. Cut-out templates may be moved about on the floor plan to determine floor space needs, and to find most efficient arrangement of equipment.

A sheet of thin tracing paper is taped over the floor plan, and lines are drawn on it to show the route used in the preparation of several menu items. Drawing lines tracing the movements of food and workers from one key work point to the next within a unit as well as from one work area or department to the next is a good check on the efficiency of the arrangement. Actual measurement of the distances can be made by passing a string over pintacks at each key point as the preparation of a menu item progresses and then measuring the string (usual scale is ¼ inch to 1 foot). At this time a check on width of aisles, work area space, location of hand washing sinks for employees, storage space for carts and trucks, and similar details is made.

The above procedures afford good checks of the adequacy of the tentative floor plan, for necessary equipment, and of working areas before the final plan is made. The space allowances for passageways between working areas, between tables, between ranges and cook's table, and between other major pieces of equipment should also be checked for adequacy. Changes and adjustments should be made on paper instead of after construction has begun, because it is costly to make revisions at that time.

Separate drawings are made by the architect for plumbing, electric, and gas installations in addition to those for the building construction. All must be coordinated and checked carefully to ensure that gas, water, and waste outlets and vents will be in the correct positions for the equipment planned. Also, the electrical wiring with convenient switch control boxes, power and regular outlets, and turn-on switches, locations, and kinds of light fixtures must be noted. Telephone conduits and outlets and wiring for computers, an intercom, public address, or TV system as decided on are indicated.

COMPUTER-ASSISTED FACILITY DESIGN PLANNING   Computer capability for graphic designing has made it possible for many organizations to use a computer for floor planning and equipment layout rather than the method described in the previous section. However, all of the preliminary studies, analyses, and team planning remain as necessary steps in computer-assisted design planning.

Riggs[8] identified several available computer programs featuring different layout characteristics that date back to 1964. Since that time various programs have been developed, each with special features for use in industry. In the 1970s, more programs were developed, and in the 1980s the computer-aided design (CAD) has grown with a focus on decreasing computation costs and increasing capabilities of computer technology.[9]

Computer-assisted facility design for food systems in the 1980s is based on an interactive graphic concept. Graphics actually refer to computer software that has been developed to assist in a schematic plan. This plan is calculated through the use of software programs utilizing the variables identified by the foodservice manager. The graphic software is generally commercially developed and will have the flexibility to allow the food manager or other technical persons to utilize an appropriate data base unique to foodservice.

There are several commercial companies that have developed software and distribute it, along with the appropriate hardware, if necessary.[9,10] Also, private consultants can be contracted to develop foodservice design and equipment layout.

Architect's Blueprints

After thorough checking of the preliminary plans by the dietitian or foodservice manager and others concerned, the architect prepares to accurate scale a complete set of drawings that are reproduced as blueprints. Details of construction, materials, plumbing, electric wiring, connections and fixtures, or equipment to be attached are indicated and coded. Side elevation drawings are included for such items as door and window finishings, stairways, and built-in or attached equipment.

In reading and checking the floor plan, one must constantly keep in mind the scale to which it is drawn. The scale should be sufficiently large to permit detailed study. The heavy, solid lines indicate the walls; the space between lines indicates the thickness of the wall; and the markings in between indicate the kind of materials, such as stone, brick, and concrete blocks. Three or four single parallel lines at a break in the wall indicate the position and size of windows. The direction in which doors open is shown by an arc described from the base of the line of the door, cutting it at a point equal to the width of the door (Fig. 9.23). Steps are indicated by parallel lines with an arrow and the words *up* and/or *down*. Dimensions of all spaces are indicated and rooms and equipment labeled. All special features are shown on the plan by symbols, for example, some electrical symbols as given in Fig. 9.25. Various architects may use different designating symbols that are explained in a legend on the drawing. The schedule on the corner of the floor plan sheet indicates wall, floor, ceiling, and woodwork finishes. The window and door schedule indicates sizes and types of these items. The use of standard-size windows and doors helps to keep their cost to a minimum. Always included on the blueprint sheet are the name and address of the facility and of the architect, as well as the date the plan was drawn and the scale used.

Specifications and Contract Documents

A set of written documents must be compiled by the architect to accompany the blueprint when presented to contractors for bid. The documents in-

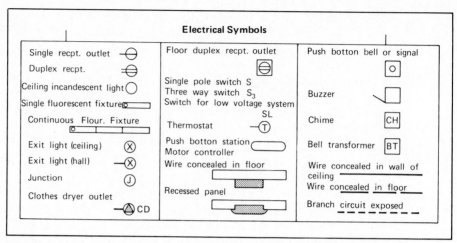

FIGURE 9.25   Electrical symbols used on blueprints to indicate type and locations of wiring and outlets.

clude: a statement of general conditions and scope of the work to be done; a "schedule of operations" with timetable for contractors to complete their work, or with penalties for failure to meet deadlines, and responsibility for installations and inspections; and the specifications for all parts of the work and for the equipment required.

The specifications include details of building such as the location of the building, type of base construction, mix of cement, size and kinds of conduits, drains, and vents, type and installation of roofing and flooring, wall finishes, hardware, doors, windows, and other construction features. Equipment specifications make up a part of this document. These details are given in Chapter 10. Generally included are brand name and model number, size or capacity, number required, and materials of construction of the equipment. In large installations separate contract documents may be made for bids for electrical work such as wiring, control switches, fixtures, and air conditioning. Plumbing contracts include details of water, sewer, and steam pipe connections and controls. Equipment specifications form the basis for another contract. All requirements must meet local and other building and installation codes, and the conditions and statements must be clearly worded so there can be no misinterpretations.

Bids, Contracts, Construction, and Inspection

When the contract documents are completed, they are duplicated and made available to any who may wish to bid on the project. It may be advertised to the public, or certain acceptable contractors and equipment dealers may be notified that the project plan is complete and they are invited to bid on it.

When bids are solicited on an open and competitive basis, the contract usually is awarded to the lowest bidder, who then works closely with the architect throughout the construction period. The foodservice manager keeps in close contact with developments and checks often with the architect. Conditions of the contract and the individuals concerned will determine to a large extent adjustments that can be made after contracts have been signed.

The actual construction time will vary from weeks to many months, depending on the type and size of building and the availability of materials, labor, and equipment. Frequent checking by the architect or a qualified representative to see that construction is progressing as specified is essential.

All construction, equipment, and installations must be inspected and approved by the architect before the facility is accepted by the organization's representative. Each item of equipment is performance tested to see that it meets specifications and claims and has been installed properly. This demonstration by a representative of the supply company to show the proper operation, care, and maintenance of the equipment should be attended by the dietitian, or foodservice manager and assistants, the kitchen supervisor, maintenance person, and the architect or representative.

Usually the various contractors guarantee necessary adjustments and some service for a specified period of time following the completion date. After the established date, all repairs and full maintenance are the responsibility of the foodservice management.

Summary

The principles and guidelines for facility design planning, whether by an individual or computer, presented in this chapter are applicable to all types of foodservice building projects.

The general considerations in making or checking floor plans are similar for different kinds of institutions, regardless of type of service, menu, clientele, and other governing conditions. The preparation and service of food are the purposes that must be kept in mind when planning a foodservice, and details that will make for increased efficiency should not be overlooked. Parts of a project that were desired but had to be eliminated at this time may be possible at lower cost at a future date if basic plans are incorporated during the construction period. For example, if either a monorail or an "Amscars" system for transporting supplies and food is anticipated in the future, the necessary overhead rails, under-the-floor wiring, or other requirements could be incorporated in the original construction of the building. Cost calculations and estimates must be based on scientific and practically proven facts, experiences, and observations.

During a planning project, most dietitians or foodservice managers would have been collecting a list of "do not forget to include" items that should be incorporated into the proposed plans. These reminders might vary from a telephone jack in the dining room to storage space for banquet tables, high chairs, reserve china, paper, and cleaning supplies, same size filters for all hoods over cooking areas for easy interchange, timers on cooking appliances, steam hose by garbage can washer, tray sizes modulated for use in refrigerator and ovens and on trucks, dumb waiters, and shelving, a bulletin board, first aid kit, time clock, and extra spare parts for emergency repair of equipment, overages on carpeting, tiles, light fixtures, and bulbs, and many more. A written list of such details provides a good check sheet to use when final plans are completed and before construction begins.

A good balance of beauty and utility in the structure, furnishings, and equipment should be maintained for successful foodservice planning. Colorful walls and floor coverings, modern lighting, streamlined, modular kitchen equipment fabricated of well-finished metals, machines with mechanical parts and motors enclosed, and the use of attractive woods and metals in dining room furniture are a few of the many features that contribute materially to the beauty of modern foodservice areas. Sanitation, ease of maintenance, noise reduction, and controlled environmental temperatures for comfort are built-in features that contribute to making a successful facility and help achieve the objectives outlined in the prospectus for the foodservice operation.

Notes

1. Webster's New Collegiate Dictionary. Springfield, MA: G. and C. Merriam Co., 1977.
2. Marriott, Robert H., Jr.: You take the high road and I'll take the low road. Western Foodservice 14(5):12, 1985.
3. Dunlap, Suzanne: Valparaiso's shift to a la carte. Food Mgmt. 19(8):84, 1984.
4. Design in 2000. Food Mgmt. 18(1):80, 1983.
5. Minno, M. P., and Bhayana, R.: Planning a new restaurant from feasibility to menu concept in 7 days. NRA NEWS 5(5): 18, 1985.
6. Kotschevar, L., and Terrell, M. E.: Foodservice Planning: Layout and Equipment, 3rd ed. New York: John Wiley and Sons, 1985.
7. Mayfield, Barbara K. General guidelines vs. actual determination of square footage requirements. J. Am. Diet. Assoc. 85:851, 1985.
8. Riggs, James L.: Production Systems: Planning, Analysis and Control. New York: John Wiley and Sons, 1981.

9. Reskow, Richard P., and Voisinet, Donald D.: McGraw-Hill CAD Curriculum. New York: McGraw-Hill Book Co., 1984.
10. FED Systems, Inc.: Food Equipment Design with Equipment Library. New London, CT, 12 Montauk Ave., 1984.

Supplementary References

American Hospital Association: Selection of a Consultant for Hospital Food Service Systems Design and Equipment. AHA Catalog No. T011, 1977.

Clark, Sam: The Motion Minded Kitchen. Boston: Houghton Mifflin Co., 1983.

Cutting Energy Costs: 1980 Yearbook of Agriculture. Washington, DC: Supt. of Documents, US GPO.

Eshbach, C. E.: Foodservice Management, 3rd ed. Boston: CBI Publishing Co. 1979.

Kazarian, E. A.: Food Service Facilities Planning, 2nd ed. Westport, CT: AVI Publishing Co., 1983.

Kilowatt counting saves energy. School Food Service Journal 37(2):18, 1983.

Lundberg, D. E.: The Restaurant: From Concept to Operation. New York: John Wiley and Sons, 1985.

Opening a restaurant. NRA NEWS:
PART 1: From feasibility to menu concept. 5:18, May 1985.
PART 2: The project planning team. 5:24, June/July 1985.
PART 3: Financing the new restaurant. 5:17, September 1985.

Pannell, D. V.: School Foodservice, 2nd ed. Westport, CT: AVI Publishing Co., 1981.

Papa, Anne: Restaurant design: Finding the right look. NRA NEWS 6(1):12, 1986.

Unklesbay, N. and Unklesbay, K.: Energy Management in Foodservice. Westport, CT: AVI Publishing Co., 1982.

Wright, Victor: Drafting by design. PC Tech Journal (for IBM computer users), 4(1):50, 1986.

CHAPTER 10

Equipment and Furnishings

Introduction

Foodservice equipment includes "kitchen, bakery, pantry and cafeteria units and other food handling and processing equipment, such as tables of all kinds and their component parts, counters, shelves, sinks and hoods."[1] Complete coverage of this broad subject area is impossible in a general textbook, but an effort is made here to include pertinent basic information that can be supplemented by current literature from the manufacturers and from observations of equipment in use.

The selection and purchase of furnishings and equipment for any foodservice are major responsibilities of the director and the staff, and the wisdom with which selection is made determines in large measure the attainment of lasting satisfaction. The efficiency of work units and the beauty of environment may be marred by poor selection and placement of furnishings and equipment, and the quality of service that an organization may render is influenced, if not limited, by these features.

The wise selection of equipment for any foodservice can be made only after a thorough study of all factors affecting the particular situation has been made. Items are available in many designs, materials, sizes, and within a wide cost range, but only those items that will help to meet the specific needs of the foodservice and contribute to its efficient operation should be purchased.

The problem of selection is so important and errors so costly that major characteristics to consider in the selection of certain basic pieces of equipment are included. Energy conservation, as it relates to the selection and operation of foodservice equipment, is discussed.

This chapter concludes with a section devoted to dining room furnishings. Basic information needed for the wise selection of dinnerware, tableware, glassware, and table covers is presented in this section.

Factors Affecting Selection of Equipment

Equipment for any foodservice should be selected on the basis of a thorough study of all major considerations. Important among these are:

1. Needs of the particular foodservice organization as determined by the menu plan and complexity of the foods included
2. Number and type of patrons to be served
3. Form in which the food will be purchased
4. Style of service and length of serving period
5. Number of labor hours available
6. Abilities of employees to do the work
7. Accessibility and cost of utilities
8. Budget and amount of money allotted for equipment
9. Floor plan and space allotments

Before final decisions are made, individual pieces of equipment should be considered as to design, materials in relation to suitability for the purpose, durability and cleanability, construction and safety, size and capacity, installation, operation, and performance, maintenance, and replacement of parts. Cost and method of purchase are also major considerations in the selection of equipment.

Determination of Needs

Sound generalizations concerning equipment needs are difficult to formulate because each foodservice presents an individual problem with an interplay of factors not exactly duplicated elsewhere. The determination of these needs, therefore, should be one of the first and most important considerations of the foodservice manager as a basis for deciding what equipment should be purchased. Each item selected must accomplish those definite tasks peculiar to the specific situation. If the installation is new, information concerning the demands to be made of the facility and the ways in which the furnishings and equipment may help to meet these demands is of primary importance in planning the layout and selecting the equipment. If the installation is already in operation and has been found to be inefficient, an analysis should be made of the layout and equipment as it exists. This study can be used as a basis to rearrange the floor plan and include any additional furnishings and equipment needed.

The menu pattern and typical foods to be served must be known in order to determine the extent and complexity of the required food preparation. Detailed analysis of the preparation requirements of several typical menus provides the best basis for estimating foodservice equipment needs for a particular situation. This procedure was pioneered by Thomas,[2] who some years ago applied many of the principles of industrial management to the solving of problems in the area of foodservice management. Thomas carefully observed and recorded the processes and times involved in the preparation of the various types and quantities of foods and the equipment used. She noted the capacity of each piece of equipment as well as the hour, length of time, and by whom it was used. Thomas employed process and equipment usage charts in recording observations. From a study of the compiled data, recommendations for desirable pieces of equipment of suitable capacities and sizes were developed for the unit under study. These same principles are followed today.

Standardized recipes that include AP and EP (as purchased and edible portion, see Chapter 5), weights of ingredients, yields, pan sizes, and portion size are invaluable aids to planning for efficient equipment. Batch size and how often a procedure is repeated are important considerations for determining equipment needs. A large mixer and both large capacity and duplicate steam-jacketed kettles or tilting frypans might be advisable, since they are used in the preparation of many menu items. An increase in the lengths of times required for certain processes for 500 over those needed for 100 portions would be necessary but not always proportional to the increase in quantities. In general, little difference in times is required for chopping various amounts of food in less than machine-capacity quantities or for mixing or cooking an increased amount of food in larger equipment. Repetitive processes such as hand rolling of pastry or batch cooking vegetables in a small pressure steamer requires almost proportional quantity, time, and space increases.

Number and Type of Patrons

The number and type of patrons are important factors in selecting the appropriate amount and kind of equipment for a foodservice. The equipment needs for the preparation and serving of a plate lunch to 500 children in a school lunchroom are quite different from those of a service restaurant offering a diversified menu to approximately the same number of people three times daily. In the school foodservice there probably would not be more than two hot entrees on the menu for any one day, but all food would have to be ready to serve within a short period of time. In the restaurant, a variety of items would be ready for final preparation over extended serving periods; also, some items would be cooked in small quantities at space intervals according to the peak hours of service. Obviously, smaller and more varied types of equipment would be needed in the restaurant than in the lunchroom. Production schedules in a shortorder operation would require duplicates of such items as griddles, broilers, and fryers, whereas a residence hall foodservice would need steam-jacketed kettles, steamers, and ovens to produce a large volume of food within a specified time period.

The number of people to be fed determines to a great extent the total volume of food that must be prepared, but numbers in themselves cannot be used to evaluate equipment needs. Estimates of numbers of persons to be served during each 15-minute interval of the serving period will provide a guide to food and equipment needs. Amount and capacity of equipment to select is based on the number served at the interval of greatest demand in relation to cooking time required for specific items.

Form of Food Purchased and Styles of Service

The form in which the food is to be purchased will greatly influence equipment needs. The selection of fabricated meats and poultry, frozen portioned fish, frozen fruits and vegetables, juice concentrates, ready-to-bake pies, and some cooked entrees, chilled citrus fruit sections, washed spinach and other greens, and processed potatoes, carrots, and apples eliminates the need for space and equipment for the usual preprepreparation and disposal of waste. Adequate facilities for short and long storage at the proper temperatures must be provided, but other equipment needs would be limited primarily to those pieces required in the final stages of production and the serving of the finished products.

Various styles of service, like self-service in a lunchroom, table or buffet service in a public dining room, or vended service, require particular kinds of equipment for their efficient functioning. Length of serving period is another factor.

Labor Hours and Worker Abilities

The labor hours available and the skill of the workers cannot be overlooked in considering the equipment needs of any foodservice. If the labor budget or local labor market is limited, usually the selection of as much labor-saving equipment as possible is warranted. Judgment must be exercised in deciding what equipment will provide for the smooth functioning of the organization and also give the best return on the investment. Will the increased productivity of employees with automated equipment compensate for the possible increased payroll and initial and maintenance costs? With the rising pay rates for employees at all levels, managers must weigh values carefully in selecting equipment they can operate successfully, efficiently, and economically to accomplish the job to be done.

Utilities

The adequacy of utilities for the successful installation and performance of commercial cooking and warming or power-driven equipment must be checked before the final decision is made on selections. Often the choice between gas, electric, or steam-heated cooking equipment demands considerable investigation of the continuing supply of the source of heat, replaceability of parts of the various items, relative costs of their operation and maintenance, and the probable satisfactions from their use in the particular situation. High-pressure steam is not always available, in which case self-generating steam units would be a necessary choice. Power-driven equipment is equipped with motors of the proper size for the capacity of the machine, but cycle and current would have to be designated so that the machine would operate properly for the wiring and power in the building.

Most institutional foodservices include one or more of each of the following: oven, range, tilting frypan, fryer, broiler, steam-jacked kettle, pressure steam cooker, coffee maker, refrigerator, freezer, ice maker, mixer with attachments, food cutter, sinks, tables, and carts. A wide variety of additional equipment may be purchased as necessity demands and money permits.

Once the equipment has been installed, care must be taken that menus are planned with consideration for its balanced use. This means that the person responsible for planning menus must be familiar with the facilities at hand and know the capacities of the equipment and the timing of processes for the amounts of food to be prepared. Demands for oven cooking beyond the capacity load may lead to much unhappiness between manager and cook, and may also encourage the production of inferior quality food or too-early preparation. Preparation timetables, equipment capacity charts, and standardized recipes that indicate AP and EP weights of ingredients, yield, and pan size for the particular setup can contribute much to effective planning for the efficient use of equipment.

The Budget

The budgetary allowance must cover not only the initial cost of the equipment but often the additional cost of installation. Available funds determine to a great extent the possible amount and quality of equipment that can be purchased at any given time. If the initial equipment budget is adequate, the choice among various pieces becomes mere determination of the superior and preferred qualities for each article desired. Sometimes the equipment budget is so limited that the food director is forced to decide between certain desirable articles and to weigh with serious thought the relative points in quality grades of the pieces believed to be essential. It is advisable then to list all the needed equipment so that unbalanced expenditure will not result. Lack of such thought or insistence on "the best" may lead to disastrous spending.

Consensus is that equipment of good quality is the most economical. Generally, if the amount of money is limited, it is better to buy a few well-chosen pieces of equipment that will meet basic needs and make additions as funds are available than to purchase many pieces of inferior quality that will need to be replaced in a short time. One the other hand, some consultants warn that because of the rapid change in the trend toward the use of prepared foods, it may be preferable in some installations to plan equipment for a short life span and early replacement until such developments are stabilized. The initial cost of equipment is influenced by the size, materials used, quality of workmanship, construction, including special mechanical features, and finish of the article. The limitation of funds may lead to the necessity of a choice as to which one or more of these points may be sacrificed with least jeopardy to the permanence of the article and satisfaction in its use.

Estimates of cost for foodservice equipment are difficult to ascertain as each operation must be considered individually. It is advisable to learn the costs of comparable situations before making tentative estimates for a new or remodeled setup.

The Floor Plan

Space allocation for the foodservice may restrict the amount and type of equipment and its placement, especially in old buildings where architectural changes are limited and in new ones where the original planning may have been ill advised regarding the functions and needs. The size and shape of the space allotted to food preparation and its relation to receiving, storage, and dining areas influence greatly the efficiency of operation and ultimately customer satisfaction, as discussed in the preceding chapter. Floor space either too small or too large to accommodate the equipment suitable and desirable for the volume of food production anticipated creates an unsatisfactory situation. In the first instance the overcrowding of work makes for confusion and frustration, limits the amount and type of preparation that can be done, and slows production. When the space is too large, much time and effort may be wasted by workers in transporting food long distances. Also, there may be a tendency to overequip with needless items simply because ample space is available. In any case a complete analysis of the real needs is necessary before an equipment investment is made.

FIGURE 10.1   A compact arrangement of modular cooking units may be fitted into a continuous framework for beauty, spacesaving, operational efficiency and maintenance of sanitation. This one includes cabinet-mounted steamers, kettles, and a tilting braising pan.   *Courtesy, Groen Division, Dover Corporation.*

Features of Equipment

General objectives and trends in current equipment developments include an increase in the number and kind of specialized items, many of which are adaptable to multiple use; function and attractiveness in appearance; compactness and efficient utilization of space to reduce labor hours and time requirements to a minimum; speed output of quality products; modular planning of matched units as shown in Fig. 10.1, mobility and flexibility of arrangement; exact engineering tolerances, effective insulation, computerized and solid-state controls (Fig. 10.2) for even temperatures and operation; built-in sanitation; and fuel efficiency. With the change in the type and amount of food preparation in the individual units has come a corresponding change in equipment to meet the particular production needs.

Design and Function

The design of equipment and furnishings for the foodservice should be in close harmony with the general plan of the building, especially in the decorative features and items such as table appointments. This is particularly noticeable in summer resorts, children's hospitals, and certain types of restaurants, where not only the modern trend of foodservice planning and interior decoration has been followed, but also some specialized idea or theme has been expressed through the design and type of furnishings selected.

FIGURE 10.2   This computerized convection oven utilizes solid-state temperature devices accurate to within one degree (± 1°F). A digital control panel replaces conventional control knobs and allows entry of exact cooking temperatures and times.   *Courtesy, Lange Manufacturing Company.*

Sensitivity to the artistic design of institutional foodservice furnishings and equipment is often more acute than to the design of similar items for the home, because of the larger size of items required and duplication in number, as in dining room tables and chairs. Generally speaking, heavy-duty equipment is designed to give a streamlined effect.

The Joint Committee of Food Equipment Standards[1] states:

> Food service equipment and appurtenances shall be so designed and constructed as to exclude vermin, dust, dirt, splash or spillage from the food zone which may be encountered under the intended use conditions and be easily cleaned, maintained and serviced.

Beauty and utility may be combined in foodservice equipment through the application of art principles and consideration of the functions of the various items by the designer. The gadget or piece of equipment may be beautiful in line and design, but it is of little value if it serves no real purpose or if an unreasonable amount of time is required for its operation or care. The design of cutlery such as a chef's knife with a heavy wide blade shaped for

FIGURE 10.3   Spoodles are designed to give the portion control of a ladle with the ease and balance of a spoon. Made of either *(a)* stainless steel with plastic handles or *(b)* entirely of high-impact plastic in a variety of capacities with perforated or solid bowls.   *Courtesy, Vollrath Company.*

cutting on a board and a long-handled cook's fork are examples of how closely design is related to use of an article. Also, the design may influence the timing, efficiency, and comfort of operation, such as the utensils shown in Fig. 10.3. These spoodles, or combination spoon and ladle, are not only color coded for portion control, but feature a handle that is designed for control and comfort.

Simplicity of design is pleasing and restful and usually means a minimum amount of care. The maintenance of high sanitation standards in a foodservice is aided by designing the equipment so that sharp corners, cracks, and crevices are eliminated and all surfaces are within easy access for cleaning, as the portable salad bar in Fig. 7.10. The more complicated items should be designed for quick disassembling of parts for machine or hand washing. The Joint Committee on Food Equipment Standards has stressed the sanitation aspect of kitchen equipment design and construction as exemplified in the following statement regarding the material and construction for legs and feet on equipment:

> Legs and feet shall be of a material of sufficient rigidity to provide support with a minimum of cross bracing and so fastened to the body of the equipment and so shaped at floor contacts as to prevent accumulation of dirt and harborage of vermin. When the outside dimension of the leg is greater than the outside dimension of the foot by ½ inch (12.7 mm) or more in the same plane, the foot shall, at minimum adjustment, extend 1 inch (25.4 mm) below the leg. All openings to hollow sections between feet and legs and equipment shall be of drip-proof construction with no openings greater than 1/32 inch (0.8 mm).

Legs and feet shall be of simple design, free from embellishments and exposed threads. Gussets, when used, shall be assembled to the equipment so as to insure easy cleanability and to eliminate insect harborage. The resultant assembly shall have no recessed areas or spaces.[1]

All equipment mounted on legs or castors, such as the salad bar in Fig. 7.10, Chapter 7, should be designed to have a minimum clearance of 6 and preferably 8 inches between the floor and the bottom surfaces of equipment, shelves, pipes, drains, or traps, to permit ease of cleaning. Heavy stationary equipment such as ranges and cabinets may be mounted successfully on a raised masonry, tile, or metal platform at least 2 inches high, sealed to the floor and at all edges. Usually this type of island base is recessed to allow for toe space beneath the equipment.

Specially designed mountings on wheels for specific purposes have become an important feature of foodservice planning for convenience, sanitation, and economical use of space and labor. Portable back-of-the-counter breakfast service units including toaster, waffle irons, and egg cookers can be transported out of the way during the remainder of the day. Dispenser units can be filled with clean trays in the dishwashing room and wheeled into position at the counter with a minimum of handling (see Fig. 10.4). Portable bins for flour and sugar are more convenient to use and easier to keep clean than built-in bins. Sections of shelves in walk-in refrigerators and dry-storage rooms mounted on wheels make for convenience in cleaning and rearrangement of storage. The importance of designing general utility trucks and dollies to fit into the places in which they are to be used cannot be overestimated.

Heavy-duty wheeled equipment such as range sections, tilting frypans, fryers, ovens, reach-in refrigerators, and the many mobile work and serving units make possible their rearrangement to adapt to changing needs at minimum cost. Often the conversion of certain spaces from limited- to multiple-use areas can be effected through the inclusion of mobile designed equipment. Also, thorough cleaning back of and underneath is made easier when the equipment is movable and accessible from all sides.

One of the outstanding improvements in serving equipment has been effected through a change in the design and construction of heated serving counters. This change from the old pattern of a given number of rectangular and round openings, far apart, in an elongated steam-table arrangement with limited fixed storage, to a condensed type with fractional size containers, has been estimated to permit up to 50 per cent greater food capacity in the same amount of space. This arrangement also makes possible almost unlimited flexibility in service through the close arrangement of a few regular 18- by 12-inch rectangular top openings into which full-size or combi-

FIGURE 10.4   Mobile self-leveling tray unit, filled at dishmachine and transported to the point of use.   *Courtesy, Precision Metal Products, Inc.*

nations of fractional-size pans of different depths may be fitted with or without the aid of adaptor bars. Hot food serving counters may be designed and constructed for two or more openings, moist or dry heat, gas or electricity, separate heat controls for individual sections or for the unit, and space below enclosed or fitted for dish storage.

The selection of inserts for this type of counter should be made to meet the demands at peak times for the best service of all the usual types of hot foods included on a menu. The number of each size and depth of pans to purchase can be determined easily by careful analysis of several sample menus, the quantities of each type of food required, and the most satisfactory size and depth of pans for their preparation and service. In most instances this will mean a relatively small number of sizes with ample duplication of those for which there will be the greatest need.

Common depths of the counter pans are 2½, 4, and 6 inches with some sizes available 1 and 8 inches deep. Capacities are listed for each size as, for example, in the accompanying table. All inserts fit flush with top openings,

One-Half Size		One-Fourth Size	
Depth (in)	Capacity (qt)	Depth (in)	Capacity (qt)
1	1¾		
2½	4½	2½	2⅛
4	7⅛	4	3⅜
6	10⅞	6	4¾
8	15		

except the 8-inch deep pans, which have a 2-inch shoulder extending above the opening. Pans of one size and depth are designed to nest together for convenient storage. Since these pans are made of noncorrosive well-finished metal, certain types of menu items may be cooked in and served directly from them, whereas other foods will need to be transferred to them for serving. Recipes can be standardized for a specific number of pans of suitable size and depth for a product and with the exact number of portions predetermined. The pan shown in Fig. 10.5 is designed with reinforced corners to add strength and prevent vacuum-sticking of stacked pans. As with most hotel pans they are available in full, half, one-third, one-fourth, and one-sixth sizes.

Size or Capacity

The size or capacity of equipment to select for a given situation is determined largely by the type of menu and service offered and the quantities of

FIGURE 10.5   A hotel pan designed to last longer, not stick together when stacked, be more comfortable to carry, provide a better steamtable seal, and be easier to clean.   *Courtesy, Vollrath Company.*

different types of foods to be prepared at one time. More pieces of heavy-duty equipment of larger capacities are required for the preparation of food for a college residence hall serving a nonselective menu at a set hour than for the preparation and service for a short-order lunch counter serving comparable or even greater numbers throughout an extended meal hour. Batch cooking, the cooking of vegetables in not more than five-pound lots, timed at intervals to provide for a continuous supply to meet the demands of the service, is far preferable to cooking the entire amount at one time and holding the cooked product through the serving period. The latter would require one or two large steam-jacketed kettles instead of a battery of small ones and would mean less effort and time for the cook, but at the sacrifice of eye appeal, flavor, crispness, nutritive value of the food served, and the satisfaction of the guests.

Large equipment, such as ranges, ovens, tilting frypans, mixers, and dishwashers, may be obtained in more or less standard sizes, with slight variations in the articles produced by different manufacturers. For example, range sections may vary a few inches in the overall measurements and the inside dimensions of ovens may differ, whereas the capacities of mixers made by most firms are comparable.

Charts are available from most manufacturers that show the capacity or output per hour for each size of machine. For example, the capacity of a dishwasher is measured by the number of dishes that can be washed in an hour. The size of mixer to purchase would be determined by the volume of a product to be prepared each mixing, the time required for mixing or mashing each batch, and the total quantity of the produce needed within a given period of time. Obviously, the size and number of pieces of each item of equipment required will depend on the needs of the particular institution.

The articles most often fabricated or built to individual specifications are those that must conform to a given size or are desired because of special material. Special orders make the equipment more expensive and often delay delivery. However, to most people the satisfaction of having a piece of equipment that exactly fits usually more than compensates for the disadvantages.

Standards of uniformity in size of small as well as large equipment have become fairly well established through the experience of users and their working with designers, manufacturers, and consultants. Many kitchens of the past have had a multiplicity of sizes of cooking utensils, baking pans, and trays that may or may not have made economical use of range, oven, refrigerator, cabinet, or truck spaces in the particular situation. An example is the large oval serving tray that would never fit on a rack, shelf, or truck. Alert foodservice directors and planning experts have come to recognize some of these problems and to note the advantages that are gained by simplification of the whole setup through improved planning for the efficient and inter-related use of the items selected.

The selection of certain "modular" items of equipment or those of uniform size has proven advantageous in quantity food operations. When a specified size pan, tray, or rack fits easily in the refrigerator, storage cabinet, serving counter, or on racks or carts, great adaptability in and economical utilization of space are made possible. Also, manpower efficiency is increased and labor hours are reduced; less floor area is required with improved use of vertical space; the use of pans and trays of the same size or in their multiple units reduces the total number and kind to buy, their cost, and the storage space needed; the number of shelves in refrigerators, cabinets, and carts can be reduced when trays and pans can be inserted at close intervals on angle runners or glides; the rehandling or transfer of foods or dishes is reduced, since the tray rack fits into any unit, either on a shelf, on glides, or in the counter; sanitation is improved through reduced handling of food or dishes, low spillage, and machine washing of trays and pans.

Common modules are the 12 by 18-inch and 18 by 26-inch trays, which are easily accessible in several materials and convenient to use. The 12 by 18-inch trays fit into standard dishwashing racks of conveyor-type machines. Cabinets, shelves, refrigerators, and carts are readily available to accommodate one or a combination of such trays. Some spaces could be sized so that either one 18 by 26 bun pan or two 12 by 18-inch trays could be used.

Another common module is space into which 20 by 20-inch dishracks would fit, for storage of cups and glasses in the racks in which they were washed.

This system merits careful consideration in planning equipment for simplified operation with maximum efficiency and economy. Each unit will continue to need a certain amount of its equipment custom built according to specification, but certainly there should be uniformity within each operation.

Materials

Materials for the various pieces of foodservice equipment should be suitable for the purpose and give the best satisfaction possible. The materials used in the equipment influence price, wearing qualities, sanitation, satisfaction, and usefulness. The weight, finish, and workmanship of the materials are important factors in determining their suitability and wearing qualities.

The Joint Committee on Food Equipment Standards has established minimum requirements for materials and construction of certain foodservice equipment items.

> Only such materials shall be used in the construction of foodservice equipment and/or appurtenances as will withstand normal wear, penetration of vermin, corrosive action of foods or beverages, cleaning compounds and such other elements as may be found in the use environments and will not impart an odor, color or taste to the food.[1]

The committee further specifies that surface materials in the food zone shall be smooth, corrosion resistant, nontoxic, stable, and nonabsorbent, and that they must not contribute to the adulteration of the food. Nonfood contact surfaces should be of corrosion-resistant material or be made so by coating, except with paint, which is not acceptable on parts of the equipment directly over and adjacent to the food zone. Solder must be nontoxic and welded areas must be equally as resistant to corrosion as the parent metal.

METALS   Metals have become increasingly important in foodservice planning. Today we depend on them for nearly everything, from structural features such as doors, flooring under steam units, and walk-in refrigerators to tables, sinks, dishwashers, and cooking equipment. A wide variety of old and well-known metals and alloys, such as copper, tin, chromium, iron, steel, and aluminum, were used in the foodservices of the past, but have been outmoded by the chromium and chromium-nickel stainless steels. At one time copper cooking utensils and dishwashers were commonly found in institutional foodservices. Their care and upkeep were high because they required frequent polishing and replacement of nickel or tin linings to prevent the reaction of foodstuffs with the copper. Such utensils were heavy to handle and were used mostly in hotels where male cooks were employed. Nickel was used considerably as a plating for equipment trim, rails of cafeteria counters, and inexpensive tableware.

Aluminum lends itself to fabrication of numerous kinds and will take a satin, frosted, or chrome-plated finish. It can be painted, etched, or engraved. It is relatively light in weight, has high thermal and electrical conductivity, does not corrode readily, and if cold-rolled, is relatively hard and durable. It is capable of withstanding pressure at high temperature, which makes it particularly well suited for cooking and baking utensils and steam-jacketed kettles. Aluminum cooking utensils often become discolored by food or water containing alkali, certain acids, and iron. Many items are manufactured from anodized aluminum that has been subjected to electrolytic action to coat and harden the surface and increase its resistance to oxidation, discoloration, marring, and scratching. Anodized aluminum is often used for items such as dry-storage cabinets and service carts and trays. Its strength and light weight are factors in its favor for mobile equipment. Aluminum may be combined with other metals to produce alloys of higher tensile strength than aluminum alone.

Cast iron is used in institution equipment as braces and castings for stands and supports, for pipes, and for large pieces of equipment such as ranges. Its use in small equipment is restricted to skillets, Dutch ovens, and griddles.

Galvanized steel and iron were long used for such equipment as sinks, dishwashers, and tables. In the process of galvanizing, a coating of zinc, deposited on the base metal, protects it to a certain extent from corrosion. The initial cost of equipment made of galvanized material is comparatively low, but the length of life is short, repair and replacement expenses are high, sanitation is low, contamination is likely, and the general appearance is undesirable and unattractive in comparison to equipment made of noncorrosive metal.

The use of *noncorrosive metals,* mainly the alloys of iron, nickel, and chromium, for equipment in food processing plants such as bakeries, dairies, canneries, and in home and institution-size kitchens has increased tremendously within recent years until at present all such units are planned with widespread usage of this material. These materials are available in forms suitable for fabrication into any desired types of equipment. If the sheets are too small for the particular item, they may be joined and welded most satisfactorily. The price is not prohibitive, so that this type of material functions in many and varied instances from decorative effects in or on public buildings to heavy-duty equipment, cooking utensils, and tableware. Improved methods of fabrication and the unprecedented emphasis on sanitation have been important factors in the high utilization of noncorrosive metals in items of equipment.

The outstanding characteristics of noncorrosive metals for foodservice equipment include permanence, resistance to ordinary stains and corrosion, lack of chemical reaction with food, attractive appearance, ease of cleaning and fabrication, and nonprohibitive price. Tests show that with proper construction and care noncorrosive metals wear indefinitely, and equipment made from them may be considered permanent investments. The strength and toughness are so high that even a comparatively lightweight metal may be used for heavy-duty items. These metals do not chip or crack. High ductility and weldability also make for permanence of the equipment made from them; thus the upkeep costs are reduced to a minimum.

Resistance to stains and corrosion is a major feature in foodservice equipment where cleanliness, appearance, and sanitation are of utmost importance. The freedom from chemical reactions of the noncorrosive metals with foodstuffs at any temperature makes their use safe in food preparation. Tests show few or no traces of metals or metallic salts present after different foods have been heated and chilled for varying periods of time in containers made of these metals.

The appearance of noncorrosive metal equipment when well made and carefully finished is satisfying and conducive to the maintenance of excellent standards of cleanliness and order. The smooth, hard surface is not easily scratched or marred, and simple cleaning methods are all that are required. There are special metal cleaners on the market, but a good cleaner and water and the usual polishing should be enough to keep the equipment in good condition. Common steel wool, scouring pads, scrapers, or wire brushes may mar the surface or leave small particles of iron imbedded in the stainless steel to cause rust stains. Darkened areas are caused usually by heat applied either in fabrication or in use and may be removed by vigorous rubbing with stainless steel wool, a stainless steel pad and powder, or a commercial heat-tint remover. To avoid heat tinting of cooking utensils, they should be subjected to no more heat than required to do the job effectively, never heated empty or with heat concentrated on a small area.

The noncorrosive alloys manufactured most often into institutional equipment are nickel-copper and the stainless steels. Monel metal is a natural alloy that contains approximately two-thirds nickel and one-third copper, with a small amount of iron. The supply is fairly limited so it is seldom selected for fabrication into foodservice equipment.

By far the greatest amount of foodservice equipment is made of some type of stainless steel. Each company producing stainless steel under its own trade name may use a slightly different formula, but the important elements are practically the same. A relatively low carbon content in the stainless steels gives high resistance to attack by corrosive agents. A chromium-nickel stainless steel alloy commonly called "18-8" (number 302) is a favorite material for foodservice equipment. As its name indicates, it contains approximately 18 per cent chromium and 8 per cent nickel with no copper present. Observations of equipment made of the noncorrosive alloys in satisfactory use and their appearance and sanitary qualities prove the value of these materials for heavy-duty equipment.

Standard Gauge. The gauge of thickness of metals is an important consideration in selecting materials for equipment. The adoption of the micrometer caliber to indicate the thickness of sheet metal in decimal parts of an inch and the abolition of gauge numbers are strongly recommended. However, the United States standard gauge is used by most manufacturers of iron and steel sheets. This system is a weight, not a thickness, gauge. For instance, number 20 United States gauge weighs 1.5 pounds per square foot, subject to the standard allowable variation. Weight always is the determining factor. That this gauge is 0.037-inch thick is secondary in the system. Numbers 10 to 14 gauge galvanized steel or 12 to 16 noncorrosive metals are most generally used for foodservice equipment. Metal lighter than 16 gauge is commonly used for sides or parts where the wear is light (see Fig. 10.6).

Finish of Metals. The surface or finish of metals may be dull or bright; the higher the polish, the more susceptible is the surface to scratches. The degree of finish of metals is indicated by a gradation in number, the larger

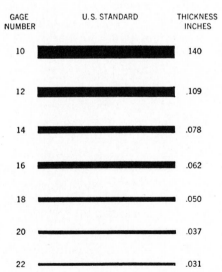

FIGURE 10.6 A diagram showing actual thickness of commonly used gauges of metals.

numbers indicating finer finish and a higher degree of polish. Standard finishes for the steels in sheet form are listed in this table.

Finish	Description
No. 1	Hot-rolled, annealed, and pickled
No. 2B	Full finish—bright cold-rolled
No. 2D	Full finish—dull cold-rolled
No. 4	Standard polish, one or both sides
No. 6	Standard polish, tampico brushed one or both sides
No. 7	High-luster polish on one or both sides

Numbers 4, 6, and 7 are produced by grinding and polishing the sheets of metal with different grades of abrasives. These original surface finishes are capable of being retained in the usual fabrication of equipment, which requires only local forming. Materials with a number 4 grind surface are more often selected for such items as table tops, sinks, and counters than are those with shiny or mirrorlike finishes.

GLASS   Glass and ceramic-lined equipment, such as drip coffee pots, is most satisfactory for certain purposes. It protects against metallic contamination, corrosion, and absorption. Glass-lined equipment is highly acid resistant and will withstand heat shock. This last quality is due to the fact that the coefficient of expansion of the glass enamel is similar to that of the steel shell. Most ceramics will break readily when exposed to extreme heat or mechanical shock.

OTHER MATERIALS   Items such as counter fronts and ends and food tray delivery carts made of mirror-finish *fiberglass* with stainless steel structural trim are available in many beautiful colors. The interior and exterior walls of the food delivery carts are molded in one piece, then insulated with polyurethane foam. The surfaces are strong, dent and scratch resistant, and light in weight. *Porcelain* (glass on steel) or *vinyl* covered galvanized steel may be used satisfactorily on outside walls of refrigerators and on counter fronts at less cost than stainless steel. The above materials contribute to a colorful and pleasing decor, reduce reflected glare of light, and are easily maintained. Detached well-laminated and sealed *hardwood* cutting boards are permissible in some cities and states.

Carts, racks, stands, and dollies made of *polycarbonate* are light in weight

FIGURE 10.7 A selection of food storage containers which stack or nest easily and are available with snap-tight covers facilitate sanitary and efficient storage and transportation of food. Boxes made from *(a)* clear polycarbonate and *(b)* white high-density polyethylene are shown. *Courtesy, Cambro Manufacturing Company.*

but capable of carrying heavy loads; they resist stains, dents, and scratches, will not rust or crack, and are easily disassembled for cleaning in a conveyor-type dishwashing machine. Side panels may be of a solid color or transparent, and most models are designed to accommodate 18 by 26-inch food boxes with fitted lids, trays, and bunpans (see Fig. 10.7a and b.). All items may be fitted with nonmarking neoprene brake wheels, and ball bearings. Reversible nontoxic, nonabsorbent polyethylene cutting boards are available for use on the worktable topped cabinets.

Construction

The construction of and workmanship on equipment determines whether or not it is durable, attractive, and sanitary. High-quality material and a perfect design for the purpose do not ensure good construction, although they contribute to it. Accurate dimensions, careful and well-finished joinings, solidarity, pleasing appearance, and ease of cleaning are important factors. Sinks, drainboards, and dishtables sloped to drain; tables and chairs properly braced; hinges and fasteners of heavy-duty materials and drawers constructed to function properly; adequate insulation where needed; and safety features are a few of the points to consider under construction. It is a necessity that all parts are easily cleanable.

Welding has replaced riveting, bolting, and soldering of both surface and understructure joinings in metal foodservice equipment. Great emphasis is placed on the importance of grinding, polishing, and finishing of the surfaces and welded joints for smoothness and to ensure against possible progressive corrosion. Mitered corners, properly welded and finished smooth, in items such as dishtables and sinks are superior to deep square corners or those filled with solder. The construction recommended for items of equipment used for unpackaged food is for rounded internal angles with a minimum continuous and smooth radius of 1/8 inch and internal rounded corners with a minimum continuous and a smooth radius of 1/4 inch for vertical and horizontal intersections and 1/8-inch radius for the alternate intersection.

The bull-nosed corner construction is used most often in finishing off the corners of horizontal surfaces such as worktables. The corner section of the top material is rounded off and made smooth both horizontally and vertically as an integral part of the horizontal surface. If the edge is flanged down and turned back, a minimum of 3/4 inch should be allowed between the top and the flange, and the same distance should be allowed between the sheared edge and the frame angle or cabinet body to provide easy access for cleaning.

To simplify construction and eliminate some of the hazards to good sanitation, fittings and parts have been combined into single forgings and castings wherever possible, and tubular supports sealed off smooth or fitted with adjustable screw-in solid pear-shaped feet have replaced open angular bracings with flange bases. In many instances, mobile, self-supporting, or wall-hung structures have replaced external framing. Several items welded or fitted together into a continuous unit may need to be brought into the facility and positioned before construction of the building is complete and while there is ample space for transporting the unit into the area.

The Joint Committee on Food Equipment Standards outlines in detail permissible methods for construction of such general parts as angles, seams, finishes of joinings, openings, rims, framing and reinforcement, and body construction. Specifically, they give construction features for special items such as hoods, water-cooling units, counter guards, doors, hardware, sinks, refrigerators, power-driven machines and their installation. Many health departments use the recommended standards as a basis for approving equipment and its installation. An example of such a standard follows. Fig. 10.8 gives the diagram.

FOOD SHIELDS   Display stands for unpackaged foods are to be effectively shielded so as to intercept the direct line between the average customer's mouth and the food being displayed and shall be designed to minimize contamination by the customer.

Shields shall be mounted so as to intercept a direct line between the customer's mouth and the food display area at the customer "use" position. The

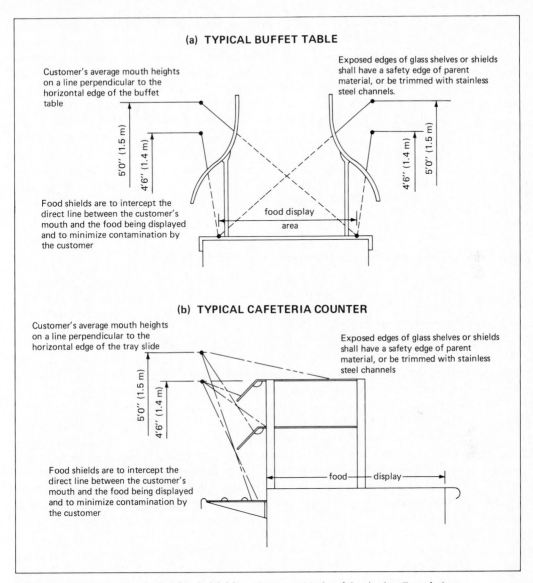

(a) TYPICAL BUFFET TABLE

Customer's average mouth heights on a line perpendicular to the horizontal edge of the buffet table

Exposed edges of glass shelves or shields shall have a safety edge of parent material, or be trimmed with stainless steel channels.

5'0'' (1.5 m)

4'6'' (1.4 m)

Food shields are to intercept the direct line between the customer's mouth and the food being displayed and to minimize contamination by the customer

food display area

(b) TYPICAL CAFETERIA COUNTER

Customer's average mouth heights on a line perpendicular to the horizontal edge of the tray slide

Exposed edges of glass shelves or shields shall have a safety edge of parent material, or be trimmed with stainless steel channels

5'0'' (1.5 m)

4'6'' (1.4 m)

Food shields are to intercept the direct line between the customer's mouth and the food being displayed and to minimize contamination by the customer

food — display

FIGURE 10.8   Standards for food shields.   *Courtesy, National Sanitation Foundation.*

vertical distance from the average customer's mouth to the floor shall be considered to be 4 feet 6 inches (1.4 meters) to 5 feet (1.5 meters) for public eating establishments. Special consideration must be given to use location conditions such as tray rails and average customer's mouth height in educational institutions and other special installations.

Such shields are to be fabricated of easy-to-clean, sanitary materials conforming to materials specifications.[1]

Safety features for the protection of workers in the use and care of equipment and for the production of safe food are important factors in the design, choice of materials, and construction of kitchen equipment. There is also a close relationship between these and the standards and controls for sanitation in a foodservice operation. Smooth, rounded corners on work surfaces, table drawers with stops and recessed pulls, automatic steam shut-off when cooker doors are opened, temperature controls, guards on slicers and chopping machines, brakes on mixers, recessed manifold control knobs on ranges and ovens, smooth, polished, welded seams, rounded corners, and knee-lever drain controls on sinks are a few examples of built-in safety in heavy-duty kitchen equipment.

Installation, Operation, and Performance

Proper installation is a necessity for the successful operation of all equipment. The best design and construction would be worthless if electrical, gas, or water connections were inadequate or poorly done. The dealer from whom the equipment was purchased may not be responsible for its installation by contract but will usually deliver, uncrate, assemble, and position the item ready for steam fitting or electrical and plumbing connections. In many cases the dealer will supervise the installation and test it out to be certain that the equipment will function properly and instruct personnel in its operation and maintenance.

Architects, contractors, and engineers are responsible for providing proper and adequate plumbing, electrical wiring, and venting facilities for the satisfactory installation of kitchen equipment according to the standards of the local building, plumbing, electrical, and sanitation codes. Water, steam, gas, and waste pipe lines and electrical conduits must be planned for each piece of equipment so that proper joinings can be made at the time of installation to avoid the necessity of extra pipe or wiring that might interfere with cleaning or placement of other equipment items.

The sanitation and safety aspects of equipment installation are important to the convenience and safety of its use and care. Sinks that drain well, wall-hung or mobile equipment that permits easy cleaning under and around it, equipment sealed to the wall, and adequate aisle clearance so that food and supplies can be transported easily and safely on carts are but a few of the considerations to make in planning installations. Refer to Fig. 10.1 for an example of combining related pieces of equipment into a single continuous unit.

The operation of each piece of equipment must be checked many times by both the contractors and service engineers before it is ready for actual use. Full instruction for the proper operation and satisfactory performance of each piece of equipment should be given to all persons who will work with it. They must know the danger signals, such as the sound of a defective motor, so that preventive measures can be taken early.

Maintenance and Replacement

The cost of care and upkeep on a piece of equipment may determine whether or not its purchase and use are justified. The annual repair and replacement of equipment should be made with consideration of the unit as a whole, and labor and operating costs should be checked constantly. If these are too high, they limit other expenditures that might promote greater efficiency in the organization. The dispersion of outlay between care and repair is important in more ways than one. Money, attention, and effort spent on care assume the continuance of the necessary equipment in use; money and effort spent on repair are often attended by a disrupted work schedule, unpleasant stresses and strains on personnel, and sometimes definite fire hazards.

Many questions arise in regard to care and upkeep costs when equipment is selected. Are parts readily available, easily replaced, and relatively inexpensive? Does the replacement require the services of a specialist, or can a regular employee be trained to do the work? Should some piece of equipment fail to operate when needed, has provision been made in planning so that operations may be carried on? Are special cleaning materials needed in caring for the equipment?

The care and repair of electrical equipment represent a major item in the maintenance cost of many foodservices. The adequate care of electric motors requires expert attention by technically trained and responsible engineers. Arrangements for such care are commonly made with the maintenance department on a contract basis, covering weekly inspection and other checkups necessary for good maintenance. Competent maintenance personnel will have a record card for every motor in the plant. All repair work, with its cost, and every inspection, can be entered on the record. If this system is used, excessive amounts of attention or expense will show up, and the causes can be determined and corrected. Inspection records will also serve as a guide to indicate when motors should be replaced because of the high cost of keeping them in operating condition.

To evaluate a piece of equipment in use, an analysis of the expenditures for care and upkeep is made, and the condition of the equipment is checked to determine if the deterioration has been more rapid than it should have been under normal usage, exposure, cleaning operations, and contacts with food and heat. A factual basis for appraising upkeep costs and depreciation of kitchen equipment can be obtained by keeping careful records on each major piece. Fig. 10.9 is a suggested method for keeping such records.

Successful maintenance of equipment requires definite plans to prolong its life and maintain its usefulness. Such plans place emphasis on a few simple procedures: keep the equipment clean; follow the manufacturer's printed directions for care and operation, including lubrication; keep the instruction card for each piece of equipment posted near it; stress careful handling as essential to continued use; and make needed repairs promptly. Some pertinent suggestions for the care of machines and instructions for their use are: the assignment of the care of each machine to a responsible person; daily inspection for cleanliness and constant supervision by the manager when in use; immediate adjustment of even minor repairs; thorough knowledge of operating directions; regular oiling and inspections; and repairs by a competent person. Printed instructions should be easily available; directions for operation with a simple diagram should be posted by the machine; and any special warnings should be printed in large or colored letters. When explaining its operation, the function and relationship of each part should be described in detail so that it is understood by the operator. There should also be a demonstration of proper use of the machine and an explanation of its value and the cost of repairs. (See Fig. 8.5, Chapter 8 for the procedure for cleaning a food slicer.) Similar directions should be formulated for each piece of equipment and made into a manual for use by employees responsible for the care and cleanliness of the various items.

The operating cost is an important feature often overlooked in purchasing equipment. In some localities electricity may be available for cooking purposes at a lower operating cost than gas, or vice versa. When all factors are considered, an electric range may be more economical in this particular instance, even though the initial cost may be more. Due consideration and investigation of the relative efficiency of various models and types are also necessary in selecting any piece of equipment.

Method of Purchase

The method of purchase of equipment varies somewhat with the institution. However, regardless of whether the actual placing of the order is done by the director of the foodservice, the purchasing agent, or the superintendent of the hospital, the preliminary procedures are much the same. All available data as to the needs and requirements of the institution are collected by the director, who is responsible for the smooth operation of the service and the

Name of Institution:_____

A. LARGE EQUIPMENT RECORD

Equipment or
Appliance Item: Purchase Date:_____

Motor Serial Number	Motor Make Model	Equipment Number	Location
Original Cost	Estimated Period of use: Months Years ☐ ☐	Make of Equipment item:	Description: Type_____ Size _____ Capacity ___ Design_____

Appraisal		Motor Specification: W V Amp. H.P. ___ ___ ___ ___	Estimated Depreciation per Month___Year___	Date fully Depreciated _____
Date	Value			

	Repairs and Replacements			
Date	Nature	By Whom	Cost	Remarks

Name of Institution _____

B. SMALL EQUIPMENT RECORD

Name of Item: Purchase
Date: Purchased
From: Location:

Style Size	Amount of Original Purchase	Quality or Grade	Uses:
___ ___	_____	_____	

Appraisal		Repairs or Replacement			Amount on hand
Date	Value	Date	Nature	By Whom Cost	

FIGURE 10.9   Suggested form for recording information on each piece of *(a)* large equipment, and *(b)* small equipment.

satisfaction of its guests. Usually representatives of different firms are willing to demonstrate equipment and to give the prospective buyer information concerning the particular piece of equipment needed. Visits may be made to various institutions to see similar models in operation. After such investigations are made and a definite idea of what is wanted is established, specifications are written and submitted to reliable firms. Written bids are then received and tabulated and a comparison is made, after which the order is placed.

The reliability of the firm from which the equipment is purchased means much to any institution. A reputable company with a record of years of successful operation usually strives to sell dependable merchandise of good quality. The company may be counted on to stand back of the guarantee and to do all possible to keep the goodwill and confidence of the customer. In their planning and engineering departments, equipment dealers employ experts whose services are always available to the prospective customer. Years of experience and constant contact with both the manufacturing and operating units in the field enable them to be of valuable assistance. Most companies keep records of the sale, service calls, and repairs of the various pieces of equipment. In return they deserve fair treatment and consideration from the director of the foodservice or the purchasing agent for the institution.

To be of value, a specification for equipment must be specific and definite. It covers every detail in relation to material, construction, size, color, finish, and cost, eliminating any question in the mind of either the buyer or the manufacturer as to what the finished product will be. If the equipment when delivered does not measure up to the specified order, it need not be accepted. If the buyer is disappointed but has permitted loopholes in the specification, and the product meets the requirements of the specification, it must be accepted. However, most firms are so desirous of selling satisfaction that they check orders carefully with the buyer to see that everything is included before the equipment is made or delivered.

The vague and the definite specifications that follow for a particular piece of equipment illustrate the difference between the two types. Specifications may be indefinite, and yet to the casual observer all points may seem to be included. After reading the second example, one can readily see the weak spots in the first.

VAGUE SPECIFICATIONS

- Item number: xx.
- Name of item: Cook's table with sink.
- Dimensions: 8 ft long, 2 ft 6 in. wide, 3 ft high.
- Material and construction: Top of this table to be made of heavy-gauge stainless steel with semirolled edge and to be furnished with one sink, 18

in. long, 24 in. wide, 12 in. deep, fitted with drain. Sink to be located 3 in. from left end of table. The under side of this table to be reinforced with channel braces. Table to be supported by 4 stainless steel tubular standards with adjustable feet. Stainless slatted shelf to rest on cross rails 10 in. above floor. Table to be equipped with one drawer, 24 in. long, 22 in. wide, and 5 in. deep. Drawer to be made of heavy stainless steel, reinforced on front facing. All joints of this drawer to be welded, and drawer equipped with ball-bearing drawer slides. This drawer to be fitted with a white metal handle.

- Price: $ . . . .

DEFINITE SPECIFICATIONS

- Item number: xx.
- Name of item: Cook's table with sink.
- Dimensions: 8 ft long, 2 ft 6 in. wide, 3 ft high.
- Material and construction: Top of this table to be made of No. 14 gauge, No. 4 grind, No. 302 stainless steel with all edges turned down 1½ in., semi-rolled edge. All corners to be fully rounded "bull-nose" construction and integral with top. Top of this table to be fitted with one sink, 18 in. long, 24 in. wide, and 12 in. deep, with all corners and intersections fully rounded to a 1-in. radius. All joints to be welded, ground smooth, and polished. Bottom sloped to drain in center. Sink to be located 3 in. from left end of table, 3 in. from each side. Sink to be equipped with 2-in white metal drain with plug and chain complete.

The under side of this table top to be properly reinforced and braced with 4-in. No. 14-gauge stainless steel channel braces welded on. Four tubular leg standards to be welded to these channel cross braces. Standards to be made of seamless stainless steel tubing 1⅝ in. outside diameter, cross rails and braces of the same material, fitted and welded together. Resting on these cross rails and braces will be a slatted bar shelf elevated 10 in. above floor. Slats to be made of No. 16 stainless steel, No. 4-grind, welded to 2-in. No. 16 stainless-steel supports. Slats 2 in. wide and bent down at ends and formed to fit over cross rails. Slatted shelf to be built in two removable parts of equal length. Leg standards to be fitted with adjustable inside threaded, stainless-steel, tubular, closed, smooth-finish feet.

Table to be equipped with one drawer, 24 in. long, 22 in. wide, and 5 in. deep. Drawer to be made of No. 16-gauge, No. 4-grind stainless steel throughout, reinforced on front facing with No. 14-gauge, No. 4-grind stainless steel. All joints of this drawer to be welded, ground, and polished. Each drawer to be equipped with nontilting, easy-glide roller-bearing drawer slides, and all metal tracks welded to under side of table top. This drawer to be fitted with a polished white metal pull handle.

· Price: F.O.B. . . . . . . $ . . . .
· Delivery date: not later than . . . .

When purchasing electrically operated equipment, it is essential that exact electrical specifications be given to the manufacturer at the time of placing the order. A motor is wound to operate on a certain voltage current, and when set up to operate on another, it may run more slowly or more rapidly than was intended, causing its output to be greater or less than its rated horsepower. There is danger of overheating and a breakdown of insulation, which will result in short circuits and the necessity for motor repairs or replacements. A three-phase motor is desirable because the absence of brushes lessens the maintenance problems. Motors of less than 1 horsepower may be used equally well on 110- or 220-volt currents, but motors of larger horsepower should be operated on a 220-volt current. Manufacturers now use ball-bearing motors, fully enclosed and ventilated, which eliminate the necessity of frequent oiling. Most motors are built especially for the machines they operate. They must be adequate in power to easily carry the capacity loads of the machines.

Selection of Some Basic Items

An analysis of the basic considerations discussed thus far helps to determine whether the selection of certain items of kitchen equipment is justified and gives attention to the mechanics of buying. Standards for various types of equipment have been mentioned. The problem of selection is so important and errors are so costly that major characteristics to consider in the selection of certain types of items will be suggested. No attempt is made to evaluate or identify equipment by trade name. The buyer may need to make a selection between the products of several competitive manufacturers or jobbers, each of whom may have quality products but with a wide variance in some details. All equipment should be a sound investment for the operator, be easily cleaned, safe to operate, and accomplish the work for which it was designed. Wise selection can be made only after an exhaustive study of all available data and observation of similarly installed equipment have been accomplished.

Manufacturers' specification sheets, brochures, and catalogs, current professional and trade journals and magazines, and the representatives of the manufacturing companies are the best sources of up-to-date information on specific items. Special features may be changed fairly often so that detailed information on certain models is soon outdated in a publication like this one.

Some points for consideration when selecting foodservice equipment, other than price, cost of operation, and maintenance, are included in the following pages to help acquaint the reader with possible features and variations of certain items. The availability of utilities and other factors might predetermine some decisions; for example, the choice between an electric or gas-heated range presents no problem if the advantages of one source of heat over the other are evident in the particular situation; instead, the problem becomes one of a choice between various models manufactured by several different firms. Space permits only a limited amount of basic information on certain fundamental items. It is expected that supplementary material will be kept up-to-date and made available in library or office files for students and foodservice operators.

Cooking Equipment

This equipment must conform to requirements for material, construction, safety, and sanitation established by groups such as the American Standards Association, American Gas Association, National Board of Fire Underwriters, Underwriters Laboratories, Inc., American Society of Mechanical Engineers, and the National Sanitation Foundation. One should be sure that parts are replaceable and service is available for all items selected as well as give consideration to original and operating costs, the effectiveness in accomplishing the task to be done, and the time and skill required for ordinary maintenance. The life expectancy requirement depends somewhat on the situation, but the selection of durable, high-quality equipment is usually economical.

ELECTRIC AND GAS FIRED EQUIPMENT   *Electrically heated* cooking equipment designed for alternating or direct current of specified voltage; rating required expressed in watts or kilowatts (1,000 watts = 1 kilowatt) per hour; wiring concealed and protected from moisture; switches plainly identified; thermostatic heat controls; flues not required for electric cooking equipment but the usual hood or built-in ventilating system necessary to remove cooking vapors and odors.

Gas fired cooking equipment designed for natural, manufactured, mixed, or liquefied petroleum fuel; adapted to given pressures; rating requirement expressed in British thermal units (Btu) per hour; individual shut-off valve for each piece of gas equipment; manifolds and cocks accessible but concealed; removable burners; automatic lighting with pilot light for each burner; thermostatic heat controls; gas equipment vented through hood or built-in ventilator instead of kitchen flue to exhaust combustible gases.

Ranges. Simple design, easily cleanable; heavy, well-braced angle iron frame; sturdy riveted or welded construction; body—sheet steel with baked-on black Japan or porcelain enamel smooth finish, or stainless steel; with or without ovens and high backs; heating elements of burners with individual controls; automatic pilot; removable drip trays to prevent spillage under elements or burners; may be mounted on casters or flush-to-wall.

Types: (1) Heavy-duty ranges—durable and well suited for large volume food-service operations with constant usage, as in hotels, large restaurants, colleges, hospitals. Approximate sizes of sections: electric—36 inches wide, 36 inches deep, 32 inches high; gas—31 to 34 inches wide, 34 to 42 inches deep, 33 to 34 inches high. (2) Medium weight or restaurant type—lighter in construction than heavy-duty and used where demands are less constant such as short-order cooking or where use is intermittent as in churches and clubs. Complete units, 6, 8, or 10 burners, or combination with fry top and/or even-heat top; 1 or 2 ovens. Approximate size 35 to 64 inches wide, 27 to 32 inches deep, 34 inches high; ovens, 26 inches wide, 22 inches deep, 15 inches high.

Tops: polished chrome-nickel-iron alloy, high strength and heat absorption qualities; resistant to warping, chipping, and corrosion; accurate thermostats provide controlled heat surfaces as desired.

1. Open or hot plate top—usually associated with short-order preparation. Heat concentrated under kettles; heating elements and grates simple in design, easily removable for cleaning; gas cones elevated so combustion and ventilation can be complete; burners can be turned on and off as needed; instant heat available; high Btu output by means of small blower to force air into burner.
2. Closed top—styled for heavy-duty continuous cooking as entire surface area is heated; various burner arrangements. For gas:—*Uniform hot top:* even heat distribution from rows of bar burners set in fire brick under smooth top; depression in brick around edge acts as duct to flue in gas range. *Graduated heat:* by means of concentric ring burners with separate controls; intense heat in center (approximately 1100°F) to low heat at edge (450°F); projections on underneath side of top help direct heat to edges. *Front-fired* (gas): row of burners under front of range top; heat concentrated at front with gradation in degrees of heat intensity toward back.
3. Fry or griddle top—even heat; solid top with edges raised to prevent overflow of grease; fitted with grease trough and drain to receptacle.

Range ovens: even heat distribution, automatic pilot and heat control; high-quality insulation; walls, top, bottom, and removable racks or shelves of smooth, durable, cleanable material or finish; sturdy counterbalanced door with nonbreakable hinges, cool handle; door to support at least 200 pounds. Designed so spillage will drain to front for easier cleaning. Approximate size: 26 inches wide, 28 inches deep, 15 inches high (inside measurements).

Legs and feet: simple design; rigid support; adjustable legs; shaped at floor contact to prevent accumulation of dirt or harborage of vermin; sealed hollow sections; minimum clearance of 6 inches between floor and lowest horizontal parts unless mounted on raised masonry island at least 2 inches high and sealed to floor.

Installation: heavy-duty range sections often joined together with other modular units as broilers and fryers to make a complete cooking unit.

Griddles. Separate griddle units to supplement or substitute for range sections; mobile griddles give use where needed, as kitchen or counter; extra-heavy, highly polished plates to hold heat and recover rapidly; even heat distribution; chromium or stainless front and ends; oversized, cool valve handles; sloped to grease drain-off. Sizes from 7 by 14 inches to 36 by 72 inches. Capacity expressed in terms of food that can be cooked at one time.

Broilers. Sheet steel of 16 gauge or better, with smooth, baked-on block Japan finish, or stainless steel; rigidly reinforced with angle support; warp-resistant heating units with radiant ceramic or alloy materials to give even heat distribution, lining of long-wearing reflective materials; spring-balanced raising or lowering device; right or left hand operation; safety stop locks; close-fitting cast-iron grids, removable for easy cleaning, adjustable over distances of 1½ to 8 inches from heat source; removable drip tray; drain to receptacle; size of grid determines capacity.

Types: (1) Unit or heavy-duty broilers—designed for large volume production and fast continuous broiling; grid area varies from 3.3 to 5.0 square feet; may be same height as range section and with high shelf above or integral with an overhead oven, heated by burners in broiler below, or mounted on a conventional range-type oven and with or without overhead warming oven. (2) Combination broiler and griddle units—suitable for small kitchen where space is limited. Fry griddle forms top of broiler and both are heated by the same set of burners but simultaneous use not recommended. (3) Salamander or elevated miniature broiler—mounted above the top of a heavy-duty closed range or over a spreader plate between units of cooking equipment. Features are similar to heavy-duty broiler except for a smaller gird area of only 1.6 to 2.8 square feet. Advantage is that it requires no floor space but may be mounted on separate legs or stand if desired. Used where small amounts of broiled foods are served. (4) Hearth-type or open-top broilers—utilize a heavy cast iron grate horizontally above the heat source. Charcoal or chunks of irregular size ceramic or other refractory material above gas or electric burners, forms the radiant bed of heat. Juice and fat drippings cause smoking and flaming that necessitate an efficient exhaust fan over the broiler. Available in multiple sections of any desired length (Fig. 10.10).

FIGURE 10.10   This countertop, underfired charbroiler has a tilting grate to draw off excess grease and to provide variable heat zones on the cooking surface. *Courtesy, U.S. Range Company.*

Fryers. Chromium-plated steel, stainless steel; automatic temperature control with signal light and timer; quick heat recovery; cool sediment zone; self-draining device; easy removal of sediment and filtering of fat; capacity expressed in pounds of fat or pounds cooked per hour; fuel input used to determine production capacity also; should fry from 1½ to 2 times the weight of fat per hour.

Types: (1) Conventional instant fat fryers—sizes from 11 by 11 to 24 by 24 in. with fat capacities 13 to 130 pounds. Models are available as free-standing, counter, or built-in, single or multiple units. (2) Pressure fryers—equipped with tightly sealed cover, allowing moisture given off during cooking to build up steam pressure within kettle; cooking accomplished in approximately ⅓ normal time. (3) Semiautomatic—speed production model equipped with conveyer to permit continuous batch cooking and automatic discharge of product as completed. (4) Convection Fryers. See Fig. 10.11.

FIGURE 10.11   Convection fryer combines convection cooking, continuous fat filtration, and heat exchanger to produce an energy efficient, highly productive piece of equipment.   *Courtesy, Hobart Corporation.*

Installation: Adequate ventilation necessary, venting into hood recommended; flue venting from fryer to general vent flue not desirable; table or workspace adjacent to fryer is necessary.

Tilting Frypan. Versatile piece of equipment—can be used as a frypan, braising pan, griddle, kettle, steamer, thawer, oven, food warmer-server; eliminates most top-of-stove cooking and provides for one-step preparation of many menu items. All surfaces, interior and exterior heavy-duty stainless steel; contoured pouring spout; one-piece counterbalanced hinged cover; self-locking worm and gear tilt mechanism; even-heat smooth flat bottom (either gas or electric); automatic thermostatic heat controls for wide range of temperatures. Available in several sizes and capacities as floor models mounted on tubular legs with or without casters, wall mounted, or small electric table mounted (see Figure 10.12); conserves fuel and labor; quick-connect installation conducive to rapid rearrangement, easy maintenance, and good sanitation. Easy to clean and reduces use of pots and pans and their washing.

Ovens. Two basic designs for heating ovens: *radiation,* in which heated air circulates around outside of heating chamber and radiates through lining, and *convection,* where heated air from heat source passes through the cabinet. All welded construction of structural steel for durable rigid frames; inner lining of 18-gauge rustproof sheet metal reinforced to prevent buckling; minimum of 4 inches of nonsagging insulation on all sides, up to 10 inches in large bakery ovens; thermostatic heat control precise between 150 and 550°F; signal lights and timer; level oven floor or deck of steel, tile, or transite (concrete and asbestos combination); well-insulated, counterbalanced doors that open level with bottom of oven to support a minimum of 150-pound weight; nonbreakable hinges; concealed manifolds and wiring; cool handles; system designed to eject vapors and prevent flowback of condensate; light operated from outside oven; steam injector for baking of hard rolls; thermocouple attachments for internal food-temperature record, and glass windows in doors available upon request.

Types: (1) Deck (cabinet)—units stacked to save space; separate heating elements and controls for each unit and good insulation between decks; decks at good working heights; 7 or 8 inches clearance for baking, 12 to 16 inches high for roasting; capacity expressed in number of 18 by 26-inch bun pans per deck; pie, cake, or baking pans should be sizes to fit multiples of that dimension; floor space requirements and inside dimensions vary with types; example of a typical one-section oven of compact design on 23-inch legs:

- Floor space requirements　　60 ½ inches wide, 39½ inches deep without flue deflector
- Inside dimensions　　42 inches wide, 32 inches deep, 7 inches high

FIGURE 10.13   Filled baking trays placed in an oven-fitted frame may be rolled directly into this convection oven from a specially designed dolly.   *Courtesy, The G.S. Blodgett Co., Inc.*

Capacity	Two 18 × 26-inch bun pans; 24 one-pound loaves of bread; 12 ten-inch pies
· Btu/hour	50,000

(2) Convection oven-forced air circulation cabinet, which employs high-speed centrifugal fan to force air circulation and guarantee even-heat distribution by an air-flow pattern over and around product in a minimum of time or from one-third to three-quarters of time required in a conventional oven. More cooking is accomplished in smaller space as food is placed on multiple racks instead of on a single deck (see Fig. 10.13).

Sizes vary with the manufacturers, but a typical convection oven measures 36 inches wide by 33 inches deep or larger models 45 inches wide by 42½ inches deep. Removable rack glides designed to accommodate 8 or 9 trays or baking sheets, 2 inches apart, thus holding more than other ovens that require greater floor space. Units may be stacked to double the output in the relatively small

FIGURE 10.13   Filled baking trays placed in an oven-fitted frame may be rolled directly into this convection oven from a specially designed dolly.   *Courtesy, The G.S. Blodgett Co., Inc.*

floor space. Convection ovens must be well insulated; may have interiors of stainless steel or vitreous enameled steel. Shelves and shelf supports lift out for easy cleaning; fitted with inside lights, timer, thermostatic heat control, glass doors or window in doors, removeable spillage pan. Quick-connect installation and addition of casters make for flexibility in arrangement. Muffle-type seal on doors for roasting and baking reduce shrinkage because of moisture retention and reduced time for cooking.

(3) Revolving tray or reel ovens—flat tray decks suspended between two revolving spiders in a ferris-wheel type of rotation; compact, space saving; welded steel, heat-tight construction; all parts highly resistant to heat and corrosion; main bearings and entire tray load supported independently of side walls; trays stabilized to keep level and sway proof; each tray equipped with individual emergency release; heavy-duty motor; smooth roller-chain drive, self-adjusting, automatic controls; example of relative dimensions; four trays, each 96 inches long by 26 inches wide; capacity, twenty 18 by 26-inch bun pans; outside, 10 feet 2 inches wide, 7 feet 4 inches deep, 6 feet 7 inches high. Small units 3½ feet deep and 6-pan units available for small foodservice operations.

(4) Rotary ovens—similar to revolving tray ovens except rotation is on a vertical axis instead of a horizontal one. Both revolving tray and rotary type ovens are most suitable for large volume baking.

(5) Microwave ovens—electromagnetic energy directed into heating cavity by magnetrons producing microwaves that penetrate food, create a magnetic field, and set up friction, causing almost instantaneous cooking of the food; energy produced at given rate is not stored nor does it heat the air surrounding or the dish containing the food (glass, china, plastic, paper); components include heating cavity of stainless steel, radio frequency generator, power supply, usually 220 volts, between 30 and 50 amperes; must pass close inspection to assure safety in use; automatic shut-off before door can be opened. Can be stacked; used extensively for fast reheating of prepared bulk or plated foods, but items may be cooked quickly and served immediately on the same dish.

(6) Combo ovens—combination convection oven, pressureless steamer, proofing cabinet, and cook-and-hold oven in a single compact unit (Fig. 10.14a).

(7) Impinger ovens—conveyorized, convection-type ovens; hundreds of high-velocity, hot-air jets focus directly on food surfaces from above and below; programmable for temperature/speed/heat zones (Fig. 10.14b).

STEAM EQUIPMENT Steam may be supplied from a central heating plant, directly connected to the equipment; or steam may be generated at point of use, which requires water connection and means of heating it to form the steam; pressures vary according to needs, with automatic pressure control and safety valve if supply is above 5 to 8 pounds per square inch; equipment of stainless steel or aluminum for rust resistance; smooth exterior and interior surfaces for easy cleaning and sanitation; timing and automatic shut-off devices; concealed control valves; steam cookers offer fast cooking in two general types.

(a)

(b)

FIGURE 10.14   *(a)* This combination steamer oven is most suited to a small operation where space is limited. *Courtesy, Groen Division, Dover Corporation. (b)* Air impingement technology is the design for this conveyorized cooking system.   *Photo
courtesy of Lincoln Food Service Products, Inc.*

Cabinet Cookers. Steam injected into cooking chamber comes in direct contact with food—to ensure clean steam supply may need to generate on the premises from tap water source instead from steam system for a group of buildings; door gaskets to seal; doors of full-floating type, with automatic bar-type slide-out shelves linked to doors; timers and automatic shut-off, and safety throttle valve for each compartment so doors cannot be opened until steam pressure is reduced; perforated or solid baskets for food; capacity in terms of number of 12 by 20-inch counter pans side by side each shelf or 10 by 23-inch bulk pans. Counter pans used both for cooking and serving.

Types: (1) Heavy-duty, direct connected steamers—compartments fabricated to form one-piece body and entire interior of stainless steel; 5 to 8 pounds per square inch with continuous steam inflow and drain-off of condensate; 1 to 4 compartments with adjustable shelves; inside dimensions 28×21 inches desirable to accommodate two 12×20-inch counter pans on each shelf, and 10 to 16 inches high. (2) Pressure cookers—operate at 15 pound steam pressure for small-batch speed cooking; reheating frozen meals or thawing and cooking frozen foods; smaller than free-venting cabinets; self-sealing inside door cannot be opened under pressure; 15-pound safety valve and 30-pound gauge; automatic timers and cutoffs. Inside capacities, from 12 to 40 inches wide, 14 to 28 inches high, 18 to 31½ inches deep; 1 to 3 cooking compartments. (3) Self steam-generating (nonpressure)—intended for installations without direct steam supply; requires water (hot preferred) connection and adequate source of heat supply to produce the steam; steam generators fit below cookers; designs and capacities similar to heavy-duty steamers. (4) Pressureless forced convection steamers—high-speed steam cookers with convection generators producing turbulent steam, without pressure, in the cooking compartment. Doors may be safely opened at any time during cooking cycle, and cooking is faster than in the conventional pressure cooker.
Installation: heavy-duty steamers of cabinet type may have pedestal support or be equipped with feet and have at least 6-inch clearance from floor, or be wall mounted to save space; install in drip pan or floor depression with drain; modular units available in many combinations with other steam equipment (Fig. 10.15).

Steam-Jacketed Kettles. Two bowl-like sections of drawn, shaped, welded aluminum or stainless steel with air space between for circulation of steam to heat inner shell; food does not come in contact with steam; steam outlet safety valve and pressure gauge; direct-connected or self-generated steam supply; full or two-thirds jacketed; stationary or tilting, open or fitted with no-drip, hinged and balanced cover (note Fig. 10.16); mounted on tubular legs, pedestal, wall brackets, or set on table. Power twin-shaft agitator mixer attachment for stirring heavy mixtures while cooking, and electrically oper-

FIGURE 10.15   Self steam-generated jacketed kettles and compartment cooker designed as a single unit for a small operation.

ated device to automatically meter water into kettle are available; may have cold water connection to jacket to cool products quickly after cooking; modular design (square jacket) for easy combining with other modular equipment to save space. Basket inserts available for removing and draining vegetables easily (Fig. 10.17).

Types: (1) Deep kettles, fully or two-thirds, jacketed—best for soups, puddings, pie fillings. (2) Shallow kettles, always full-jacketed—suitable for braising and browning meats, stews; prevents crushing of under layers of food as in deep type. (3) Trunnion or tilting kettles—mounted on trunnions with tilting device and pouring lip for easy unloading; either power-driven or manual mechanism; self-locking devices to secure kettle in any position; large floor models, or small units mounted to table to form battery; used on deep or shallow-type kettles. Capacities: from 1 quart to 80 gallons; up to 20-quart size suitable for table mounting and rotation vegetable cookery. (4) Stationary types for liquids or thin mixtures—tangent outlet for straight-flow drain-off; capacities: from 10 to 150 gallons.
Installation: kettle set for easy draw-off of food, and drip into grated drain in floor or table; mixing swivel faucet over kettle to fill or clean; table models at

FIGURE 10.16   Steam-jacketed kettle cover actuator assembly. Counter-balanced spring tension holds cover securely tight *(a)*, or open *(b)* in any position for safe easy
use; cover removable for cleaning. Suited for all types of
kettles either floor or wall mounted, stationary or tilting.   *Courtesy, Groen Division, Dover Corporation.*

height convenient for workers; adequate voltage or gas supply for self-generating models.

Fig. 10.18 shows equipment designed to be used in the cook/chill or
cook/freeze foodservice systems. This specially equipped kettle with the inclined agitator has a three-inch draw-off valve for pumping food into Cryovac
casings. The casings are quickly sealed and chilled in a cold water bath. Packaged food is then held at refrigerator or freezer temperature until rether-
malized for service.

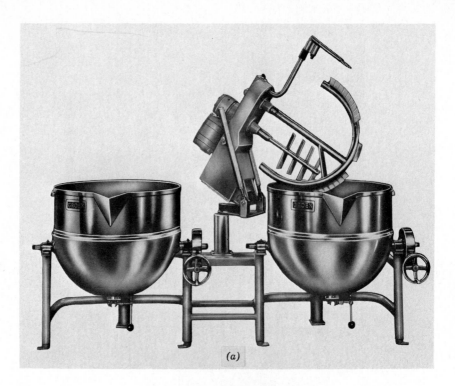

(a)

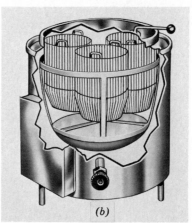

(b)

FIGURE 10.17   Steam-jacketed kettle showing *(a)* swivel power mixer attachment assembly mounted on extension of back leg of trunniontype kettle; *(b)* cross-section view of triple basket insert for holding and draining vegetables cooked in kettle.   *Courtesy, Groen Division, Dover Corporation.*

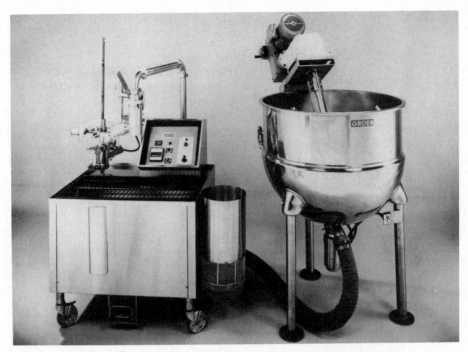

FIGURE 10.18   Designed to be used in a cook-to-inventory meal production system this equipment includes the agitator kettle, a pump/filling station, and a tumbling chiller/cook tank.   *Courtesy, Groen Division, Dover Corporation.*

Noncooking Equipment

POWER OPERATED   Modern foodservices depend upon motor-driven machines for rapid and efficient performance of many tasks. Safety precautions are necessary. Capacity charts for all types of machines are available from manufacturers and distributors. Motors, built-in according to capacity of machine, must carry peak load easily; specify voltage, cycle, and phase; three-phase is usually used for three-quarters horsepower or larger; sealed-in motors and removable parts for ease of cleaning.

Mixing Machines. Bench models for use on tables, counters, back bars, and floor models; 3- or 4-speed transmission, ball-bearing action; timed mixing control with automatic shut-off; action designed for thorough blending, mixing, and aerating of all ingredients in bowl; electrically controlled brake; possible to change speeds while in action on some machines; durable washable finish as stainless steel or anodized aluminum. Bowls: heavily tinned steel, or stainless steel (see Fig. 10.19).

FIGURE 10.19   Mixers are available in many sizes and capacities. Thorough mixing of ingredients is made possible by the planetary action of the beater or whip.   *Courtesy, Blakeslee.*

Standard equipment: one bowl, one beater, one whip; other attachments available as bread hook, pastry knife, chopper, slicer, dicer, oil dripper, bowl splash cover, dolly, purchased separately; most models have one or two adapters with smaller bowls, beaters, and whips that may be used on same machine. Capacities: standard, 10, 12, 30, 60, 80, and 140 quarts. Example of one size: 60-quart machine, mashes 40 pounds potatoes, mixes 50 pounds pie dough, mixes 24 quarts muffin batter; approximately 24 inches wide, 40 inches deep, 56 inches high.

Choppers, Cutters, Slicers. Some foodservices meet their needs for chopping, slicing, and shredding through the use of mixing machine attachments; others need specialized pieces of equipment in certain work areas. Various sizes and capacities of such machines are available in pedestal or bench models or mounted on portable stands. A typical slicer is shown in Fig. 10.20. All should be made of smooth, noncorrosive metals, have encased

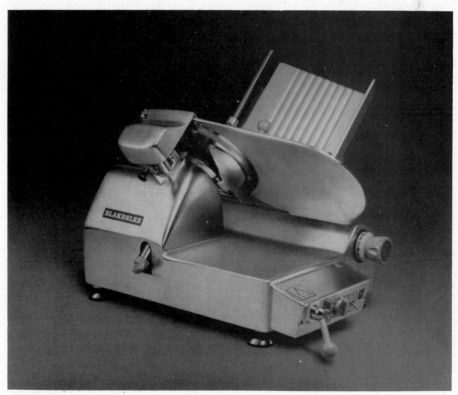

FIGURE 10.20   A slicer with an angle-fed trough.   *Courtesy, Blakeslee.*

FIGURE 10.21   Automatic portion control scale slicer is adaptable to operate with most late model gravity feed automatic slicers. It is designed to shut off the slicer when a preset weight of thinly sliced meat drops onto the scale platter.   *Courtesy, E. L. Sly Co., Portland, Oregon.*

motors, safety protectors over blades, and parts removable for cleaning and should slice in horizontal or angle-fed troughs. Fig. 10.21 illustrates how a slicer and portion control scale may be combined into one piece of equipment.

Vertical Speed Cutter Mixer. High-speed vertical cutter-mixer (Fig. 10.22), gray enamel cast iron base, stainless steel or aluminum bowl; blades move at 1,750 rpm giving increased product yield and quality as well as speed over conventional mixing. Mixes, cuts, blends, whips, creams, grates, kneads, chops, emulsifies, and homogenizes. Counterbalanced bowl cover interlocks with motor; easy tilt design for emptying. Mounted on tubular steel frame equipped with casters for portability or permanent installations; variety of cutting blades, shafts, and baffles for specific uses. Capacities: 25, 40, 60, 80, and 130 quarts; 40-quart model handles 80 pounds ingredients in one load. Cuts 40 pounds frozen meat and blends for meat loaf in 40 seconds; 12 heads lettuce in 3 seconds.

FIGURE 10.22   High-speed cutter-mixer knife blades move at 1750 revolutions per minute. Prepares foods for cooking or serving in seconds.   *Product of Hobart Corporation.*

Refrigerators. Detailed information in Chapter 9. Central or self-contained units; water or air-cooled compressors; walk-in, reach-in, pass-through, cabinet convertible temperatures; efficient nonabsorbent insulation; tight-fitting doors, strong no-sag hinges, strong catches; all surfaces and parts cleanable. *Reach-in:* fitted with tray glides to accommodate standard tray sizes, or removable wire or slatted stainless steel shelves (note Fig. 10.23). *Walk-in:*

FIGURE 10.23   Convenient unit refrigerator: exterior surfaced with thermal bonded vinyl in choice of colors, interior silver-tone white vinyl; doors same as outside finish or sliding glass; 3-inch thick glass fiber insulation; may be fitted with pan slides or shelves and 5-inch swivel casters.   *Product of Hobart Corporation.*

portable, sectional, slatted metal shelving. Some reach-in models may be detached from motor unit to provide portable, temporary refrigerated storage.

> *Counter units:* individual compressors for salad, frozen dessert, milk storage areas; self-leveling dispensers for cold or freezer storage and service. *Ice makers:* central and self-contained units; cubes, tubes, flakes, capacity, measured in output per hour; many models and sizes are available. *Water coolers:* glass filler or bubbler faucet; capacity: depends on cooling volume per hour and size of storage tank; designed for convenient storage of clean glasses.

Dish and Utensil Cleaning Equipment. (1) Pot and pan cleaners. *Manually controlled power scrubbing brush,* cleans and polishes; multiple use with accessories, extension cords, scouring brushes, buffers; requires no extra space. *Water agitator attachment for pot soaking sinks;* loosens cooked-on food; can be installed with limited space. Dishwashers, pot and pan washers, glass washers. Stainless steel, welded construction; operation control, manual or automatic. This type of equipment is discussed in detail in Chapters 8 and 9 (see Figs. 8.9 and 8.15).

Dishwashers: bench or floor models; single or multiple tank; semi- or fully automatic operation; rack or conveyor type for continuous racking (see Fig. 10.24 a, b, c); doors or curtains; automatically timed conveyor speed; separate temperature controls for rinse, wash, and final rinse; automatic detergent dispenser; parts removable for cleaning; inspection door for easy access to wash and rinse compartments; scrapping, prerinse and blower-type assemblies available; water—pressure, temperature, hardness, pipe size; waste disposer. Model designed especially to accommodate trays is illustrated in Fig. 10.25.

> Capacity expressed in number of pieces washed per hour, many sizes from 1-tray bench model, 22 inches long, 23 inches wide up to heavy-duty conveyer machine, approximately 30 feet long. Trend is toward smaller units to conserve space.
>
> Racks: chrome plated or stainless steel, plastic-coated, removable and adaptable dividers; or all-plastic, light-weight, space-saving nesting racks. Open divided racks for cups, glasses; designed for stacking in storage.
>
> Conveyors: linked metal, plastic, or metal tipped with plastic or nylon projections to hold dishes in inclined position.

Waste Disposers. One system for the disposal of waste may solve the problem in a given situation, but, in many cases, it may be feasible to combine two or more of the following methods.

Unit disposers for food waste at vegetable and salad preparation, sinks, and dish scrapping areas eliminate the need for garbage can collections, storage,

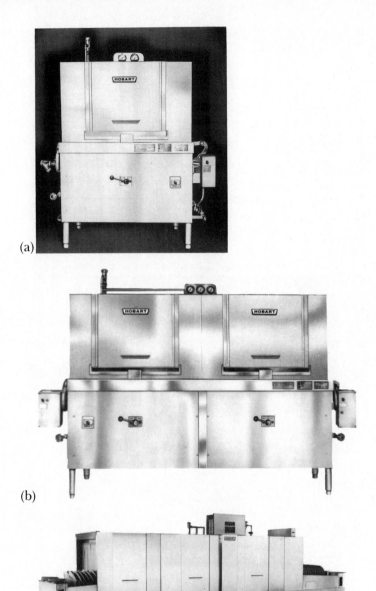

FIGURE 10.24 Examples of *(a)* single tank, *(b)* double tank, and *(c)* conveyor-type dishwashers. *Courtesy, Hobart Corporation.*

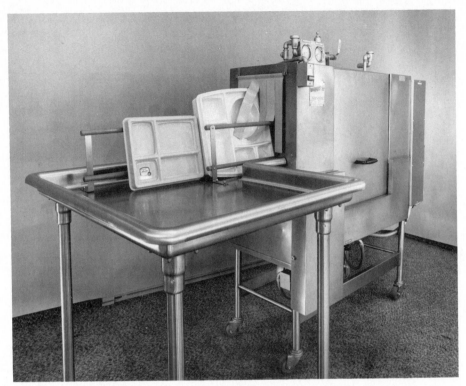

FIGURE 10.25   Machine designed especially for washing trays.   *Courtesy, Insinger Machine Company.*

and outside pickup unless their installation and use are prohibited by environmental controls. All waste paper, cardboard cartons, wood crates, plastics, tin cans, broken china, and glassware (and garbage) might need to be discharged into dumpster bins for pickup if incineration of burnable waste is restricted by antipollution regulations in the community.

Can and bottle crushers are capable of reducing this type of disposable bulk up to 90 per cent and cut labor costs, refuse space, and cost of pickup. Capacities of models vary from 50 cans and bottles per minute to 7,500 per hour. Design of such a crushing mechanism is shown in Fig. 10.26.

The use of *compactors* to reduce the volume is a convenient and economical aid to the disposal of all waste in many foodservices. One model with 13,000 pounds of force can compact paper, milk cartons, cans, bottles, food scraps to a minimum 5-to-1 ratio or as high as 20-to-1, depending on the combination of materials. Discharge of the compacted material, up to 50 pounds,

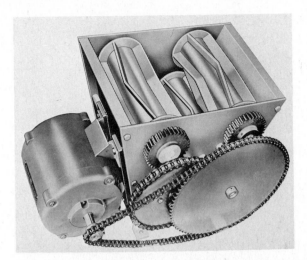

FIGURE 10.26   Rugged crushing mechanism of can
and bottle crusher. Rollers set in "v" design prevent clogging and progressively reduce cans to smallest bulk possible. *Courtesy, Qualheim, Inc.*

into a poly bag or carton on a dolly makes it ready for short-time storage
and haulaway. Most machines operate on a 120-volt, 20-amphere outlet, have
safety interlocks throughout for operating protection, and a sanitizing-deo-
dorizing spray that may be released at each return stroke of the compaction
ram to avoid any objectionable odor from the compacted mass (Fig. 10.27).

The *pulping system* reduces the volume of disposable materials such as food
scraps, paper, plastic, and cooked bones up to 85 percent, depending on the
mix. Cans, silverware, and some glass are tolerated, but are automatically
ejected from the pulping tank into a trash box. Durable teeth on a rotating
disc and cutters pulp the material in the tank. It is then circulated to a pow-
erful waterpress above, reducing the pulp to a semidry form that is forced
into a discharge chute to containers for removal as low-volume waste. The
water from the press recirculates to the pulping tank. This equipment is
available in several sizes. It may be incorporated into the dishwashing system
or other area where pulpable waste originates (see Figs. 10.28 and 8.7).

Transport Equipment. Usually powered equipment for transport of food
and supplies within a foodservice is kept to minimum distances by careful
planning of area relationships. A thorough study of the advantages, capabilities, and maintenance factors should precede the selection of a system for a
particular situation. Also, automatic and emergency shutoffs, enclosed but

FIGURE 10.27   This mobile, hydraulic trash compactor can reduce trash to 1/10 of its original size and features a compactor dolly for ease of unloading of the compacted trash.   *Courtesy, Precision Metal Products, Inc.*

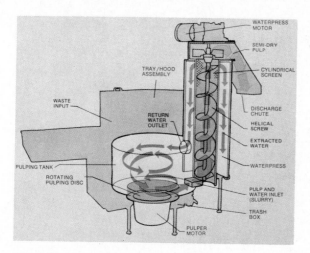

FIGURE 10.28   Diagram showing how pulpable waste
may be reduced in volume and form.   *Product of Hobart
Corporation.*

easy access to working parts, safety, and cleanability are important features
to consider.

Conveyors and Subveyors. Reverse for two-way service; emergency brakes;
safety guards; automatic stop and start with removal of tray, or continuous
flow. *Conveyors:* horizontal transportation; stationary or mobile units for flexibility of tray or food assembly. *Subveyors:* vertical conveying, used where
space may be limited on a single floor and work or serving units are on
different floors.

Monorail and Driverless Vehicles. These require special equipment and
installations; reduce labor and hand-pushing of carts; speedy; relatively expensive to install. Monorail requires overhead rail and "Amsco" system, a
special electronic track under the floor. Cars of the latter are monitored
from a control panel; powered by batteries; directed over the track to locations on the same floor or to a bank of special elevators that automatically
open and close on signal and exit on the assigned floor.

NONMECHANICAL KITCHEN EQUIPMENT

Tables and Sinks. Often fabricated by specification order to fit space and
need; stainless steel, No. 12 or 14 gauge. No. 4 grind; welded and polished
joinings; rounded corner construction; seamless stainless steel tubular supports with welded cross rails and braces of same material; adjustable inside
threaded stainless steel rounded or pear-shaped feet; worktables may be fit-

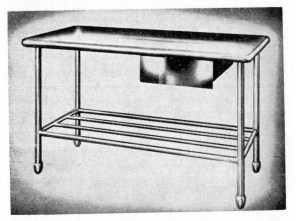

FIGURE 10.29   Kitchen worktable. Note simplicity of
design, rounded edges and corners of top, smooth joinings of tubular supports, and rounded feet or may be fitted with casters.   *Courtesy, C. Blickman, Inc.*

ted with ball-bearing rubber-tired casters, 2 swivel and 2 stationary, brakes
on 2 casters.

For *tables:* Top of one sheet without seams; edges; integrally finished, rolled
edge, raised rolled edge where liquids are used, turned up as flange or
splashback and with rolled edge. Legs and feet: tubular, welded or seamless
metal; adjustable; simple design; provide a minimum of 6 inches of space
between bottom of unit and floor; drawers: operate on ball bearings, equipped
with stop, removable. Undershelves: stationary bar, slatted, solid, removable
sections; sink or bain-marie; note Fig. 10.29.

Dimensions: standard, length 48, 60, 72, 84, 96, 108, 120 inches; width 24, 30,
36 inches; height, 34 inches; other dimensions by individual specification.
Types: *Baker's tables*—fitted with drawers; separate storage bins as specified.
Salad tables—with or without refrigerated work space and storage, sinks. *Sandwich tables*—refrigerated storage for fillings: removable cutting boards. *Dish tables*—well-braced sturdy understructure; 3-inch upturned and rolled edges, higher
if joined to wall; scrap block, waste drain, sinks for soaking, over-and-under
shelves, rack return, tray rest; adequate space for receiving, soiled dishes, clean
dishes, preflush.

For *sinks:* one, two, three compartments; all-welded seamless construction,
drainboard and splashback integral from one sheet of metal, rolled edges;
corners fully rounded with 1-inch radius, coves spherical in shape at inter-

section of corners; bottom of each compartment scored and pitched to outlet; outlet recessed 5 inches in diameter, ½-inch deep, fitted with nonclog waste outlet; partitions: two thicknesses formed of one sheet of metal, folded and welded to bottom and sides of sink; provision for overflow; drainboards pitched to drain into sink; drainboards supported by channel braces to sink legs or wall-bracketed, if longer than 42 inches usually supported by two pipe legs at end away from sink; removable strainer at waste outlet; external lever control for outlet valve; stationary or swing faucets.

> Dimensions, standard single compartment, 20, 24, 30, 36, 48, 60, 72 inches long, 20, 24, 30 inches wide, 14, 16 inches deep; two-compartment, 36, 42, 48, 54, 60, 72 inches long, 18, 22, 24, 30 inches wide, 14, 16 inches deep. Others by individual specification; 38-inch height convenient for sinks.

Storage Cabinets, Racks, Carts. Cabinets and racks stationary or portable. Open or closed; shelves: attached, removable, adjustable, tray slides; sturdy construction for use; solid floor; bolted or welded; doors, hinged or side sliding, side sliding removable, suspension hung. Both stationary or portable types may be heated or refrigerated. Size determined by needs and space.

Scales. Heavy-duty *platform scale* built into floor of receiving room area for weighing in supplies and food; weight indicator should be plainly visible from both front and back. *Exact-weight* floor or table models in storeroom, ingredient room, bakeshop, and where recipes are made up. *Portion scales* for weighing individual servings where needed. All types of scales are now available with electronic (L.E.D.) readouts, locking in accurate weight almost instantly on an easy-to-read screen, as in Fig. 10.30.

Cooking Utensils. Strong and durable to withstand heavy wear; nontoxic material; resistant to chipping, dents, cracks, acids, alkalis; cleanable; even heat spread; highly polished metal reflects heat, dull metal absorbs and browns food more readily in baking; variety of sizes of sauce pans, sauce pots, stock pots, frypans, roast and bake pans; *aluminum heavy-duty*—double-thick bottoms, extra-thick edge, *semiheavy*—lighter weight, uniform thickness, rolled edge; *stainless steel*—uniform thickness, spot heats over direct fire. Small equipment as pudding pans, pie and cake pans, quart and gallon measures, mixing bowls of lighter weight metals. Pudding and counter pans selected to fit serving table, refrigerator, and mobile racks for flexibility of use: 12 by 20-inch-size recommended. Clamped on lids cut spillage losses in transporting prepared foods.

Cutlery. High-carbon tooled steel or high-carbon chrome-vanadium steel; full tang construction; compression-type nickel-silver rivets; shapes of handles and sizes of items varied to meet needs; handle and blade weight balanced for easy handling.

FIGURE 10.30   An electronic portion control food scale gives accurate weight almost immediately on a large L.E.D. readout. This model is shown with an AC adaptor and optional foot pedal control.   *Courtesy, Pelouze Scale Company.*

Serving Equipment

COUNTERS   Attractive, compact, efficient arrangement designed for specific foodservice; welded and polished in one piece; hot and cold units well insulated; easily cleaned; separate temperature controls for each unit of heated section; counter guard shields for open food display sections; portable or built-in self-leveling dish and tray storage may be desired; adequate tray slide to prevent accidents.

SERVING UTENSILS   Variety of sizes of ladles, long-handled spoons, perforated, slotted, and solid; spatulas; and ice cream dippers; selected to give predetermined portions size. Capacity or size marked on ladle handles and on dippers.

Special counter equipment: Convenient arrangement; easily operated automatic heat controls. Coffee maker—urn or battery vacuum makers with cup storage near; toasters, egg cookers, grills with hoods; temporary storage cabinets for hot cooked foods, rolls—controls for temperature and moisture content; freezer cabinet unit for ice creams; bread dispensers; milk-dispensing machines.

SELF-LEVELING DISPENSERS Counterweighted springs bring platform to uniform level upon removal of item; for foods, dishes, containers; heated, refrigerated, or freezer storage; mobile, stationary, or built-in; open or closed frames of stainless, galvanized, carbon steel or aluminum; noncorrosive springs. Tube type: for plates, saucers, bowls; chassis type; accommodates square or rectangular trays, or racks, empty or filled; adjustable to vary dispensing height (see Fig. 10.31).

COFFEE MAKERS Coffee-making equipment falls into two general types: (1) urns for making large quantities of coffee when many people are served in a short period of time, and (2) small electronic automatic brewing units for a continuous fresh supply of the beverage. Requirements are fairly simple in either case, but important to the making of an acceptable product: glass or stainless steel liners for urns, glass or stainless steel decanters for the automatic brewing machines; fluted paper filters; controlled hot water temperature, coffee and water measurement, infusion time, brewing speed and holding temperatures; easily cleaned. Installation with quick-disconnect utilities outlets provide for easy relocation of equipment (see Fig. 10.32). The use of freeze-dry coffee simplifies the process, reduces time and labor, and eliminates the necessity of discarding coffee grounds.

MOBILE FOOD SERVING CARTS Specialized equipment for transporting bulk or served food some distance to the consumer; well-insulated, automatic temperature controls; engineered for ease in moving and turning; circumference bumper guards; designed for easy cleaning; may require high voltage outlets; combination heated, nonheated, low temperature and refrigerated sections; beverage dispensers and other accessories as found on serving counters (see Chapter 7 for details).

The selection of foodservice equipment by any arbitrary rule would be unwise and ill advised. Each operation must be studied to determine the real needs and purchases made accordingly. *The foregoing statements are suggested as a guide only in helping to recall basic considerations regarding various items of equipment.*

FIGURE 10.31   Mobile self-leveling china dispensers may also be specified with heating mechanisms.   *Courtesy, Precision Metal Products, Inc.*

FIGURE 10.32   Coffee dispenser uses brewed liquid coffee concentrate to produce regular and decaffeinated coffee.   *Courtesy, Pasco Packing Company.*

Energy Conservation

According to the National Restaurant Association, energy management programs and the wise selection of equipment can result in savings of up to 20 per cent on utility costs for the average foodservice establishment.

An energy management program requires the constant participation of every employee in the operation. Inservice training and incentive programs should be set up to ensure the cooperation of all involved. Some general guidelines for conserving energy in foodservice operations that should be included in any program are given in Chapter 5.

Using too large equipment at less than full capacity is one of the most common energy wasters. This includes but is not limited to dishwashers, ovens, griddles, fryers, ranges, steam-jacketed kettles when operated with partial loads and being left on between loads.

Routine maintenance and cleaning of equipment are essential components of an energy reduction program. Weak or broken door springs on ovens and refrigerators may reduce efficiency by 35 per cent. Carbonized grease and cooking residue on griddle plates can reduce cooking efficiency by 40 per cent.[3]

Utility companies often offer free equipment service adjustments, energy audits, and assistance in establishing effective energy management programs. Following is an example of information that may be obtained from a utility company.

> HOW MUCH ENERGY DOES IT SAVE . . . To use OPEN BURNER RANGES instead of Hot Tops?[4]
>
> You are way ahead in conserving fuel and reducing operating costs when you use OPEN BURNER RANGES. Tests show dramatic savings in fuel consumption when OPEN BURNER RANGES are compared to Hot Top Ranges.
>
> - Similar quantities of water boil in up to *one-third less time* on the OPEN BURNER RANGE.
> - Boiling similar quantities of water requires up to *55% less fuel* on the OPEN BURNER RANGE.
> - Hot Tops must be preheated. Preheat takes 30 to 60 minutes. The gas flame on the OPEN BURNER RANGE comes on instantly when you need it. *No preheat necessary!*
>
> Tests show additional energy can be conserved no matter what kind of range top you have.
>
> - Covering pans reduced energy consumption
>   —on OPEN BURNER RANGES, covering pans reduced consumption up to 20%.
>   —on Hot Tops, covering pans reduced energy consumption up to 35%.
> - Heating larger quantities of food can be done more efficiently than heating smaller quantities of food.
>   —on OPEN BURNER RANGES, BTU consumption per pound was reduced up to 19% when the quantity of water heated was doubled.

—on Hot Top Ranges, BTU consumption per pound was reduced up to 20% when the quantity of water heated was doubled.

Other energy conservation suggestions for use of equipment in food service establishments follow.

- Ventilation systems, air conditioning, heating:
  Make-up air for hoods; use thermostatically controlled unheated and unrefrigerated air.
  Use heat recovery systems in hood; heat exchangers for hot water and/or comfort heating.
  Use evaporative coolers (swamp coolers) to comfort-condition kitchen air (do not use refrigerated air).
  Size air-conditioning units and comfort heaters accurately for climate area; limit size of heaters for kitchen area to take advantage of heat from cooking equipment.
  Use economizer cycle systems (use of outside air when cool enough to eliminate need for refrigerated air).
  Place air-conditioning and furnace filters in an easily accessible location to ensure frequent scheduled cleaning or replacement.
  Insulate heating and air-conditioning ducts adequately and completely, using two inches of insulation.
  Zone and wire air-conditioning and furnace units to permit zone control of unoccupied areas.
  Install covered and locked thermostats, 68° for heating, 78° for cooling.
  Use time clocks to decrease utility consumption by mechanical equipment in off-peak periods.
- Water heating:
  Locate water heater in close proximity to major use.
  Insulate all hot water lines.
  Size water heating equipment accurately; do not undersize or oversize; use quality equipment.
  Install spring-loaded faucet valves or spring-loaded foot controls to limit hot water waste.
  Use quality valves to minimize dripping faucets.
  Consider solar-assisted and/or waste heat exchanger water heating systems to preheat water.
  Use single system, high-temperature water heating equipment and automatic mixing valves.
  Use water softening equipment to soften water in areas where water is hard.

- Dishwashing:
  Size dishwasher to handle average maximum requirements.
  Install easily accessible switch to permit shut down of equipment in slack periods. Consider chemical dishwasher for small establishments.
- Cooking equipment:
  Be selective in specification of equipment offering greatest efficiency and flexibility of use.
  Careful planning can save on operating and initial equipment costs. Do not overestimate equipment requirements. Specify thermostatically controlled equipment whenever possible.
- Ranges: Specify open top burners—they require no preheat and offer maximum fuel efficiency as compared to center fired and front fired hot tops, or even heat tops. Open burners reduce the air cooling load as there is minimal heat radiation when cooking operation is completed.
- Convection ovens: Versatile and perform most baking/roasting operations in shortest period of time.
- Steamers: Self-contained (boiler); high production at minimal operating cost.
- Grooved griddle: Replaces the underfired broiler; minimizes air pollution problems; operates much more efficiently than underfired broilers and places less of a load on air cooling systems; generally has greater cooking capacity.
- Broilers: Underfired—minimize specification—reasons stated in grooved griddles. Overfired—preferred over underfired. More efficient, faster, no pollution problems. Compartment over broiler provides use for waste heat as plate warmer, finishing foods, browning, cheese melting (may be used for these purposes in lieu of salamander).
  Salamanders/cheese melters: Specify those employing infrared ray radiation; they reach full operating temperature within seconds, are efficient, can be turned off when not in use.
- Braising pans/tilting skillets: A versatile volume production piece of equipment that can serve many cooking operations—fry, boil, braise, roast, steam, food warmer. Consider caster equipped pans and installation of additional gas outlets near serving lines, banquet facilities, and such to obtain maximum utilization of this equipment and reduce gas consumption.
- Fryers: Floor fryers provide maximum production capabilities, have self-contained power oil filter units for ease and speed of filtering, which prolongs oil life. Consider inclusion of multiproduct programmed computers; they are available built into the fryer and will provide consistently high-quality fried products with novice operators; lowers labor, food, and oil costs. Specify more than one size of fryers; full production capacity

and standby or nonpeak period smaller capacity fryers; save on initial equipment cost; fuel costs and oil costs.

Dining Room Furnishings

A dining area that is attractive and appealing does much to make patrons feel comfortable and adds to the enjoyment of the food they are served. The foodservice director may be responsible for the selection of some of the furnishings, especially for the dinnerware, tableware, and glassware. The services of an interior designer or decorator may be employed, however, to help create the desired atmosphere through selection of the appropriate style and type of tables and chairs, window treatment, and a color scheme that will coordinate all furnishings into a harmonious effect.

Basic information needed for the wise selection of dinnerware (dishes), tableware (knives, forks, spoons), glassware, and table covers is presented here. Specialized assistance likely will be sought for the purchase of furniture, drapes, curtains, and other furnishings. All furnishings should be pleasing, durable, serviceable, and easy to maintain.

Dinnerware

There are many choices of materials used in making dishes for today's foodservice market, including china, glass, and melamine or other plastic ware or combinations of other materials kept secret by their manufacturers. Dinnerware suitable for foodservices varies with the type of service given. A club or luxury restaurant may wish to use as fine a china as may be found in the homes of its patrons. On the other hand, a school foodservice needs more durable ware to withstand the hazards attendant on its use. Fast food establishments usually find disposable dinnerware best fills their needs.

CHINA

Types of China. There are three types of china: vitrified, semivitrified, and pottery. Of these, only vitrified is considered durable enough for use in most foodservices.

Vitrified china, also known as porcelain, is made of excellent quality clay free from iron, with flint and feldspar added. These materials plus water can be shaped and fired to a high temperature for at least 60 hours, which fuses the mixture into a homogeneous body that is durable and virtually nonabsorbent. At this point, the shaped piece is known as "bisque." A notable improvement in making vitrified china was effected by the introduction of a metallic ion "alumina" into the body of the materials. This enabled the industry to make a thinner, whiter, stronger piece of china with greater edge chip resistance, greater impact strength, and smoother body that has faster surface cleanability than china made without alumina.

The U.S. Bureau of Standards has established three standards for vitrified china for institutional use:

1. Thick—5/16 to 3/8 inches thick (which is quite heavy)
2. Hotel—5/23 to 1/4 inches thick, with a rolled underedge
3. Medium-weight—sold on the market as "banquet" weight; thinner than hotel weight and has straight edges

The Bureau also tests and sets limits for moisture absorption for each size piece, and tests for durability by use of chipping, impact, and breakage tests under stated conditions. Fig. 10.33 shows a resistance-to-breakage test being conducted by one china manufacturer to ensure that government standards will be met.

It is essential that the buyer recognize that weight does not mean strength

FIGURE 10.33   The resistance to breakage of china may be measured accurately.   *Courtesy, Syracuse China Company.*

and long life for china. Durability and strength are far more directly related to the quality of materials used and the methods of manufacture employed than they are to weight.

The thick china is commonly used for lunch counter service or other situations where extra heavy service is demanded of the table appointments. It is clumsy to handle and apt to be unattractive in appearance. All hotel-weight china except cups have a roll under the outer edge that gives the effect of weight and also lessens chipping on the upper side of the plate. This type of china is well adapted for use in institutions such as hospitals, residence halls, and restaurants. It is highly resistant to shock, easy to handle, and available in many designs and colors. Banquet-weight china is used extensively in exclusive restaurants, clubs, and the private room service of hospitals. It resembles more closely household dinnerware.

Vitrified heat-resistant ware of good quality is nonabsorbent, stainproof, and withstands high temperatures without crazing or breaking. Items are available in a variety of attractive colors and designs and include coffee pots, teapots, casseroles, ramekins, and individual pudding or pie dishes.

Semivitrified china is a good quality earthenware that has been fired insufficiently to obtain vitrification. This treatment results in a soft body, which is, therefore, porous and absorbent. Semivitrified china has been given a glaze that seals and finishes the dish, but the glaze may be sensitive to heat shocks and checks easily. The design may not be permanent as it is applied after the china is glazed and fired in making semivitrified and semiporcelain china.

Decoration. Three methods are used to put color, designs, and decorations on china:

1. Lining—a line design applied to the edge or rim of the dish by machine; only one color may be used.
2. Printing—any type of design may be applied by this stamping or printing-on process.
3. Decalcomania process is used when two or more colors in the design are desired.

After the colored design has been applied on vitrified china by whatever method, the item is dipped into a glaze and fired at a high temperature. The glaze is a molten glass that is applied as a coating to the shaped, fired, and decorated dish and is fused to it. This process seals the surface of the bisque, covers and protects the design and further strengthens the body, makes the surface smooth, and is then highly resistant to chemicals and to cracking, crazing, or marring by physical shock.

Certain colors such as some blue pigments and the application of gold trim are affected by high temperatures of the firing of the glaze, so may be applied after the glazing process. This design over the glaze is not as satisfactory as under glaze for institutional foodservice use in most situations. The colors and gold that are put on top of the glaze are less durable and wear away faster than those that are put on under the glaze and protected by it.

Factors in Selection of China. The things to consider in selecting china are its weight, the color and design, budget, availability of replacement, shapes, sizes, and capacities. In addition, in purchasing china, "firsts" the most perfect pieces that can be selected from each run of the kiln after the firing process, are the most desirable. They are free from warping, chips, faults in the glaze, thin or uneven glaze, large scars on the underside from the pins on which the china was held during firing, and uneven or poorly applied designs. Other pieces are graded as "seconds" or "thirds," depending on the degree of imperfection. Warped plates are detected by rolling several plates on edge simultaneously. The warped ones show up plainly in the rolling in contrast to the first selection. Close inspection of each piece by experienced workers completes the grading process.

The *color and design* of the china selected should be in harmony with the overall motifs and general atmosphere desired in the dining area. Pigments and processes have been so perfected that at the present time there is practically no limit to the color and design possibilities of china. Conservative but attractive designs enhance the beauty of any dining room and ordinarily do not detract from interest in the food. Colors primarily used for the body of china are white, off-white or ivory, and buff or tan. These complement natural food colors and serve as a good background for them. Design colors should harmonize. Gaudy and naturalistic designs in the center of plates seem to leave little room for food. Also, such designs may add 5 to 25 per cent of the cost of each plate. On the other hand, an inexpensive design may be created with a colored edge for the dominant note.

That the choice of china is influenced by the size of the budget is evident. Not infrequently the budget limits the choice to the china with the simple border pattern, which may or may not have artistic appeal. Managers need to weigh values of beauty and durability along with cost in the selection of china. Interest in and demand for good design in less expensive china has influenced manufacturers to produce such items.

Another factor that may influence choice is the available designs for which *replacements* may be obtained within a reasonable time period. Stock types of patterns are usually available for immediate shipment. Specially made china, such as that having a monogram or crest, must be ordered weeks in advance. This fact must be considered along with the relatively higher cost of such special china in selecting a pattern for any specific service. Even open-stock types of patterns may be discontinued with limited notice; so when the initial selection is made, the possibility of replacements with identical china or that similar in type should be considered.

Another consideration in selecting china is the *shape* of the pieces for there are many different ones on the market. Plates are available with a wide flat 1 to 1½-inch rim; Econo-Rim, which is ¼ to ⅜-inch rolled under edge, designed to save space on trays and in storage and give extra strength to the edge; and coupe-shape, which is a no-rim design with the body of the plate scooped or slightly concave. Cups are made in a low, wide shape and in a taller, slender shape with a much narrower opening, which holds heat in the beverage longer and stores easier than the more open shape. In addition, mugs of all sizes and shapes, some footed and some not, have become popular in many foodservices and eliminate the need for saucers.

A wide range of *sizes and capacities* of china is available and may vary somewhat from manufacturer to manufacturer. The present trend in purchasing is to limit the number of different size dishes, supplying one size for several uses. For example, instead of buying both 4-inch bread and butter plates and 6-inch salad/dessert plates, a 5-inch plate to satisfy both uses may be purchased. Or, instead of ordering different size bowls for soup, cereals, and similar items, one size is purchased for all. This simplification is advantageous from the standpoint of service, inventory, dishwashing, replacement, and storage.

The size of plates is the measurement from outer rim to outer rim, and that is the size specified when ordering. Cups, bowls, sugar bowls and creamers, and pitchers are specified by capacity in terms of ounces.

Amounts to Purchase. The quantity of dinnerware to be purchased for equipping a foodservice depends on many factors: the seating capacity and total number of people to be served, the length of the serving period, the type of menu and the price of the meal, the kind of service, the dishwashing facilities and whether they are used intermittently or continuously, and the caliber and speed of the employees. Other factors not to be overlooked are the variety of sizes of each item to be stocked and the frequency of use of the piece. For example, if only one size plate is purchased for multiple use as a bread and butter, salad, and underliner, fewer total pieces would be required than if three different-size plates had been selected. Also, a larger number of coffee cups used many times a day must be purchased to provide a margin of safety than would be necessary for bouillon cups that may be used only once or twice a week.

Any listing of quantities must be determined by the needs of a particular institution and not by a set formula. The following suggestions for the number of each item of dinnerware needed per customer in a foodservice using an intermittent dishwashing cycle might be used as a basis for initial planning.

Item	Number Per Customer
Cups	1.25
Saucers	1.25
9-inch plates	1.0
5-inch plates	0.66
Bowls, cereal	0.5
Sauce dishes	0.5

Care. China has a much longer life when handled carefully and cleaned properly. It is believed that most breakage is caused by china hitting against china, and that 75 to 80 per cent of all breakage occurs in the soiled dish and washing area. Careful training and supervision of the personnel do much to prevent breakage and keep dishes looking bright and clean. Procedures to reduce the number of times a piece of china is handled will assist also in this. Examples are to separate and stack soiled dishes into like kinds before taking them to the dishroom for washing, and to store clean cups and glasses in the racks in which they are washed. Rubber plate scrappers and collars on openings in scrapping tables not only decrease noise but help to reduce breakage of dishes. Also helpful are the use of plastic and other synthetic coated metal dishracks and plastic or nylon pegs on dishmachine conveyors.

Suitable washing compound, proper temperature of wash and rinse waters, in addition to careful attention throughout the scrapping, washing, and stacking and storing of clean dishes contribute to the length of life of china.

The soiled dishes, scrapped and ready for the machine, are placed on belts or in racks, so that all surfaces are exposed. Sorting and stacking dishes into piles of the same kind and size will help to reduce breakage. The loading of one type of dishes in the racks or on the conveyor belt speeds washing at both the loading and unloading ends of the machine and ensures better wash action, since there is no overlapping of larger dishes to block the spray. After the washing and rinsing, the china is air dried. Plates of like size are stacked carefully so that the bottom rim of one does not mar the surface of the plate beneath it. Cups and glasses are stored in the wash racks, stacked on dollies, and wheeled to the unit where they will be used next. Plates and bowls likewise may be placed directly from the dishmachine into self-leveling mobile units or onto dish storage trucks where they remain until needed. Thus breakage is lowered through reduced handling, and fewer labor hours are required for this one-time handling as opposed to storing dishes in a cupboard and then having to remove them when needed.

Generally, breakage is highest on small plates, saucers, and fruit dishes; they are often stacked too high and slide off the trays or carts; handles are broken from cups; and the edges of large heavy plates may be chipped if stacked carelessly. As a means of reducing breakage through carelessness, it is advisable to make a frequent inventory of stock in circulation. Thus the workers become aware that a constant check of breakage is being made. Often a price list of china is posted, so the total loss to the foodservice through breakage is made known to the workers. Supervisors, too, should try to determine how and where breakage is occurring, if it seems unreasonably high, and then include corrective procedures in training sessions held for those workers involved in dish handling.

Replacement of china may be made as breakage demands, or provision may be made for a stockroom supply ample for the probable yearly need. In this case replacement may be made of the storeroom stock following the annual inventory. Managers should be aware of the supply of dishes in circulation and an ample quantity made available so service will not be slowed because of a lack of clean dishes when needed.

GLASS DINNERWARE   A popular dinnerware made by the Corning Glass Company is a basic glass in which a percentage of the sand used in its manufacture is replaced with aluminum powder. The resulting dinnerware is strong, thin, well-tempered, has a smooth surface, and is highly resistant to stains, heat, scratching, and breakage. It is available in a variety of sizes, shapes, and decorative designs on a white background. The cost is less than that of some high-quality vitrified china dinnerware. The amounts to order and the care of Corning dinnerware is comparable to china.

PLASTIC DINNERWARE   The introduction and availability of synthetic compounds for molded dinnerware has given competition to china and glass for use in some types of institution foodservices. The history of the development of a suitable and highly acceptable product has been a long one.

Celluloid (1868), an early synthetic thermoplastic compound and a forerunner of modern plastics, was made of cellulose nitrate and camphor. Its nonresistance to heat, high inflammability, and camphor odor and flavor made it unsuitable for dishware. In the next period of development (1908), phenol and formaldehyde were incorporated into a thermosetting compound that was capable of being molded under pressure and heat into forms that would retain their shapes under mechanical strains at well above the temperature of boiling water. This type of compound has had wide and varied usage, but because of its odor and unattractive brownish color, its use in the foodservice industry was limited mainly to counter and serving trays. The substitution of urea for phenol made it possible to produce a white compound of great strength that would take colors well. The basic cost of this material was high; therefore, it was often made into thin dishes suitable only for picnic or limited use and that could be sold for a reasonably low price.

During World War II, it was found that melamine could be combined with formaldehyde to give a tough resin that could withstand the demands on it in high-altitude flying equipment. This type of melamine plastic compound is now used in the production of dinnerware, often called Melamine Ware.

The first heavy-duty dinnerware made of melamine-formaldehyde compounds contained a chopped cotton cloth filler. The products had a high tensile and impact strength but were unattractive and limited to a low color range. Compounds made by blending long-fiber, high-grade paper stock with melamine resin and colorfast pigments are used in the production of dinnerware at the present time. This material is known as alpha-cellulose-filled, melamine-formaldehyde, thermosetting molding compound, and the products made from it are available in a wide range of colors and designs.

The melamine compound undergoes chemical change in the molding process under pressure of some 3,000 to 3,500 pounds per square inch at 335°F, which gives the dinnerware pieces a smooth lustrous surface, resistant to scratching, chippage, breakage, detergents, and grease. Also, it is not affected by the hot water used in dishwashing. Because the color pigment is thoroughly blended with the compound before molding, there is no fading of the finished product.

The permanent decoration of melamine dinnerware is made possible by opening the press when the material has just been shaped and adding a melamine-impregnated overlay, with the lithographed side placed down onto the dish. The mold is closed and, during the cure, the overlay becomes an integral part of the base material, and the resulting product has a smooth wear-resistant and protective glaze over the design.

Factors in Selecting Plasticware. The U. S. Department of Commerce has established standards for heavy-duty type of melamine dishes. Foodservices should specify that the ware being purchased complies with Commercial Standards (CS) 173-50 that relate to thickness, resistance to acids, boiling water, dry heat, and the finished product.

Sample pieces of plasticware may be purchased or requested for testing before an order is placed. Special attention should be given to balance and to any marring of the surface by normal cutting and use.

The original cost of plastic dinnerware may be somewhat higher than for medium-weight china, but the replacement costs are estimated to be only about one-tenth of that for china. Differences in shape, density, and balance in design account in some measure for the price range in melamine ware. Competition is keen between the molding companies to produce items from this common basic material that are attractive in color and design and that meet the needs of the food industry. A price quotation from several companies should precede purchase.

The choice between melamine or the long-accepted china dinnerware may pose problems for the prospective buyer. The light weight of melamine, which is about one-third that of ordinary dinnerware, its low breakage, minimum handling noise, and attractive colors make it especially acceptable in many types of foodservice operations, especially in hospitals and other health care facilities, and in school foodservices.

One disadvantage of melamine may be staining and difficulty in cleaning, although improvements in manufacture have reduced this as a major problem. Although melamine products possess low thermal conductivity, thus eliminating the need to preheat them for service, they may present some dishwashing problems. This ware does not air dry quickly and may remain damp for storage. Bacteriological tests on such dishes, however, indicate no cause for concern over this condition.

Care. The same care in dishwashing as described for china should be followed for plasticware dishes. However, the staining of cups may require the extra step of soaking them to remove the stain. China cups may also require this step.

Many manufacturers of melamine dinnerware have successfully incorporated stain-resistant compounds into the thermosetting resin, which prevents much of the objectionable staining and adds to the life of this type of dinnerware. The development of new washing compounds and closer attention to washing techniques have eliminated the problem somewhat. Alkaline detergents are recommended for washing. Abrasives cannot be used successfully on plastic surfaces; therefore, chemical rinses must be depended on, preferably those without chlorine. Some users believe that frequent cup replacement is the answer and is justly compensated by the high resistance to breaking, chipping, cracking, and crazing under ordinary conditions, the lightness of weight, the low noise level in handling, the attractive coloring and luster, and the relatively low upkeep and replacement costs.

Amounts to Purchase. The initial stock of plastic dinnerware is comparable to that given for china. Sizes of dishes are also comparable. Another guide for amounts of dinnerware to select for the average foodservice would be an allowance of three times the number of dining room seats for items such as bread and butter plates, salad dishes, dinner plates, saucers, fruit and/or cereal dishes, and four times for cups. The amounts of these and other items would depend much on the menu pattern and other conditions mentioned earlier.

DISPOSABLE DINNERWARE   One-time use items for table service are available in many different materials: paper, plasticized paper, clear or colored thin plastics, styrofoam, and aluminum foil among them. They are available in a wide range of sizes, shapes, colors, and quality by weight. Some are made for use with cold foods only; others withstand considerable heat, making them suitable for oven or microwave use, and for serving hot foods.

The selection of disposable dishware over other types may well be justified, especially for any foodservice using the assembly/serve system, and for fast food, carry-out businesses.

Factors in Selection. Consideration should be given to initial and replacement *costs* of conventional dinnerware, space and equipment for dishwashing, and labor for handling in comparison to the initial and repeat cost of paper or plastic; and its *disposal* and *acceptability* by the persons to be served. In any case, it is well for all foodservices to have ready access to some disposable dishware for times of emergency.

Disposal of large quantities of "disposables" poses problems in some situations. The availability on premises of a large trash compactor is a necessity to handle this waste without undo bulk.

Quantities to purchase are determined by the amount of space to store the large cartons of paper or plastic goods, the relative closeness to a marked supply, and, of course, the number of persons to be served in a given period of time and the menu items offered.

Tableware

The most satisfactory type of eating utensils for institutions is that which has been designed and made especially for heavy duty. Such ware falls into two classes: *flatware* of the usual array of knives, forks, and spoons; and items such as teapots, sugar bowls, pitchers, and platters, known as *hollow ware* if made of silver. All must be durable and serviceable and at the same time attractive in line and design. Silver and stainless steel tableware are the two types used, and the decision to select one or the other will depend largely on the type of foodservice, the tastes of the clientele served, and the amount of money available for this expenditure and upkeep.

SILVER TABLEWARE

Silverware. Quality silverware has been used in discriminating foodservices because of the demands for and interest of the residents or clientele in attractive service. It lends dignity and charm to dining tables, perhaps because of the association of the idea that silver, a precious metal, is found where people know and appreciate gracious, comfortable living. Some knowledge of the manufacture of silverware will help the foodservice manager make a wise decision in the selection of this item.

"Blanks" serve as the basic forms for flatware as well as hollow ware. They are made of 18 per cent nickel silver, a metal that gives the utensil the needed strength and resistance to bending or twisting to which institutional silverware is often subjected. The design, shape, and thickness or weight of the blanks should be conducive to heavy wear and beauty.

Nine pounds per gross is the standard weight of blanks of ordinary teaspoons sold for public service. The principal weights of blanks used are: heavy, 10½ pounds; regular, 9 pounds; medium, 7½ to 8 pounds. The 9-pound blanks are desirable for hospital tray service, whereas the 10½-pound patterns may be advisable for heavy-duty silverware for certain commercial restaurants and cafeterias. The weight of the blank used influences the price of the silverware.

Flatware blanks are stamped, graded, and rolled until they are the corresponding size of forks or spoons. They are then placed in various presses, and the fork tines or spoon bowls are shaped. In the next step they are struck with the pattern die, after which the edges are trimmed and smoothed down so that the articles resemble the finished products. Forks should have well-designed tines, durable and heat treated, to give maximum strength, and both forks and spoons should have heavy reinforced shanks to give the best wearing qualities. After being cleaned and polished, the articles are ready for plating with the silver.

The steps in the manufacture of knives prior to plating differ from those in the making of blanks for forks and spoons. The 18 per cent nickel-silver base was found to produce a blade that bent easily and refused to take an edge sharp enough for practical use in cutlery. Stainless steel has become widely used for knife blades, and noncorrosive alloys have been made that prove satisfactory as the base for solid-handle knives that are to be plated. The popular hollow-handle knife, made with the 18 per cent nickel silver as the base of the handle, has been largely replaced by the one-piece stainless steel knife with the plate handle. An improvement in the design of knives was the change in style from the long blade, short handle to the short blade, long handle type that permits the user to press down with the forefinger on the back of the handle instead of on the narrow edge of the steel blade.

For better qualities of flatware there is an intervening step between the making of the blank and its plating. Reinforcements of an extra disc of silver are made on blanks at the point of greatest wear: the heel of the bowls of spoons and the base of fork tines (see Fig. 10.34). Such treatment is referred to as *overlay, sectional plate,* or *reinforced plate,* and increases many times the length of wear.

FIGURE 10.34   Plated silver should be reinforced on the points of greatest wear.   *Courtesy, Oneida, Ltd.*

The plating of silverware is accomplished by electrolysis. Pure silver bars or ingots are placed around the side of a plating tank, and the articles to be plated are hung in the solution in the tank. By means of an electric current, the silver passes from the bars and is deposited on the blanks, the length of time and the strength of the current determining the amount of silver deposited.

After the articles are removed from the plating tank, they are sent to the finishing rooms. Better grades are burnished, or rubbed under pressure with a round pointed steel tool, to harden and smooth out the plate. It is then polished and colored. The better qualities of silverware are given extra burnishing. The various finishes are: butler or dull finish, hotel finish or medium bright, and bright, which are obtained by using different types of buffs and polishing compounds and by carrying the polishing process to different degrees.

The plating of institution silverware is heavier than for the silverware generally used in the home, the most common institution ware being known as *triple plate,* or three times full standard. In triple plate, 6 ounces of pure silver have been applied to 1 gross of teaspoons, with other items in proportion—for example, tablespoons with 12 ounces of silver to the gross. A much lighter plating known as *full standard* carries a deposit of 5 ounces of pure silver to the gross of tablespoons and only 2½ ounces to the gross of teaspoons. *Half standard,* as its name implies, carries half the amount of silver deposit of full standard. Full standard plate quality is the lightest grade recommended for use in institutions.

The leading manufacturers of silver plate generally make, under their own trade name, a better quality of silver plate than those noted above. An example of such silverware is heavy hotel teaspoons, which weigh 11½ to 12 pounds per gross. An extra-heavy plate deposit is used on 10½-pound blanks in their production. Usually the silver overlay on tips and backs of bowls and tines is invisible on any 10½- and 11-pound qualities. The heavy finely finished metal blanks, the heavy plating standard, and the fine finish of this quality of silverware make the initial cost greater than the ordinary commercial grades of plate, but the cost is offset by the long wearing qualities and satisfactory service of the various items.

Hollow Ware. Silver hollow ware items such as serving bowls, platters, sugar bowls, creamers, pitchers, teapots, and coffee pots are made from the same materials as for flatware and are plated in similar manner to varying qualities. The bodies of the various items are die-shaped, and the several pieces for each are assembled and hand soldered by expert craftspeople before plating. The quality of materials and workmanship and the design determines cost.

Features to consider in selecting hollow ware include: sharp corners are to be avoided; short spouts are easier to clean than long ones; simple designs are usually more pleasing than ornate ones and easier to clean. However, plain silverware may become badly scratched with ordinary handling; hence a pleasing, simple design that breaks the smooth surface may be more practical than plain silver. Simplicity is always the keynote of good taste.

Standard designs and patterns are often made individual by stamping or engraving the name, crest of the organization, or a special decorative motif on the otherwise plain surface. If silverware is to be stamped, the stamping should be done on the back of the item before it is plated. The name of the manufacturer is stamped on the bottom.

Silver hollow ware may seem an extravagance, but when the cost is considered over a period of years, it may be more economical than china or glassware. Furthermore, the satisfaction and prestige gained through its use are not to be discounted.

Care. The care of silverware has much to do with its appearance and wearing qualities. Careful handling prevents many scratches. The following procedure is suggested for cleaning silverware and keeping it in good condition: sort, then wash in a machine to which has been added the proper cleaning compound, at a temperature of 140 to 150°F, and rinse thoroughly. A final dip in a solution with high-wetting properties prevents spotting of air-dried silver. It is advisable to presoak flatware or wash immediately after use. If washed in flat-bottom racks, the silver should be scattered loosely over the rack surface, sorted after washing, placed into perforated dispensing cylinders, and rewashed to ensure sanitization. If silver is sorted into cylinders before washing, the handles of the utensils are down so that all surfaces of knife blades, fork tines, and bowls of spoons will be subjected to the wash and rinse processes. Care must be taken not to overcrowd the containers. The washed silver is left in the cylinders to dry. This system is convenient, especially in self-service units, because clean dispensing cylinders may be inverted over those used in washing, turning the silver upside down so handles are up, and placed on the counter without handling of the clean silver.

Tarnishing of silver occurs readily when exposed to smoke or natural gas, or comes in contact with rubber, certain fiber, or sulphur-containing foods. Detarnishing is accomplished quickly and easily by immersing the silver, placed in a wire basket, into a solution of water plus a cleaning compound containing trisodium phosphate in an aluminum kettle reserved for this purpose.

The tarnish (oxide) will form a salt with the aluminum, and all tarnish will be removed through a mild electrolytic action. The cleaning compound also cuts and dissolves any grease or dirt on the silver. The silver is left in the solution *only long enough to remove the tarnish*. It is then rinsed in boiling water and dipped in a solution of high wetting qualities. Burnishing machines are used for silver polishing in large foodservices. Care must be taken to see that the machine is not overloaded and that there are enough steel shots of various sizes in the barrel of the machine to be effective in contacting all surfaces to be polished. Also, the right amount of proper detergent must be added to the water in the burnishing machine to produce the required concentration of the solution. There can be no set rule about the frequency of detarnishing and polishing; each foodservice must set up its own standards.

STAINLESS STEEL TABLEWARE   Stainless steel tableware has gained wide acceptance for heavy-duty tableware in many foodservices. The flatware is fairly inexpensive, is highly resistant to heat, scratches, and wear, and will not rust, stain, peel, chip, or tarnish. It stays bright indefinitely with ordinary washing and offers a wide selection of attractive designs from which to choose. Flatware in stainless steel is available in light, standard, and heavy weights. Cheap quality stainless steel utensils have appeared on the market, but they are not really suitable for most establishments. These are made from rolled sheets of the metal and are die-stamped into desired shapes. The resulting pieces are the same thickness throughout and have poor balance, and fork tines and bowls of spoons are too thick to pick up food easily. This quality should be avoided.

Good quality ware is rolled and tapered as needed to give good balance and to be comfortable in the hand. A test for good balance is to place a fork or a spoon at the base of its bowl or tines on an index finger; the utensil should balance equally between handle and bowl or tines. In poor quality, the bowl or tines will overbalance the handle and the utensil will fall off the finger.

Another consideration in selecting stainless steel tableware is the size and shape of the handles. Older persons particularly find it difficult to hold a slim handle and much prefer a wider, easier-to-grasp shape and size.

Water pitchers and individual teapots of stainless steel are considered a lifetime investment, although the initial cost is high in comparison to these items in ordinary glass or pottery. The same methods of sorting, washing, and drying are recommended for stainless steel tableware as for silver.

Amounts of Tableware to Purchase   The menu to be offered determines what items of tableware the foodservice must supply. It is more difficult to calculate the quantities of each piece to stock. As with dinnerware, the trend in use of flatware is toward as few different pieces as possible. For instance, knives and forks of dessert size can be used for many purposes and are usually preferred to knives and forks of dinner size. Dessert spoons may be used for soup and serving spoons as well as for certain desserts.

A good quantity estimate of flatware for cafeterias is twice the seating capacity for all the flatware items required. Should the dishwashing facilities be limited and the turnover of patrons rapid, this quantity might need to be increased to three or even four times the seating capacity. For table or tray service, 3 teaspoons per cover, 3 forks, using a dessert fork for all purposes, and 2 knives per cover usually are sufficient. All other items are estimated on the basis of 1½ per cover, or according to the needs as for banquet or special party service. This may call for limited quantities of specialized items such as oyster or fish forks, bouillon spoons, butter spreaders, or iced tea spoons.

On the basis of total investment in tableware, an estimate found to be about average is that 2½ per cent of the budget for all foodservice equipment is required.

Glassware

Glassware is a major item of purchase for dining room furnishings for foodservices, since it is easily broken and replacement is frequent. It is usually more economical to purchase good quality glassware than inexpensive types.

Glassware is classed as lead or lime glass, depending on the use of lead or lime oxide in the manufacturing process. Lead glass is of better quality, is clearer, and has more brilliance than lime glass, which is less expensive. Articles of glass are made from a molten compound, formed by blowing them into shape by machine or hand processes or by pressing molten glass into molds by means of a machine. The blowing method is the more expensive and produces a thinner glass of finer texture, higher luster, and clearer ring. Hand-blown lead glass is superior to all other glassware because of its brilliance, light weight, and variety of styles. Lime-blown glassware possesses these characteristics in a lesser degree, is less expensive, and is used extensively in institutions. It is usually machine blown. The style, color, and decoration determine the cost of manufacture of blown-glass articles.

Pressed lime glass is used in many institutions. It is serviceable, and better qualities of it are comparatively free from bubbles and cloudiness. Moreover, it is relatively inexpensive and may be obtained in many styles. A good quality of glassware should be selected for the institution, regardless of whether pressed glass or blown glass is to be used. Desirable characteristics are clearness, luster, medium weight, freedom from such defects as marks and bubbles, and a clear ring. Also, it should be designed so that it is not easily tipped over.

Glassware must pass boiling and shock tests without showing signs of corrosion, chipping, scumming, or cracking in order to meet federal specifications. In making the boiling test, articles are suspended for 6 hours in boiling water in a closed container with vent. The shock test is made by immersing articles in tap water at 18.5°C $\pm$ 2½° (65°F $\pm$ 5°) for a 10-minute period, then suddenly transferring them into boiling water. This procedure is repeated five times. Not all the glassware sold meets federal specifications, and there is no labeling to indicate which, if any, is of that quality.

The sizes of glassware used most commonly in institutions are glasses of 5- or 6-ounce capacity for fruit juice, glasses of 9- or 10-ounce capacity for milk and water, and glasses of 12- or 14-ounce capacity for iced tea. A wide range of sizes and shapes must be stocked for bar service.

Goblets and footed dessert dishes are other items of glass selected for some foodservices. Portion size of specific menu items will determine the capacity size required for these items.

CARE OF GLASSWARE   Glassware to be washed is sorted and often washed in a separate dishwashing machine from that used for other dishes, or in glasswasher built for that purpose. If glassware must be washed in the same machine used for dishes, it should be segregated and washed first while the water is entirely free from grease and food particles, or left until after the dishes are finished and the soiled water is replaced by clean. In either case, with a rack machine, all items to be washed are placed upside down in racks after they are transported from the dining room and remain in the same racks to wash and drain, and are then loaded onto carts for transport to the point of storage or use without rehandling.

Glassware should be under constant scrutiny to maintain in service only those pieces that are not chipped, cracked, clouded, or scratched in appearance. Filmed glasses may be caused by low rinse pressure and volume, too short rinse cycle, nonaligned spray jets, and a hard water precipitate. Tea stains may be removed by using a chlorinated detergent in the glass washing machine. Water spots may be caused by slow drying or the need for softening the rinse water. The effect of an otherwise attractive dining service may be spoiled by damaged or poorly washed glassware on the tables.

The breakage of glassware in institutions is often high and results from careless handling and storage, choice of improper designs for heavy service wear, use of poor quality of glassware, and subjection to high temperature during washing. The shape of the glass has much to do with the breakage anticipated. Straight side tumblers that can be stacked are a decided breakage hazard, and there are patented shapes available that make it impossible to stack tumblers. Many styles of glassware curve in slightly at the top so that the edges will not touch when they are set down together, the contact coming at a reinforced part away from the edge of the glass. Other styles have reinforced edges at the top, advertised as making them more highly resistant to chipping. This feature is also found around the foot of some stemmed ware.

AMOUNTS TO PURCHASE   The amount and kind of glassware to supply vary as for tableware and dinnerware. Choice is based primarily on the menu, type of service, seating capacity and rate of turnover, dishwashing facilities, skill of persons employed in dish handling, and whether scheduling is continuous or intermittent. However, since glassware is more fragile than other tableware, it is well to have an ample stock on hand of the most frequently used items: tumblers, fruit juice glasses, and sherbert or dessert dishes (if glass ones are used). A suggested rule for quantities to purchase is two pieces for each person to be served; one piece in use and one-half in the dishroom, plus 50 per cent of that total in reserve in the stock room.

Table Covers

One other furnishing to consider is the type of covering, if any, to be used on the dining tables, or trays if that type of service is used. Many table top surfaces are attractive, durable, and suitable for use without a cover. Simplicity and informality in dining have made this custom popular, and it does reduce laundry costs.

For many people much of the charm of a foodservice is conditioned, if not determined, by the use of a clean tablecloth of good quality, freshly and carefully placed. Paper napkins and place mats and plastics have replaced cloth in many foodservices for convenience and economy. Whatever the choice, the cover should be of a type and color appropriate for the facility, contribute to the total atmosphere of the room, and be harmonious with the dishes to be used.

CLOTH TABLE COVERS　　In some localities, tablecloths may be rented from local laundries, thus relieving the foodservice of purchasing and storing this item. However, if cloths are to be purchased, there are many materials from which to choose: pure linen, union, rayon, cotton, cotton mercerized, or linenized damasks, and polyester-cotton blends.

Cotton fibers may be used in combination with linen or rayon in the union damasks to produce durable and satisfactory table coverings and napkins. Rayon and cotton blend table napkins are highly resistant to wear and often superior to all-cotton or all-linen napkins in appearance and breaking strength. Cotton is used alone in plain cotton, mercerized, or linenized fabrics. The last two fabrics are so treated after being woven that a permanent finish is produced to give the cloth characteristics similar to linen. The wearing quality of cotton fabrics is better than that of linen, less loss in strength occurs through laundering, and cotton does not lint. Linen gives satisfaction in use, is attractive, and lintless.

Because of the high initial and maintenance costs of both linen and cotton cloths, those of a 50-50 blend of polyester and cotton with a no-iron finish are rapidly replacing the former in other than the most sophisticated foodservices. Polyester yarns are used in the making of lace cloths as well as the plain woven ones.

Tablecloths may be purchased in white, in colors, or in white with colored borders or designs. Colored linen is popular as place mats and luncheon cloths for breakfast and luncheon services. Colored linens are used to help create "atmosphere" in many dining rooms. Fabrics may be purchased by the yard and made up for the specific size tables of the individual establishment, or the cloths may be purchased ready-made.

The size and shape of the tables will determine the *sizes* of cloths needed. The cloth should be large enough to hang 7 to 12 inches below the table top at both sides and ends, with allowances made for shrinkage according to the material selected. The usual sizes of tableclothes are 52 by 52 square, 60 by 80 inches, 67 by 90 to 102 inches or longer, depending on the length of banquet tables. Some places use a table-size top over the regular cloth for frequent changes and so reduce laundry costs.

Common sizes for cloth dinner napkins in institutions are 18, 20, or 22 inches square.

PAPER PLACE MATS AND NAPKINS　　The range of colors and designs available in paper products is so large that selection of appropriate covers should be relatively easy. Size is dependent upon the size of tray for tray service. For use on table tops, 12 by 18-inch mats provide generously for each cover, although the 11 by 14-inch size is frequently used. Often the name, logo, or design of the foodservice may be imprinted on the mat and/or napkin, which serves as good advertising for the establishment.

Summary

Prospective foodservice managers as well as those already employed in the field should have a "working" knowledge of equipment and furnishings—construction, materials suitable for various uses, something of the sizes or capacities available, and how to relate that information to meeting the needs of the individual foodservice. Wise selection and proper care of the many items that must be provided for efficient operation of the foodservice should result in economies for the organization and a satisfied working crew who have been supplied with the correct tools to accomplish their tasks.

Notes

1. National Sanitation Foundation: Standard No. 2 for Food Service Equipment. June 1982.
2. Thomas, Orpha Mae Huffman: A Scientific Basis for the Design of Institution Kitchens. New York: Teachers College, Columbia University, 1947.
3. Mitchell, T.: How-to's of energy efficiency. Western Foodservice. 8:13, 1983.
4. Southern California Gas Company: How much energy does it save? 1985.

Supplementary References

ANON: Growing importance of equipment planning. Hospitals 58(21):100, Nov. 1, 1984.

AVERY, A. C.: Careful planning creates equipment energy savings. Restaurant and Institutions 95(44):157, Feb. 20, 1985.

AVERY, A. C.: A Modern Guide to Foodservice Equipment. Boston: CBI Publishing Co., 1980.

HYSEN, P.: Let the buyer beware. Food Mgmt. 3:111, 1983.

KAZARIAN, E. A.: Foodservice Facilities Planning, 2nd ed. Westport, CT: AVI Publishing Co., 1983.

KOTSCHEVAR, L. H. AND TERRELL, M. E.: Foodservice Planning: Layout and Equipment, 3rd ed. New York: John Wiley and Sons, 1985.

National Sanitation Foundation: 1985 Annual Listing of Food Service Equipment, 1985.

National Sanitation Foundation: 1986 Annual Listings Special Categories of Equipment, Products, and Services, 1986.

SCRIVEN, C. AND STEVENS, J.: Food Equipment Facts. New York: John Wiley and Sons: 1982.

ZACCARELLI, H.: Making a good habit of maintenance. Cooking for Profit. 8:8, 1983.

Organization and Administration of Foodservices

CHAPTER 11

Organization and Management

Introduction

The American society is composed of a variety of interdependent, overlapping organizations. In order to function effectively, organizations must be properly designed. This chapter examines the basic principles of organizational structure.

Organizations need competent managers to be able to meet their objectives both efficiently and effectively. The growing complexity of organizations today means a greater need to examine them as a whole. Using the systems approach a manager can diagnose situations and choose the proper fits between subsets of the organization. The contingency approach leads management to apply different basic guidelines depending on the particular situation. Recent drops in productivity suggest that greater attention be paid to the quality of work life. The quality of work life approach promotes greater productivity through greater attention to the needs of both individual workers and groups.

To accomplish the common managerial functions of planning, organizing, staffing, directing, coordinating, reporting, and budgeting, a manager engages in a variety of activities that can be grouped into three basic categories: interpersonal relationships, information processing, and decision making. The three categories can be further divided into ten observable working roles. In this chapter the functions and roles of managerial work are explored. The skills required to perform these various functions and roles are also discussed.

The chapter concludes with a discussion of some important management tools. The organization chart is a map of the organization. The organization manual with its job descriptions, job specifications, and job schedules goes even further as a model of the organization.

Organization

Theories of Organization

Organization for management is as old as human society and grew out of a common interest and combined effort to accomplish a common goal. Through the years many theories have been proposed, particularly since the early part of the twentieth century. Most of them fall into three categories: classical or traditional, human relations, and the modern or systems approach.

CLASSICAL   Classical organization theory rest on several premises—that division of work is essential for efficiency, that coordination is the primary responsibility of management in the organization of work, that the formal structure is the main vehicle for organizing and administering work activities, and that the span of control sets outside limits on the number of people responsible to a given manager.[1] Other principles that emerged are: (1) the scalar principle, in which authority and responsibility flow in a direct line vertically from the highest level of the organization to the lowest, (2) delegation, in which decisions are delegated to the lowest competent level, (3) unity of command, which specifies that each person should be accountable to only one superior, (4) the functional principle, based on specialization of work, and (5) the line and staff principle, in which support and advisory activities are provided for the main functions of an organization. Classical organization theory continues to have great relevance to basic managerial problems, but it has been criticized as too mechanistic and not recognizing the interaction of groups and the decision-making processes in the formal structure.

HUMAN RELATIONS   The human relations theory evolved from the effort to compensate for some of the deficiencies of the classical theory. Where classical organization advocates focus on tasks, structure, and authority, human relations theorists have introduced the behavioral sciences as an integral part of organization theory. They view the organization as a social system and recognize the existence of the informal organization, in which workers align themselves into social groups within the framework of the formal organization. Many human relations theorists hold that employee participation in management planning and decision making yield positive effects in terms of morale and productivity.

SYSTEMS APPROACH   The systems approach, introduced in Chapter 2, is defined as a set of interdependent parts that work together to achieve a common goal. According to Beach,[2] there are several important systems concepts that apply to organizations. Being predominantly open systems, human organizations interact with various elements of their environment. (For example, a hospital dietary department interacts with many external groups such as patients, customers, medical staff, hospital administration, and some regulatory agencies. The department, in turn, affects the external groups with which it interacts).

Beach also discusses other systems concepts that apply to organizatons.[2] For example, organizations tend toward a dynamic or moving equilibrium. Members seek to maintain the organization and to have it survive. They react to changes and forces, both internal and external, in ways that often create a new state of equilibrium and balance. *Feedback* of information from a point of operation and from the environment to a control center or centers can provide the data necessary to initiate corrective measures to restore equilibrium.

Organizations and the world of which they are a part consist of a *hierarchy of systems*. Thus, a corporation is composed of divisions, departments, sections, and groups of individual employees. Also, the corporation is part of larger systems, such as all the firms in its industry, firms in its metropolitan area, and perhaps an association of many firms from many industries such as the National Restaurant Association or the American Hospital Association.

Interdependency is a key concept in systems theory. The elements of a system interact with one another and are interdependent. Generally a change in one part of an organization affects other parts of that organization. Sometimes the interdependencies are not fully appreciated when changes are made. A change in organization structure and work flow in one department may unexpectedly induce changes in departments that relate to the first department.

Systems theory contains the doctrine that the whole of a structure or entity is more than the sum of its parts. This is called *wholism*. The cooperative, synergistic working together of members of a department or team often yields a total product that exceeds the sum of their individual contributions.

Systems theory helps organize a large body of information that might otherwise make little sense. It has made major contributions to the study of organization and management in recent years. Systems theory aids in diagnosing the interactive relationships among task, technology, environment, and organization members.

In contrast to the classical models of organization, the systems approach has shown that managers operate in fluid, dynamic, and often ambiguous situations. The manager generally is not in full control of these situations. Managers must learn to shape actions and to make progress toward goals, but they know that results are affected by many factors and forces.

Systems theory has become popular in the last twenty-five years or so because of its apparent ability to serve as a universal model of systems, including physical, biological, social, and behavioral phenomena.

Organization Structure

Beach[2] defines an organization as "a system, having an established structure and conscious planning, in which people work and deal with one another in a coordinated and cooperative manner for the accomplishment of recognized goals." The formal organization is the planned structure that establishes a pattern of relationships among the various components of the organization. The informal organization refers to those aspects of the system that arise spontaneously from the activities and interactions of participants.[3]

According to Dale,[4] whenever several people are working together for a common end, there must be some form of organization; that is, the tasks must be divided among them and the work of the group must be coordinated. Otherwise there may be duplication of effort or even work at cross purposes. Dividing the work and arranging for coordination make up the process of organization, and once that is completed the group may be described as "an organization."

Certain steps are necessary in developing the framework of an organization structure if goals of an enterprise are to be accomplished and the workers' talents developed to their fullest potential. These steps may be summarized as follows:

1. *Determine and define objectives.* The purpose of every organization dealing with personnel is to accomplish with the efforts of people some basic purpose or objective with the greatest efficiency, maximum economy, and minimum effort, and to provide for the personal development of the people working in the organization. Specifically, a foodservice has as its goal the production and service of the best food possible within the financial resources. It is important that these objectives and the plans and policies for their achievement be presented in writing and understood by all responsible.

2. *Analyze and classify work to be done.* This is accomplished by dividing the

total work necessary for the accomplishment of overall goals into its major parts and grouping each into like, or similar, activities. Examination of the work to be done will reveal tasks that are similar or are logically related. Such classification may be made by grouping activities that require similar skills, the same equipment, or duties performed in the same areas. There are no arbitrary rules for grouping. In a foodservice the activities could be grouped as purchasing and storage preparation and processing, housekeeping and maintenance, and service and dishwashing. Each of these groupings might be broken into smaller classifications, depending on the type and size of the enterprise. With the increasing complexity of foodservice organizations and the trend toward centralization of certain functions, the organization structure takes on new dimensions and must consider the total management structure as well as the organization of its individual units.

3. *Describe in some detail the work or activity in terms of the employee.* This step is discussed in more detail later in this chapter under "Job Description."

4. *Determine and specify the relationship of the workers to each other and to management.* The work should be grouped into departments or other organizational units, with responsibility and authority defined for each level. It is generally understood that each person assigned to a job will be expected to assume the responsibility for performing the tasks given him or her and that each person will be held accountable for the results. However, persons can be accountable only to the degree that they have been given responsibility and authority. Responsibility without authority is meaningless. An assignment should be specific and in writing. For an organizational structure to become operational, of course, requires the selection of qualified personnel, provision of adequate financing and equipment, and a suitable physical environment. No successful organization structure remains static. It must be a continuing process that moves with changing concepts within the system and with changing conditions in its environment.

Application of the principles of organization and administration to a specific situation should precede any attempt at the operation of a foodservice unit. A detailed plan may be outlined for use as a guide in initiating a new foodservice of any type or for reorganizing one previously in operation.

Types of Organizations

Two types of authority relationships most often found in foodservice systems are line and line and staff. Large, complex operations may be organized on a functional basis.

LINE   In the line organization, lines of authority are clearly drawn, and each individual is responsible to the person ranking above him or her on the organization chart. Thus, authority and responsibility pass from the top-ranking member down to the lowest in rank. In such an organization structure each person knows to whom he is responsible and, in turn, who is responsible to him.

Organization line structure can grow in two directions, vertically or horizontally. Vertical growth occurs through the delegation of authority, in which the individual at the top delegates work to her immediate subordinates, who redelegate part or all of this work to their subordinates, and so on down the line. For example, the director of a growing cafeteria operation may add an assistant manager, thus creating another level in the chain of command. When the distance from the top to bottom becomes too great for effective coordination, the responsibilities may be redistributed horizontally through departmentalization. In establishing departments, activities are grouped into natural units, with a manager given authority and accepting responsibility for that area of activities. There are several ways of dividing the work, but, in foodservices, the most usual are by function, product, or location. The work may be divided into production and service; in dietetics, by administrative, clinical, and education; in a central commissary, by meat, vegetable, salad, and bakery departments; or by individual schools in a multiunit school foodservice system.

Advantages of the line organization include expediency in decision making, direct placement of responsibility, and clear understanding of authority relationships. A major disadvantage is that the person at the top tends to become overloaded with too much detail, thus limiting the time that he can devote to planning and research necessary for development and growth of the organization. There is no specialist to whom one can turn for help in the various areas of operation.

LINE AND STAFF   As an enterprise grows, the line organization may no longer be adequate to cope with the many diversified responsibilities demanded of the person at the top. Staff specialists, such as personnel director, research and development specialist, and data processing coordinator, are added to assist the lines in an advisory capacity. The line positions and personnel are involved directly in accomplishing the work for which the organization was created; the staff advises and supports the line. A staff position also may be an assistant who serves as an extension of a line officer. The potential for conflict exists between line and staff personnel if there is not a clear understanding of the lines of authority. For example, if a staff specialist recommends a change in procedure, the order for the change would come from the line staff. Friction may arise if a strong staff person tries to overrule the manager or if the manager does not make full use of the abilities of the staff.

FUNCTIONAL   Some writers consider functional authority as staff and others consider it a distinct type in itself. Functional authority exists when an individual has delegated to her a limited authority over a specified segment of activities. In a multiunit foodservice company, for example, the responsibility for purchasing or for menu planning and quality control may be vested in a vice president who then has authority over that function in all units.

Management

Organizations need competent managers to be able to meet their objectives both efficiently and effectively. The return that organizations realize from human resources will be determined, in large part, by the competence of their managers.[5]

Theories of Management

In this era of constant societal change and what have been described as "turbulent times,"[6] three management trends have emerged. *The systems approach,* described earlier in this chapter, gives managers a way of looking at the organization as a whole that is greater than the sum of its parts. The systems manager recognizes the contribution of each part to the whole system and that a change in one part will impact other parts of the system. This approach allows a manager to diagnose and identify reasons for a situations occurrence.

The *contingency approach* holds that managerial activities should be adjusted to suit the situation. Factors within the situation such as characteristics of the work force, size and type of organization, and its goals should determine the managerial approach that is used.

The most recent approach was introduced in the late 1960s. *Quality of work life* (QWL) represents an attempt to increase productivity by providing greater opportunity for satisfaction of human needs in the workplace. QWL is discussed in greater detail in Chapter 14.

Functions of Management

The basic purpose of management has been recognized as the leadership of individuals and groups in order to accomplish the goals of the organization.

In 1916, Fayol,[7] a French mining engineer/manager, recognized that managerial undertakings require planning, organization, command, coordination, and control. Gulick[8] developed the following seven major functions of management: planning, organizing, staffing, directing, coordinating, reporting, and budgeting. Various combinations of these functions with some modifications, deletions, and additions are found in modern management texts.[9]

POSDCORB, the acronym created from the names of the seven functions described by Gulick, is widely accepted as describing the basic framework of the manager's job. Some disagreement does exist as to whether these functions are common to all levels of management. Others believe that even more functions should be included. Leading, actuating, activating, motivating, and communicating are concepts often fitted into the POSDCORB framework. That there is a degree of overlapping is evident in the functions themselves and in the efforts to classify them.

PLANNING   The planning function, described by Gulick[8] and still relevant today involves developing in broad outline the activities required to accomplish the objectives of the organization and the most effective ways of doing so. Planning is the basic function and all others are dependent upon it. The objective of planning is to think ahead, clearly determine objectives and policies, and select a course of action toward the accomplishment of the goals. Day-to-day planning of operational activities and short- and long-range planning toward department and institution goals are part of this function. Overall planning is the responsibility of top management, but participation at all levels in goal setting and development of new plans and procedures increases their effectiveness.

Forecasting is an important factor in effective planning for the future operating program of any company. Predictions of trends for the immediate and distant future based on an objective study of past and present situations usually are more reliable than mere guesses. Outside or external factors, such as social, economic, political, and other environmental conditions, are involved in forecasting, as are internal factors, such as size of plant and productivity of the personnel. A study of the interrelationships of such factors and their effects on the business, from data such as personal incomes, population growth, cost of living, and technological developments in food and equipment, should help the food manager to interpret possible future needs for personnel, physical facilities, and other budgetary items. A high degree of accuracy in forecasting is difficult to attain because of the uncertainties of the future. However, forecasting has merit in that it requires creative thinking, provides some helpful information, and may call attention to current problem areas within the organization. Examples of forecasting in foodservices are given in Chapter 5 on production planning and control and Chapter 15 on financial management.

ORGANIZING   Organizing includes the activities necessary to develop the formal structure of authority through which work in subdivided, defined, and coordinated to accomplish the organization's objectives. The organizing function identifies activities and tasks, divides tasks into positions, and puts like tasks together to take advantage of special abilities and skills of the workers and to use their talents effectively. Perhaps the chief function of the organizing process is the establishment of relationships among all other functions of management.

STAFFING   Staffing is the personnel function of employing and training people and maintaining favorable work conditions. The basic purpose of the staffing function is to obtain the best available people for the organization and to foster development of their skills and abilities. Chapter 12 discusses this important management function.

DIRECTING   Directing requires the continuous process of making decisions, conveying them to subordinates, and assuring appropriate action. Delegation of responsibility is essential to distribute workloads to qualified individuals at various levels. Whoever delegates a responsibility should not fail to do so with detailed instructions as to what is expected of the subordinate and the necessary authority to carry out the responsibilities. If a subordinate is not given sufficient authority, the job is merely assigned, not delegated.

A very important part of the directing function is the concern with employees as human beings. Studies have shown that most people work at only 50 to 60 per cent efficiency, and some investigators place this figure as low as 45 per cent. The alert manager is aware that through careful, intelligent guidance and counseling and by effective supervision, the worker's productivity may be increased as much as 20 per cent. This may mean the difference between financial success and failure of an enterprise.

COORDINATING   Coordinating is the functional activity of interrelating the various parts of work for smooth flow. In order to function effectively, organizations must be properly designed. Division of work is usually accomplished through departmentation, or specialization by function, product, client, geographical area, number of persons, or time. Different methods of coordination are required for different types of departmentation. As stated in Chapter 2, management's role in the systems approach in one of coordinating. This requires recognition of the need of all the parts and decisions made based on the overall effect on the organization as a whole and its objectives.

REPORTING   Reporting involves keeping supervisors, managers, and subordinates informed concerning responsibility through records, research, reports, inspection, and other methods. Records and evaluations of the results of work done are kept as the work progresses in order to compare performance with the yardstick of acceptability.

BUDGETING   Budgeting includes fiscal planning, accounting, and controlling. Control tends to ensure performance in accordance with plans and is a necessary function of all areas of foodservice. This necessitates measuring quantity of output, quality of the finished product, food and labor costs, and the efficient use of workers' time. Through control, standards of acceptability and accountability are set for performance. A good control system prevents present and future deviation from plans and does much to stimulate an employee to maintain the standards of the foodservice director. The budgeting function should be one of guidance, not command. It is concerned with employees as human beings with interests to be stimulated, aptitudes and abilities to be directed and developed, and comprehension and understanding of their responsibilities to be increased (see Chapter 15).

Skills of Managers

The most widely accepted method of classifying managerial skills is in terms of the three-skill approach initially proposed by Katz.[10] He identified *technical, human,* and *conceptual* skills as those that every successful manager must have in varying degrees, according to the level of the hierarchy at which the manager is operating. Katz contended that managers need all three skills to fulfill their role requirements, but the relative importance and the specific types within each category depend on the leadership situation.

Based on the concept of skill as an ability to translate knowledge into action, the three interrelated skill categories may be briefly summarized as: (1) technical, performing specialized activities, (2) human, understanding and motivating individuals and groups, and (3) conceptual, understanding and integrating all the activities and interests of the organization toward a common objective. Technical skills are usually more important than conceptual ones for lower level managers. Human skills are needed at all levels of management, but are relatively less important for managers at the top level than the low level. Conceptual skill becomes more important with the need for policy decisions and broad-scale action at upper levels of management.

Managerial Activities and Roles

Whereas a number of studies have investigated the personal styles and characteristics of managers, relatively few have researched what managers actually do in fulfilling job requirements. After reviewing and synthesizing the available research on how various managers spend their time, Koontz[11] reported that Mintzberg designed a study to produce a more supportable and useful description of managerial work. Mintzberg's resulting role theory of management has received attention as a useful way of describing what managers do. Mintzberg[12] defined a role as an organized set of behaviors belonging to an identifiable position. He identified ten roles common to the work of all managers and divided them into interpersonal (three roles), informational (three roles), and decisional (four roles). Although the roles are described here individually, in reality they constitute an integrated whole. In essence, the manager's formal authority and status educe interpersonal relationships leading to information roles and these, in turn, to decisional roles.

The three *interpersonal* roles of figurehead, leader and liaison devolve from the manager's formal authority and status. As *figureheads,* managers perform duties of a symbolic, legal, or social nature because of their position in the organization. As *leaders,* managers establish the work atmosphere within the organization and activate subordinates to achieve organizational goals. As *liaisons,* managers establish and maintain contacts outside the organization to obtain information and cooperation.[12]

The three *informational* roles of monitor, disseminator, and spokesperson characterize the manager as the central focus for receiving and sending of nonroutine information. In the *monitor* role, managers collect all information relevant to the organization. The *disseminator* role involves the manager in transmitting information gathered outside the organization to members inside. In the *spokesperson* role, managers transmit information from inside the organization to outsiders.[12]

The four *decisional* roles are entrepreneur or initiator, disturbance handler, resource allocator, and negotiator. Managers adopt the *entrepreneurial* role when they initiate controlled change in the organization to adapt and keep pace with changing conditions in the environment. Unexpected changes require the manager to perform as a *disturbance handler.* As *resource allocators,* managers make decisions concerning priorities for utilization of organizational resources. Finally, managers *negotiate* with individual or other organizations.[12] These interlocking and interrelated roles are shown in Fig. 11.1.

Tools of Management

Directors of foodservices commonly use the organization chart as a means of explaining and clarifying the structure of an organization. They also use job descriptions, job specifications, and work schedules as devices for the clear presentation of personnel and their responsibilities to top management and to employees. These mechanical or visual means are indispensable in the able direction and supervision of a foodservice, and for convenience they

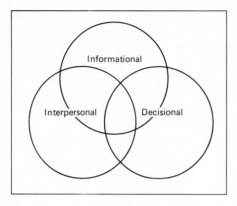

FIGURE 11.1   Interlocking and inter-related roles of managers.

may be called *tools of organization and management*. Performance appraisal as a tool of management is discussed in Chapter 12.

ORGANIZATION CHART   The chart of an organization may be considered the first tool of management. It presents graphically the basic groupings and relationships of positions and functions. The chart presents a picture of the formal organization structure and serves many useful purposes, but it does have some limitations. Whereas lines of authority are depicted on the chart, the degree of authority and responsibility at each level is not shown. Informal relationships between equals or between people in different parts of the organization are not evident. For this reason, job descriptions and organization manuals are valuable supplements to the organization chart.

The organization chart usually is constructed on the basis of the line of authority, but it may be based on functional activity or a combination of the two. Functions and positions are graphically presented by the use of blocks or circles. Solid lines connecting the various blocks indicate the channels of authority. Those persons with the greatest authority are shown at the top of the chart and those with the least at the bottom. Advisory responsibility and lines of communication often are shown by use of dotted lines. Organization charts for a small and a large hospital are shown in Figs. 11.2 and 11.3, and for a college foodservice in Fig. 11.4.

JOB DESCRIPTION   A job description is an organized list of duties that reflects required skills and responsibilities in a specific position. It may be thought of as an extension of the organization chart in that it shows activities and job relationships for the positions identified on the organization chart. Job descriptions are valuable for matching qualified applicants to the job, for orientation and training of employees, for performance appraisal, for establish-

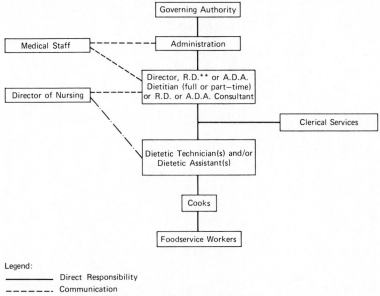

Legend:

—————— Direct Responsibility

– – – – – –. Communication

—.—.—.— May be designated as having advisory responsibility

*The need for full—time, part—time, or consultant R.D.(s) and lines of communication will be dependent on type, complexity of patient care. and the systems of food service provided by the health care facility.

**R.D. The registered trademark for Registered Dietitian

For a group care facility of 100 or more beds a full—time Director, R.D. is reommended. A part—time Director, R.D. for 75—100 beds facility and for less than 75 beds an R.D. or A.D.A. Consultant are also recommended. The Director usually assumes the responsibilites assigned to Clinical and Administrative R.D.s.

FIGURE 11.2   Organization chart for the department of dietetics in a hospital or other group care facility of less than 150 beds.*   *Courtesy, The American Dietetic Association.*

ing rates of pay, and for defining limits of authority and responsibility. They should be written for every position in the foodservice and should be reviewed and updated periodically. In many organizations, the job descriptions are incorporated into a procedure manual or kept in a looseleaf notebook for easy access.

Job descriptions may be written in either narrative or outline form or a combination of the two. The format probably will vary according to the job classification; for example, the work of the foodservice employee is described in terms of specific duties and skill requirements, but the job description for the professional position is more likely to be written in terms of broad areas of responsibilities. Most job descriptions include identifying information, a job summary, and specific duties and requirements. The initial job descriptions for a new facility would reflect the responsibilities delegated

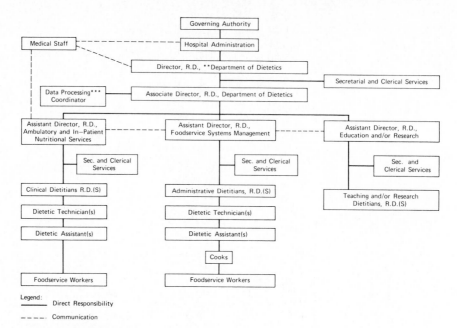

FIGURE 11.3 Organization chart for the department of dietetics in a large hospital (500 beds or more), health center or other group care facility.* *Courtesy, The American Dietetic Association.*

to each position on a trial basis and subject to early revision. In the case of an established unit, they are developed from information obtained from interviews with employees and supervisors and from observations by the person responsible for writing the job description. A *job analysis*, in which all aspects of a job are studied and analyzed, may be conducted first to collect information for the job description.

The job description in Fig. 11.5 may be useful as a guide. The exact content and format, however, will vary according to the position being described and the needs and complexities of the institution.

JOB SPECIFICATION   A job specification is a written statement of the minimum standards that must be met by an applicant for a particular job. It covers duties involved in a job, the working conditions peculiar to the job, and personal qualifications required of the worker to carry through the as-

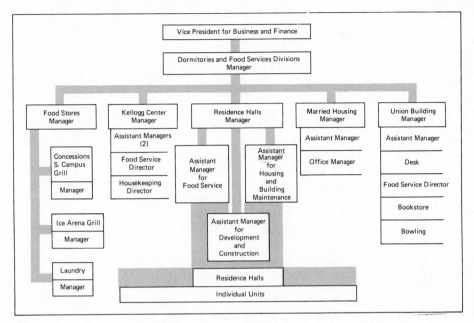

FIGURE 11.4   Organization chart for a large housing and foodservice system. *Courtesy, Michigan State University.*

signed responsibilities successfully. This tool is used primarily by the employing officer in the selection and placement of the right person for the specific position. Many small institutions use the job description as a job specification also (see Fig. 11.6.).

WORK SCHEDULE   A work schedule is an outline of work to be performed by an individual with stated procedures and time requirements for his or her duties. It is important to break down the tasks into an organized plan with careful consideration given to timing and sequence of operations. Work schedules are especially helpful in training new employees and are given to the employee after the person has been hired and training has begun. This is one means of communication between the employer and employee. Work schedules should be reviewed periodically and adjustments made as needed to adapt to changes in procedures.

An example of a work schedule for a cafeteria worker is given in Fig. 11.7. For food production employees, the individual work schedule would outline in general terms the day's work routine, but would need to be supplemented by a daily production schedule giving specific assignments for preparation

---

JOB DESCRIPTION

Job title: First Cook   *Date:*   September 2, 19____
Job code: 2–26.32 Dept. 10   *Location:*   Kitchen of University Cafeteria
Job summary
   Prepares meats and main dishes, soups and gravies for noon meal.
   Cleans and washes small equipment used in cooking.
   Keeps own working area clean.
Performance requirements
   Responsibilities: responsible for the preparation of meat and main dishes,
   soups and gravies to be served at a stated time.
   Job knowledge: plan own work schedule, know basic principles of quantity
   food cookery and how to use certain equipment.
   Mental application: mentally alert.
   Dexterity and accuracy: accurate in weighing and measuring of food ingre-
   dients and portions.
   Equipment used: food chopper, mixer, ovens, ranges, steam cooker,
   steam-jacketed kettle, fryer, broiler, meat slicer.
   Standards of production: preparation of foods of high quality in specified
   quantities.
Supervision
   Under general supervision of dietitian.
   Gives some supervision to assistant cooks.
Relation to other jobs
   Promotion from: Salad maker or vegetable preparation worker.
   Promotion to: Foodservice supervisor (if education and ability warrants).
Qualifications
   Experience desirable but not required.
   Education and training.
     Technical or vocational training: none.
     Formal education: grammar school.
     Ability to read, write, and understand English.

FIGURE 11.5   Job description; write up for a cook's position. Job description should be available for all positions in the department.

of the day's menu items and prepreparation for the next day. A more detailed discussion of production scheduling is included in Chapter 5.

Van Egmond[13] suggests three basic types of work schedules: individual, daily unit, and organization. Because the individual schedule on a daily basis would be too time consuming for most managers, she recommends the daily unit schedule shown in Fig. 11.8.

The organization work schedule gives the standing assignments by half hour periods for all employees in chart form. It does not relate specifically to the day's menu. This type of schedule shows graphically the total work-

---

JOB SPECIFICATION

Payroll title: First Cook
Department: Preparation Department   *Occupational code:*   2–26.32
Supervised by: Dietitian
Job summary: Prepares meat, main dishes, soups, and gravies for noon meal.
Educational status: Speak, read, write English. Grammar school graduate or higher.
Experience required: Cooking in a cafeteria or restaurant 6 months desirable but not required.
Knowledge and skills: Knowledge of basic principles of quantity food preparation; ability to adjust recipes and follow directions; ability to plan work.
Physical requirements: Standard physical examination.
Personal requirements: Neat, clean; male or female.
References required: Two work and personal references.
Hours: 6:30 a.m. to 3:00 p.m., 5 days a week; days off to be arranged; 30-minute lunch period.
Wage code: Grade 3.
Promotional opportunities: To foodservice supervisor.
Advantages and disadvantages of the job: Location, environment, security.
Tests: None.

FIGURE 11.6   Job Specification. Example of a typical format used for each job in the department.

load and its division among employees, but would not be effective unless accompanied by daily assignments or a production schedule.

SCHEDULING OF EMPLOYEES   Workers may be scheduled successfully only after thorough analysis and study of the jobs to be done, the working conditions, and the probable efficiency of the employees. The menu pattern, the form in which food is purchased, the method of preparation, and the total quantity needed are important factors in determining the amount of preparation time and labor required to produce and serve meals in a given situation. Good menu planning provides for variation in meal items and combinations from day-to-day, with a fairly uniform production schedule. Workers cannot be expected to maintain high interest and to work efficiently if they have little to do one day and are overworked the next.

Analysis of several sample menus in terms of total labor hours and the time of day required for the amounts and types of preparations is a basic consideration in determining the number of employees necessary in any foodservice. The total estimated work hours required to cover all activities within the organization divided by the number of working hours in the day

```
┌─────────────────────────────────────────────────────────────────────────────┐
│                WORK SCHEDULE FOR CAFETERIA COUNTER WORKER                     │
│  Name: _____        Hours: 5:30 to 2:00 p.m.           │
│                                           30 min for breakfast                │
│                                           15 min for coffee break             │
│                                                                               │
│  Position—Cafeteria Counter Worker—No. 1   Supervised by: _____        │
│  Days off: _____             Relieved by: _____        │
│                                                                               │
│  5:30 to 7:15 A.M.:   1.  Read breakfast menu                                │
│                       2.  Ready equipment for breakfast meal                  │
│                           a.  Turn on heat in cafeteria counter units for hot foods, grill, dish │
│                               warmers, etc.                                   │
│                           b.  Prepare counter units for cold food             │
│                           c.  Obtain required serving utensils and put in position for use │
│                           d.  Place dishes where needed, those required for hot food in dish │
│                               warmer                                          │
│                       3.  Make coffee (consult supervisor for instructions and amount to be │
│                           made)                                               │
│                       4.  Fill milk dispenser                                 │
│                       5.  Obtain food items to be served cold: fruit, fruit juice, dry cereals, │
│                           butter, cream, etc. Place in proper location on cafeteria counter │
│                       6.  Obtain hot food and put in hot section of counter   │
│                       7.  Check with supervisor for correct portion sizes if this has not been │
│                           decided previously                                  │
│                                                                               │
│  6:30 to 8:00 A.M.:   1.  Open cafeteria doors for breakfast service          │
│                       2.  Check meal tickets, volunteer lists, guest tickets, and collect cash │
│                           as directed by supervisor                           │
│                       3.  Replenish cold food items, dishes, and silver       │
│                       4.  Notify cook before hot items are depleted           │
│                       5.  Make additional coffee as needed                    │
│                       6.  Keep counters clean; wipe up spilled food           │
│                                                                               │
│  8:00 to 8:30 A.M.:   Eat breakfast                                          │
│                                                                               │
│  8:30 to 10:30 A.M.:  1.  Break down serving line and return leftover foods to refrigerators │
│                           and cook's area as directed by supervisor           │
│                       2.  Clean equipment, serving counters, and tables in dining area │
│                       3.  Prepare serving counters for coffee break period    │
│                           a.  Get a supply of cups, saucers, and tableware     │
│                           b.  Make coffee                                     │
│                           c.  Fill cream dispensers                           │
│                           d.  Keep counter supplied during coffee break period (9:30–10:30) │
│                       4.  Fill salad dressing, relish, and condiment containers for noon meal │
│                                                                               │
│  10:30 to 11:30 A.M.: 1.  Confer with supervisor regarding menu items and portion sizes │
│                           for noon meal                                       │
│                       2.  Clean equipment, counters, and tables in dining area │
│                       3.  Prepare counters for lunch:                         │
│                           a.  Turn on heat in hot counter and dish warmers     │
│                           b.  Set out tea bags, cream, ice cups, glasses       │
│                           c.  Place serving utensils and dishes in position for use │
│                       4.  Make coffee                                         │
│                       5.  Fill milk and clean dispensers                      │
│                       6.  Set portioned cold foods on cold counter            │
│                                                                               │
│  11:30 A.M. to        1.  Open cafeteria doors for noon meal service          │
│  1:30 P.M.:           2.  Replenish cold food items, dishes, and silver as needed │
│                       3.  Keep counters clean; wipe up spilled food           │
│                       4.  Make additional coffee as needed                    │
│                                                                               │
│  1:30 to 2:00 P.M.:   1.  Turn off heating and cooling elements in serving counters │
│                       2.  Help break down serving line                        │
│                       3.  Return leftover foods to proper places              │
│                       4.  Serve late lunches to doctors and nurses            │
│                       5.  Clean equipment and serving counter as directed by supervisor │
│                                                                               │
│  2:00 P.M.            Off duty                                               │
└─────────────────────────────────────────────────────────────────────────────┘
```

FIGURE 11.7   Work schedule for a counter worker in any type of cafeteria.

WORK SCHEDULE

MENU:
LASAGNA CASSEROLE   BUTTERED FRENCH BREAD
TOSSED SALAD   MILK
CHILLED PEACH HALVES

Time	Manager 7 1/2 hr	6-Hr Assistant	5-Hr Assistant	4-Hr Assistant
7:30– 8:00	Make coffee or tea for teachers			
8:00– 8:30	Help with lasagna sauce	Prepare lasagna		
8:30– 9:00	Lunch count—Tickets		Dip up fruit and refrigerate	
9:00– 9:30				
9:30–10:00	Teachers' salads		Wash vegetables for salad	
10:00–10:30	Cut bread and butter	Prepare bread crumbs for fried chicken tomorrow		Cut up vegetables for salad
10:30–11:00			Put out desserts	Set up line—napkins, straws, dishes
11:00–11:30	Eat lunch—20 min	Eat lunch—20 min	Eat lunch—20 min	
	Put food on steam table	Put food on steam table	Wash pots and pans	Mix salad for first lunch
11:30–12:00	Cashier	Serving / Set up for next line	Serving / Help in dishroom	Back up line / Dishroom
12:00–12:30	Serving	Serving / Set up for next line	Cashier / Help in dishroom	Back up line / Dishroom
12:30– 1:00	Serving	Serving / Put away food	Cashier / 10 min break	Back up line / Dishroom
1:00– 1:30	Count money—10 min break / Help to clean tables	10 min break / Clean tables	Clean steamtable	Eat lunch (eat on own time)
1:30– 2:00	Prepare reports	Clean up		Clean dishroom
2:00– 2:30	Place orders			Help with kitchen cleanup
2:30– 3:00	Take topping out of freezer and put in refrigerator for tomorrow			

FIGURE 11.8   Sample work schedule for school foodservice employees.   *Courtesy, Dorothy Van Egmond, School Foodservice, Westport, CT: AVI Publishing Co.*

would give an indication of the number of full-time employees needed. However, careful attention must be given to time schedules so that each employee will be occupied during his or her hours on duty. Certain preparations or service duties may require a reduction in the estimated number of fulltime workers and the addition of some part-time ones during peak periods in order to maintain the desired standards at an even tempo. A graphic presentation of the estimated work hours needed for each job helps to clarify the problems of scheduling and the distribution of the workload (Fig. 11.9).

Working conditions such as the physical factors of temperature, humidity, lighting, and safety influence the scheduling of personnel and affect their

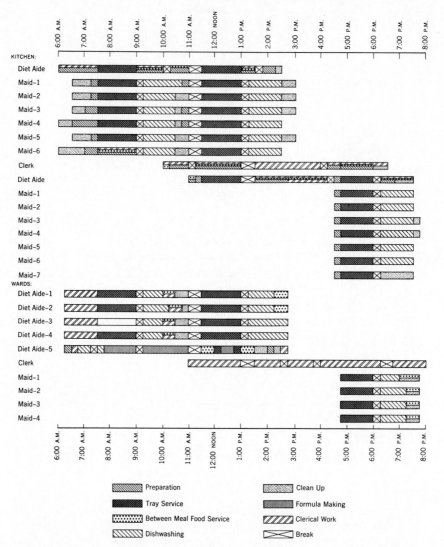

FIGURE 11.9   Bar graph used to detail employee time schedules and task assignments for patients' foodservice. Total time spent on each separate task may be easily calculated.   *Courtesy, King County Hospital System, Seattle.*

performance. Of particular importance is the amount and arrangement of equipment. The distance each employee must travel with his or her work area should be kept at a minimum in order to conserve the individual's energy and time. Use of mechanical devices in the processing and service of food may decrease the total labor hours needed and increase the degree of skill and responsibility of employees. Arrangement of work areas for efficient operation cannot be overemphazied.

A work distribution analysis chart of the total activities within a department will show where tasks may be eliminated, combined, or modified in the overall picture. One must be sure that the activities are so organized and combined that efficient use is made of the labor hours of each individual worker. Studies may be made to determine a good standard for each procedure, such as the time required for the average worker to combine and shape 25 pounds of ham loaf mixture into loaves in pans for baking. The standards set for each procedure should be such that the workers in a particular organization will be able to maintain them. The standard time should be established at a level that the average employee could do 20 to 30 per cent more work without undue fatigue.

Written schedules clarify the responsibilities of workers and give them a feeling of security. It is wise to include a statement indicating that additional duties may have to be assigned from time to time. However, work schedules must be kept flexible and adjustments made as needed to adapt to the daily menu. Also, the introduction of new food products may decrease the amount of time needed for prepreparation as well as the time of cookery; likewise, additional processes may become necessary.

Information pertaining to the broad subjects of organization and management is voluminous. Only basic concepts with limited application are included in this chapter. The following chapters discuss some special areas of concern to persons in the management of foodservices. Supplementary reading of current literature is advised to become acquainted with newer developments as they evolve.

Notes

1. HAIMANN, T. AND SCOTT, W. G.: Management in the Modern Organization, 3rd ed. Boston: Houghton Mifflin, 1978.
2. BEACH, D. S.: Personnel: The Management of People at Work, 5th ed. New York: Macmillan, 1985, p. 68.
3. KAST, F. E. and ROSENZWEIG, J. E.: Organization and Management: A Systems Approach, 3rd ed. New York: McGraw-Hill Book Co., 1979.
4. DALE, E.: Management: Theory and Practice, 4th ed. New York: McGraw-Hill Book Co., 1978.
5. BOYATZIS, R. E.: The Competent Manager. New York: John Wiley and Sons, 1982.
6. DRUCKER, P. F.: Managing in Turbulent Times. New York: Harper & Row, 1980.
7. FAYOL, H.: General and Industrial Management. London: Sir Isaac Pitman and Sons, 1949.

8. GULICK, L.: Notes on the Theory of Organization. *In* Gulick, L. and Urwick, L., eds.: Papers on the Science of Administration. New York: Columbia University Press, 1937.

9. HUSE, E. F.: The Modern Manager. St. Paul, MN: West Publishing Co., 1982.

10. KATZ, R. L.: Skills of an effective administrator. Harvard Bus. Rev. 52:90 (Sept./Oct.), 1974.

11. KOONTZ, H.: *The management theory jungle revisited.* Acad. of Mgmt. J. 5:175, 1980.

12. MINTZBERG, H.: The Nature of Managerial Work. New York: Harper & Row, 1973.

13. VAN EGMOND-PANNELL, D.: School Foodservice, 2nd ed. Westport, CN: AVI Publishing Co., 1981.

Supplementary References

BAIRD, S. C., AND SYLVESTER, J.: Role Delineation and Verification for Entry-Level Positions in Foodservice Systems Management. Summary and Final Documents. Chicago: The Amer. Diet. Assoc., 1983.

ELLIOTT, T.: Profitable Foodservice Management (nine manuals in series), S. Barnes, ed. Washington, DC: National Restaurant Assoc., 1984.

How to Prepare a Restaurant Operations Manual. Washington, DC: National Restaurant Assoc., 1982.

KEISER, JAMES: Principles and Practices of Management in the Hospitality Industry. New York: CBI/Van Nostrand Reinhold, 1983.

Standards of Practice: A Practitioner's Guide to Implementation. The American Dietetic Association Council on Practice, Quality Assurance Committee. Chicago: The Amer. Diet. Assoc., 1986.

CHAPTER 12

Staffing and Managing Human Resources

Introduction

Staffing and managing human resources involves all the methods of matching tasks to be performed with the people available to do the work. Recruiting, hiring, placement, orientation, training, performance appraisal, promotion, transfer, discipline, dismissal, supervision, decision-making, and grievance handling are all intertwined in this process. Each of these subjects is discussed in this chapter.

An important aspect of the staffing function is the establishment, acceptance, and enforcement of fair labor policies within an organization. Four ideas in which policies are generally established are discussed: wages and income maintenance, hours and schedules of work, security in employment, and employee services and benefits. Major federal legislation that impacts these organizational policies is included in each section. The chapter concludes with a discussion of labor-management relations including relevant legislation and the impact of unionization on foodservices.

Staffing

Foodservice has been called the ultimate people business. As the single most important resource in any enterprise, the human factor is the key to success. The ability of foodservice managers to understand people, recognize their potential and provide for their growth and development on the job is of inestimable worth in helping to create good human relations. Realization by workers that they are useful and important to efficient functioning of the business contributes to their sense of responsibility, ownership, and pride in the organization. Increase in pay alone does not buy good will, loyalty, or confidence in self and others. Often only simple changes or considerations such as beautification of the work area, elimination of safety hazards, rearrangement of equipment, modification of work schedules, or even cheerful words of appreciation and encouragement produce incentives with resultant increased and improved quality output. Mutually understood and accepted objectives and policies of the foodservice and well-defined channels of communication also contribute significantly to high-level employer-employee relationships.

Levering[1] lists a number of characteristics beyond good pay and benefits that are common to those companies considered best to work for in America. These include: encouraging open communication, flowing up and down; promoting from within; stressing quality, fostering a sense of employee pride in output; allowing employees to share in profits; reducing distinctions between ranks; creating as pleasant a workplace environment as possible; encouraging employees to be active in community service; helping employees save by matching funds they save; and making people feel part of a team. The presence of these characteristics results in a good workplace climate and low turnover of good employees.

Staffing is not simply a synonym for employment. Staffing includes all the methods of matching requirements of tasks to be performed with skills available. Hiring, placement, promotion, transfer, job design, and training are all intertwined in this process. People must be hired and promoted who can be trained to perform the necessary tasks. And training must be designed around the needs of the employees and the organization. Staffing may be thought of as an integrated system for moving people into, through, and eventually out of the organization. The components of an integrated staffing system are shown in Fig. 12.1.

A detailed plan of organization for a foodservice indicates the number and types of human resources needed, presents their distribution among the various work areas of the service, and shows their work schedules, the provision made for their training, and the responsibilities assigned to each. Far more difficult than the formulation of such a plan on paper is its inauguration in actuality. Then all the neat little blocks on the chart designating individuals assigned certain responsibilities become persons with diverse energies and loyalties, egocentric ideas, and unclarified codes of values, some skillful, others not, some with acceptable food standards, and others apparently totally lacking in this regard. Left to chance, the introduction of the

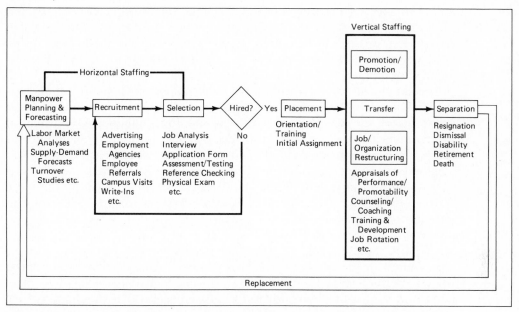

FIGURE 12.1   Components of an integrated staffing system. Reprinted by permission. *ASPA Handbook of Personnel and Industrial Relations, by Dale Yoder and H. G. Heneman, p. 4–3, copyright © 1979, by Bureau of National Affairs, Inc., Washington, D.C.*

human element into an orderly plan is likely to plunge it into chaos. With wise selection, intelligent and adequate direction, and careful supervision, the human element vitalizes and enriches the plan.

Foodservices in many large companies have personnel departments responsible for the staffing function. In such organizations the dietitian or foodservice director works closely with the personnel department. However, in many small foodservices, personnel management responsibilities are assumed by the director of that department. Thus the director may be responsible for the organization plans, the procurement, placement, induction, on-the-job training, and supervision of all employees in the department.

Management of human resources presents unique problems that can be solved only by persons with an understanding of human nature, a respect for the personalities of others, and an appreciation of the labor requirements and employment opportunities of the company. Insight into and respect for the rights of all individuals in an organization is the responsibility of the person in charge. These time-honored rights include: (1) the right to be treated as an individual and respected as a person, (2) the right to have a voice in one's own affairs, which includes the right to contribute to the best of one's own abilities in the solution of common problems, (3) the right to recognition for one's contribution to the common good, (4) the right to develop and make use of one's highest capabilities, and (5) the right to fairness and justice in all dealings with one's supervisors.

As soon as employed, a worker becomes a member of the group and begins to share in forming that intangible but all-important element termed group morale or group spirit. An understanding, cooperative, and helpful worker contributes to group morale; an irritable, carping, complaining, and obstructive worker destroys it. Many organizations have learned through sad experience how very great a destructive force one malcontent member can exert on group spirit. Since discipline of workers who are a disturbing force or their elimination from the work group is neither easy nor pleasant, the selection of those who will build morale rather than destroy it is of great importance in the choice of staff.

The skill, craftsmanship, dependability, and regularity of workers and their contribution to group morale may determine their selection as a present worker. Certain other things indicate probable contributions in the future. Capacity for growth, desire for self-improvement so that they may render greater service, ambition for promotion, and identification with the firm are all important in the selection of a work force for tomorrow. However, not all people are equally desirous of assuming responsibility and carrying a project to conclusion. This is true also of workers who are unwilling to face problem solving. Some people are overdependent and eager to avoid directing themselves or others.

After the foodservice director has considered personnel needs, what the service has to offer in return should be considered. Everybody works smarter when there's something in it for them. Part of the reward will be made with money. Adequate compensation and steady employment are basic to any satisfactory employer-employee relationship.

Another part of the compensation may be intangible; that is, just as employees contribute to the morale of the group spirit of the service, so the administration will contribute to their sense of personal satisfaction. The provision of meaningful work and the recognition of achievements are important motivational elements.

A third part of the compensation will be the opportunity to do a good job. Full instructions as to accepted procedures and standards and adequate on-the-job supervision are vital to satisfactory performance by workers. Only then will they experience pride in their accomplishments and attain and maintain a high level of performance on the job.

The job should provide opportunity for growth and a reasonable chance for promotion. Workers should have an opportunity to make their service a creative experience. They should be encouraged to regard improvement in techniques as possible and welcome and to feel that suggestions toward this end will be cordially received. They have a right to expect fairness in dealing with management, freedom from misrepresentation and misinformation about the employing organization, a reasonable opportunity for continued education, promotion when earned, and provision for satisfying recreation.

The foodservice director should synthesize the two points of view—the employer's and the employee's—into an adequate, functioning personnel program. Such a program should be characterized by wise selection, careful placement, adequate supervision, and education for the present job and for the future; fair employment policies; services desirable for the comfort and welfare of employees; and the keeping of records that will facilitate the evaluation and revision, if needed, of the management program.

The Employment Process

Organization charts indicate the number of workers needed in each department of a foodservice, and job descriptions and job specifications outline the specific conditions under which each employee will work, the job requirements, and the training and other personal qualifications deemed desirable. Such information affords the foodservice director charged with personnel management an inventory of employment needs.

Recruitment

The next step is to survey the sources of labor supply and determine which one or ones shall be used to bring the open positions to the attention of the best qualified prospective employees. There should be active recruitment of minority group members if the institution is to stay in line with public policy. Labor sources are many and varied, dependent somewhat on which sources are available locally and on the general labor market. Most sources may be classified as either internal or external.

INTERNAL SOURCES   Promotion of employees to a position of higher level, transfer from a related department or unit, and rehiring of a person formerly on the payroll are examples of internal sources. Promotions or transfers within an organization help to stimulate interest and build morale of employees when they know that on the basis of measured merit they will be given preference over an outsider in case of a good vacancy. Caution must be taken to ensure that the individual has the necessary personal attributes as well as training and experience for the position open and that equal opportunity employment regulations have not been violated.

An indirect internal source of labor is a present employee who notifies friends or relatives of vacancies and arranges for an interview with the employer. This means of recruiting labor has advantages and disadvantages. Present employees generally prefer working with those who are congenial, and a pleasant spirit within the group may be built by utilizing this source of labor supply. On the other hand, personal ties may be stronger than business loyalties, and inept, unskilled workers may be highly recommended by relatives and friends. Furthermore, a strongly clannish feeling among the workers may lead to an unfortunate generalized reaction against any disciplinary measure, however well justified. The many phases of this situation should be considered before extensive use is made of this source of labor.

EXTERNAL SOURCES   Some foodservice organizations may plan to fill many vacancies by promoting from within, but eventually replacements will be needed to fill the depleted ranks. The most common external sources are the press, employment agencies, schools, and labor unions.

Advertising. Newspaper advertising is a means of reaching a large group of potential applicants. Such advertisements cite the qualifications desired; otherwise a mass of applicants may respond, none of whom are qualified. Definite statements as to desired training and experience in the foodservice field tend to limit the applicants to possible candidates. Details concerning salary, sick leave, time schedule, and vacations are much better left until the personal interview. The advertisement should state whether application is to be made first in person or by letter.

Employment Agencies. Private employment agencies have long served as a means of locating labor. Usually they are supported by a registration fee charged those seeking employment. They generally provide a preliminary "weeding out" of would-be applicants, eliminating the obviously unfit from consideration. Often these agencies tend to deal with specialized groups in the professional or technical areas and are of most value to those seeking employees on the managerial level.

Federal, state, and local employment agencies are a significantly important labor source. The value of these agencies has increased since they have studied the employer's needs and set up machinery to test aptitudes and skills of the workers. Such procedures benefit the foodservice managers endeavoring to reduce turnover to a minimum and develop stability of employment.

School. In some localities vocational and technical school offering training for the food industry have excellent prospects from among the graduates. The adequacy of their specific preparation for this work may greatly shorten the period of preliminary training necessary.

Another source, important in the foodservices of college and universities, is the student employment office of the college. Utilizing this type of labor offers financial assistance to worthy students and often provides experience to those majoring in food systems management. Perhaps the greatest advantage of student employees to the college dietitian is their availability for short work periods during the peak of the service load. However, the labor cost is high because of the inexperience of the workers, and the labor turnover is great, thus requiring the expenditure of much energy in introducing new workers to the jobs. The short work periods necessitated by student classroom assignments make the planning of work far more complicated than when full-time employees are used. The immaturity and inexperience of the worker may result in a waste of food supplies and labor hours unless constant and thorough supervision is provided. The maintenance of high food standards and acceptable service is often much more difficult with student employees than with carefully chosen, well-trained employees of long-time service.

Labor Unions. In institutions where employees are unionized, the labor union may be an important source for workers.

Selection

After the prospective workers have been recruited, the next step is for the employer to select the most able person available for the particular opening. The cost of hiring, training, and discharging or transferring a worker is too great to allow many mistakes in the employee procurement process. Failure at this point is far more expensive than is commonly recognized.

Recognition of the heavy initial cost of employment means, when the labor market permits, a trend toward careful selection of each appointee.

APPLICATION FORM   The application form plays an important role in the employment of any worker. The information requested should be phrased in direct simple statements pertinent to the particular job in which the applicant shows interest, and questions raised should be easily answered. Obviously, quite different information would be required of the person applying for the position of administrative dietitian than for one who expects to be a counter worker. However, both application forms, when completed, must contain biographical data that will provide the employer with all the facts necessary not only to determine the fitness of the applicant for the job, but also to compare the qualifications of all applicants. The Fair Employment Practice laws adopted by many states make it illegal to ask questions that would be discriminatory because of race, religion, sex, or national origin. After the employee has been hired, such information can be obtained for the individual's personnel records. The dietitian or manager should check with the personnel department or other authoritative source regarding restrictions in the application form and the interview. References of former employment usually are requested and should be checked.

INTERVIEW   The purposes of the selection interview are: (1) to get information—not only all the facts, but attitudes, feelings, and personality traits that determine "will-do" qualifications, (2) to give information—although it is essential that the interviewer know all about the applicant, it is just as essential that the applicant know all about the establishment and the job, and (3) to make a friend—treat an applicant with the same courtesy that you would give to a customer, for every applicant is a potential customer.

The direct personal interview is advantageous in that the interviewer has the opportunity to become acquainted with the applicant and to observe personal characteristics and reactions that would be impossible to learn from an application form or letter. Also, the great majority of employees of a foodservice are persons relatively untrained, whose qualifications cannot be ascertained in any other way than by a personal interview and possible communications with previous employers. Documents that could be termed credentials are rarely available; therefore, the personal interview becomes of great importance in making a wise choice. In filling administrative positions, the personal interview serves as a final check on the fitness of a person whose credentials have been considered carefully.

The applicant should be treated as a person whose concern with the decision is as real and vital as that of the employing agency. The job should be discussed in relation to other positions in the foodservice to which the job might lead. Reasonable hopes for promotion should be discussed and fringe benefits should be presented. Appraisal of the job specifications in terms of the applicant's own fitness should motivate self-direction toward either self-placement or self-elimination.

The development of a successful technique in interviewing requires thought, study, and experience. Some interviewing suggestions include these *do's:*

Do's 1–16

1. Have a purpose and a plan for the interview—a guided interview pattern.
2. Have and study carefully, an analysis of the job, a job description, and a job specification.
3. Provide a private place for the interview, free from interruptions and distractions.
4. Put the applicant at ease; establish confidence and a free and easy talking situation.
5. Use the pronoun *I* very, very sparingly; *we* is much better.

6. Listen with sincere and intensive interest.
7. Do ask questions beginning with *what, why,* and *how.* Useful phrases to keep in mind are:
   Would you give me an example?
   For instance . . .
   In what way . . .
   Suppose . . .
8. Do safeguard personal confidences.
9. Do strive to learn not only what the applicant thinks and feels, but *why the applicant thinks and feels that way.*
10. Do be pleasant and courteous.
11. Do strive to be a good sounding board or mirror for the applicant's expressions of attitudes, feelings, ideas.
12. Do ask questions that encourage self-analysis.
13. Do prod, search, and dig courteously for all the facts.
14. Maintain an attitude of friendly interest in the applicant. Make a friend and a customer even though you do not hire the applicant.
15. Do make notes for record purposes either during or after the interview.
16. Do, immediately after the interview, write a summary of it on the interview form in the space provided.

Don'ts 17–31

Suggestions of things to avoid in interviewing include these:
17. Do not interrupt the applicant.
18. *Do not talk too much.* Talkative interviews usually are failures.
19. Do not rush the interview. This is not only discourteous, but it results in failure of the interview.
20. Do not ask leading questions. If the question is so worded that the answer you want is apparent to the applicant, you are actually interviewing yourself.
21. Do not ask questions that can be answered only with either yes or no.
22. Do not merely talk when the applicant has finished a statement. Use such responses as "I see," "I think I understand," or "What else can you add to that statement?"
23. Do not agree and do not disagree. Be interested but noncommittal.
24. Do not argue, or else the interview is finished.
25. Do not lose control of self or the interview.
26. Do not get in a rut. Do not leave any impression with the applicant that the interview is routine and perfunctory.
27. Do not "talk down."
28. Do not express or imply authority. The good employment interview is a free and easy exchange of attitudes and ideas between equals.

29. Do not jump to conclusions. The purpose of the interview is to get information. Appraisal and conclusions will come *after* the interview.
30. Do not preach or moralize. This is not the purpose of the interview.
31. Do not interview when either you or the applicant is upset.

PERSONNEL RECORDS   After an agreement on employment terms has been reached, a record of appointment is made. This becomes the nucleus of the records of the activity and progress of the worker within the organization. Records may be kept on data-processing cards, in card files, or in looseleaf form. Included among the items listed on the forms are name, address, name of spouse, number of children, other dependents, educational background, former employment (including company and length of time), date of hiring, job assigned, wage rate, whether or not meals are included, absences with reasons, adjustments in work and wages, promotions, demotions, or transfers with reasons, and information concerning insurance and health benefits. Such complete records are useful in indicating the sense of responsibility and the serious intent of employees, and as a basis for merit ratings, salary adjustments, or other benefits.

TESTS   Impressions of the prospective employee gained in the interview and from the follow-up of references are admittedly incomplete. They may be checked or replaced by tests of various types, the most common being intelligence, trade, and aptitude. Any type of testing to be of value must be done by a person well qualified by education and experience for this specialized function of personnel management.

The physical fitness of an applicant for a foodservice appointment is highly important. A health examination should be required of all foodservice workers. Only physically fit persons can do their best work. Quite as important is the need for assurance that the individual presents no health hazard to the foodservice. Managers are well aware of the devastation that might result from the inadvertent employment of a person with a communicable disease.

The Worker on the Job

Orientation

The induction of the newly employed worker to the job is a most important phase of staffing. Smith[2] outlines ten steps to be included in an orientation program that are designed to challenge the new employee's interest and elicit support for the goals and objectives of the company.

1. Introduction to the company. Introductions are simply a matter of who the company is, where it has been, and where it is going. The key is to make the new employee feel good about the company and begin to instill the pride of belonging, being a part of the company.

2. Review of important policy and practice. Policy review will vary from company to company, but certainly must include standards of conduct, performance standards, and introductory (probation) period of employment, discipline policy, and safety.

3. Review of benefits and services. A review of benefits is crucial. It is not so important to sell a benefits program and all its virtues as it is to communicate what is provided and at what expense.
   Employees need to appreciate the cost of benefits, and you should be able to relate the percentage of payroll spent on their behalf.
   Additionally, discuss services that the employee might not construe as a benefit, such as a credit union, parking, food, medical care, discounts, and social recreational services.

4. Benefit plan enrollment. Complete necessary benefit enrollment forms with assistance and with the assurance that the employee understands his or her options. Provisions should be made to allow the employee to discuss plan options with a spouse before making a commitment.

5. Completion of employment documents. Payroll withholding, emergency information, picture releases, employment agreements, equal employment opportunity data, and other relevant and appropriate documents must be completed.

6. Review of employer expectations. This deals with employer-employee relationships. Discuss teamwork, working relationships, attitude, and loyalty. A performance appraisal form makes a good topical outline for a discussion of employer expectations.

7. Setting of employee expectations. If employees meet company expectations, what can they expect from the company? Training and development, scheduled wage and salary reviews, security, recognition, working conditions, opportunity for advancement, educational assistance programs, counseling, grievance procedures, and other relevant and appropriate expectations should be detailed.

8. Introduction to fellow workers. Introduce people a few at a time to let the names be assimilated. Use of name tags is helpful and so is the buddy system. Assign someone to be mentor to the new employees, to introduce them around, take them to break periods, have lunch with them. A few days is usually enough introduction time.

9. Introduction to facilities. Take a standard tour of the facility. This is more effective if you break it into several tours. The first day tour the immediate work area and then expand the tour on subsequent days until the facility is covered.

10. Introduction to the job. Have your training program in place. Be prepared and ready to get the employee immediately involved in the work flow.

Training

After the individual worker has been properly introduced to the job, there still remains the need for training through qualified supervision, especially in the initial period of employment. Familiarity with established operational policies and procedures, presented by management in a well-organized manner, can do much to encourage the new worker and help in gaining self-confidence. Generally, advantages of a good training program include reduction in labor turnover, absenteeism, accidents, and production costs, and an increase in the maintenance of morale, job satisfaction, and efficient production at high levels.

The first step in establishing a training program is to decide when training is needed. Next, determine exactly what needs to be taught and who should receive that training. Goals should be established for the program and an outline developed containing the steps required to help meet those goals.[3]

ADULT TRAINING   The unique characteristics of adult as learners must be considered when planning for on-the-job training. Children learn for the future and to advance to the next level of learning. Adults, however, learn for immediate application or to solve a present problem. For this reason, they require practical results from the learning experience. Other distinguishing characteristics of the adult learner are: a reduced tolerance for disrespectful treatment, the preference for helping to plan and conduct one's own learning experiences, and a broader base of life experiences to bring to the learning activity.[4]

GROUP TRAINING   Often training can be given efficiently and economically through group instruction. This type of teaching saves time for the instructor and the worker, and also has the advantage of affording the stimulus that comes as the result of group participation. In a foodservice, basic group instruction concerning the policies of management is practical and valuable. Among the areas that might be included are the history and objectives of the organization, relationships of departments and key persons within the particular department, the operational budget as it affects the workers, the preparation and service of food, the sanitation and safety program, and the principles and values of work improvement programs.

Perhaps the most important psychological principle of group training is the use of well-prepared teachers instead of a fellow worker who may have had successful experience in a limited area. Often the stimulation and the inspiration given to the employee by an able instructor are highly motivating and more important in the development of the individual worker than the immediate mastery of routine skills. Tools found to be of value in such a instructional program are audio and visual aids, including films and television, illustrative material, such as posters, charts, and cartoons, and demonstrations in which both the instructor and the employees participate. Spending time and money merely showing films in group training classes is wasteful unless the workers have been alerted to the points of emphasis, time allowed for discussion after the presentation, and follow-up through application on the job. Other psychological principles of group education cannot be considered here, although they should be understood by those in charge of such programs.

ON-THE-JOB TRAINING   Some large foodservice organizations have inaugurated rather extensive programs to provide on-the-job training of employees, with highly satisfactory results. Important among the objectives of such programs are: to reduce time spent in perfecting skills for the production and service of attractive, wholesome food of high quality at reasonable cost, to avoid accidents and damage to property and equipment, and to promote good understanding and close working relationships among employees and supervisors. In these programs emphasis is given to certain requirements common to all good job instruction, such as job knowledge, manipulative skills, human relations, adaptability, and ability to express oneself. These requirements are necessary for the instructor to be an effective teacher, able to do an effective job of instruction.

Teacher preparation for instruction to be given on the job and teaching steps include, first—to get ready to instruct:

1. Break down the job—list principal steps, pick out the key points.
2. Have a timetable—how much skill you expect your pupil to have and how soon.
3. Have everything ready—the right tools, equipment, and materials.
4. Have the workplace properly arranged—just as the worker will be expected to keep it.

And second—to instuct:

1. Prepare the worker. Put the worker at ease. A frightened or embarrassed person cannot learn. Find out what is already known about the job. Begin where knowledge ends. Interest the worker in learning the job. Place the

worker in the correct position so that the job won't be viewed from the wrong direction.

2. Present the operation. Tell, show, illustrate, and question carefully and patiently. Stress key points. Make them clear. Instruct slowly, clearly, and completely, taking up one point at a time—but no more than the trainee can master. Work first for accuracy, then for speed.

3. Try out the worker's performance. Test by having the worker perform the job under observation. Have the worker tell and show you, and explain key points. Ask questions and correct errors patiently. Continue until you know the worker knows.

4. Follow up the worker's performance. Let the worker perform alone. Check frequently, but do not take over if you can give the help needed. Designate to whom the worker goes for help. Encourage questions. Get the worker to look for key points as progress is made. Taper off extra coaching and close follow-up until the worker is able to work under usual supervision. Give credit where credit is due.

A job breakdown is the analysis of a job to be taught and a listing of the elemental steps of what to do and the key points of how to do them. This serves as a guide in giving instruction so that none of the necessary points will be omitted. Fig. 12.2 is an example of a job breakdown for making change. There should be a job breakdown for every task and/or job to be performed in the organization.

Slide-tape programs for individual instruction in work methods and procedures have proven to be satisfactory, and although their preparation is time-consuming, the results appear to justify their use. Slides showing correct techniques are accompanied by oral examinations on tape. For techniques involving motion or rhythm, videotaping may be helpful.

Encouragement of the worker by the supervisor during the first days on the job and during the training period is important in stabilizing interest and sustaining a sense of adequacy. Informal interviews may serve as a means of determining points on which help is needed, as well as those in which ability is most marked. Every expression of friendly, courteous interest is appreciated by the worker and aids in a successful adjustment to the new environment.

In addition to the satisfaction attained by establishing pleasant employer-employee relations, the right induction of the new worker has a dollar-and-cents value that cannot be overlooked. An employee who is unhappy, disinterested, and discontented will tend to look for placement elsewhere after a short experience with the company. Then all the money, time, and effort spent in obtaining and introducing the employee to the job will have been lost, and a similar expenditure must be made before another worker can be assigned the task.

Job: Making Change

Equipment and Supplies   Money and Cash Register

Important Steps	Key Points
REGISTER FIRST—WRAP AFTERWARDS	
1. Accepts money from customer.	1. State amount of sale* "out of" amount received from customer.
2. Place customer's money on plate.	2. Stand in front of cash register. Do not put bill in drawer until after change has been counted.
3. Record the sale on cash register.	3. Check amount recorded on viewer.
4. Count change from till.	4. Begin with amount of sale picking up smallest change first up to amount received from customer.
5. Count change carefully to customer.	5. Start with amount of sale—stop counting when amount is the same as the customer gave.
6. Place customer's money in till.	6. Close the drawer immediately.
7. Deliver change, receipt or sales slip, and merchandise to customer.	7. Say *Thank You*. Let customer know you mean it.

*Including tax (state and federal).

FIGURE 12.2   Job breakdown for making change at the cash register. Important steps are "what to do"; key points are "how to do."

Performance Appraisal

For maximum effectiveness from the work force, every employee should know what is expected and how he or she is performing on the job. Workers are entitled to commendation for work well done and to the opportunity to earn greater responsibility, either with or without increased remuneration. One of the responsibilities of management and supervision is the performance appraisal, and then management has an obligation to communicate this information to each worker regarding individual progress. The personal development of and efficient production by each worker is of concern to management, but an individual worker cannot be expected to improve if evaluations are not made known or counsel is not made available for assistance. Performance appraisals are used to determine job competence, need for additional training or counseling, and to review the employee's progress within the organization. Ratings made objectively and without prejudice furnish valuable information that can be used in job placement, training, supervision, promotion, and replacement. Careful selection and placement and proper training of employees for their particular responsibilities are prerequisites to a successful evaluation program. The performance appraisal may be accomplished by several methods, including rating scales, checklists, narrative evaluation, personal conferences, or management by objectives.

There are few if any objective standards that can be used for measuring subjective personal characteristics such as character, reliability, and initiative. Yet these traits, as they relate to the capabilities, efficiency, and development of each employee, are important to an organization. Such characteristics must be appraised in some way if management is to have an intelligent basis for classifying workers according to rank or grade and thus help to provide a standard for salary increases, promotions, transfers, or placement into a job for which the worker is well suited.

Rating procedures have been developed that provide a measurement of the degree to which certain intangible personality traits are present in workers and of their performance on the job. Care should be taken to design the scale to meet the objective desired. Will this estimate of the relative worth of employees be used as a basis for rewards or recognitions or as a tool for explaining to workers why they may or may not be making progress on the job? In the hands of competent administrators, the rating form could be designed to obtain information to accomplish both purposes.

Distinguishable personal traits most likely to affect performance are honesty, initiative, judgment, and ability to get along with other workers. Examples of qualities on a rating charge are: quality of work, quantity of work, adaptability, job knowledge, and dependability.

These so-called rating scales, from which the variously known merit, progress, development, or service ratings are derived, are not new in industrial management, although few are directly applicable to institutional foodservices. Some administrators prefer a system of gradation checking where each quality, factor, or characteristic may be marked on a scale ranging from poor to superior, or the reverse, with two or three possible levels within each grade. For example:

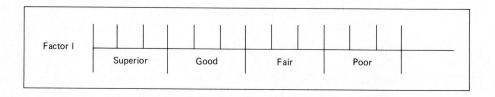

Another format might describe the grade for each factor listed.

Fig. 12.3 is an example of a rating scale with definitions of the various

EMPLOYEE PERFORMANCE REVIEW RATING

NAME_____DATE _____

PRESENT JOB _____DEPARTMENT_____

PAY RANGE_____ TO _____

CURRENT RATE_____ NEW RATE _____

REVIEW PERIOD FROM_____TO_____
                                    Date   Date

REASON
FOR REVIEW: □ PROBATIONARY □ ANNUAL □ SPECIAL_____
                                                                    Explain

Date to be returned to Personnel Department _____

PART I

The purpose of the Employee Performance Review is twofold.

1. To identify the areas in which the employee is proficient, to encourage more effective utilization of known and demonstrated strengths, and to apply these proficiencies to the best advantage in accomplishing the objectives of the job and the department.
2. To identify areas in which improvement is desirable and to assist the employee to plan and execute a program of study, practice and/or discipline to develop total competency in the job.

It is the responsibility of the employee's supervisor to do the utmost to see that these purposes are accomplished. With this in mind, make every effort to state your comments so that they are constructive and positive.

It is important to remember that a rating of "Successful Performance" represents the performance level of a fully competent employee who is successfully performing all job duties and responsibilities and is doing a good job. Performance levels either above or below "Successful Performance" should be fully documented in Part II with regard to what was done to merit the rating given.

Indicate your evaluation of the employee's performance on each of the factors below by placing a ($\sqrt{}$) at the proper place on each scale.

FIGURE 12.3   Scale for review of employee performance.   *Courtesy, Lincoln General Hospital, Lincoln, Nebraska.*

For your convenience the midpoint on the rating scale has been indicated *but* it is important to remember that the evaluations criteria have been weighted. Therefore, the relationship between the score checked on the rating scale and the amount of the merit increase is minimal (a score of 5 on the rating scale does not mean a 5 percent increase).

KNOWLEDGE OF WORK: Consider the knowledge and understanding the employee has regarding the job. Does the employee know the methods or techniques to be used? Does the employee know the reasons for the procedure to be followed? Does the employee know the purpose of the job and what is required to be accomplished and how it contributes to the objectives of the department?

Evaluate:

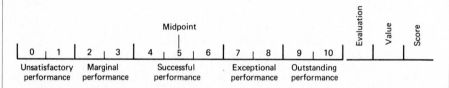

QUALITY OF WORK: Consider the accuracy, thoroughness and neatness with which the employee accomplishes the assigned work. Does the employee approach the work methodically? Is the employee economical with work time and materials used?

Evaluate:

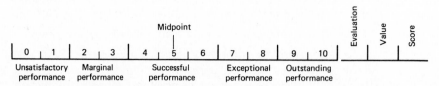

QUANTITY OF WORK: Consider the volume of work done under everyday conditions. Does the employee normally complete the work schedule or assignments? Does the employee work fast enough to accomplish the assigned share of the work? More than the assigned share?

FIGURE 12.3 *(Continued)*

Evaluate:

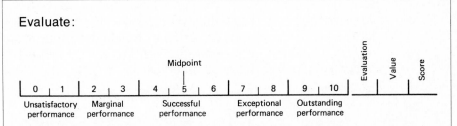

DEPENDABILITY: Consider the extent to which the employee can be depended on in the job. Is the employee punctual? Is the employee on the job when scheduled? To what extent does the employee require supervision? Does the employee inform the appropriate person if late, absent, or unable to complete the assigned work task?

Evaluate:

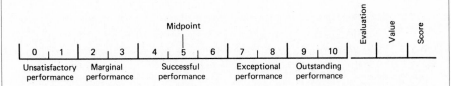

COMPATIBILITY: Consider the extent to which the employee's attitude toward the work, the responsible supervisor, and the hospital are compatible with the objectives of the hospital. Is the employee cooperative, easy to work with? Is the employee's attitude toward patients and fellow employees friendly and cooperative? Where contacts outside the hospital are required in fulfilling job responsibilities, does the employee represent the hospital with confidence and discretion? Does the employee conform to the personal grooming standards?

Evaluate:

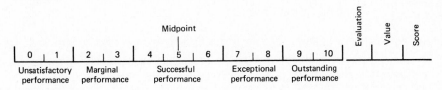

INITIATIVE: Consider how well the employee applies the knowledge of work. Is the employee a self-starter who makes frequent practical

FIGURE 12.3 *(Continued)*

suggestions? Does the employee proceed on assigned work voluntarily and readily accept suggestions? How much does the employee rely on others in getting started on assigned work? How effectively does the employee share acquired skills with others?

Evaluate:

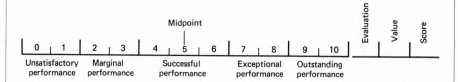

SAFETY: Consider the extent to which the employee is aware of unsafe practices and conditions in the work setting. Is the employee quick to sense possible hazards and then to take the appropriate steps to get them corrected? How careful is the employee insofar as safe work practices are concerned with regard to regular work assignments? Does the employee always follow the established work procedure for assigned tasks?

Evaluate:

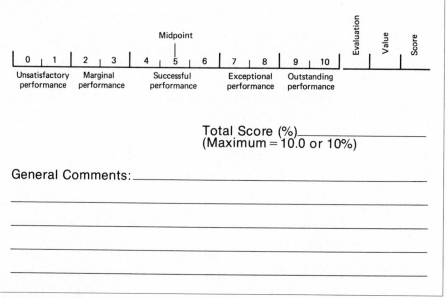

Total Score (%)_____
(Maximum = 10.0 or 10%)

General Comments:_____
_____
_____
_____
_____

FIGURE 12.3　(*Continued*)

PART II

The purpose of this section is to present the employee a well-conceived and workable program for:

1. Optimum application of known and demonstrated strengths and;
2. Study, practice, and/or discipline to develop competency in the areas requiring improvement. Be specific. Formulate benchmarks, attainable objectives so that the employee can recognize accomplishment and be aware of growth.

Knowledge of Work: _____

_____

_____

_____

Quality of Work: _____

_____

_____

_____

_____

Quantity of Work: _____

_____

_____

_____

_____

Dependability: _____

_____

_____

_____

_____

Compatibility: _____

_____

_____

_____

FIGURE 12.3   *(Continued)*

Initiative: _____

Safety: _____

Prepared by _____
               Name   Title   Date

Department head _____
                     Name   Date

FOR EMPLOYEE: My signature on this form indicates that I have reviewed my performance evaluation as presented on this form and a copy has been given to me.

                             For Probationary Rating ONLY
                               Recommended for:

                               ☐ Permanent Status

                               ☐ Extension of Probation

_____
Signature   Date   ☐ Termination

FIGURE 12.3   *(Continued)*

factors attached for use of the rater. Fig. 12.4 shows one of a different format.

One of the original purposes of management by objectives (MBO) was to simplify and overcome the limitations of the more traditional performance appraisal. This approach emphasizes the setting of measurable performance goals that are mutually agreed on by the employee and the immediate supervisor. At stated intervals the employee's progress toward the goals is assessed by the employee and the superior. Participation by employees in the performance appraisal process has resulted in favorable perceptions regarding the performance appraisal interview as well as positive performance outcomes.[5]

Regardless of the rating systems selected, the person making the ratings should be well qualified for the responsibility of evaluating people. Usually the immediate supervisor is in a position to do the best job, since this person can observe activities continuously. However, adequate instructions are needed as to the purpose and values of the program so that follow through with assistance will be provided when needed. Also, a thorough explanation and understanding of the factors to be rated is necessary to avoid misinterpretation of the forms or failure to meet the intended standards. The person who is charged with the responsibility of rating employees must be able to be objective and evaluate individuals in terms of the factors to be rated, should be guided by the pattern of performance instead of isolated happenings, should communicate fairly and accurately what is observed, and should be consistent from one time to the next. These are prime requisites of the rater.

An interview is a vitally important part of the performance appraisal process. The purpose of the interview is to provide information and set goals. It should be scheduled in advance and both employee and supervisor should be prepared. The proper atmosphere for two-way communication must be established. The supervisor should begin with a statement of purpose and then encourage the employee to participate in the dialogue. Total performance, both positive and negative, should be discussed. The evaluation stage of the interview should conclude with a summary and documentation of the interview for the employee's file. In the second stage of the interview, the emphasis should be on setting mutual goals, including personal growth and formulating follow-up procedures.[6] The employee should never be left in doubt of the rating given, or what must be done to change or improve if there is need to do so.

Promotions and Transfers

On the basis of sound ratings by members of staff, the dietitian or foodservice manager is fairly able to predict the probable future development of

Associate Rating Form: Kitchen Worker

1. *Job Skill* (Max. points: 25)

   Consider job performance and skill. Does he keep up with his work and keep his station clean, make all products uniformly; is he waste conscious, economical; does he work quietly and reasonably fast, refrain from visiting with fellow associates while on duty?

Excellent	25
Good	20
Average	15
Fair	10
Poor	5

2. *Cooperation* (Max. points: 25)

   Consider attitude. Does he respond quickly to a call for assistance from a fellow associate? Does he have a spirit of willingness? Is he receptive to change and new ideas? Will he accept new suggestions regarding his work?

Excellent	25
Good	20
Average	15
Fair	10
Poor	5

3. *Sanitation* (Max. points: 10)

   Consider health regulations: "No Smoking—Wash Hands When Leaving Rest Rooms." Does he keep: paper, trash, liquids, vegetable leaves, and other foreign materials off floor, hot foods hot, and other food under refrigeration?

Excellent	10
Good	8
Average	6
Fair	4
Poor	2

4. *Care of Equipment* (Max. points: 10)

   Does he: keep equipment clean and everything returned to proper place, know correct way to operate ovens, steamers, mixers, and other appliances?

Excellent	10
Good	8
Average	6
Fair	4
Poor	2

5. *Safety* (Max. points: 10)

   Does he work safely and is he safety conscious? Does he correct or report all hazards that may cause an accident? Does he know whereabouts of fire extinguisher and how to use it?

Excellent	10
Good	8
Average	6
Fair	4
Poor	2

6. *Appearance* (Max. points: 10)

   Consider personal cleanliness and neatness. Does he seem to enjoy his work? Is he clean of body? Are clothes clean and appropriate?

Excellent	10
Good	8
Average	6
Fair	4
Poor	2

7. *Attendance* (Max. points: 10)

   Consider regular daily attendance and promptness. Does he return from 10 minute breaks and meal periods on time?

Excellent	10
Good	8
Average	6
Fair	4
Poor	2

FIGURE 12.4   An example of a rating form designed for evaluating a kitchen worker. Comparable forms could be made applicable for each classification of worker.

various members of the organization. In the application of a rating scale, one group may stand high. In it will be found the people deserving the stimulus and encouragement of promotion. The term *promotion* commonly implies an increase in responsibility and salary. Sometimes promotion carries only the opportunity for experience in a desired field. It may mean shorter hours and greater assurance of security. Regardless of the nature of the promotion, it is an expression of appreciation of an individual's worth.

Often a worker found unfit for one job may do well in another. The apparent lack of fitness may arise in the supervisory relationship or in contacts with coworkers. Personal prejudice against a particular type of work or physical inability to do the job may be the cause. In some cases a minor shift may enable the worker to become a contented and valuable employee. Transfer of an employee who is not finding satisfaction in the current job to another opening within the organization offering a different challenge or opportunity has salvaged many workers. Different jobs may present wide variation in skill requirements, which makes possible the transfer of workers if necessary. Relative levels of difficulty should be considered in placement and in replacement. Continued training of the employee in this new position is critical to the success of a relocated worker.

Discipline

Discipline is required when other measures have failed to make sure that workers perform according to accepted standards. Leadership must first ensure that work rules are clear, reasonable, fair, reviewed regularly, and consistent with the collective bargaining agreement. Rules must be disseminated to employees orally and posted in a visible location. And they must be enforced promptly, consistently, and without discrimination. Leadership must set a good example by complying with all rules and requirements.[7]

Any disciplinary action must be undertaken with sensitivity and sound judgment. The supervisor should first thoroughly investigate what happened and why. As a general rule, disciplinary action should be taken in private. Personnel policies usually fit the severity of the penalty to the severity of the infraction, with the steps in progressive discipline ranging from an informal talk, oral warning or reprimand, written or official warning, disciplinary layoff, demotion or transfer, to discharge.[8]

As an aid to supervisors, Metzger[9] proposed the "hot stove" analogy to disciplinary action. Experiencing discipline should be like touching a hot stove. The burn gives advance warning, is immediate, consistent, and impersonal. Advance warning—everyone knows what will happen if you touch a hot stove. Employees should know what is expected of them. Immediate—the burn is immediate. Discipline should not be hasty, but should be taken as soon as possible after the infraction. Consistent—the hot stove burns every time. Disciplinary action should be taken every time an infraction occurs. Impersonal—whoever touches the stove is burned. The act not the person should be disciplined. After disciplinary action, the employee should be treated as before.

Dismissals

If employee is terminated without the consent of the employee, the act is termed dismissal. An individual may be discharged because of failure to perform assigned duties, but this should be the final step and should follow counseling, warning, or possibly disciplinary layoff. Each person discharged from a foodservice should be given a terminal or "exit" interview in which strong points are recognized and the reasons for dismissal are dispassionately reviewed. If the situation merits that the employee be recommended for another position, aid should be given in the placement problem. In any event the discharged employee should not leave the service without having had a chance to speak regarding the dismissal and without being made aware, if possible, of the fair deal given by the supervisor.

Opinions differ regarding the discussion of a dismissal with other employees. If there is a possibility that the incident may foster a sense of insecurity among the group, a presentation of the facts, not necessarily full and complete, may be desirable from the standpoint of group morale. Often employees understand far more of such situations than the director believes.

Supervision

Supervision encompasses coordinating and directing the work of employees to accomplish the organization's goals. In small foodservice systems, the total supervisory function may be the responsibility of the dietitian or manager. In larger systems, the supervision of the day-to-day technical operations may be delegated to foodservice supervisors, dietetic technicians, or cook-managers. The dietitian or manager is thus able to concentrate on planning, policy and goal setting, and interdepartment relationships, and on solving overall problems of the department. In a large department, the director, chief dietitian, or other administrator may delegate these management functions in part to other professionally trained staff.

When responsibility and authority are delegated, management must provide guidance so the supervisor understands the limits of authority; that is, what decisions can be made without consultation and what actions can be taken on one's own. Management has a responsibility for training supervisors so they can solve problems and meet emergencies.

The supervisor represents both management and employees. In a foodservice unit, as with industry in general, the supervisor is one of the key persons in the organization. The supervisor is the one to whom the employees look as a representative of management, whereas to management the supervisor represents the working force. Both groups, therefore, are interested in the quality of the supervision as represented by this staff member. The supervisor must be able to: (1) interpret the objectives and policies of the company to the employees in such a way as to encourage their cooperation and elicit their confidence, and (2) inspire and lead employees as evidence through fair and intelligent dealing with them and through the personnel program.

Throughout an employee's term of service from the first days to the last, supervision should play a large part in relating the employee to the task and to coworkers. When the probation period is past and the employee is regarded as a member of the permanent staff, familiar with the task and able in its performance, supervision is still necessary to maintain interest and provide for personal growth. To a large extent, recognition and approbation by superiors remain potent incentives to the average worker. The supervisor must accept the responsibility of finding and using incentives that lead to sound development. Adjustments in work assignments to meet changes in the individual's abilities and interests are wisely made only when supervision is adequate, both in kind and amount.

ROUTINE SUPERVISION   Routine supervision will vary with the situation, but it is, for the most part, a matter of personal contact reinforced through checking by observations, records, and charts. Routine supervision may consist each day of greeting employees by name, checking for cleanliness, appearance, and state of health, checking menus and work schedules, making work assignments, explaining to employees any instruction they seem not to understand, checking continuously for quality and quantity of production and service, inspecting for sanitation of work areas and equipment, and, in general, maintaining good working conditions. The supervision of personnel is too often left to chance or to the "free time" that never seems a part of the foodservice manager's busy day. To avoid the hit-and-miss contact with employees, the wise supervisor sets aside a certain time each day for checking on the work in progress and for stimulating interest and cooperation in the individual and in the group. Schedules are needed for checking daily, weekly, and periodic jobs. Checking at the end of the day to see that the work as scheduled has been carried out completes the "routine" supervision.

Decision Making

Much of the supervisor's time is spent in making decisions and solving problems. Decision making can be thought of as the generic process, whereas problem solving is one type of decision making that applies to a specific situation.

The ability to make decisions in a timely and logical manner is an important skill for supervisors to possess. Better decisions are likely to be made when a number of steps are followed in the proper sequence. These are: (1) define the problem—nothing is as useless as the right answer to the wrong question, (2) analyze the problem, (3) develop many alternatives—brainstorm and then think them through considering the consequences of each, (4) choose the alternative with the most positive consequences and the least negative consequences, and (5) follow up and appraise the decision.

Handling Grievances

The wise supervisor gives active supervision; that is, the wise supervisor does not sit at a desk waiting for employees to come with problems. The wise supervisor foresees and is prepared to meet possible difficulties instead of merely waiting for something unpleasant to happen. Grievances are not always expressed in verbal or written form. Supervisors should be alert for symptoms of unexpressed dissatisfaction such as excessive absenteeism, decline in quantity or quality of work, change in attitude, or indifference.

Many grievances can be settled by the supervisor and employee on an informal basis. If the employees are unionized, the contract includes formal grievance procedures, which usually include presentation of the grievance in writing (see Fig. 12.5) and an attempt to settle the dispute at the first-line supervisory level. If this is not possible, the grievance moves through higher levels of authority until settled.

Staff Conferences

Regular staff conferences, department meetings, and the use of rating scales are all valuable in personnel direction. Continued effort to relate workers to their tasks and to the organization as a whole is often expressed in conferences scheduled at regular intervals by the supervisor. At these conferences, points of general interest are presented and suggestions for improvement of the foodservice are exchanged. Knotty problems, such as waste, breakage, and low production, that have not been mastered by direct supervisory approach may yield to solution as the interest and awareness of the whole group is focused on them. Never should a staff conference be used for disciplinary action for certain members of the group. As previously stated, the adult worker, like the schoolchild, rarely benefits from public reprimand and unkind ridicule.

In addition to group contact, time should be taken by the supervisor for

LINCOLN GENERAL HOSPITAL
LINCOLN, NEBRASKA
GRIEVANCE CONTROL FORM

1. _____
　　　　(Name)　　　　　　(Position Title)　　　　(Dept.)　　　　(Employment Date)

　　_____　　　　_____
　　　　　(Supervisor)　　　　　　　　　　　　　　　　(Department Head)

2. *Nature of Dissatisfaction:* (Be specific in writing up the dissatisfaction. Be sure to state who is involved, what happened, where did it occur, what were the circumstances, how did it happen, and what is the solution being sought.) _____

　　_____

　　_____

　　_____

3. *The Final Settlement Was:* (Resolution at what step; what was the recommended solution and all other pertinent information significant to the solution.) _____

　　_____

　　_____

　　_____

4. *Action Taken:*

*Work Days	Step	Date	Action Taken By:	Schedules Met (Yes/No)	**Work Days	Resolved (Yes/No)
2	I	_____	_____ (Supervisor, Verbal)	_____	2	_____
2	II	_____	_____ (Department Head, Verbal)	_____	2	_____
5	III	_____	_____ (Grievance Committee, Written)	_____	2	_____
4	IV	_____	_____ (Administrator, Written)	_____	2	_____

Comments: (Regarding any exceptions made at any step) _____

_____

_____

_____

Any of the time limits specified in the procedure may be extended by mutual agreement of the parties involved.

**In the event that the employee fails to appeal the decision to the next step in the grievance procedure within two (2) working days, the employee will be deemed to have accepted the decision and waived the right to further appeal.*

FIGURE 12.5　Form for written record of a grievance and action taken.　*Courtesy, Lincoln General Hospital, Lincoln, Nebraska.*

a talk with each individual worker at least once a week. All employees want to feel that someone is interested in them as an individual and recognizes their present and potential worth to the organization.

Labor Policies and Legislation

Policies are guides for future action. They should be broad enough to allow some variation in management decisions at all levels, yet offer guidelines for consistency in interpretation and commit personnel to certain predictable action. Policies should not be confused with directives or rules. Policies are adopted to provide meaning or understanding related to a course of action; directives and rules are aimed at compliance.

An important aspect of personnel management is the labor policies accepted and put in force. This is true regardless of the size of the organization. There is an old saying that when two men (or women) meet, there is a social problem; when one undertakes a task at the other's behest, there is a labor problem; and when wages are paid for this labor, there is an economic problem. The policies controlling the approach to these problems have slowly developed as civilization has grown and as the number of workers has increased. They have been formed, reformed, and revised due, particularly in recent years, to legislation enacted at federal, state, and local levels.

Policies relating to personnel are known as labor policies. Procurement policies may be related to preferred sources to be used for obtaining applicants, instruments such as tests to be used in selection, or a ratio of employees, such as women to men or minority to major racial groups to be hired. Policies for development of personnel may concern the type of training programs the company will offer, whether or not fees or tuition for continuing education will be paid, time to be allowed from work for personnel to attend classes or meetings, and the bases for promotions and transfers.

Those policies regarding compensation have to do with wages scales to be followed, vacation, sick leave, and holiday time pay to be given, bonus or profit-sharing plans to be offered, and group insurance or other benefits available to the personnel.

Integration polices refer to a recognition or not of labor unions, the way that grievances and appeals will be handled, or the degree of employee participation to be permitted in decision making.

Maintenance policies are about the services to be provided for employees' physical, mental, and emotional health. They may be related to safety measures, compensation for accidents, retirement systems, recreational programs, or other services, all of which are a part of the institutional plan.

Once policies have been developed and accepted, they should be written. The wise employer of today makes available to every worker a copy of the labor-management policies presented in a company handbook. This publication may be an impressive volume of many pages and elaborate illustrations or a few mimeographed sheets, but whatever its format, the contents should include information that the worker wants to know about the organization and that the employer wants him or her to know. Employees are not interested in cooperating as members of the team without understanding the policies, especially as these affect them. They want to know what is expected of them and to be kept informed of their accomplishments, the basis for promotion, for wage increases, fringe benefits, opportunities for steady work, and the possibilities of any seasonal layoffs.

From the standpoint of the employee, labor policies should be explicit in their provisions for a fair rate of pay, for promotions and transfers, for stabilization of employment, and for ways of keeping jobs interesting so that life will not become mere dull routine. They should offer provisions for fair disciplinary action among employees, recognition of industrial health hazards and provisions for their control, participation in the formulation of future plans and policies of the company, usually expressed by demands for collective bargaining, and certain fringe benefits.

Managers wish to have employees informed of policies about the goals and objectives for which the organization is in business, the products and services offered, the effect of high productivity as a benefit to both the employee and the company, cost-expenditure ratios and how they affect profits and resulting benefits, and the relationships desired with the public and with other departments of the organization.

There is general agreement on the list of topics that the employer has found must be covered in labor policies conducive to productive management and those desired by employees as vital to satisfactory working conditions. The ones cited by both—wages and income maintenance, hours of work, schedules and overtime provisions, security in employment including transfers and promotions, safe and otherwise satisfactory working environment, insurance, retirement, or pension plans, equal employment opportunities, and fair employment practices and civil rights—may be regarded as the major issues in labor policies for most foodservice operations.

These topics can be grouped under four headings: wages and income maintenance, hours and schedules of work, security in employment, and employee services and benefits. Major federal legislation applicable to employment in the private sector is included as appropriate under each of the following discussions.

WAGES AND INCOME MAINTENANCE   From the point of view of the worker, the most important characteristic of the wage, the take-home pay received for labor performed, is its purchasing power. This represents the measure of the wants that the worker is able to satisfy and largely determines the adequacy of his or her standard of living, sense of financial security, and identification of self as a worthy and responsible member of the community. In the past, foodservices, like other service organizations, have tended to offer an annual wage rate below that necessary for a fair standard of living. This situation has improved as desirable policies on wages have been adopted and as state and federal laws have been enacted.

The formulation of satisfactory policies regarding wages and other income maintenance is contingent on many factors, among them: (1) the desire and intent of the company to pay fair wages to all employees and at the same time to maintain just control over labor costs, (2) recognition of the relationship between the duties and responsibilities of various jobs within the organization and the wages paid, and (3) acknowledgment of individual differences in experience, ability, and willingness to take responsibility. Management has the obligation to reflect such differences in the wage scale established for a particular job and to communicate freely with the workers on these points. Policies based on such considerations will lead to a systematic classification of jobs and wages that could be developed jointly by the employer and the employees. It would then be possible to express the value or worth of each job in terms of wages.

The application of the wage policy to kitchen and dining room personnel would lead to certain groupings, such as:

1. Busers, pot and pan washers, dishwashers
2. Workers in preliminary or prepreparation
3. Foodservice groups, including counter workers and waiters or waitresses
4. Cook's assistants and second cooks; dining room host or hostess, cashiers
5. Cooks, including meat, vegetable, salad, and pastry cooks
6. Supervisors on the nonprofessional level

A wage differential will exist between groups. Civil service and labor unions as well as many other organizations have established steps within each wage level or grade so that employees who merit wage increases may be given such recognitions for superior service, although not qualified for advancement to a higher grade or job category.

The *Fair Labor Standards Act* of 1938, also known as the Federal Wage and Hour Law, was first enacted to help eliminate poverty, to create purchasing power, and to establish a wage floor that would help prevent another depression. The minimum wage set at that time was $.40 per hour! Gradually over the years, the base was increased. The Act was amended in 1966, and, under new provisions, most foodservice employees were included for the first time. The minimum wage that year was $1.60, and the law included provisions for gradual increases that would continue as cost of living increased. The Act applies equally to all covered workers regardless of sex, number of employees, and whether they are full- or part-time workers.

The *Equal Pay Act*, a 1963 amendment to the Fair Labor Standards Act, prohibits employees from discriminating on the basis of sex in the payment of wages for equal work for employees covered by the act. It requires employers to pay equal wages to men and women in their employ doing equal work on jobs requiring equal skill, effort, and responsibility that are performed under similar working conditions.

Another provision of the Fair Labor Standards Act of special interest to commercial foodservice managers relates to wages for tipped employees. Tips received by an employee may be considered by the employer as part of the wages of the employee, but cannot exceed 50 per cent of the applicable minimum rate. A "tipped" employee is a worker engaged in an occupation in which the worker customarily and regularly receives more than $20 a month in tips.

Many foodservice operations employ student workers; this is especially true in colleges and universities, schools, retirement homes, and other homes for congregate living. Minimum wage laws adopted by various states may make provision for compensation at an adjusted rate below the federal standard. Usually students who work less than 20 hours per week are not affected by provisions of such laws.

Unless specifically exempt by this law, all employees must be paid at least one and one half times the employee's regular rate of pay for all hours worked in excess of 40 hours in a work week of 7 days. Extra pay is not required for Saturday, Sunday, holiday, or vacation work.

All foodservice managers should become familiar with the state and federal laws regulating minimum wages for their various classifications of employees. Information may be obtained from the nearest office of the Wage and Hour Division of the U.S. Department of Labor.

Unemployment compensation is another piece of federal legislation that, in addition to regular pay for work on the job, partially assures income maintenance. This nationwide system of insurance to protect wage earners and their families against loss of income because of unemployment was first established under the Social Security Act of 1935. The purpose of this insurance is to provide workers with a weekly income to tide them over periods of unemployment between jobs. Persons covered must have been employed for a specific period of time on a job covered by the law, who are able and willing to work, and who are unemployed through no fault of their own.

Unemployment insurance is a joint federal-state program, operated by the states with the assistance of the U.S. Department of Labor. Each state has its own specific requirements and benefits. Basically, employers pay a tax based on their payrolls. Benefits to unemployed workers are paid out of the fund built up from these taxes. In most states firms employing three or four or more workers during 20 weeks in the year must participate. Each state law specifies conditions under which workers may receive benefits, the amount they receive, and the number of weeks they may draw benefits. In most states, the employer alone contributes to this fund; in only a few do employees make payment to it. Thus, unemployment compensation is an added payroll cost for many foodservice managers and an added benefit to the employees.

HOURS AND SCHEDULES OF WORK   The 40-hour work week established under the Minimum Wage and Hour Law is generally in use throughout the United States. Some organizations have adopted a 37½ or a 35-hour week and some, such as nursing and rest homes, which are exempt under this legislation, may have a 48-hour week. Time worked beyond this and within a 7-day or a 14-day period as specified under the law requires extra compensation, as previously noted.

The schedule of specific hours of the day when each employee is to be on duty should be carefully considered by all foodservice managers. As discussed, many different factors enter into the planning of satisfactory schedules. Employers have a responsibility for scheduling their employees so that their time at work will be as needed and will be used to best advantage to help control labor costs. Split shifts are almost a thing of the past; straight shifts are usually preferred. An 8-hour day, 5 days a week is common practice also. However, some organizations have experimented with variations, notably a 10-hour day and 4-day week to allow a 3-day off-duty period for the employees and a 12-hour day, 3-day week. Most foodservice organizations have not found this scheduling practical because of the nature of the work to be done.

In addition to the needs of the employer and the organization, consideration is given to the employee and to stipulations in union contracts, if in effect, when planning scheduled time on and off duty for each member of the staff. Most state labor laws require break times for meals and between meal rest periods for employees, which is a further consideration when planning schedules to cover work that must be done. Familiarity with these regulations is a necessity for the manager.

SECURITY IN EMPLOYMENT   One of the major concerns of the working world in recent years is equal opportunity for employment for all those who wish employment and are qualified. Equal employment opportunity has been the topic of much legislation, beginning with the consideration of civil rights.

The *Civil Rights Act of 1964* stipulates that "No person in the United States shall, on ground of race, color, or national origin be excluded from participating in, be denied the benefits of, or be subjected to any program or activity receiving Federal Financial assistance." Title VII under this act extended the provision to include prohibition of discrimination "by employers, employment agencies and labor unions."

Thus, employees who are in covered positions are entitled to be free of unlawful discrimination with regard to recruitment, classified advertising, job classification, hire, utilization of physical facilities, transfer, promotion, discharge wages and salaries, seniority lines, testing, insurance coverage, pension and retirement benefits, referral to jobs, union membership, and the like. All potential employees have equal opportunity, regardless of background.

The *Age Discrimination in Employment Act of 1967* promotes the employment of the older worker, based on ability instead of age. It prohibits arbitrary age discrimination in employment and helps employers and employees find ways to meet problems arising from the impact of age on employment. The act protects most individuals who are at least 40 but less than 65 years of age from "discrimination in employment based on age in matters of hiring, discharge compensation or other terms, conditions, or privileges of employment."

Legislation has been effected in many states and cities to prohibit discriminatory employment practices against persons because of their race, color, religion, national origin, or ancestry. These are designated as fair employment practice laws and have as their intent in barring of undemocratic practices in American industry. A Public Accommodations law, when in effect, requires that service be given in an equal manner to anyone.

As may be seen, our economic society is characterized by many areas of friction in industry. Students of labor are quite generally agreed that in no area is there an economic problem more important to human beings than security of job tenure, which means assurance of the satisfaction of physical needs, a place in the esteem and affection of others, an opportunity for self-expression, and a chance to enjoy leisure. The three risks that more than any others tend to make the position of most wage earners in industry insecure are unemployment, physical impairment, and old age. The definition for unemployment used by the Bureau of Census in making its enumeration is: "Unemployment may be described as involuntary idleness on the part of those who have lost their latest jobs, are able to work, and are looking for work." This definition is obviously narrow, because it excludes all those persons who are unwilling to work, are unemployable because of physical or mental defects, or are temporarily idle for seasonal causes. However, the definition covers the group whose unemployment usually arises from conditions inherent in the organization and management of industry.

Problems of tenure must concern all persons charged with the direction of the foodservice industry. Fortunately, foodservices on the whole lend themselves to steady employment, and many managers take pride in the long tenure of large numbers of their workers. Sometimes, however, the workers' acceptance of tenure as a matter of course brings definite problems such as laxity and inefficiency in the performance of assigned tasks and lack of interest in improved practices. Standards of performance in some instances have been lowered as security of employment has been assured. Personnel policies should cover such contingencies.

EMPLOYEE SERVICES AND BENEFITS   Benefits that employees receive often represent 15 to 25 per cent of wages earned. Some of these are so taken for granted that they are scarcely realized or appreciated by those who receive them. Yet, if such services were not provided, the lack would be acutely noticed. Managers recognize the humanistic desirability of making available certain programs and services in addition to a fair wage for their employees' comfort and well-being. A less altruistic point of view may cause managers to offer those same benefits in order to compete in the job market and attract desirable applicants.

Extra benefits, sometimes called "fringe" benefits, fall into three general groups: health and safety, economic, and convenience and comfort. The first *health and safety,* is an important basic factor in all personnel problems. This matter affects social and economic life, being of interest not only to the employee but to the employer and the public as well. Time lost because of illness and accidents is expensive for both management and labor, results in lowered production and increased losses for the employer, and directly affects the income of the employee. Maintaining the good physical condition of employees is economically desirable as well as necessary for achievement of the many goals of the department. Also, dietitians and managers of any foodservice recognize that the health of the worker may affect the health of the public through both direct and indirect contact. Additional discussions regarding the importance of good health for the foodservice employee are given in Chapters 5 and 8.

Safe working conditions are of first importance to employer and employee alike. A foodservice does not present the identical hazards found in any other industry, but duplicates some of those found in several. Falls, burns, shocks, and cuts are possible, as they are in any other place where mechanical equipment is used. It is the responsibility of the manager to see that safeguards are maintained, that the equipment is kept in safe condition, and that all working conditions are safe and clean.

The *Occupational Safety and Health Act* (OSHA) of 1970 has forced managers to look critically at working conditions and to bring any that are undesirable up to a standard demanded by law. Every employer covered by the law is required to furnish employment and places of employment that are free from recognized hazards that are causing or are likely to cause death or serious physical harm, and must comply with all safety regulations promulgated by the Secretary of Labor in accordance with the provisions of the act.

Another benefit for employees is provided for in the *Workmen's Compensation Insurance* program. This legislation is administered by the states, and the liability insurance premiums are paid for by employers. Workmen's compensation laws are based on the theory that the cost of accidents should be a part of production costs, the same as wages, taxes, insurance, and raw materials.

This insurance covers employers' liability for the costs of any accident incurred by an employee on or in connection with the job. The workers must show that they were injured on the job and the extent of their injuries. Compensation laws state the specific amount of payment allowed for each type of injury in addition to hospital, surgical, and, in case of death, funeral expenses. All foodservice directors will need to determine, through their state department of labor, who can be covered by Workmen's Compensation, the methods of payment, and the amount of benefits to which the worker is entitled.

Health and accident insurance plans provide some assistance to employees who may become ill or who are injured off the job. Fear of injury or illness is the cause of much worry, even when an insurance plan is available to employees. Without it, many workers would be in financial straits, trying to pay medical and hospital bills on their own.

Many forms of health and accident insurance are available for groups. In some cases the company alone pays for it for the employees; in others it is jointly borne by the company and those who participate in it. Through labor union efforts and the efforts of concerned managers, more and more health services are being made available to employees, many at employer expense. Some of these include dental care, mental health counseling, vision care, and prescription drugs.

The extent to which foodservices provide these benefits to employees usually depends on the size of the organization and the facilities it has available, for example, the emergency room of a hospital, and the concern of those at the decision-making level.

The second group of employee services and benefits are those labeled *economic*. Most of the programs discussed so far provide some economic benefit to workers, even if indirectly. All insurance plans undoubtedly could be put under this classification instead of putting some under health and safety. However, benefits to be discussed in this economic group have a direct monetary value in returns to the employee; the employer carries the cost of some, and others are shared by the employer.

Social Security benefits are provided by the *Social Security Act,* a nationwide program of insurance to protect wage earners and their families against loss of income due to old age, disability, and death. A designated percentage of the salary of each employed person must be withheld from his or her wages and the same amount from the business added to the Social Security Fund, or to a comparable retirement-system fund if a nonprofit type of organization is involved. Provisions and benefits of Social Security change from time to time, so details soon become outdated. Managers must keep in touch with their local Social Security office to be informed of current changes.

Other economic benefits offered by some organizations to their employees may include group life insurance programs, profit-sharing plans, and pensions or retirement plans. All of these add to the economic security of those who continue in the service of a particular organization long enough to build a fund that is significant for them after regular employment ceases, either because of retirement or death. Vacations, holidays, and sick leave, all with pay, are other forms of fringe benefits for personnel. Properly administered, they are of advantage to the organization as well.

Employee convenience and comfort benefits make up the third group of fringe benefits. Services provided for the comfort or convenience of employees comprise a long list and include, among others: adequate rest and locker rooms, meal service available to employees often at reduced or at-cost levels, free medical service on an emergency basis, credit unions, and recreational facilities. Educational tuition or fees for personnel to attend workshops or classes for self-development and skill development are also among these. Various foodservices participate in many of these or in different ones for their employees. In turn, these benefits help in building a loyal, contented working group with high morale.

Labor legislation, as discussed, is directed toward establishing socially desirable channels of behavior to be observed by labor and management. Whatever the purpose of labor legislation, the federal, state, and local laws have been the chief means by which an enlightened public conscience has expressed its concern with the health, safety, and general well-being of the worker on the job. The method of expressing this interest differs among the states. Full information on each specific situation is important because requirements for various industries may differ widely. For the most part, foodservices are controlled through state laws. They become subject to federal laws when they engage in interstate commerce or under conditions just discussed. Local laws may regulate the sanitation standards, but they seldom take labor policies under their scrutiny.

Although many of the labor laws enacted are directed toward the protection of specific groups, the regulations applicable to all workers are well established. Familiarity with federal, state, and local laws applying to foodservice employees is obligatory for every foodservice administrator and manager. Only then can labor policies be of benefit to both the worker and his or her organization and be put into action for implementation.

Labor-Management Relations

Dietitians and foodservice managers are concerned with problems arising from directing employees' activities, that is, in handling the people who must translate the policies, procedures, and plans into action. When groups of people work together, there is always potential for conflict. Some people must manage and some must carry out the technical operations. Everyone wants more of whatever will improve his or her position. The closer the relationship between the employee and manager, with open and free discussion on both sides, the less danger there is for grievances to arise.

Many foodservices are so small that the relationship between employer and employee is immediate and direct. Under such circumstances discussion of points of mutual concern is possible right in the place of work. Direct face-to-face contact tends to develop a sense of real association and mutual interest. Employees with a somewhat complete picture of a relatively small business may see their job in relation to the whole. Many services, on the other hand, are so large that there is limited personal contact between employer and employee. Workers may feel there is little chance for the individual to be recognized as an important person in the organization. Also, they may not have an overall view of the business that would make possible self-evaluation of their own jobs in terms of the whole. Workers engaged in a limited phase of total large-scale production may find that they lack the direct contact that tends to humanize employer-employee relationships in a small foodservice.

Legislation

Managers who are not attuned to these concerns of employees, who do not recognize that a small complaint or conflict that may arise is probably a symptom of a deeper problem and fail to investigate and correct the situation, are opening the door for labor unions to come in to represent the employees better.

Over the years much legislation has been enacted to attempt to balance the power between labor and management. The *National Labor Relations Act* of 1935 was pro-labor in its intent; workers in many situations had been exploited by management during depression years just preceding passage of the bill. Terms of the act regulate unfair management practices, and prohibit management from interference with their employees joining a union and from discrimination against those who do join.

The *Taft-Hartley Labor-Management Relations Act* in 1947 was pro-management, to offset the power and unfair practices that labor unions seemed to have acquired since 1935. Among other things, it prevents unions from coercing employees to join, outlaws the "closed shop," and makes it illegal for unions to refuse to join in collective bargaining. The law created the National Labor Relations Board (NLRB) to administer the provisions of the act, to remedy unfair labor practices whether by labor organizations or employers, and to conduct secret ballot elections in which employees decide whether unions will represent them in collective bargaining.

Further legislation in 1959 was the *Labor-Management Disclosure Act*, which is in the interests of both labor and management, but is especially pro-individual labor union member. It contains a bill of rights for union members and requires disclosure of union trusteeship practices through a specified reporting system.

Employees of hospitals operated entirely on a nonprofit basis were exempt from the original National Labor Relations Act. However, the amendment to the NRLA brought nonprofit hospitals under the provisions of the act. In such situations dietitians may be called on to defend their positions as "management" instead of as "labor."

There are numerous reasons for employers to become the target of union organizing attempts or for employees to turn to a union. Chief among these reasons are poorly developed or administered personnel policies and practices, or a breakdown in some facet of employer-employee relations. A number of steps should be taken by managers long before organizational attempts begin. Most important among them is a review of personnel policies and employee relations, making every effort to maintain good personnel practices, put policies into writing, and communicate them to employees with frequent reviews and discussions. What the employee, the manager, the company, and the union can and cannot do during a union organizing drive is outlined by Metzger.[9]

The impact of unionization on foodservices may be great for those who are naive in the ways of collective bargaining. Legal counsel to assist in negotiating a fair, workable contract for both labor and management is to be encouraged. If unionization is to become a reality, it is important to create a favorable climate for cooperation, to make sure that the negotiator understands the economic as well as the administrative problems of a foodservice operation, such as scheduling required to cover meal hours, the services necessary, especially to patients in health care facilities, the equipment to be used, and the prices charged in relation to the labor costs.

Certain rights of management may be lost when unionization takes place, since some of the authority but little of the responsibility will be shared with the union. Some of the freedoms lost are the right to hire, discharge, change work assignments and time schedules, set wages and fringe benefits, change policies without appeal, discipline workers without being subject to appeal to the union, and receive and act on grievances directly. The loss of the right to use volunteer workers in the department may also be realized.

It is imperative, therefore, that the collective bargaining agreement contain a management rights clause. "There are two major categories of management rights clauses. One is a brief, general clause not dealing with specific rights, but with the principle of management rights in general. The other is a detailed clause, which clearly lists areas of authority which are reserved to the management."[10]

Certain cost increases will be noted also: for time loss from the job by the person selected to be the union steward, and the cost of management support to the union based on a given sum per member per month in contributions.

The nature of labor organizations and the method they use differ according to the understanding and goals of the leaders and members, their convictions as to remedies needed, and by legal and other forms of social control. Ordinarily, management and organized labor have different approaches to solving their problems. This often leads to long hours of negotiations before a satisfactory mutual agreement can be reached. It is important that each group try to see the other's viewpoint with fairness and with an honest belief in the good faith of the other.

Notes

1. Levering, R., Moskowitz, M., and Katz, M.: The 100 Best Companies to Work for in America. Reading, MA: Addison-Wesley Publishing Co., 1984.
2. Smith, R. E.: Employee orientation. Pers. J. 63:46 (Dec.), 1984.
3. Haig, C.: A line manager's guide to training. Pers. J. 63:42 (Oct.), 1984.
4. Puckett, R. P.: Training—A how-to-do-it. *In* Rose, J. C.: Handbook for Healthcare Food Service Management. Rockville, MD: Aspen Systems Corp., 1982.
5. Odiorne, G. S.: MBO II. Belmont, CA: Fearon Pitman Publishers, Inc., 1979.
6. Baker, H. K. and Morgan, P. I.: Two goals in every performance appraisal. Pers. J. 63:74(Sept.), 1984.
7. McGregor, D.: The Human Side of Enterprise. New York: McGraw-Hill Book Co., 1985.

8. U.S. Department of Labor: Federal Labor Laws and Programs. Bulletin 262. Washington, DC: Employment Standards Administration, Division of Employment Standards, 1971.

9. Metzger, N.: The Health Care Supervisor's Handbook, 2nd ed. Rockville, MD: Aspen Systems Corp., 1982.

10. Metzger, N. and Pointer, D. D.: Labor-Management Relations in the Health Service Industry. Washington, DC: Science Health Publications, Inc., 1972.

Supplementary References

ANON: A checklist of qualities that make a good boss. Nation's Business 72:100(Nov.), 1984.

CAMERON, D.: The when, why and how of discipline. Pers. J. 63:37(July), 1984.

CARROLL, S. J. AND SCHNEIER, C. E.: Performance Appraisal and Review Systems. Glenview, IL: Scott, Foresman and Co., 1982.

CARROLL, S. J. AND TOSI, H. L.: Organizational Behavior. Chicago: St. Clair Press, 1977.

CHARNOV, B. H.: Management Report: Appraising Employee Performance. NY: Caddylak Publishing, 1985.

DAVID, H.: Helping cast-off managers. Nation's Business 72:51(Aug.), 1984.

FRENCH, W. L.: The Personnel Management Process, 5th ed. Boston: Houghton Mifflin, 1982.

FRENCH, W. L., KAST, F. E., AND ROSENZWEIG, J. E.: Understanding Human Behavior in Organizations. New York: Harper & Row, 1985.

HARRIS, P. R.: Management in Transition. San Francisco: Jossey-Bass, Inc., 1985.

HERSEY, P. AND BLANCHARD, K.: Management of Organization Behavior, 4th ed. Englewood Cliffs, NJ: Prentice-Hall, Inc., 1982.

HESHIZER, B. P. AND GRAHAM, H.: Discipline in the nonunion company: Protecting employer and employee rights. Pers. 59:71(Mar/Apr), 1982.

HUFFMIRE, D. W.: Learning to share the load. Nation's Business. 72:51(Aug.), 1984.

LeBOEUF, M.: The Greatest Management Principle in the World. New York: G. P. Putnam's Sons, 1985.

MOWDAY, R. T.: Strategies for adapting to high rates of employee turnover. Human Resource Mgmt. 23:365(Winter), 1984.

MUNN, JR., H. E. AND METZGER, N.: Effective Communication in Health Care. Rockville, MS: Aspen Systems Corp., 1981.

MYERS, M. D.: Every Employee a Manager, 2nd ed. New York: McGraw Hill Book Co., 1981.

ODIORNE, G. S.: Strategic Management of Human Resources. San Francisco: Jossey-Bass, Inc., 1984.

PERSSON, L. N.: The Handbook of Job Evaluations and Job Pricing. Washington, DC: Bureau of Law and Business, Inc., 1982.

ROSE, J. C.: Handbook for Healthcare Food Service Management. Rockville, MD: Aspen Systems Corp., 1982.

SILVERMAN, S. B. AND WEXLEY, K. N.: Reaction of employees to performance appraisal interviews as a function of their participation in rating scale development. Pers. Psych. 37:703(Winter), 1984.

STRAUSS, G. AND SAYLES, L. R.: Behavioral Strategies for Managers. Englewood Cliffs, NJ: Prentice-Hall, Inc., 1980.

U.S. Department of Labor, Manpower Administration. Handbook for Analyzing Jobs. Washington, DC: U.S. GPO, 1972.

WITZY, H. K.: The Labor-Management Relations Handbook. Boston: Cahners Books, 1975.

YODER, D. AND HENEMAN, H. G., JR., EDS: ASPA Handbook of Personnel and Industrial Relations. Washington, DC: Bureau of National Affairs, Inc., 1979.

CHAPTER 13

Administrative Leadership

Introduction

As administrative leaders, those individuals who assume the management of foodservice organizations will be successful to the degree that they are willing to assume responsibility and are able to maintain good human relations. Goals and objectives of the department cannot be attained by the administrator alone; working satisfactorily through other people constitutes the major part of the job.

Most people would assume that without administrative leadership no organization could achieve its goals and plans. This assumption is generally valid, but what is meant by administrative "leadership"? In this chapter the difference between leadership and management is discussed, and the characteristics displayed by managers and leaders in administrative positions are compared.

The topic of leadership effectiveness is of special interest. An historical view of leadership is presented tracing the evolution of effective leadership theories from the era of scientific management to the present-day systems concept and contingency approach. The major contributions of each period are summarized.

Communication is a key part of effective leadership. Some of the barriers to successful communication are described as well as some techniques to improve in this area.

Although profit and productivity are still major goals of administrative leadership, social and professional responsibility have assumed equal importance. This chapter concludes with a discussion of the social and professional responsibilities required by administrative leaders in today's foodservice industry.

Administrative Leadership

Leadership, like the concept of management, means different things to different people—ranging from being the first to initiate a change to inspiring bravery on the battlefield. This fact has caused many to use other, more definitive terms, such as activating or influencing. At times, leadership and management have been used synonymously. However, leadership is essentially the business or activity of trying to *influence* people to strive willingly to attain the goals and plans of the organization. Management, on the other hand, is the function of running an organization from a conceptual or policy standpoint. Leadership may then be defined as working with people to get them willingly to produce the results the leader wants or needs to accomplish.[1]

Abraham Zaleznik,[2] a professor of social psychology of management, writes that managers and leaders are very different kinds of people who differ in motivation, personal history, and how they think and act. Managership and leadership require different responses to different demands, and there are situations when each is required. In order to see how the roles of leaders and managers differ, some of the characteristics of each are tabulated in Fig. 13.1.

Koontz and O'Donnell suggest that subordinates will respond to authority alone to do the bare minimum to maintain their jobs. But "to raise effort toward total capability, the manager must induce devoted response on the part of subordinates by exercising leadership."[3]

Leadership has been viewed as a special form of power involving relationships with people. These relationships are developed when leaders successfully fuse organizational and personal needs in a way that allows people and organizations to reach levels of mutual achievement and satisfaction. This can be an exceedingly difficult task. Each employee is different with different motivations, ambitions, interests, and personalities. As a result, each must be treated differently. Work situations differ. How managers can handle these divergent factors effectively has been the subject of study for many years, and such research, both past and present, can be used to improve managerial leadership effectiveness.

The Traditional Leadership Role

SCIENTIFIC MANAGEMENT   The era of "scientific management" was founded on the belief that the main common interest of both the organization and the employee was money, and only money. The manager's role consisted of

Manager	Leader
How They View Themselves:	
Managers have a strong sense of belonging to their organizations.	Leaders see themselves as separate from their organizations and the people of their organizations.
Managers see themselves as protectors of existing order with which they identify.	Leaders have strong personal mastery which impels them to struggle for change in existing order.
How They View Their Function:	
Managers work through other people within established organizational policies and practice to reach an organizational goal. They limit their choices to pre-established organizational goals, policies, and practices. Managers are concerned with process.	Leaders question established procedure and create new concepts. They inspire people to look at options. They are concerned with results.
Personality:	
Managers have a strong instinct for survival.	Leaders seek out risks, especially where rewards seem high.
Managers can tolerate mundane, practical work.	Leaders dislike mundane tasks.
Relationships:	
Managers relate to people according to their role, that is, boss, employee, peer, and so forth.	Leaders relate to people in an intuitive and empathetic way.
Primary Concern:	
Managers are concerned with achievement of organizational goals.	Leaders are concerned with achievement of personal goals.
Place in Organization:	
Managers are supervisors, department heads, administrators. They are usually considered higher echelon.	Leaders may be found at any level in the plan of organization from technician to highest echelon.
Power:	
Managers derive power from their positions.	Leaders derive power through personal relationships.

Goals:	
Managers are concerned with pre-established, organizational goals. Their personal and subgoals arise out of necessity to conform to organizational structure, rather than a desire to change.	Leaders are concerned with personal goals. They are not comfortable with the status quo of established organizational goals and policies. They enjoy innovating.

FIGURE 13.1   Some characteristics of managers and leaders.   *Tamel, Mary E. and Reynolds, Helen:* Executive Leadership. *Englewood Cliffs, NJ: Prentice-Hall, Inc., 1981, p. 59. Used with permission.*

issuing orders, handing out rewards, meting out punishment. The founders of the scientific management theory, such as Frederick W. Taylor and Frank and Lillian Gilbreth, were primarily concerned with the best method and "right wage" for doing the job. The employee was viewed as a machine or tool. This type of thinking met the needs of the day. But times change. The practices of the scientific management movement began to be questioned in the late 1920s.

HUMAN RELATIONS APPROACH   The turning point came as a result of the Hawthorne studies. Western Electric Company conducted some experiments at their Hawthorne plant outside Chicago to determine the relationship between physical working environment and productivity. Lighting was one variable tested. Researchers were surprised to find that no matter how they varied the intensity of the lighting, productivity increased. They concluded that the level of performance had nothing to do with the lighting intensity but rather was a result of the interest shown in the worker as a person rather than as a machine. The "human relations" era was born. Human relationists such as Mayo, Maslow, Roethlisberger, and Dickson brought a more tolerant approach to the supervision of people—consideration of the individual and an understanding of why people work. The theory was good. The implementation, in many cases, was poor.

Newer Approaches to Leadership

THEORY X AND Y   The human relations movement began to lose favor in the early 1950s. McGregor[4] introduced his Theory X and Theory Y analysis of leadership strategies, suggesting that the basic attitude of a manager toward employees has an impact on job performance. He divided these supervisory attitudes into two categories—"Theory X" and "Theory Y." Theory X atti-

Theory X: The Traditional View of Direction and Control

Assumptions:

1. The average human being has an inherent dislike of work and will avoid it if possible.
2. Because of this human characteristic of dislike of work, most people must be coerced, controlled, directed, threatened with punishment to get them to put forth adequate effort toward the achievement of organizational objectives.
3. The average human being prefers to be directed, wishes to avoid responsibility, has relatively little ambition, wants security above all.

Theory Y: A New Theory of Direction and Control

Assumptions:

1. The expenditure of physical and mental effort in work is as natural as play or rest.
2. External control and the threat of punishment are not the only means for bringing about effort toward organizational objectives. People will exercise self-direction and self-control in the service of objectives to which they are committed.
3. Commitment to objectives is a function of the rewards associated with that achievement.
4. The average person learns, under proper conditions, not only to accept, but to seek responsibility.
5. The capacity to exercise a relatively high degree of imagination, ingenuity, and creativity in the solution of organizational problems is widely, not narrowly, distributed in the population.
6. Under the conditions of modern industrial life, the intellectual potentialities of the average person are only partially utilized.

FIGURE 13.2   Two sets of assumptions about human nature. *McGregor, D.: The Human Side of Enterprise. New York: McGraw-Hill Book Company. Copyright © 1985. Used with permission.*

tude was held by the traditional and "old-line" managers. Theory Y was the attitude held by the emerging manager of the 1960s and 1970s. These two sets of assumptions about human nature and human behavior are listed in Fig. 13.2. However, again implementation was the problem. Managers trained in Theory Y management found that, in many cases, the resulting job performance was not the desired level or quality.

SITUATIONAL MANAGEMENT   The work of Reddin, Fiedler, Blake, and Mouton, and others culminated in the theory that effectiveness as a leader depends on a multiplicity of factors, not only human behavior and motivation. The situational approach to management concentrates on the theory that leadership effectiveness is a function of the individual leader (including traits and personalities), that leader's subordinate (including attitude toward working, socioeconomic interests, and personality), and the situational variables involved.

More recent studies delineated two dimensions of leadership effectiveness—concern for the task and concern for the people who do the task. Analyzing various leadership styles in view of these two dimensions, Blake and Mouton[5] developed the managerial grid as a method of determining how a leader can behave and successfully manage people. The term leadership style was believed ideal—high concern for people and high concern for production. However, it was soon found that some of the other leadership styles were equally effective and that some managers using a team leadership style were not effective. In the late 1960s, the theory that leadership effectiveness is contingent upon not only leadership style but the attitude and outlook of the follower and the situational constraints came to be accepted.

CONTINGENCY THEORIES OF LEADERSHIP   Basically, contingency theory holds that there is no one "best" style of leadership but that style must be adjusted to fit the situation. Effective leadership in any given situation is dependent on a number of circumstances: The situation—how structured is the task involved, whether or not the leader has any power as perceived by subordinates, and how well the leader gets along with subordinates. Fiedler[6] developed a continuum identifying possible states of each of the three factors. He concluded that in very "favorable" or in very "unfavorable" situations for getting a task accomplished by group effort, the task-oriented management style works best. In intermediate situations, the human relations style is more successful.

In 1958, Tannenbaum and Schmidt[7] wrote a now classic article, "How to Choose a Leadership Pattern," in which they described how a manager should successfully lead his organization. Fifteen years later, they reconsidered and updated their original statements to reflect new management concepts and societal changes. The revised continuum of manager-nonmanager behavior is shown in Fig. 13.3.

The total area of freedom shared by managers and nonmanagers is constantly redefined by interactions between them and the forces in the environment. The points on the continuum designate types of managers and nonmanager behavior that are possible with the amount of freedom available to each. This continuum allows managers to review and analyze their own behavior within the context of alternatives available. It is important to recognize that there is no implication that either end of the continuum is

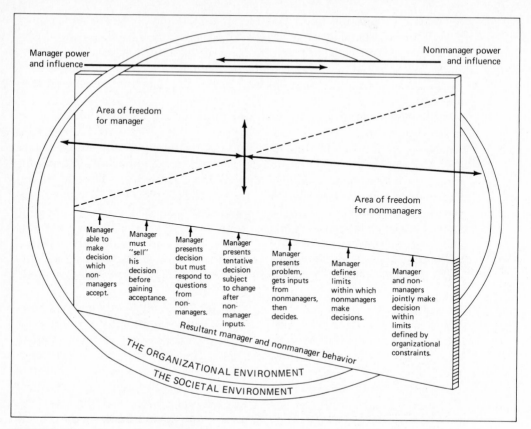

FIGURE 13.3   Tannenbaum-Schmidt's continuum of manager-nonmanager behavior.   *Tannenbaum, R. and Schmidt, W. H.: How to choose a leadership pattern.* Harvard Business Review, *51(3):162. Copyright © 1973 by the President and Fellows of Harvard College; all rights reserved. Used by permission.*

inherently more effective than the other. The appropriate balance is determined by forces in the manager, in the nonmanager, and in the particular situation. The model also suggests neither manager nor nonmanager has complete control. The nonmanager always has the option of noncompliance, and managers can never relieve themselves of all responsibility for the actions and decisions of the organization. It is probable that most people are unable to operate within a narrow band of preferred ways of leading and tend to use these styles over and over. Self-development and training should be directed to a wider range of styles for use in the appropriate situations.[7] Ideally, persons in foodservice management positions should accept as a per-

Early Managers—The Employee as a Dependent

Scientific Management—1910 to 1926

Taylor and Gantt	The one best way
F. and L. Gilbreth	"Efficiency" and work simplification

Human Relations—1926 to 1947

Mayo	Employees must be treated like people, not machines
Roethlisberger and Dickson	
Maslow	Satisfaction in work

The Behavioral Scientists—1947 to 1967

McGregor	Under the right conditions, people will manage themselves
Argyris	
Likert	People work best when their social and psychological needs are met
Drucker	
Herzberg	

The New Thinkers—1967 to 2000

Vroom	The situation, the type of work, and the type of manager all determine the most appropriate management style
Fiedler	
Levinson	
Heilrigle and Slocum	There is no "one best way"
Sayles	

FIGURE 13.4   A sumary of the historical view of leadership.

sonal philosophy that their human resources are their greatest assets and that to improve their value is not only a material advantage but a moral obligation as well.

The historical view of leadership and the contributions of each of the periods is summarized in Fig. 13.4.

Effective Communication

In a study conducted in 1980,[8] the number one training need of managers was found to be communications. The estimates of time spent communicating by managers range from 70 percent and up. One leadership model shows the central function of communication for leadership effectiveness (Fig. 13.5). In this model communication is the glue that binds the behavior between leader and follower. The messages transmitted between them present the styles, attitudes, values, motives, skills, and personality variables that are possessed by the leader. The amount of control exerted will vary depending on the situation, task, personnel, and the interrelationships of these compo-

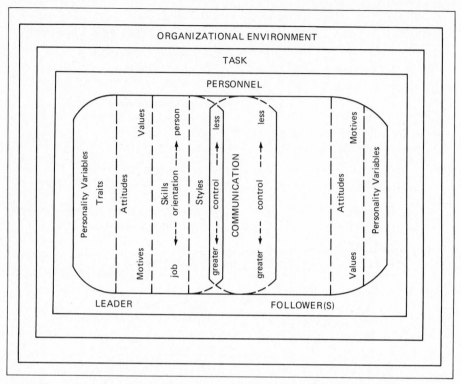

FIGURE 13.5   Model of leadership effectiveness. *Koehler, J. W., Anatol, K. W., and Applbaum, R. L.,* Organizational Communication, *2nd ed. New York: Holt, Rinehart and Winston, 1981. Used by permission.*

nents.[9] As this model dramatically illustrates, communication is a key part of effective leadership.

DEFINITIONS   Communication is defined as the transmittal of meaning from one individual to another. For a leader to lead, directions must be followed. For directions to be followed, they must be understood. The best plans will fail if the communication is not comprehended. It is almost certain that no message will be transmitted or received with 100 percent accuracy. The average employee remembers:

10–15% of what (s)he hears
15–30% of what (s)he hears and sees
30–50% of what (s)he says

> 50–75% of what (s)he does
> but (s)he remembers
> 75% of what (s)he does with proper
> instruction

Proper instruction includes use of all of the senses—hearing, seeing, saying and doing, and then repeating it all again.

BARRIERS TO GOOD COMMUNICATION   Some of the barriers to communication have to do with the language used, differing backgrounds of the sender and receiver, and the circumstances in which communication takes place. The receiver hears what he or she expects to hear and may "shut out" or ignore what is not expected. There is a tendency to infer what is expected even when it has not been communicated. Senders and receivers have different perceptions based on their different backgrounds. It is important to consider where the other person "is coming from." Receivers evaluate the source and will interpret or accept communication in light of that evaluation. A trusted and respected leader will have more open channels of communication than a leader who does not command trust and respect. Conflicting information is often ignored. Different people will attach different meanings to different words. The sender or communicator must carefully choose words that convey the meaning in such a way that the receiver understands. Verbal cues are often ignored. Body language and facial expression often say more than the words they accompany. A receiver who is emotionally upset often stops listening in order to think about what he or she will say next. Noise and the environment often form a physical barrier to communication. There is a right place and a wrong place to conduct good communication. There is a right time and a wrong time.

IMPROVING COMMUNICATIONS   Communication is not a one-way process. One of the most important parts of effective communication is to listen to the reply—either words, facial expression, body language, or even silence. The evaluation of "feedback" can tell much about how the message has been received. Empathy or the ability to put yourself in the receiver's shoes in a conversation can also be crucial to mutual understanding. Ten suggestions for improving communications specifically geared to the foodservice industry are offered by Eshbach.[10]

1. Know what you want to say and be sure of what it means to you. If you are not sure of what you mean, you cannot expect other people to know what you want them to know or to do. It is hard enough to get understanding without adding handicaps.

2. Know as much as you can about your audience, their educational level, their interests, attitudes, skills, and abilities. Information of this kind can help you make what you have to say more readily understood by those with whom you are communicating.

3. Try to put yourself in the place of the person with whom you are communicating and consider what you have to say as you think he or she would. This is hard to do, but it is well worth the effort. Relate what you have to say to things that you know are of interest or concern to your listeners.

4. Give attention to the people who are communicating with you. Being a good listener can mean a great difference in the effectiveness of communication.

5. Make communication a two-way street and not two one-way streets. If people have an opportunity to ask questions and check to see if what they heard is what is meant, communication will be much more effective.

6. Recognize the limitations of the various communication methods. Dashing off a memorandum is not the best way to communicate in all circumstances and situations.

7. Remember that many factors affect understanding by other people of what you say and write. Some factors may be more important at one time than at another time.

8. Do not try to impress people with big complicated words. Research shows that even people of high intellectual levels pay better attention and react more effectively to messages that have shorter, simpler words. Many people do not have time to try to determine the meaning in long-word material. Make the correct choice of words. Some words are general with many different meanings. Others are specific with less chance of being misunderstood. The meaning people get from words is closely related to their experiences and the meanings they have come to associate through those experiences with the words. So, meaning differs among people.

9. People's opinions are not always based on reason and logic. Often logical statements of fact do not result in their correcting their views and agreeing. Instead, they strengthen their determination to continue holding the view that they have, and they make greater efforts to find new reasons to support those views.

10. Above all, recognize your need to improve communications, want to improve your communication, and work hard at it. The foodservice industry, and other industries as well, would find communication a far less serious problem if more people were willing to admit that they are not doing a good job of communicating and really tried to do something about improving it.

MODES OF COMMUNICATION   The lines of communications within an organization should be clearly established. The modes of communicating are many and varied; a variety of them will be used within a foodservice department. An employees' handbook is a good starting point for managers to communicate with their personnel. Group meetings to discuss policies, rules, and procedures are important and effective when well planned. Bulletin board notices, memos, and posters provide another means of communication, but must be kept up-to-date and must be changed frequently to provide the desired impact.

An informal means of communicating found in every organization is the "grapevine." If managers do not communicate adequately or give complete information to employees, particularly in regard to an anticipated change, rumors begin. "What you do not tell me, I assume to be bad" is the usual attitude of those who are not "in the know." To avoid misapprehension, mistrust, and fear that can arise from false rumors, managers should be as frank and open as the situation allows. This helps build confidence, loyalty, and good morale among the working group.

At the administrative level, much of communicating is accomplished through the use of analytical tools of management science. Routine reports generated for managers' analysis, simulation techniques as a basis for decision making, and certain planning and other functions may be carried out through use of a computer. Operations Research (OR), Performance Evaluation and Review Techniques (PERT), and Management by Objectives (MBO) are a few of these tools used by managers for communicating data and information at upper levels in the organization.

Social and Professional Responsibility

The major goals of administrative leadership in the scientific management era were profit and productivity. Today, leadership in organizations involves a number of social responsibilities as well. Among these are compliance with equal opportunity in personnel matters, minimizing environmental pollution, energy conservation, employee health and safety, compliance with consumer interests, and the overall image of the organization in the community. Many of these are controlled by governmental regulatory agencies and legal mandates.

Professional responsibility is outlined in various professional codes of ethics. The American Dietetic Association[11] has recently implemented Standards of Professional Responsibility (Fig. 13.6) for its members. Professional associations in foodservice and dietetics have devoted much time and thought to areas of social responsibility and professional image in recent years in an effort to take a proactive stance rather than a reactive approach to the rap-

Standards of Professional Responsibility

and

Review Process for Alleged Violations

THE AMERICAN DIETETIC ASSOCIATION

Introduction

The American Dietetic Association joins the ranks of other professional associations that have adopted a voluntary, enforceable code of ethics. This code, called Standards of Professional Responsibility, challenges all members to uphold ethical principles. With implementation of the enforcement process on January 1, 1985, a fair system is established to field complaints about members from peers or the public, notify members of complaints, and allow members a chance to respond.

The first code of ethics in the professions was adopted by the American Medical Association in 1848. Since that time, many other professional societies have established codes to protect consumers, other professionals, and third parties such as insurers, from improper conduct.

The American Dietetic Association's first Code of Ethics was published in 1956 for the guidance of the membership. In 1976, an ad hoc committee of the House of Delegates was named to work on the most recent revision of the code to encompass changes in the profession and in society as a whole. After several years of work, the revised code, the Standards of Professional Responsibility, was adopted by the House of Delegates in October 1982. The Standards became effective January 1, 1984. Enforcement was targeted for 1985.

The Ethics Committee of the House of Delegates is responsible for reviewing and updating the Standards and for implementing the enforcement procedures. The committee also educates members and the public about the ethical principles contained in the Standards. Support of the code of ethics by each member of the Association is vital to guiding our professional actions and to strengthening our credibility.

Standards of Professional Responsibility of The American Dietetic Association

Preamble

A profession has the opportunity to set ethical standards that will benefit society and the profession. Members of The American Dietetic Association, engaged in diverse roles in the practice, education, and research of dietetics have voluntarily developed Standards of Professional Responsibility, which reflect the ethical principles of the dietetic profession and outline obligations of the member to self, client, society, and the profession.

FIGURE 13.6   *(Continued)*

1. The American Dietetic Association member provides professional service with objectivity and with respect for the unique needs and values of individuals.
   - *The member avoids discrimination on the basis of factors that are irrelevant to the provision of professional services, including, but not limited to, race, creed, sex, and age.*
   - *The member provides sufficient information to enable clients to make their own informed decisions.*
2. The American Dietetic Association member accurately presents professional qualifications and credentials.
   - *The member uses "R.D." or "registered dietitian" only when registration is current and authorized by the Commission on Dietetic Registration.*
   - *The member permits use of his/her name for the purpose of certifying that dietetic services have been rendered only if he/she has provided or supervised the provision of those services.*
3. The American Dietetic Association member remains free of conflict of interest while fulfilling the objectives and maintaining the integrity of the dietetic profession.
   - *The member advances and promotes the profession while maintaining professional judgment, honesty, integrity, loyalty, and trust to colleagues, clients, and the public.*
   - *The member promotes or endorses products only in a manner that is neither false nor misleading.*
4. The American Dietetic Association member assumes responsibility and accountability for personal competence in practice.
   - *The member maintains knowledge and skills required for continuing professional competence.*
   - *The member recognizes the limits of his/her qualifications and seeks counsel or makes referrals as appropriate.*
   - *The member adheres to accepted standards for his/her area of practice.*
5. The American Dietetic Association member complies with all applicable laws and regulations concerning the profession, but seeks to change them if they are inconsistent with the best interests of the public and the profession.
6. The American Dietetic Association member presents substantiated information and interprets controversial information without personal bias, recognizing that legitimate differences of opinion exist.
7. The American Dietetic Association member maintains the confidentiality of information.
8. The American Dietetic Association member conducts him/herself with honesty, integrity, and fairness.
   - *The member makes and fulfills professional commitments in good faith.*
   - *The member who wishes to inform the public and colleagues of his/her services does so by using factual information. The member does not advertise in a misleading manner.*
   - *The member makes all reasonable effort to avoid bias in any kind of professional evaluation.*

FIGURE 13.6 *(Continued)*

- *The member provides objective evaluation of candidates for professional association memberships, awards, scholarships, or job advancements.*
9. The American Dietetic Association member accepts the obligation to protect society and the profession by upholding the Standards of Professional Responsibility and by reporting alleged violations of the Standards through the defined review process of The American Dietetic Association.

Philosophy Statement to Accompany the Standards of Professional Responsibility

The Standards of Professional Responsibility approved by the Board of Directors are the result of several years of effort by the Ethics Committee.

Widespread review and input from members, extensive legal scrutiny, and strong staff support all contributed to the development of the professional standards. It now seems appropriate to review the thinking behind these efforts. What is the purpose of a code of professional ethics? Such a code is designed to guide the professional, enhance the profession's image, and strengthen credibility with those it serves. The Standards of Professional Responsibility should intensify the member's sensitivity to and awareness of what constitutes ethical conduct. They should protect the public and the professional from unscrupulous practitioners.

ADA members who commented on early drafts of the code of ethics were insistent that it be meaningful and enforceable. They rejected high-sounding phrases with little substance. An enforcement process was mandated by vote of the House of Delegates and the Board approved the Standards accompanied by a review mechanism for alleged violations.

Because the disciplinary segment is the most difficult aspect of code development, it may assume greater-than-deserved emphasis. In our preoccupation with dealing with violators, we must not lose sight of the code's function as an educational tool for dietitians.

Great care has been taken to develop legally appropriate standards and a detailed procedure for review of alleged unethical acts. The Ethics Committee encourages members to use the code in a positive manner, recognizing the high motivation and professional responsibility of our membership.

If further information is desired, contact the administrator, Division of Policy Administration, at ADA headquarters.

Review Process for Alleged Violations of the Standards of Professional Responsibility of The American Dietetic Association

Underlying Principles

Two considerations are basic to the review process for resolving complaints of alleged unethical practice.

1. The Review Process will be conducted in strict confidence, and the rights of a member who allegedly has violated the Standards of Professional Responsibility will be protected throughout.

FIGURE 13.6 *(Continued)*

2. The Review Process will result in either dismissal of the complaint, acquittal of respondent, or disciplinary action taken against a member.

Procedures for Review Process

1. *Complaint*

   A complaint that a member has allegedly violated the Standards of Professional Responsibility of The American Dietetic Association will be submitted in writing on the appropriate form to the Ethics Committee in care of the administrator, Division of Policy Administration, of The American Dietetic Association, at ADA headquarters.

   The complaint must be made within one year of the date that the complainant first became aware of the alleged violation.

   The complainant (person making complaint) need not be a member of The American Dietetic Association. Complaints may be brought by a member or a nonmember against a member.

   The complaint will contain details of the nature of the activities complained of, the basis for complainant's knowledge of these activities, and names, addresses, and telephone numbers of all persons involved or who might have knowledge of the activities, and whether the complaint has been submitted to a court or a state licensure board. The complaint will also cite the section(s) of the Standards of Professional Responsibility allegedly violated.

   The complaint will be signed and sworn to by the complainant.

2. *Preliminary review of complaint*

   The chairman of the Ethics Committee, legal counsel of The American Dietetic Association, and the administrator of the Division of Policy Administration will review the complaint to determine if all the required information has been submitted by the complainant and whether an ethics question is involved.

   If a complaint is made regarding an alleged violation of the Standards of Professional Responsibility and a similar complaint is already under consideration regarding the same individual by a state board of examiners of dietitians or in a court of law, the Ethics Committee will not process the complaint it has received until the state board or court outcome is known.

3. *Notice to the respondent and response*

   Within two weeks of the determination that further action should be taken, the chairman of the Ethics Committee will notify the respondent (person against whom the complaint is made) that a complaint has been made.

   The notice will be sent from the Division of Policy Administration via registered mail. The respondent will receive a copy of the complaint including the name of the complainant, the Standards of Professional Responsibility, the Review Process, and a Response to Complaint form.

   The respondent will have thirty days from receipt of the notification in which to submit a response.

FIGURE 13.6 (*Continued*)

If the Ethics Committee does not receive a response, the chairman of the Ethics Committee or his/her designee will contact the respondent by telephone. If contact with the respondent is still not made, two written notices will be sent. Failure to reach the respondent will not prevent the committee from proceeding with the investigation.

4. *Investigation and disposition*
The Ethics Committee of The American Dietetic Association will review the complaint and the response.

Within 90 days of initial notification of the respondent, the committee will reach a decision as to the disposition of the complaint, either: (1) that the complaint and response, jointly, do not present an ethics issue, or (2) that the Ethics Committee of The American Dietetic Association conduct a hearing.

The Ethics Committee of The American Dietetic Association will notify the complainant and the respondent of the decision.

5. *Preparation for hearing*
The Ethics Committee of The American Dietetic Association will notify the respondent and the complainant by registered mail of the date, time, and place of the hearing.

Hearings will be held twice a year: One at the time of the Annual Meeting, and another no later than eight months after receipt of a complaint.

The respondent may request a copy of the investigative file and will be allowed at least one postponement.

6. *Hearings*
The chairman of the Ethics Committee of The American Dietetic Association will conduct a closed hearing before the Ethics Committee and legal counsel of The American Dietetic Association. The parties shall have the right to appear to present witnesses and evidence; to cross-examine the opposing party and adverse witnesses; and to have legal counsel present.

Legal counsel for the parties may advise their clients, but may participate in the hearings only at the discretion of the chairman; they may be excluded from the hearings at any time.

The American Dietetic Association will bear the costs for the hearing committee, The American Dietetic Association legal counsel, and any other parties called by The American Dietetic Association.

The respondent and the complainant will be responsible for expenses incurred in their attendance at the hearing their legal counsel, and any witnesses they choose to call.

Five members of the Ethics Committee consitute a quorum. Two-thirds (⅔) of the members voting will determine the final outcome.

A transcript will be prepared.

FIGURE 13.6 (*Continued*)

7. *Decision and recommendation*

The Ethics Committee of The American Dietetic Association will render a written decision specifying the reasons therefore and citing the provision(s) of the Standards of Professional Responsibility that has/have been violated. The committee will specify one of the following:

A. that the respondent be acquitted; or

B. that the respondent be censured, suspended, or expelled from The American Dietetic Association.

Censure—An official written reprimand expressing severe criticism or disapproval of a particular type of conduct or action. Censure carries with it the possibility of removal from office at the national, state, and district level and from committee membership.

Time frame—not applicable.

Suspension—Temporary loss of membership and all membership privileges for a specified time with the exception of entitlement to coverages under health and disability insurance. Malpractice insurance will not be renewed during the suspension period.

At the end of the specified suspension period, membership privileges are automatically restored.

Time frame—specified time to be decided on a case to case basis.

Expulsion—Removal from membership and a loss of all privileges.

Time frame—may apply for reinstatement after a five-year period has elapsed, with payment of the reinstatement fee.

Must meet membership requirements in effect at the time of application for reinstatements.

The findings and action of the Ethics Committee of The American Dietetic Association will be sent to the respondent and the complainant within sixty (60) days after the hearing.

8. *Appeals*

Only the respondent may appeal an adverse decision to The American Dietetic Association Appeals Committee.

During the appeals process, the membership status of the respondent remains unchanged.

A. *Recourse to the Appeals Committee.* To request a hearing before the Appeals Committee, the respondent/appellant shall notify the administrator of Affiliate Relations at ADA headquarters, by registered mail, return receipt requested, that the member wishes to appeal the decision. This notification must be received within thirty (30) calendar days after receipt of the letter advising the respondent/appellant of the Ethics Committee's decision.

1) The appeal must be in writing and contain, as a minimum, the following information:

a. The decision being appealed

b. The date of the decision

FIGURE 13.6 (*Continued*)

    c. Why the individual feels the decision is improper

    d. The redress sought by the individual.

       If the appeal does not contain the information listed above, it will be returned to the individual who will be given ten (10) calendar days to resubmit. Failure to furnish the required information within ten (10) calendar days will result in the appeal being cancelled.

2) Upon receipt of this notification, the administrator of the Division of Policy Administration shall promptly notify the chairman of the Appeals Committee that the respondent/appellant is appealing a decision made by the Ethics Committee.

3) The Appeals Committee chairman shall acknowledge the appeal and request a copy of the relevant written information on the case from the administrator of the Affiliate Relations Department.

B. *Procedures for appeals.* The objective of the hearing is to consider all pertinent evidence and consider all pertinent arguments to permit the Appeals Committee to make a sound and just decision.

  1) *Composition of Appeals Committee.* The Appeals Committee shall consist of an Appeals Committee member serving as presiding officer two members selected from the Appeal's Panel, one technical advisor from the ADA headquarters staff, and The American Dietetic Association legal counsel.

  2) *Participants at hearings.*

    a. The complainant/appellee, the respondent/appellant and the chairman of the Ethics Committee will be invited to participate in the appeals hearing.

    b. The parties may have legal counsel present, who may advise their clients, but may participate in the hearings only at the discretion of the chairman. They may be excluded from the hearings at any time.

    c. Attendance at the hearing will be limited to persons determined by the presiding officer to have a direct connection with the appeal.

  3) *Conduct of the hearing.* The three parties involved in the appeal will be given the opportunity to state why the decision of the Ethics Committee should be upheld, modified, or reversed.

  4) *Scope of Review.* The Appeals Committee will determine whether the Ethics Committee committed procedural error that affected its decision. In reviewing the Ethics Committee's decision, the Appeals Committee shall consider only the transcript of the hearing and the evidence presented to the Ethics Committee, and whether the Ethics Committee's decision was contrary to the weight of the evidence presented to it. The Appeals Committee may also determine whether there is new and substantial evidence that was unavailable at the time of the Ethics Committee's Hearing.

  5) *Record of hearing.* The Appeals Committee shall prepare a written decision stating the reasons therefor. A transcript will be prepared.

  6) *Decision of Appeals Committee.*

    a. The decision shall be to affirm, modify, or reject the decision of the

FIGURE 13.6 *(Continued)*

Ethics Committee or to remand the case to the Ethics Committee with instructions for further proceedings.

  b. Decisions of the Appeals Committee will be final.

9. *Notification of adverse action*

   If the respondent is censured, suspended, or expelled by the Ethics Committee and does not appeal the decision, the chairman of the Ethics Committee will notify the appropriate American Dietetic Association organization units and the state dietetic association within thirty (30) days after notification of the final decision.

   In the event the respondent appeals a decision to censure, suspend, or expel him/her from the Association, and the Ethics Committee decision is upheld, similar notification will be made by the chairman of the Ethics Committee.

   Disclosure of adverse action of the Ethics Committee, following final appeal, will be published in the *Journal of The American Dietetic Association* and the *ADA Courier.*

10. *Record keeping*

   A. Records will be kept for a period of two years after the disposition of the case in the Department of Affiliate Relations.

   B. Records of those acquitted will be sealed. Information will be provided only upon written request and affirmative response from Association legal counsel.

Adopted by the Board of Directors, April 20, 1983. Revised and adopted by the House of Delegates, October 14, 1984. Revised and approved by the House of Delegates Executive Committee on July 26, 1985.

Confidentiality Procedures

The following procedures have been developed to protect the confidentiality of both the Complainant and the Respondent in the investigation of a complaint of an alleged violation of the Standards of Professional Responsibility:

1. The need for confidentiality will be stressed in initial communications with all parties.
2. Committee members will refrain from discussing the complaint and hearing outside of official committee business pertaining to the complaint and hearing.
3. If the Hearing on a complaint carries over to the next committee, the complaint will be heard by the original committee to hear the complaint.
4. Communication with ADA witnesses will be the responsibility of the committee chair or staff liaison.
5. Witnesses who testify on behalf of ADA will be informed of the confidentiality requirements and agree to support them.
6. The committee chair will stress the importance of confidentiality, on the record, at the time of the hearing.

FIGURE 13.6   (*Continued*)

7. To ensure confidentiality the only record of the hearing will be the official transcript and accompanying materials which will be kept at the ADA offices. All other materials that were mailed or distributed to committee members should be returned to ADA staff at the Hearing along with any notes taken by Committee members.

Approved by the House of Delegates Executive Committee on recommendation of the Ethics Committee, March 16, 1986.

FIGURE 13.6 Standards of Professional Responsibility of The American Dietetic Association. Copyright © 1985, The American Dietetic Association. *Reprinted by permission from* Journal of the American Dietetic Association, *Vol. 83:702, 1983.*

idly changing needs of society (see the supplementary references at the end of this chapter).

Functional Responsibilities and Skills Required

Certain basic responsibilities are common to all foodservice administrators in whatever type of organization they may be employed. Most of the ones that are specific to foodservice are discussed in detail in other chapters of this book. They include:

- Establishment of goals, objectives and standards
- Personnel selection, education, and welding an effective staff
- Overall planning and delegation of work to be done; scheduling of workers
- Purchase of food, equipment, and supplies according to specification
- Planning for physical facilities and equipment needs
- Supervision of all technical operations: production, delivery and service of food, sanitation, safety, security
- Financial planning and control

These responsibilities may be classified under the functions of management given in Chapter 11.

Effective administrative leadership is a professional responsibility. Some of the key characteristics of successful—and thus professionally responsible—leaders are given by Lester:[12]

(1) Sense of responsibility—This may mean sometimes subordinating personal desires to the needs of the organization or the profession; (2) Technical and

professional competence—The input of others to make decisions may provide guidance, but the final decision will require personal technical and professional knowledge and skills; (3) Enthusiasm—Honest, genuine enthusiasm for the goals and plans of the leader are vital to the generation of commitment and enthusiasm on the part of employees. New directions and unfamiliar areas should be sought without reluctance; (4) Communication skills—Communication is one of the vital linking processes that holds the organization together. It is a key variable in leadership effectiveness. Verbal, written, and nonverbal communications should be understood and utilized effectively. Active listening, avoiding distortion, is a key to good communication; (5) High ethical standards— Ethics are the basis of all group interaction and decision-making processes. Therefore, they play a key role in the leadership function. Professional ethics require leaders to maintain high standards of personal conduct in all situations so that employees may rely on their actions. Integrity is demonstrated when concern for company interests is greater than personal pride; (6) Flexibility— Leaders must have the ability to take whatever comes along and thrive on it. This requires an understanding and acceptance of the fact that no two people or two situations are ever exactly alike. Approaches must be adapted. Change and stress must be understood and managed; (7) Vision—An ability to see the organization as a whole made up of interdependent and interrelated parts; to see where it is going and how it can get there is necessary for effective leadership. Leaders with ideas and images that can excite people and develop timely and appropriate choices will inspire those they lead.

Nine specific suggestions for the improvement of the professionalism of the administrative dietitian or foodservice manager are:

1. Increase your confidence in use of management skills such as communications, planning, evaluation of services offered through reading, study, and practice.
2. Memorize facts important to the fiscal accountability of the operation. Be prepared to cite figures such as cost per patient day, productivity (meals per manhour) in order to reinforce your department's needs.
3. Select continuing education activities that are interesting and challenging enough to make you feel more alive and creative as a person.
4. Establish a daily study period, even if it is only ten minutes long.
5. If speaking up for yourself and your department is difficult or very uncomfortable, take an assertiveness training course.
6. Keep a daily log. Each time you change activities, jot down the starting time and nature of the task. After a week or two, review your activities and estimate the relative amount of time spent on each. Then decide which functions you would like to spend more time or less time on. Delegate simpler tasks so that you have more time for more difficult, demanding (therefore, more rewarding) tasks.

7. Set specific professional objectives for a one-year period. Establish a timetable for achieving them and write down your plans for achieving them.
8. Keep a log of trials, successes, problems, and insights. As goals are achieved, set new ones.
9. Publicize your successes. Don't be so modest.
10. Give seminars and workshops for groups within and beyond your institution. Show your community your talents and capabilities.

Summary

Persons who will successfully administer foodservice departments in the future will be those who are committed to a philosophy of service, who refresh and update their knowledge and skills to keep pace with ever changing situations, and who continually strive to improve conditions for their organization and personnel. Further, they will develop a marketing plan to promote their foodservice and to be cognizant of the fact that the foodservice managers themselves are the marketing agents for good public relations for their organization, both in the work setting and in the community.

Notes

1. Steinmetz, L. L., and Todd, H. R.: First-Line Management. Rev. ed. Dallas, TX: Business Publications, Inc., 1979.
2. Zaleznik, A.: Managers and leaders: Are they different? Harv. Bus. Rev. 55:67 (May/June), 1977.
3. Koontz, H. and O'Donnell, C.: The functions of the manager. *In:* Principles of Management. New York: McGraw-Hill Book Co., 1968.
4. McGregor, D.: The Human Side of Enterprise. New York: McGraw-Hill Book Co., 1960, pp. 38–44.
5. Blake, R. R. and Mouton, J. S.: The Managerial Grid. Houston, TX: Gulf Publishing Co, 1964.
6. Fiedler, F. E.: Engineer the job to fit the manager. Harv. Bus. Rev. 43:119, 1965.
7. Tannenbaum, R. and Schmidt, W. H.: How to choose a leadership pattern. Harv. Bus. Rev. 51(3):162, 1973
8. Greene, J. P.: People management: New directions for the 80s. Admin. Mgmt. 62:22 (Jan.), 1981.
9. Koehler, J. W., Anatol, K. W. E., and Applbaum, R. L.: Organizational Communication, 2nd ed. New York: Holt, Rinehart and Winston, 1981.

10. Eshbach, C. E.: Foodservice Management, 3rd ed. Boston: CBI Publishing Co, 1979.
11. Standards of Professional Responsibility of The American Dietetic Association. Chicago: The Am. Diet. Assoc., 1984.
12. Lester, R. I.: Leadership: Some principles and concepts. Personnel J. 50:868 (Nov.), 1981.

Supplementary References

McCLELLAND, D. C. AND BURNHAM, D. H.: Power is the great motivator. Harv. Bus. Rev. 54(2):100, 1976.

MISSHAUK, M. J.: Management Theory and Practice. Boston, MA: Little, Brown and Co., 1979.

NEWMAN, W. H. AND WARREN, E. K.: The Process of Management, 4th ed. Englewood Cliffs, NJ: Prentice-Hall, Inc., 1977.

PLACHY, R. J.: Leading vs Managing: A Guide to Some Crucial Distinctions. Mgmt. Rev. 80:58 (Sept.), 1981.

POWERS, T. F.: Introduction to Management in the Hospitality Industry. New York: John Wiley and Sons, 1979.

CHAPTER 14

Work Improvement and Productivity

Introduction

Productivity, the ratio between output and input, can be used as a measure of work improvement. Any attempt at work improvement must take into consideration the people involved. An understanding of human nature on the part of management and improvement in the overall quality of work life are necessary components of any productivity improvement program.

Increased production with less human effort has been an objective in the foodservice industry for years. Some methods for designing effective and efficient ways of accomplishing work are included in this chapter. This work design must consider improved job content, a safe and healthy work environment, and efficient and effective work methods.

Each of these requires a careful study of existing conditions before any change is implemented. The study of work methods begins with the establishment of standards. The method employed may then be analyzed using one of several techniques. Work simplification is one such technique for identifying and eliminating the uneconomical use of time, equipment, materials, space, or human effort.

A step-by-step procedure for implementing a work improvement program is outlined. One very important step requires that the job be broken down into its component parts in detail. This may be accomplished by work sampling, a pathway or flow diagram, operation and process charting, or micromotion studies. Each is discussed briefly.

What Is Productivity?

The successful and efficient day-to-day operation of a foodservice is a constant challenge to its management group. No foodservice system can afford to remain static for long, but must keep pace with the socioeconomic changes and technological developments in food and equipment and their effects on the overall pattern of operation. Changes in consumer attitudes and behavior, labor and energy costs, regulatory considerations and the general business environment have created new and challenging problems. The present-day foodservice consumer shows a much greater awareness of economic value and sanitary requirements and demands quality food and efficient service at a reasonable price.

Increased production with less human effort has long been an objective in industry. Interest in the designing of work systems to convert human work practices to machines was a contributing factor to the Industrial Revolution. Since then the development has not been steady, but today we rely heavily on mechanization and automation to increase productivity and develop manpower effectiveness. Current high material and labor costs make it imperative that every effort be made to study the work design and perfect efficient operation if high standards of production and quality of products are to be maintained at a reasonable cost.

Simplification of tasks and techniques designed to decrease fatigue of workers are effective aids to good management that are accorded wide recognition and attention by both managers and workers in the foodservice field.

Increased productivity and employee satisfaction are frequently considered to be the overall objective of work design. Many definitions have been given for productivity, but essentially in foodservice management, it is a measure or level of *output* of goods produced or services rendered in relation to *input* in terms of time (labor hours, minutes, or days), money spent, or other resources used.

In order to relate such diverse quantitative units of measurement as number of meals and amounts of service, pounds of materials, labor hours, BTUs, and capital equipment, they may be expressed in dollar values. The resulting formula is a profitability ratio that must be greater than one to produce a profit.[1]

According to one author, a crucial problem facing many companies is their inability, because of competition (and cost containment) to recover increases in the cost of materials, labor or other resources by raising prices. They are unable also to decrease the cost of the resources or substitute others. Therefore, if the profit margin is to be maintained or increased, productivity must be improved.[1]

In a hospital foodservice, productivity is measured using productivity indicators such as: meals per worked hour, meals per paid hour, meal equivalents per worked hour, meal equivalents per paid hour, transactions per worked hour, and transactions per paid hour.[2] When measured for successive periods, these indicators show a trend. Comparisons may also be made between similar institutions.

The QWL Approach

Quality of work life (QWL) is a term that has been used to describe values that relate to the quality of human experiences in the workplace. QWL is affected by a composite of factors on the job, including factors that relate to work itself, to the work environment, and to the employee personally. People are the key factor in improving productivity. If productivity is to be improved, both the nature of people and of the organizations in which they work must be understood. Bain[3] agrees that people are the highest order of resources and, as such, are responsible for controlling and utilizing all other resources.

Bennett[4] agrees and goes one step further, stating that if the source of improving the productivity position of an organization is directly traceable to people, then it follows that the achievement of a better bottom line of productivity must be *everybody's* business. Managers must be capable of utilizing the human resources of the organization and use a systems approach to productivity improvement in which all members of the organization are involved.

Increased productivity means motivation, dignity, and greater personal participation in the design and performance of work in the foodservice organization. It means developing individuals whose lives can be productive in the fullest sense.

A study[5] of 195 U.S. companies found that management ineffectiveness was by far the single greatest cause of declining productivity and that the only successful effort to raise productivity was an integrated QWL approach.

Quality of work life is a multifaceted concept. Incentive plans such as a contingent time-off plan under which the company agrees to award specific time off if the workers perform at an agreed-upon level have been successful in improving productivity.[6] Such factors as reducing worker fears, providing opportunity for advancement, implementing job enrichment by adding responsibility, budget, or staff to the job, allowing the exercise of professional skills, and improving communication skills also aid in increasing productivity.

A classic study[7] conducted by behavioral science researchers a number of years ago found that a particular leadership style was more effective in increasing productivity and employee satisfaction. The characteristics of this style of leadership are: (1) general supervision rather than close, detailed supervision of employees, (2) more time devoted to supervisory activities than in doing production work, (3) much attention to planning of work and special tasks, (4) a willingness to permit employees to participate in the decision-making process, and (5) an approach to the job situation described as being employee centered, that is, showing a sincere interest in the needs and problems of employees as individuals, as well as being interested in high production.

Increased involvement of workers in their organizations has received much attention in the last few years. Today's workers no longer want to be separated from responsibility. Productivity appears to be maximized when there exists a unity of purpose and a feeling of ownership among all employees. This unity is created when the greatest possible responsibility is given to the lowest possible levels of the organization; compensation systems are designed so that all employees are salaried with incentive earnings tied to competence and performance; the greatest degree of involvement and consensus is sought from all levels; and management exhibits the unity they feel with the employee.[8]

In addition to these characteristics, improvements in resources (supervision, methods, and technology) so as to facilitate greater effectiveness and reduce frustrations seem effective in improving productivity and employee satisfaction.[9]

The quality of work life approach, in essence, attempts to replace the typical adversary relationship between management and employees with a cooperative one.[10] Key words of QWL are cooperation, trust, involvement, respect, rapport, and openness.

Work Design

The overall objectives of work design are to increase productivity and employee satisfaction. The specific objectives are to improve the content of the job, provide a safe and healthy work environment, design a staff of fit people, optimum work environment, and effective and efficient work methods.

JOB CONTENT   Job content in foodservice systems is being improved through automation of the production and distribution systems. Food factories and commissary-type operations employ large-volume machinery in long, integrated production runs to prepare one specific product at a time. This system makes possible a more orderly pace and usually more desirable working hours.

Another approach to changing job content is to delegate some parts of the job to less skilled employees. The ingredient room where foodservice employees weigh, measure, and assemble all the ingredients for each production formula is an example of this downward shift of responsibility. The use of support personnel such as dietetic technicians and assistants is another example.[11] Delegation of this type must be done carefully. It is a complex process requiring skill in planning, organizing, and controlling. The different needs and abilities of employees must be effectively managed.

SAFETY AND HEALTH   To provide a safe and healthy work environment is both economically and sociologically important. From an economic standpoint, accidents and job-related illnesses are extremely costly in terms of productivity. The safety and health of the work force is the responsibility of its management and is discussed further in the sections that follow.

EQUIPMENT DESIGN   Kazarian[12] states that: "Probably the greatest change that will be evident in the future planning of foodservice facilities is the physical arrangement of spaces and equipment to increase the productivity of workers." Avery[13] says:

> In order for the equipment and workers to combine productively, one must call on the science variously known as ergonomics, human factors, or human engineering. This may be defined as adapting tasks, equipment and working environment to the sensory, perceptual, mental, and physical attributes of the human worker. The employee works best if his equipment is designed for the job to be done, his capabilities, and if it is well placed in pleasing surroundings.

To maximize productivity in foodservice, Avery sets forth these principles of human engineering:

1. Design and arrangement of equipment should be such that the equipment's use requires a minimum application of human physical effort.
2. Only essential information should be provided for the equipment, and this should be presented when and where it is required with maximum clarity. It should be arranged in a step-by-step order.
3. Control devices on equipment should be easily identified, minimum in number, logical in placement, and in consonance with displays in operation. They should relate precisely to the functions they control.

4. Equipment should be designed to provide maximum productivity while utilizing the worker's physical and mental attributes most effectively. It should take into account the dimensions of the worker and his or her strengths.

5. Equipment should be selected on the basis of need in utilizing specific ingredients to prepare a selected menu, grouped in most used combinations, and arranged in order of most frequent interuse proceeding from left to right. Those tasks demanding the greatest skill should be grouped around the worker having these skills, and his or her movements to provide for his or her needs should be minimal.

6. The environment in which the foodservice worker operates should be designed and controlled to allow him or her to be most productive, comfortable, and happy with his or her job. This control involves consideration of lighting, facility and equipment coloration, temperature, humidity, noise, smells, facility design, floor conditions, and safety, among others.

WORK ENVIRONMENT   One of the goals of human engineering is the prevention of fatigue. The manager of a foodservice may find that fatigue or tiredness of some workers, with a resultant drop in their energy, enthusiasm, and production output, is due to external factors beyond his or her control, such as irregularities in the home situation, extraordinary physical exertion away from the job, or a nutritionally inadequate food intake. However, within the organization and while the workers are on the job, there are unlimited opportunities to study causes of fatigue and correct them if possible.

Certain psychological factors such as attitude because of disinterest in and boredom with the job, dislike of the supervisor, or a low rate of pay may contribute to the fatigue and low output of some workers, but such situations often can be improved through changes in personnel policies and their administration. Emphasis in this section is relative to the environmental and physical factors on the job affecting fatigue and work improvement methods.

With a given set of working conditions and equipment, the amount of work done in a day will depend on the ability of the worker and the speed at which he or she works . . . The fatigue resulting from a given level of activity will depend on such factors as (1) hours of work, that is, the length of the working day and the weekly working hours, (2) number, location, and length of rest periods, (3) working conditions such as lighting, heating, ventilation, and noise, and (4) the work itself.[14]

The amount of reserve energy brought to the job varies with individuals. Some workers can maintain a fairly even tempo throughout the day, whereas others tire rather quickly and need to rest periodically to recoup nervous and physical energy. Short rest periods appropriately scheduled tend to reduce fatigue and lessen time taken by employees for personal needs.

Lighting, heating, ventilation, and noise are environmental factors that often contribute to worker fatigue. Satisfactory standards for the lighting of kitchen areas is 35 to 50 foot-candles on work surfaces with reflectance ratios of 80 for ceiling, 30 to 35 on equipment, to a minimum of 15 for floors. Temperature and humidity influence worker productivity. A desirable climate for food preparation and service areas is around 68 degrees to 72 degrees F in the winter and 74 degrees to 78 degrees F in summer with relative humidity 40 to 45 per cent.[13] Higher temperatures tend to increase the heart rate and fatigue of most workers. Air conditioning in hot and humid locales is considered a necessity, whereas in some parts of the country a good fan and duct system is satisfactory to give an air change every two to five minutes. Hoods over cooking equipment provide for the disposal of much heat and odor originating from these units. Noise has a disturbing and tiring effect on most people. Effective control of the intensity of noise within a foodservice area is possible through precautionary measures such as installation of sound-absorbing ceiling materials, the use of rubber-tired mobile equipment and smooth-running motors, and training the employees to work quietly.

Much has been written about the value of the study of physical facilities and the procedures followed in specific jobs, aimed at increasing efficiency in the operation of a foodservice. A thorough analysis of a floor plan, on paper or in actuality, would provide facts on which to base decisions regarding changes needed in order to make the most compact arrangement possible, yet provide adequate equipment in an efficient arrangement.

WORK METHODS　In order to design the most effective and efficient work methods, existing methods must first be studied. A very important part of the manager's job is the establishment and maintenance of standards by which performance can be judged. Standards are criteria against which results are judged.

Foodservice managers and administrative dietitians have responsibility for determining the standards for their own department, standards of time, quantity, quality, and cost. How much work of what quality is to be accomplished in what length of time and at what cost? Managers must be able to answer these questions realistically and provide the information for the workers if any degree of competence and *high productivity* are to be achieved. Otherwise, employees develop their own standards and may never reach their own potential or produce at an acceptable level. Managers who allow this to happen have lost control of operations; events then control the manager.

Standards are derived from objective, the statements of what is to be achieved. Behavioral objectives relate specifically to what an individual should be able to do as a result of the learning process. Such objectives usually form the basis of a training program and give specific measures for trainee attainment. And although workers learn proper techniques and procedures throughout training program, actual work experience usually is necessary for them to develop speed and accuracy in completing a given task. This is where preestablished standards are necessary so the employees will know exactly what is expected of them and so a goal is provided for them to attain. An example of a behavioral objective for a kitchen worker is "the employee will be able to make and wrap 90 sandwiches in 30 minutes."

Time and quantity studies must be made within a given foodservice department in order to establish desirable standards for that department with its own equipment, space arrangement, facilities, and procedures. These variables make it difficult if not impossible to have universal standards among foodservice organizations. The employee who knows she is expected to make 45 sandwiches in 15 minutes, or 3 sandwiches per minute, is much more apt to respond to meet the challenge of a goal to be reached than the employee who is told to "just work as fast as you can."

Each operation or task to be performed requires similar questions to be asked and answered. Actual time studies may be made in order to arrive at realistic time-quantity standards. Quality and cost standards come from the knowledge of the dietitian or foodservice manager, who must have acquired this from his or her basic education and preparation for the position. Standards for personnel to which applicants can be compared include minimum acceptable qualities necessary for adequate performance of the job duties. These standards or qualifications will be stated in job specifications for use by those who select personnel. (See Chapter 11 for more on job specifications.)

Although no one can set standards for someone else's department, results of some research studies may prove helpful as a guide to foodservice managers undertaking a standards-setting project. Pedderson[15] gives a formula for determining how long it takes to accomplish a given task, using the following symbols:

a = the "least" amount of time to do a given task
b = the "most" amount of time to do a given task
m = the most "likely" time to do a given task

To calculate the most "probable" (allowable in the schedule) amount of time it will take to do a given task, use the formula:

$$\frac{a+4m+b}{6} = \text{Probable time required}$$

Let us say, for instance that we want to know how much time should be allowed to mop a heavily obstructed 1600-square foot institutional kitchen. A sloppy, cursory job will take 20 minutes.

$$a = 20 \text{ (minutes)}*$$

An extremely thorough job will take 120 minutes.

$$b = 120 \text{ (minutes)}*$$

The job, done adequately, will most likely take 45 minutes.

$$m = 45 \text{ (minutes)}*$$

Using the formula,

$$\frac{a + 4m + b}{6} = \frac{20 + (4 \times 45) + 120}{6} = \frac{20 + 180 + 120}{6} = \frac{320}{6} = 53\tfrac{1}{3} \text{ minutes}$$

Knowing that the most probable time to mop the floor is 53 ⅓ minutes, we will allot that amount of time daily to that task.

*Derived from actual time study of cursory, thorough, and adequate sampling.

Bartscht and coworkers[16] made comprehensive time studies of tasks performed in hospital dietary departments. The methodology that they developed can be used as a formula by other hospital dietary managers to calculate the amount of time required to perform a task in their own department, based on distances to be traveled.

Other studies throughout the years have given suggested standards in terms of number of labor minutes required for one meal served. These ranged from a low of 4 or 5 minutes for some school foodservices, to 9 or 10 minutes for college and industrial cafeterias, up to 18 to 20 labor minutes per meal including supervisory time in hospitals. Greater efficiency (lower number of minutes required) is usually achieved when a larger number of meals are served as compared with a small organization serving few meals. Foodservice managers may wish to make a study of their own operations and develop a standard for themselves based on number of labor minutes needed for each meal serviced.

School foodservice standards for personnel staffing have been suggested.[17] These are stated in terms of number of labor hours needed for number of lunches served, as in the table.

Number of Lunches Served	Meals Per Labor Hour	Total Hours
Up to 100	9½	9–11
101–150	10	10–15
151–200	11	15–17
201–250	12	17–20
251–300	13	20–22
301–350	14	22–25
351–400	14	25–29
401–450	14	29–32
451–500	14	32–35
501–550	15	35–36
551–600	15	36–40
601–700	16	40–43
701–800	16	43–50
801+	18	50+

Worker efficiency in foodservices is estimated to be from 40 to 55 per cent. Although the nature of the work involved in preparing meals for specified periods of the day, causing uneven workloads, may be part of the reason for such low productivity as compared with that in other industries, foodservices can no longer afford the luxury of inefficiency. Labor costs are too high, and every means possible should be used to improve productivity.

Productivity is sometimes equated with efficiency. Kaud[2] proposed this formula for expressing work efficiency.

$$\text{Efficiency \%} = \frac{\text{earned (standard) hours}}{\text{actual (worked) hours}} \times 100$$

The time the worker actually performs necessary work may be determined through the use of the management tool, work sampling (see later in this chapter under "methods for Work Improvement Study").

WORK SIMPLIFICATION   Detailed studies of activities within an organization often reveal that cost and time requirements are high because of unnecessary operations and excess motions used by the workers in performance of their jobs. When proper adjustment are made in both the physical setup and the work procedures, the conservation of energy of the workers, increased production, and a reduction in total manhours should result. Such studies have proved highly effective in the simplification of effort in both repetitive and nonrepetitive activities and apply either in a new situation or where long-established procedures have become accepted practices.

What has become known as "work simplification" began in the late 1920s. An industrial engineer, Allan H. Mogensen, developed the philosophy as a result of his work at Eastman Kodak. He found that workers were

> creative at thwarting his attempts to prescribe more efficient methodology and, when not under surveillance, would develop more productive methods that would enhance their rewards. He reasoned that this creativity could be harnessed in a way that would enable every employee to be her own industrial engineer.[18]

The slogan, "Work Smarter, Not Harder," emerged.

Work simplification is more than a technique or set of how-to-do-its. It is a way of thinking or a philosophy that there is always a better way. The emphasis is on the elimination of any uneconomical use of time, equipment, materials, space, or human effort.[16] Conservative estimates are that through an effective work simplification program, foodservice worker productivity can be increased as much as 20 to 50 percent.

Employee interest, understanding, and cooperation are essential to the successful operation of a work simplification program. Thinking through and planning before starting any task is necessary if it is to be accomplished efficiently and in the simplest manner possible. The elimination of wasted effort is easy once the worker becomes "motion conscious," learns to apply the principles that may be involved, and sees objectively the benefits of changed procedures. Such benefits may be evidenced by lessened fatigue of workers, safer and better working conditions, better and more uniform quality production, and possibly higher wages through increased production. Agreement and understanding of the objectives and realization that benefits will be shared mutually by workers and management are factors for success. The solicitation and incorporation of suggestions for job improvement methods from the workers are conducive to enthusiastic interest and participation by them. Usually any employee resistance to change in established work routines can be overcome by the proper approach of management before and after the inauguration of a work simplification program. The selection of personnel qualified by personality and training for leadership in this work is of prime importance to its implementation.

MOTION ECONOMY   The same principles of motion economy adopted by engineers many years ago are applicable in a foodservice operation. Analysts and supervisors need to have an understanding of these principles and the ability to interpret them to workers effectively before job breakdown studies and revision in procedures, arrangement of work area, and equipment are inaugurated. A listing of these fundamental principles of motion economy is given in Fig. 14.1.

Practical application of most of these principles can be made easily in the foodservice field and will lead to increased efficiency, that is, reduction in the motion and time required for the job, and to a steady output of production with less fatigue on the part of the worker. A few specific examples of application follow.

- *Principles 1, 2, and 3.* To serve food onto a plate at the counter, pick up plate with left hand and bring to a center position while right hand grasps serving utensil, dips food, and carries it to the plate, both operations ending simultaneously; when panning rolls, pick up a roll in each hand and place on pan.
- *Principle 6.* Stir a mass of food easily and with minimum fatigue by grasping the handle of a wire whip (thumb up) and stirring round and round instead of pushing the whip directly back and forth across the kettle. Principles 5 and 7 are applied also in this same example, since greater force may be gained easily at the beginning of the downward and upward parts of the cycle.
- *Principle 8.* Gain and maintain speed in dipping muffins or cupcakes through the use of rhythmic motions; use regular and rhythmic motions in slicing or chopping certain vegetables and fruits with a French knife on a board.
- *Principles 8 and 10.* Equip and arrange each individual's work area so that body movements are confined to a minimum in his job performance.
- *Principle 11.* Store mixing-machine attachments and cooking utensils as close as possible to place of use; remove clean dishes from washing machine directly to carts and lowerator units that fit into serving counter; store glasses and cups in racks in which they were washed; cook certain foods in containers from which they will be served.
- *Principle 12.* Install vegetable peeler at end of preparation sink so that peeled potatoes can be dumped directly into the sink; install water outlets above range and jacketed kettles so utensils may be filled at point of use.
- *Principle 14.* For breading foods, arrange container of food to be breaded, flour, egg mixture, crumbs, and cooking pan in correct sequence so that no wasted motions are made.
- *Principle 16.* Provide some means of adjusting height of work surface to the tall and short worker; include one or two adjustable-height stools in list of kitchen equipment.
- *Principle 18.* Provide knee lever-controlled drain outlets on kitchen sinks; install electronic-eye controls on doors between dining room and kitchen.

PRINCIPLES OF MOTION ECONOMY

A check sheet for motion economy and fatigue reduction

Use of the Human Body	Arrangement of the Work Place	Design of Tools and Equipment
1. The two hands should begin as well as complete their motions at the same time.	10. There should be a definite and fixed place for all tools and materials.	18. The hands should be relieved of all work that can be done more advantageously by a jig, fixture, or a foot-operated device.
2. The two hands should not be idle at the same time except during rest periods.	11. Tools, materials, and controls should be located close to the point of use.	19. Two or more tools should be combined wherever possible.
3. Motions of the arms should be made in opposite and symmetrical directions, and should be made simultaneously.	12. Gravity feed bins and containers should be used to deliver material close to the point of use.	20. Tools and materials should be pre-positioned whenever possible.
4. Hand motions should be confined to the lowest classification with which it is possible to perform the work satisfactorily.	13. "Drop deliveries" should be used wherever possible.	21. Where each finger performs some specific movement, such as in typewriting, the load should be distributed in accordance with the inherent capacities of the fingers.
5. Momentum should be employed to assist the worker wherever possible, and it should be reduced to a minimum if it must be overcome by muscular effort.	14. Materials and tools should be located to permit the best sequence of motions.	22. Levers, crossbars, and hand wheels should be located in such positions that the operator can manipulate them with the least change in body position and with the greatest mechanical advantage.
6. Smooth continuous motions of the hands are preferable to zigzag motions or straight-line motions involving sudden and sharp changes in direction.	15. Provisions should be made for adequate conditions for seeing. Good illumination is the first requirement for satisfactory visual perception.	
7. Ballistic movements are faster, easier, and more accurate than restricted (fixation) or "controlled" movements.	16. The height of the work place and the chair should preferably be arranged so that alternate sitting and standing at work are easily possible.	
8. Work should be arranged to permit easy and natural rhythm whenever possible.	17. A chair of the type and height to permit good posture should be provided for every worker.	
9. Eye fixations should be as few and as close together as possible.		

Source. *Ralph M. Barnes*, Motion and Time Study, *Sixth Edition, Wiley, New York, p. 220, 1968.*

FIGURE 14.1

WORK IMPROVEMENT PROGRAM   Improvement in any work program is contingent on a study of the environmental factors and the activities of the workers in meeting the objectives of the organization. Such a study may involve one or more jobs in an organization. The usual approach for analysis and revision of a job method is:

1. Select the job to be improved. What needs improvement most? A bottleneck job is the best one to start thinking about. Jobs that require much time or that require much worker movement for materials, tools, and such are also good choices.
2. Break down the job in detail. Get in the habit of seeing every job as: make ready—the effort and time put into getting the equipment, tools, and materials with which to work; do—the actual productive work; and put away—the clean up or disposal following the "do." Analyze each operation, noting procedure, equipment used, distance moved, and time required. Some methods for performing this step are discussed in the next section.
3. Challenge every detail. Ask these questions of the entire job and of every part of the job. *What* is done? *Why* is it done at all? Is it necessary? *Where* is it done? Why is it done there? Is this the right place for it? Where is the best place? *When* is it done? Why is it done then? Is there a better time? *Who* does it? Why does this person do it? Is he or she the right person? *How* is it done? Why is it done this way? Is there a better way? Is there an easier way? Also question the materials, tools, and equipment that are being used. A form such as that shown in Fig. 14.2 is useful for this step.
4. Develop a better method. The process- or activity-activity analysis chart affords opportunity to study any job objectively and to evaluate the efficiency of performance. Checks can be made easily to determine the necessary and the excess operations, where and how delays occur, the distances either product or worker must travel, and where changes can be made.
5. Put the new method into effect. Teach the new method and follow up with proper supervision. Continue to seek new and better ways to do the job.

Much of the analysis or breakdown of jobs is accomplished through motion and time studies. Barnes[14] defines motion and time study as:

> the systematic study of work systems with the purposes of (1) developing the preferred system and method—usually the one with the lowest costs; (2) standardizing this system and method; (3) determining the time required by a qual-

Situation Studied   _Lettuce Chopping_   Date   _9–17–81_

Why Studied   _To improve efficiency of the process_   Study by   _Gregoire/Palacio_

Where   _Kramer Food Center Salad Area_   _31.03_ minutes/occurrence

How Often Repeated per Year   _690_   _21410.7_ minutes/year

	What is achieved?	What would happen if it weren't done?	What could be done and still meet requirements?	What should be done?
Purpose	Lettuce is chopped for salads	There would be no tossed salads	Lettuce could be bought chopped	Lettuce should be chopped at the facility
	Where is it done?	Disadvantages of doing it there:	Where else could it be done?	Where should it be done?
Place	Salad area	Don't always have enough heads of lettuce to fill barrels of chopped lettuce	Veg. Prep (downstairs) **Advantages of doing it elsewhere:** Barrels could be filled to capacity.	Salad area for control and better use of existing space.
	When is it done? Before:	Disadvantages of doing it then:	Advantages of doing it sooner:	When should it be done?
Sequence	Each meal After: Lettuce is cleaned	Requires set-up and clean-up three times a day	Clean-up and set-up only once **Advantages of doing it later:** Lettuce would be fresher	Once a day
	Who does it?	Why that person?	List two others who could do it.	Who should do it?
Person	Student salad employee	Assigned to students because this job is routine and disliked by full-time employees	Veg. Prep employee Salad foodservice worker	Salad foodservice worker
	What equipment and methods are used? **Equipment:**	Disadvantages of equipment:	How else could it be done?	How should it be done?
Means	Cutting board French knife **Method:** Manual chopping	Somewhat dangerous **Method:** Slow, tedious	Purchase chopped Manual lettuce chopper VCM–Meat slicer **Advantages:** Faster, safer	VCM

FIGURE 14.2   Critical examination of the process of lettuce chopping. Example of how such a study is recorded on a suitable form.

ified and properly trained person working at a normal pace to do a specific task or operation; and (4) assisting in training the worker in the preferred method.

METHODS FOR WORK IMPROVEMENT STUDY   The breakdown of job activities may be made in various ways and recorded appropriately for analysis, study, and evaluation. Among the possibilities are work sampling, pathway or flow diagram, operation and process charting, and micromotion studies. The objective is to be able to gain a complete and detailed picture of the process, regardless of the method of recording.

Work sampling is a tool for fact finding and often is less costly in time and money than a continuous study. It is based on the laws of probability that random samples reflect the same pattern of distribution as a large group. The primary use of work sampling is to measure the activities and delays of people or machines and determine the percentage of the time they are working or idle instead of observing the detailed activities of a repetitive task. The shorter and intermittent observations are less tiring to both the worker and the observer than continuous time studies; several workers can be observed simultaneously; interruptions do not affect the results; and tabulations can be made quickly on data-processing equipment, although neither management nor workers may have the knowledge of statistics involved. This process is sometimes known as random ratio-delay sampling.

A *pathway chart* or *flow diagram* is a scale drawing of an area on which the path of the worker or movement of material during a given process may be indicated and measured, but with no breakdown of time or details of the operation. Measurement of the distance traveled as the worker moves about in the performance of a task is made by computing the total length of lines drawn from one key point to another simultaneously with the worker's movements and multiplying by the scale of the drawing. A more convenient method is to set up pins or string supports at key points on a scale drawing of the worker's area and wind a measured length of string around the supports as the worker progresses from one position to another.

Operation charts may be used as simple devices to record, in sequence, the elemental movements of the hands of a worker at a given station, without consideration of time. A diagram of the work area might head the chart with the observed activities of both hands listed in two columns—left side for left hand, and right side for right hand. In such a chart, small circles usually are used to indicate transportation and large circles to denote action. Analysis of the chart gives a basis for reducing transportation to the lowest degree possible and for replanning the work area and procedures. It is important that both hands be used simultaneously and effectively. A chart showing the procedures used in making a pineapple and cottage cheese salad is given in Fig. 14.3. The lettuce cup had been prearranged on the plate.

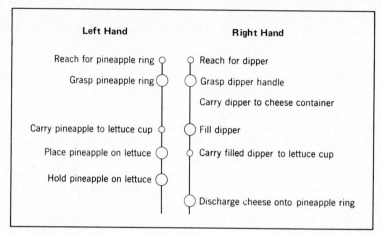

FIGURE 14.3   Operation Chart showing movement of the two hands in making pineapple and cottage cheese salad.

The *process chart* is a fairly simple technique for recording and analyzing the breakdown of a job. It presents graphically the separate steps or events by the use of symbols for a given process so that the entire picture of the job can be condensed into compact yet easily interpreted form. A process chart may present either *product analysis,* which shows in sequence the steps that a product goes through, or *person analysis,* which is a study of what the person does. Many different symbols were used by the Gilbreths when they devised this method of recording job activity years ago. Today, for most practical purposes, only four or five symbols are used that simplify and list quickly the steps or activities in a process. The symbols often used are:

$\bigcirc$ = operation or main steps in the process
$\Rightarrow$ = transportation or movement
D = delay
∇ = storage or hold
$\square$ = inspection such as examination for quality or quantity

Symbols may be arranged in a vertical line in sequence or, as in the activity-analysis charts (Figs. 14.4 and 14.5), with lines drawn from one symbol to another in each succeeding step. This method of charting makes for ease in checking time and in determining the number of repeats in any process as a basis for their reduction through revision of the method.

Without benefit of an elaborate process chart form, a simple listing of the procedures and times used in the preparation of a menu item can be made

PROCESS CHART					
Present ☒ Proposed ☐					
1951 – H.Q. Davidson				FILE NUMBER page	
SUMMARY	No.	TIME ( )	TASK or JOB : Dishwashing Procedure, Operations I Scrapping Trays		
OPERATIONS ○	1,546				
INSPECTIONS ☐	0		DEPT. ' 10th Floor Pantry		
MOVES ⇨	99		EQUIPMENT, TOOLS' etc. : Scrapping counter, prerinse counter with disposal unit, trash can, carts, cloth		
DELAYS ⅅ	70				
UNITS PRODUCED: 70 trays		1½ hr.	OPERATOR Pantry Maid A		
TOTAL DISTANCE MOVED			ANALYST	DATE March 20, 1963	

Descriptive Notes	Activity	Dist.	Time	Analysis Notes
Rinses cloth at sink.	☒☐⇨ⅅ			Damp cloth is used to wipe trays
Carries cloth to scrapping table.	○☐⇨ⅅ	8' 6"		
Brings loaded cart into pantry from hall.	○☐⇨ⅅ	5' 6"		Positions cart at left of operator. Each cart holds 6-9 trays.
Moves to side of table.	○☐⇨ⅅ			
Takes tray from cart and places on scrapping table.	☒☐⇨ⅅ			
Moves around in front of table.	○☐⇨ⅅ	1' 0"		Convenient position for working.
Changes position of tray.	○☐⇨☒			
Places tray on stack of empty trays.	☒☐⇨ⅅ			
Pulls menu from tray.	☒☐⇨ⅅ			
Places name card on tray at extreme right of scrapping table.	☒☐⇨ⅅ			Name cards in stacks by sections.
Picks up salt and pepper with left hand.	☒☐⇨ⅅ			
Places salt and pepper on tray with name cards.	☒☐⇨ⅅ			
Empties coffee pots into disposal.	☒☐⇨ⅅ			
Places empty coffee pots on prerinse counter.	☒☐⇨ⅅ			
Picks up plate and scrapes waste into disposal.	☒☐⇨ⅅ			
Adds plate to stack on prerinse counter.	☒☐⇨ⅅ			
Picks up creamer and empties contents into disposal.	☒☐⇨ⅅ			
Places creamer on prerinse counter.	☒☐⇨ⅅ			
Places cup and saucer on prerinse counter.	☒☐⇨ⅅ			Saucers stacked.
Removes glasses from tray and empties contents into disposal.	☒☐⇨ⅅ			
Places empty glasses upside down in wash rack on prerinse counter.	☒☐⇨ⅅ			
Picks up bowl with right hand.	☒☐⇨ⅅ			
Transfers bowl to left hand.	○☐⇨☒			Unnecessary handling.
Scrapes waste food from bowl with spoon into disposal.	☒☐⇨ⅅ			Rubber scraper better tool.
Stacks bowls on prerinse counter.	○☐⇨ⅅ			

DEPARTMENT OF INDUSTRIAL ENGINEERING—THE OHIO STATE UNIVERSITY

FIGURE 14.4   Process Chart of tray scrapping as observed in a hospital floor-service pantry.

PROCESS CHART

Present ☐ Proposed ☒

1951 - H.Q. Davidson   FILE NUMBER   page

SUMMARY		No.	TIME ( )	TASK or JOB	Dishwashing Procedure, Operation I : Scrapping Trays
OPERATIONS	◯	1,024			
INSPECTIONS	☐	2		DEPT.	: 10th Floor Pantry
MOVES	⇨	13		EQUIPMENT, TOOLS' etc. :	Scrapping counter, prerinse counter with disposal unit, trash can, carts, pan, rubber scraper
DELAYS	D	0			
UNITS PRODUCED: 70 trays			1 hr. TOTAL	OPERATOR : Pantry Maid A	
TOTAL DISTANCE MOVED 117 feet				ANALYST :	DATE: April 3, 1963

Descriptive Notes	Activity	Dist.	Time	Analysis Notes
Rinses cloth at sink and fills pan with water.	⊗☐⇨D			Cloth is rinsed several times during operation.
Carries cloth and pan to scrapping table.	◯☐⊗D	7' 0"		Pan of water at counter reduces trips to sink.
Goes to silver storage unit.	◯☐⊗D	4' 9"		
Gets rubber spatula from drawer.	⊗☐⇨D			
Returns and places spatula on scrapping table.	◯☐⊗D	5' 0"		
Brings loaded cart into pantry from hall.	◯☐⊗D	5' 6"		Pre-positioned tray on scrapping counter facilitates placement of name cards, and salts and peppers.
Takes tray from cart and places on scrapping table.	⊗☐⇨D			
Picks up salt and pepper and places on tray at extreme right of worker.	⊗☐⇨D			
Places name-card holder with menu on same tray.	⊗☐⇨D			Menu pulled after name-card holder is on tray while hand is in position. Drops menu on table; all menus later put into trash can at one time.
Scrapes waste food from bowl with rubber scraper.	⊗☐⇨D			
Stacks bowls on prerinse counter.	⊗☐⇨D			All refuse from one tray scraped into one dish; then, into disposal.
Places silver in rack on prerinse counter.	⊗☐⇨D			
Removes glasses from tray, empties contents into disposal.	⊗☐⇨D			
Places glasses upside down in wash rack on prerinse counter.	⊗☐⇨D			
Empties coffee pot and creamer into disposal, transfers directly to dish rack.	⊗☐⇨D			Both hands used simultaneously. Movements combined or continuous wherever possible.
Removes paper tray-cover, folds once and places in trash can.	⊗☐⇨D			
Wipes off bottom of tray, places on stack than wipes off top of tray.	⊗☐⇨D			Handling of each tray reduced to a minimum.
Reaches to cart for next tray.	⊗☐⇨D			
Operations repeated until all trays are scrapped.	◯☐⇨D			
	◯☐⇨D			

DEPARTMENT OF INDUSTRIAL ENGINEERING—THE OHIO STATE UNIVERSITY

FIGURE 14.5   Process Chart of same operation as Fig. 14.3 after a study and revision of the original procedures had been made. By changing the sequence of operations and moving the tray cart near the working area, the operations, moves, and delays were reduced materially.

and used to improve either the physical setup or the method, for example, the observance of the cook mixing and portioning meat balls, beginning at the worktable.

A *micromotion study* is a technique whereby movements of the worker may be photographed and recorded permanently on film. This method affords

Procedure Chart

Approximate Distance (ft)	Time (min)	Description of Operation
6	9:00	Fasten bowl and beater in position on mixer.
15	9:01	Go to refrigerator for milk, ground meat, and other weighed recipe ingredients (use cart).
15	9:035	Return to mixer.
3	9:04	Place seasonings, eggs, milk, and cut-up bread in mixer bowl.
	9:05	Mix slightly (observe).
	9:06	Add meat and mix to blend (observe).
3	9:075	Remove beater and take to wash sink.
5	9:085	Lift bowl of meat mixture to low bench near worktable.
50	9:09	Assemble portion tools and pans.
	9:10	Portion onto pans with number 12 dipper.
	9:25	Complete portioning.

a more accurate presentation of detail than others, and projection for analysis may be made at different rates of speed. In addition, the time of each movement may be recorded.

A detailed motion breakdown of the activities portrayed on micromotion film is easily made and recorded in graphic form by use of *therbligs,* expressed through letter, line, or color symbols. The word *therblig,* formed by spelling Gilbreth backward but retaining the original order of the last two letters, was coined by Frank Gilbreth at the time he introduced the system of breaking down, into 17 subdivisions or elements, basic hand movements employed in job performance. The therbligs are: search (Sh), select (St), inspect (I), transport empty (TE), grasp (G), hold (H), transport loaded (TL), release load (RL), position (P), preposition (PP), assemble (A), disassemble (DA), use (U), avoidable delay (AD), unavoidable delay (UD), plan (Pn), and rest (R).

Most often letter symbols are used in recording the breakdown of a procedure, for example, cutting a cake.

P	Place cake on table in position to cut.
TE	Move right hand toward knife rack.
Sh	Look over supply of knives.
St	Decide knife to use.
G	Take knife in right hand.
TL	Move knife to cutting position above cake.
U	Cut cake.

Any human activities may be analyzed by this system as a basis for eliminating the unnecessary and excess motions in the formulation of an improved method of procedure.

The chronocyclegraph is a photographic technique to show motion patterns of hands in performing rapid repetitive operations. It is made by attaching lights to the hands, which show as dotted lines on the finished photograph. The entire workplace must be included in order to study the relationship of the worker and direction of his or her hand movements to the work setup. Complete calculation of velocity and acceleration of hand motions is limited by the two-dimensional factor in this technique.

Applications of Work Improvement

Analysis of the data accumulated in the study of the work situation and the methods used in a foodservice may show that certain changes could be made immediately, whereas others involve time, money, and an educational program for the workers. No one set of rules can be used to bring about the desired improvements, but through the cooperative effort of management and worker groups, many things can be made possible. A few suggestions for making improvements follow.

One of the first steps in a job improvement plan is to try to *eliminate unnecessary operations, delays, and moves* without producing deleterious effects on the product or worker. Habit plays an important part in the work routines of people, and it is easy for them to continue in the old pattern; for example, even though the improved methods of processing dehydrated fruits eliminates the necessity of soaking before cooking, some cooks might continue to soak them. A common example of good practice is to have one person fill and deliver storeroom requisitions once a day instead of each cook going to the storeroom for single items as needed.

Operations may be combined as in the making of certain types of sandwiches when the butter could be combined with the spread mixture and all applied in one operation instead of two. Other examples of simplified practice are the one bowl method of combining ingredients for cakes, and cutting a handful of celery stalks at one time on a board instead of singly in the hand.

A *change in sequence of operations* to make the most efficient use of time and equipment and to reduce distance is important. Instead of trying to pare and cut dry, hard squash, put it into the steamer for a short time until the hard cover softens; then it can be pared and cut quickly and easily.

The *selection of multiple-use equipment* reduces to a minimum the items needed. A mixing machine with all of the chopper, slicer, and grinder attachments might be more desirable for a given situation than the purchase of a chopping machine in addition to the mixer without attachments. Where and when the item will be used will determine its best location. A mixing machine to be used in one department only should be located convenient to that center of activity, whereas a machine shared by two departments would be located between the two but nearest and most accessible to the department requiring the heaviest and most frequent usage. Duplication of some equipment may be compensated in reduced labor hours required for certain jobs.

Equipment may be relocated or removed entirely to facilitate a more direct flow of work in any area. To reduce "searches" a definite place should be provided for every item, and in a well-regulated foodservice everything will be kept in the designated location except when in use. This storage location or pre-positioning of the items should be convenient to the center of their first use; for example, the bowls, beaters, and attachments for the mixing machine should be stored next to or underneath the machine, the cook's cutlery stored in a drawer or on a rack at the cook's table, and clean water glasses returned to the water cooler in the wash racks for storage. Some kitchens may have retained a meat block, even though pan-ready meats are now used. Others may have more range space than is needed for modern cookery. In either case, the removal of certain equipment would provide space for more efficient utilization. Some kitchens may need additional equipment to provide adequate physical facilities for satisfactory operation. Most kitchen machines are designed as labor-saving devices and can do many times the amount of work that could be accomplished by hand in a comparable time and should be used whenever feasible. Improvements in design and operation of kitchen machines influence the method of operation. Automatic timing and temperature-control devices release the worker for other duties more than was possible when frequent checking and manual control were necessary.

The *reduction of transportation or movement of materials and equipment* often can be made through rearrangement of equipment, mobile equipment, and the use of carts to transport many items at one time. The relation of the receiving, storage, and preparation areas requires careful planning to be sure that the flow of the raw product through preparation and service is kept direct and in as condensed an area as practicable. Some delays in operation may be avoided by the installation of additional equipment, by a change in the sequence of operation, such as the assembly-line technique in pie making, by the training of the workers to use both hands at one time and to practice certain shortcuts in preparation, or by a better understanding of the timing standard for various processes.

The *use of a different product* could become a deciding factor in changing the method of procedure. The present tendency is toward the increased use of preprepared foods. Peeled carrots, processed potatoes, peeled and sectioned citrus fruit, frozen fruits and vegetables, basic mixes for baked products, freeze-dried shrimp, and pan-ready poultry are only a few such items that definitely change the preliminary procedures necessary in many food production jobs.

Consideration of these suggestions and other factors peculiar to the situation provides a basis for outlining an improved method that can be tried and reevaluated for further streamlining. An example of the advantages to be gained from such a revision are indicated in the summaries at the tops of Figs. 14.4 and 14.5.

Every foodservice director should develop an attitude of "high productivity" in every phase of the operation. The constant seeking of ways for employees to become more productive and then training them to follow such procedures will bring desired results. With the emphasis on financial accountability in today's market, high productivity is essential for success. Time for study and research into the organization's work design, and then making necessary work improvement applications should be high priorities on the manager's schedule.

Notes

1. Brayton, G. N.: Simplified method of measuring productivity identifies opportunities for increasing it. Industrial Engineering 15:49 (Feb), 1983.
2. Kaud, F. A.: Productivity: Measures and improvement approaches. *In* Rose, J. C., ed.: Handbook for Health Care Food Service Management. Rockville, MD: Aspen Systems Corp., 1984.
3. Bain, D.: The Productivity Prescription. New York: McGraw-Hill Book Co., 1982.
4. Bennett, A. C.: Productivity and the Quality of Work Life in Hospitals. Los Angeles: American Hospital Publishing, Inc., 1983.
5. Judson, A.S.: The awkward truth about productivity. Harvard Bus. Rev. 60:93 (Sept./Oct.), 1982.
6. Lockwood, D. L. and Luthans, F.: Contingent time off: A nonfinancial incentive for improving productivity. Mgmt. Rev. 73:48 (July), 1984.
7. Kahn, R. L., and Katz, D.: Leadership practices in relation to productivity and morale. *In* Cartwright, D., and Zandar, A., eds.: Group Dynamics Research and Theory, 2nd ed. New York: Harper & Row, 1960.
8. Miller, L.: Tearing down the barriers between management and labor leads to increased productivity and greater profits. Mgmt. Rev. 73:8 (May), 1984.
9. Katzell, R. A. and Yankelovich, D.: Work, Productivity, and Job Satisfaction. New York: The Psychological Corp., 1975.
10. Konz, S.: Work Design: Industrial Ergonomics, 2nd ed. Columbus, OH: Grid Publishing, Inc., 1983.
11. Matthews, M. E.: Productivity studies reviewed, trends analyzed. Hospitals 49:81 (Dec. 16), 1975.

12. Kazarian, E. A.: Foodservice Facilities Planning, 2nd ed. Westport, CN: AVI Publishing Co., 1983.

13. Avery, A.C.: A Modern Guide to Foodservice Equipment. Boston: CBI Publishing Co., 1980.

14. Barnes, R.M.: Motion and Time Study—Design and Measurement of Work, 7th ed. New York: John Wiley and Sons, 1980.

15. Pedderson, R.: Motivation and worker productivity. *In* Wilkinson, J., ed.: Increasing Productivity in Foodservice. Boston: Cahners Books, 1973.

16. Bartscht, K. G., Bayha, F. H., Molhoek, D. G., and Kausler, G. J.: Hospital Staffing Methodology Manual, MM-3 Dietary. Ann Arbor, MI: Community Systems Foundation.

17. VanEgmond-Pannell, D.: School Foodservice, 3rd ed. Westport, CN: AVI Publishing Co., 1985.

18. Myers, M. S.: Every Employee a Manager. New York: McGraw-Hill Book Co., 1981.

Supplementary References

BARUCCO, H.: Fear and productivity: More closely related than we think. Mgmt. Rev. 70:23 (Jan.), 1981.

BERKE, E.: At last an easy route to productivity: Communication. Mgmt. Rev. 72:5 (Nov.), 1983.

CURTIS, S. R. AND MESSERSMITH, A. M.: Job function time allocations of school food service directors. School Food Service Research Review 10(2):87, Fall 1986.

HAIMANN, T. AND HILGERT, R. L.: Supervision: Concepts and Practices of Management, 2nd ed. Cincinnati: South-Western Publishing Co., 1977.

KANTER, R. M. AND STEIN, B. A.: Ungluing the stuck: Motivating performance and productivity through expanding opportunity. Mgmt. Rev. 70:45 (July), 1981.

LAGGES, J.G.: The role of delegation in improving productivity. Pers. J. 58:776, 1979.

LAWLER, E.E.: Creating high involvement work organizations. *In* Flamholtz, E. G., ed.: Human Resource Productivity in the 1980s. Los Angeles: Institute of Industrial Relations, University of California, 1982.

PALMER, J.D.: The logic and logistics of commissaries. Cornell H.R.A. Quarterly 25:104 (May), 1984.

SARTAIN, A. Q. AND BAKER, A. W.: The Supervisor and the Job, 3rd ed. New York: McGraw-Hill Book Co., 1978.

THE WALL STREET JOURNAL. January 3, 1974, p. 11.

CHAPTER 15

Financial Management

Introduction

Financial planning and accountability for the foodservice organization is a major responsibility for the manager. Cost effectiveness is essential for a successful operation, especially with today's economy and competitive market, whether for a restaurant, hospital, school or college foodservice, or some other.

Every person responsible for the financial management must know, day by day, what transactions have taken place and how they compare with established goals. Otherwise, downward trends may not be detected in time to take corrective action before financial disaster occurs.

The primary purpose of this chapter is to provide information necessary for managers to be able to: (1) plan a budget, (2) set up a system of records that will provide financial operating data, (3) use records to prepare financial reports, (4) review and evaluate data from the records and reports by comparing them with budgeted figures, and (5) know what kinds of corrective action can and should be taken to keep financial operations in line with anticipated and desired goals.

Basic information required for this kind of cost control and good financial management is the same whether a computerized or manual system is to be used. Decision making regarding objectives and goals, cost justification, control measures, and corrective action to take when needed remains a personal activity and responsibility of the foodservice manager.

Financial Planning

Good financial planning and management are essential for the success of every foodservice operation. Knowledge of the techniques used to control costs and to provide data for sound financial decision making is a management must. The following four actions are basic to achieving financial maturity on the part of the manager, and when followed should provide the guide to achieving the success desired:

1. Setting financial goals or standards to be attained, usually through a planned budget
2. Knowing what is being accomplished through a system of records to provide pertinent data on current operations
3. Using the data from the records to evaluate progress toward reaching the set goals, best done through daily, monthly, and yearly reports that compare actual achievement with the standard
4. Taking any corrective measures necessary to bring operations in line with those desired

The financial goals of various foodservices differ. Some are in business to make as large a profit as possible; others are nonprofit but seek to provide the best possible food and service that their financial resources allow. In all situations, however, some type of financial plan is a key to achieving desired departmental goals. Without such a guide, problems may arise before management is aware of them and could lead to financial downfall.

The financial plan most commonly used is a budget that all foodservice organizations should prepare and use as a guide for maintaining a sound, healthy organization. Such planning is, of course, done within the policies of the organization.

Budgets

A budget is a forecast of future needs. It covers the planned activities of the department for a given period of time, usually the fiscal or calendar year, and should be arranged in some orderly manner. Budgets are often thought of as a *financial* plan, but foodservice budgets include operating data as well, the number of meals to be served, and labor time requirements.

Budgets are based on factual data from past records of income, expenditures, census and labor hours used, and a consideration of any anticipated changes that may affect future operations. This method alone, however, may focus too much on desired additions to the budget unless there is a cost evaluation made to justify both past and newly planned expenditures.

For any foodservice that is just beginning operation, a detailed budget will not be possible, of course. Since the service has not operated previously, there will be no records of past operations available on which to base a plan. An established goal of percentage of income to be spent for food (see daily food cost reports) can serve as a general guide for the first few months of business, however, and compared daily with actual operations.

With the current emphasis on cost containment and better management of all resources, it is important that foodservice managers understand the budget planning process and techniques used to prepare a realistic budget. Too many managers operate without a budget as a guide because it is time-consuming to prepare, predictions are difficult, and perhaps have incomplete records to provide the necessary data. The value of a budget and the budgeting process must be clearly understood and accepted by management. Otherwise, if one is planned at all, it may be an empty gesture, and the budget not used for its intended purpose.

VALUE OF A BUDGET   To some, the word *budget* has the connotation of curtailed spending and inflexibility, and is, therefore, undesirable. This is not true. Instead, a budget is a valuable management tool used as a guide for allocation of resources and for comparison with actual operations, the basis for financial control.

The advantages of budget planning and budgets are many and far outweigh any possible disadvantages. They include:

1. Budget planning forces those in management positions to seriously consider the future directions and development of their department, and to reaffirm old or establish new financial goals. All those with decision-making authority in the department should be involved in budget planning and contribute to final decisions made.
2. The budget planning committee's review of previous expenditures provides an evaluation process and a base for justifying future requests for funds.
3. A budget is an important control device. It gives a standard for comparison against actual transactions. Deviations from the anticipated (budgeted) are known and can be corrected or justified as they occur.
4. The use of the budget helps prevent problems from arising that could cause financial difficulties. Through study of their department's current operating trends and desired goals, managers are alerted to such problems.

5. Since those involved in planning establish priorities of need, they should be committed to staying within the limits they were responsible for setting.
6. A budget provides a goal for achievement. Employees made aware of those goals are apt to feel responsibility toward meeting them.
7. A budget provides for continuity in the event of a changeover in management.

Disadvantages of budgeting and budgets are minor compared with the positive results of having a budget for a guide. However, disadvantages may include:

1. A budget that is rigid may be ignored as unworkable. Budgets should be flexible and adjustable according to changing situations.
2. Budget preparation requires time and takes personnel away from regular management activities.
3. Unless the entire managerial staff is in support of budgeting and cooperates in preparation and use of the budget, the process may be only a gesture and have limited value.
4. Departments within the organization may vie with each other for funds, which could cause undesirable competition and problems.

TYPES OF BUDGETS   Although there are many types of budgets, all have the same focus: to determine how much money (or other resources) will be available to be used, and then to allocate that amount fairly to cover various expenses plus a margin for profit.

Following are descriptions of some types of budgets used by foodservice managers and some terms used in the budgeting process.

Operating budget, as the name implies, is a plan for operating the foodservice, including both financial forecasts for income and expense items and the numbers of customers (guests, patients, students, and so on) and the projected labor hour requirements. Accurate historical data from records and reports must be available in order to project reliable forecasts. If new equipment is needed, an **equipment budget** with costs and priorities may be included. Likewise, a **facilities remod-** eling or repair budget section may be a part of the total budget plan. A separate **labor budget** that details the number of labor hours or days and total personnel needs with labor cost totals is also a budget component. A **sales** budget or forecast of number of meals the operation expects to serve and the dollar volume of income is especially valuable to the profit-type organizations.

Fixed budget is one based on a fixed annual level or volume of transactions such as the number of meals served, number of hospital patient days, or similar classification, and computed with the projected average rate figure, as cost per meal.

Flexible budget   considers the ranges from high to low activity figures rather than averages as with the fixed budget. This type of budget gives "flexibility" in operating, but may be more difficult to use as a control than the fixed budget.

Zero-based budget   requires managers to justify in detail each request for funds and to re-evaluate all activities each year. There is no carryover from previous years, so each new budget begins with a "zero" balance.

Project budgeting   is a process of costing each activity that affects the budget and ranking them in priority order as to the cost benefits to be derived. Often alternative plans are given for two or three levels of service that could be offered, the current level and one higher and one lower. For example, the dishwashing activity presently requires three employees and 96 labor hours. Could this activity be accomplished with fewer people and/or fewer hours, or will more time be required? The latter is a higher level of service and will cost more. Managers and supervisors at all levels must be involved in collecting such cost data and making decisions regarding priorities. The department director must view requests as a whole and not by separate activity categories. Project budgeting lends support to the overall operating or financial budget, but does not replace it.

Steps in Budget Planning

As can be realized from the description of budgets, they are time-consuming to prepare and require thought-provoking effort on the part of all who are involved. A timetable should be set up for various phases of data collection and planning. The schedule must allow ample time for careful completion of the project so it can be evaluated and approved well in advance of the beginning of the next fiscal period. Budget planning as a joint endeavor represents many points of view. Final agreement by that group should ensure a fair allocation of funds for the goals to be met.

The steps involved in arriving at a good, carefully planned budget are outlined according to Minno and Bhayana:[1]

There are three distinct phases, each one deriving information from the one before:
• the evaluation phase, which makes sense of your restaurant's past performance and identifies those factors that may influence the future,
• the planning phase, which uses the information compiled during the evaluation to forecast the budget, and

• the control phase, which uses the budget cost during planning to keep track of monthly performance.

More specifically, these steps usually are found in planning the foodservice financial budget:

1. Collect operating data from current and past records and reports of income and expense, and census (see later in this chapter under "Financial Operations: A System of Records and Reports").
2. Study those data and evaluate them against departmental goals. Information reviewed should cover actual operating and budget variance figures from the previous three or four years with justification or explanation of variances; income and expense trends; sales reports and sales statistics; menu, prices, customer selection, portion sizes, and food cost per portion; such labor statistics as the number of employees, their duties, schedules, and wage rates.
3. Discuss and analyze any and all factors that may affect future operations. These include both external (outside your control) and internal (within your control) influences that can be identified as having a possible effect on foodservice costs or activities in the future. Examples of *external* factors: the local economy, actions by government (change in taxes or laws), changes in utility costs, new construction that might bring in new business or divert traffic and so reduce patronage, or increases in competition. Examples of *internal* factors: a planned addition to the facility that will change the number of persons to be served; a change in type of foodservice system as from conventional to assembly/serve; converting to computerized record keeping; change in hours of service to better accommodate patrons.
4. Discuss and plan for new goals or activities desired, such as a remodeling project, purchasing new equipment, or a new service, possibly catering, to be offered. These are all considered in light of anticipated changes and current prices.
5. Set priorities and make decisions as to what can be included in the budget for next year. In establishing budgetary priorities the director must weigh the relative desires and needs of each unit, search out nonessentials, decide if any items could be provided at a lower cost, plan for upkeep and expansion of the plant, and provide for the development and increase of personnel. Even though the income may remain approximately the same year after year, careful appraisal of past expenses should be made whenever a new budget is prepared in order to prevent overspending for some items to the neglect of others quite as important. In a period of rising costs some allowance should be made to take care of replacement furnish-

ings and equipment, since depreciation is calculated on the original cost of these items.

The *financial budget* must reflect the objectives and policies of the organization for which it is planned. For example, the school foodservice has as its objective the serving of good food at a minimum cost. The foodservice may pay for food, labor, and laundry only, while the school subsidizes the overhead and operating costs. In such a case, the percentage of income spent for food is, rightly, very high. The foodservice budget of a college residence hall that is helping to pay for retirement of bonds is necessarily quite different from one whose physical plant and equipment are not encumbered. In each situation, the proportion of the income spent for various expense items will vary with the size and type, objectives, and policies of the individual foodservice.

The budget planning committee has responsibility for making decisions as to what expense items can be included in the budget with a fixed income, or how the income can be expanded, if it is a variable income, to cover the cost of the items of expense deemed essential. Forward-looking managers establish priorities and plan an orderly way of achieving these goals, even if it means looking beyond the next year's budget.

6. Write the budget for presentation. Although there is no established format for the formal write-up of the budget, it contains an organized listing of expected income, classified as to sources, and the classified list of all expense items. Usually a form similar to the one shown in Fig. 15.1, is

Budget Work Sheet—Income and Expense

	Estimated Last Year		Actual Last Year		Anticipated Changes		Estimated Next Year	
	Total	%	Total	%	+	−	Total	%
Income								
Regular Sales								
Special Meals								
Other (Itemize for specific Foodservice)								
Total								
Expenses								
1. Food								

FIGURE 15.1   Budget planning worksheet, adaptable for use in any foodservice.

	Estimated Last Year		Actual Last Year		Anticipated Changes		Estimated Next Year	
	Total	%	Total	%	+	−	Total	%
2. Salaries and wages:								
Regular employees								
Student or part-time employees								
Social security tax								
Other taxes								
Fringe benefits								
Total								
3. Services:								
Laundry								
Utilities								
Telephone								
Exterminator								
Garbage and trash disposal								
Total								
4. Supplies, repairs, and maintenance:								
Cleaning supplies								
Paper supplies								
Office supplies								
Equipment repairs								
Miscellaneous supplies								
Physical plant								
Total								
5. Housing:								
Amortization or rent								
Taxes								
Interest								
Depreciation								
Insurance								
Repairs								
Total								
Grand Totals								
Excess of income over expenses								

FIGURE 15.1 *(Continued)*

Sources of Income	Income Past Period	Anticipated Increase	Anticipated Decrease	Anticipated Income
Board fees				
Cafeteria receipts				
Guest meals				
Special meals				
Catering				
Special food orders				
Miscellaneous				
Total				

FIGURE 15.2   Income sources and detailed information for use in budget planning.

used as a work sheet to organize data in the budget. Writing the budget continues, following these steps:

a. List all sources of expected income. Sources vary according to type of foodservice. Fig 15.2 illustrates those for a college residence hall where income comes from student board fees. Commercial operations derive income from cash sales. Record this year's dollar figures for each of the sources of income and then the anticipated changes for the next budget period. Calculate and record the total expected income.

b. Classify and list the items of expense with the cost calculated for each. Basically these are food, labor, overhead (fixed costs as amortization or rent, taxes, insurance), and operating costs (as utilities, telephone, paper goods). Specific items vary somewhat for various types of food-services. Fig. 15.1 shows one such chart of accounts, as the listing is called. The National Restaurant Association has provided comparable information for commercial operations in its Uniform System of Accounts for Restaurants.[2]

c. Add other pertinent data as number of meals served, labor hours—total and per meal served, last period, expected changes and new totals.

d. Prepare a justification for requests for new funds.

e. Review and make any changes necessary.

f. Write the budget in final form with any cost benefit statements attached. If the budget is to be forwarded to a higher administrator for approval, an explanation of certain items will prove helpful for good understanding of requests.

g. Use the budget! Once the budget has been approved, it should be *used.* The yearly budget figures are divided into appropriate time periods for comparative purposes. For example, a calendar month may be used for those with year-round operations. Schools may wish to use a 20-school-day period, since holidays and vacations result in more or fewer operating days some months, making comparisons unrealistic.

A form similar to the one illustrated in Fig. 15.3 should be designed or provided for recording the budgeted figures. At the close of the month or other time period used, the actual operating figures are recorded from the income, expense, and census records for easy comparison. A quick glance at this comparative report will show any discrepancies between anticipated and actual business. If there are any deviations, some type of corrective action is

Name of Food Service

Month _____ , 19 _____

	Number of Meals	Food Cost		Payroll Expense		Other Costs and Expenses	
	Total for month	*Total for month*	*Per meal served*	*Total for month*	*Per meal served*	*Total for month*	*Per meal served*
Budgeted							
Actual							
Over + − Under							

Cumulative for Year to Date

	Jan.	Feb.	Mar.	April	May	June	etc.
Budgeted							
Actual							
Over + − Under							

FIGURE 15.3   Budgeted figures are compared with actual operating figures for management control of finances.

called for. The data on the comparative form should be used in connection with information from the daily food cost report, profit and loss statements, discussed later in this chapter for evaluating activities and deciding what actions to take.

Following are Minno and Bhayana's "recipe" for budgeting and Kaud's explanation of the budget.

The Step-by-Step Budgeting Recipe

Step one—The evaluation phase

1. Evaluate the sales generators.
2. Evaluate the competition.
3. Evaluate community activities.
4. Evaluate other economic factors.
5. Evaluate the restaurant's internal financial data.

Step two—The planning phase

1. Plan the sales.
2. Plan food cost and beverage cost.
3. Plan payroll cost.
4. Plan controllable expenses.
5. Plan other expenses.
6. Plan the profit level.

Step three—The control phase

1. Control through comparisons of actual results to budgeted amounts.
2. Control through evaluating significant variances and determining causes of the variances.
3. Control through timely actions upon significantly unfavorable variances.[1]

Kaud[3] said:

> It is generally agreed that the proper design and use of the budget process is one of the most effective management tools because it does the following:
>
> • States goals and objectives in a quantifiable manner.
> • Serves as a communication and commitment device for management.
> • Acts as a measurement tool and feedback for corrective action.
> • Points out deficiencies.
> • Forecasts when shortages might occur.

Financial Operations: A System of Records and Reports

Knowledge of the day-to-day financial transactions and an awareness of "where the money is going before it is gone" is an ongoing responsibility of the foodservice director. The use of records is essential for providing readily available operating data. No foodservice operation, regardless of size, can long exist without the definite information that records provide to guide present operations and as a basis for future financial planning and control.

Records, like all forms of control, vary with the type, size, and policies of the institution, so that the management must ascertain what information is desired and how it may be obtained with the least expenditure of effort, time, and money.

Most foodservice organizations today utilize the computer for much of their record keeping and reporting. Data required for computer input is essentially the same as that for noncomputerized record keeping; forms and procedures vary. Good manual control and decisions on what information should be provided by computer are prerequisites to a good computerized control system. Designing appropriate forms for data organization is the first step in setting up either a manual or computerized system.

Records for Control

Records deemed essential for a noncomplex foodservice operation include those for controlling the major phases of the operations. These essential records may be classified as those for procurement and receiving, storage and storeroom control, production and service of food, number of people served, cash transactions, operating and maintenance, and personnel. More specifically, these include:

> Purchasing and receiving records
>> Purchase order
>> Invoice
>> Receiving record
>> Purchase record
>> Summary of purchases record
> Storage and storeroom records
>> Storeroom control

Requisition or storeroom issue records
Perpetual inventory
Physical inventory
Food production and service records
    Menu
    Standardized recipes
    Portion control standards
    Production schedule and leftovers report
    Menu tally
Dining room/patient room records
    Census reports: number of meals served
    Regular and special meals' count
Income/expense records
    Cash sales register reports
    Guest checks
    Cash disbursement records for all expense items
Personnel records (related to cost control)
    Time card/payroll records
    Work schedules
    Fringe benefits record

Illustrations of record forms are given in the chapters appropriate for each topic: menu planning (Chapter 3), purchasing and storage (Chapter 4), production (Chapter 5), and staffing (Chapter 12). Only census and income/expense records are presented here. Since these are given as examples only, each foodservice director will want to design forms for his or her own department according to the specific situation. However, these examples may aid in determining what information should be included.

DINING ROOM/PATIENT COUNT RECORDS   A record of number of people served is vital for forecasting purchasing and production needs. Also, the data from a census report are necessary for determining per meal costs, average sales per person, and the distribution of meals served to various categories of consumers for each meal of the day.

A form designed for recording the census should be large enough to include figures for the entire month (or other accounting period) and for each category of consumers. A sheet of paper may be divided horizontally into the days in the operating period, and vertically into the meal periods per day with the classification of groups served. Fig. 15.4a and b give examples of typical census report forms for two types of foodservices. If more detailed information is desired, patient meals could be divided into "regular" and "special" diets, and personnel meals into "staff" and "employees."

Monthly Census Report

Name of Organization _____

Date _____ Month _____ 19 ____ Year

| Day/Date | Regular Guest Count | | | Totals | | Employee Meals | | | Totals | | Special (Catering) Functions | | | Totals | | Grand Totals | |
	Break-fast	Lunch	Dinner	Today	To Date	Break-fast	Lunch	Dinner	Today	To Date	Break-fast	Lunch	Dinner	Today	To Date	Today	To Date
Su 1																	
Mo 2																	
Tu 3																	
—																	
Tu 31																	

FIGURE 15.4(a) Census record keeping form adaptable to commercial foodservice. The "To Date" figures are cumulative for the month.

	Patient Meals					Personnel Meals					Patient and Personnel
MONTHLY MEAL CENSUS											
Hospital						Date _____ 19 ___ mo.					

Date	Break-fast	Lunch	Dinner	Total Meals Today	To Date	Break-fast	Lunch	Dinner	Total Meals Today	To Date	Total Meals Today	To Date
1												
2												
3												
—												
30												
31												

FIGURE 15.4(b)   Meal census summary sheet suitable for health care facilities.

Information to be recorded on this form comes from cash register reports for personnel and guest meals; dietary count of patient meals and of meals served at any special functions.

Special Meals Records. A record of details of special meal functions is necessary for foodservices that cater to special groups in addition to their own regular meal service. A hospital, college residence hall, or industrial foodservice may be requested to cater for an occasional special group, whereas it is a common occurrence for several parties to be scheduled at the same time in a hotel or college student union. Each may have a different menu and demand specialized service, for which they pay accordingly. In all cases it is necessary to have definite policies and procedures outlined that can be followed through from the planning to the billing of the charges in order to ensure successful and satisfactory operation. Fig. 15.5 is a typical agreement form for special group meetings and meals with a record of price and total charges and number of people served.

INCOME AND EXPENSE RECORDS   A record of daily transactions is essential for preparation of monthly financial statements. Managers must know the sources and amounts of income, and where that income goes. Several records are needed to provide that information in a simplified way.

Sales and Cash Receipts. Even small operations such as school lunchrooms handle some cash, and businesslike procedures are needed for an accounting of the money. Cash registers provide a relatively safe place for money during serving hours and also provide accurate data on number of

Name of Foodservice

Organization _____   Function _____

Date _____ Time _____   Arranged by _____

Room_____   Address _____

Number Guaranteed_____ Served _____   Phone No._____

Price _____   Booked by _____ Date _____

Total Charge _____   Approved by _____

Menu

Details

Setup

Speaker's Table

Flowers

Music

Public Address

Tickets

Misc.

Guarantees are not subject to change less
than 24 hours in advance of party. We
are prepared to serve 10% in excess of the
number guaranteed.

Accepted_____

Union Office_____

Copies: Manager
Food Director
Catering
Maintenance
Kitchen
Accounting

FIGURE 15.5   Special meals agreement form also serves as record of number
served.

sales and total cash received. Larger organizations may use cash registers of varying degrees of sophistication including electronic point-of-sales (POS) computer terminals. These produce summary printouts and proofs of cash collected, which can replace the use of the cash register record shown in Fig. 15.6. The POS terminal can be programmed to provide as much information and detail as management desires. This may include among other things:

- Number of sales
- Total sales dollars by cash, check, credit card
- Tax collected
- A total customer count of those who paid by cash and a count by number of those customers who received meals other than by the cash system
- The total number of servings for each type of food, such as entrees, vegetables, desserts, salads, and beverages (menu tally).
- The dollar volume for each type of food sold

Also the computer can:

- Printout an itemized receipt for each customer.
- Calculate automatically the change to be returned to the customer and print the transaction on the receipt.
- Report productivity by hour or shift and totals.

A record of income from other than cash sales and of payments made for all expense items is also essential. A *cash receipts and disbursements* book is used by bookkeepers to record these transactions. Also, they may be kept by computer. Sample forms of the two parts of the cash record are given in Figs. 15.7a and b. These should be filled in daily, posting the disbursements amounts from bills received and paid by check; the cash received from the cash register reports and report of any other cash payment received. Much of this bookkeeping and record keeping is computerized in today's foodservices (described in more detail in Chapter 16). However, the data and information presented here are basic for either manual or computer record keeping.

No records, however carefully designed, will be of value unless they *are kept daily, are accurate, and are used by management.*

Financial Accountability

Accountability for expenditures made with the company's or institution's money is not assured by merely keeping records. The data and information provided by the records just described will be of no value unless they are *used* in ways to analyze and improve the financial situation. To do that, cer-

Form 7158

FOOD SERVICE

REPORT OF CASH RECEIVED

Report No.

Dep't. No.

Page of

Period from to Incl.

(Unit)

Present Reading	Less: Previous Reading	Difference	Void	Register Sales	Tax on Register	Over Short	Description	Validated Receipt	Code
							REGISTER 1		
							TOTAL 1		
							REGISTER 1		
							TOTAL 2		
							REGISTER 1		
							TOTAL 1		
							REGISTER 1		
							TOTAL 2		
							REGISTER 1		
							TOTAL 1		
							REGISTER 1		
							TOTAL 2		
							TOTALS		

Receipt No.	Received from (Name and Description)	Date of Charge or Period Covered	Received on Account (Tax Incl.)	Other Receipts
	TOTAL CASH RECEIVED			

Signed

Supt. or Manager

Total Deposit

FIGURE 15.6 Cash report form. To be filled in by cashiers using cash registers.

tain reports are first prepared using data from the records. Essential ones are: a Daily Food Cost Report; a Monthly Report, or Profit and Loss Statement; a Yearly Summary Report; and Comparative Reports of Operations.

Reports

DAILY FOOD COST REPORT   A simple daily food cost report as illustrated in Fig. 15.8 is prepared from four records: the cash receipts record of *total*

Cash Receipts Record (a)

Name of Organization _____   Month _____ 19 _____

Date	Total Amount Received	Food Sales	Beverage Sales	Accounts Paid	Misc. Sales	Other Source	Amount
				Source of Income			
1							
2							
3							
4							
—							
31							
Totals							

Cash Disbursements Record (b)

Name of Organization _____   Month _____ 19 _____

Date	Name of Account	Check No.	Amount Paid	Food	Beverages	Supplies	Utilities	Payroll	Rent
				Classification of Expense Accounts					
1									
2									
3									
4									
—									
31									
Totals									

FIGURE 15.7 *(a)* Sample cash receipts and *(b)* cash disbursements forms for financial control. Income sources and expense accounts will vary with type of operation. Totals on each form are posted to the appropriate classification column.

income from sales for the day, the *census record* of number of people served, the *storeroom issues* record, and the *invoices for perishable foods,* issued directly to the kitchen and not kept on inventory (known as direct purchases). A total of storeroom issues and direct purchases gives the cost of food for the day.

This is the most valuable of the three reports as a management tool because it provides up-to-the-minute information about sales, food costs, and

UNIVERSITY COMMONS
DAILY FOOD-COST REPORT

Year_____

Day and Date	Tuesday May 1		Wednesday May 2		Thursday May 3		Friday May 4		Saturday May 5		Sunday May 6	
	Census	Sales	Census	Sales	Census	Sales	Census	Sales	Census	Sales	Census	Sales
Income and Census:												
A. From cafeteria sales (Cash register report)												
B. From parties (Charges)												
C. Total today												
D. Total to date												
E. Cumulative total for month												
Food Cost:												
F. Food cost today												
G. Total food cost to date												
H. Cumulative total for month												
Food-cost percentage												

FIGURE 15.8 Daily food cost report form; used continuously for each accounting period, usually a calendar month. Food cost percentages are calculated on the cumulative totals; the one for the last day is the average for the month.

number of people served. Expenses other than food usually are not included in the daily report, since they do not fluctuate as greatly as food costs. Food is the item of expense that needs to be watched most closely by the dietitian or manager.

The relationship between food cost and income expressed in terms of per cent is the most significant single figure to be observed. This percentage figure is found by dividing the cost of food used today by the income for today. For example, if the income from sales (or budgeted allocation) is $1,280 and the food cost is $530:

$$\frac{\text{Food Cost} - \$530}{\text{Income} - \$1,280} = .414 \times 100 = 41.4\%$$

41.1% is the food cost percentage, or
percent of income spent for food

By looking at this figure, the manager can quickly tell whether or not it meets the standard set for his or her operation. Each foodservice sets its own food cost percentage standard based on the type of organization, its goals, characteristics, and expenses. A luxury restaurant with elaborate service and high overhead may set 20 to 25 per cent of the sales for food as its standard. Other expenses and profit take up the other 75 to 80 per cent of the income.

On the other hand, a school foodservice where some of the foodservice overhead is paid by the school and where labor costs are not excessive, 50 to 60 per cent may be the standard for food. Although the percentage is much higher, the actual amount spent for food is considerably lower, since the income per meal is so much greater in the restaurant than in the school.

Whatever food cost per cent is established, it should be based on careful analysis of past expenditures and on other costs to be met. It also should reflect a fair return in the form of food that is satisfying to the customers who provide the income. Consideration must be made for some excess of income over expenditure to the extent that the goals and philosophy of the organization expect.

In addition to the daily food cost calculation, *cumulative* figures for the month are important (see Fig. 15.3). The sales and food cost figures for the first day of the month are added to those of the second; the total of the first two days is added to the third day's figures, and so on throughout the month.

The cumulative (rather than daily) figures should be used to determine the food cost percentage, because they tend to average out the "ups and downs" of a single day's operation and give the picture of operations to-date. If the food cost per cent figure varies from day-to-day within reasonable limits, there is little cause for concern. It is the cumulative or average figure, calculated each day, that should be in line with the desired food cost per-

SUMMARY OF DAILY FOOD COST EXPENSE BY PRODUCTION AND SERVICE UNITS

Month _____ , 19_____

Day and Date		Main Production Unit	Vegetable Preparation	Salad Unit	Bakery	Serving Counter	Totals	
							Today	To Date
Mon. 1	Direct purchases							
	Storeroom issues							
Tues. 2	Direct purchases							
	Storeroom issues							

FIGURE 15.9 Charges for raw food issued to production and service units may be accounted for by use of this record form.

centage. Variations in it indicate the need for investigation to determine the reasons.

The *daily* cumulative food cost report is so valuable because it shows deviations from the budget at the time they occur and corrective action can be taken *at once*. An end-of-the-month report (profit and loss statement) shows deviations that occurred sometime during the month, and any action taken will not bring expenditures in line for that month.

Another daily report that will help managers pinpoint and evaluate expenditures is the record of charges for *raw* food sent to various production and/or service units. For example, large foodservice operations distribute food to a pantry, salad unit, and cafeteria among others. On a form as in Fig. 15.9, the direct and storeroom issue costs are recorded. This information shows trends in unit spending and also may be used for comparison with income generated from production in each unit. These figures also provide a helpful productivity analysis.

A record of cost of *prepared* food sent from a main production center to various service units as in a hotel to its coffee shop, main dining room, catering and room service, or in a large medical center to its patient areas, visitors/staff cafeteria, and perhaps separate children's, psychiatric, rehabilitation, and other hospital units is another necessary cost control record.

The charge for food prepared and sent to these units may be based on the number of portions issued, or on total weight or volume of the food. In either case, precosting with current prices of the various menu items is the preliminary step. A form for recording these daily issues and charges may be developed by the dietitian or foodservice manager so that the appropriate transfer of charges may be made.

The daily food cost report, although more or less approximate, usually is sufficiently accurate to pinpoint trouble spots before serious financial reverses can occur. If a detailed breakdown of costs each day is important to the manager, a computer program may be planned to make such information quickly available. A computer printout of essential data from the previous day's transaction can be on the manager's desk each morning for study and evaluation. As with all reports, the daily food cost report, of whatever form, provides a working tool for foodservice managers, who are expected to know how to use it.

PROFIT AND LOSS STATEMENT   The profit and loss report is a summary comparison in dollars and cents of the income with *all* expenses of the department to determine the amount of profit or loss for a given period. Usually it is prepared at the end of each calendar month. In schools, however, the accounting period may be the number of operating days per year divided into equal periods of about 20 or 25 days each. This gives a basis for better comparison of operations from period to period. The profit and loss statement shows the true cost of food used based on purchases, adjusted with inventories, and all other actual expenditures.

The figures for preparing this statement are taken from the cash ledger, income and disbursements, and from the beginning and ending physical inventory figures. A simple summary of the profit and loss statement is:

> Income (sales)
> Less: Cost of food sold
> Equals: Gross profit
> Less: Labor, overhead, and operating costs
> Equals: Net profit or loss

The "cost of food sold" in the profit and loss statement is determined by adjusting the cost of food purchased during the month with the beginning and ending inventories for that month:

Purchases   (Figure obtained from vendors' end-of-month statements verified by manager's check on daily invoices)

+ Beginning inventory (Value of goods on hand in the storeroom available for use. Figure obtained from costed inventory taken

on *last* day of preceding month, which becomes the
beginning inventory the *first* day of the month, the
next day)

= Cost of goods available to be used
− Ending inventory   (Value of goods on hand on the last day of the
month; goods not used during the month but avail-
able for use in the next month)

= Cost of goods used

An example of a typical profit and loss statement is given in Fig. 15.10.
Percentage ratios of the major items of expense and of the profit to the sales
are included for better interpretation of operations, as dollar and cents figures in themselves have little meaning here. The percentage figures are determined by dividing each expense item *by* total income. That is, the percentage of income that is spent for food, labor, other expenses, and a profit,
or if expenses exceed income, a loss.

As with the daily food cost report, a cumulative statement of profit and
loss, recorded month by month, together with the budgeted figures gives
comparative data for the manager's use.

If this report is to be effective, it must be completed and available as early
in the month as possible, and certainly no later than the tenth of the month.
Reports coming to the food manager's desk a month or six weeks after the
end of the operating period will have little or no control value at that late
date. The amount of profit or loss should be no surprise, however, to the
manager who has used the daily reports to "keep a finger on the pulse of
operations."

Large organizations where foodservice is but one of several departments,
such as hospitals, colleges and universities, and hotels/motels, have their own
bookkeeping departments. However, in most situations the foodservice manager generates his or her operating data for closer control and speedier,
more complete reports than may come from a central business office. They
do provide good checks on each other, however, and managers of both departments will be well informed about needs and requests presented in the
budgeting process.

ANNUAL REPORTS   No discussion of reports would be complete without
mention of a yearly or *annual report* of the dietary or foodservice department. Such a report usually is prepared for higher administrative officials
and provides a resume of the activities and accomplishments of the year just
completed as well as plans and hopes for future developments. Although an
annual report contains statistical data, it should be much more than a mere

COLLEGE COMMONS
PROFIT AND LOSS STATEMENT

April, 19___
(Operating days, 22)

			Per cent of Sales
Sales	$26,476.72		
Less: sales tax	1,040.00		
Net sales		$25,436.72	100.00
Cost of food sold			
Inventory—April 1	1,976.05		
Freight	35.16		
Purchases	10,632.07		
	12,643.28		
Less: inventory April 30	2,258.99		
Net cost of food sold		10,384.29	40.82
Gross profit on food		$15,052.43	59.18
Labor:			
Regular employees	4,651.48		
Student employees	3,081.51		
Supervision	2,479.53		
	10,212.52		40.15
Operating expenses:			
Social security tax	386.96		
Other taxes	291.16		
Maintenance and repair	590.06		
Utilities	757.56		
Supplies (cleaning, paper, office)	766.73		
Laundry	527.39		
Depreciation on equipment	600.00		
	3,919.86		15.41
Total labor and operating expense		14,132.38	
Excess of income over expenses		$ 920.05	3.62

FIGURE 15.10   Monthly profit and loss statement for a college foodservice unit.

listing of facts and figures. It is the interpretation of these data that makes the report significant to those who read it.

The preparation of such a report usually requires staff participation and planning together as a group. It calls for creative thinking and provides opportunity to dream while forecasting ways in which the department can be improved, not just next year by two, five, or ten years hence. If there is a specific message the managers wish to convey, such as the need for enlarging or remodeling the facility, the report should emphasize that theme for maximum impact.

The cumulative profit and loss statements, census reports, and other records of income and expense are the bases for the financial part of an annual report. Comparisons should be made of the actual and budgeted figures for the year and explanations given for increases or decreases. Often the presentation of these data in graphic form, such as a pie chart illustration of the expenditure of the income dollar, will be more quickly understood than the mere statement of words. The use of bar graphs to show comparisons and the plotting of income or census figures month by month on a graph are other examples of effective reporting.

Information on the personnel situation should be included also, since the cost of labor is high. Administrators are interested in percentage of turnover, promotions, length of service, and outstanding achievements of the staff and employees. Reasons for terminations of employment are important, too; they may help to point out some weakness in the organization. Interpretations of labor hours worked in terms of ratios to meals served, income received, or other comparisons of special significance may well be included.

The physical plant and the equipment changes or repairs that have been made as well as anticipated needs in all areas of operation should be reported. Any situation that calls for a major expenditure of money requires explanation and justification.

The annual report also includes a summary of accomplishments or goals reached during the period. Special problems encountered and solved, unusual occurrences or services rendered, and the projected plans for the future complete an annual report.

"Ten Commandments of a Good Report" were written some time ago but are pertinent today and should be helpful to foodservice managers in preparing annual reports. They are:

1. Organize record keeping so the information can be used to make up reports *on time* and in time to be meaningful.
2. Practice the art of being brief and to the point.
3. Learn to distinguish between important and unimportant data.

4. Be accurate both in narrative as well as in graphic presentation.
5. State the case clearly and concisely in language that will be understood.
6. Employ techniques that will simplify the data—if in statistical form, use a small unit that has more meaning.
7. Relate to a standard for comparison, such as a budget or preestablished goal; otherwise, reports for top management will have little meaning.
8. Have the courage to report all facts, both favorable and unfavorable, and be honest in giving them.
9. Do not be afraid to dramatize reports by using: arrows or symbols to point out significant facts; colored pencils to underline; red type to emphasize important points; charts and graphs to make data more meaningful.
10. Keep in mind that the value of the report will be balanced against the data it contains. The report should be such that it will motivate the right person to take the right action at the right time.

FACTORS AFFECTING COST CONTROL: EVALUATION OF OPERATIONS   A critical step in achieving a good financial position involves the manager making follow-up decisions and taking actions after review of the records and reports. If operations are in line with the budget plan, no action is indicated. If, however, costs are excessively high and profits not what were predicted, a review of the many factors involved in cost control is called for. There are many alternatives to the approach used by some managers who are untrained to cope with this situation and who think first of raising prices, reducing portion size, or lowering quality of food purchased. These may be required actions at some time, but not as the first stroke.

Managers with professional preparation and experience will search for causes of deviation from the expected from among the many factors that have a bearing on overall expense. These include every activity in the department from the physical arrangement and layout of equipment to customer satisfaction, and everything in between. A brief review of some of these factors to be evaluated when seeking to contain costs is given here.

FOOD COSTS   Food is the most readily controlled item of expenditure and the one subject to greatest fluctuation in the foodservice budget. If control of food costs is to be effective, efficient methods must be employed in planning the menu, purchasing, storing, preparing, and serving good. The expenditures for food vary greatly from one type of institution to another and often for institutions of the same type because of the form of food purchased, the amount of on-premises preparation, geographic location, and delivery costs.

In spite of the variation in the amounts spent for food, the underlying bases of food cost control are the same for all types of foodservice units. The effectiveness of control is determined by: the menu, menu pricing and establishing selling price, the purchasing, receiving, storage, and storeroom control procedures, methods used in the production of food, including pre-preparation, cooking, and use of leftovers; portion size and serving waste; and the cost of employees' meals.

Menus. Menu planning is the first and perhaps the most important step in the control of food costs. The menu determines what and how many foods must be purchased and prepared. Knowledge of these food costs, as well as labor time/cost to prepare, and the *precosting* of the menu to determine whether or not it is within budgetary limitations are essential for control procedure. Menu planning is discussed in detail in Chapter 3. Some questions managers should answer, however, in reviewing this procedure, include:

- How many choices are offered in the menu?
- What are they?
- How many of each item are selected/sold today and over a period of time?
- What items are profitable and preferred by customers and what ones should be eliminated?
- Could foods be better merchandised either through word descriptions on menu cards or on the food displays on cafeteria/buffet lines?

The extent of the number of choices of each menu influences food costs. Menus that provide extensive choices require preparation of many kinds of foods, several of which may not be sold in quantities sufficient to pay for their preparation. If widely diversified selection is offered, the investment of too large a sum in food or labor for its preparation may result. Also, it may result in carrying an extensive inventory of small quantities of food items, or of foods infrequently used. Both are costly.

Foodservice managers should remember also that although menus are made some days or even weeks in advance, they must be adjusted daily to the inventory of food on hand and to local market conditions. Waste can be prevented only by wise utilization of available supplies, which helps to keep food costs under control and adds to variety of the menus.

Menu Pricing and Establishing Selling Price. One important responsibility of foodservice managers is to determine a sound basis for establishing the selling price for food. Haphazard methods can lead only to financial disaster, dissatisfaction of the patron, or both. Perhaps this lack of intelligent planning is one of the major factors contributing to the high percentage of failures in the foodservice business each year.

Even those institutions with budgeted funds that "serve" rather than "sell" meals (such as health care facilities, student residence halls, government or privately supported institutions, or homes for various groups) should have some system for pricing the food served. Managers may ask: is the way we price our food and/or menus the best or most profitable method, or is there a better way?

Foodservices use a variety of methods for determining a selling price. The most common method is based on the raw-food cost of menu items plus a "markup" to give a selling price appropriate for the type of organization and the desired food cost percentage level that the foodservice wishes to maintain.

The *raw-food cost* is found by costing the standardized recipe for each menu item. An example of a costed recipe is shown in Fig. 15.11. Storeroom purchase records provide the price of ingredients to use in costing the recipes. Many foodservices have the costed recipes and storeroom records on computer with programs to update recipe costs as ingredient prices fluctuate, to provide accurate, current data.

The *markup* is determined by dividing the desired food cost percentage level that the foodservice wishes to maintain, into 100 (representing total sales or 100 per cent). The resulting figure is called the "markup factor" by which the raw-food cost is multiplied to obtain a selling price. To illustrate: Assume the foodservice wishes to maintain a 40 per cent (of income) food cost:

$$\frac{100 \text{ (represents total sales)}}{40 \text{ (per cent of income for food)}} = 2.5$$

2.5 is the markup factor.

Cost of the recipe in Fig. 15.11 is $.2687 \times 2.5 = \$.672$, or .70, the suggested selling price.

The markup factor cannot be used alone, however, to calculate selling price. There are many "free" items given with a meal that must be added in—salt, pepper, condiments, sugar and cream, jams, jellies and sauces, for examples. These do not show up in recipe costing, but they must be accounted for.

Also, it is imperative that the food manager know not only the raw-food cost of menu items but also the cost of the many hidden losses in preparation, cooking, and serving, which if not controlled add appreciably to the total food cost. Overproduction and unavoidable waste likewise add to the costs, and the wise manager will analyze all of these, control what is possible, and consider the other in the establishment of selling prices. To compensate for these "unproductive and hidden costs," many foodservice managers add

Name of Product *Quiche Lorraine*

Size of Pan *12 × 20 × 2*

Yield (Total Quality) *2 pans*

How Portioned *4 × 6 : 24/pan*

Size Portion *7 oz.*

Date Prepared *5-19-75*

No. of Portions *48*

Prepared by *K. L.*

NUMBER OF SERVINGS: *48*

INGREDIENTS	E. P. Weight	Measure	A. P. Weight	Measure	Unit Price	Cost
Flour, Pastry			3 lbs. 2 oz		.21/lb	6562
Salt, Cooking			2 oz		.058/lb	0072
Shortening			1 lb 12 oz		.73/lb	1 277
Water		2½ c				—
Onion, Chopped	4.2 g.		4.5 oz		.225/lb	063
Milk		1 gal.			1.89/gal	1 89
Swiss Cheese, Grated			2 lb		2.29/lb	4 58
Eggs, fresh, whole		3 doz			.68/doz	2 04
Mustard, dry			½ oz		.92/lb	0287
Ham, ground (optional)	1 lb 4 oz				1.89/lb	2 362

Procedure:

Total Cost *$12.904*

Portion Cost *.269*

FIGURE 15.11   Costed recipe is the basis for establishing selling price.

10 per cent (or some such standardized amount) to the recipe cost before markup. Thus in the illustration given, the suggested selling price of $.70 would be changed:

Raw-food cost of $.2687 × .10 = .0269
+ .2687 = $.2956
× 2.5 = .739, or .75, a more realistic selling price.

Pricing of table d'hote, selective, elective, or other combination menus usually found on printed menus in commercial foodservices follows the same procedure as illustrated. However, all items that are served together at one price (as meat, potato, vegetable, salad, and beverage) are costed, and total raw-food cost is obtained before the markup factor is used to calculate the selling price.

Obviously, the exact markup price cannot be used when a fraction or an "awkward" number results. Such numbers are rounded off to the nearest reasonable figure; $1.87 might become $1.90 or even $2, for example.

Another method, called "demand-oriented pricing," is based on what the customers perceive the value/cost should be and what they are willing to pay for what they receive. This is also known as "what the traffic will bear." Prices are set as high above raw-food cost as the customers will pay, and without lowering the number of sales on the item. Close control and watch on sales with good records to support pricing decisions are necessary.

Sometimes managers set their selling prices to be comparable with their competitors. This is unrealistic if used as the only basis, for there are too many variables in each operation. This method may be used for a single food item, perhaps for a cup of coffee, but it is not a "scientific" way of pricing.

These two methods, demand-oriented and competitive pricing for establishing a selling price, have been questioned by some foodservice managers, especially in these times of soaring labor and operating costs. Overhead costs remain about the same regardless of the menu and do not vary from day-to-day. Labor costs are affected by the menu, however, as preparation time is different for each item of food. Roasts and steaks, for example, usually are high cost foods but require relatively little labor time to prepare. Stew and quiche, traditionally lower cost items, require much more time to prepare. It seems logical to some operators, therefore, to base selling prices on labor cost plus raw-food cost. In this way all customers share more equally in the expenses of the foodservice. This method is called "prime cost" pricing because food and labor are the primary expense items in the budget. Together these two items of expense usually make up 70 to 85 per cent of the total of all expenses, depending on the type of organization. The markup in this case is figured on the prime costs:

$$\text{Sales:} \quad \frac{100}{70} = 1.43 \text{ or } \frac{100}{80} = 1.25$$
$$\text{Food} + \text{Labor:}$$

instead of the 2.5 used in the traditional method example given previously.

To utilize the prime cost system requires accurate records of labor time spent in preparing the various foods. The amount of labor time used multiplied by the employee's wage rate will give this cost of labor.

An example of pricing by this method and by the conventional for steak and for quiche shows:

Conventional Method	*Prime Cost Method*
at 33⅓% food cost	at 33⅓% food cost
markup = 3x	+ 46⅔% labor cost
plus 10% of raw food	80% prime cost
cost	Markup = 1.25x

STEAK

Raw-Food Cost	1.80	Raw-Food Cost	1.80
+10% Hidden Cost	+.18	+ Labor Cost	
	1.98	of 5 min.	
×Mark Up	×3	@ 12.00/hr.	+1.00
	5.94		2.80
		or ×Mark Up	×1.25
Selling Price =	6.00	Selling Price =	3.50

QUICHE

Raw-Food Cost	.850	Raw-Food Cost	.85
+10% Hidden Cost	+.085	+ Labor Cost	
	.935	of 20 min.	
×Mark Up	×3	@ 12.00/hr	+4.00
	2.805		4.85
		×Mark Up	×1.25
Selling Price =	2.80		6.06
			or
		Selling Price =	6.00

Because of customer perception of value/cost, it is doubtful that many portions of quiche would be sold for $6 in the same foodservice where steak is sold for $3.50. At the same time, management could likely apply the "demand-oriented pricing" to the steak item in the prime cost method, because customers would be willing, and expect, to pay more for a steak than for quiche.

The conventional method, with management decision making to adjust certain costs from time to time, is used by a majority of foodservice directors.

Purchasing. Food purchasing is fully described in Chapter 5. However, when managers are reviewing and evaluating overall expenses, purchasing methods should be included. Some questions that may be asked in this evaluation are:

- Is the person responsible for food quality the one who does the purchasing or writes the specifications for food purchases?
  There must be close cooperation and good working relations between the food buyers and production manager if two people are responsible for these activities.
- Has a strict set of specifications been developed and followed in ordering/purchasing?
  A rigid set of specifications for quality of food to be purchased, detailed enough to make competitive bidding possible, statements of exact amounts needed, and, finally, a report of condition of the foods received are requirements for successful control of costs at this point, whatever the purchasing method.
- If the foodservice is small, has consideration been given to group purchasing?
  There is a trend toward this by schools, small hospitals, and health care institutions. By banding together and pooling food and supply orders, considerable savings can be realized through larger volume purchases. Although savings can be shared, it entails cooperative decision making and joint agreement on specifications for quality, form of food, and size of purchase units in order to be successful.
- Has the buyer visited the market and studied market conditions and trends recently?
  The market is ever changing and the buyer must keep abreast of new developments and learn what best suits the needs of the foodservice and at the most advantageous price. Specifications may need to be changed from time to time according to market trends. Certain costs are controlled through wise purchasing by an informed, capable buyer who is alert to ever changing market conditions and has a knowledge of new products as they become available.

Receiving. Losses may easily occur at the point of receiving goods if management is negligent about checking in orders as they are received. This task may be entrusted to an assistant, but should be someone with managerial authority. Questions to be considered when evaluating this procedure include:

- Are all incoming items checked against the purchase order at the receiving dock?
- Are the quantity and quality of goods received exactly as specified? Checking on deliveries will make vendors aware that the manager is alert and, therefore, exercise more care in filling orders correctly. Weighing of foods as they are received may make the difference between an acceptable food percentage and one that is out of line. The vendor should be notified at once of any discrepancy and correction made either through an adjustment in the bill or delivery of the additional amount needed to complete the order.

Storage and Storeroom Control. Protection of the company's large investment of money in the food after it is purchased and received contributes greatly to overall cost control. It has been said that one should buy only the amount that can be used at once or stored adequately. Furthermore, one should store only what is essential for limited periods of time because unnecessarily large inventories tend to increase the possibility of loss through spoilage, waste, pilferage, or theft.

In the overall assessment of costs, managers can well review their food and supplies inventories and inventory turnover, and question:

- What is the value of our inventory in relation to cost of goods sold? The turnover rate? That is, how many times are the goods in the storeroom used and replenished during a certain period of time?

The rate is determined by dividing the cost of goods sold by the value of the ending inventory (from the profit and loss statement). A turnover of three to five times a month is fairly average for many foodservices, although this varies considerably. A small fast food restaurant in a large city may have a high turnover of inventory, for foods are used quickly and deliveries can be made frequently. A large university, on the other hand, that is located in a somewhat geographically isolated area may keep a large inventory of staple items to carry through a school year, and so the inventory turnover would be very low.

If the turnover rate is excessively high, it may indicate a shortage of funds to purchase in sufficient quantities, and small amounts that are used almost at once are purchased. This is an expensive method. It may also limit the foodservice's credit rating and ability to buy competitively.

If the turnover rate is low, probably too much stock is remaining on the storeroom shelves too long, or many items are not being used. Managers should check the inventory from time to time and include on the menu those items that need to be "moved" before they deteriorate and cause "waste" cost.

- Is there evidence of pilferage or theft from the storeroom? If so, what procedures are used to control access to the storeroom? to teach employees to respect the institution's property and develop within them an attitude of protecting it?

As discussed in Chapter 4, certain procedures for good storeroom/stock control are essential to prevent excessive costs due to loss by various means. A locked storeroom is of prime importance. A controlled storeroom is one in which one person is held accountable for the merchandise it contains. It is kept locked, and issues are made only on written requisition, signed by the person to whom authority for ordering has been given. No one should be permitted to enter the storeroom except the people accountable for it. Locks may need to be changed from time to time as lost keys are easily duplicated.

- Is the storeroom arranged in an orderly and logical manner that makes it easy for the clerk to rotate stock on a "first-in, first-out" basis? And can goods be located quickly for issue, thus keeping labor time/costs for this activity to a minimum? (See the storeroom index suggested in Chapter 4.)

- Are correct temperatures being maintained in refrigerators, freezers, and dry storerooms to keep foods in best possible condition and prevent rapid spoilage?

A daily check of the temperature readings on thermometers in refrigerated storage areas should be made routinely. Correct temperatures and humidity for optimum storage of various perishable foods, fresh, frozen, and cooked, are discussed at length in Chapters 4 and 6. Suffice to say here that storage areas for canned and staple foods must be well ventilated and cool if spoilage is to be kept at a minimum. Other foods such as flour need adequate circulation of air to retain their good quantity and flavor. The use of metal containers for rice, dry beans, and similar products to prevent infestation by rodents and insects is also essential for waste reduction and cost control in the storage areas.

Food Production: Preparation, Cooking, and Leftovers Control. Foodservice managers are well aware of the many costs and potential losses that can occur in the production of food for service. See Chapter 5 and 6 for details.

A management review of activities in this area of the operation might include these questions:

- Is a set of standardized recipes provided and used by the employees? Have recipes been adjusted for best results if a change in brand or quality of ingredients has occurred? Have any new employees been adequately trained to follow the recipes properly?

- Has consideration been given to setting up a *central ingredient room* (if one is not now in use) and exact quantities of ingredients issued to each preparation unit as a control measure?

The proper use of standardized recipes will do much toward reducing errors in preparation that could result in financial losses. Ingredients inaccurately weighed and measured may yield unsatisfactory products that cannot be sold. Slight excesses in nonbasic ingredients above actual requirements, few additional pieces of fruit, an extra spoonful of nut meats or olives, or a little more cream than is necessary soon make an appreciable difference in the total cost of a product. Some foodservices have found good control resulting from the use of a central ingredient room. This requires training one person to be responsible for weighing and measuring all ingredients to be processed by the cooks. Since only these amounts are issued to the kitchen, it reduces to a minimum the possibility of the cooks using incorrect amounts.

- Is the equipment available in the production area adequate and efficient for best results? Does some need to be replaced or repaired? Have employees been trained to use equipment properly and so reduce waste? Excess waste in preliminary preparation of foods may result from leaving vegetables in a peeler too long, and therefore wearing away edible portions of that food, cutting off too much of the tomato ends, or trimming meat carelessly. Natural losses due to shrinkage of foods during the cooking period should not be overlooked; however, these can be reduced to a minimum by controlled oven or cooking temperatures. The cook who sets the thermostat at 400°F to "speed up" the cooking of the roast produces a loss in volume as well as in quality of food, and therefore a loss of dollars in sales. Preparation losses may be due to unskilled, inexperienced personnel who have not been trained, inadequate supervision, or lack of proper equipment; these are all *management* caused, and yet they are management responsibility. Preparation losses are examples of seemingly small channels of waste but, by the end of a month can make a large contribution to an unsatisfactory financial statement. Such waste cuts into profits and should be avoided.

- Are records of previous sales of menu items used as a guide in forecasting production?

Reducing the amount of leftover prepared foods is another step toward cost containment. The manager's ability to forecast accurately the number of portions that will be used or sold is critical and should not be based on guesswork or left to the cooks to decide how much to prepare. Rather, the use of records to show *amounts prepared, amounts sold or used,* and *amounts left* gives a realistic basis for estimating quantities required the next time an item is served. A suggested form for this type of record keeping is shown in Fig. 5.1. Reviewing such records kept for a span of time may reveal that some menu items never sell well, and so may be omitted. Circumstances on any given day can alter customer choices, however, so weather, day of the week, and similar situations should also be considered.

Portion Size and Serving Wastes. An established portion size is a part of the standardized recipe, the basis for costing and setting the selling price. The size of a portion or serving to be offered to the consumer is a management decision. The number of shrimp of a particular size to be served in a shrimp cocktail, the number of pieces to be cut from a pie or cake, or the number of ounces of a filling for a sandwich are examples.

When evaluating this production activity for possible cost savings, managers should answer such questions as:

• Have portion sizes been established and made known to employees? Are portion-size lists posted in appropriate serving areas for reference use? Have employees been trained to serve the proper amount? Have they been provided with appropriate serving equipment to give the correct portion?
Standardized portions or portion control is important not only in the control of costs but also in creating and maintaining guest or customer satisfaction and goodwill. No one likes to receive a smaller portion than other customers for the same price, so all portions must be uniform. The use of standardized recipes is of little value if, after the food is prepared, the person who is serving it does not know or does not follow the directions for obtaining the exact number of portions from a given quantity of prepared food. An overly generous employee can raise costs appreciably without detection.

One means of assuring standardized portions is to know size and yield of all pans, measures, ladles, and other small equipment used in the serving. For example, if one gallon of soup is to yield 16 one-cup servings, there must be accurate measurements both of the original quantity and the amount taken up in the ladle. A one-cup ladle should be provided for the server's use, and not a three-quarter cup or some other size, to obtain the standard portion. Other appropriate-size serving equipment should be used for other food items. Fig. 5.7 illustrates a standard portion listing such as could be posted for employee reference on sizes to serve.

Employees' Meals. The trend over the last several years has been away from providing meals to employees as part of their compensation. Foodservice employees traditionally were provided with their own dining area in or off the kitchen and given meals when on duty. Today, however, most larger foodservices pay adequate salary for employees to purchase their own meals (or otherwise provide for themselves) in the regular employees' cafeteria. Sometimes employees are given a discount on their meals or are charged "at cost" prices rather than the usual marked up selling price.

The philosophy of management regarding employees' meals, to charge or not for them, varies with the individual institution. Managers should question the present policy in view of overall cost control. If meals are provided, the value of them must be determined for use in the financial statement.

The value of food consumed by employees should be of real concern to management in attempting to better control both food and labor costs.

On the average, the expense of providing meals for employees may be estimated as 4 to 5 per cent of total food cost. Although 4 to 5 per cent of total food cost or 1 to 3 per cent of total sales may seem an insignificant figure, these amounts can have a decided bearing on a financial statement.

Meals provided as part of employees' compensation should be handled as a labor cost, not food cost, in the profit and loss statement. A cost determination of the value of the meals is made by management, and the total of all employees' meals is deducted from the "cost of food sold" and added to "labor" as an employee benefit to reflect their true place in financial accounting. Since 1967, when the restaurant business came under the Fair Labor Standards Act, employees' meals cost (if given as part of compensation) may be used to give the employer a credit in determining the cash wage. Refer to the Uniform System of Accounts for Restaurants.[2]

LABOR COST CONTROL   Labor costs represent a major component of the total foodservice expense in most organizations today. Until recent years, food was first in importance and labor second. Together food and labor made up around 75 per cent of the total expense. With ever-increasing wage rates and employee benefits, it now is estimated that labor constitutes 50 to 70 per cent of the total, as an overall average.

However, there are so many variables in each situation that even "averages" have little meaning. Restaurants with full table service in luxurious surroundings and French-style service will have quite a different labor cost than a serve-yourself buffet operation. In the first case, the income per meal may be $20; in the second, $2.95. The labor cost may be 50 per cent in each case: $10 for labor in the luxury restaurant and $1.48 in the self-service establishment. But each shows the same *percentage* of income spent for labor. Dollar figures need to be closely monitored in any evaluation, and managers should not rely on percentages only.

Production employees can prepare more servings of most menu items with little extra time expenditure; supervisors can handle a somewhat larger volume of trade within their time on duty; and probably no additional office help would be required as the volume of business increases. Good managers should be able to determine when additional labor is required to handle increased volume. But generally speaking, the greater the volume of business, the greater the returns on labor dollars spent. Labor costs are less controllable than food costs, and their percentage of payroll costs to sales fluctuates with sales. It is impractical if not impossible to change the number of employees day by day in proportion to the number of customers, patients, or students, as one might change the menu to meet fluctuating needs. Therefore, it is necessary to consider ways to get full returns from the payroll dollar.

Labor should not be considered a fixed expense, because it is influenced by many conditions, some of which can make for greater productivity, reduce costs, and give management a "full day's work for a fair day's pay." These conditions include: the type of operation and extent of services offered, the hours of service, the menu pattern and the form in which the food is purchased, the physical plant—the size and arrangement of the preparation and serving units and their relation to each other, and the working conditions, the amount, kind, and arrangement of labor-saving equipment, the personnel program and policies regarding selection, training, and scheduling of employees, the amount and adequacy of supervision, the wage scale and fringe benefits given and rate of turnover, and the standards that are to be maintained in production and service.

Many of these factors are discussed in previous chapters, especially in Chapters 12 and 14. They are mentioned here again, however, as specific situations to be evaluated as managers seek ways to reduce labor costs.

Type of Foodservice System. The various types of systems and the labor required in each are described in Chapter 2. Foodservice organizations faced with excessively high labor costs might investigate the feasibility of converting to another, lower labor requiring system. Or if a complete conversion is not possible, consideration could be given to the use of more preprepared frozen food items, thus reducing labor time/cost for food production.

Type and Extent of Services Offered. The extent of service offered within the organization affects total labor costs. In cafeterias, for example, the patrons may carry their own trays and bus their own soiled dishes, or if table service is used, the ratio of servers to guests varies as does the cost of labor. If the menu and service are simple, one waiter is able to serve many guests. When the formality of dining calls for personalized service and several echelons of dining room employees from the maitre d' to the head waiter or waitress, servers, wine steward, coffee server, and bus persons, it is easy to understand the high cost of labor in such establishments.

Managers can well study the cost benefits of services offered and decide whether or not changes could be made to effect savings.

Hours of Service. The hours of service determine the number of "shifts" of personnel as well as the total number of labor hours required to accomplish the work. The hospital cafeteria that is open 7 days a week and serves 4 or 5 meals daily—breakfast, lunch, dinner, night supper, and 3 A.M. lunch for the night workers—demands a larger complement of employees than does the school lunchroom that serves only one meal per day for 5 days. The restaurant open 24 hours a day, 7 days a week has a different labor scheduling than the one that is open for business 10 or 12 hours a day for 6 days a week. Each situation will have a different labor cost expense.

Records of patronage and sales by 15-minute time segments throughout the serving period provide valuable data for management when evaluating labor needs and scheduling. Electronic or computer point-of-sales (POS) cash registers provide such data; small foodservices may use a simple form such as shown in Fig. 15.12 for posting such data. Use of a graph as in Fig. 15.13 helps managers answer questions such as:

- Is there enough business and income at certain hours to justify being open at that time?
- Could the hours of service be adjusted for greater profitability?

Name of Foodservice

Date ———— AM	Number of Customers	Amount of Sales	Average Sales	Labor Hours	Labor Cost
7:00–7:15					
7:16–7:30					
7:31–7:45					
(etc.)					

(Breakfast label along left side)

FIGURE 15.12 Records of census and sales by time segments give managers data helpful for evaluating and scheduling personnel.

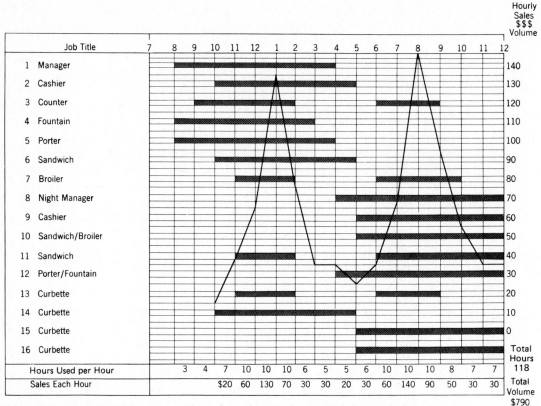

FIGURE 15.13   Graphic presentation of employee's time schedule in relation to volume of sales in one restaurant.   *Courtesy of Ohio State Restaurant Association.*

- Do employees' scheduled times of duty need to be altered in view of the patronage level?
- What might be done to generate more sales at slack periods?
- Could employees perform additional tasks at any slack times to improve productivity?

Physical Plant: Size and Equipment Arrangement. An efficient kitchen arrangement and a convenient location are positive factors in labor cost control. Facility planning and layout are discussed in detail in Chapter 9. The foodservice manager may not be the one responsible for the kitchen plan, but if he or she "inherited" one that is poorly arranged, some changes may be called for. A study may answer:

- How much inconvenience and waste of human energy is actually caused by poor placement of equipment? Studies can be conducted to provide management with information on present employee activity, which in turn may suggest need for change. Step-by-step procedures for work simplification, pathway, and operations studies, all of which may be used for the purpose suggested here, are given in Chapter 14.

    One such study[4] determined that restaurant employees spent 27 per cent of the workday in walking an average of over 2 hours out of the 8-hour day. This represented a cost of 18 per cent of the annual payroll and may indicate a need for improved layout of equipment. A better work plan to keep employees from having to move away from their own work areas, or move so much within their own areas, may be developed. One cook in a small, older kitchen was found to "travel" 6.2 miles in one 8-hour period because water was not accessible over the cooking equipment, requiring her to walk some distance to obtain it. The installation of a water pipe and faucet at the point of use saved hours of time and great deal of energy. Other simple changes may be made that would improve labor costs and, likely, employee morale.

- If an ingredient room is not used, could one be set up? The implementation of a central ingredient room could reduce travel time of certain employees; an evaluation of storeroom issuing procedures may reveal too many employees going to the storeroom for their own supplies rather than having one stockroom employee deliver to each production unit.

- Are pieces of equipment that are shared by two units placed conveniently for efficient working? Equipment that must be shared by two units or two employees may not be in a convenient location for both. Studies of the layout and kitchen arrangement will reveal such situations that could be improved for convenience and efficiency.

The amount and adequacy of available labor-saving equipment bears a relationship to the number of labor hours required to accomplish a given piece of work. It must be questioned, however, whether *all* labor-saving equipment really reduces labor cost. Even though large volumes of food can be processed more quickly with the use of power equipment, certain hand operations may be more efficient when small amounts are involved. The time required for using and cleaning an electric cutting machine, for example, may be much greater than that required for chopping a few onions by hand.

The complexity of the equipment may require the services of highly skilled and well-trained employees to operate it. Although the use of the equipment reduces the number of labor hours, the wage rate of the operator may be so high as to increase the total labor cost. Adequate equipment conveniently arranged for the use of the worker is important if unnecessary labor costs are to be avoided. A saving is evident not only in labor costs but also in the energy and the increased satisfaction of the workers when units are designed for efficient operation.

Menu and Form of Food Purchased. Many questions can be asked about the menu and form of food purchased as they affect overall labor costs. (Various types of menus are presented in Chapter 3.)

- Could a change to a different menu type from the one presently used reduce labor time/cost?
  Adopting a cyclic menu, for example, provides a basic pattern for the manager to follow instead of planning "from scratch" and so reduces administrative time spent on this activity. Also, with cycle menus, employees become proficient in preparing certain food combinations after several repetitions and so reduce preparation time required. As the menu is the center of activity of the institution kitchen and service areas, so it is a major controlling factor in determining the number of employees required and the skill they must possess. The skill required of a cook in a school lunchroom with its simple food and limited menu varies considerably from that expected of the chef in an exclusive restaurant with gourmet foods and elaborate preparations demanded by its clientele. The labor time required in each case would be quite different, as would the wage rate demands.
- Are too many choices or too many unpopular ones on the menu?
  Careful analysis of menu items and their popularity and sales appeal serves as the basis of eliminating items that result in leftover wastage as well as the labor costs involved. The cutting, chopping, recombining, and other processes involved to make the product salable a second time adds significantly to total labor costs.
- Have dishwashing costs been considered in the menu plan? The menu determines not only the number of labor hours for its preparation but also the number of dishes and pieces of silverware required to serve it, and hence to be washed. Too, the dishwashing labor hours will be increased when difficult-to-wash dishes are used, such as individual custard or casserole dishes that require soaking and special handling.
- Are labor requirements considered in planning the forms of food to buy? The amount of "built-in" labor purchased with the food influences the labor hours required for preparation. The purchase of convenience foods certainly changes the labor requirements, but may add to the food cost. Some managers have found that certain foods usually purchased pre-

packaged, such as individual packets of jams, jellies, catsup, mayonnaise, mustard, and salad dressings, could be purchased in bulk and prepackaged on the premise at cost savings. Often there are "lull" times in certain employees' schedules that can be utilized to portion such foods. Labor cost is neither increased nor decreased, but some food cost reduction is noted. Studies to determine the exact labor time and cost involved in the preparation plus the raw-food cost of both forms of the food and a careful comparison of the two total costs give a preliminary basis for decisions on which form to buy.

Personnel Policies and Productivity. Labor is a commodity that cannot be purchased on short notice. And no organization can expect to have an efficient working force if the people in it are not carefully selected and placed in positions for which they are best fitted by native ability, training, and experience. The determination of the work to be done and the number of labor hours needed to do it are discussed in Chapter 12 and are basic to the control of labor costs. In addition to the initial cost involved in finding, selecting, and training an employee, the investment each year in wages should be an incentive to the managers to select employees with great care. And so, turnover would be kept at a minimum and replacement costs reduced. In this overall evaluation of labor costs, manages may well study the turnover rate and review policies regarding selection and training, wage scales, and the number, kind, and cost of employee benefits for possible clues to excessive labor costs.

However, the most important aspect of labor costs probably is employee productivity. And as noted in Chapter 14, management ineffectiveness is the single greatest cause of declining or poor productivity. Foodservice managers can well ask themselves:

- Have definite production standards been established for employees to achieve? See Chapter 14 for examples.
- Do the employees *know* the standards after they are set, and are they *trained* in proper procedures, based on principles of motion economy discussed in Chapter 14, to attain the standard? These, coupled with a Quality Work Life (see Chapters 11 and 14) approach and attitude of management, should make workers more productive and so reduce labor costs.
- How much is spent for overtime work? Can it be justified? One other policy to be scrutinized is that relating to overtime work/pay. Unless some control procedures are followed, overtime work may be "abused," and the resulting costs can throw the labor budget out of balance. Prior authorization for any overtime work should be required. Thus, the supervisor

knows of overtime costs and can try to minimize this expenditure through better scheduling or redistribution of workloads.

Employees' Time Schedules. A review should be made of employees' time schedules, and the question asked whether each employee is on the job at the right times.

• Have any circumstances changed to affect the time a job should be carried out, yet the time schedule remained unchanged?
• Is waste time or unproductive time found?

One new manager reported finding that one dishwasher was scheduled for duty at 6:30 A.M., but breakfast service didn't start until 7 A.M. and no special duties were assigned until the first soiled dishes came to the dishroom! Such an extreme example probably would not be duplicated, but it may emphasize the need to look for payments made for poor scheduling and unproductive time that increase labor expense.

Supervision. Supervision is a major factor in the labor cost picture. The effects of good or bad supervision cannot be underestimated when evaluating total labor cost. *Good* supervision assures adherence to established policies and rigid control of work schedules and standards, and influences employee morale; productivity is high and management receives fair returns on the labor dollar invested.

Too often, however, administration views supervision costs as excessive and attempts to cut labor costs by replacing competent, well-trained supervisors with inexperienced, immature ones. Sometimes an experienced but unqualified person is promoted from the ranks to assume supervisory duties at a relatively low cost. Rarely does such replacement prove satisfactory. Neither the inexperienced nor the experienced untrained worker is able to see the full view of the foodservice operation. Usually the costs begin to rise until any slight saving entailed in the employment of an untrained director is absorbed many times over. Money spent for efficient supervision brings high returns in economic value to the organization. There is no substitute for good supervision.

OPERATING AND OTHER EXPENSES   Control should not end with consideration of food and labor costs only; 12 to 18 per cent of the departmental budget probably will be used for other items classified as overhead and operating expenses. These include utilities, laundry and linen supplies, repairs, replacement and maintenance, telephone, printing, paper goods, office supplies and cleaning materials, depreciation, rent or amortization, and insurance and taxes.

In addition, there is a real concern for conservation of energy resources within all foodservice establishments. Not only does conservation meet a national need, but it also helps to reduce departmental operating costs.

Maintenance and Repair. A planned maintenance program with the services of a maintenance engineer helps prevent breakdowns, extends the life of the equipment, and is usually a cost-effective procedure. The manager should ask:

- What has been the cost of repairs and maintenance of major equipment over the last several months?
- Could replacement of an old piece of equipment be financed with little more outlay of money than repairs are costing? Purchase of a new, energy efficient model would help reduce utility costs also.
- Are employees trained to report at once any broken equipment? Early repairs can effect good savings, especially on leaky faucets, thermostats out of calibration, and noisy electrical motors.
- Is some one person on the premises responsible for the maintenance and servicing of all equipment? Is this scheduled at definite time intervals and reports of findings given to management? Preventive maintenance is the key to cost control.

Breakage. Excessive breakage quickly adds to operating costs.

- Is a record kept of china and glassware breakage?
- What are the replacement costs?
- Are employees made aware of the cost of replacing an item they break? A chart of such costs posted in the dishwashing room is an effective means for emphasizing the need for care.
- Have employees been trained in proper dish handling procedures and then supervised to be sure that those procedures are used to keep breakage at a minimum?

Laundry and Linen. Accurate accounting for these items helps control costs.

- Do employees have free access to the clean linen supply? Or are issues of clean towels, aprons, uniforms, and such made at stated times from a locked supply cabinet? Making employees responsible for their own supply by exchanging soiled for clean usually helps hold costs in line.
- Does the foodservice have use of an on-premises laundry service, or is it contracted out? Have terms been renegotiated recently?

Supplies. Supplies include paper goods, cleaning compounds, dishwasher detergents, office supplies, and similar items. Although they may be considered "small" in relation to other costs, any waste is costly, and the manager should ask:

- Are specific quantities of cleaning compounds issued to the workers so they will not go by the rule that "if a little is good, more is better" and use too much? Managers should include in the directions for performing a cleaning chore, the exact quantity of the compound to use. No guesswork.
- Who has control of the paper goods supply? These items should be issued on requisition as are food supplies so the cost can be accounted for and stock controlled.

Other operational problems that can affect the total overall financial picture include cash register shortages, bad checks, storeroom losses, and pilferage throughout the foodservice. It is essential to establish and maintain controls that will eliminate and/or reduce such occurrences.

Energy and Utility Costs. The energy "squeeze" of several years ago made most foodservice managers and equipment manufacturers well aware of the need for conservation. New equipment designs are energy efficient, and managers continue to seek ways to conserve and to reduce utility bills. Fig. 15.14 shows energy use per square foot of floor space by various commercial operations. The energy use by restaurants (probably typical of all foodservices) far exceeds that of others in this category and emphasizes the need for conservation. Energy-efficient equipment is discussed in Chapter 10; built-in energy efficient layout and design in Chapter 9; and ways of saving energy in storage and production of food in Chapters 4 and 6. Some suggestions are given or repeated here to alert management to the areas for review and evaluation when seeking ways to lower operating costs. One of the best means is to make employees aware of the many simple ways they can help while carrying out their own assignments. Perhaps a chart as in Fig. 15.15 will dramatize for them where the largest uses occur.

A few of the many ways that energy costs savings can be made are outlined in Chapters 4 and 10 and are not repeated here. In a campaign to reduce energy costs that is effective, however, managers must know how much the cost savings have been. Comparison of utility bills, month by month, will give this information, which should be passed along to the employees. Praising them for the results of their efforts to conserve or pointing out ways to bring about further reductions is important. Without the cooperation of everyone in the department, it is difficult to keep these operating costs under control.

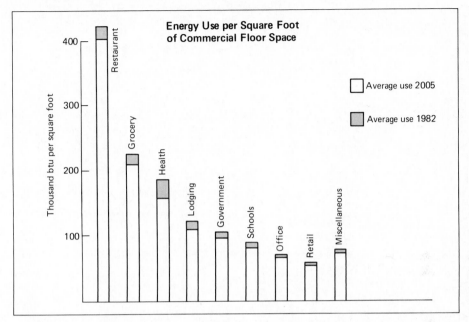

FIGURE 15.14   Restaurants in Oregon used more energy than other types of commercial enterprises and are predicted to do so in years ahead.   *From State of Oregon First Biennial Energy Plan, 1985–1987, prepared by Oregon Department of Energy.*

Management Decision Making for Financial Control

Use of the financial reports on a day-to-day basis alerts managers to changes in income and expenses as they occur. This daily report should trigger a search for answers regarding the department's operations that affect overall costs, as discussed in this chapter. A study of operations should be an on-going activity of managers seeking greater cost containment. Comparative cost studies show trends and serve as a basis for forecasting and budget planning. All of these are financial management tools.

Analyses of the profit and loss statement in its three parts—income, expenses, and profit—provide keys for future action. Managers want to know whether income (sales) are increasing or decreasing and why? How can revenues be increased? What innovative or new services could be offered to generate additional income? Health care institutions particularly are seeking cost-saving and revenue-producing programs and to meet federal intervention.

If food costs are increasing, is it because more people are being served so larger quantities of food are used, or have food prices increased? These

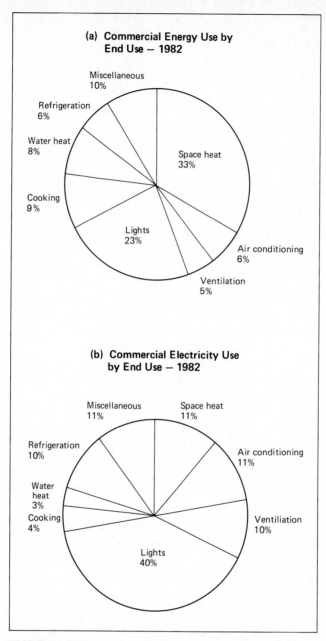

(a) Commercial Energy Use by End Use — 1982

Miscellaneous 10%
Refrigeration 6%
Water heat 8%
Cooking 9%
Space heat 33%
Lights 23%
Air conditioning 6%
Ventilation 5%

(b) Commercial Electricity Use by End Use — 1982

Miscellaneous 11%
Space heat 11%
Refrigeration 10%
Air conditioning 11%
Water heat 3%
Cooking 4%
Ventiliation 10%
Lights 40%

FIGURE 15.15   *(a)* Commercial energy use by end use; *(b)* commercial electrical use by end use. These two illustrations show total energy and electrical use in commercial establishments in Oregon. Any foodservice could prepare similar charts to point out areas of greatest need for conservation.   *From State of Oregon First Biennial Energy Plan, 1985–1987, prepared by the Oregon Department of Energy.*

factors affect the overall ratios of income to expense, and will change the percentage figures in the profit and loss statements. Managers should know whether such changes are good or bad for the operation and how to cope.

Other comparisons and ratios may be made as a guide to financial management. Some of these are productivity indicators discussed in Chapter 14.

In other cases for small institutions, as stated by a nursing home consultant, "the financial record keeping and analysis are less detailed primarily due to time constraints (and many other duties) of the dietary manager. As a consultant, I watch the *bottom line* figures (total food and total labor), and as long as they are within budget and my menu is being followed, I don't insist on a lot of detailed cost accounting."[5]

One significant figure for commercial operations to watch is the average check, determined by dividing the total sales by the number of customers. If expenses increase, the average check and total sales should increase proportionately to cover the cost rise.

Another analysis to make is the dollar amount of revenue generated per seat in the dining room, and the seat turnover per meal period. The higher the turnover, potentially more income can be realized. Managers should watch this trend.

The third part of the profit and loss statement is the profit or loss figure and per cent. Some institutions speak of this as "retained earnings" or "excess of income over expenses." However, managers must consider what is an appropriate profit for their type of operation. This decision is based on other financial data from the balance sheet of the organization, that is, total net worth and assets.

A more in-depth study of such reports than is provided in this text is required by managers to make sound judgments on some of these fundamental concerns. The reader is directed to the bibliography and supplementary reading lists at the end of this chapter. Several references are given for each of several types of foodservices that provide additional information and may prove helpful to the manager charged with financial accountability.

Notes

1. Minno, M. P. and Bhayana, R.: Restaurant budgeting: Step by step. NRA NEWS 40:21, (Nov.), 1984.
2. Horwath and Horwath: Uniform System of Accounts for Restaurants, 5th ed. National Restaurant Assoc., Washington, DC, 1983.
3. Kaud, F. A.: Financial Management of the Hospital Food Service Department. Chicago: American Hospital Publishing, Inc., 1983, p. 13.
4. Labor Utilization and Operating Practices in Table Service Restaurants. USDA Marketing Research Report No. 931, Superintendent of Documents, Washington, DC, 1971.

5. Henderson, Pat, R. D. Dietetic Consultant, Seattle, WA, personal correspondence, 1985.

Supplementary References

AMERICAN SOCIETY FOR HOSPITAL FOOD SERVICE ADMINISTRATORS: Preparation of a Hospital Food Service Department Budget. Chicago: American Hospital Association, 1978.

BELL, DONALD: Food and Beverage Cost Control. Berkeley: McCutchan Publishing Corp., 1984.

COLTMAN, M. M.: Financial Management for the Hospitality Industry. Boston: CBI Publishing Co., 1979.

DITTMER, P. R. AND GRIFFIN, G. G.: Principles of Food, Beverage and Labor Cost Controls for Hotels and Restaurants, 3rd ed. New York: Van Nostrand Reinhold Co., 1984.

Food Service Guide for Health Care Facilities. California Licensing and Certification Division, State Dept. of General Services, P.O. Box 1015, North Highlands, CA 95660.

JERNIGAN, B. S.: Guideline for energy conservation. J. Am. Diet. Assoc. 79:459, 1981.

KAUD, F. A., MILLER, P., AND UNDERWOOD, R. F.: Cafeteria Management for Hospitals. Chicago: American Hospital Association, 1982.

KEISER, J. AND KALLIO, E.: Controlling and Analyzing Costs in Food Service Operations. New York: John Wiley and Sons, 1974.

NINEMEIER, JACK.: Managing Food Service Operations (A systems approach for healthcare institutions). Hillside, IL: Dietary Managers Association, 1984.

PEPPER, MICHAEL (Editor): Menu Planning and Cost Control. Peoria, IL: Bennet Publishing Co., 1984.

REID, R. D.: Foodservice and Restaurant Marketing. Boston: CBI Publishing Co., 1983. (chapter on Menu Pricing)

STOKES, JUDY: Cost Effective Quality Food Service, 2nd ed. Rockville, MD: Aspen Systems Corp., 1985.

UNKLESBAY, NAN AND UNKLESBAY, KENNETH: Energy Management in Foodservice. Westport, CT: AVI Publishing Co., 1982.

CHAPTER 16

Management Information Systems (MIS)

Introduction

Every organization has an information system, a subsystem in the overall structure. It is a network of communication that converts data generated by activities of the operation into meaningful information to be used by management as a basis for decision making.

Foodservice managers need efficient, timely and accurate methods for producing desired information, and they are turning more and more to computer technology for this purpose. A well-organized manual system of keeping records and reports is the basis for developing a good computerized system.

This chapter presents information on the use of computerized data processing as a foodservice information system. Certain computer terminology, considerations to be made in selecting a suitable computer system, including programs, and some applications to foodservice administration are given. This information should aid managers who wish to change from a manual to a simple computerized information-producing system. Success of any such system depends on its design in relation to departmental needs and goals and the extent to which management uses the information provided.

Description of MIS

Management information systems are networks of communication that provide management with information about the organization activities and serve as a basis for decision making.

As defined in Chapter 2, an information system is a subsystem of the overall organization. It is the collection of people, machines, ideas, and activities that gather and process data to provide formal information needed. All subsystems operate with inputs, processing operations, and outputs, and information systems are no exception.

Most often management information systems are thought of as computerized data processing. That is increasingly true, and ultimately the foodservice organization that does not utilize a computer system will be at a distinct disadvantage. However, MIS includes other modes for providing information that are used alone or in conjunction with computers. The computer is only a tool for running the MIS more effectively and efficiently.

All organizations have information systems. Some are informal, as the grapevine, opinions, gossip, and hearsay; other are formal, such as written policies and procedures, and records and reports. Although both types may be necessary, only the formal information system is a valid basis for decision making. As noted in the discussion on records and reports in Chapter 15, information must be current, accurate, complete, clear, timely, and accessible when needed in order to be of greatest value to the manager. The department's MIS must be designed to meet those requirements.

Any successful information system must be well organized and developed on the basis of wants and needs of the individual foodservice operation. MIS is a total process in which data are provided and refined to give desired information to management at all levels. To attain this goal, specific objectives as to what the formal information system is to accomplish must be stated and the information to be provided identified.

Usually, information systems are designed to:

> Monitor progress.
> Track trends.
> Assess performance.
> Consider alternatives.
> Make decisions.
> Take corrective action needed.

In other words, an MIS facilitates the management functions of planning, organizing, delegating, leading, and controlling.

It should be pointed out that *data* are raw facts that in themselves have little or no meaning. They must be translated into a meaningful form for whoever is to use them. Thus, data are transformed into information. For example, the data on a census report tells the number of people served on a given day or a monthly total. Those figures alone have little meaning, but become important information to the food buyer or production manager who uses that data to decide how much food to buy or to be prepared, or to the manager who compares the census data to the income to determine the degree of financial success achieved for a certain time period, and provides a basis for deciding whether or not any remedial action is required.

Since so much data are generated in any business, too much for most managers to cope with in the raw form, it is necessary that the data be screened, synthesized, compared, and analyzed according to the needs of a particular foodservice operation.

Although there are endless methods for producing information from data, Burch, Strater, and Grudnitski[1] tell us there are ten steps or operations taken to convert data into information, whatever mechanism is used:

1. Capturing—recording
2. Verifying—checking data
3. Classifying—into specific categories meaningful to the user
4. Arranging or sorting—predetermined sequence (an inventory file, for example)
5. Summarizing—combining data
6. Calculating—mathematics/logical manipulation of data (as figuring employees' pay or customers' bills)
7. Storing for later retrieval
8. Retrieving—searching and gaining access to
9. Reproducing
10. Disseminating/communicating to final user—report, disc, screen, and so on.

These steps may be accomplished by computer or manually. Selection of a system to perform the functions is of major concern to today's foodservice manager. For a discussion of the manual procedures for designing and keeping records and preparing reports, see Chapter 15. Informal information systems such as oral communication through group meetings, individual counseling, and training programs are discussed in Chapter 12. Written information provided through policy and procedure books, quality assurance evaluations, operating standards, and employee appraisals, also presented in this text, are a part of the total information system. In this section, data on the basics for selection and use of a computerized management information system and some of the applications to the foodservice are given.

MIS by Computer Systems

Computers are being used to some degree almost universally today, although foodservice organizations have been slower than other industries to convert to their use, especially for decision-making support. The primary function of computers is to record data that are created with every transaction and convert them into usable information in a matter of seconds or minutes instead of the days or weeks it takes to do so manually. It is important to recognize that the computer MIS is only as good as the manual system employed. Also, computers do not constitute the entire MIS, but are supplemented with other modes of communication.

Technological developments in computer design bring new types and models to the market almost daily. With the advent of microcomputers, the desktop personal computers, the price range is now within the budget of most foodservice departments. These machines can perform functions that formerly were almost prohibitively expensive when done by mainframe computer for many foodservices. And because of their wide availability and the competitive computer market, the price of automation has been greatly reduced. Foodservice computer systems have been, and can be, designed to handle a wide variety of programs. And whereas the foodservice manager does not need to be a computer scientist or have programming skills, a degree of computer literacy is necessary to recognize and utilize what a computer can do. Basic information, terminology, and foodservice applications presented here may serve as an aid in the selection of an appropriate computer system and programs to meet specific needs or in talking with computer analysts who may be employed to assist with computerization. However, a study of the market for available computer models and programs at any given time is essential to make sure selections will be current and the best available for the price.

Types of Computers

Computers have commonly been classified into three categories—mainframe, minicomputer, and microcomputer—based primarily on size and memory capacity. The classical descriptions of these are:

- *Mainframe:* the very large, full-scale computers that require specially designed rooms to house them and specialists to operate and keep them in repair. These are appropriate for very large organizations and usually are shared by many departments, or time-leased to outsiders, which may result in time lags in obtaining the desired output. Cost is upward of a million dollars, but capabilities are extensive, and computer time available to many users at once. Terminals at remote locations connected with the computer may be used to enter data or call for programs stored, and to receive printouts.

- *Minicomputer:* somewhat smaller and less costly than the mainframe, but with many of the same characteristics. Developed later than the mainframe, it has features that make it more flexible in programming. This type is often used for research projects with large quantities of data to process, or used by large business organizations. The cost range is wide, $25,000 and upward.
- *Microcomputer:* small, desk-top, single-user type (including personal computers). Price range approximately $2,000–$5,000 (or more). Great variety of makes and models; capable of providing most information required by a foodservice department. Units may be interconnected or linked to provide a more complex, automated foodservice information system (see Fig. 16.1).

Although these computer classifications are still used, they are no longer as useful and definitive to explain the capabilities of the computer. There are now numerous makes and models within each category from which to choose. All computers have been reduced in size over the years since World War II. Memory size has brought about the development of a class of computers, the supercomputer, which has greater memory than has generally been available.

Probably the biggest change has been in the availability of new peripherals (see later under "Computer System Requirements" for definitions) for all classes and/or categories of computers. A microcomputer, for example, may now be hooked up to a whole series of other microcomputers to form a local area network (LAN), to an expanded memory hard disc, or even to mainframe computers. Other new peripherals are being developed continuously for computers of all sizes. There are voice-activated, touch-sensitive devices, optical scan devices, and a variety of new printers.

Although all of these may make information gathering, storage, retrieval, and dissemination easier, one of the outstanding developments combines the technologies of a personal microcomputer with the telephone, and is known as the *telecomputer*. This instrument is capable of transmitting and receiving voice and electronic data and information. Data are transmitted through a digital display telephone equipped with a hands-free speakerphone. Although this is not an information *producing* system, it does provide for rapid interdepartmental or outside transmission of data or information. Fig. 16.2

FIGURE 16.1   Typical microcomputer suitable for foodservice establishments.   *Copyright 1986. Courtesy, Dytran Computer Systems, Inc., Beaverton, Oregon.*

shows the components of a sophisticated voice and data display system that
can be interconnected throughout the building.

Computer System Requirements

Most students today are conversant with computers and their use so need
little more introduction to them. Some foodservice managers, however, may
wish to become more familiar with terms used in discussing and selecting
computers. A brief review of this terminology and requirements of a computer system follows:

COMPONENTS   The parts or elements of a computer system that make it
functional include the following.

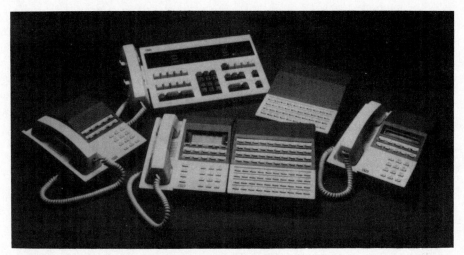

FIGURE 16.2   Digital voice/data communication system provides a range of flexible configurations from 20 to 240 stations, internally as a local area network (LAN), or externally to remote areas. Provides simultaneous voice and data display capability. GTE Starlog™ Communication System.   *Courtesy, GTE Communications System Corp., Phoenix, Arizona.*

Hardware   is the computer equipment itself.

Software   is a series of instructions fed into the computer that tells it to perform certain functions (the program); also is output from a printer.

Central Processing Unit   (CPU) is the calculation or "brains" of the computer. It directs the flow of data (information) within the computer and controls the processing of it according to instructions given by the program used.

Memory   or the temporary storage unit; capacity of the computer is measured in binary digits or *bits*. Eight bits grouped together form a *byte,* which represents one character, letter or number, used in coding data. The greater the number of bytes specified for a computer, the larger it is and the greater the amount of data it can store and process at one time. *Kilobite* (K) equals 1,000 bytes of memory, so a 64K computer can store about 65,000 characters, or 35 typed pages.

RAM (random-access memory) is data stored on chips and is erasable and changeable. It is entered by "loading" the computer from a tape or diskette, or from a keyboard.

ROM (read-only memory) is permanently fixed data or programs supplied by the manufacturer and cannot be changed.

Input   is the data fed into the computer (software) and the *device* or equipment used to feed the data into the computer (hardware). Devices for mainframes and minicomputers are: terminal key board or keypunched (coded) cards, or data stored on magnetic or paper tapes; and for microcomputers: discs, cassettes, solid-state cartridges, or terminal keyboard. Newer inputs include voice input, touch devices, and optical scanners.

Output is the information given out after the data have been processed (software), and the device used for presenting the results (hardware). Mainframe and microcomputers have the same equipment for output:
Printer—prints out a permanent copy
Display screen—temporary display
CRT (cathode ray tube)
VDT (video display terminal)
Voice output

Peripherals are the parts of a computer system other than the basics just de-

scribed; also used to refer to accessory parts of the system not essential to its operation. Some of the more common peripherals are:
Graphics tablet and *plotter* for generating graphs, charts, and designs.
Color graphics capacity device for obtaining colored designs.
Joysticks or "game" paddles for manually directing or controlling a "pointer" or beam of light to a particular area on a display screen.
Modem, a device that connects a computer to telephone lines to transfer messages to other computers; electronic signals from the computer are transformed to audible tones that can be transferred over the telephone lines to another computer at remote or nearby locations; especially valuable for accessing data bases and obtaining information not stored locally.

ER COMPUTER-RELATED TERMINOLOGY:

Data base—a file of related data, stored item by item, that can be added to, changed, or deleted, and can be used by any user who has access to the file. Some data base files are prepared and stored by the user; others are available for purchase.

Computer program—a set of instructions to be used directly or indirectly in a computer and designed to bring about a certain result. Must be expressed in a form "understood" by the computer.

Types of **processing** include:
Batch processing—data held and verified for accuracy by the computer be-

fore being used to change or update permanent files.
Real-time processing—immediate processing of data to update files as soon as data are entered in a terminal.

Types of **printers** for output onto paper, producing **hard copy** include:
Dot-matrix printers that produce characters by means of dots that form patterns.
Letter-quality printers that produce characters by means of a single impact similar to a typewriter.
Laser printers that produce typewriter-quality printout.

Diskette or **floppy disc:** a flexible magnetic-coated device resembling a phonograph record that is used to store information; the most commonly used means of permanent storage for microcomputers. Available in 8-inch, 5-¼ inch, and, most recently, 3-¼ inch sizes.

Micro chip or **microprocessor:** a tiny silicon flake containing microscopic electronic switches connected by wires of metal film; designed as the "heart" of microcomputers, combines memory with logic. The ¼-inch square chip can hold a million electronic components and is virtually weightless.

Spreadsheet: an electronic version of a multicolumnar bookkeeping sheet used for processing large volumes of numeric data to be analyzed according to predefined relationships; used, among other things, as an aid in decision making by showing likely results of "what if" certain changes were to be made.

Converting to a Computer and/or Computer System

Many questions need to be answered by any foodservice manager who wishes to "computerize" his or her department's activities. Much time, thought, and study are required before the decision is made to install a computer system. Expectations of benefits to be derived often exceed the commitment a manager is willing to make to prepare for computerization. However, for the manager who understands specifically what is desired, what may be expected, and what must be done to achieve desired results, success is usually assured. Many organizations find it money well spent to employ a reputable computer analyst to carry out the search for hardware and software and to set up a suitable system to meet their specific needs.

A foodservice manager who has a well-organized and functioning system of records and financial reporting will be able to understand computer processing and convert to it much easier than one who does not have such data readily available. A computer analyst must have such detailed information in order to design a computer system.

The first question to be addressed is what type of computer will be used? For those foodservices that are a part of a large organization with its own mainframe computer, time may be allocated for foodservice use. Then programs can be developed for use with that computer, usually with the help of a computer programmer. For other foodservices, the purchase and use of a microcomputer and perhaps programs that have been developed by others present a different situation. Since mainframe computers preceded the advent of microcomputers, much has been written and published about programming foodservice activities for mainframe processing. The supplementary references at the end of this chapter direct attention to such information.

Microcomputers are crowding the workplace today, so instead of using the huge, sometimes intimidating mainframe computer with its programmers and processors, foodservice managers can now control and disseminate information for themselves on their own "friendly" personal computers. Or work can be done on the micro and transferred to a mainframe for storage. Selecting appropriate hardware and software is the challenge.

PREPARING FOR COMPUTERIZATION

1. Spend time studying to become knowledgeable about what the computer industry and software companies have to offer. Some references given at the end of the chapter provide a starting place. Become familiar and comfortable with using computer terms.
2. Study your own operation and decide what it is you would really like to have a computer do or what would benefit most from automation. Write down these computer goals—both general and specific. Examples of a general goal might be: to improve the cost-effectiveness of the department, or to be able to redirect staff time now used for routine bookkeeping tasks. More specific goals could be: to maintain the perpetual inventory, or to calculate the payroll.

SELECTING OR PREPARING SOFTWARE PROGRAMS

Begin a search to investigate the availability of software programs that are designed to meet the identified needs of your organization. It is estimated that there are some 150–200 companies producing programs designed for foodservice and dietary use. One good way to locate this information is to attend trade shows and/or professional meetings where hardware and software vendors exhibit their products. Another is to subscribe to computer-related periodicals (*Journal of Dietetic Software* carries some foodservice programs). Write to the companies featured, requesting information. Also, many courses in basic computer use are offered at community colleges, by computer companies, and others. Enrollment in such a course will prove most worthwhile for the uninitiated. Anther important source is one's colleagues who are using computers at their workplace and can give good assistance.

Fetter[2] discusses guidelines for evaluation of computer software and has developed an evaluation form (Fig. 16.3) that is helpful for recording the details of each program reviewed in the search process. Although designed specifically for education programs, it is readily adaptable to other types. Two other comprehensive sets of forms were developed by Byrd-Bredbenner and Pelican for nutrient analysis programs and educational programs. These may be of interest to some readers (see Supplementary References). Of special concern in the evaluation of programs are its:

Evaluation of Computer Programs*

I. Product Title:_____

    Author/Publisher:_____

    Publishing/Copyright Date:_____

Computer

Developed for:_____

Unit Cost:_____

II. Type of Program Format (check appropriate description):

    Diskette:___   Text:___

    Cassette:___   Other:___

    Module:___

III. Target Population (check appropriate description):

    A. Students   ___   Grade Level:___   Ability Level: ___

    B. Teachers   ___

    C. Administrators___

    D. Other_____   (Describe: _____)

IV. Resources Needed:

    A. Cassette Recorder___

    B. Disk Drive_____

    C. Printer_____

    D. Other_____   (Describe: _____)

V. Type of Program: (check all that apply)

    A. Administrative Aid___   F. Simulation_____

    B. Drill and Practice____   G. Testing_____

    C. Educational Game___   H. Tutorial_____

    D. Entertainment_____   I. Word Processing___

    E. Problem-Solving_____   J. Other_____(Describe: _____

                                               _____)

VI. Appropriateness:

    A. Are the stated objectives of the course being met by this product?   Yes_____ No___

    B. Can materials be used with other than the stated population?   Yes_____ No___

    C. Can materials be used to accomplish other than the stated goals?   Yes_____ No___

    D. Is the product adaptable to various teachers or situations?   Yes_____ No___

    E. Are alternative learning opportunities suggested/provided for?   Yes_____ No___

    F. Is there a definite need for this particular product in teaching the course?   Yes_____ No___

VII. Content:

    A. Is the content of this instructional material sufficient in quantity to adequately cover the

       topic as provided in the syllabus?   Yes_____ No___

    B. Is the content of this instructional material sufficient in quality to adequately cover the

       topic as provided in the syllabus?   Yes_____ No___

    C. Does the instructional material provide adequate quantity and quality of additional

       content to provide for remedial instruction?   Yes_____ No___

    D. Does the instructional material provide adequate quantity and quality of additional

       content to provide for enrichment exercises for individuals?   Yes_____ No___

(Continued on Next Page)

FIGURE 16.3   Form for evaluating computer software programs.   *Courtesy, W. R. Fetter and Educational Technology, March 1984.*

VIII. Organizational and Technical Components: (rate each of the following items)

	Exc.	Good	Fair	Poor
A. Instructions are clear, concise, and understandable	___	___	___	___
B. Content is accurate	___	___	___	___
C. Presentation of material is consistent with accepted practices	___	___	___	___
D. Reading level is appropriate for intended users	___	___	___	___
E. Program motivates learner	___	___	___	___
F. Program employs positive feedback and reinforcement	___	___	___	___
G. Program handles learner input errors effectively	___	___	___	___
H. Program helps student develop correct response	___	___	___	___
I. Program employs the following techniques: (rate each that applies; leave other items blank)	___	___	___	___
1. Graphics	___	___	___	___
2. Color	___	___	___	___
3. Sound/Music	___	___	___	___
4. Voice	___	___	___	___
5. Time Display	___	___	___	___
6. Score Display	___	___	___	___
7. Personalized Responses	___	___	___	___
8. Other (Describe)	___	___	___	___

IX. Technical or Teacher's Manual:
A. Is a manual included with the product? Yes ___ No ___
B. Does the manual indicate the necessary qualifications of teachers for using the product effectively? Yes ___ No ___
C. Does the manual describe the necessary support system needed for effective use of the product? Yes ___ No ___
D. Does the manual list field data on the product's effectiveness as an instructional aid? Yes ___ No ___
E. Does the manual list field data on typical users of the product? Yes ___ No ___
F. Does the manual suggest a typical setting or time frame for product usage? Yes ___ No ___

X. Evaluation: (of learners)
A. Are instruments for the evaluation of learners included with the product? Yes ___ No ___
B. If YES, do the instruments meet the course objectives and the stated objectives of the materials? Yes ___ No ___
C. If NO, can evaluation instruments be easily developed which will accomplish the evaluation of the learner meeting the course objectives through use of the product? Yes ___ No ___

XI. Product Revision: Is there evidence that the product has been regularly revised and updated? Yes ___ No ___

XII. Narrative Comments: Use this space to make any comments concerning any question on the evaluation form. Please refer to *both* the section number *and* question letter when making comments.

_____
_____
_____
_____
_____
_____
_____
_____
_____
_____
_____
_____
_____

FIGURE 16.3 (*Continued*)

1. Appropriateness
2. Cost
3. Flexibility
4. Availability/delivery schedule
5. Revision policy and service support

Berst[3] advises: "you evaluate software in three distinct stages: first the documentation, then the support, and finally the program itself." *Documentation* is the user's manual. Without complete directions it is difficult to get full value from the program. Manuals should be well organized, easily understood, and provide a sample printout, and a picture of the video display as it would look. Many programs can be eliminated from consideration if those features do not appear in the manual. Berst says that most good documentations contain six elements: *Overview* or description of the program; *tutorial* section giving step-by-step instructions; a *command* summary, or brief review, of the instructions for follow-up reference; *technical section* that outlines the program logic for benefit of a programmer's use in case the program needs to be changed; *trouble-shooting* section that tells how to "get back on track" after making mistakes; and an *index* that is comprehensive and complete.

The *support* aspect of software evaluation refers to the service and assistance that the company selling the program will give. Look for one that will correct bugs. A *hotline* to the company provides a means of talking to an expert; a *warranty* will replace defective disks and refund money paid if the program will not run on your machine, even though it was stated as being compatible. Other types of support may be offered in addition, such as a trade-in allowance on old software when a new one comes out, and a company-trained local dealer who may give assistance if needed.

Finally, evaluate the *program* itself in terms of matching or providing information and/or the needs outlined by the foodservice manager. Good programs are easy to use; they "talk" to the user in English, not in code numbers; they are set up to warn the user to follow certain steps so obvious mistakes are avoided; and they are standardized, that is, consistent throughout in commands, keys for same use, and location of data on the screen.

Some companies do not allow a program to be previewed before purchase for fear of "pirating." In this situation the foodservice manager may wish to locate and talk with persons who are using the program to help determine its appropriateness. It is too costly to buy a program only to find it does not provide the information needed.

Critical evaluation of software programs, both of the general program characteristics and the subject matter content, is extremely important. Remember that no program is perfect. The manager should decide how much he or she is willing to compromise, or how a program can be adapted for a particular operation.

Develop your own program if suitable preprepared programs are not available on the market. Some foodservice managers have the knowledge and ability to do their own computer programming. Others will work with a systems analyst to design the program desired. If this is the case, a clear presentation of the foodservice operations and transactions involved is essential for providing needed background information. Copies of written records and reports used and a step-by-step description of the procedures for obtaining data on the records and how they are used are also important. Having a well-organized system of records as outlined in Chapter 15 is the basis for developing a good computerized program.

Additionally, Wheeler[4] suggests that if dietitians wish to develop a computer-assisted instruction (CAI) program, they need a CAI development team. The team should include an instructional designer (educational expert), a computer programmer, and the dietitians themselves as the content experts. She stated that from her own experience a good rule of thumb is that it takes 50–150 hours of design effort for each hour of CAI materials developed.

When a preliminary program is ready, a "walk through" is a good test for errors before putting it into final form. Describing each piece of information in the data base as to who will use it, where and how it flows from one user to the next is part of this testing process to smooth out the program before putting it into operation.

SELECTING A MICROCOMPUTER   Select a microcomputer or system that is compatible (can be used) with the program you designed or purchased. By having the software available first, the manager knows what makes of computers can be used, and so narrows the choices, which makes selection easier. If the organization is large and has other computers with which this new one may interface, be certain it is compatible with the others.

Features to evaluate and conditions to consider in making the selection and before purchasing a microcomputer include:

- Explore all local outlets to find dealers who carry the make and model you need. A local dealer is available to help set up or install the equipment and give follow-up support, which is not possible through a mail-order company.
- Compare makes and models available in relation to their capability and cost. As costs increase, capabilities or memory should increase and provide faster processing. Remember that the basic cost of the computer may be only the beginning of costs involved in making the system functional.

A significant investment must be made in the computing process after the initial purchase. There is much overhead involved in installing and operating the system. The purchase price of a personal computer is just the beginning of the user's expenses—not the end. Therefore, in comparing prices, include the prices of all of the extras: paper, cables and wiring for installation, peripherals desired, printer ribbons, and so on, and, of course, service charges. Some companies may help set up a small computer at no extra charge, but complex systems with interacting units may cost thousands of dollars to install and make operable.

- Investigate the reputation of the companies that can provide equipment you need. How long have they been in business?
- How extensive are their sales? Do they give good support to users of their equipment? Have other users been satisfied with the service received? Is the company dependable?
- Ask about a warranty. What does it cover and for how long?
- Is a trade-in possible if a change in computer or system is desired?
- After making a selection, ask the vendor for a written statement of purchase/sales conditions agreed upon.

INSTALLING THE SYSTEM   Prepare the site for the computer and schedule installation. Preparation for placing a personal computer or single-unit microcomputer may require providing only a table or desk and space for storing discs, paper, and such. Or considerations may include designating an entire room for the system with its peripherals and accessories. Some installation of electrical wiring and placement of cables may be necessary before hardware and software can be put into place.

Employees who will spend much of their working day in front of a microcomputer deserve a comfortable setup, one that will prevent stiff necks, back pain, eye strain, and related problems. Guidelines have been developed related to ergonomics, that is, the design of computer space for efficiency and comfort. Fig. 16.4 illustrates the positioning of equipment to meet those guidelines for correct relationships between user and components of a personal computer.

IMPLEMENTING THE SYSTEM   One specific person in the department should be given the time and responsibility for overseeing the installation of the equipment and implementing the program. This may be the foodservice manager or some other person who is knowledgeable and who can be given time to stay with the project until it is fully operable. This person should be charged with training all who will use the computer system. *Training* is the key to success in converting to a computer system. Permit ample time for

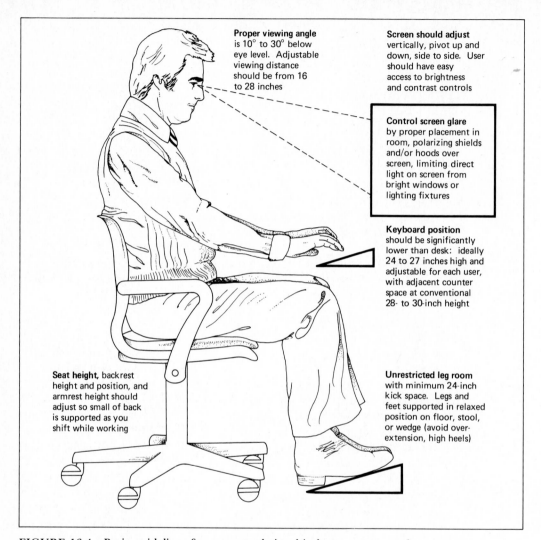

Proper viewing angle is 10° to 30° below eye level. Adjustable viewing distance should be from 16 to 28 inches

Screen should adjust vertically, pivot up and down, side to side. User should have easy access to brightness and contrast controls

Control screen glare by proper placement in room, polarizing shields and/or hoods over screen, limiting direct light on screen from bright windows or lighting fixtures

Keyboard position should be significantly lower than desk: ideally 24 to 27 inches high and adjustable for each user, with adjacent counter space at conventional 28- to 30-inch height

Seat height, backrest height and position, and armrest height should adjust so small of back is supported as you shift while working

Unrestricted leg room with minimum 24-inch kick space. Legs and feet supported in relaxed position on floor, stool, or wedge (avoid over-extension, high heels)

FIGURE 16.4   Basic guidelines for correct relationship between user and computer components, designed to ease physiological strain of person using computer: Ergonomics.

this training, for even knowledgeable people need time to really learn the system.

It is not necessary to implement all of the programs at once. In fact, putting the system into operation one step at a time, and maintaining audit checks against existing records to prove the accuracy of the computer program, is more satisfying for building user confidence. Problems do occur in initiating new computer systems. It takes time and patience to iron them out. Close scrutiny of the implementation process and good training of the workers should help minimize any difficulties encountered.

Foodservice Computer Application

The computer's primary function over the years has been to process operating data into usable information. Early computer programs in foodservice organizations, utilized for many years, have been expanded and interfaced until there are many new applications for them today.

Foodservice computer information systems may be classified into six basic program categories:

1. Menu planning and analysis
2. Inventory and purchasing control
3. Production control (including ingredients and recipes, forecasting, and scheduling
4. Food cost accounting
5. Sales control
6. Labor productivity and payroll

In addition, computer capabilities are used for decision-making support through simulation and various data manipulation programs, for graphics designing of floor plans, equipment layouts, and similar projects. And although robots may be thought of as "equipment," they are computer controlled and programable, and so are included here. Some specific applications of computer uses in certain types of foodservices are mentioned.

The components of each of the six basic program categories with inputs, outputs, and capabilities are outlined below, adapted from unpublished work by Adams.[5] The foodservice manager must be prepared to provide all of the input data listed in order for a computer program to be developed or a suitable one purchased for implementation. A good, manually operated system of records and reports is the basis for obtaining the required data. Supplementary references at the end of this chapter will lead readers to more information and detail.

Menu Planning and Analysis

INPUT

1. Recipe file—listing of all recipes (menu items) in use, stored in computer memory or data file (see Fig. 16.5).

Code Number	Recipe Name	Portion Size	Cost/Serving
	* * * * Starch Items * * * *		
400041	MASHED POTATOES	3 OZ	$0.029
400050	DUCHESS POTATOES	3.5 OZ	$0.124
400100	POTATO/CARROTS IN BROTH	7 OZ	$0.282
400131	BAKED POTATO WEDGES	3 OZ	$0.086
400173	TATOR TOTS OR FR FRIES	3 OZ	$0.086
400175	BUTTERED WHOLE POTATOES	3 OZ	$0.107
400181	PARSLEYED POTATOES	3 OZ	$0.108
400185	HASH BROWNS-OVEN FRIED	3 OZ	$0.116
400190	PAN FRIED POTATOES	3 OZ	$0.093
400220	CREAMED POTATOES	4.5 OZ	$0.119
400225	CREAMED PEAS & POTATOES	6 OZ	$0.160
400262	HOT GERMAN POTATO SALAD	3.5 OZ	$0.217
400301	SCALLOPED POTATOES	3.5 OZ	$0.072
400305	BUTTERED RICE	3 OZ	$0.039
400424	MACARONI SALAD	3 OZ	$0.203
400467	POTATO SALAD	3 OZ	$0.101
400581	BUTTERED NOODLES	3 OZ	$0.061
410306	BREAD DRESSING	3 OZ	$0.086
410705	GLAZED SWEET POTATO	4 OZ	$0.166
410710	SWEET POTATOES & APPLES	4 OZ	$0.165
420107	BAKED BEANS	3 OZ	$0.063
421804	BLACKEYED PEAS	3 OZ	$0.027

FIGURE 16.5   Portion of a recipe file by food groups with costs per serving, used by computer for menu planning.   *Courtesy, Cook-Ware™, Dytran Computer Systems, Inc. Copyright 1986.*

2. Food inventory item file with costs—a listing of the food inventory, item by item with current price of each
3. Nutrient data base
4. Constraints—frequency of menu item use; cost limitations; color, texture, flavor, and shape of foods

OUTPUT

1. Menu printed for specified time period that meets objectives prescribed

OTHER CAPABILITIES

1. Computer selects menu items that are within the desired constraints; substitutions are possible.

2. Recipes/menus are costed to provide base for establishing a selling price.
3. Computer can interact with POS (Point of Sales) registers for menu talley data and analysis for eliminating unpopular items.
4. Computer can plan patient special diets (health care facilities).
5. Total nutritional values calculated for a meal and/or for the day.
6. Menu index—to reference menus however desired: by date, meal, cycle, (see Fig. 16.6) month or week, or by index number.

INVENTORY AND PURCHASING CONTROL

INPUT

1. Master item file—a list of all items carried in stock (food and supplies) in computer memory
2. Maximum and minimum stock levels established for each item in master item file
3. Inventory transactions:
   a. Orders—total amount for each item by vendor
   b. Goods received—by item, vendor, and cost
   c. Storeroom issues

OUTPUT

1. Master food and supplies item file—printout of all items in each file; example in Fig. 16.7
2. Daily report of purchases
   a. Printout of all items ordered
   b. Printout of goods received—item, amounts, cost
3. Daily storeroom issues report—printout of items and amounts issued (from inventory) with cost for each item
4. Perpetual inventory update—items received, added to inventory; items issued subtracted and printout new master item file
5. Purchase order or recommended buy list—computer identifies items below minimum-quantity standard and generates a purchase order printout to bring stock up to maximum (Fig. 16.8)

OTHER CAPABILITIES

1. Purchase summaries—by item with total cost by week, month or year, or by vendor with total purchases from each (to be used for forecasting futures purchasing)
2. Issue summaries—total cost of issues, by category, to various service units (for charging costs to specific units; to track spending trends; to use to compare with income generated from each unit)

MENU CYCLE WEEK : 1
DAY OF WEEK :Sunday
MEAL :Breakfast

MASTER CYCLE MENU PLANNER

Cook-Ware™

DATE: _____

COST PER MEAL: $ .40

```
* * * * * * * * * * * * * * *        * * * * * * * * * * * * * * *
*         REGULAR DIET          *    *      CALORIE CONTROLLED DIET    *
* HAM & CHEESE SCRAMBLE (3.25 OZ) *  * SCRAMBLED EGG (2 OZ=1) HAM *
* MALT O MEAL^COLD CEREAL (1/2C) *   * (1OZ=1)                    *
*                                *    * MALT O MEAL (1/2C^4 OZ=1 EX) *
* CRANBERRY JUICE (4 OZ)         *    *                            *
*                                *    * LC CRANBERRY JC (1/2C^4 OZ=1EX) *
*                                *    * TOAST (1 SL=1EX) LC JELLY PKG *
* COFFEE, HOT TEA, 2% MILK       *    * MARG PAT (1=1 EX)          *
* BUTTERED TOAST (1 SL) JELLY PKG *   * 2% MILK (1C^8 OZ=1 EX)     *
* * * * * * * * * * * * * * *        * COFFEE, HOT TEA            *
                                      * * * * * * * * * * * * * * *
```

1-Entree ——→
2-Starch ——→
3-Vegetable ——→
4-Salad ——→
5-Dessert ——→
6-Soup/Other ——→
7-Beverage ——→
8-Bread ——→

```
* * * * * * * * * * * * * * *        * * * * * * * * * * * * * * *
*       2 GM SODIUM DIET        *    *       LIBERAL BLAND DIET    *
* S.F. SCRAMBLED EGG (3 OZ)     *    * HAM & CHEESE SCRAMBLE (3.25 OZ) *
* MALT O MEAL^COLD CEREAL (1/2C) *   * MALT O MEAL^COLD CEREAL (1/2C) *
*                                *    *                            *
* CRANBERRY JUICE (4 OZ)         *    * CRANBERRY JUICE (4 OZ)     *
*                                *    *                            *
*                                *    *                            *
* COFFEE, HOT TEA, 2% MILK       *    * COFFEE, HOT TEA, 2% MILK   *
* BUTTERED TOAST (1 SL) JELLY PKG *   * BUTTERED TOAST (1SL) JELLY PKG *
* * * * * * * * * * * * * * *        * * * * * * * * * * * * * * *
```

1-Entree ——→
2-Starch ——→
3-Vegetable ——→
4-Salad ——→
5-Dessert ——→
6-Soup/Other ——→
7-Beverage ——→
8-Bread ——→

```
* * * * * * * * * * * * * * *        * * * * * * * * * * * * * * *
*         PUREED DIET           *    *      30-40 GM FAT DIET     *
* PUREED HAM & CHEESE SCRAMBLE *     * F.F. SCRAMBLED EGG (2 OZ)  *
* MALT O MEAL^COLD CEREAL (1/2C) *   * MALT O MEAL^COLD CEREAL (1/2C) *
*                                *    *                            *
* CRANBERRY JUICE (4 OZ)         *    * CRANBERRY JUICE (4 OZ)     *
*                                *    *                            *
* COFFEE, HOT TEA, 2% MILK       *    * COFFEE, HOT TEA, SKIM MILK *
* BUTTERED TOAST (1 SL) JELLY PKG *   * UNBUTTERED TOAST (1SL) JELLY PK *
* * * * * * * * * * * * * * *        * * * * * * * * * * * * * * *
```

1-Entree ——→
2-Starch ——→
3-Vegetable ——→
4-Salad ——→
5-Dessert ——→
6-Soup/Other ——→
7-Beverage ——→
8-Bread ——→

```
* * * * * * * * * * * * * * *
*      2.4-4.5 GM SODIUM DIET     *
* SCRAMBLED EGG (3 OZ)           *
* MALT O MEAL^COLD CEREAL (1/2C) *
*                                *
* CRANBERRY JUICE (4 OZ)         *
*                                *
* MARG PAT (1)                   *
* COFFEE, HOT TEA, 2% MILK       *
* BUTTERED TOAST (1 SL) JELLY PKG *
* * * * * * * * * * * * * * *
```

```
* * * * * * * * * * * * * * *
*     MECHANICAL SOFT DIET      *
* HAM & CHEESE SCRAMBLE (3.25 OZ) *
* MALT O MEAL^COLD CEREAL (1/2C) *
*                                *
* CRANBERRY JUICE (4 OZ)         *
*                                *
*                                *
* COFFEE, HOT TEA, 2% MILK       *
* BUTTERED TOAST (1SL) JELLY PKG *
* * * * * * * * * * * * * * *
```

FIGURE 16.6 Example of a menu, filed by *cycle index* in computer.
Courtesy, Cook-Ware®, Dytran Computer Systems, Inc. Copyright 1986.

Inventory Control System

Cook-Ware™
Food Item File

Stock Number	Description	Qty-On Hand	Cost/Buy Unit	Buy-Unt Unit	Issue Unit	C.F.	Use-Wgt Grams	Min/Max Levels	On Order	Date	Vendor	Loc
01104	Corn beef, cooked 4/5#	11	$ 1.76	lbs	lbs	1	453	20/40	190	01/01/1980	Lady1	1
01147	Beef, stew cut 10#	30	$ 1.75	lbs	lbs	1	453	40/60	0	06/15/1982	Koncen	2
01180	Beef patty, ground 5/1#	1	$ 1.80	lbs	lbs	1	454	40/120	0	06/15/1982	Koncen	2
01201	Hamburger, bulk 5#	10	$ 1.35	lbs	lbs	1	453	40/200	0	06/15/1982	Burton	2
01228	Beef bones	10	$ 0.20	lbs	lbs	1	456	15/40	0	06/15/1982	Koncen	3
01252	Dried beef	0	$ 0.00	lbs	lbs	1	453	0/0	0	/ /		
01279	Cube steak 3 oz	0	$ 0.00	lbs	ind	6	85	0/0	0	/ /		
01325	Beef roast (inside)	0	$ 1.79	lbs	lbs	1	453	45/135	0	06/15/1982	Test vendr	3
01341	Corned beef	0	$ 0.00	lbs	lbs	1	453	0/0	0	/ /		
01342	Beef short ribs	0	$ 0.00	lbs	lbs	1	453	0/0	0	/ /		
01343	Beef brisket	0	$ 0.00	lbs	lbs	1	453	0/0	0	/ /		
02071	Fish square 3 oz	0	$ 0.00	box	ind	6	453	0/0	0	/ /		
02089	Cod fish 3 oz 6#	0	$10.54	box	lbs	6	453	35/70	0	06/15/1982	Koncen	4
02313	Fish cakes 2 oz	0	$ 0.83	lbs	ind	8	57	180/720	0	06/15/1982	Koncen	3
04073	Pork chop 4 oz	0	$ 0.00	lbs	lbs	1	453	0/0	0	/ /		
04146	Pork steaks 5 oz	0	$ 1.49	lbs	lbs	1	453	55/145	0	06/15/1982	Koncen	4
04341	Ham patty 20#box	161	$37.40	box	ind	160	86	180/360	0	02/16/1984	Pisc	1
04405	Ham roll, fresh 3/10#	0	$ 1.62	lbs	lbs	1	453	45/135	0	06/15/1982	Graves	1
04499	Chopped ham, canned	1	$ 1.45	lbs	lbs	1	453	24/100	0	06/15/1982	Pisc	1
04529	Ham roast, fresh	0	$ 1.35	lbs	lbs	1	453	50/150	0	06/15/1982	Koncen	1
04588	Sausage bulk 6#	0	$ 1.65	lbs	lbs	1	453	12/18	0	06/15/1982	Grav	1
04642	Sausage pty 1.5 oz 8/6#	0	$63.84	case	ind	512	43	360/100	0	06/15/1982	Graves	1
04677	Sausage link 1 oz 6#	0	$10.31	box	ind	96	28	150/100	0	06/15/1982	Grav	1
04707	Polish sausage 10#	0	$ 1.53	lbs	lbs	1	453	20/30	0	06/15/1982	Graves	1

FIGURE 16.7 Sample section of a master food item file; note that it shows costs and size of units as purchased (Buy), unit in which item is issued from storeroom and the minimum/maximum stock levels, and quantity on hand. *Courtesy Cook-Ware™, Dytran Computer Systems, Inc. Copyright 1986.*

Inventory Control System

Cook-Ware™
Listing of Items below Min.

Stock Number	Description	Qty-On Hand	Cost/Buy Unit	Buy-Unt Unit	Issue Unit	C.F.	Use-Wgt Grams	Min/Max Levels	On Order	Date	Vendor	Loc
01104	Corn beef, cooked 4/5#	11	$ 1.76	lbs	lbs	1	453	20/40	190	01/01/1980	Lady1	1
01147	Beef, stew cut 10#	30	$ 1.75	lbs	lbs	1	453	40/60	0	06/15/1982	Koncen	2
01180	Beef patty, ground 5/1#	1	$ 1.80	lbs	lbs	1	454	40/120	0	06/15/1982	Koncen	2
01201	Hamburger, bulk 5#	10	$ 1.35	lbs	lbs	1	453	40/200	0	06/15/1982	Burton	2
01228	Beef bones	10	$ 0.20	lbs	lbs	1	456	15/40	0	06/15/1982	Koncen	3
01325	Beef roast (inside)	0	$ 1.79	lbs	lbs	1	453	45/135	0	06/15/1982	Test vendr	3
02089	Cod fish 3 oz	0	$10.54	box	lbs	6	453	35/70	0	06/15/1982	Koncen	4
02313	Fish cakes 2 oz	0	$ 0.83	lbs	ind	8	57	180/720	0	06/15/1982	Koncen	3
04146	Pork steaks 5 oz	0	$ 1.49	lbs	lbs	1	453	55/145	0	06/15/1982	Koncen	4
04341	Ham patty 20#box	161	$37.40	box	ind	160	86	180/360	0	02/16/1984	Pisc	1
04405	Ham roll, fresh 3/10#	0	$ 1.62	lbs	lbs	1	453	45/135	0	06/15/1982	Graves	1
04499	Chopped ham, canned	1	$ 1.45	lbs	lbs	1	453	24/100	0	06/15/1982	Pisc	1
04529	Ham roast, fresh	0	$ 1.35	lbs	lbs	1	453	50/150	0	06/15/1982	Koncen	1
04588	Sausage bulk 6#	0	$ 1.65	lbs	lbs	1	453	12/18	0	06/15/1982	Grav	1
04642	Sausage pty 1.5 oz 8/6#	0	$63.84	case	ind	512	43	360/100	0	06/15/1982	Graves	1
04677	Sausage link 1 oz 6#	0	$10.31	box	ind	96	28	150/100	0	06/15/1982	Grav	1
04707	Polish sausage 10#	0	$ 1.53	lbs	lbs	1	453	20/30	0	06/15/1982	Graves	1
05185	Chicken, fine cooked	1	$ 1.60	lbs	lbs	1	453	40/120	0	06/15/1982	Koncen	1
05312	Chicken, diced 6/5#	1	$ 2.40	lbs	lbs	1	453	30/120	0	06/15/1982	Koncen	1
05576	Chicken fryer 8 cut/lb	1	$ 0.89	lbs	lbs	1	453	65/260	0	06/15/1982	Grav	1
05771	Turkey 60/40 2/10#	1	$ 1.10	lbs	lbs	1	453	25/100	0	06/15/1982	Graves	1
05894	Turkey breast, cooked	10	$14.60	lbs	lbs	20	453	25/75	0	06/15/1982	Lady	1
06203	Hot dogs 2 oz	20	$ 1.26	lbs	ind	8	57	180/360	0	06/15/1982	Pisc	1
06408	Beef liver 10#box	1	$11.70	box	ind	50	75	180/200	0	06/15/1982	Lady	1

FIGURE 16.8 Computer-generated listing of food items below the minimum standard stock level. This calls attention to items to be reordered. *Courtesy, Cook-Ware®, Dytran Computer Systems, Inc. Copyright 1986.*

3. Physical inventory form—printout of items in inventory to use for recording actual count of goods on hand; example in Fig. 16.9
4. Perpetual-physical inventories comparative report—printout of differences found between computer-stored perpetual inventory and physical inventory, item by item; used by management to reconcile reports
5. Recipe-ingredient cross reference—printout of all ingredients on inventory (food item file) and an accompanying list of all recipes that contain each food item (major ones); aid in identifying recipes in which a particular ingredient is no longer available or has changed form; may call for recipe adjustment or restandardization
6. Inventory location file (for foodservices with multistorage units: warehouse, daily stores, refrigerator, freezer)—can be used to identify location of all items and by order in which they were received; aid in inventory taking and proper costing of items

Physical Inventory Form

Location Code: _____ , 19 _____

month

Classification Code	Code No.	Item	Issue Unit	Quantity on Hand	Unit Price	Total Cost
Beverages						
0000	0001	Coffee	lbs			
	0002	Hot chocolate powder	2 oz packet			
	0003	Iced tea bags	each 1 gal			
	0004	Tea bags	100/box			
Cereals, prepared						
0100	0101	All-Bran	1# box			
	0102	Ass'td indiv.	50/cs			
	0103	Barley	1# pkg			
(etc.)						

FIGURE 16.9   Example of a computer-generated form for use in taking physical inventory. Food items in stock are pre-printed on form.

PRODUCTION CONTROL (RECIPES, INGREDIENTS, FORECASTING, SCHEDULING)

INPUT

1. Master food item (ingredient) file (with prices and yields)—stored in computer memory
2. Standardized recipe file, by name, classification (breads, desserts, meats, etc.), listing ingredients; procedures including preparation time, weight and/or volume of ingredients; and number and size of servings—stored in computer memory
3. Daily production forecast—number of servings to be prepared of each menu item (recipe)
4. Conversion file—to automatically convert food items from units in which purchased into units as used in recipes (e.g., baking powder purchased in 10-pound cans but used in ounces or tablespoons in recipe)

OUTPUT

1. Production schedule—printout of adjusted recipes to be used in the amount (number of servings) required; one recipe per page if desired (Fig. 16.10)
2. Storeroom issue request—printout of items to be issued from storeroom as required to produce recipes on the day needed
3. Advance freezer withdrawals—printout of any frozen foods called for in recipes to be used in days ahead. Alerts storeroom workers to remove frozen foods from freezer to refrigerator to defrost in time for use
4. Advance preparation lists—printout of recipes that require advance preparation, to alert cooks to schedule these items (as gelatin) far enough in advance to have them ready when needed
5. Recipe cost update—as new purchases are made, current costs in food item inventory file used to cost recipes whenever desired

OTHER CAPABILITIES

1. Daily production—time schedules for kitchen employees based on input detail of preparation procedures, time of service, equipment availability, and employees' time schedules
2. Interfaces with POS registers to report flow of sales of various menu items and triggers need for additional foods to be prepared (with batch cookery)
3. Production forecasts—based on historical census data for specific days of the week, seasons, holidays, or other

```
SNELL HALL                        OREGON STATE UNIVERSITY
09/30/86

                              Recipe Costing

170100
CLAM CHOWDER
DINNER/SUPPER          SOUP                         NUMBER OF SERVINGS 100


ATTRIBUTES—    WHITE           MILD           LIQUID     hot
               4 DAYS SEPARATION


ESTIMATED—     WEIGHT OF A SERVING                 7.69 OZ
               VOLUME      6.00 FL OZ
               RECIPE YIELD   75.00 LB
```

Food Code No.	Ingredients	Quantity	Unit	Weight Cooked	Cost/ Ingredient
2500	Milk, whole	3.00	gallon	12.00	2.125
2400	Margarine	3.75	pound	3.75	1.560
5290	Flour	1.75	pound	1.75	.319
4354	Potatoes frozen	3.00	pound	3.00	.630
4426	Onions chopped	2.50	pound	2.50	.533
1200	Clams canned	28.75	pound	28.75	32.123
0	Water	3.00	gallon	10.80	0
5482	Salt	1.00	ounce	.06	.002
5470	Pepper	7.50	gram	.02	.016

```
Calculated recipe yield        62–63 lb        Total food cost          $37.31
Calculated weight of a serving  10.02 oz        Food cost per serving    $  .373
               (raw)
```

FIGURE 16.10   Example of computer-costed recipe; one taken from complete recipe file.

FOOD COST ACCOUNTING (RECORDS AND REPORTS)

INPUT

1. Daily transactions of sales, census, storeroom issues, and purchases received, total income and expenditures
2. Desired markup percentage

OUTPUT (SPREADSHEET SOFTWARE BEST USED FOR THESE REPORTS)

1. Daily foodcost report and analysis (spreadsheet program utilized)
2. Cumulative food cost report with percentage of income spent for food
3. Sales per hour (or other time period) and by salesperson
4. Monthly profit and loss statement
5. Summaries of transactions for various time periods

OTHER CAPABILITIES

1. Transaction entries programmed to automatically update general ledger accounts (accounts receivable and payable)
2. Comparative reports of food cost data with other time periods
3. Precosting (cost of recipes used for menu of day plus other meal costs—paper goods, condiments and accompaniments/garnishes—compared with postcosting (waste in preparation and cooking considered); postcost based on beginning inventory plus purchases, minus ending inventory, and should equal real cost.

SALES AND CASH CONTROL

INPUT

1. Guest check information: table number, number of guests at table, check number, and server's code number, entered on a POS register or ECR (electronic cash register)
2. Guests' food orders
3. Individual charges for menu item
4. Cash sales report

OUTPUT

1. Guests' checks automatically calculated and totaled
2. Guests' orders displayed on screen on back-of-house computer or print-out of the order may be given for cooks to fill orders (interfaced with POS register). No order should be prepared before this.
3. Menu item talley of sales—for evaluation of menu mix and popularity
4. Total cash intake from sales, and total income per server
5. Automatic calculation and dispensing of customers' change
6. Reconciliation of actual cash on hand with records of cash transactions

OTHER CAPABILITIES

1. Develop sales and other expense budgets or analyses as in Fig. 16.11
2. Sales by time segments throughout serving period, by server or service unit

Inventory Control System

Cook-ware™
Expense Analysis Sheet

Facility: _____   Reporting Period: _____

Date: ___/_____/_____   Filed by: _____

| # LINE | GENERAL DESCRIPTION | $ DOLLAR AMOUNT $ |

** MATERIAL EXPENSE **

1 Inventory value at beginning of reporting cycle: _____
       (note posting report for values)
2 Total purchase for period (note posting report):   _____
3 Sub total (add #1 + #2)   _____
4 Value of inventory at end of reporting period: _____
       (note posting report for values)
5 Total inventory expense (subtract #3 − #4):   _____

** SALARY EXPENSE **

6 Total dietary salary expense for period: _____
7 Dietary supervisory salary expense for period: _____
8 Dietary consultant expense: _____
9 Total dietary labor expense (add #6 + #7 + #8):   _____

** MISCELLANEOUS EXPENSE **

10 Miscellaneous dietary expense during period: _____
11 Cafeteria sales during period: _____
12 Number of cafeteria meals served to non-residents: _____
13 Total resident census (daily census × #days/period):   _____
14 Total resident meals served (#13 − #12):   _____
15 Total dietary expense (#5 + #9 + #10 − #11):   _____
16 Total dietary cost per resident per day (#15 / # 14)   _____

FIGURE 16.11   Data for analyzing expenses and census to be filled in as indicated.   *Courtesy, Cook-Ware™, Dytran Comptuer Systems, Inc. Copyright 1986.*

3. Special transactions as tax, employees' meal discounts, catering sales, payment by credit card, tip credits calculations
4. Revenue from sales data automatically posted to a general ledger; used for income statement and financial reports

LABOR PRODUCTIVITY AND PAYROLL

INPUT

1. Employee time-on-duty—"in/out" record data
2. Employee identification codes
3. Job codes with wage information
4. Work schedules for each employee
5. Employees' personal data stored
6. Income Data

OUTPUT

1. Individual and total payroll reports automatically entered in accounts payable ledger
2. Paychecks generated
3. Amount of time employee(s) spends on various tasks; total time calculated
4. Productivity indicators calculated
   a. Income/employee
   b. Labor hours/task (establish standards)
   c. Sales/labor dollar

OTHER CAPABILITIES

1. Productivity history for each employee
2. Labor budget variances from actual
3. Prepare labor budget; predict future demands
4. Labor cost for each menu item and per serving of prepared foods (aid in establishing selling prices)

OTHER COMPUTER USES

Robots. According to Adams and Messersmith,[6] an accepted definition of robots is that given by the Robot Institute of America: "a reprogrammable, multifunctional manipulator, designed to move material, parts, tools or specialized devices through variable programmed motions for the performance of a variety of tasks." They say:

> The key words of this definition are *reprogrammable* and *multifunctional,* for those characteristics distinguish a robot from automated machinery. Although automated equipment, sometimes mistaken for robotic technology, becomes outdated when the specific job for which it was designed is discontinued, a robot can be (computer) reprogrammed and retooled to perform an entirely different job function."[6]

Adams and Messersmith indicate the industrial-type robot is more suitable for use in the foodservice industry than is the mobile/personal robot. The industrial robot "is composed of a power/drive unit, such as the arm, wrist, and end effector or hand, and a control system such as a computer and feedback sensors." The end effector is the part that can be changed quickly to perform different job functions or tasks.

Some possibilities identified for foodservice use of robots include: loading/unloading, lifting product and stocking shelves; steam cleaning carts and such; loading/unloading racks from dish machines; chopping, dicing, and slicing with equipment; stirring, filling, sorting/picking operations; feeding materials into equipment; metering of ingredients; loading delivery carts (trayline); delivering supplies from storage to production areas and from production to service areas.

Although robots are not being utilized to a great extent in foodservice operations at present, the potential is there. If labor shortages and high costs intensify, the use of computerized robots may provide a solution for the future. Any possible negative effects on human productivity should not be overlooked.

Graphic Design. Computer use for floor planning and equipment arrangement is a growing application in the foodservice industry. As described in Chapter 9, computer-aided design (CAD) software programs are on the market to assist managers with designing projects. These programs allow for the use of specific variables, identified by the foodservice director, that are appropriate for one particular project/facility (see references at end of Chapter 9).

Data bases unique for facility designing are available also for any who may wish to utilize one for their own project planning. Some foodservice directors may utilize their own computer graphic tablet and plotter to develop their own schematic drawings. *Simulation* of proposed features of the facility, such as planning cafeteria configurations, are often used as a basis for considering alternatives and for decision making.

Decision-making Support. The majority of foodservice computer applications in use at present tend to be for routine accounting functions. However, the potential of the computer for more management decision-making and problem-solving support should be emphasized. The current challenge is to focus on *management* of information and not merely on its manipulation.

Decision-support systems have to be individualized for each user since each need is unique. The information compiled is processed in whatever form the manager requires. Several possible alternatives resulting from a particular decision may be generated to aid the manager in making a wise choice. These are know as "what if" situations and show the overall effect a change

		Name of Foodservice		
Date _____		Day of Week _____		
Meal	Time Segments	Sales for Period	Number of Customers	Average Check
Breakfast	7:00–7:29	32.20	35	.92
	7:30–7:59	65.10	62	1.05
	8:00–8:29	68.85	81	.85
	8:30–8:59	33.12	46	.72
	9:00–9:29	34.85	41	.85
	9:30–9:59	19.32	28	.69
Total/Averages:		253.44	293	.865
Continental Breakfast/ AM Break	10:00–10:15	40.50	54	.75
	10:16–10:30	32.30	38	.85
	10:31–10:45	45.08	49	.92
	10:46–11:00	13.49	21	.69
Total/Averages:		135.95	162	.839
Lunch	11:00–11:29	178.25	65	2.75
	etc.			

FIGURE 16.12   Simple spreadsheet used for analyzing sales by time periods.

may have on the system's operation before it is put into effect. Several processes may be used to achieve this result.

"*Electronic spreadsheets* are used primarily in financial planning and budgeting decisions . . . . The operator alters the sales data in a budget or financial plan and the computer shows the likely results of decisions based on the new assumptions."[7] Spreadsheets also may be used to support purchasing choices, employee scheduling, inventory control, and menu analysis. Fig. 16.12 shows an example of a simple spreadsheet output.

Kasavana[8] describes *menu engineering* as "a series of processes through which management can evaluate current and future menu pricing, design, and content decisions." The 12-step procedure in menu engineering focuses on *menu mix* or customer demand for each item, and *item pricing* analysis to determine the profit contribution of all menu items. "It provides a quantitative measurement scheme for evaluating success in menu and related decision areas." These include answers to questions such as: What is the potential food cost for a given menu? At what price level and mix of sales does a (restaurant) foodservice maximize its profits? Which current menu items require replacing, repricing, or repositioning on the menu? How can the success of a menu change be evaluated?

Analyses can be achieved through use of the electronic spreadsheets or by matrix mathematical computations. Matthews and Norback[9] describe this technique in discussing a new approach to the design of information systems for foodservice management. They state that:

> Because a change in any part of the foodservice system will have an impact on other parts of the system, the most critical need for effective managment is the integration of information presented . . . . This requires that the foodservice data be organized before those data are put into the computer . . . . Matrices can provide this organization . . . . A matrix is a rectangular arrangement of numbers, in which the position of the entry within the rows and columns of the matrix gives the entry meaning.

The computer can be programmed for mathematical computations. It integrates various pieces of data about each resource used (inputs) that has a bearing on the problem to be solved (output). The output provides management with the information on which to base a decision as to the "best" action to take. "Best" is based on the organization's goals and limitations. It is up to management to initiate the action called for and to ascertain that it is integrated into the activities of the operation. This follow-up function cannot be performed by computer!

One type of computer program helpful to managers who wish easy retrieval of specific bits of information, or seek answers to questions by direct searching of data bases, is known as the "conversational" method. The user converses with the computer in foodservice terms that the computer can understand. Some examples of the kind of information that can be retrieved in this conversational manner are:

1. The impact on cost and other resource use of exchanging one menu item for another in the menu plan
2. The impact on cost of changing ingredients in a recipe
3. The pattern of use for a specific ingredient over a range of meals
4. Ingredient amounts in stock and anticipated orders for replenishing supplies
5. Labor productivity information for individuals and the work force
6. Budgetary comparisons—planned to actual
7. Conversational menu planning—building a menu cycle plan and simultaneously testing it against budgetary and other constraints
8. Anticipating the consequences to the foodservice of price changes of ingredients or changes in a labor contract.[9]

Managers of specific types of foodservice operations will find other needs that can be met with these decision-support computer systems. Applications seem to be limited only by the creativity of management.

Summary

Management information systems have become sophisticated, accurate, and more timely since the development of microcomputer technology. Manual computations and record keeping that require hours of clerical time can now be accomplished in minutes, after a computer program has been designed or purchased and a computer system installed.

New types of computers and programs are marketed almost daily and open new possibilities for management support. Predictions for the future include more decision-support systems that integrate several types of computing (word processing, data processing, query languages, and more), which are presently used separately, into one unit. Dietitians and managers will be able to utilize this tool in their workplaces to maintain a cost-effective operation. The organizational structure of foodservice may change, with a flattening of the management pyramid and fewer levels between top and first-line management. With access to data formerly denied, supervisors may participate in greater decision making and so be better informed.

Harris[10] says that the future will bring better organized communication with voice-store-forward telephone systems that avoid time-wasting repeat calls; electronic mail exchange that simultaneously transmits memos, reports, and drafts; teleconferencing to link remote managers to one another to help save time and reduce costs. Computers can be used to monitor production flow and quality and so free supervisors for more training, coaching, negotiating, and worker counseling and planning.

Other trends seem to be toward more voice-operated machines that allow, for example: customers to place their own orders and receive change and receipt automatically; computer hookups between service units in one foodservice system as in large school foodservice operations, medical centers, or restaurant chains; computerization of the human resources system—recruitment, training, placement (matching characteristics for success with those of applicants), and retention; and improved decision making at all levels by combining the organization's data with external economic sociological and technological factors for forecasting. These applications, as well as others not mentioned here, are in use to some degree in some foodservices today; many more are sure to come.

Any information system is only as good as its design and use. In planning a management information system, remember the desired result: placing data into a *meaningful context* for those who are to use it, *disseminating* the information to the right people *when needed,* and making certain that the data are *complete, accurate,* and *free of bias.* Only when this is accomplished will the MIS have achieved its greatest potential value in the foodservice operation.

Notes

1. Burch, J. G., Strater, F. B., and Grudniski, G.: Information Systems: Theory and Practice, 3rd ed. New York: John Wiley and Sons, 1983, pp. 7–8.
2. Fetter, W. R.: Guidelines for evaluation of computer software (with an evaluation form). Educational Technology 24:19 (March) 1984.
3. Berst, Jesse: The ABC's of evaluating packaged software. Interface Age 8(2): 35, 1983.
4. Wheeler, Madelyn L.: (Personal correspondence, 1985) Coordinator, Research Dietetics, Diabetes Research and Training Center, School of Medicine, Indiana University, Indianapolis.
5. Adams, Elaine: Computer Usage in Food Systems. Unpublished graduate work, Food Systems Management Department, College of Home Economics, Oregon State University, Corvallis, 1984.
6. Adams, E. A. and Messersmith, Ann: Robots in food systems: A review and assessment of potential uses. J. Am. Diet. Assoc. 86(4):476, 1986.
7. Patterson, John and Alvarez, Roy: Computer systems for food-service operations. Cornell HRA Quarterly 26(1):132, 1985.
8. Kasavana, M. L.: Computer Systems for Foodservice Operations. New York: Van Nostrand Reinhold Co., 1984, pp. 153, 155.
9. Matthews, M. E. and Norback, J. P.: A new approach to the design of information systems for foodservice management in health care facilities. J. Amer. Diet. Assoc. 84(6):675, 1984.
10. Harris, P. R.: Management in Transition. San Francisco: Jossey-Bass, Inc., 1985, pp. 162–63.

Supplementary References

JOURNAL ARTICLES

BOZYMSKI, MICHAEL: Computers in foodservices: The crucial link. Restaurant Business 84(8):151, 1985.

BRONSON, RICHARD: Computer simulation: What it is, how it's done. BYTE 9(3):95, 1984.

BRYD-BREDBENNER, C. AND PELICAN, S., editors: Software programs. J. Nutr. Ed. 16:77, 1984.

BURROWS, F.: Spreadsheets and sales. Food Management 20(10):16, 1985.

COLDWELL, R. M.: The computer as a teaching tool. J. H. Econ. 74(3):45, 1982.

DWYER, JOHANNA et al.: Computerized dietary analysis systems: A comprehensive view. J. Amer. Diet. Assoc. 83(4):421, 1983.

Facts about inventory control, computer style. Rest. and Inst. 95:60, July 10, 1985.

HIEMSTRA, S. J. AND VAN EGMOND-PANNEL, D.: Computer applications in school foodservice. School Food Service Research Review 8(2):86, 1984. (computers in foodservice)

HOLMES, Z. A.: Microcomputer simulation helps teach food science problem solving. Food Tech. 38(12):114, 1984.

INGERSON, S.: Computers and you! School Food Service J. 39(7):134, 1985.

KASAVANNA, M. L.: How to buy a computer (7 tips for first-time computer buyers). NRA News 4(4):25, 1984.

MANDIGO, T. R.: Develop a data base for daily specials. Independent Rest. 47(6):23, 1985.

NORBACK, J. P. AND MATTHEWS, M. E.: Data structures for integrating quality and cost factors in a foodservice operation. Journal of Food Protection 44(5):364, 1981.

PACKER, C. L. et al.: Which major systems? On which type of computer? Hospitals 58(23):81, 1984.

PERRON, MARY: Dietary analysis in food software. Hospitals 58(7):76, 1984.

SAWYER, CAROL A.: Comprehensive food-service software in the classroom. Cornell HRA Quarterly 26(2):71, 1985.

WHEELER, L. A. AND WHEELER, M.L.: Review of microcomputer nutrient analysis and menu planning programs. M.D. Computing 1(2):42, 1984.

BOOKLETS AND PERIODICALS

COMPUTERS IN NUTRITION EDUCATION. J. Nutr. Ed. 16(2): 1984. (Excellent reference issue including listing of software companies as of that date.) 1736 Franklin Street, Suite 900, Oakland, CA 94612.

Hi-Tech Hospitality (a monthly journal of technology for the hospitality industry). Hi-Tech Publications, Inc., 12416 Hymeadow Drive, Suite Two, Austin, TX 78750–1896.

HOOVER, L.: Computers in Nutrition, Dietetics and Foodservice Management: A Bibliography, 2nd ed. Dept. of Human Nutrition, Foods and Food Systems Management, College of Home Economics, 217 Gwynn Hall, University of Missouri, Columbia, MO 65211, 1983. ($6 per copy)

HOOVER, L. W. AND PERLOFF, B. P.: Model for Review of Nutrient Data Base Software Capabilities. (same address as above)

INSTRUCTIONAL COMPUTING AT THE COLLEGE LEVEL. Pipeline (a publication of CONDUIT), PO Box 385, Iowa City, IA 52244.

Journal of Dietetic Software. PO Box 2665, Norman, OK 73070. (quarterly)

BOOKS

AMERICAN MANAGEMENT ASSOCIATION: The 1985 Report on Information Centers. 135 W. 50th Street, New York, NY 10020.

HANSEN, R. H.: The Why, What and How of Decision Support. New York: Am. Mgmt. Assn. (AMA Membership Publication Division), 1984.

HICKS, J. O.: MIS: A User Perspective. St. Paul: West Publishing Co., 1984.

JARRETT, I. M.: Computer Graphics and Reporting. New York: John Wiley and Sons, 1983.

MELTZER, M.F.: Information—The Ultimate Management Resource: How to Find, Use and Manage It. New York: AMACOM, 1981.

PELLIGRINO, T. W.: Selecting a Computer-Assisted System for Volume Food Service.
Chicago: Am. Hospital Publishing, Inc., 1986.

RILEY, M. J.: MIS. Oakland, CA: Holden-Day, Inc., 1981.

WILLIS, J. AND MILLER, M.: *Computers for Everybody,* 2nd ed. Beaverton, OR: Dilithium Press, 1983.

SOFTWARE PROGRAM SOURCES (SELECTED)

Advanced Analytical Computer Systems (restaurant programs for microcomputers), 11777 San Vicente Blvd., Suite 525, Los Angeles, CA 90049.

The CBORD Group, Inc., Suite 300, First Bank Building, The Commons, Ithaca, NY 14850.

Comcater International, Inc., 65 S. Main Street, Pennington, NJ 08534. (accounting and control system)

Computerized Management Systems, 1039 Cadiz Drive, Simi, CA 93065.

Dietary/Food Management System (DFM) by Medical Software Systems Company, 4812 SW Ninth Street, Des Moines, IA 50315.

Dietary Systems, Inc., Suite 216, 2161 Newmarket Parkway, Marietta, GA 30067.

Dietetic Com-Pak, University of Missouri Hospital and Clinics, Department of Nutrition and Dietetics, Columbia, MO.

National Educational Media, Inc. (NEM) (audiovisual training and education programs for foodservices, etc.), 21601 Devonshire St., Chatsworth, CA 91311.

National Semi Conductor Corp., PO Box 58112, Santa Clara, CA 95052-8112. (Data Checker/DTS—management reports and control systems)

Nutrition Consultants, Inc., Box 1513, Norman, OK 73070. (recipe scaling)

Nutrition Services, Division of Health Development, Inc., 1165 West Third Avenue, Columbus, OH 43212.

The Ohio State University Hospitals, Department of Dietetics, 410 W. 10th Avenue, Columbus, OH 43210–1128. (nutrient data base and other programs)

Restaurant Menu Management from Viking, Inc., 910–500 Boulevard, Rice Lake, WI 54868. (food cost monitoring)

USDA Nutrient Data Bases: U. S. Department of Commerce. Distributed by National Technical Information Service, 5285 Port Royal Road, Springfield, VA 22161. (price: $100)

Index